Praise for *The Chosen and the Damned*

"I have taught Native American history for thirty years and have always maintained that, despite the injustice and the horror of it, we are not looking at a case of attempted genocide. Silverman's book made me change my mind. It is a powerful work of the highest order."
—**Camilla Townsend, author of** *Fifth Sun: A New History of the Aztecs*

"Drawing on deep research, weighing evidence carefully, and refusing easy answers, Silverman places Indigenous peoples at the core of Americans' ideas about race and national identity—and therefore at the core of the national story. Especially in these times when fundamental historical meanings are deeply contested, everyone should read this wise, humane, and disturbing book." —**Daniel K. Richter, author of** *Before the Revolution: America's Ancient Pasts*

"From colonial times to present-day controversies about 'Who is an Indian,' David Silverman traces the central role of Native Americans in the ugly, messy, and violent history of race and racism in America. Euro-Americans developed a collective identity as 'civilized Whites' that drove and justified the destruction and dispossession of 'savage Indians'; Indigenous peoples adopted 'Indian' as a shared identity that distinguished them from and bolstered resistance to their genocidal and land-hungry oppressors. Readers may be discomfited by this bold and sweeping history, or take issue with some of its interpretations, but no one should ignore it." —**Colin G. Calloway, author of** *The Indian World of George Washington: The First President, the First Americans, and the Birth of the Nation*

"An eye-opening and masterfully crafted book. David J. Silverman dismantles the myth that Native peoples were a doomed race, while insisting that their stories are the core of the American story." —**Andrew Lipman, author of** *Squanto: A Native Odyssey*

"In this powerful and wide-ranging work, David J. Silverman weaves discussions of race formation and racism into a highly readable narrative history of North America's Indigenous peoples. A powerful, important, and provocative book that will force considerations of the many paths not taken in American history." —**Michael Leroy Oberg, author of** *Native America: A History*

"An ambitious and convincing book that lays bare the way White Europeans and Americans, for over four hundred years, have used White constructs of race, white supremacy, and racism as ideological justifications for genocidal actions and policies against American Indians. Full of woe, violence, race-making, racism, and Native resilience, this is the story at the heart of America." —**Robbie Ethridge, author of** *From Chicaza to Chickasaw: The European Invasion and the Transformation of the Mississippian World, 1540–1715*

"David Silverman writes with clarity and grace about complex, sensitive, and often sorrowful events. *The Chosen and the Damned* gives readers powerful new insights into the history of racialist and racist ideas in America." —**James D. Rice, author of** *Tales from a Revolution: Bacon's Rebellion and the Transformation of Early America*

BY THE SAME AUTHOR

This Land Is Their Land: The Wampanoag Indians, Plymouth Colony, and the Troubled History of Thanksgiving

Thundersticks: Firearms and the Violent Transformation of Native America

Ninigret, Sachem of the Niantics and Narragansetts: Diplomacy, War, and the Balance of Power in Seventeenth-Century New England and Indian Country
(coauthored with Julie A. Fisher)

Red Brethren: The Brothertown and Stockbridge Indians and the Problem of Race in Early America

Faith and Boundaries: Colonists, Christianity, and Community Among the Wampanoag Indians of Martha's Vineyard, 1600–1871

THE CHOSEN AND THE DAMNED

NATIVE AMERICANS AND THE MAKING OF RACE IN THE UNITED STATES

DAVID J. SILVERMAN

BLOOMSBURY PUBLISHING

NEW YORK · LONDON · OXFORD · NEW DELHI · SYDNEY

BLOOMSBURY PUBLISHING
Bloomsbury Publishing Inc.
1359 Broadway, New York, NY 10018, USA
50 Bedford Square, London, WC1B 3DP, UK
Bloomsbury Publishing Ireland Limited,
29 Earlsfort Terrace, Dublin 2, D02 AY28, Ireland

BLOOMSBURY, BLOOMSBURY PUBLISHING, and the Diana logo
are trademarks of Bloomsbury Publishing Plc

First published in the United States 2026

Copyright © David J. Silverman, 2026
Maps created by Ortelius Design

All rights reserved. No part of this publication may be: i) reproduced or transmitted in any form, electronic or mechanical, including photocopying, recording, or by means of any information storage or retrieval system without prior permission in writing from the publishers; or ii) used or reproduced in any way for the training, development, or operation of artificial intelligence (AI) technologies, including generative AI technologies. The rights holders expressly reserve this publication from the text and data mining exception as per Article 4(3) of the Digital Single Market Directive (EU) 2019/790.

Bloomsbury Publishing Plc does not have any control over, or responsibility for, any third-party websites referred to or in this book. All internet addresses given in this book were correct at the time of going to press. The author and publisher regret any inconvenience caused if addresses have changed or sites have ceased to exist, but can accept no responsibility for any such changes.

ISBN: HB: 978-1-63557-838-6; EBOOK: 978-1-63557-839-3

Library of Congress Cataloging-in-Publication Data is available

2 4 6 8 10 9 7 5 3 1

Typesetting by Six Red Marbles India
Printed in the United States by Lakeside Book Company

To find out more about our authors and books visit www.bloomsbury.com
and sign up for our newsletters.

Bloomsbury books may be purchased for business or promotional use. For information on bulk purchases please contact Macmillan Corporate and Premium Sales Department at specialmarkets@macmillan.com.
For product safety–related questions contact productsafety@bloomsbury.com.

To Julie A. Fisher

CONTENTS

	A Note on Terminology and Style	ix
INTRODUCTION	A Memorial by the Chosen to the Damned	1
CHAPTER ONE	Loss of Faith	31
CHAPTER TWO	Race Wars	71
CHAPTER THREE	"Undistinguished Destruction"	109
CHAPTER FOUR	Whitewash	149
CHAPTER FIVE	"Exterminate Them!"	193
CHAPTER SIX	"A Race of Tenants"	241
CHAPTER SEVEN	Visions in an Age of Systematic Racism	285
CHAPTER EIGHT	Choosing	333
EPILOGUE	Transitions	367
	Acknowledgments	379
	Abbreviations	381
	Notes	383
	Index	477

A NOTE ON TERMINOLOGY AND STYLE

As a study of race-making, this book is also a study of racial terminology. Readers are bound to encounter racial labels and ideas that they find unfamiliar, at best, and offensive, at worst. I include such language, almost always as part of quotes from primary sources, as evidence for how race worked in historic times and places. Readers should take as given that my quoting and discussing of racial slurs and outdated racial labels does not represent my approval.

I capitalize all racial terms, including "Indigenous," "Native," "White," and "Black." The reason is that these words, though formally adjectives in some contexts, functioned historically as nouns. This book traces parts of that history. My editorial judgment on this issue has been influenced by Nell Irvin Painter's essay "Why 'White' Should Be Capitalized, Too" (*Washington Post*, July 22, 2020). For stylistic simplicity, I do not put these racial labels in quotation marks. Nevertheless, this book demonstrates the point of such quotation marks, which is to signal that racial groups are products of the human imagination rather than actual biological entities.

Considerations of style also guide my decision not to put the words "civilize," "civilization," "civility," "mixed-bloods," and "full-bloods" in quotation marks or precede them with qualifiers on most of the occasions that they appear in the text. To do otherwise would become endlessly repetitive and distracting. Let me be clear that I do not subscribe to the value judgments inherent in these terms.

I use "Indian," "Native," and "Indigenous" interchangeably, though I employ "Indian" the most, for two main reasons. The first is that the majority of Native American people whom I know personally or have encountered through professional events and media continue to favor the term. Over the course of centuries, their people have appropriated this misnomer and made it a source of pride, which this book will explore. Not all Indigenous people in the United States follow this practice, but my sense is that "Indian" remains the label of choice in most Native circles, as illustrated by its continued use in Native-run institutions like the National Congress of American Indians and *Indian Country Today*. My second reason is that "Indian" remains an official term in United States law and government, as illustrated by the agency name of the Bureau of Indian Affairs and the designation of "Indian country."

For the most part, I use widely familiar tribal names, but readers should be aware that some of those labels are not what Indigenous people call themselves. For example, I refer to the Diné people as Navajos and the Anishinaabeg people as Ojibwes. My reason is that most readers will find the vast range of even common tribal names to be challenging. When I sense that an Indigenous people's preferred name has begun to enter the mainstream, as in the cases of Haudenosaunee (instead of Iroquois) and Ho-Chunk (instead of Winnebago), I employ that term. I favor the tribal plural (the Shawnees) instead of the tribal singular (the Shawnee) to be consistent with the way I refer to other groups of people and to avoid conveying a false sense that tribal groups were centralized polities.

I refer to the Bureau of Indian Affairs variously—Indian Office, Indian Department, Indian Service—in accordance with historical practice, until 1947, when its current name became official.

Any underlined or italicized material within quotation marks appeared thus in the original source. I have also left dates as they appear in the original sources instead of adjusting the dates of the Julian calendar in use among the English before 1752 to fit the modern Gregorian calendar.

I have modernized spelling and punctuation in quotes to allow readers to focus on the meaning of the words rather than their exotic forms.

Citations appear at the end of each paragraph. I have identified the source to which a given quote belongs by including a portion of that quote after the source's page numbers.

INTRODUCTION

A Memorial by the Chosen to the Damned

Imagine yourself as an immigrant from Europe, full of hope and worry, completing the Atlantic crossing to America in the early twentieth century. As your vessel enters New York Harbor, you join the anxious passengers above deck for a first look at the coast of your new home. You scan the horizon and among the first things that catches your eye is that statue, symbolizing the United States' welcome of you into its society of freedom and opportunity. Nowadays, we take for granted that Lady Liberty has always fulfilled that role since her dedication in 1886, but in 1913 a group of White business elites and politicians planned to upstage her with another grand monument, closer to the mouth of the harbor. A towering figure of an Indigenous man would be perched at Fort Wadsworth, at the northeastern tip of Staten Island overlooking the narrows with Brooklyn, to hail incoming ships to shore. It was to be known as the National American Indian Memorial. Congress and two presidents gave their approval, and a ceremonial groundbreaking took place on February 22, 1913, to great fanfare. But it was never built. Nevertheless, this failed project represented the centrality of Native people to White Americans' conceptions of themselves as a superior race and their nation as a vehicle for human progress, regardless of the devastation they had wreaked on an entire continent of Indians.

A bizarre partnership between Rodman Wanamaker, scion of the Wanamaker department store family in Philadelphia and New York, and Joseph K. Dixon, the Wanamaker organization's education director, was the drive behind the memorial. Rodman's father, John, had an abiding fascination for American Indians stemming from his boyhood love of Henry Wadsworth Longfellow's 1855 narrative poem

The Song of Hiawatha. In it, Longfellow tells of the epic adventures and tragic romance of a fictional Ojibwe warrior from the Great Lakes. A purely Indian world unfolds across the generations until the White people's arrival, whereupon the hero bids farewell to his tribe and canoes away toward the setting sun. "Listen to their [the newcomers'] words of wisdom," he intones as he shrinks into the distance. "Listen to the truth they tell you." The meaning for Wanamaker was that White Americans should take pride in their nation's history as the triumph of civilization over savagery while lamenting the awful but necessary toll this progress had taken on Indigenous people. He passed down this lesson and his admiration for Longfellow's classic to Rodman, who, in turn, immersed himself in other legends of White Americans' Manifest Destiny to expand and thrive and Indians' tragic fate to vanish. James Fenimore Cooper's *Last of the Mohicans* and Buffalo Bill Cody's Wild West Shows were among his favorite iterations. The Wanamakers showed their empathy for the supposedly disappearing Indian by employing students from the Carlisle Industrial Indian School at their Philadelphia store during "work outings" designed to assimilate the young Natives into the dominant White society.[1]

Dixon had taken a curious route into the Wanamakers' employ, one that exemplifies that behind the American celebration of the self-made man is the reality that too many of those figures were and are mere hucksters and blowhards. He began his adult life as a Baptist minister until sexual and financial impropriety cost him his career and first marriage. He then became a lecturer for the Eastman Kodak Company, manufacturer of camera equipment and film, which brought him to the Wanamakers' attention and ultimately earned him the directorship of their stores' educational programs. Dixon styled himself an expert on Indians, apparently by virtue of having lived close to the reservations of the Potawatomis, Kickapoos, Iowas, Sauks (or Sacs), Foxes, and Kaws during his higher education at the Leavenworth Normal School in Kansas. It was enough to convince Rodman to sponsor Dixon to lead one photographic expedition after another to Indian country in the name of preserving for the White public the memory of Native people before they were gone altogether. Wanamaker was particularly concerned with enlightening the immigrant masses so visible outside his stores, who, he feared, would drag down the nation unless their social betters schooled them on the historic values that made America great. Indians, or at least Dixon's images of Indians, would be the foundation for that education, just as *The Song of Hiawatha* and other frontier myths had been for the Wanamakers.[2]

In 1908, Dixon's team visited the Crow reservation in Montana to photograph the people's lifeways, or, rather, what Dixon and the White American public fantasized their lifeways to be. Many of the Crows had long since taken up ranching, White people's clothing, and Christianity, but Dixon had his subjects change into ceremonial regalia like feathered headdresses and buckskin leggings to perform for the camera at shooting a bow and arrow, riding horseback, and staring contemplatively into the distance. These were the kinds of activities that, unlike the Indians' actual daily routines, the White public had come to associate with Indian authenticity through anthropology, literature, visual arts, and especially the recent outpouring of Hollywood movies. This perspective defined any of the Indians' adaptations to modern life as cultural loss, including their concessions to unrelenting government efforts to force White ways on them. The catch-22 was that if Indians changed to meet the demands and opportunities of the real world, they would sacrifice their claim to be Indians, and if they refused to do so, they would wither away. Dixon also hired Crows to act in a movie performance of *The Song of Hiawatha*, now set in the Great Plains rather than the Great Lakes. After returning East, Dixon combined this film, his still photos, and a self-written lecture into a single show, which he exhibited to an estimated four hundred thousand people who visited the Wanamaker stores, as well as to children in hundreds of schools across New York City and Philadelphia. Dixon and Rodman Wanamaker interpreted the zeitgeist of the day perfectly. There seemed to be no limit to the White public's craving for pageants of Indian primitiveness, however fictional, as a tonic to America's growing might, urbanization, and industrialization.

Drunk with celebrity, the next year Dixon headed another Wanamaker expedition, this time to stage what he pronounced "The Last Great Indian Council." Assisted by the federal government's Indian Office, Dixon had reservation agents from across the West send twenty-one elderly men, all of whom Dixon styled as chiefs, to meet on the site of the 1876 Battle of the Little Bighorn, also on the Crow reservation, where the Lakotas and Cheyennes had decimated the U.S. Seventh Cavalry commanded by George Armstrong Custer. There were representatives from the Crows, Gros Ventres, Comanches, Northern and Southern Cheyennes, Umatillas, Apaches, Blackfeet, Oglala Lakotas, Yankton Dakotas, and Kiowas. These figures were supposed to sit together in ceremonial regalia, smoke, and reflect on the buffalo days of old, the golden era before the arrival of the White people. Dixon touted this meeting as one last "splendid moment" in which the Natives could be "really Indians again." Then they would make a final peace with one another before riding off into the sunset, literally, while the cameras clicked away. As Dixon framed things, this spectacle would allow White Americans to witness the final example of the genuine Indian warrior, who, when faced with the civilizational choice "to make himself over or die," determined "he would not yield." The book featuring Dixon's photographs projected the result of the Indians' traditionalism. It was titled *The Vanishing Race*.[3]

The day-to-day lives of the councilmen disproved Dixon's maxim "that the Indian, as a race, is fast losing its typical characters and is soon destined to pass completely away." For a number of them, living like a "real Indian" in 1909 meant worshipping in church, working as a policeman, rancher, or farmer, and taking the train to conduct business in Washington, D.C., or other Eastern cities. They had agreed to participate in Dixon's production because they thought it was a diplomatic opportunity to improve their actual *futures*. Pretty Voice Eagle, of the Yankton Dakotas, used the occasion to ask Dixon, whom he misjudged as "a man of influence," to lobby the government to fulfill its treaty obligation "to give us good horses and good wagons." Bull Snake, of the Crows, wanted Dixon to inquire after the status of his government pension. Dixon had no interest in such mundane business. He, like the era's more famous photographer of Indians, Edward S. Curtis, wanted his subjects to conform to the role of unadulterated primitives belonging to the past. The national American myth that Indians were fated by God and nature to waste away before White civilization had no room for actual Indians adapting to modernity. Therefore, the White public either ignored them or dismissed them as inauthentic. Recognition as real Indians required playing to the stereotype.[4]

Joseph K. Dixon's photograph of the Great Council of Chiefs *Skirting the Sky Line* was just one of several images of them fading into the distance. Courtesy of Denver Public Library Western History Collection.

The backing of a who's who of elites for the next Wanamaker and Dixon initiative, the National American Indian Memorial, reflected the nearly universal agreement in White America with these principles. The plan originated at a grand dinner in 1909 hosted by Wanamaker in honor of Buffalo Bill and quickly gained the support of the nation's most powerful men. The project's supervisory committee included such luminaries as former U.S. president Theodore Roosevelt, future president Franklin Delano Roosevelt, railroad magnate Cornelius Vanderbilt, Wall Street baron J. P. Morgan, steel tycoon Andrew Carnegie, newspaper mogul William Randolph Hearst, and author-publisher Ralph Pulitzer. It did not occur to Wanamaker and Dixon to consult actual Indians, but the memorial did receive the endorsement of the Improved Order of Red Men, an elite Whites-only fraternity whose members paraded about in Indian costumes and addressed one another using faux Indian titles. President William Howard Taft's approval led Congress to pass a bill in 1911 setting aside land at Fort Wadsworth, on Staten Island, for the venture. The stipulation, however, was that the memorial should be built exclusively with private funds. That requirement would prove to be the scheme's undoing.[5]

These grandees backed Wanamaker and Dixon because they, like the overwhelming majority of White Americans, shared the ideology that God had damned Indians to extinction to make way for His chosen people, the Whites of the United States. Now that the process was almost complete, it was left to Whites to carry on the Indians' nobler virtues in their stead. In other words, the conquerors, as an act of charity and nobility, would claim the identity of the conquered and thereby become small-*n* native Americans themselves. As Dixon explained in his characteristically melodramatic prose, "the original Americans deserve a monument. They have moved majestically down the pathway of the ages, but it culminates in the dead march of Saul." Consequently, "our only hope, if we wish to keep the Indian, is to carve a statue of him in stone, or mold his figure in bronze." Dixon's vision was for the memorial to include a classical Greek-style building containing a museum of Indian artifacts, his photographs, and a research library. A life-size statue of a Plains Indian warrior on horseback would stand at the lower end of a long staircase leading to the entrance of the museum, which itself would be flanked by two statues of bison, that other vanishing American icon. The main feature would be a 165-foot-tall male Indian in bronze standing on a pedestal resembling an Aztec pyramid rising out of the museum. The Indian's left hand would hang at his side gripping a bow and arrow, to symbolize "that he is through with his war weaponry." The right hand would reach upward "with the two fingers extended toward the open sea" in "the universal peace sign of the Indian."

Dixon's proposed design for the National American Indian Memorial. From the cover of *Ceremonies Attending the Official Inauguration of the National American Indian Memorial at Fort Wadsworth, Harbor of New York, February 22, 1913* (n.p.).

It was supposed to represent the Indians' "perpetual welcome to the white man when he first came to these shores."[6]

The notion that Indians had conceded to European colonization so the newcomers could later form the United States had become a stock feature of White American public memory by the early twentieth century. It was the basis of the myth of the first Thanksgiving, in which friendly Indians take the Pilgrims into their care, seal the relationship with a feast, and then fade into the mist. In the Mid-Atlantic, the equivalent tale was of the Delaware Indians' peacefully ceding their country to Pennsylvania's Quaker founder, William Penn. In the South, it was the young Powhatan princess, Pocahontas, saving the Englishman John Smith from execution at the hands of her chieftain father and thereby allowing the colony of Virginia to continue. In the West, it was another Indian maiden, Sacajawea, guiding the Lewis and Clark expedition to the Pacific to permit the United States to claim the continent from sea to shining sea. These stories were so foundational to White people's sense of national history that they all appeared in the art of the United States Capitol rotunda. The point of the National American Indian Memorial was to introduce generations of new Americans, just as they were about to set foot in the country, to the legend of Indians peacefully conceding to colonialism. As Rodman Wanamaker explained to Taft, the great Indian statue would serve as a beacon "to all those coming to this land of liberty and freedom, recognizing also the welcome which the Red Man gave to the White Man when our forefathers first came to these shores."[7]

The problem, of course, was squaring this fairy tale with the colossal violence that had accompanied White expansion across America. The solution offered by American cultural productions, ranging from the scholarship of the historian Frederick Jackson Turner to scores of Hollywood films, was that the frontier struggle to tame the wilderness and the savages had transformed effete European settlers into intrepid, individualistic Americans. In other words, Indians, even in their resistance, had contributed to the greatness of White America. Part of Wanamaker's urgency to expose recent immigrants to this creed was that few of them thought of themselves or others in the racial terms that Americans took for granted. To become true Americans, they needed to learn that they were White people; that Whites, by virtue of their superiority, now dominated the continent and its darker-hued populations, particularly Blacks; and that Indians had for the most part vanished as part of God's will "in the name of progress," as Wanamaker's hero, Buffalo Bill, so often put it.[8]

The memorial's groundbreaking dramatized these ideas just as assuredly as the structure was supposed to embody them. Held in drizzling rain on George Washington's birthday, the event featured Taft, in the final days of his presidency, as the main guest of honor, joined by members of his cabinet, the governor of New York State, the mayor of New York City, military officers, and many other eminent invited guests. Several chiefs from Dixon's Last Indian Council were there, too, along with some other Indians who had interrupted tribal business in Washington, D.C., to attend. Taft's speech, given in full view of the Native guests, praised the monument as "perpetuating the memory of the succession from the red to the white race in the ownership of the Western Hemisphere." It was "the story of the march of empire westward and the progress of Christian civilization." Taft finished by digging up one scoop of dirt with a silver spade provided by Rodman Wanamaker, and then another with an ancient Indian stone axe previously excavated from the site. Next up was the Northern Cheyenne elder Wooden Leg, whose shovel was a buffalo thigh bone brought in from the Plains. The Indian delegates then sang a war song (which one, from which tribe, the accounts do not say), and signed or marked a pledge of allegiance to the United

States to express their supposed agreement that "the Indian is fast losing his identity in the face of the great waves of Caucasian civilization, which are extending to the four winds of the country, and we want fuller knowledge, in order that we may take our places in the civilization which surrounds us." Finally, the Indians hoisted Old Glory while a military band played a song specially composed by the Wanamaker stores' musical director, Irvin Morgan. He titled it "The Indians' Requiem," a genre usually meant to be played at a Mass for the dead. Symbolically, Dixon and Wanamaker had roped the Indian delegates into performing at their own funeral.[9]

The proceedings were also an opportunity for White people to congratulate themselves for their magnanimity in triumph. As the event's printed program asked rhetorically, where else but America would such an edifice be built "by a civilized nation to a race of primitive people"? The victors' nobility toward the vanquished might very well have been unprecedented. "So far as can be learned," Dixon waxed, "never before in the history of mankind has a monument been erected to a race of people," never mind a conquered one.[10]

Indians at the groundbreaking showed no interest in ushering in their own demise or applauding White people for erecting an Indian statue as compensation for their destruction of so many actual Indians. Austin Red Hawk, an Oglala Lakota, delivered a speech about "my strong belief that we," Indians, "were created by the Great Spirit to live in this country," contrary to the ceremony's insistence on their doom. White people had long argued that God destined them, as civilized Christians, to spread at the expense of Indian savages. Indians across the centuries had countered that the Creator had made Indians and Whites separately and put them each on their own continent to follow their distinctive ways of life. Therefore, Whites should return to Europe or, at the very least, leave Indians alone, and Indians should shun the White people's culture as pollution. Red Hawk refrained from elaborating those points given the spirit of the occasion, but his Indian counterparts would have understood the reference.[11]

The Indian representatives also rejected White characterizations of them as primitive relics by spending the day after the proceedings in a tour of New York City, taking the subway to the American Museum of Natural History, the Bronx Zoo, Grand Central Terminal, and the Woolworth Building, and then a ferry to the Statue of Liberty. They even witnessed a firehouse drill. Everywhere they went, crowds followed, jostling to catch a look at "real Indians." For Whites, one of the purposes of hosting such delegations was to overawe Indians with the scale, wealth, and power of American society, but sometimes the efforts backfired. In this case, one unidentified member of the Native troupe found it sad that such an obviously rich community had paved over so much green earth. The implication was that perhaps Whites stood to learn as much from Indians as Indians did from them.[12]

Later that week, the Native delegates visited the Office of Indian Affairs in Washington, D.C., where they made it clear that they saw the groundbreaking as a diplomatic council rather than as the last rite for their race. The Crow chief, Plenty Coups, told Commissioner Frederick H. Abbott, in English, that he thought the event was meant to symbolize "it is friendship from now on." The Brulé Lakota chief Hollow Horn Bear, a veteran of the Battle of the Little Bighorn, believed the point was to demonstrate that the "open road for happiness and prosperity among my people is to join hands with the white brother, and receive into our own lives the civilization and education that he offers and join with our white brothers in supporting the flag." He conceded that this agenda was the only way forward given that "the white people" had "driven me into certain places, the reservations, small places where I am penned up." The Blackfeet leader, Mountain Chief, who in 1871 had been the intended target of a massacre by American troops, hoped participation in the groundbreaking would serve "as our protection," which the tribes expected but rarely received from the United States despite its treaty obligations. He also complained that there was too much turnover among reservation agents and in the federal Indian Office, which made it difficult to cultivate and sustain productive relationships. Clearly, none of these men thought their people were about to ride off into the sunset.[13]

The sharpest criticism of the memorial came from the Society of American Indians (SAI), a recently founded organization of formally educated, professional Indians who largely favored dismantling the reservations and encouraging Indians to assimilate into White society while retaining pride in their Native heritage. They saw the memorial, and all the rhetoric of Indian primitiveness and imminent extinction surrounding it, as a rejection of their progressive examples, never mind of the history of the United States brutally subjugating Native people and forcing White civilization and Christianity on them. The Seneca anthropologist Arthur C. Parker wrote in the society's journal that "the irony of building a gigantic statue to a race of men who have been so grossly injured by the evils of civilization cannot but be apparent to those who think even superficially." To him, the whole exercise was "a flagrant insult." The SAI's Chauncey Yellow Robe, a Brulé educator, likewise denounced the memorial as a "degrading, demoralizing, and degenerating" romanticization of savagery, akin to stereotypes of Indians in the movies and Wild West shows. He took even greater offense at the depiction of Indians as a disappearing race when they were struggling and sometimes succeeding at recovering from the damage the United States had inflicted on them. "The Indian wants no such memorial monument," proclaimed an indignant Yellow Robe, "for he is not yet dead."[14]

Precious few White Americans, Dixon foremost among them, were open to this critique given how central the idea of Indians being damned to extinction was to their self-conception as a White nation of chosen people. Furthermore, Dixon, like so many other cultural producers, profited by trafficking in imagery of vanishing Indians, in his case through the sale of his photographs, his books, and tickets to his shows. To that end, he followed up the groundbreaking with an audacious plan for a new photographic expedition to Indian country. Traveling by private train, Dixon and his team would visit eighty-nine reservations over the course of six months, beginning in Oklahoma, across the Southwest to California, up the coast to the Pacific Northwest, and then back east across the Rocky Mountains, North-Central Plains, and Great Lakes before concluding in New York. At each stop, the reservation agent would have Indians dressed in regalia raise the stars and stripes from the groundbreaking at Fort Wadsworth and sign their own pledge of allegiance to the United States. Next, they would hear patriotic pep talks by Rodman Wanamaker and President Woodrow Wilson played on a phonograph donated by Thomas Edison, and an in-person lecture by Dixon. Finally, they would lower the original flag and raise a new one to fly over the reservation forever more. Dixon imagined that this pageantry would inculcate Indians with loyalty to the United States and represent the country's commitment to "justice and fair play to the Indian." He went so far as to claim that the flag-raising ceremony would change the very "destiny of a whole race of people" and establish Rodman's reputation as the Abraham Lincoln of the Indians. Of course, Dixon would capture it all on film to drum up donations for the memorial.[15]

Several Indians refused to follow Dixon's script, some because they feared this private expedition was an official event to trick them into surrendering yet more of their territory. After all, reservation agents were involved, and the proceedings centered on an American flag, a recording of President Wilson, and a swearing of fealty to the United States. Furthermore, accompanying Dixon was Major James McLaughlin of the Department of the Interior, who had overseen several Indian land cessions, earning him the nickname "the man who goes around bothering his friends for more land." Other Indians believed that the ceremony would make them citizens, which most of them still were not because acquiring that status first required them

"Rodman Wanamaker" (actually Joseph K. Dixon) and the Great Council of Chiefs at the groundbreaking for the National American Indian Memorial, Fort Wadsworth, New York, February 22, 1913. Courtesy of Library of Congress.

From left to right: Cheyenne chief Wooden Leg, Cheyenne chief Two Moons, Joseph K. Dixon (though credited as Rodman Wanamaker), Crow chief Plenty Coups, Crow chief Medicine Crow, Crow Indian White Man Runs Him, Oglala Sioux chief Jack Red Cloud, and two unidentified headdressed men.

to receive an agent's approval that they were versed enough in White ways to take up reservation land as private property. In fact, the blanket granting of citizenship to Indians would not take place until 1924, sometimes over the opposition of Native people who saw it as a breach of tribal sovereignty and an unwanted tax burden.[16]

Dixon anticipated grateful Indians welcoming him at every reservation, but instead many Natives were indifferent, obstructive, or committed to their own agendas. At one of the expedition's first stops, at Pawhuska, Oklahoma, the Osages grew so bored with the preliminary speechifying that half of them left before the actual flag raising took place. The Kickapoos refused Dixon's instruction to bow their heads in fealty before the outstretched American banner so he could take their photo. Few Indians could be found at reservations along Puget Sound because they were off taking advantage of the season's fish runs. In any case, the Tulalip agent explained, there was no chance of convincing them to appear in regalia because "the pageantry and romance of paint and feathers has passed away from our Indians long ago . . . The primitive costume is not now to be seen, much less worn." Plenty of Navajos attended Dixon's ceremony but spent their time complaining that the reservation agent,

"Flag-raising ceremony," Crow Creek Reservation, South Dakota, October 5, 1913. Courtesy of Indiana University Museum of Archaeology and Anthropology and the Trustees of Indiana University, Item 1974-44-4386.

backed by 125 cavalrymen, had recently "forced his way into their homes, taking boys and girls prisoners, and marching them off to school"—so much for Dixon's claim about the country's justice and fair play toward Indians. The greatest pushback came at Isleta Pueblo, where the leaders protested "that they received more kindness, justice, and sincere treatment under the Mexican flag than under the American flag, that they preferred the Mexican flag."[17]

Formally educated Indians denounced the expedition as nothing more than a racist publicity stunt. The student newspaper of the Chilocco Indian School in Oklahoma charged that Dixon's main purpose was to stage pictures of old primitives, not to improve Indian lives. Arthur C. Parker agreed, disparaging Dixon as a "circus manager" of a "theatrical affair" having nothing to do with real Indian life but just "a white man's ideas." Joseph Craig, a Cayuse from Oregon, wanted Dixon to quit popularizing the image of Indians as relics and instead tell that they "refuse to die." The key to a better future for Native America had less to do with Indians changing than for "the white man" to give them "common justice."[18]

No Shirt, the leader of the Walla Walla people of Washington State, had tried to voice his criticism of White Americans' treatment of Indians when the flag-raising expedition reached his reservation, but Dixon refused to let him speak. Instead, No Shirt had the reservation agent put his speech to paper for delivery to the Commissioner of Indian Affairs. In it, he shared his people's belief that the Creator would destroy the world someday, an idea that had periodically galvanized Indians in the Pacific Northwest since at least White Americans' first appearance among them. Showing the clear influence of Christian teachings, No Shirt believed that these end times would include a day of judgment on which the Creator would ask, "Where is the red man that I once created?" White people, No Shirt predicted, would answer "that the red men are ignorant while they were living on earth, that they do not deserve the enjoyment, that they should all be condemned," just as they so often said about Indians in the here and now. But the Creator would chastise the Whites, "Everyone was created by me, that no one should be condemned by another person, except myself." The point, No Shirt stressed, was that "I, the red man, should respect you, and you, the white men, should respect us . . . I have as [much] right to live in this world as you have." That respect included honoring one another's distinct ways of life, as the Creator intended. No Shirt, like so many other Indigenous people, agreed with White Americans that Indians and Whites belonged to different races, but rejected the premise that these races were hierarchically ranked, or at least that Whites were superior. As such, he would not raise Dixon's flag.[19]

Dixon's plans for the National American Indian Memorial went nowhere, despite the Wanamakers' vast outlays on the expeditions to Indian country and Dixon's thousands of photographs, dozens of miles of movie footage, countless lectures, and boundless bombast. White people gradually tired of Dixon's act, and then World War I diverted their attention from him entirely. The showman had hoped to raise $1.5 million for his memorial, but by 1922 his fund contained a measly $143.10. Though Rodman could have easily made up the difference, his interest had shifted to the design of flying boats that would allow businessmen like him to travel between America and Europe with ease. In effect, the flag-raising expedition was Dixon's last claim to fame. Afterward, he was the one who vanished into obscurity. Indians remained, committed to their futures despite the oblivion toward which Whites were so eager to usher them.[20]

We should resist the temptation to dismiss the National American Indian Memorial as little more than the quixotic fantasy of a self-promoter with a fabulously wealthy patron, and instead take seriously the view of its supporters that it would symbolize dominant American values and the arc of American history. We should also heed Indian opposition to these principles. The racial terminology and viewpoints that permeated discussions of the project were the result of three centuries of genocidal struggle between Native Americans and Euro-Americans, and they would continue to resonate for a century afterward amid equally dire conditions.

The most convincing framework for understanding the historic relationship between the White conquest of Native America and race-making is a field of academic inquiry known as Settler Colonial Studies. This school of thought has been criticized (justifiably, in my view) for some of its proponents' furious and even antisemitic castigations of Israel as the modern embodiment of colonial evils, but those extremes should not negate this theory's important contributions to understandings of race-making. Associated most closely with the scholarship of the late anthropologist Patrick Wolfe, Settler Colonial Studies makes a critical distinction between two types of colonies. It defines "extractive" or "franchise colonies," such as most European colonies in nineteenth- and twentieth-century Africa and southern Asia, as those in which the imperial power plunders a foreign land's wealth while leaving its Indigenous population in place as labor. Then there are "settler colonies," to which an imperial nation sends colonists (or settlers) to displace the Indigenous people and seize their land. The goal (or project) of settler colonies, in other words, is to eliminate the Natives in order to take their territory, whether by removing them, exterminating them, subjugating and absorbing them, or, in the case of the United States, a combination thereof.[21]

Settler colonial societies justify this land-driven exploitation by inventing racial ideologies that posit their own people's superiority and the Natives' inferiority. When the process of elimination is more or less complete, the settlers appropriate Indigenous identity (think of Indian sports team monikers and Halloween costumes in the United States) as the final stage of making the conquest seem natural or God-ordained.

Settler Colonial Studies posits that the multifaceted process of Native elimination in the United States should be understood as structural genocide. I agree. Given that some readers will find my use of the term "genocide" to be jarring and even offensive because the American events in question did not take the form of the most familiar example of this crime against humanity, the Nazis' quick industrial mass murder of Jews during World War II, here I wish to pause to explain my thinking.

Let us first come to a shared understanding of this loaded word. The term "genocide" was coined during World War II by the Polish lawyer Raphael Lemkin to describe Nazi atrocities. His lobbying, combined with an international commitment to prevent future horrors of this kind, led to the United Nations' 1948 Convention on the Prevention and Punishment of the Crime of Genocide. The convention, with the United States as a signatory, agreed on an official definition of that crime, which read:

> Genocide means any of the following acts committed with intent to destroy, in whole or in part, a national, ethnical, racial or religious group, as such:
>
> (a) Killing members of the group;
> (b) Causing serious bodily or mental harm to members of the group;
> (c) Deliberately inflicting on the group conditions of life calculated to bring about its physical destruction in whole or in part;
> (d) Imposing measures intended to prevent births within the group;
> (e) Forcibly transferring children of the group to another group.

Lemkin argued that genocide had taken place in innumerable colonial contexts, including North America. A growing corpus of carefully reasoned, thoroughly documented studies supports his contention, though the issue is still a matter of dispute.[22]

There is a scholarly consensus that the United States and its citizens perpetrated at least several discrete genocidal acts against Indigenous people, but some scholars refute that these events constituted a program, largely because there was never an explicit imperial or national policy to wipe out Indigenous people entirely. I see things differently. Consider, for instance, the following long list of mortal actions and inactions committed against Indians by White Americans and their governments over the course of four centuries, all of which I discuss in this book: waging total war with the express purpose of exterminating one Native society after another; forcibly removing tens of thousands of Eastern Indians from their homelands without adequate resources for their welfare during the journey West despite widely reported results in the early stages of this fifteen-year process that about a quarter of them would die along the way; purposefully decimating the bison to starve recalcitrant Indians—including women, children, and the elderly— onto federal reservations; failing to provide adequate food, medical care, housing, clothing, and opportunity on these reservations in full knowledge that these conditions led to widespread economic destitution, ill health, and early death; seizing Indians' vast lands based on the promise of smaller protected reservations, then breaking up those reservations into private property tracts and dissolving tribal governments even after it was clear that these policies led to pervasive Indian homelessness and even more abject poverty, malnutrition, and premature death;

seizing Indian children from their families and restricting them to White supremacist boarding schools with the stated purpose of alienating them from their tribes, cultural heritage, and loved ones; creating conditions in those schools that produced alarming rates of malnutrition, deadly disease, and abuse, and failing to reform even in the face of critical investigations; tolerating the widely reported decades-long pattern of Whites in the towns and counties bordering reservations poaching the Indians' resources, preying on their addictions, raping the women, subjecting them to abusive police violence, and sometimes even murdering them in the open; more generally, subjugating Indians to White authority and then failing to extend them the protection of the law, which is most glaring today in the crisis of missing and murdered Indigenous women; the federal government, energy companies, and mining corporations consciously poisoning the environments of reservations across the country during the Cold War, resulting in the early deaths of untold numbers of people and shocking health disorders among survivors; failing, to this very day, to clean up many of the leftover Superfund sites from these activities; in the mid- to late twentieth century, using social services to remove Indian children from their families at rates that eclipsed any other American population based on racial double standards, then fostering or adopting those children to Whites in awareness that the children would be alienated from tribal society and despite the high risk of physical, sexual, and psychological abuse; sterilizing as many as a quarter of Native women of childbearing age who sought care from federal Indian Health Service hospitals and their contracting partners in the 1970s and possibly earlier, often by threatening to take the women's existing children from them, and sometimes without the women's consent; and covering up the totality of this sordid history by reducing it to an act of Manifest Destiny or, more recently in several states and at federal military academies, banning the teaching of the subject altogether because it makes some White people uncomfortable.[23]

    I dissent from the argument that because there was never an explicit consensus among national leaders to exterminate the entire race of Indians, therefore the aforementioned pattern of atrocities did not constitute a genocide. As we shall see, in every one of these examples, White authorities and American society as a whole had ample information about the harm their actions and inactions were doing to Indians, and rarely did anything about it. That apathy extended from the view, evident in the campaign for the National American Indian Memorial, that Indians were damned to extinction and thus any harm they suffered in the interests of God's chosen people, White Americans, was just fate. Equally important, there were almost always perpetrators at every rank of American society who openly advocated for eliminating Native people, not just as tribes, but as a race, almost always with an eye toward seizing their land. People with such genocidal views have exercised very real power in the United States, including in shaping the country's racial discourse, throughout much of its history. It is a wrenching but critical lesson that every citizen should confront.[24]

There are almost as many definitions of race as there are studies of race, but the one I find most compelling is from the sisters Karen E. Fields and Barbara J. Fields, the first a sociologist and the second a historian. The Fieldses describe race as "the conception or the doctrine that nature produced humankind in distinct groups, each defined by inborn traits that its members share and that differentiate them from members of other distinct groups of the same kind but unequal rank." They stress that race is no more than "folk belief," not science, and, thus, there is no such thing outside of human imagination as "accurate racial identity," "racial mixture," "unmixed race," or "racial purity." As we shall see in this book, the "folk belief" of race existed among European settlers and Native Americans well before the rise of biological race science in the nineteenth century. During the seventeenth century, it existed even before Europeans began calling themselves Whites and Natives began calling themselves Indians. What made these early folk beliefs racial was the contention that opposed groups of people were innately, not just culturally, different and irreconcilable.[25]

Whereas race is a human fiction, racism is quite real. The Fieldses define racism as "the theory and the practice of applying a social, civic, or legal double standard based on ancestry and the ideology surrounding such a double standard . . . Racism is first and foremost a social practice, which means that it is an action and a rationale for action, or both at once." Note the emphasis here on the circular relationship between racial thought and racism. Racial thought justifies racism, which, in turn, produces the unequal results that seem to confirm invented racial categories. In other words, the action (racism) produces evidence of the imagined thing (race).[26]

Over time, this mutualism contributes to making race appear natural and, therefore, results in its being taken for granted or unquestioned. This is when race becomes, as race theorists put it, hegemonic. Think, for example, of the widespread and longstanding assumption in American society that Indians are unsuited for modernity or even extinct, which is partially a result of Whites relegating tribal societies to remote reservations, robbing them of their most profitable resources, and repeatedly depicting them in popular culture in antiquated feathered headdresses and on horseback. Think also of the historic White assumption of Black inferiority, which justified policies and customs that relegated Blacks to inferior segregated education, housing, and jobs, and permitted the White majority to exploit Blacks with impunity. White racial ideology then blamed Black inferiority for the resulting high rates of poverty, unemployment, crime, broken families, and low education. The cause of this inequality was racism, not race, but ingrained racial ideology reversed people's sense of causation and led them to accept it as simply the inherent order of things.[27]

Indoctrinating people with racial ideology conditions them to take for granted one group's privilege and another's degradation, even destruction. As this book will discuss, sometimes the spreading of racial ideas was explicit, as in political movements, calls to arms, religious preaching, science, education, and literary and visual arts. At other times, the messaging was more subtle. For instance, having Indians segregated on isolated, impoverished reservations taught that they were not meant for modernity, whereas Whites were. Society's expectation that Indians, like Blacks, should behave deferentially toward Whites, or, for that matter, that White police could and should treat any Indian in a White neighborhood as a potential criminal, reinforced White superiority and Indian inferiority without requiring anything to be said. The same went for repeatedly seeing Indians in menial jobs or selling trinkets on the street at tourist sites, and Whites practically monopolizing all forms of prestigious employment. The cumulative effect was to make these arrangements seem like the God-given order of things. Race might be instrumental—invented and maintained by human beings to achieve their worldly ends, such as, in the White American case, land—but its operation in society is so multivalent that its believers are often unaware of its function or how it came to be. This book tells that intertwined story.

At the onset of the colonial era, European settlers did not yet conceive of themselves as Whites, but as Christians. Their transition to a racial identity would require decades of violent campaigning to subjugate Native people and appropriate their territory, multiple largely unsuccessful missionary campaigns, and the development of a slave system in which Euro-Americans initially targeted Indians as well as Africans. Racial thinking was also a response to Indians and Blacks becoming Christian in sufficient numbers to challenge Europeans' exclusive claim to that status. Colonists and their descendants defined being White as having the privilege, by virtue of embodying Christianity and civility, to lord it in these ways over Indians and Blacks, Christian or otherwise.

Yet Europeans already had the label "Indians" to apply to Indigenous people from the start of colonization. Furthermore, they possessed a firm conviction that the Native American way of life was savage. First and foremost, Indians worshipped what Europeans considered to be false gods, at best, and the Devil, at worst. To Christian Europeans, it followed that Indian life was full of sinful behaviors. For instance, the Natives' lack of private property and generous sharing of resources, while admirably charitable, discouraged the hard work that led to personal accumulation, and thus produced sloth. Indian men seemed the laziest of the lot because their main duty was to hunt, which Europeans viewed as a leisure activity, while Native women labored at cultivating crops (a male responsibility in Europe) and raising children. Furthermore, Europeans judged that Indians had no law, given their lack of a formal judicial system and written rules, and therefore weak standards of morality, most evident in the Indians' sexual liberty. Europeans denounced Indian warfare as cowardly and cruel because it featured guerrilla raids, mutilation (particularly scalping) of the dead and dying, and taking of captives for torture (particularly in the cases of men) and forced adoption (especially in the cases of women and children). To Europeans, the gulf between their own civility and Christianity and the Indians' savagery and paganism seemed cavernous.

The question was whether it could be bridged. From the very beginning of the colonial era well into the twentieth century, settlers debated if Indians were capable, by their very "nature," of Christian, civilized living under White law. The answer yes meant that Indians were entitled to the protection of their lives and at least some of their land. There were always religious and political elites at a safe distance from the bloody warfare of the frontier who insisted that Indians could and should change. They also considered it to be the moral duty of Whites, as cultural superiors, to force this transformation. Their goal was to eliminate Indian communities as distinct cultural entities and eventually as political ones, too, while preserving and absorbing Indigenous people as individuals. By contrast, frontier settlers, who had the greatest desire to conquer Native territory, repeatedly denounced this vision as not only naïve but also dangerous because it promoted empathy for a savage enemy. Living as they did on the front lines of ferocious Indian resistance to equally vicious colonial land lust, White frontiersmen rejected the ability of Indians to shed their supposed barbarity. Instead, they called for the Natives' outright extermination, going so far as to argue that God himself had damned Indians to make way for His chosen people, White civilized Christians. They dismissed Christian Indians as fakes who used their disguise to act as spies and subversives. Therefore, they, too, had to die. When White authorities opposed the indiscriminate slaughter of Indians, sometimes frontiersmen rebelled against them, as occurred repeatedly during the colonial and early national eras and sometimes even later.

Throughout the entire four centuries discussed by this book, Whites disagreed among themselves about whether culture or bodily essence was responsible for the supposed inferiority of Indian people and imagined superiority of Whites. Even individuals were inconsistent about where they stood, sometimes in a single conversation. Consequently, it is impossible to locate a time when most of American society held one view or the other, though there were fleeting moments when one opinion or another was ascendant enough to shape policy. The more important point is the persistence of the tension itself. The narrow spectrum of White opinion, with exterminationists on one side and White supremacist assimilationists on the other, encouraged culturalists, racists, and people in between to accommodate one another. They were able to do so because, they fundamentally concurred that Whites were superior to Indians (whether culturally or innately), Whites were entitled to seize more or less whatever Indian land they wanted, and Indians could either accept White rule and adopt White culture or face the dire consequences.

Though the violent racial genocide advocated by frontiersmen never became universally accepted in White society, it drew widespread support, particularly in wartime, even among elites. Politicians who courted Western votes and/or had speculative profits at stake in displacing Indians from their territory either encouraged the mob or at least stayed out of the way. Calls to exterminate Indians sometimes emanated from the highest ranks of the military, never mind among common troops. In every era, there were newspapermen, novelists, and other shapers of public opinion, in the East as well as the West, who whipped up passions in favor of destroying Indians. Some ministers demonized Indians as biblical Canaanites whom White Christians, as God's new Israelites, were permitted to destroy. In the nineteenth century, some university scientists even adopted the frontiersmen's view that Whites and Indians were fundamentally different, with Whites destined to prosper and rule, and Indians doomed to extinction. Historians tend to emphasize how American elites created race through their influence over the law, law enforcement, religion, and formal knowledge. This approach makes sense when the subject is Black slavery and segregation, because rich White planters and their allies did indeed exercise enormous formal power to institutionalize race in accordance with their economic interests. But when it came to Indians, lower-class Whites living on the Western margins were the drivers of race-making because they had the greatest economic and security stakes in it. The general trend was of educated elites following the lead of the bigoted masses.

Indigenous people, for their part, had no conception of themselves as "Indians" or of the newcomers as "Whites" when the colonial era began. Yet they would also adopt this terminology as they began to perceive colonists and then White Americans as a unified threat to a shared Indigenous way of life. In other words, Indian resistance to colonial domination was a spur to race-making among Indians and settlers alike.

Native people's definitions of "Indian" and "White," however, rarely followed those of Euro-Americans. Across time and space, Indians defending their autonomy, lands, and even lives argued, like No Shirt, that the Creator put different kinds of people on different continents to follow their special destinies. Therefore, Indians should enjoy the liberty to live in their own way on their own land independent from White people. Indians widely castigated Whites as Christian hypocrites consumed by greed, underhandedness, and violence. The pattern of Whites persecuting even Christian Indian allies was their most powerful piece of evidence. Some Indians went so far as to claim that ancient Native values made them better Christians, or just better people, than Whites.

Whereas these features of the American debate over race had emerged as early as the seventeenth century, White people's contention that they were chosen by God to dominate the continent and that Indians were damned to extinction, so evident at the memorial groundbreaking, was barely a hundred years old. The first signs of it appeared during the era of the Revolution and the early republic, when White Americans' expansionism led them to declare that if Indians did not become Christian and civilized and accept the jurisdiction of the United States, Whites were entitled to drive them out by any means necessary, including extermination. Yet the United States did not yet possess the strength to fulfill this bluster, for though it boasted three to four million people, compared to the low hundreds of thousands of Indians east of the Mississippi, poor finances and poorer internal navigation limited its military reach west of the Appalachian Mountains. By the late 1820s and '30s, however, the United States had both the numbers and the means to force nearly the entire Indian population to the west of the Mississippi. Proponents of Indian Removal, under the leadership of President Andrew Jackson, devised a new racial rationale positing that the vulnerabilities of savage Indians meant they would degenerate into drunken poverty and go extinct if allowed to remain in contact with superior White civilization. Therefore, forcing Indians West was for *the Indians'* own good, rather than just good for White profits. As ever, a parallel argument was that God wanted his chosen people, Whites, to possess the land in the interest of spreading Christianity and civility. Some Indians pleaded that many of them were already civilized Christians, that they were willing to live surrounded by Whites if they could continue to do so under their own governments, and that the United States had pledged in formal treaties to honor their boundaries. Others revived the old argument that the Great Spirit never intended for Indians to adopt White norms in the first place, but instead willed them to remain on their ancestral lands to live in their ancestral fashion. None of it mattered as long as Whites wanted their land.

By the mid-nineteenth century, Whites were also overrunning the western half of the continent. In this phase of the conquest, specifically during the U.S. wars against Mexico and the Plains tribes, Whites refashioned the belief that they were chosen and Indians were damned into a new form, Manifest Destiny. It held that the Lord willed White Americans not only to expand but also to possess the entire continent of North America and even territory beyond so they could spread Christianity, democracy, and economic opportunity. Any resulting Indian and Mexican losses were a necessary sacrifice for this civilizational progress. Given that the option no longer existed to remove Indians west, the only way to avoid a catastrophe, White policymakers contended, was to force Indians onto reservations, protected islands of Indian land amid a sea of Whites. The rationale, like the argument for Jacksonian Indian Removal, was that Indians in contact with Whites either suffered a quick, violent death at the hands of settlers or a slow descent into poverty, alcoholism, and dispiritedness because they could not cope with the challenges of civilization. Reservations would not only shield Indians from those destructive forces but also provide them with the instruction and material resources to become Christian and civilized themselves, which was their only hope to survive in the long run. If the Natives resisted confinement to reservations, Whites would eradicate them, for they were a threat to White settlers and destined to perish anyway amid the crush of White society.

Shortly, Western Whites coveted reservation land as well, and just as assuredly this greed, coupled with Eastern humanitarian impulses, gave rise to a new instrumental racial argument: Whites had the duty to force Indians to conform to civilization because otherwise they would waste away until extinct. This program involved shipping Indian children to boarding schools for brutal lessons in assimilation, dividing the Indians' communal reservations into smaller private-property tracts and selling the surplus to Whites, and dissolving tribal governments in favor of putting Indians under the direct authority of Whites. White advocates of this experiment rationalized that if forced assimilation resulted in Indian poverty and death, the fault was the Natives' own inherent inferiority, for God and reason demanded a Christian, civilized society of private property and democratic law to triumph over savagery. If the Indians successfully assimilated, they would no longer be known as Indians but as Whites. Either way, Indians were destined to disappear. These ideas continued to resonate in 1913 at the National American Indian Memorial groundbreaking less because men like Dixon and Wanamaker wanted Indian land for themselves than because their society's culture had encouraged them from childhood to think this way. Racial ideology allowed White Americans to make sense of the stunning contrast between their power and population, which had reached one hundred million people and stretched across North America, and the sorry condition of American Indians, who had fallen to a nadir of barely two hundred thousand, down from many millions when the colonial period began, without having to confront the responsibility of their society past and present.[28]

Throughout the twentieth century, Indians regrouped and marshaled their own racial arguments to counter the White insistence that they were inevitably bound for extinction or assimilation. Some of them wielded the old argument of separate divine race creations and destinies. Others moderated that the best choice was for Native people to bend to unavoidable White pressures without breaking with cherished traditions, values, tribal loyalty, and their relatively new sense of Indian identity. Elite Indians educated in boarding schools that had been dedicated to destroying Indian identity and culture came out of the experience, ironically, with an education and perspective that empowered them to form national organizations dedicated to fostering Indian race pride. Later in the century, young Native activists and lawyers would rally around the principle of Red Power to assert tribal sovereignty as a moral and constitutional right and the need for Indigenous people to embrace their cultural heritages and racial identities. They also aspired to awaken White people to the dark truths of the United States' centuries-long assault on their people.

Despite attributing Indian decline to God's plan or nature, generations of White Americans have been responsible for numerous explicit extermination campaigns against Indigenous people, subjugation of Native people to servitude and slavery, destruction of Native economies, traffic in liquor, environmental devastation of Indian country, and unwillingness to treat subjugated Native people with basic justice and dignity. They also played a significant indirect role in the Indians' decimation by epidemic diseases, so often cited as evidence that Indian population collapse was a faultless accident. For instance, there are only a few (though some) documented cases of Whites intentionally spreading epidemic diseases like smallpox among Native people, but Whites were the main vectors. Furthermore, the strains of colonial expansion on Native people (such as malnutrition, the crowding of Indians into defensive sites and refugee camps, and the linking of far-flung communities through the trades of fur and Indian slaves) contributed to lethal outbreaks of epidemic disease. The subsequent reduction of Native populations was a significant precondition to conquest and a factor in White people's sense of superiority. Likewise, Whites were not the main cause of destructive intertribal wars, but they often encouraged these conflicts in a strategy of divide and conquer, and the weaponry they traded to Indians contributed mightily to the loss of life. One of the purposes of racial ideology was to obviate all these horrors and absolve Whites of their role in them.[29]

Racial ideology and the White exploitation of Native people were mutually reinforcing. If God intended Whites to possess the land to spread civilization, and Indians to disappear to make way, then for Whites to denigrate and despoil Indians and dismantle their tribes was just fate running its course. The resulting destitution of Native people, in turn, justified further abuse of them because it served as evidence that they did not belong in the modern world. The position of some Native people in favor of assimilation, as represented by the Society of American Indians during the project to build the National American Indian Memorial, was an emergency response to the very real threat that Whites would eliminate Native people once and for all. Progressive Indians could see no other way forward because Whites had given them little other choice.

The centuries-long White American genocide against Indians indelibly involved race-making, yet those conjoined histories have never been told together with sufficient chronological, geographical, and thematic breadth, or with an eye toward including Native people as central actors. Until the 1970s, the history of race focused overwhelmingly on what Whites thought about and did to Blacks in the contexts of slavery and Jim Crow, to the near exclusion of Indians. The importance of White-Black history was undeniable, but its singularity had as much to do with the politics of modern American society as with how the past unfolded. In the twentieth-century United States, African Americans were much more populous, visible to White society, and politically powerful than Native Americans, including when it came to demands to have their history addressed. Ongoing White oppression of Blacks and subsequent Black inequality remained salient national issues begging historical context. Indians, by contrast, were largely invisible to the majority of Americans because of their small population, isolation on reservations, and anonymity as Indians whenever they lived in mainstream society as regular, modern people. They were easy to overlook, and those White Americans who preferred patriotic myth to hard-nosed history had good reason to ignore them. As such, the history of American race relations, as scholars once styled it, remained overwhelming a White-Black story.

Within these parameters, scholars tended to argue that racial ideas remained nascent or inchoate (what they called "protoracism") until intellectuals in the late eighteenth and especially nineteenth centuries gave it their stamp of authority. Racial ideology, according to this view, was an elite production of science, theology, high politics, literature, and fine art. The thoughts and actions of lower-status Whites, such as smallholding farmers, ranchers, miners, common soldiers, local officials, and newspapermen, hardly factored. Yet these were the very kinds of people at the vanguard of the nation's conquest of Indian country and, as such, often the greatest proponents of genocidal anti-Indian racism. Scholarship also tended to ignore the racial opinions of non-Whites, whether Indians or Blacks, even though they had plenty to say in response to White racial theories. History treated people of color as mere objects of elite White power.[30]

A great deal has changed in the study of race in the past fifty years as an extension of global decolonization, the American civil rights movement, and the diversification of the scholarly ranks. Critically, scholars no longer view race as real in a biological sense. Rather, they see it as a product of history, of human beings categorizing one another as discrete descent groups and giving those categories social, cultural, economic, and political meaning based on struggles for power. That is to say, scholars agree that race is not a matter of skin color, blood, or some other physical essence, but is purely a human construct for human purposes. That construct has taken various forms across time and place. To uncover the purposes is most of the battle to understand why historical actors defined race in the ways they did, because race is usually instrumental—a tool designed to achieve certainly worldly ends.

In turn, the number of scholars who depict historic race-making mostly as a top-down phenomenon is shrinking. The growing view is that race-making involved people of all descriptions engaged in war, slavery, captivity, law, policy, religion, trade, gender relations, vernacular speech, popular culture, education, art, literature, and more. The racial meanings generated by these activities were the result of people pursuing their own immediate material, cultural, and political interests rather than just of intellectual debate. Scholars no longer assume that the masses automatically followed the lead of elites, or that the thinking of everyday people, including Indians, is unknowable even within the limits of the documentary record. Furthermore, modern scholars treat the actions and experiences of those populations as relevant. Both top-down and bottom-up dynamics are at play.[31]

Furthermore, historical scholarship on race in America no longer takes White identity for granted or treats Blackness as the only racial identity requiring explanation. Instead, Whiteness is now seen as a historical phenomenon whose invention, institutionalization, and periodic redefinition begs scrutiny. These processes, scholarship now emphasizes, have always involved people of color.[32]

Indians are still largely peripheral to the scholarship of race in American history, but there has been considerable effort to move them toward the center. There were still only a few important historical studies that examined elite White views of Indians as late as the 1970s and '80s. As Indian tribes became more visible and assertive in the 1990s and early 2000s, however, historians began to explore how White identity emerged in specific colonial times and places during warfare with Indians, how Indian people generated their own racial ideas under the pressure of White expansion, and even how some Indian groups developed racial systems to hold Blacks as slaves. The current scholarly focus is on race-making and genocide by settler colonial regimes, an approach that has opened up fresh interpretations of the United States, but that risks minimizing Indian agency and historical contingency (the recognition that things could have gone differently) in favor of teleology (an all-encompassing narrative of inevitability). I write deeply influenced by this perspective but acutely aware of its limits.[33]

The primary argument of this book is that Indians always have been and remain central to the history of race-making in America, and that this history has unfolded in the context of a structural genocide. I also submit that a sizable portion of the major events in Native American history from the colonial period onward were shaped by the historical actors' racial ideologies and interpreted by them in terms of race. These episodes contributed to the ongoing development of racial thinking and the social, political, and cultural arrangements that defined America's racial divisions. I am not contending that Indians are more important than or equally as important as Blacks in American racial history. Nor am I trying to recast American racial history fundamentally as a White-Indian affair. Rather, I submit that American racial history, including the history of Whiteness, is woefully incomplete and distorted without discussing Indigenous people and the particular hell they suffered.

We need this history in order to understand America's present. Modern racial identities, particularly Indian and White, are products of it. So, too, is the violent, conspiratorially minded White nationalism that has surged since 2016 under Donald Trump. Several historians have recently highlighted that White nationalism is hardly new in America. Yet there is still little appreciation for how deeply its historic antecedents are rooted in White encounters with Indians. As we shall see, for instance, American history exhibits a pattern of White mobs attacking government agents and installations, including capital cities, when authorities obstructed popular violence against Indians.[34]

Equally important, grappling with this history is a step toward greater public understanding of Indians in the modern United States. Contrary to White predictions surrounding the National American Indian Memorial, Native people did not disappear. Instead, they have persevered and evolved and forced the United States to adjust with them. They are not going anywhere. Many of their communities are thriving and becoming more visible and economically and politically influential. Yet too many Americans cannot understand who these people are because they have not been taught anything about them other than stereotypes. To move forward together productively and respectfully, we need honest, informed discussions of race and its history. This book is my attempt.

A few caveats. The professional historian's mission is to recover a complex history in as much of its complexity as possible. It has nothing to do with cultivating national pride or discouraging it. The reader's emotional response to that history, including fears (justified or not) about the consequences of confronting it, is neither here nor there. The history recounted in these pages is not patriotic or emotionally uplifting, though I see it as essential to understanding the American past more clearly and charting a future of which we can be proud.

The point of this book is to educate and illuminate, not to make people who identify as White feel guilty, though that might very well be the result in some cases. I hope this account will help readers understand how and why they think of themselves as belonging to racial groups in the first place. I also want to demonstrate the centrality of this thinking to the way the United States and its self-identifying White citizens have behaved toward Indigenous people over the centuries.

Other readers might take issue with my effort to render historical Native people three-dimensionally, as people with agency and flaws, rather than as pure victims or hapless innocents. I subscribe to the principle that my job as a historian, and my commitment to taking Native Americans seriously in the here and now, requires depicting Indigenous people in the same complex manner as all other groups of people. These pages show Indians not only on the receiving end of White racism but also themselves committing acts of violence, racism, religious zealotry, and exploitation. I present a substantial amount of primary source evidence to illustrate that Indians had a tradition of thinking in terms of blood identity, which qualifies the current scholarly truism that blood-quantum ideology was simply a colonial invention imposed on Native people to rob them of their land. This book also features Indians repeatedly disputing Whites in contending that races should be separate rather than hierarchically ranked, and, somewhat contradictorily, asserting that White people's qualities were repugnant whereas Indian characteristics were honorable. Equally important, I address how Indians used resistance and accommodation, tradition and reinvention to preserve what was most important to them and adapt to the challenges of their times. My point in treating Indian historical actors in this rounded fashion is not to excuse or minimize their victimization, but, again, to try to recover a complex history in as much of its complexity as possible. The facile polemic of absolute oppressors versus the absolute oppressed, which is too common in contemporary academic circles, saps history of its contingency and surprise. The same goes for depictions of Indians in American history writing, creative arts, and popular culture as either bloodthirsty barbarians or (far more common nowadays) noble savages akin to Adam and Eve before the Fall. American racial history has profound lessons for our times, but we must guard against trying to force it to adhere to our contemporary preoccupations and politics.

My hope is that the reader of this book will agree with me that race and racism in the United States and its colonial predecessors have involved American Indians, as actors and objects, to a far greater degree than we have hitherto appreciated. It is high time for a reckoning.

CODA

For the past decade, each October, Native Americans and their supporters have held an annual celebration of Indigenous Peoples' Day on Randall's Island, in the East River of New York City, a short distance from the point where the National American Indian Memorial was supposed to be built. Each year, the crowd, typically numbering several hundred people, gathers in a circle to watch Indigenous dances to the sounds of drums, rattles, and singing, and listens to speeches about modern issues affecting Native communities. It includes Indigenous people from all corners of the United States, who see themselves collectively as Indians, and even other parts of the globe. They all consider one another as compatriots. Outside the circle, vendors sell Indian foods, art, craftwork, and literature. Back in 1913, the groundbreaking ceremony for the National American Indian Memorial involved White authorities, including the president of the United States, declaring unequivocally and, indeed, triumphantly that Indians were on the brink of extinction. A century later, here are Indians practically on the same location celebrating their triumph over that doom and everything White Americans had done to make it come true.[35]

Though the point of this event is to celebrate Native America, it overlaps with protests against Columbus Day by Indigenous people and their supporters. Christopher Columbus was not the discoverer of a New World, protesters assert. Rather, he was the first and one of the worst of many colonial destroyers of an Old World of Indigenous civilizations. On his voyages to the Americas, his men murdered, raped, enslaved, kidnapped, and otherwise brutalized Native people with abandon, a horrific pattern other colonists continued throughout the hemisphere. To lionize Columbus, the demonstrators contend, is to celebrate the genocide of Native America, and they will not permit that exercise to go unanswered. Answer it they have: Their actions have included parading on horseback through midtown Manhattan while calling on the crowds and cameras to take heed of Native people and afford them greater dignity. Another year, they gathered at the American Museum of Natural History to demand more respectful exhibits and the removal of a statue of Theodore Roosevelt, whose voluminous writings routinely denigrated Indians in crass racial terms, and whose presidency marked the height of the United States' forced assimilation policies toward Indians.[36]

Certainly, many of the protesters are local. In New York City alone, over 180,000 residents identify as American Indian or Alaska Native, with most of them originating from other parts of the country. Nearby Long Island is the home of the federally recognized Shinnecock and Urcachaug tribes, and the bordering state of Connecticut boasts the federally recognized Mashantucket Pequots and Mohegans. In upstate New York, federally recognized tribes include the Mohawks, Oneidas, Onondagas, Senecas, and Tuscaroras. These groups have scratched, clawed, litigated, and organized since the dark days of the late nineteenth and early twentieth centuries, when their existences truly hung in the balance, to become stable, even flourishing, modern Indian nations on tiny parcels of what is left of their ancestral territory. Many of them run profitable tribal enterprises that include gaming, hospitality, and museums. They offer tribal citizens housing, medical services, educational assistance, and, not least, forums in which to teach, learn, and experience the people's distinct cultures, including language. They steadfastly defend their sovereign rights to land, self-governance, and cultural self-determination, and often fight to recover some of what the states and White neighbors have stolen from them over the generations. Clearly, the groundbreaking ceremonies for the national memorial were premature in anticipating the extinction and even just the submission of Indigenous people.[37]

If the National American Indian Memorial had been built back in 1913, doubtless modern Indigenous Peoples' Day protests would take place there. The memorial, after all, was meant to represent false ideologies of race that damned Native people to extinction, trumpeted their conquerors as God's chosen people, and turned the Indians' genocide into a saga of human progress. However misguided, these beliefs and the behaviors they justified have profoundly shaped our world. This book explores how.

CHAPTER 1

Loss of Faith

The earliest colonists in North America did not want to think of their enterprise as brute conquest, but rather as the bestowing of Christianity and civility on savage pagans, with the ultimate goal of incorporating them. Virginia's royal charter proclaimed that its mission was the "propagating of Christian religion to such people, as yet live in darkness and miserable ignorance of the true knowledge and worship of God." This transformation, the colony's organizers imagined, would "in time bring the infidels and savages, living in those parts, to human civility, and to a settled and quiet government" under the English. The Massachusetts Bay Colony similarly declared that its "principal end" was to "win and incite the Natives of the country to the knowledge and obedience of the only true God and savior of mankind and the Christian faith." Western Europe already had a long record of bloody expansion across Iberia, Ireland, the Canary Islands, the Caribbean, and South and Central America. Nevertheless, practically every new colony insisted that if it only did a better job than its predecessors of presenting the superiority of Christianity and civility, awed Indigenous people would submit of their own accord.[1]

Indians had their own visions of a shared future with Europeans that did not involve subjection to the religion and rule of these foreigners. The Powhatans' leader, Wahunsenacawh, expected the English of Jamestown to abide by his authority, trade him weaponry and copper, and provide military backing against his Native enemies. His effort to absorb the newcomers *into his polity* included capturing and ritually adopting their leader, John Smith, in 1607, after which he referred to Smith as his "son." Years later, in 1621, the Wampanoag sachem (or chief) Ousamequin, better known today as Massasoit, aided the struggling *Mayflower* colonists in exchange for their military support and trade. Decades later, Ousamequin's son, Pumetacom (or King Philip), remembered his father as having performed the role of a "great man" in his care of the "little child" of Plymouth. Native people made similar efforts to transform the newcomers into metaphorical kin and allies in practically every early colonial setting.[2]

Little did any of these historical actors know that some of their offspring would come to see and treat one another as fundamentally different and hostile, as "savages," "cutthroats," "bloody barbarians," "long knives," and, eventually, as Whites and Indians. The racial identities that emerged from the religious and military contest for America have existed for so long that they seem natural. But race is not the product of nature. It is a human invention for human purposes. The purpose of Europeans in America, in addition to spreading Christianity, was to build profitable and secure colonies, which, in the English case, depended on the appropriation of Native land and labor and the crushing of any resistance. The English eventually justified their subjugation, dispossession, and even destruction of Indigenous people by developing two mutually defined racial ideas: first, that "Indians" were fundamentally savage, and, second, that they, as Whites, were fundamentally Christian and civilized. Native people's answer was to appropriate the identity of Indians, particularly when rallying opposition to colonial aggression. In fact, they tended to identify as Indian before their colonial neighbors called themselves White. Over time, Native Americans also referred to Europeans as Whites, but not because they shared the colonial view that Whites were superior. Instead, Indians of all descriptions routinely castigated Whites as congenitally underhanded, hypocritical, and merciless.

Though most Native people developed a racial worldview in opposition to colonization, others did so in the context of taking colonists at their word that embracing Christianity and civility would lead to friendship. The most desperate Native people hoped that these reforms would save them body and soul from the horrors colonialism had unleashed, only to meet disappointment at almost every turn. Among the greatest influences on race-making in colonial America was the unwillingness of most Europeans and more than a few Indians to give this Christian experiment a reasonable chance to succeed.

The harsh reality of violent struggle in place of the colonial fantasy of Christianizing, civilizing, and absorbing Native people made the seventeenth century a time of precedent in the history of American race-making. It was during this century that colonists began to wage genocidal warfare against Indigenous people based on explicit racial justifications, a pattern their descendants and other newcomers from Europe would continue into the late nineteenth century. This era also saw the first instances of land-hungry and scared frontier colonists and their successors rebelling against government when it obstructed their indiscriminate violence against Indian friends as well as foes. Such developments contributed to the emergence of "White" identity in opposition to "Indian" by the close of the century. Too often, we overlook this era as a racial watershed because the action pivots unexpectedly on Indian-colonial relations instead of on Black slavery, and the drivers of race-making are the lower orders of society rather than the elites. Furthermore, the historical actors of this age used language and logics that modern people often struggle to grasp. If we open our minds to evidence of the unexpected, the seventeenth century emerges as a foundational time not just for European settlement, but for a new American racial order in which race rationalized land theft, not just human bondage.

INFLUENCES

Europeans called America a "new world," but they arrived with strong preconceptions about the people there that would influence their later notions of race. Europeans thought of themselves collectively as Christians, followers of the one true faith, and of Europe as Christendom, despite sometimes violent struggles for dominance between Catholics and Protestants and even between Protestant denominations. This mindset gave Europeans an unmistakable sense of superiority, but also of some moral obligation to outsiders. Christianity emphasized that all humankind was created and governed by a single omnipotent God and descended from a pair of original parents, Adam and Eve. Furthermore, Christianity was a proselytizing religion, which commanded its followers to bring unbelievers into the fold.[3]

Yet the fact that Native Americans were not Christians but instead animists meant that Europeans viewed them as heathens, pagans, and barbarians, with few claims to the dignity to which Christians were entitled. For all of the Christians' infighting, they viewed one another as coreligionists deserving of some humanity. The example during the Middle Ages of the Muslims' prohibition against holding fellow believers in slavery had convinced Christians to follow suit. Yet Europeans put no such limits on themselves in "just wars" fought against pagans who rejected the offer to submit to Christian rule. Like the conquering Romans who had brought Christianity and civility to the rest of ancient Europe, now it was Western Europe's turn to spread grace and order throughout the pagan world, by force if necessary.[4]

To Europeans, the binary of civility and savagery paralleled that of Christianity and paganism. Savagery, as Europeans defined it and as they applied it to Indians, had mostly to do with a people's deficiencies. Europeans imagined that savages lived in a state of near anarchy, without formal laws, government, religious institutions, or multitiered social hierarchies. How could it be otherwise? After all, the thinking went, savages' lack of reading and writing meant that they had no books, archives, universities, sacred texts, sophisticated bureaucracies, censuses, tax records, formal laws, and the like. North American Indians did not even possess the wheel, metallurgy, or draft animals. Crude technology and a lack of authority to protect personal property supposedly also meant that savages wanted for permanent homes, fenced-in fields, and other labor-intensive improvements. Savages owned nothing because they could keep nothing in the absence of law and order, or so Europeans presumed. Therefore, savages had no incentive to work, stored little food, and sometimes went days without eating until they managed to catch something wild. They relocated with the seasons in pursuit of whatever bounty nature offered freely, producing next to nothing and giving little thought to the future. Europeans judged that, among Indians, the men were particularly lazy. When they were not abroad hunting, warring, or trading, Indian men seemed only to lounge about the village smoking and talking while the women did everything else, including tending to the crops. Europeans viewed farming as men's work. To Europeans, savagery was a world without godly discipline, which was to say, the Devil's kingdom.

Europeans also contended that savages lacked any notion of sin and had no shame of their bodies, exposing torsos and limbs that civilized people diligently kept covered. In turn, sexual license trumped the values of premarital chastity and monogamous lifelong marriage. Worse still, Europeans believed that savages unrestrained by Christianity openly practiced cannibalism, incest, abortion, infanticide, and wife beating. Bloodthirsty and brutish, savages were thought to make no distinction between combatants and noncombatants in war, and to torture their captives sadistically. When the *Mayflower* landed in New England in the winter of 1620–21, the passengers feared, as William Bradford recounted, that they were in "continual danger of the savage people: who are cruel, barbarous, and most treacherous" and "delight to torment men in the most bloody manner that may be . . ." All this before they had actually met any of the locals.[5]

Early colonists who wrote about Indians through firsthand experience tended to qualify these harsh opinions, at least initially. Figures such as John Smith of Virginia, Edward Winslow of Plymouth colony, and Roger Williams of Rhode Island stressed that Indians had a capacity for European-style living insofar as they exhibited some social stratification, village living, customary law, religious thought, and ethics, even if they still fell short of the civilized mark. Thus, the moral imperative of colonization, to raise pagan savages to Christian civility, and, with it, the economic imperative to appropriate Indian land, had prospects for success. These observations also served to convince prospective colonists and investors in colonial enterprises that Europeans who migrated to America would not themselves degenerate into savagery. European thinkers widely subscribed to an "environmentalist" view that attributed differences between human societies and even physical appearances to geography and climate, which caused some trepidation in those considering overseas adventures. It reassured them to learn that Native people were not inveterate barbarians but had the potential to improve. Some accounts even went so far as to claim that the Indians' dark complexions were a result of their oiling otherwise light skins and exposure to smoke and the sun, rather than an inherited characteristic. The point was that Europeans who migrated to America did not need to fear turning into dark-hued barbarians but could instead focus on Christianizing and civilizing the Natives.[6]

To some Christian thinkers, the Indians' very lives, not just the fate of their souls, depended on their converting to Christianity and civility. God, it appeared, punished the Indians with devastating epidemic diseases for their pagan savagery and to make way for Christians. Europeans had no other way of understanding why contagions like smallpox, which had been previously unknown in America, appeared so suddenly among the Indians to such devastating effect. After various plagues in 1616–19, 1622, and 1633–34 swept off massive numbers of southern New England Indians while leaving the newly arrived English relatively unscathed, colonial spokesmen found their explanation in God's providence. "For the Natives, they are all near dead of the smallpox," marveled John Winthrop, governor of the Massachusetts Bay Colony, "so the Lord hath cleared our title to what we possess." The colonist Thomas Morton agreed that the depopulation had to be "the hand of God" to permit "the English Nation" to settle the land "and erect in it temples to the glory of God." The catastrophic toll of foreign epidemics on Native America was one of the most significant disasters in modern world history, both for the millions of lives it claimed and for weakening Indian resistance to colonialism. The New England phase of this apocalypse was the earliest example of Euro-Americans interpreting the die-off as evidence that they were chosen and Indians were damned, with land as the prize.[7]

Indians had their own understandings about Europeans that extended partially from prophecies of the arrival of potent strangers. A Powhatan shaman claimed that well before the first colonists landed at Jamestown, the ancestors taught that "bearded men should come and take away their Country and that none of the original Indians be left, within . . . a hundred and fifty" years. Likewise, when the missionary John Eliot visited the Wampanoags of Cape Cod in the 1640s, one of them remembered that long ago he had dreamt of a man clad in black, like Eliot, carrying a great book, the Bible, preaching that a great spirit would punish the Indians for their sins. Belief in such visions helped Native people come to terms with the vast uncertainties of early contact.[8]

Despite some wariness, Indians were drawn to the Europeans' material wealth and sophisticated technology. The newcomers dazzled Indians with magnets, magnifying glasses, compasses, and spring clocks that ran by themselves. Mostly, though, Native people focused on the staples of the fur trade: brightly colored cloth, thick wool blankets, iron knives and axes, copper kettles, scissors, thimbles, needles, colored glass bottles, and, of course, firearms. The Indians' fascination with European goods is evident in the names they first gave to the newcomers: Coat Men, Sword Men, Cloth Makers, Iron People, and Knife Men, but not, for the meantime, Whites. Clearly, the primary importance of these strangers to Indians was in the goods they had to offer.[9]

Indians were no different from Europeans in favoring their own customs and values over others'. Whereas Europeans criticized Indians as lazy, Natives saw themselves as prioritizing community life and Europeans as consumed by endless toil and worry. The Indians' religion denounced by Europeans as Devil worship was to Native people communion with fellow spirits of a single Creator embodied in animals, plants, elements, cardinal directions, and geologic forms. Europeans denounced Indians as bloodthirsty and cruel, but Indians found European ways of violence, particularly imprisonment, just as repulsive as the Europeans found theirs. What Europeans criticized as Indian disorder, Indians defined as freedom. Colonists occasionally took Indians on visits to Europe to convince them of Christendom's superiority, but few of the Natives were impressed and some were outright disgusted. A Mi'kmaq reportedly asked a French Jesuit, "Why now, do men of five or six feet in height need houses which are sixty to eighty?" He preferred his people's ability to follow seasonal resources to the Europeans' mundane, sedentary life. Other Indigenous people were appalled at Europe's crassly unequal distribution of wealth. A Montagnais (Innu) wondered why the beggars of Paris "did not take the others by the throat and set fire to their houses." He "thought that [this inequity] was due to a lack of charity, and blamed us greatly, saying that if we had some intelligence, we would set some order in the matter, the remedies being simple." However impressive

Indians found Europeans' technological achievements, they judged that the cost was a tyranny of church, state, and greed.[10]

Yet if Indians preferred their ways over Europeans', their notion of "we" was far narrower. Whereas Europeans claimed membership in a vast greater Christendom of many millions, Natives belonged primarily to clans of hundreds of people, local communities the size of villages, and more generally to tribes, confederacies, and multinational council fires numbering at most in the low tens of thousands of people. Real and metaphorical kin, including foreign allies, were "we." The rest of the world, whether strangers or enemies, were "they," lying outside the spectrum of mutual responsibilities. Roger Williams had conversations with the Narragansetts and Wampanoags in which "they have often asked me why we call them Indians, Natives, &c., and understanding the reason [say] they will call themselves Indians, in opposition to the English." John Eliot had a similar exchange with the Massachusett Indians, who wondered "why the English call them Indians because before [the English] came [the Indians] had another name?" The Natives' puzzlement had less to do with finding an equivalent word in their languages for "Indians" than with the concept itself. They had never thought of themselves in such a broad manner.[11]

Unlike colonizing Christians, Indians had no religious or political dictates to convert Europeans but instead followed the maxim of live and let live. Thus, when Europeans pressured Indians to bend to their ways, they came off as rude and even hostile. This principle confronted European missionaries practically everywhere they went in Indian country. Jesuits in New France reported in 1616, "All your arguments, and you can bring a thousand of them if you wish, are annihilated by this single shaft which they [the Indians] always have at hand... (They say,) 'That is the savage way of doing it. You can have your way and we will have ours.'"[12]

The Indians' metaphysical reason for this social principle was that the two peoples' respective spirits had created them separately for separate purposes. The Narragansetts, according to Williams, "deny not that English man[']s God made English Men, and the Heavens and Earth there [in old England]! yet [contend that] their Gods made them, and the Heaven and Earth where they dwell." The Europeans' Creator had given them "clothes, books, etc.," whereas the Narragansetts' spirits taught them to hunt game and cultivate corn and beans. Indians did not go so far as to say that they and Europeans were incapable of living like each other. When Indians and European colonists exchanged children, as they sometimes did, it was with the expectation that the youngsters would learn the languages and customs of the host people and later serve as intermediaries. The same principle applied to war captives adopted into the

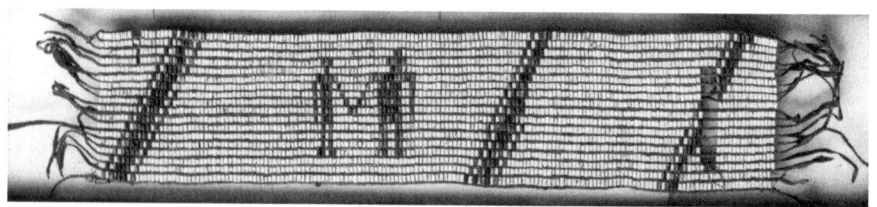

Lenape (Delaware) wampum belt of alliance believed to have been presented to William Penn by the sachem Tamanend at Shackamaxon (present-day Fishtown, Philadelphia), 1682. Courtesy of New York State Archives.

community. Indians assumed that when foreigners went through the ritual process of joining the group, they would follow that community's distinct, divinely created way of life and identity. Their old selves were supposed to be transformed.[13]

European and Indian philosophies of human diversity could not have been more incompatible. Most Europeans equated difference with inferiority. They tended to group people into binaries such as Christian versus pagan and civilized versus savage, with the positive terms applying to Europe and the negative ones describing most of the rest of the globe. Consequently, Europeans felt justified in treating people they viewed as savage pagans, including Indians, with contempt and violence. They also assumed that their own ways were so obviously superior as to be irresistible to savages. By contrast, Indians attributed differences between groups to separate divine creations. Unlike Christians influenced by the concepts of grace and sin, Indians did not prejudge whether a foreign people's idiosyncrasies were inherently good or bad, though they often came to the latter conclusion, but waited to see whether the strangers applied them to productive or destructive ends. Thus, Indians usually approached the earliest Europeans they contacted with great hospitality if also caution, to enlist their aid and avoid provocation. These assumptions, though always subject to revision based on experience, would have profound influence on the two groups' interactions and mutual conceptions during their American encounter.

REACHING OUT

It took years before English colonial authorities began to follow through on their pledges to Christianize and civilize Indigenous people. There was no designated missionary class in the Protestant English colonies during the seventeenth century, only ministers or religious lay people with other full-time jobs and familial

obligations (as Protestant clergy could marry). Any aspiring missionary had to not only learn the language of the Indigenous people he targeted, but also earn their permission to preach to them. Securing this consent was difficult because it was plain that Christianity and colonial political influence went hand in hand. Furthermore, in the relatively centralized Indian polities of the Chesapeake region and New England, where the English first settled, chiefly and priestly authorities were heavily intertwined, and religious ceremonies underpinned social and political solidarity. Christianity therefore threatened the order of things, which made it appealing only to Indians who were disaffected, disillusioned, or contrarian.

By contrast, the Catholic colonies of Spain, in the cases of Florida and New Mexico, and France, in the case of New France, made missionary work foundational to Indian relations from the start. In this, the Catholic powers had several major advantages over the English even as they, too, confronted Indian resistance. Their countries' marriage of church and state meant their Christianizing had ample government support. Additionally, Catholic religious orders like the Jesuits and Franciscans provided an unmarried class of professional missionaries. Both Catholic powers parlayed these advantages, plus the threat of Spanish force and the French promise of trade and alliance, into religious enterprises that reached far into Indian country, well beyond colonial population centers. By the mid-seventeenth century, Spanish missions stretched across the Florida panhandle and along the Rio Grande of New Mexico, while French missions extended from Maine and the Canadian Maritimes in the east, up the St. Lawrence River, and into the Great Lakes and upper Mississippi River Valley. The geographic reach and military and economic strength of the Catholic colonies rested on tens of thousands of Indians who were part of these systems.[14]

The nearly constant hostilities between Virginia and the Powhatans from 1609 to 1614 foreclosed any missionary work. Yet when Wahunsenacawh's daughter, Pocahontas, accepted baptism and marriage to John Rolfe while a captive of the English, it produced a peace that cracked open the door to evangelization. One of Pocahontas's instructors, the Reverend Alexander Whitaker, criticized fellow Englishmen who had come to doubt Indians' capacity for Christianity in the course of seizing their land, for he argued that Native people "have reasonable souls and intellectual faculties as well as we; we all have Adam for our common parent." By 1620, the lay Englishman George Thorpe had begun to act on this principle, preaching to nearby Powhatans and advocating for the creation of an Indian college. Most colonists, however, considered him to be on a fool's errand, with Thorpe complaining that "there is scarce any man among us that does so much afford them [the Indians] a good thought in his heart and most men with their mouths give them nothing but maledictions and bitter execrations."[15]

An even bloodier clash, the Pequot War of 1636–37, was the spur to missionary outreach in New England. In it, the English killed hundreds of Pequot innocents and enslaved most of the rest, which so terrified other Indians that some of them began hosting missionaries as a sign of goodwill. Other Natives gave Christianity a hearing because they had been devastated by successive waves of unfamiliar epidemic disease ever since the English arrived and wanted to know why they were so singularly affected. The colonists' honest answer was that Christians followed the one true God, who protected them and smote His enemies. Meanwhile, colonial New England's leaders felt the sting of criticism from London that they had slaughtered so many Indians before converting any of them.

The result was the largest evangelical campaign in the history of England's North American colonies. By 1670, a long roster of English and Native missionaries had contributed to nearly five thousand Wampanoag, Massachusett, and Nipmuc Indians' self-identifying as Christians and forming several congregations led by ordained Indian preachers and elders. The colonies designated sixteen Christian Indian communities as "praying towns," with land protected from English encroachment as long as the Indians upheld Christian living. A number of these places contained day schools that taught literacy in local Algonquian languages put to writing for the very first time. A handful of Indian boys even attended Harvard College, taking their classes upstairs from a printing press that was running off the entire Bible and other religious tracts in the Wampanoag tongue. One praying Indian went so far as to predict that "in forty years more, some Indians would all be one English, and in a hundred years all Indians here about would so be."[16]

Yet the Indians' adoption of Christianity had the ironic effect of producing new divisions between them and the colonists. In 1652 Massachusetts ruled that Indians "brought to civility" could live in colonial towns "according to the custom of the English," but hardly any Natives took up the offer, preferring life alongside their own people, in their own communities, under their own governance. There was also a conspicuous lack of marriages between the two groups. Sex and reproduction occurred, certainly, between colonial fur traders and Native women, and in English households with Indigenous servants or slaves, but colonists tended to keep such activity quiet and discourage it officially. Sometimes it was difficult to tell whether a common Christianity was drawing the two people closer together or driving them further apart.[17]

Social relations framed by shared religion were far more prevalent in the Catholic colonies, albeit often in exploitative contexts. The Spanish of New Mexico routinely forced Indian women servants and slaves into concubinage. Formal marriage, however, remained uncommon. In short time, New Mexico's locally born population was majority mestizo, or of mixed descent. The Spanish colonies had a baroque system of racial categorization for mixed people, but applying it was like trying to nail jelly to the wall. In official settings, hardly anyone would tell the truth about their backgrounds. Instead, they tried to distance themselves from their Indian and African heritages in pursuit of legal recognition of blood purity, *limpieza de sangre*, or Whiteness.[18]

The French also engaged in formal and informal sexual relationships with Native people to a far greater degree than the English, especially in the context of the fur trade. French fur traders operated deep in Indian country, where a Native wife from an influential family was essential for protection and profit, never mind physical comfort. Untold numbers of these relationships occurred *à la façon du pays* (in the fashion of the country), some lasting only a season or two, others for years and even lifetimes. Occasionally, the couples sanctified these relationships if the woman was baptized. Such formal marriages were rare—there appear to have been only sixty-five during the whole colonial era—but among the Illinois Indians they were common enough to contribute to a series of long-term French-Indian settlements. In turn, there arose a Métis (mixed) population numbering several hundred or more. The French example demonstrates that when religion and trade bound Natives and newcomers together, and Indian alliances were worth more to Europeans than land, coexistence was possible. Those conditions, however, were becoming all too rare in the English colonies.[19]

THINGS FALL APART

In short order, English designs on Indian land and Native resistance overwhelmed the colonies' founding aspiration to bring Indians to Christianity, civility, and European rule. It had been bad enough for the Powhatans when they realized that Virginia would never bow to their authority or trade them the guns they wanted, but then the colony's discovery of a profitable tobacco crop and importation of thousands of indentured servants to cultivate it threatened to dispossess them entirely. Their response came in March 1622, as Wahunsenacawh's brother, Opechancanough, led them in a surprise blitz against Virginia's dispersed plantations that wiped out a third of the inhabitants in a matter of days. Facing the very real possibility of their own destruction, the English launched a merciless counteroffensive fueled by racial animus.[20]

Calls to "exterminate" Indians now replaced earlier pledges to Christianize, civilize, and absorb them. Members of the Virginia Company, which sponsored the colony, contended that the Powhatans' slaughter of the English "without remorse or pity" exposed them as "miscreants," a "viperous brood," and "creatures ... (I cannot call them men) no character of God in them." A number of Company men decided that Indians and other dark-skinned people were "descended of the cursed race of Cham (or Ham)" the son of the biblical Noah, who was condemned with his descendants in the nation of Canaan to be "a servant of servants." The poet Christopher Brooke would not grant the Powhatans even this degraded status. He posited, rather, that after the biblical flood they "sprung up like vermin of an earthly slime ... fathered by Satan, and the sons of hell." As "errors of nature, of inhumane birth, the very dregs of garbage," the only fate they deserved was "extirpation."[21]

A fanciful depiction of the Powhatans' surprise 1622 attack on Virginia by the European artist Matthäus Merian the Elder, based on an earlier engraving by Theodor de Bry.

Recasting the Powhatans as subhuman justified a total war in which the English killed all Indians within reach and tried to starve the remainder by ruining their crops and villages every planting season. Colonists even lured Powhatan leaders to a peace conference where they served them poisoned wine and then put them to the sword. A truce in 1632 turned out to be just a pause. Two years later, the English finished building a six-mile palisade across the peninsula between the James and York Rivers to consolidate their territorial gains and mark any unescorted Indian inside as an enemy to be shot on sight. Unwilling to wait for the next land grab, in 1644 Opechancanough launched another onslaught that killed perhaps five hundred colonists in just two days. Yet Virginia's population had grown too large to defeat through such means. In took only until 1646 for the same total war tactics that had proven so effective earlier to force the surviving Powhatan communities to surrender.[22]

The passions unleashed by the war ushered in a new racial geography defined by a frontier line between English and Indian territories policed by a deputized colonial public. Virginia declared that "it shall be lawful for any person to kill any Indian" found without an English-issued badge south of the York River, north of the James, and east of the falls. Apparently, some colonists interpreted this ruling too liberally, for in 1649 the assembly negated it, citing the "rashness and inadvisedness of diverse persons." That same session, the legislature also prohibited colonists from kidnapping and enslaving Indian children, which had been occurring "to the great scandal of Christianity and of the English nation . . . rendering religion contemptible and the name of Englishmen odious . . ."[23]

War and the race hatred it generated also wrecked New England's experiment in Christian coexistence. Back in 1636, the Pequot sachem, Sassacus, had warned the Narragansetts and Mohegans that if they joined the English "strangers" against his people, they would be the next targets in the colonial long game of divide and conquer. Now, with the Pequots vanquished, the Narragansett sachem, Miantonomo, realized that Sassacus had been right. He responded with a grand tour of the Indian communities of Long Island Sound, "soliciting them to a general war against both the English and the Dutch." Miantonomo's appeal was that henceforth Native peoples should be "all Indians as the English are, and say brothers to one another; so must we be one as they are, otherwise we shall be all gone shortly." Yet his campaign went nowhere because rival sachems distrusted the Narragansetts and remained committed to the independence of their respective polities. They still did not see themselves as Indians.[24]

Miantonomo's call for Indian unity resonated more loudly after the English-allied Mohegans executed him in 1643 (at the colonists' urging) because it grew inescapable that the colonies posed an existential threat to all Native people. First Ninigret, the sachem of the Niantics and Narragansetts, and then Wamsutta and Pumetacom, sachems of the Wampanoags, began the painstaking process of trying to form a multitribal, anticolonial coalition, leading to five war scares between 1653 and 1671. Each time the peace held, but the pattern could not go on forever. Finally, in June 1675, Pumetacom led his followers against the English, explaining "that they [Indians] were as good to be killed as [to] leave all their livelihood." In other words, Indians facing landlessness, subjugation, and enslavement had nothing left to lose.[25]

Shortly, colonists' treatment of neutral Indians as enemies within swelled the ranks of the resistance. The Nipmucs of central Massachusetts, the so-called Friend or River Indians of the Connecticut River Valley, and the Abenakis of Maine took up arms only after the English demanded that they surrender their weapons. The Narragansetts joined them after colonists responded to their refusal to hand over Wampanoag noncombatants with a vicious "preemptive" strike on their Great Swamp Fort in December 1675. It was only by a hair's breadth that the Mohegans, Pequots, and Christian Wampanoags of Cape Cod and Martha's Vineyard managed to avoid the same fate by providing support for the colonies from the very start of the war. Otherwise, the English created a self-fulfilling prophecy that "the plot is general (if not universal) among the Indians."[26]

Even Christian Indians faced English Indian-hating amid the terror of war. Militiamen accused allied Indian warriors of acting as a fifth column by feeding the enemy intelligence and deliberately misfiring in combat. Meanwhile, colonists in exposed Massachusetts towns like Chelmsford and Concord were quick to blame Indians from nearby praying towns for enemy actions. Seizing on the public's fear, a privateer named Samuel Moseley formed a motley brigade of furloughed prisoners, servants, and teenagers that devoted as much effort to menacing Christian Indians as it did to pursuing hostile forces, including seizing them captive for sale into overseas slavery. English authorities hardly knew what to do, torn as they were between suspicion of Indians as a whole and concern that "innocent Indians" were vulnerable to "the rash cruelty of our English." Their solution was to inflict more suffering on the victims. Massachusetts first ordered the praying Indians confined to their towns on punishment of death, then imprisoned them in a concentration camp on barren Deer Island in Boston Harbor. Plymouth followed suit by removing local Christian

Indians to Clark's Island and warning Christian Wampanoags not to leave Cape Cod or else face their own Moseleys.[27]

Some Bostonians went so far as to call for the Christian Indians on Deer Island to be put to the sword. When the missionaries John Eliot and Daniel Gookin dared to protest that this "spirit of enmity and hatred" was "without cause," street mobs called for their heads, too. As Gookin characterized these dark times, the "animosity and rage of the common people" had made the name "praying Indian" an epithet, as if there was "no distinction between one Indian and another." "Hence it was," he lamented, "that all Indians are reckoned to be false and perfidious."[28]

In fact, the English treated the Indians in resistance even more brutally. Not only did the colonies give bounties for Indian scalps, in the first case of its kind, but the war effectively began with Plymouth governor Josiah Winslow mounting the severed head of an Indian spy before his door, and it ended with Plymouth piking Pumetacom's head outside the town gate to rot for the next twenty years. The fighting probably would have ended far earlier than it did, in the estimation of the Plymouth soldier Benjamin Church, if the colonies had not enslaved so many Indians who surrendered, which discouraged other war-weary Indians from following suit. Even the close of active combat did not remove the risk of Englishmen shooting down any Indians they found hunting in the woods, wandering the roads at night, or even just picking berries in groups of women and children in broad daylight. Colonial society saw every Indian as the enemy.[29]

Colonial authorities also brutalized the one Englishman, a Rhode Islander named Joshua Teft (or Tift) suspected to have supported the enemy Indians, as a warning to others that civilized people should never turn savage. English forces captured Teft among the Narragansetts at the Great Swamp Fight, whereupon accusations began pouring in that he was a traitor. Teft pleaded that he had been nothing more than an unfortunate captive of the Narragansetts, but nobody believed him. Ruling that Teft was guilty of high treason for having "apostatized to the Heathen," as Increase Mather put it, a military court sentenced him to be hanged, quartered, and his head impaled.[30]

War produced a new racial order in New England, just as it had previously in Virginia, in which the English appropriated the land and labor of all Indians, whether enemies or allies. Henceforth, the surviving Wampanoags, Pequots, and Mohegans would have to cede the colonists land whenever they demanded it, toil for them as debt peons, and provide them with soldiers for their wars against the French and other Indians. Their reward was the right to scrape by on mere slivers of their once extensive homelands. The racially segregated nature of these places was evident in the colonists' names for them, like "Indian Neck," "Indian Hill," or "Indian Town." Though most Native survivors of King Philip's War were already Christians or soon would be, their status as Indians marked them as second class or worse in colonial society. The Pequots complained of their colonial neighbors in 1725, "We see plainly that their chiefest desire is to deprive us of the privilege of our land, and drive us off to utter ruin ... they threaten us if we don't hold our tongues, to beat our brains out." The English kept a clear conscience by insisting, in the words of the Rev. John Thomas of Long Island, that the "true nature" of Indians was to be "sottish, debauched, and incapable of any instruction." To all but a few romantics, the New England colonies' founding vision of Christianity and civility uniting English and Indian peoples was dead. "God land," which the dissident Roger Williams had once accused his Puritan neighbors of worshipping as an idol, had triumphed once and for all.[31]

Colonial New Englanders emerged from the war more convinced than ever that they were a chosen people. English leaders attributed the war to God punishing them for their sins and testing their faith, rather than to legitimate Indian grievances. In fact, when King Philip's War began, one of the first actions by Massachusetts was to pass a series of sumptuary laws to discourage wayward behavior and ease God's judgment. These measures banned men from wearing long hair, women from "following strange fashions in their apparel," and unmarried couples going riding together unchaperoned "upon pretense of going to lecture," among other provisions. The colonies' victory in the war convinced the Boston minister Increase Mather that these steps had worked, that "God has let us see that he could easily have destroyed us by such a contemptible enemy as the Indians ... But God has wasted the heathen, by sending the destroying angel among them." Just as the Lord once led the nation of Israel out of slavery and into the promised land, now He had "graciously and gloriously begun our salvation ... Let him bring health and cure unto this Jerusalem." This conquest ideology, that God chose Christian Europeans and their descendants to possess the land of "the heathen," would be renewed by every subsequent generation of White Americans during its respective Indian and foreign wars, becoming known as Manifest Destiny in the 1840s and American exceptionalism more recently.[32]

The same Indian-hating that strained colonial society in New England during King Philip's War nearly pulled English Virginia apart in Bacon's Rebellion of 1675–77. Whereas New England survived its civil tumult partly because it was closely integrated through clustered settlements, religion, deference to authority, and widespread access to land, Virginia society was alienated, dispersed, and deeply stratified. The vast majority of its population consisted of indentured servants toiling under contracts that ran as long as seven years. Corrupt political elites acquired so much of the best acreage that nearly everyone else had either to rent farms from their social betters or strike out west, beyond the fall line, where Indians remained a threat but their lands beckoned. A dearth of ministers, isolated plantations, and a lack of towns meant that there were few institutions to bind the people together. To top it all off, the governing class imposed heavy taxes on struggling small planters, then lined their own pockets with impunity. No wonder that Governor William Berkeley had already warned King Charles II that Virginia was a powder keg waiting to explode. "Consider us," he pleaded, as "a people pressed at our back with the Indians, in our bowels with servants... How miserable that man that governs a people, where six parts of seven at least are poor, indebted, discontented and armed."[33]

When war broke out in 1675 between Virginia and the Susquehannocks, who had recently moved south into the Potomac River Valley, many colonists did not trust the government in Jamestown to manage it. But something had to be done. Thomas Matthew remembered of those days, "no man stirred out of door unarmed" for fear that "these brutish and inhumane brutes" had "devised a hundred ways to torture and torment those poor souls whose... fate it was to fall into their unmerciful hands." The people demanded that Berkeley authorize them to form their own militia units, like Moseley's in New England. When he refused, probably out of as much concern for the safety of Virginia's elites as for innocent Indians, the people felt abandoned— that is, until Nathaniel Bacon rose to the fore.[34]

Bacon was one of the first of an American archetype, the White racial demagogue who whips up the masses by declaring that they are the real victims of the dark-complexioned people their society exploits. These firebrands accuse governmental elites who are supposed to defend the people of disdaining them as rabble and protecting their enemies out of political or economic self-interest. Descriptions of Bacon by his contemporaries could apply to any one of these figures through the centuries. He had inherited wealth and status from his father in England, and had enjoyed numerous advantages in Virginia as cousin to Berkeley's wife, yet somehow he always felt aggrieved. In front of an audience, he possessed "so much cunning and subtlety that the people's minds became quickly flexible and apt to receive any impression..." After suffering a Susquehannock attack on his plantation that killed an overseer, Bacon called on the people to "adventure our lives... [rather] than to be sneakily murdered in our beds" by "such a notorious, cruel, and declared enemy... a most bloody and barbarous enemy." The crowd responded with roars of approval, shouting, "A Bacon! A Bacon!"[35]

The Baconites' explicit self-identification as a racial group lagged behind their blanket hostility toward Indigenous people. They did not rally together as "Whites," a term that remained uncommon in Virginia for another fifteen years, but rather as "the people" and "the country." They consisted primarily of Englishmen, but also of a fair number of other western Europeans from a variety of Protestant denominations. They were not just the "ruder sort" or "giddy-headed multitude," as their opponents charged, but included a number of planters and political officers, whose hatred of Indians superseded whatever concerns they had about the mobilization of their subordinates. There were even some Black slaves among the Baconites, a portion of whom probably had no choice in the matter, others of whom might have acted out of a shared fear of Indians and ambition to gain their freedom.[36]

Yet if Bacon's men did not explicitly identify as White, their movement was decidedly racial in its view of Indians as an undifferentiated, inferior group deserving of extermination. As a report to London explained, the rebels "look upon all Indians alike, and (they [Indians] being all of a color) [the colonists] make no distinction between enemies and friends." The "common cry" was "we will have war with all Indians . . . we will spare none." Bacon "greatly cheered and animated the people" by declaring that "our design" is "to ruin and extirpate all Indians in general," the so-called common enemy. Any authorities who stood in the way became the common enemy, too.[37]

The Baconites' defiance of Berkeley's prohibition against attacking Indians turned Virginia's race war into a civil war. Bacon's army struck first against the Occaneechis south of the James River, killing dozens and setting their fortress town ablaze even after Occaneechi warriors raided a Susquehannock camp and turned over the captives as a show of good faith. The drama then shifted to Jamestown, where the Virginia House of Burgesses was meeting, with Bacon as one of its members. Berkeley and the assembly rejected calls to commission Bacon to lead a general Indian war because they followed the principle that "we ought not to involve the innocent with the guilty," only to capitulate after Bacon marched five hundred of his men into the capital. Berkeley then retreated to the east side of Chesapeake Bay, declared Bacon a "rebel," and raised his own forces, including, unwisely, a number of Indians. With this, Bacon denounced the governor and his supporters as traitors, then returned to hunting Indians. Initially, Bacon's army turned its rage against the Pamunkeys, a small Powhatan community that had lived peacefully as a tributary to Virginia since the war of 1644–46 and had nothing to do with the Susquehannocks. Bacon's men killed several of the Pamunkeys and captured forty-five. Next, the Baconites marched against Berkeley's loyalists, plundering their estates and taking their wives captive to use as human shields in a siege of Jamestown, which they burned to the ground. Nothing was going to stand in the mob's way of killing Indians, enslaving them, and taking their land.[38]

Nothing, that is, except Bacon's dying of dysentery just ahead of the arrival of well-armed tobacco ships and redcoats to restore law and order. Royal commissioners charged with investigating this debacle could hardly believe that so many "inconsiderate sort of men" had refused to see that "amicable Indians" were their best first line of defense when warring against other Natives. Instead, the Baconites claimed that the colony's so-called friend Indians were playing a double game and that "it was impossible to distinguish one nation [of Indians] from another." Royal officials had their blinders as well. They wanted to believe that only the "vulgar" or "ruder sort" had rallied to Bacon, but in fact his Indian-hating had broad support. The extermination of Indians and appropriation of their territory was the closest thing colonial Virginia had to a unifying principle.[39]

Bacon's death and the suppression of his remaining forces did not end this racial passion so much as temporarily quell and then redirect it. Initially, the royal commissioners dismissed as "wild" demands from Virginia's county governments for "an immediate war with all Indians in general." Virginia's tributary Indians, including Pamunkeys, Mattaponis, and Chickahominies, tried to protect themselves by signing 1677's Treaty of Middle Plantation, in which they conceded to subjugation in exchange for a guarantee of their lives and a portion of their lands, but they could not have put much faith in that pledge. Colonists continued to menace local Natives on the grounds that they knew "not one Indian from another" and "our tributaries may on the slightest occasion prove as bad as bandits." If the Indians resisted this exploitation, as in 1704, when the small community of Nanziattico Indians on the Rappahannock killed a colonist and his family after years of unaddressed grievances, the backlash was merciless. Virginia executed most of the Nanziattico men, sentenced the rest of the people to slavery, and sold the adults away to Antigua. Bacon was long dead, but the fear, hatred, and greed that drove his movement continued to animate the colony's vicious exploitation of Native people for decades to come.[40]

The Spanish and French colonies no less than the English engaged in brutal conflicts with Indians in which they castigated the enemy as bloodthirsty savages, but their dependence on Indigenous subjects and allies did not transform those passions into generalized Indian-hating. In 1680, a mass uprising by the Pueblo Indians, in reaction to the Spaniards' forcible imposition of Catholicism and exploitation of Indian labor, drove the Spanish out of New Mexico for twelve years. By the 1690s, the Spanish were back, but with the realization that they would have to wield their power with a much lighter hand. Though New Mexico remained active in purchasing and capturing Indigenous slaves from the hinterland, its authorities demanded less from Pueblo communities than formerly in matters of religion, labor, and tribute to avoid another costly revolt. In the case of New France, the colony engaged in bloody warfare against the Haudenosaunees on and off throughout the seventeenth century due to its alliances with the Haudenosaunees' tribal enemies, including the Ottawas and Wyandots. Furthermore, New France acquired a small number of Indian slaves through diplomatic presents and purchases from the colony's Indigenous allies. Yet the colony was so dependent on those allies for the fur trade and defense, and so desirous to convert them, that it could not begin to imagine subjecting Indians as a whole to slavery or other forms of violent repression. Race in colonial America was instrumental, a tool used to achieve larger economic and political goals. When racial prejudice did not serve those purposes, it remained inchoate or limited.[41]

Race hatred against Indians gained greater traction in the English colonies because it promoted the English ends of seizing Indian land, crushing Indian resistance, and enslaving Native survivors. Whereas the Spanish and French colonies remained lightly populated and economically and militarily dependent on Indigenous people, the English colonies' population exceeded that of local Natives within a matter of decades, permitting an economy premised not on trade with Indians but on displacing them from their territory. Furthermore, murderous Indian-hating was sometimes all that seemed to unite the religiously and politically fractious English colonies. That went double once King Philip's War and Bacon's Rebellion introduced a new source of Indian-hating premised on the notion that large-scale Indian resistance was not just God's providential judgment or a common Indigenous reaction to shared colonial pressures, but the instigation of those the English viewed as the Devil's servants: the Catholics.

SATAN'S MINIONS

During the late seventeenth century, English colonists' racial hostility toward Indians increasingly fed on their anxieties about real and fantastical Catholic-Indian conspiracies. Protestants and Catholics had fought for more than century for religious and political supremacy in Europe and, increasingly, the rest of the globe. This contest had kept England in a state of near constant turmoil since the late 1500s, never more so than after the 1685 ascension of James II. James, a barely closeted Catholic leading an overwhelming Protestant country, tested the limits of his rule by seeking rapprochement with France, led by the imperial Catholic king Louis XIV. Then he twisted the screw by revealing his own faith. The English tolerated this state of affairs only because James had no heirs and therefore the crown was likely to pass to his Protestant daughter Mary, wife of Prince William of Orange of the Netherlands. Yet when James sired a son, in 1688, England faced the unthinkable reality of a Catholic succession and the possibility of the king reestablishing the Church of Rome.

In America, English Protestants shuddered that the next imperial war might unleash the Catholic empires and their Indian converts on them, and some of them feared that this nightmare had already begun to materialize. A number of conspiratorially minded New Englanders sensed that "vagrant Jesuit priests" were behind King Philip's War. Likewise, shortly after Bacon's death, some of his supporters began to whisper that Governor Berkeley's opposition to them had been orchestrated by Maryland's Catholic proprietor, Lord Baltimore, whom they suspected of plotting with French Jesuits to have their Indian followers sack Protestant colonists. King James's short-lived decision in 1686 to consolidate the unruly Northern colonies into a single Dominion of New England under royal authority made some colonists think that their own king might be in on the scheme, for Protestants commonly associated centralized, arbitrary government with Catholic tyranny.[42]

William and Mary's 1688 invasion of England and ascension to the throne has since been known as the Glorious Revolution because it was bloodless and welcomed by the majority of English people, but its inglorious effect in the colonies was to unleash a fresh wave of Indian-hating attached to fear of Catholic intrigue. While the result of the revolution in England was still uncertain, rebels in Massachusetts arrested the Dominion governor, Sir Edmund Andros, on the charge that he had been plotting with the Wabanakis and Haudenosaunees (both of whom hosted French Jesuit missionaries) and the government of New France to have the French navy strike Boston from the east in coordination with an army of Indians and French Canadians from the north and west. Andros's supporters dismissed these and numerous other inflammatory accusations as the "foolish and nonsensical stories" of "the ignorant multitude." Yet clearly New England Protestants were terrified that the devilish forces of their world, Indians and Catholics, were converging in apocalyptic fashion to destroy their godly republic. In other words, English colonists' apprehension of Indians had become inextricable from their anti-Catholicism.[43]

Maryland's Protestant majority (which outnumbered Catholics twenty-five to one) had long resisted the authority of the colony's Catholic proprietor, Lord

Baltimore, and suspected that English Jesuits in the colony were more concerned with recruiting Indians as Counter-Reformation warriors than saving their souls. Now they were sure. They interpreted raids by the distant Senecas against the local Piscataways and Nanticokes not as intertribal politics but as part of a wider campaign to "cut off the Protestants." Rumors described shadowy Indians trafficking letters between Baltimore's agents and the French, thousands of Indian warriors massing at the edges of the colony, and the government collecting the people's guns for repair as a ploy to disarm Protestants before the Catholic invasion. By the summer of 1689, Baltimore's nemesis, John Coode, had formed the Association for the Defense of the Protestant Religion against the imagined Catholic-Indian threat. It went on to defeat pro-government forces and remove all Catholics from power. The Protestant Associators also put local Indians on notice that the slightest provocation would bring the ire of the mob upon them, too.[44]

Nowhere did conspiratorial thinking prove as fatal as in Massachusetts, where the people had long envisioned themselves as God's chosen ones but now seemed under a multipronged assault by the Devil and his French and Indian minions. Anxieties were already running high after years of imagined popish plots and the uncertainty of whether William and Mary would restore the old Massachusetts charter of local rule and Puritan privilege. When Wabanakis rose up again following the withdrawal of Andros's troops, striking as far south as the Massachusetts–New Hampshire border, the stress was too much for the fractious town of Salem to bear. In 1692, the nightmarish visions of a group of young girls sent the community and eventually the surrounding county into a panic that a number of pious grandmothers were witches in league with Satan. Some of the original accusers were orphans from Maine working as servants in Salem homes after having lost their parents to attacks by Wabanakis carrying French guns and wearing crucifixes. The anguished girls testified that the Devil had appeared to them in the form of a black Indian, like Wabanakis painted for war. This delusion not only contributed to the judicial killings of twenty people, and proceedings against 144, but also reinforced the colonial ideology of King Philip's War that Indians were the tools of Satan and his other foot soldiers, the Catholics.[45]

CHRISTIAN INDIAN SLAVES

The principle that Christianity was meant for all people was what brought the Reverend Francis Le Jau to South Carolina in 1706. As an Anglican missionary with the Society for the Propagation of the Gospel, which evangelized dissenters and the unchurched in the English crown's overseas dominions, Le Jau had spent five years in the Caribbean island colony of Montserrat struggling to win the sugar planters' consent for his instruction of their slaves. Then, as if seeking greater frustration, he decamped for South Carolina. The colony's European population was split into Protestant denominations of Anglicans, Quakers, Huguenots, Baptists, and Puritans. Slaves actually outnumbered free people, the only case of its kind in the mainland English colonies. Though most of these poor souls originated from Africa (largely via the West Indies), a sizable minority were Native Americans, whose intertribal enemies had captured and sold them to the English. Free communities of so-called Settlement Indians, such as the Pee Dees, Winyaws, and Cusabos, could also be found interspersed among the English of the coastal plain. Far more powerful Indigenous nations—Westos, Savannahs, Yamasees, Catawbas, Creeks (Muskogees), and Cherokees—some with populations in the tens of thousands, hemmed in the colony to the north, west, and south. Colonists feared them as potential enemies even as they depended on their trade in Native slaves and deerskins. Le Jau considered it his duty to bring all these groups to the Church of England and civilized living.[46]

The difficulty of pursuing these ideals became clear as Le Jau settled into his parish at Goose Creek, just north of Charles Town (or Charleston), one of the most ruthless, if also wealthy, neighborhoods in all of colonial America. The political power and riches of the leading Goose Creek Men depended on the traffic in slaves, whether selling Indian captives abroad or buying Africans and Indians to grow rice in Carolina's malarial wetlands. Large numbers of these planters had lived previously

The seal of the Society for the Propogation of the Gospel in Foreign Parts. Note the Indigenous people on the shore welcoming Christianity. Courtesy of Chronicle/Alamy.

in the flourishing sugar colony of Barbados, where they convinced themselves that it was just to hold African and Indian people in lifetime, heritable slavery under miserable conditions. The rationale was that these slaves owed their lives to their masters, for their original tribal captors would have killed them outright if no one had wanted to buy them (they did not dwell on whether the existence of a market for those slaves had motivated the captive-taking in the first place). Others invoked the biblical curse of Cham to contend that Africans and Indians were fated to slavery. Some Christian-minded planters grasped at the excuse that bondage would expose their slaves to saving grace. Such ideas were utterly novel given that slavery had practically disappeared in western Europe over the previous three centuries. This kind of thinking was an invention of Europeans in colonial America to justify their exploitation of others.[47]

Planters revised these attitudes as their interests dictated. In Barbados, no sooner had some slaves received baptism than they began petitioning for freedom to test the colonists' principle that Christians should not hold one another in bondage. One planter response was to reduce the use of "Christian" as a general term for "European" in favor of "White," for whereas dark-skinned people could become Christians, it was much more difficult for them to claim Whiteness. Barbados thus became the first place in the English empire where Europeans referred to themselves as White people. The practice spread over subsequent decades, reinforced by the White identity that colonists were forging in the cauldron of colonial-Indian wars, becoming common in South Carolina and Virginia by the late 1600s, New England by the early 1700s, and Pennsylvania by the 1730s.[48]

A growing number of planters insisted that "Negro" slaves of whatever ancestry should not and even could not become Christians because they were not fully human. The term "Negro" derived from the Portuguese and Spanish words for *black*, but not all "Negro" slaves were African. A significant minority of them throughout the Atlantic colonies were Indian, either sold to colonists by other tribes or taken by colonists as prisoners of war. In Barbados and Bermuda, for instance, their numbers included New England Indian captives from King Philip's War. The reason colonists were open to enslaving both Africans and Native Americans was because they wanted cheap agricultural labor, but the rationalization was that both populations were foreign pagan savages, or, as they were becoming collectively known in a state of slavery, Negroes. If "Negro" and "slave" had become synonymous in plantation colonies, so had slavery and dehumanization. During a stint on Barbados in the 1670s, the Anglican missionary Morgan Godwyn reported hearing colonists opine that "I might as well Baptize a Puppy, as a certain young Negro," that the sacrament "was to one of those [slaves] no more beneficial than to her black Bitch [or dog]," and even "that the Negroes, though in their figure they carry some resemblances of manhood, yet are indeed no men." To Godwyn, these were blasphemous ideas. He agreed, however, with another planter response to the problem of slave baptism, which was simply to legislate that this ritual did not confer freedom.[49]

By the time Le Jau arrived in South Carolina, the contagion of race had also spread there. Le Jau opened a night school for the religious instruction of slaves, but the overwhelming majority of planters would not permit their subordinates to attend. Some masters worried that slaves would use their excused absence from work to plot revolt. Others believed "that after their slaves are baptized they are no longer servants, they say, but free," despite a 1712 law stating otherwise. Most planters, however, echoed the crass racism of White Barbadians. Le Jau wrung his hands that "many masters can't be persuaded that Negroes and Indians are otherwise than beasts, and use them as such." These same colonists adopted "a praying posture" during church services, but clearly, Le Jau judged, "they do not love their neighbor."[50]

Le Jau was equally despondent at White South Carolinians' denial of basic humanity to their victims in the Indian slave trade. This sordid enterprise involved colonists recruiting Native tribes to raid one another for captives, whom colonists would then purchase for munitions, liquor, and cloth. South Carolina was not alone in this practice. Virtually every other colony, whether English, French, or Spanish, also trafficked in Indian slaves to one degree or another. But the scale in South Carolina was unprecedented, involving not just dozens or hundreds of slaves, as was typical elsewhere in the North American colonies, but tens of thousands, with many more left dead along the way. By the early 1700s, most Indians within several hundred miles of Charles Town were involved in this horror as perpetrators, victims, or both. South Carolina's own proprietors, from their headquarters in England, denounced the colony for inducing Indians "through [their] covetousness of your guns, powder, and shot and other European commodities to make war upon their neighbors, to ravish the wife from the husband, kill the father to get the child and to burn and destroy the habitations of these poor people." Yet they were powerless to stop it.[51]

How could the Christian God not take offense given that Carolinians enslaved not only pagans but also thousands of Catholic Indians from the missions of Spanish Florida? For centuries, Europeans had subscribed to the principle that Christians should not enslave other Christians. European slave traders operating in Africa, and their customers in the Americas, skirted this rule when they purchased captives seized from the Catholic kingdom of Angola, but they could plausibly deny that they knew anything about the origins of these prisoners. The same could not be said for Carolinians who not only bought Catholic Indians from Native sellers, but also frequently organized and participated in the slave raids themselves. One slaver, Thomas Nairne, admitted that while "kniving Indian towns in Florida" he noticed that "these people have had Christian churches among them for an 100 years past" and that the Indians' language "is enriched with an abundance of Spanish words, particularly those pertaining to religion." When these Indians reached South Carolina, still other colonists discovered that there were "many grown persons among them [who] had been baptized by Spanish priests, and have Christian names."[52]

The slave traders could not have cared less, and hardly anyone in authority bothered to oppose them. The lone voice of protest came from the Quaker governor John Archdale in 1695, after he learned that four slaves held by Carolina's Yamasee Indian allies "profess'd the Christian Religion as the Papists do; upon which I thought in a most peculiar manner, they ought to be freed from Slavery." He intervened just before Carolinian slave traders bought these figures and resold them to the Caribbean, "as was usual," and instead returned them to Spanish officials in St. Augustine. Yet when Archdale sailed off to England a year later, his cause left with him.[53]

South Carolinians' willingness to enslave Indigenous people from Florida had nothing to do with hostility toward the Indians' Catholicism or doubts about the legitimacy of their conversions. The colonists' only rationale was that they were Indians. The English did not enslave the Spaniards captured in these raids. In fact, officials in Carolina rewarded Indians for delivering them Spanish prisoners for redemption. The fact was that the slavers felt confident that they could get away with enslaving Catholic Indians, whereas if they had enslaved Spaniards it would have sparked a diplomatic crisis among European kingdoms. The slave trader James Moore even became South Carolina's interim governor. The English felt no obligation to treat Indians with humanity, regardless of their Christianity or subjecthood to European sovereigns.[54]

Le Jau saw God's judgment at work when surrounding Indians finally struck back against the exploitation of the slavers, traders, and planters, first in the Tuscarora War of 1711–13, then again in the ferocious Yamasee War of 1715–16, which almost pushed the English back into the sea. Le Jau believed that the Lord was using the Indians as a rod to punish Carolinians for "our crying sins and scandalous and presumptuous transgressions of divine, ecclesiastical, and humane laws." Yet such wars were the very moments in which the sins Le Jau decried gained potency through people vocalizing and acting out their notions of race. Le Jau watched in horror as Carolinians, like Virginians and New Englanders before them, sought to not only defeat but extirpate their Indian opponents. "We think to destroy the whole nation," he bemoaned, "that is, kill the men and make the women and children slaves. This is our way of war upon the like provocations."[55]

Carolina's leadership galvanized this destruction by invoking normally latent racial prejudices against Indians, even as the colony recruited Indians as allies for the campaign. For instance, the government issued public declarations that Indians were "cruel and barbarous . . . for they spare neither age nor sex, but those who are so miserable as to fall into their hands can expect nothing but death by torturing from their cruelty and barbarity." Officials attributed the Indians' uprising not to any actual grievances but to the notion that "Indians are so addicted to war and bloodshed and so long accustomed to it that it's almost impossible for them to abstain from it." Demonizing Indigenous people in these ways freed colonists to act as inhumanely as they accused the Indians of doing. As Le Jau's contemporary the Reverend Gideon Johnston observed, "our military men are so bent upon revenge and so desirous to enrich themselves by making all the Indians slaves" that "they kill without making the least distinction between the guilty and the innocent."[56]

The Tuscarora and Yamasee Wars quickened the trend toward skin color rather than religion or culture (such as dress, hairstyle, and ornamentation) symbolizing a person's social roles and geographic place in the colonies. Having learned the hard way that the Indian slave trade put South Carolina's security at risk, the planters turned away from this enterprise and headlong toward the importation of Africans, whose home societies on the other side of the Atlantic Ocean were in no position to retaliate against the colony. Economic considerations also played a role in this shift, as Carolina's Indian wars coincided with growing efficiencies in the transatlantic slave trade that made African captives more available than ever. Furthermore, Carolina's victory in the wars produced a spike in demand for bound labor to cultivate the vast tracts of land seized from defeated Indigenous enemies. As boatload after boatload of Africans arrived to toil alongside enslaved Indian prisoners of war, the colony tightened its systems to keep these captives subjugated. During the early eighteenth century, Carolina followed Barbados, Jamaica, and Virginia in prohibiting any "negro or other slave" from traveling without a pass, gathering in groups, resisting White abuse, testifying in court against White people, claiming freedom through baptism, or selling property. "White people," by virtue of being White, could do all of these things and more, including kill recalcitrant slaves with impunity.[57]

Subtly, the law's repeated use of terms like "negro or other slave" redefined Indian bondspeople and their Afro-Indian offspring as Black, which Whites had made synonymous with "slave." As Godwyn had observed decades earlier in Virginia and Barbados, "these two words, *Negro* and *Slave*" had "by custom grown homogenous and convertible; even as *Negro* and *Christian*, *Englishman* and *Heathen*, are by the like corrupt custom and partiality made *opposites*." If to be a slave was to be Black or Negro, then an Indian slave could also be Black or Negro. It was no unthinking decision; the South Carolina Assembly revealed its purpose in a 1715 tax on slaves that eliminated official use of the racial category "mustee." "Mustee" was an Anglicized version of the Spanish word *mestizo*, referring to Indians mixed with either Whites or Blacks. Given that the new law taxed Black slaves at a higher rate than Indian ones, questions arose about how to categorize slaves who descended from both groups and/or from European-Indian parents. In order to avoid such "doubts and scruples," and, undoubtedly, to raise more tax revenue, the act ordered that "all and every slave who is not entirely Indian shall be deemed a negro." By the 1720s most census reports from South Carolina stopped counting Indian or Afro-Indian slaves in favor of lumping them together with the majority as "Black" or "Negro." Through such actions, colonists gradually defined White people as free, Christian, and civilized, with liberty of movement, Black people as nothing more than slaves under constant White supervision and discipline, and Indians as savage pagans living beyond the civilized pale, regardless of the myriad ways that actual people blurred and contradicted those roles.[58]

The evidence of such boundary-crossing was everywhere. It could be found, certainly, in the growing number of slaves and even free people of color who exhibited physical signs of White ancestry despite laws and customs that prohibited sex and marriage across the color line. It could be found in cases in which White women gave birth to "bastard" children fathered by Blacks or Indians, and in subsequent colonial laws that forced the children of these relationships and sometimes their mothers into servitude and other degraded statuses. It was present in the examples of British fur traders who, like their French counterparts, married Native women (especially among the Creeks and Cherokees), lived with the women's people, and abided by their customs. On rare occasions, fur traders brought the children from these relationships to be baptized or formally educated in colonial society, with the obvious expectation that other colonists would grant the youngsters at least grudging acceptance. Doubtless the long-term ambition of such fathers was that inculcating their Anglo-Indian progeny with colonial values and methods would enable them to parlay their Indigenous family ties into private claims to Native land, in addition to ongoing advantages in the trade.[59]

Yet the colonies did not legally recognize either fur trade relationships or the legitimacy of the children they produced—some colonies, like North Carolina, prohibited marriages of any sort between Europeans and Indians—even as officials understood the utility of these arrangements. Furthermore, at this early stage, White fathers rarely had much influence over their children by Native women. As the Carolinian fur trader John Lawson observed, the southeastern Indians' matrilineal and matrilocal customs, in which children identified with their mother's clan and lived with her and her kinfolk, meant "it ever seems impossible for the Christians to get their children (which they have by these Indian women) away from them; whereby they might bring them up in the knowledge of the Christian principles." Whatever aversion Southeastern Indians had toward Whites from colonial society, they considered the "mixed" offspring of Native women to be full members of their groups, particularly when those mixed offspring spoke the people's language, abided by their customs, and identified with them. The upside for colonists was that they did not have to deal with the complexity of these people as long as they stayed with the Indians.[60]

The Cherokees, Creeks, and Catawbas negotiated their own place in this developing racial system by agreeing to return any runaway "negroes" they found in exchange for payment of a musket and coat per fugitive. In the event of slave revolts, Charles Town compensated Indians for every Black scalp they delivered. As one South Carolinian acknowledged, his colony's plan for security was "to make the Indians and Negroes a check upon each other, lest by their superior numbers we should be crushed by the one or the other." Carolina also used its leverage in trade to continue to stoke intertribal warfare, which had proven so critical in the colonists' victories in the Tuscarora and Yamasee Wars. "It is always the maxim of our governments upon the continent to promote war between Indians of different nations," explained Governor Robert Johnson, ". . . for in that consists our safety; being at war with one another prevents their uniting against us." No wonder Le Jau thought that God poured down his wrath on South Carolina.[61]

The New England colonies and Pennsylvania eventually banned the importation of Indian slaves from Carolina, explaining that they were "of a malicious, surly, and revengeful spirit, rude and insolent in their behavior, and very ungovernable," which was more than mere prejudice given that Indians sometimes were the sources of slave unrest. In 1708, an Indian named Swaney, who had lived in bondage to William

Hallet Jr. of Long Island since he was four years old, killed Hallet, his wife, and his five children with an axe, apparently at the urging of an enslaved Black woman in the house. Afterward, colonial authorities executed Swaney and a number of his Indian and Black supposed accomplices. A mere four years later, in New York City, a group of slaves set fire to several buildings and then ambushed Whites who arrived to douse the flames. The rebels, twenty-one of whom authorities later executed and six of whom committed suicide, included not only Blacks identified as "Comarantee" and "Pappa" but also "Indians" and "Spanish Indians." The Spanish Indians had been arguing futilely for months that they should never have been enslaved in the first place because they had been captured as free Christian subjects of Spain.[62]

BLOODTHIRSTY ENEMIES

Between 1689 and 1763, imperial warfare between Britain, France, and Spain came to dominate eastern America, subsuming Indian-colonial wars and shaping the participants' racial views of themselves and their enemies. In the Northeast, the New England colonies, New York, and their Indigenous allies (Wampanoags, Narragansetts, Mohegans, Pequots, and others) repeatedly battled the French and their Native allies (Wabanakis, Western Abenakis, Catholic Mohawks, and occasionally Great Lakes tribes) for control of the Canadian Maritimes, northern New England, and the Lake Champlain–Lake George corridor. In the South, it was South Carolina and Georgia against, first, Spanish Florida and its Indigenous allies (Guales, Timucuas, Yamasees, and others from the missions) and, second, French Louisiana and the Choctaws. Though the imperial wars are remembered today for French and Indian raids on exposed British colonial outposts, and several mostly failed English attempts to conquer Quebec, they should also be recognized for their powerful influence in race-making, including a gruesome new form of racial violence.[63]

During the imperial wars, British colonists graphically expressed race hatred toward Indians through scalp bounties. Scalping, involving the cutting, removal, and preservation of a portion of the hair and skin from an enemy's head, had been customary throughout most of Native North America since time out of mind. Indigenous people treated scalps as honors of war, and often mounted these trophies on poles, stretched out on hoops, or sewn into warrior regalia. Taking a scalp also served as a last blow to the enemy, as it was believed to interfere with the passage of the soul to the afterlife. In the last several decades, a false myth has developed that Europeans taught scalping to Indians, not vice versa. What is true is that Europeans adopted and promoted this Native practice through bounty payments. They also made it a generator for mutually hostile White and Indian identities.⁶⁴

Though Europeans commonly decapitated and quartered egregious criminals and prisoners of war, they judged scalping to be "unchristian, inhumane, and barbarous," as Governor Jonathan Law of Connecticut put it. Colonists quickly set aside their scruples, however, based on the rationale expressed by a New York official that "we should deal exactly with them as they do by us, destroy and scalp as they do." After rewarding Indian allies for scalps during King Philip's War, the New England colonies began to offer payment to colonial soldiers and even civilians. Massachusetts passed a scalp bounty in 1689 and then again in 1703, during which the award rose from eight to one hundred pounds, more than twice the average annual income of a Boston artisan, or just below thirty thousand dollars in current U.S. money. New York followed suit in 1696, soon to be joined by nearly every British colony during the Seven Years' War in the 1750s. This was no fringe activity: Colonial authorities advertised these bounties in newspapers and broadsides and displayed enemy scalps in the halls of government.⁶⁵

Indian scalps became distinctive symbols of colonial community pride and hatred of Native people, particularly in New England. Whites throughout the region celebrated in 1724 after colonial forces destroyed the Abenaki town of Norridgewok, on the Kennebec River in Maine, and returned home with the scalps of twenty-six Indians and the town Jesuit priest, Sebastian Rale. During that same war, John Lovewell became a local celebrity for leading two separate scalp-hunting companies, one of which entered Boston in March 1725 parading ten Abenaki scalps before adulating crowds. New Englanders celebrated Lovewell's exploits not only in his day, but also for generations, as in poems authored by Henry Wadsworth Longfellow, Henry David Thoreau, and Nathaniel Hawthorne, and the application of his name to a town and mountain in Maine and a pond in New Hampshire.⁶⁶

Even Lovewell's stardom could not eclipse that of the Massachusetts scalping heroine Hannah Duston. Duston turned tragedy into fame in 1697, when, as a forty-year old mother of nine, Abenakis seized her from the town of Haverhill, on the border with New Hampshire, in an attack that killed twenty-seven people, including Duston's infant. Seemingly destined to a long captivity or ignominious death, two weeks later Duston led two of her fellow prisoners in tomahawking and scalping ten of their captors as they slept (including six Abenaki children). The trio then escaped by canoe down the Merrimack River until they reached home, where they received a bounty of fifty pounds for their grisly trophies, amounting to two years' wages for a common farm laborer. The Reverend Cotton Mather immediately published Duston's story as an example of Christian faith and resiliency in the face of devilish savagery, and other authors, including Hawthorne and Thoreau, followed in subsequent centuries. Statues of Duston erected in the nineteenth century still stand in Haverhill and Concord, New Hampshire. Both of them depict her with a tomahawk in hand, and the one in Concord features a bundle of scalps. The axe head with which she reportedly did the deed remains on display at Haverhill's Buttonwoods Museum, like a religious relic sanctifying the violence of the community's past.[67]

The bounty system obviously carried the grave risk that unscrupulous scalp hunters would target unsuspecting Native allies rather than enemies. Thus, the law typically required bounty hunters to report where they had been and who they had struck before receiving their pay, though just how strictly these provisions were enforced is unknown. What is certain is that colonial governments paid bounties for the scalps of not just Indian men, but women and children as well, with the unmistakable purpose of exterminating entire groups of people, or at least driving those groups out of the areas patrolled by the scalp hunters. In a rare critique of scalp bounties published in New York City in 1755, the anonymous author posed the question of "whether the putting old men, women, and children to death, from whom no resistance can be dreaded, be not murdering in cold blood?" The answer was obvious, which raised another poignant query, "What must strangers think of such a law?"[68]

Left: The statue of Hannah Duston on the town green at Haverhill, Massachusetts, town green. Right: Junius Brutus Stearns, *Hannah Duston Killing the Indians*, 1847. Courtesy of Colby College Museum of Art, Gift of R. Chase Lasbury and Sally Nan Lasbury.

This example aside, there was less debate in colonial society about the indiscriminate murder of Indian innocents than about British and French colonial governments buying the scalps of their White Christian enemies. Officials in New France explained to their superiors back home that Indians would not fight the English with sufficient vigor if rewarded only for captives, who were difficult and risky to transport. The British protested that scalping was too "barbarous" to apply to "Christians," failing to acknowledge that many of their Native enemies in northern New England and Florida were Christians, too. Occasionally, British colonies offered bounties for French as well as Indian scalps, as in the case of New York in 1746, but usually they targeted only Catholic missionaries and "Canadians dressed like Indians." Otherwise, the Earl of Loudon, commander-in-chief of Britain's forces in North America, denounced scalping as a "barbarous custom" to which the French should not be subjected.[69]

The rise of print in British America, especially the publication of captivity narratives, reinforced the scalp bounty's racial messages of White heroism, civilization, Christianity, and resiliency versus Indian savagery and paganism. Beginning with the story of Mary Rowlandson's Indian captivity during King Philip's War, these accounts at once titillated and horrified readers. They typically opened with the protagonist experiencing the terror of an Indian raid, marked by the slaughter of men, women, and children alike and destruction of hard-earned property. Cotton Mather, who published several of these stories, depicted Indian assailants as sadistic monsters who delighted in smashing the skulls of infants and cutting the throats of children in front of their helpless parents. The warriors then hauled the captive survivor off into the woods for a long journey to a French or Indian town, "unapproachable kennels" and "habitations of cruelty," as Mather styled them. Along the way, the prisoner suffered a daily cycle of mourning, abuse, starvation, and demoralization at the hands of "the heathen," "cruel and bloodthirsty savages," and "furious tawnies." Fortunately, survival offered the possibility of redemption, and having one's story printed. In New England, these narratives provided models of Christians maintaining their faith amid trials, and subsequent salvation in this world and the next. Elsewhere, captivity narratives were far less concerned with religious edification, particularly as the eighteenth century progressed, but maintained the basic structure of contrasting White civility and victimhood, on the one hand, with Indian savagery and bloodlust, on the other. More than 250 captivity narratives were published before the year 1800, and another 2,000 circulated in manuscript. Whereas colonists on the frontier faced the actual risk of captivity by Indians—there were some sixteen hundred cases in New England

Cover page of *A Narrative of the Captivity, Sufferings, and Removes of Mrs. Mary Rowlandson* (Boston: John Boyle, 1773).

alone between 1689 and 1754—it was captivity narratives and their accompanying oral histories that brought the danger into the homes and consciousness of White society as a whole.[70]

In the eighteenth century, newspapers performed a similar function, but with the additional role of reporting Indian atrocities in far-off places involving other "White people." Between 1704 and 1755, the *Boston News-Letter* published at least ninety-seven accounts of Indian depredations in Maine or the Canadian Maritimes, and dozens of similar stories from the Southern colonies. Likewise, during King George's War (1744–48) and the Seven Years' War (1754–63), New York newspapers were filled with shocking reports of Indian atrocities from North Carolina, Georgia, and especially Pennsylvania, afflicting not just Englishmen, but British colonists from a variety of religious and ethnic backgrounds, with whom readers would sympathize as fellow Whites. The stories' increasing use of that identifier made the connection plainly.[71]

Even outside of war coverage, newspapers contained plenty of material treating Indians as a single degraded group in contrast to the dignity of White people. There were the ubiquitous ads for the return of runaway Indian and mixed Indian servants and slaves, which assumed that colonists, as fellow Whites, would serve as a de facto deputy police force to monitor people of color on behalf of the property interests of colonial elites. Newspapers also commonly published stories about dysfunctional so-called Settlement Indians beset with drunkenness, stupidity, domestic violence, infanticide, and suicide, the more outrageous the tale the better. In November 1733 an "awful and affecting account" appeared in the *Boston News-Letter* about how an Indian couple from the praying town of Natick, John Pittomee and his wife, had left their three children at home alone, only for the oldest child, a girl of twelve or thirteen, to kill and eat her toddler brother. She confessed to colonial authorities after they began investigating the boy's disappearance. Yet, six weeks later, his intact body was found in the woods, dead from starvation and exposure after he had wandered off and gotten lost. Even a preteen Indian girl had enough exposure to colonial prejudice to know that White people would believe her extravagant nightmare.[72]

She did not need to read the newspaper to absorb such bigotry. It was everywhere, including in everyday sayings in which colonists invoked Indians to stigmatize certain behaviors. Anglicans in West New Jersey complained that they had nowhere to attend church but Quaker meetings, "which are as bad as the Indians' [assemblies], there's nothing but powwowing and conjuring to raise a devil." A critic of religious nonconformists in Providence, Rhode Island, denigrated them as "so rude and void of all sense of religion, that they are only distinguishable from the wild and barbarous Natives by their language and color." Anyone who lived remote from churches and courts might be said to be "in danger of becoming like the Indians themselves, without a God in the world." Such turns of phrase, associating Indians with the Devil, wildness, and godlessness, had become basic features of colonial speech.[73]

Most of the Indians' stories about race went unrecorded, but they tended to surface in the context of debates over whether the rivalry between the British and French was a ruse to distract from a more fundamental split between Indian and White peoples. Already, Indian-colonial warfare, intertribal conflicts, and disease had either destroyed or atomized several prominent groups throughout the East—Wampanoags, Narragansetts, Western Abenakis, Munsees, Susquehannocks, Piscataways, Powhatans, Tuscaroras, Yamasees, and many others—and seriously weakened others like the Mohicans, Shawnees, and Delawares. Larger confederacies such as the Haudenosaunees, Cherokees, Catawbas, and Creeks absorbed Indigenous populations too small to defend themselves, and tried to dominate the rest, but now colonial expansion and imperial warfare put their future in doubt as well. In fact, increasingly Indians judged that their very existence hung in the balance because the British and French, fellow Whites, both wanted to exterminate them.

As early as 1687, with tensions rising between the imperial powers, the Onondagas of the Haudenosaunee Confederacy told authorities from New York that they feared a joint conspiracy of the French and English, "for they are both of one skin, meaning they are both white skinned and not brown as the Indians are." Just two years later, the frontier town of Albany went on high alert based on a rumor that the Abenakis and Mohawks were discussing whether "to wage war against the Christians, as they understood the Christians intended to exterminate all the Indians; and that it become therefore necessary for all the Indians to unite against the Christians." Alarms warning of a "general insurrection of the Indians" sounded again in 1700, 1711, 1719, and 1733. Each time, Haudenosaunee leaders explained that the Indians were making defensive preparations because "they had been informed that the English and French had resolved to join together to destroy the Five Nations in order to divide their land" and more generally "that the white men designed to cut off the Indians."[74]

Such accusations led to a growing consensus among Indians to keep a "league of neutrality" between the imperial powers. As the Mohicans contended in several intertribal conferences, "the white people, with whom we respectively live in alliance, are about to enter into a war. We only destroy ourselves by meddling in their wars." The Onondaga chief, Canasatego, could not help but notice that as the White population grew, Indian numbers shrank, and therefore Indians should "be more careful before they destroyed one another again." Yes, the Mohawks affirmed, "let the white people determine their disputes themselves." Equally to the point, if Indians helped the British prevail over the French, "it would be of means to enslave themselves for then the English would make no more account of them than they do now of the River or Long Island Indians." In years to come, the Indian call to disengage from White people would involve the rejection of not only serving as military proxies for the imperial powers, but also all forms of White influence.[75]

DEATH OF A DREAM

The missionary William Andrews, who evangelized the Mohawks for the Society for the Propagation of the Gospel (SPG) after ten years preaching to colonists in Virginia, unwittingly found himself at the front edge of this burgeoning racial movement, and it poisoned his faith that Indians should join White people in Christianity and civilized society. The New York that greeted Andrews in 1712 bore a number of similarities to Le Jau's South Carolina. It was a remarkably heterogeneous place, with colonists from a dozen different religious and ethnic origins, and slaves constituting a fifth of the people in New York City. The vast majority of slaves in colonial New York were Africans, but a sizable minority were Natives, some of whom had arrived via Carolina. Trade with Indians was every bit as important to New York's economy as to its Southern counterpart. Indians from as far away as the western Great Lakes brought beaver pelts by the thousands to the Hudson River town of Albany for transshipment to Europe. At the same time, New York, like Carolina, remained constantly alert to the threat of the neighboring Catholic power, New France in this case, and its Native allies. It was with an eye toward solidifying New York's relationship with the Haudenosaunees that Andrews agreed to become the chaplain of Fort Hunter, a rustic military post among the Mohawks, forty miles west of Albany.[76]

Like Le Jau, Andrews initially saw himself as being in the vanguard of not only the British Empire but also Christ's kingdom, "with the hopes of doing some good among those poor, dark, ignorant creatures." Yet he found that most of colonial society had already given up such hope. No sooner had he reached Albany than Dutch colonists tried to discourage him that Indians "could never become good Christians" because "they were so much addicted to drunkenness, whoredom, and stealing." Andrews would not hear of it, not yet. Though he conceded that Indians could be "slothful and lazy enough," he blamed their vices, particularly drinking, on the colonists' own bad examples. Thus, he poured himself into his missionary work, including studying the Mohawk language so he could translate the *Book of Common Prayer* and teach Mohawk children to read and write in their own tongue. This was the most ambitious Indigenous literacy program since the translation of the Bible into the Wampanoag language in seventeenth-century New England. Additionally, Andrews preached to the Mohawks midweek and every Sunday. He reveled that "some of them are hearty and sincere in their Christian profession." For a brief moment, he could actually envision the Mohawks reaching his standards and merging with colonial society.[77]

The problem was that his Mohawk charges already had decades of experience with French Jesuit and Dutch Reformed missionaries, during which many of them had developed a strong distaste for Christianity. Years earlier, the opposition of traditionalist Mohawks had convinced hundreds of their Catholic tribesmen to split off and move closer to the French settlements on the St. Lawrence. Most Mohawks thought no better of Protestantism, despite their political ties to the English. Andrews's sponsor, the Society for the Propagation of the Gospel, heard that the Mohawks had "great prejudices to [against] our religion" because of "the English unjust encroachment upon their lands . . . They can't believe that we wish them a place in heaven when we deny them a place on earth." The Mohawks also "hated Christianity" because they "waste away and have done so ever since our first arrival among them (as they themselves say) like snow against the sun."[78]

During Andrews's tenure in Mohawk country, calls for a pan-Indian resistance arose again through the auspices of the Tuscaroras, who, after fighting a losing war with North and South Carolina, took refuge with the Haudenosaunees and became their sixth nation. The Tuscaroras, according to Andrews, insisted that Indians needed to unite and "make war upon the Christians" (meaning colonists) or else they were next because "the Christians were intended to cut them all off." A number of Mohawks agreed, and threats against Andrews's life mounted in turn, alongside accusations that he schemed to poison Mohawk children under the guise of baptizing them. It seemed to Andrews that, all of the Haudenosaunees, influenced by the Tuscaroras, "now take all occasions to find fault and quarrel [with colonists], wanting to revolt."[79]

Within two years, the Mohawks and Andrews had developed a mutual antipathy. Little by little, Mohawk students stopped attending Andrews's lessons because the parents considered such instruction to be "a useless thing," the crowds at his meetings thinned, and those who continued to show often did so as an excuse to buy liquor from the unscrupulous traders that loitered about Fort Hunter. In the summer of 1717, a Seneca man even burst into Andrews's quarters with a gun, threatening to shoot him "for denying him and his wife the sacrament, for which I had reason enough, being both great drunkards, guilty of Sabbath breaking, and cruelty in biting off a prisoner's nails that was lately brought here, and making offerings and consulting the devil."[80]

Feeling vulnerable, unappreciated, and frustrated, Andrews scribbled one racist screed after another to justify his meager results to his superiors in London. At first, he just derided the Mohawks as "a poor, ignorant, silly people who will do anything for advantage and have little esteem." A few months later, he drew deeper from the well of racist tropes to charge that "the very smell of them is offensive, being so greasy and nasty" and that "when they are sober they are quiet enough, but when drunk like mad men." Experience had disabused him that Indians as a whole were fellow children of God. In truth, he admitted, "the best character that I can give of the Indians of this nation so of all the others, is that they are a sordid, mercenary, beggarly people having but little sense of religion, honor, or goodness among them, living generally filthy, brutish lives. They are poor and beggarly through their own sottishness, sloth, and laziness . . . They are of an inhumane nature." Meanwhile, his Indian charges continued to condemn White Christians as land-grabbing hypocrites. Andrews concluded that his skeptics had been right all along, there was "little or no room for hopes of ever making them any better than as they are, heathens. Heathens they are and heathens they still will be." Shortly after penning these words, Andrews resigned his position and returned to Virginia, where, given the colony's near extirpation of local Indigenous people and marginalization of the rest to practical invisibility, he could reasonably hope never to have to deal with Indians again.[81]

Andrews's dream of bringing Indians to Christianity and civility was dead, the latest casualty in a colonial process that had already killed this founding colonial vision in one place and person after another. To be sure, the idea kept reviving and staggering onward, zombie-like, partly because colonial religious and political leaders saw it as their God-given duty, but also because they had no other moral justification for what had become an undeniably murderous conquest. Additionally, there were always some Indians so desperate in the face of colonial exploitation that they turned to Christianity as a last-ditch attempt to salvage some land and even life itself and perhaps make sense of it all. Yet, by Andrews's time, everyday White people commonly derided the notion of Christianizing and civilizing Indians as an elite fantasy that threatened their own dreams. To them, the only significant consequence of Indian evangelization would be to obstruct their appropriation of the Indians' country, which, contrary to their charters, was their real purpose for being in America. They proved over and over again that they would not let anyone stand in the way of this goal, not imperial officials, not their local political and religious leaders, and certainly not Indians. This was White American populism at work, and it would not stop until it had achieved the near total dispossession and obliteration of the continent's Indigenous people. The Natives could not unite as Indians fast enough. They would try, however, over and over again, displaying a will to survive every bit as resolute as their White adversaries' ambitions to exterminate them and seize their land.

CHAPTER 2

Race Wars

By the late 1760s, Indians throughout eastern America feared that the dark elements of colonialism were about to combine into an overpowering storm that would sweep them from the earth. Over the previous century, the population of the British colonies had expanded dramatically, from less than 150,000 in 1660 to some half a million in 1710, to nearly 1.5 million in 1760. Meanwhile, the Native population east of the Mississippi River had plummeted due to epidemic disease, intertribal warfare, colonial warfare, and slaving from its previous unknown heights to less than half a million. Colonists took advantage to expand from their Atlantic beachheads into the rich agricultural land approaching the Appalachian Mountains, and there appeared to be no end in sight. Britain's triumph in the Seven Years' War (1754–63) had won it France's vast American claims, which was consequential even though Indians still considered the land to be theirs alone. The Anglo-American assumption that Indians would be unable to defend their territory without France's help contributed to a surge of Whites across the Appalachian Mountains into the Ohio country (home of the Shawnees, Delawares, Mingos, Miamis, Wyandots, and others), Cherokee country, and Creek country. These intruders provoked Indians endlessly, expected to displace them entirely before too long, and were quick to call for their extermination whenever they resisted. Imperial and colonial officials bemoaned the chaos but frequently had profits at stake in it, for if White squatters could harass Indians out of their lands or incite a war to the same end, the elite's land corporations had a better chance of collecting on their speculative investments, including selling that territory back to the original interlopers. The Indians' superiority in forest warfare—and desperation—meant that sometimes they were able to reverse the White advance, but only temporarily. Their entire way of life, in which people lived with extended kin, ruled themselves, put only light pressure on the land, and engaged with the spirits of the surrounding world, faced utter destruction.[1]

The young, Connecticut-born Presbyterian missionary Samuel Kirkland learned about the Indians' apprehensions firsthand during a visit to the Senecas in spring 1765. Kirkland's aim was to convince Indians that their worldly comfort and eternal salvation required them to become Christian and civilized, but many Senecas had already concluded that this agenda was *against* the sacred order of things and led only to woe. One man named Onoonghwandekha explained that the Bible "was never made for Indians." The Great Spirit had already taught the Senecas to memorize, not write down, everything they needed to know. Consequently, Onoonghwandekha argued, "if we receive this White man and attend to the book which was made solely for White people, we shall become a miserable, abject people." As proof, he pointed to Indians who had adopted Christianity under colonial pressure, only for the English to reduce them to poverty and degradation, even servitude. "This will be the condition of our children and grandchildren in a short time if we change or renounce our religion for that of the White people," he warned. "We shall soon lose the spirit of true men. The spirit of the brave warrior and good hunter will no more be discovered among us. We shall be sunk so low as to hoe corn and squashes in the field, chop wood, stoop down, and milk cows like Negroes among the Dutch people." Missionaries faced this critique nearly everywhere they went in Indian country. How were they supposed to convert Indigenous people who believed, as the missionary David Brainerd put it, that "'twas not the same God [that] made them who made us," that the two peoples were "not of the same make and original"?[2]

Indians living near the coast under colonial subjugation largely agreed with Onoonghwandekha's assessment of their condition. The people of the tiny Choptank community on Maryland's eastern shore, which was one of the only groups of Natives left in the colony, described themselves as "dead and dispersed . . . [a] remnant . . . pitiful." They remembered "when there were great numbers of us Indians and but few White people in this nation, we enjoyed our privileges, profits, and customs in quiet, but it is quite contrary now." Their colonized existence, like that of other so-called Settlement Indians, was an endless succession of "malicious and hateful treatment" at the hands of "White people," including schemes to appropriate their meager lands and force them and their children into bondage.[3]

Not even Natives who lived up to Whites' civilized standards were immune from this debasement. In the mid-1770s, a cross-section of Christian Indians from southern New England and Long Island, including Narragansetts, Mohegans, Pequots, Niantics, and Montauketts, decided to form a community they called Brothertown and flee their colonized homelands for a new a start in the territory of the Oneidas, in what is now upstate New York. This remote location, they hoped, would both insulate them from colonial pressure and provide an opportunity to evangelize other Native people. Though these goals might seem to have been at cross-purposes, the Brothertown Indians did not view it that way at all. Led by a team of preachers who had attended English boarding schools, they believed that God wanted Indians to become civilized Christians, but that this course was impossible with underhanded White Christians as neighbors. Their leading light, the Mohegan minister Samson Occom, used a parable of "a poor Indian boy" to capture the trials he and his people faced on a daily basis in colonial society. This boy, as Occom told it, was "bound out to an English family" that beat him bloody for the least faults and often no fault at all. "Most of the time," the semifictional boy bewailed, his master abused him simply "because I am an Indian." "I can't help that God has made me so," Occom appealed, switching back to the first person. "I did not make myself so." Better to escape the endless indignation of life among White Christians for refuge among the Oneidas, who, though pagans, at least "look upon us to be as the same blood," as expressed by Occom's son-in-law, the Mohegan Joseph Johnson.[4]

The widely held Indian principle that Native people were of the "same blood" and fundamentally different from Whites contributed to the equally common belief that the Great Spirit had originally put Native people in America and Whites in Europe because he wanted them to pursue distinct ways of life. Europeans had violated His plan by crossing the ocean to America. Now, Indians demanded a halt to White encroachment on their lands and were prepared to fight back if necessary. As the Senecas urged the Delawares and Shawnees in 1767, "Brethren, those lands are yours as well as ours. God gave them to us to live upon, and before the White people shall settle them for nothing, we will sprinkle the leaves with their blood, or die every man of us in the attempt."[5]

To do nothing was to accept death anyway. The militants reasoned, as the British general Thomas Gage understood, "that as the White people have advanced from the coast, the original Natives have been destroyed, and of the numerous Nations which formerly inhabited the country possessed of the English, not one is now existing." With the Whites "drawing closer and closer" to the interior tribes, "they see it must soon be their turn to be exterminated." Moderate Indian leaders repeatedly bowed to colonial demands for more territory in the futile hope that, by currying favor with White authorities, this time, the line would hold. Yet most Indians had determined that there was no end to White people's greed at Indian expense. Their great fear, they told the British Indian agent Sir William Johnson, was that "we design shortly to fall upon and destroy all the Indians in alliance with us." Put in modern terms, Indians feared that White people had marked them for genocide.[6]

They were not wrong. "Backcountry" or frontier Whites, after suffering brutal retaliatory Indian raids for the better part of fifteen years and returning that violence blow for blow, were increasingly unwilling to make fine distinctions between Indian enemies and allies, Christian and civilized or not. They intended to protect themselves, or so they believed, and seize vast Indian territories in the process, by treating every Indian as hostile. When provincial authorities pleaded with the White people of Lancaster County, Pennsylvania, to stop murdering local "friend Indians," the killers answered that it was "dangerous to our frontiers to suffer any Indians of what tribe [what]soever to live within the inhabited parts of this province, while we are engaged in an Indian war; as experience has taught us that they are all perfidious." The country people's excuse for slaughtering Native women and children was that Indians were "cruel monsters" and "lest out of the serpent's egg . . . his fruit should be a fiery flying serpent."[7]

These ideas encouraged race war. After all, when Whites and Indians alike proclaimed that they were fundamentally different groups by God's design, and that the other was an evil, existential threat, it was an invitation to violence without limits. Such thinking justified Whites in their assaults on Indian land and autonomy, and galvanized Indians to unite in defense, but achieving those ends required mass murder. The legacy of this dark era was not just the blow to ideas rooted in religious faith and basic humanity that Indians and Whites could coexist, but the unleashing of mutual brutality that included a White campaign of genocide against Indigenous people.

DEBATING RACE

By the early eighteenth century, Native people throughout the East were busy probing the differences between Indians and Whites and the reasons for those distinctions, which eventually crystalized into their ideology for race war. All of them had suffered violent displacement at colonial hands, or witnessed it among their neighbors. Some of the survivors gathered in multiethnic refugee centers along the

Susquehanna River and its tributaries, roughly a hundred miles west of Philadelphia, where the Haudenosaunees granted them protection in exchange for their defending the southern approach to Haudenosaunee territory and providing way stations for Haudenosaunee warriors. This collection of people included Shawnees from all over the East, Delawares from New Jersey and Pennsylvania, Mohicans from western New England, Piscataways (or Conoys) and Nanticokes from Maryland, Tutelos from Virginia, Tuscaroras from North Carolina, and still others. Their shared colonial ordeals gave them much to discuss and consider.[8]

Their racial conversations also took place with colonists of every description, especially government officers and missionaries. Each diplomatic crisis or negotiation for land doubled as an opportunity to debate the nature of the two peoples and whether their differences could be narrowed. The same was true of missionary encounters, which occurred with greater frequency in this era than probably any period since the rise of Jesuit and Puritan evangelical campaigns in the seventeenth century. Congregationalist and Presbyterian missionaries fanned out through the Northeast following the Great Awakening of the 1730s and '40s and the opening of the Reverend Eleazar Wheelock's Connecticut boarding school to train Englishmen and Indians to spread the gospel. Their ranks included the colonists John Sergeant, Gideon Hawley, David Brainerd, Jonathan Edwards, and Samuel Kirkland, as well as the Mohegans Samson Occom, Joseph Johnson, and Samuel Ashbow, and the Montaukett David Fowler. Soon, they were joined in the field by the Moravians, a pietistic Protestant denomination from Germany with an American headquarters in Bethlehem, Pennsylvania, north of Philadelphia. Probably no one explored racial theories with Indians more deeply than these figures. Eventually, they also found themselves on the frontlines of a race war.

Inevitably, these racial exchanges included Indian critiques of White people, focusing on their Christian hypocrisy, greediness, and ingratitude. An unidentified Indian passing through Bethlehem in 1744 said "that he wanted to have nothing to do" with Christianity, "for he saw that even if many Indians and White people observe the Sabbath, they were still as wicked as them [non-Christians]." David Brainerd's experience was that Indians tended "to look upon all the white people alike, and to condemn them alike for the abominable practices of some . . . [They] have observed to me, that the white people lie, defraud, steal, and drink worse than the Indians" despite their claims to moral superiority as Christians. For Native people whose core ethic was generosity to the community, Christianity among Whites seemed to promote abominably selfish behavior.[9]

Additionally, White people seemed to have no sense of obligation to Indians, despite the history of Natives sustaining them when they first arrived in America. Echoing Pumetacom's critique of New England colonists on the eve of King Philip's War, Hudson River Indians in a 1754 conference reminded the English of a time when the "the White people were but small, [and] we were very numerous and strong." Past generations of Indians, "seeing the White people so few in number, lest they should be destroyed, took and sheltered them under their arms . . . we defended them in that low state, but now the case is altered[.] You are numerous and strong, we are few and weak; therefore we expect you will act by us in these circumstances as we did by you." The Delawares made the same point in the 1760s, when they told New Jersey officials, "Some of our old men can remember when the English were weak and few, and the Indians strong and many. We nursed them up in our bosoms and treated them as friends. We are glad our friendship hath continued so long, and hope it will always endure." Yet, with the population of the Mid-Atlantic colonies alone having climbed to more than 420,000, overwhelming the Indians' numbers, they feared it would not, which was why they invoked this memory in the first place. Native people complained at length that colonists would routinely "use them with ill language and call them dogs, etc. They take this unkindly, because dogs have no sense or understanding whereas they are men, and think that their brothers should not compare them to such creatures."[10]

The issue was more than just ingratitude, but an overall lack of basic social values that Indians had come to associate with Whites as a whole. "They wonder that the white people are striving so much to get rich," observed the Moravian missionary John Heckewelder, "and to heap up treasures in this world which they cannot carry with them to the next. They ascribe this to pride and to the desire of being called rich and great." Indians stressed that their own ancestors lived happily without such things and the endless worry about money that plagued Whites and made them so aggressive. The fact of the matter, as the South Carolina trader James Adair commented, was that Indians "think as meanly of the whites, as we possibly can do of them," adding, they "have an inexpressible contempt of the white people," calling them "nothings," "accursed people," "swine eater," "a swarm of tame fowls," and "ugly white people."[11]

The differences between Indian and White peoples seemed so fundamental that some Natives believed invisible forces lurking in colonial towns made them sick. After twenty Oneidas died of disease following an embassy to Philadelphia in 1749, the tribe's leaders concluded, "the evil spirits that dwell among the White people are against us and kill us." They cited this tragedy to reject an invitation to Virginia, explaining that "as you live much deeper within the settlements of the White people, the evil spirits must needs be more numerous, and of course will be destructive to us." Other Native people contended that the dissimilarity between Indians and Whites meant that Indian witchcraft "cannot hurt the White people," even though White spirits could harm Indians.[12]

In diplomacy, Indians sometimes tried to shrink these yawning divides by comparing their alliances with the colonies to the joint possession of a single body. This metaphor appeared most frequently in Native relations with Pennsylvania, following a precedent set in the earliest meetings between the Delawares and William Penn. Decades later, in 1723, the Conestogas, Delawares, and Shawnees recalled Penn's words that it was not enough for their people and his merely to join hands. "We must all be one half Indian and the other half English," they remembered Penn telling them, "being as one flesh and one blood under one head." As in the case of the great man / little child metaphor, soon other tribes began employing this analogy. Cherokees visiting London in 1730 proposed to the British, "tho' we are red and you are white, yet our hands and hearts are joined together." Such appeals became more urgent with every passing year as the metaphorical body began falling apart, in the hope that the words would magically stitch it back together.[13]

Natives tended to refer to themselves collectively as "Indians" and "Red people" and to colonists as "White people" or "Christians" in these racial discussions. Their use of "Indians" was probably not a matter of White interpreters taking liberties, as if, for example, a Native orator called his community "the people" in an Indigenous

Gustavus Hesselius, *Lapowinsa*, 1735. Courtesy of the Historical Society of Pennsylvania.

language and the scribe wrote "Indians" in English. Eighteenth-century writings produced by the literate Christian Wampanoags of Cape Cod and Martha's Vineyard in their own language use the words "Indians," "Ingun," and "Indiansog" (the latter featuring the Algonquian plural suffix "sog"). Colonial translations of Indians referring to themselves as "red" probably are equally reliable. The historian Nancy Shoemaker has argued convincingly that the notion of Indians as "red" originated with Native people in the Southeast like the Creeks and Cherokees in the 1720s, then spread to other Indians and Whites. Southeastern tribes traditionally categorized their towns and chiefs as either "Red" (symbolizing war) or "White" (symbolizing peace). "Red" and "White" representatives would sit on opposite sides of council fires and "Red" and "White" towns would compete against each other in the great ball game, the forerunner of lacrosse. Thus, when Europeans called themselves "White," particularly in diplomatic settings, Southeastern Indians dealing with them were culturally conditioned to respond by self-identifying as "Red." If there were cases of colonial interpreters mistranslating Native speakers' terms for themselves, they likely involved substituting "Indians" for "Red people." In most Southeastern Native languages, the word for "Indian" contains a reference to red, as in the Creek word for Indian, *esté-cāté*, which literally translates as "man red." "We are red people," proclaimed the Chickasaw headman Suckatoby in 1758; "I am a red man." Doubtless some Indians would have appreciated that their self-identification as red carried the implicit threat in their cultures that they were ready for war.[14]

It is possible that some interpreters translated Indian references to "Christians" as "Whites," but a greater certainty is that Indians increasingly used that color term as the eighteenth century progressed. "White man" is "the name they [Indians] give to any European," Georgia's Patrick Mackaway commented in a 1735 letter to England. At least one Wampanoag-language writing by a Wampanoag source identifies a female colonist as *wompessue*, or "white woman." The Delawares recalled that when the English landed in Virginia, Indians initially called them *Wapside Lenape*, or White people. Yet as hard experience began to reveal differences among the *Wapside Lenape*, the Delawares created more specific labels for them. They referred to Mid-Atlantic colonists as *Schwaannack*, "which signifies salt beings, or bitter beings . . . to express contempt as well as hatred or dislike, and to hold out the white inhabitants of the country as hateful or despicable beings." By contrast, Virginians were *Mechanschican*, or Long Knives, in an obvious allusion to their murderous land lust. "Long Knives" eventually became a common Indian appellation for frontier Whites in general, for the same reason it applied to Virginians.[15]

Whereas in the late seventeenth century, Indians sometimes referred to the British as White but not the French and Spanish, by the early eighteenth century they began to apply "White" to Europeans as a whole. One example comes from a 1726 Cherokee-Creek-English conference in Charles Town, South Carolina, in which the Cherokee leader, Long Warrior, began by referring to the gathered Indians collectively as "the red people... our flesh is both alike" and to the English as "White People." But then he asked of the Creeks, "Why do you go to the French and Spaniards... How can you go to so many white people?" More than just a reference to complexion, Indians increasingly used "White" to mean a descent group with discrete character traits. That is to say, they applied the word racially.[16]

The same is true for the rare recorded instances in which Indians mentioned Black people. In the 1640s, Roger Williams recorded that the Narragansett word for African, *Suckáutacone*, meant "a coal black man." A century later, at least one Wampanoag document used "Legroo" in place of "Negro." The meanings Indians associated with such terms tended to be negative. In 1702, a Hudson River sachem named Sackquaans took particular offense that a Mohawk had been killed by four Blacks because he judged that "Negroes... have no courage nor heart." In the Southeast, where the enslavement of Blacks took place on a larger scale, Indigenous people revised their origin stories to have the spirits create Indians or Whites first with superior qualities and Blacks last with the least desirable ones. The Reverend Hugh Jones of Virginia went so far as to claim that Indians "hate, and despise the very sight of a Negro." Native people made plenty of derisive statements to support that assertion, but those examples are offset by equally numerous cases in which Indians engaged in friendly relations with Blacks, including adopting them into their families and permitting them to hold prominent roles in their communities. The ambiguity stems from Native people's lack of investment in these attitudes, for at this point it was Whites, not they, who wanted to degrade Black people in order to justify enslaving them. For the meantime, Natives had far greater stakes in understanding the nature of Whites—and themselves.[17]

CREATION AND SALVATION

Since the beginning of the colonial era, Indians and missionaries had debated endlessly whether Indians could and should become Christian and civilized, the political agendas of missionaries, and the openness of White society to Indians who reformed. Those issues took on added importance in the mid-eighteenth century because it seemed as if Indians' very existence was at risk as the two peoples marched toward race war. Colonial hatred of Christian Indians, which had surfaced irregularly in the seventeenth century, had, by the eighteenth, become pervasive in British American society even in peacetime, in lockstep with colonial designs on Indian territory. In the mildest expression of this animus, Whites merely discouraged Indians from heeding their missionaries and missionaries from doing their work in the first place. Colonists near David Brainerd's mission community of Crosswicks (modern Trenton, New Jersey) tried to frighten his Delaware charges that "my design was to gather together as large a body of them as I possibly could, and then sell them to England for slaves." When the Moravian missionary Henry Rauch arrived in America in 1740, Whites in New York City told him not to bother evangelizing Indians because they were "a set of debauched beings among whom no European could dwell in safety." Rauch and the Moravians persevered by launching two missions to the Mohicans east of the Hudson River, only for local colonists to drive the missionaries and their most devoted followers out of the region to Pennsylvania. The unfortunate truth, explained Rev. Samuel Hopkins of West Springfield, Massachusetts, was that most White people subscribed to the principle, "let us not be at any cost and pains to gain the friendship of such a perfidious crew" as Indians, "but let us destroy them all."[18]

Indians also had "deep-seeded jealousies" of missions as wedges for the spread of White settlement, never mind culture. They "are always afraid of some design forming against them," Brainerd wrote in frustration; "they have no reason to think that the white people are now seeking their welfare." The Haudenosaunee community of Jeningo suspected even the Mohegan missionary, Samuel Ashbow, as a colonial front man, telling him "that they are very unwilling that your English should get footing among them lest by & by they root them out as they have done in New England," to Ashbow's own people, in fact.[19]

The wretched state of most Christian Indians gave rise to a common Indian argument that Christianity and civility were not meant for their kind. Sir William Johnson, who lived among the Mohawks and managed Britain's diplomacy with the northeastern tribes, heard from Indians "that it appears to them to have been ordained from the beginning that the white people should cultivate the arts, and themselves pursue hunting, that no other way of life is agreeable to them, or consistent with their maxims of policy and frame of their constitution, if it may be so called." Indians who had tried to adopt the White people's way of life "have hitherto derived no advantage from it. That on the contrary they are poor, abject, full of avarice, hypocrisy, and in short have imbibed all our vices, without any of our good qualities and without retaining their former abilities for gaining a subsistence in the only way they conceive that nature intended they should." Johnson used the words "ordained," "constitution," and "nature" deliberately because many Indians believed that they were conditioned both culturally and physically for their traditional way of life. Therefore, if they became civilized Christians, it "would be followed by their annihilation as a people."[20]

Missionaries, White and Indian alike, countered that this view had it backward, that *avoiding* annihilation *required* Indians to adopt Christianity and civility. Of course, missionaries had always cited this goal as the moral imperative for colonization, but the worldly stakes had become much higher by the mid-eighteenth century. Whites were forcing their way inland in such massive numbers that it no longer seemed possible for Native people to resist them for long. If Native people would not learn to make do with less territory, Whites were just going to seize it from them and annihilate those who fought back. The missionaries' argument was that a "respectable" life of sedentary living and intensive farming marked by plow agriculture and animal husbandry performed by males would allow Indians in the path of colonial expansion to cede their vast hunting grounds and prevail on White migrants to accept them as neighbors. Otherwise, predicted the missionary Gideon Hawley in 1763, "it will be as rare to hear or see an Indian within that vast country, as it is to find an Indian in Connecticut."[21]

Indians understood this logic even as they searched for alternatives to it. Haudenosaunees responded to Hawley that they were "sensible to the grasping disposition of the white people. They say now that the white people have surrounded them and they have, as they express it, only an island left and by and by they are quite afraid they will be quite drove off from their lands." Some of them hoped that adopting Christianity would persuade Whites to permit them to retain portions of their home territory. As the Oneidas of Kanawalohare told Samson Occom, their interest in learning "the right way of God" and putting "all our sins and all our heathenish ways and customs... behind our backs" had everything to do with their wish "that none may molest or encroach upon us." Despite the poor record of this strategy among the Indians of New England, it seemed to be the only peaceful option.[22]

Yet even Occom could not find acceptance among Whites, despite his status as a formally educated, ordained minister who spoke English and lived in what colonists judged to be a civilized manner. In October 1763, one of Occom's missionary colleagues, David Crosby, got into an argument in a Middletown, Connecticut, tavern with two men he overheard saying that the only way to "Christianize the heathen" was "powder and ball," or force of arms. When Crosby protested, the men responded by asking whether he would be willing "to marry an Indian squaw" (or woman), which left him sputtering because he knew the answer was no. While Crosby tried to compose himself, one of his antagonists continued, probably in a cruder manner than recounted, "I am so well acquainted with human nature as to know the irreconcilable aversion that white people must ever have for black." Consequently, missionary programs were "altogether absurd and fruitless . . . so long as the Indians are despised by the English we may never expect success in Christianizing of them." The two men agreed "that for their own parts, they could never respect an Indian, Christian or no Christian, so as to put him on a level with white people on any account, especially to eat at the same table. No—not with Mr. Occom himself, be he ever so much a Christian or even so learned." These sentiments were so widespread that an Anglican minister advised the Mohawk Joseph Brant, a student of Wheelock's, not to travel through New York City because White people there "heartily cursed" Indians "as deserving all to be extirpated."[23]

Even missionaries widely expressed disdain for Native people, including Christians. Brainerd judged the Indians he evangelized to be "unspeakably indolent and slothful," with "little or no resolution or ambition. Not one in a thousand of them has the spirit of a man." He had no appreciation for the wide-ranging, exhausting hunting expeditions or brave roles as warriors of the men he disparaged. Amid John Sergeant's proselytization of the Mohicans, he derided Indians as "a people difficult to be reformed from their own foolish, barbarous, and wicked customs,"

Jonathan Spilsbury, *Samson Occom* mezzotint, 1768, after Mason Chamberlain, *The Reverend Samson Occom*.

including a "base, ungrateful temper." Wheelock required his Native students and graduates to subordinate themselves in correspondence with him as "your worthless servant," "your good for nothing Indian servant," and even "a despicable lump of polluted clay as is enclosed in this tawny skin of mine." Wheelock aimed to save Indian souls, but Indians in the here and now would have to perform ceremonial racial deference and self-degradation to avail themselves of his Christian teaching.[24]

There were limits to the amount of devaluation that Christian Indians would tolerate from Whites. When the evangelical fervor known as the Great Awakening swept through Rhode Island and Connecticut in the late 1730s and early 1740s, Native participants initially attended preaching alongside Whites at White-run churches, but soon they began to chafe at their fellow Christians' insistence on racial hierarchy. It was difficult for Native believers to square the movement's emphasis on the equality of all souls with the humiliation in church of having to sit in a segregated section at the back or in the balcony. Nor could they reckon why colonial evangelicals would tolerate the preaching of unlettered White people filled with the spirit, but not that of Indians. The hypocrisy stung deeper when Whites who claimed Christian fellowship with Indians continued with their schemes, as the Pequots characterized it, "to dispossess them of all their Lands & so turn them adrift, or make Servants of them." Eventually, most Narragansetts, Mohegans, Pequots, and Niantics split off to form "Indian" churches built on the ethic of compassion for the poor and weak. As one Narragansett parried an English critic: "This is the way that we Indians have to get to Heaven. You white people have another way. I don't know but your way will bring _you_ there, but I know that our way will bring _us_ there."[25]

MURDEROUS

The growing consensus among Whites and Indians that they belonged to two fundamentally opposed groups featured in a string of cases in which White frontiersmen murdered Indians in cold blood, sometimes out of suspicion that they were enemies, but more often just because they were Indians. What was most disturbing of all, to Indians and colonial authorities alike, was how frequently White frontier society obstructed the arrest and trial of these killers. In the early seventeenth century, when Indians were important economic partners and a military threat, colonial governments in New England, at least, sometimes arrested, tried, and executed colonists for the murder of Indians, despite widespread settler resistance to it. Yet, by the mid-eighteenth century, the balance of power had shifted considerably. Indians remained formidable at the edges of colonial settlement, but they no longer had the military might to threaten the colonies' existence or the economic clout to force colonists to think twice before acting. Furthermore, colonial society had expanded beyond the range of the government's authority. In this context, colonists at every level of frontier society challenged the principle that White murderers of Indians should face justice, or even that they had committed a crime at all. Fairer-minded Eastern elites who dared to oppose the mob faced its wrath, too. Conditions were eerily similar to Virginia and Maryland in the era of Bacon's Rebellion.[26]

Such turmoil is normally associated with Pennsylvania in the 1760s, but the pattern actually began with the "Wiscasset case" in Maine more than a decade earlier. In December 1749, a group of White sailors made an unprovoked attack on a small, unthreatening band of Penobscot and Norridgewok Wabanakis, killing one man and wounding two others. Official attempts to bring the murderers to trial came to naught in the face of opposition by armed mobs with blackened faces and a White public that refused to provide any assistance. As one exasperated magistrate explained to distant superiors in Boston, there was "a spirit almost universally prevailing" in Maine "amongst those who live the most exposed to the Indian enemy in wartime . . . to secure murderers from the hands of justice."[27]

Eventually, a handsome fifty-pound reward led to the recovery of the accused killers, Samuel Ball and Benjamin Ledite, far to the south in Massachusetts, and revealed their personal histories of violence with Indians. Before taking work as sailors, both men had been soldiers in Maine pursuing scalp bounties. Furthermore, Ball's father had been killed by Indians. This history also helps to explain Maine colonists' unwillingness to hold them accountable for their crime, for practically everyone had suffered personally in their ongoing fight to wrest the Eastern country from Indigenous people.[28]

Colonists had lectured the Wabanakis for years about the superiority of English justice over "private revenge," but this was the wrong case on which to rest that argument. The Wabanakis waited patiently as authorities postponed the trial several times out of concerns for safety—just finding judges was difficult given the intimidation of the crowd. But their forbearance ran out after Ball managed to escape from jail and a local jury found Ledite guilty, not of murder but just assault, for which he received only a short whipping. Finding no redress from White courts answerable to a White public that, by and large did not consider killing Indians an offense, the Wabanakis took matters into their own hands and launched a new round of attacks on outlying White settlements.[29]

Massachusetts responded in what had become its customary way, issuing yet another scalp bounty promoting the wanton murder of innocents. Seeking this reward, on July 2, 1755, the colonist James Cargill led a company against the Penobscots, killing and scalping a family of three known for helping to keep the peace. Next, Cargill's men ambushed a Penobscot peace delegation on its way back from a conference at St. George's Fort, scalping nine. This affront to basic diplomatic protocols got Cargill arrested and tried, but also, like others before him, acquitted. Furthermore, it *enhanced* his reputation among fellow Whites to such an extent that he received an appointment as a militia colonel. As for the Penobscots, they withdrew northward and continued their campaign from there, which Massachusetts answered by raising the bounty against them to three hundred pounds per scalp, worth a breathtaking eleven years' wages for a farm worker, or some eighty thousand dollars in modern currency. The reward was sufficiently enticing to convince even the Reverend Thomas Smith of Falmouth, Maine, to join a scalp posse.[30]

If the Wiscasset case portended a new era of racially motivated White violence against Indians, the Seven Years' War (1754–63) solidified it. During this conflict, Indians allied with the French struck isolated colonial farmsteads and exposed villages throughout northern New England and New York and along the length of the Appalachian foothills from Pennsylvania to Georgia. Delawares, Shawnees, and Mingos killed or captured upward of six thousand colonists in the Allegheny country around Pittsburgh during these years. In the South, Indians also targeted slaves for capture, particularly those, according to South Carolina governor James Glen, "as had the least tincture of Indian blood in them." The Indians' resistance left British colonists everywhere terrified and full of vengeance.[31]

Even Whites who did not experience Indian assaults directly read about them in sweeping, sensationalist newspaper coverage. A representative and widely reprinted screed by Captain Benjamin Cordon of South Carolina demonized Indians as a whole as "Savages, a pack of hell hounds! Who have no idea of mercy! Whose glory is the most horrid barbarities and whose thirst for blood is insatiable; who can tear the tender infant from the mother's breast, take it by the heels, dash its head against a stump, and throw the brains in the mother's face, with the most brutal rites and ceremonies!" Anyone who turned to the papers for war news might question whether Indians were human at all.[32]

White society's blanket hostility toward Indians made diplomacy with them difficult and sometimes impossible. Lieutenant Governor Spencer Phips of

By His Honour Spencer Phips, Esq. . . . (Boston: printed by John Draper, 1755).

A proclamation by Massachusetts governor Spencer Phips of a bounty put on the scalps of the Penobscots. Courtesy of the Massachusetts Historical Society.

Massachusetts could not invite Native leaders to treat for peace without the risk of his troops "suddenly firing on any scattering Indian or Indians that may be met with." Even when Native ambassadors managed to arrive safely, colonial politicians' discriminatory treatment of them tended to leave them with more grievances, not fewer. In 1764, the Massachusetts legislature refused to meet with a visiting delegation of Abenakis because, Governor Francis Bernard complained, "the Indians were thought to be too contemptible and insignificant to deserve so public a notice from this government." Bernard understood that the only way to negotiate an end to the war was "if they were treated in such a manner as would show that we did not neglect or despise them."[33]

As in previous wars, colonists and British troops subjected even Indian allies to this sort of degradation. Though the Stockbridge Mohicans of western Massachusetts were Christians and volunteered men for the British service at an exceptionally high rate, General Jeffery Amherst expressed "as bad an opinion of those lazy rum-drinking scoundrels as anyone could have." He was just echoing the prejudices of the colonists he was assigned to protect. In 1753, a White jury acquitted one man and found another guilty only of manslaughter for murdering a Stockbridge Indian who had confronted them on the correct suspicion that they were horse thieves. The following year, nearly a thousand militiamen poured into Stockbridge town from the surrounding countryside after two local White children were found killed by enemies long since gone. The frustrated troops turned their rage against the Mohicans by "calling them by hard names" and "threatening their destruction." The next spring "some vile persons" exhumed a fresh Stockbridge Indian grave and scalped the corpse, possibly with the intent of collecting a bounty, and certainly to express the deepest contempt. Indians suffered these types of provocations practically wherever and whenever they were in contact with colonial society. As Sir William Johnson related, during the 1760 campaign, a White soldier "imprudently cursed an Indian who was passing by his tent, saying that on our return from Canada we should soon extirpate all of their color." Little did the soldier know that this Indian understood English. After news of this threat spread through the Native ranks, seven hundred warriors threatened to abandon the campaign, saying "that they did not think, they should have been insulted for accompanying us."[34]

The abuse grew so intolerable that the Cherokees turned from friends of the British into enemies. In spring 1758, a band of Cherokees quit the British siege of French Fort Duquesne and headed for home southward along the east side of the Shenandoah Mountains. Though this territory was presumably friendly, soon they found themselves in a running battle with White Virginians for whom the notion of Indian allies was an oxymoron, particularly when those allies stole their horses and killed their hogs for food. White militiamen murdered upward of forty Cherokees, some of whom they scalped, which among Indians was a declaration of war. Then the survivors returned to Cherokee country to discover that their kin had been struggling in their absence with White South Carolinians poaching on their hunting grounds and redcoats stationed at Fort George assaulting the women. The Cherokees aimed to settle the score with a series of brutal raids against White settlements, but British authorities would not let the matter rest there. Instead, they took over thirty Cherokee political delegates hostage until the tribe surrendered any of their men who had killed Whites. This diplomatic breach was an "unpardonable injury," made infinitely worse when soldiers slaughtered the captives in the midst of a Cherokee attack to free them. Unwilling to suffer such indignities, the Cherokees struck back with a campaign "to kill all the white men" that forced the abandonment of Fort Loudon, deep in Cherokee territory, and reached within seventy-five miles of Charles Town (now Charleston).[35]

The British response was ruthless, though North Carolina governor Arthur Dobbs's proposal to capture Cherokee women and children and sell them as slaves to the West Indies does not appear to have been taken up. In June 1761, twenty-six hundred British and colonial troops fought their way into the heart of Cherokee country and destroyed seventeen towns, torched more than fifteen hundred acres of crops, and displaced between a third and half of the tribe's population. The soldiers had orders to execute any prisoner who fell into their hands. Unable to take this punishment, the Cherokees sued for peace and ceded half of their Lower Towns' hunting territory to get it. This so-called Cherokee War laid bare the hard truth that White societies allied with Indians only out of short-term self-interest. Their long-term goals were to drive Indigenous people off the land and seize it, justified by the prevailing idea that Indians were savages, beasts, and monsters. If Native people, including allies, dared to mount a defense, Whites were prepared, in the words of Virginia's commissioners to the Cherokees, to "cut them off from the race of mankind."[36]

Murderous racial tensions reached their highest pitch in Pennsylvania, an irony given that the colony's founder, William Penn, had promised to keep the peace by treating Indians with justice, which is how White Americans have preferred to remember the story. Yet Penn's romantic vision was impossible to achieve. It was premised on the Delaware Indians' ceding and then permanently abandoning their lands in exchange for payment, whereas the Delawares originally believed that land sales were a step toward joint occupation and friendship. They certainly did not anticipate a massive migration of Europeans that would drive them out of their country. By 1710, Pennsylvania was already home to 25,000 people, and by 1760 its population had reached nearly 180,000, or just 70,000 shy of the estimated total number of Indians east of the Mississippi River. This surge first pushed the Delawares west to the Susquehanna River, and then another two hundred miles west to the Ohio. The Delawares and their Shawnee allies could plainly see that if they did not fight back, there would be no end to White people's displacements of them.[37]

During the Seven Years' War, Indian attacks on Pennsylvania's frontier settlements were brutal and unpredictable, though sometimes the choice of targets was to avenge previous insults and injuries. In just the year of 1755–56, Delawares and Shawnees, some of them speaking German and English, killed at least 326 Pennsylvania Whites and took at least 125 captive, with most of the violence centered in the Susquehanna Valley. The Philadelphian botanist John Bartram noticed that the same Indians who destroyed "all before them with fire, ball and tomahawk" knew their victims formerly as "almost daily familiars at their houses, eat, drank, cursed, and swore together [and] were even intimate playmates." Not anymore.[38]

Yet, in the face of this crisis, Pennsylvania's leaders did practically nothing, which led the frontier people to charge them with being Indian lovers and even traitors. The actual cause of this inaction was that Pennsylvania's governor had little power independent of the legislature, and the Quaker-dominated assembly would not authorize funds for defense or a scalp bounty unless the Penn family agreed to pay taxes on its exempt proprietary lands. Furthermore, the Quakers genuinely believed that honest diplomacy and justice would bring the warring Indians to peace in a manner consistent with Quaker pacifism. Western colonists, though, interpreted this impasse as the Quakers' valuing Indians more than them, for it was an open secret that city Quakers commonly loathed Scots-Irish Presbyterian frontiersmen as White savages. With every Indian strike, the country people grew more determined to force the government either to protect them or permit them to defend themselves. When the colony's interpreter to the Indians, Conrad Weiser, passed through the western counties in 1755, a furious mob held up his party at gunpoint to demand "that they should have a [governmental] reward for every Indian which they kill." The legislature finally gave in to this demand the following year under the threat that a frontier army was preparing to attack Philadelphia.[39]

Nevertheless, the legislature took few other defensive actions. Rather, it supported a Quaker initiative to have a "Friendly Association" negotiate with the warring Indians through "pacific measures," including redressing their grievances and reopening trade. The association contended that, "though [the Indians] are savage, and inexpressibly cruel to their enemies, they are not void of a large share of natural understanding; [and] have, in many cases, clear sentiments of justice and equity..." Frontier militants used the occasion of a peace treaty held in Lancaster in June 1757 to express their disgust toward these friendly principles. While the delegates were in session, up rode a procession of country people carting "four dead bodies [of White people], one of which was a woman with child... scalped and butchered [by Indians] in a most horrid manner," which they "laid before the door of the courthouse for a spectacle of reproach to everyone there."[40]

Indians had already gotten the message. The previous year, Scaroyady, an Oneida headman and Iroquois League representative to Pennsylvania, had complained to provincial officials that Indians "are not secure anywhere. At present your people cannot distinguish foes from friends; they think every Indian is against them; they blame us all without distinction... the common people to a man entertain this notion, and insult us wherever we go." No wonder that Indians in the Ohio country heard "a great many bad stories about the English: that they put the Indians to death that were left in the Province—that they destroyed all the Indians on the Susquehanna." Indians carried this dread almost anywhere they went in the British colonies, but particularly while traveling the so-called Warrior's Path that cut through Pennsylvania, Maryland, and Virginia, where Whites tended to shoot first and ask questions later. Such "unbrotherlike behavior," at best, left Indians "greatly disgusted," but, at worst, heightened their fear that colonists "aim at their entire extirpation."[41]

SEPARATE CREATIONS, PROPHETIC MOVEMENTS

Indians throughout the eastern half of the continent responded with a new iteration of the old idea that individual nations had their own spiritual creators and divinely ordained ways of life. This time, however, they applied that thinking to Indians, Whites, and Blacks as discrete groups. They interpreted the afflictions plaguing Indians, including disease, land loss, the decline in game animals, and alcohol abuse as the Great Spirit's punishments for deviating from the proper course of Indian behavior in favor of White ways. Corrupted Indians would suffer an even worse lot in the next life, in the form of eternal torments like the ones Christians imagined in hell. If Indians wanted to restore the Great Spirit's favor and return to the good times of the ancestors, they needed to purge themselves of White influences and follow a set of new pan-Indian rituals, communicated by the Great Spirit to religious seekers through visions.[42]

This message restored a sense of power to Indians overwhelmed by the colonial onslaught. The goal of slowing down or even rolling back White encroachment no longer depended on an unsolvable puzzle of politics, military strategy, and resources, but on Indians' relationship to the Great Spirit. Suddenly, the impossible became possible, dreams could become reality. The added benefit was that, as Native people pursued their reforms, they were simultaneously cultivating Indian solidarity, which, in reality, was their best long shot to preserve their independence and way of life from the threat posed by Whites.

Here was both a revival and a reformation, a mix of old and new means to restore an idealized past and chart a more viable future. Indians had always used visions to direct cultural and political changes, but this time the message came from a "Great Spirit" with obvious similarities to the Christian God. The directive was to return to the ways of the ancestors, but the very notion of a distinct, divinely ordained Indian way of life was an innovative response to the common threat of colonialism. The Great Spirit's chastisements for Indians who had strayed from that path awakened them to the need to band together, as Indians, to reform their lives, recover their spiritual power, and seize back control of their homeland. It is for that reason that scholars call this movement Nativism.

The incubators of Nativism were the multitribal settings of the Susquehanna and Ohio River Valleys and the Haudenosaunee communities that claimed authority over them. In the run-up to the Seven Years' War, Indians from these places repeatedly expressed that the Creator did not intend for Whites to live in America, and certainly not west of Pennsylvania's Blue Mountain range. At the Lancaster Treaty of 1744, the Onondaga spokesman, Canasatego, lectured delegates from Maryland and Virginia that "our ancestors came out of this ground, and their children have remained here ever since. You came out of the ground in a country that lies beyond the seas. There you may have a just claim, but here you must allow us to be your elder brethren, and the lands to belong to us long before you know anything of them." Canasatego's Haudenosaunee counterpart, Gachradodow, agreed, citing as evidence the "different colors of our skins, and of our flesh ... The Great King might send you over to conquer the Indians, but it looks to us that God did not approve of it; if he had, he would not have placed the sea where it is, as the line between us and you." Within a decade, these arguments were common among Indigenous people everywhere on the frontlines of White encroachment. The Seneca leader Tanaghrisson, for instance, informed the French that the forks of the Ohio (modern Pittsburgh), the epicenter of imperial tensions, was not a prize for the contending European powers. "Both you and the English are white," he underscored, "therefore the land belongs to neither one nor the other: But the Great Being above allowed it to be a place of residence for us [Indians]." If White people did not halt their incessant clamoring for land, the Great Spirit would empower Indians to give them a harsh reminder of his original intent.[43]

The Great Spirit also threatened to unleash his wrath on Indians who adopted White ways, whether Christianity, alcohol consumption, or selling territory. As early as 1737, a "seer" from the town of Otsiningo on the Susquehanna proclaimed that the Great Spirit had driven away the Indians' game animals because he was offended at them for drinking rum bought with deerskins. If they did not halt their transgressions, he would "wipe them from the earth." Twelve years later, Moravian missionaries heard that a Nanticoke living along the Susquehanna had a vision in which the Creator said that "he had made brown and white people. To the brown, he had given the Sacrifice, which they were to offer to him if they had not acted properly . . . to the white people, he had given the Bible." Indians should not "go the same way" as Whites because "if [Indians] associated with them, [the White people] would devour them all." By the Seven Years' War, Nanticoke adherents of this vision were circulating an illustration of Indian drunkards in hell boiling in a kettle, one of the most common trade goods from Whites. Another prophet on the Susquehanna, named Wangomen, posited that the Great Spirit had separate afterlives for Indians, Whites, and Blacks. White people, in their hell, suffered punishment "for making beasts of the Negroes," whereas Indians burned for the sin of adopting White ways. As to why, an unidentified Delaware woman in the Susquehanna town of Wyoming explained that alcohol was poison for Indians because the Great Spirit meant it only for Whites. The Oneida leader Saghughsuniunt summed up these ideas when he told colonial representatives at Lancaster in 1762, "I am not as you are; I am of a quite a different nature from you."[44]

Of the half a dozen or so Native seers who preached such messages during the 1750s and '60s, none were as influential as the Delaware named Neolin. The location of his home village of Tuscarawas Town, in what is now eastern Ohio, spoke to the Delaware people's numerous displacements over the previous century at the hands of the Dutch, English, and Haudenosaunee. Yet the Delawares and Shawnees remained "always in fear" in their new home, too, because the Whites kept coming.

But then Neolin had a vision that gave them hope. In it, he journeyed to Paradise and met with the Master of Life, who emphasized that he loved Indians, but hated their adultery, polygamy, infighting, alcohol abuse, dependence on White people's goods, and sales of their ancestral territory. The Master of Life thundered, "This land, where you live, I have made it for you and not for others. How comes it that you suffer the whites on your lands? Can't you do without them?" The obvious answer was yes, and thus the solution, according to the Master of Life, was to "drive them out, make war upon them. I do not know them at all, they know me not, and are my enemies, and the enemies of your brothers. Send them back to the land which I have created for them and let them stay there." If Indians followed this command, they would recover the safety and abundance their ancestors had enjoyed. If they did not, the Master of Life would continue to smite them in this life and the next.[45]

Whites in Indian country were alarmed by the sudden popularity of Neolin's vision. James Kenny, a trader in Pittsburgh, worried that his profits would suffer because the "Imposter" had convinced Indians that "the right way to heaven" was to swear off "all the sins and vices which the Indians have learned from the White people" and instead "live without any trade or connections to the White People, clothing and supporting themselves as their forefathers did." The concern of the Moravian missionary Christian Frederick Post was that Neolin "had a vision of heaven where there was no White people but all Indians, and wants a total separation from us." This rejection of Christianity included a revival of pagan rites. Twice a day, Neolin's followers would use a stick, marked by notches, to direct their prayers to the Master of Life and meditate on the right road to heaven. Kenny's understanding was that "at their towns [they] make feasts it's said now every day and perform their new devotions by dancing, singing, and sometimes all kneeling and praying . . ." During these ceremonies Neolin would call on the people to think about the damage Indians had done to themselves "by looking upon a people of a different color from our own, who had come across a great lake, as if they were part of ourselves; by suffering them to sit down by our side, and looking at them with indifference, while they were . . . taking our country from us." "This," Neolin instructed, pointing to a map with the route to heaven, is "our only avenue."[46]

There was a militant undertone to this cultural revitalization, for if purification required Indians to rid themselves of White influences, did it not also demand the elimination of White people? Kenny assumed so, which led him to predict that another war was right around the corner. According to the Moravian missionary John Heckewelder's informants, Neolin promised that once Indians reformed, "then

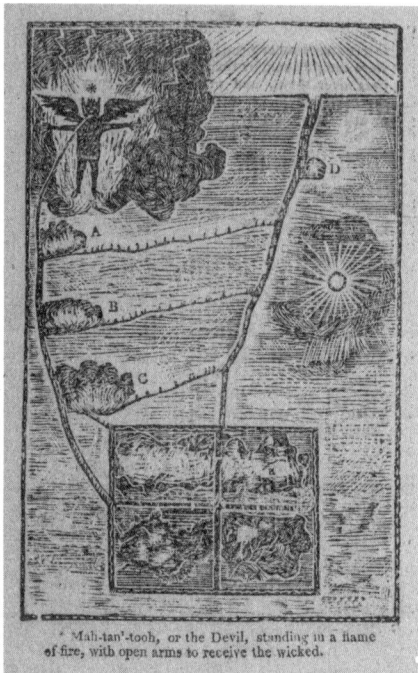

*Mah-tan'-tooh, or the Devil, standing in a flame of fire, with open arms to receive the wicked.

A page from Archibald Loudon, *A Selection of Some of the Most Interesting Narratives, of Outrages, Committed by the Indians in Their Wars with the White People* (Carlisle, PA: A. Louden, 1808–11). Courtesy of the American Antiquarian Society.

Neolin's depiction of his dream of the Master of Life, drawn by Pennsylvania's John M'Cullough after his captivity during Pontiac's War.

will the Great Spirit give success to our arms; then he will give us strength to conquer our enemies, to drive them from hence, and recover the passage to the heavenly regions which they have taken from us." A White captive of Indians in the Ohio country heard Neolin promise "that by following his instructions, they would, in a few years, be able to drive the white people out of their country." Some of Neolin's adherents differentiated between the British, whom they reviled, and the French, whom they said they loved and wanted to return to Indian country. Other Indians found this distinction specious. Both camps, however, took Neolin's preaching as the ideology for race war, or, more specifically, for Indian unity in the face of an ongoing race war instigated by Whites, particularly the British.[47]

CHILDREN OF THE GREAT SPIRIT

The signing of the Treaty of Paris, in February 1763, might have ended the great war between Britain and France, but it represented a new phase in the ongoing race war between Indians and Whites for control of the interior of eastern America, particularly the Ohio country. When news arrived that the French had ceded to the British all the land between the Appalachians and Mississippi River with the exception of New Orleans, which went to Spain, Indians were gobsmacked. They had never surrendered any of this land to the French in the first place because they always understood them to be guests, not sovereigns. Thus, they counseled the British that peace depended on red-coated post commanders behaving courteously and generously toward Indians, just as the former French occupants had usually done. They also wanted the soldiers to prevent colonists from settling around western forts. They got neither of these things. British officers, following the lead of General Amherst, treated Indians contemptuously by insulting visitors to their faces and sometimes physically assaulting them. Meanwhile, growing numbers of colonists began to squat near Fort Pitt, convinced that the soldiers would intimidate Indians into accepting their presence. Not least of all, Amherst ended the tradition of granting Indians free blacksmithing services, ammunition, and other diplomatic gifts, and placed new restrictions on colonial traders to regulate the Indians' access to munitions. "I am fully convinced the only true method of treating those Savages is to keep them in a proper subjection," Amherst wrote to Colonel Henry Bouquet. Keeping them short of powder and shot would teach them that "it is certainly not in their power to affect anything of consequence against us."[48]

An unprecedentedly broad coalition of Indian peoples inspired by prophets like Neolin soon made him eat his words. Beginning in May 1763, warriors from across the Great Lakes and Ohio country began sacking British forts and raiding farmsteads farther east in a campaign since known as Pontiac's War, after the name of the Ottawa war chief, a follower of Neolin's, who led the resistance around Detroit. Within a matter of weeks, the warring Indians captured eight weakly defended posts scattered between western Pennsylvania and Lake Michigan. They also put two stout forts, Detroit and Pitt, and Pitt's satellite, Fort Ligonier, under siege for six months, and menaced shipments of supplies and reinforcements that went to and from Fort Niagara. Another theater of this war saw the Delawares and Shawnees renew their raids on Whites in western Pennsylvania, Maryland, and Virginia, sometimes as far east as the Susquehanna River and even the Lehigh River Valley, a mere sixty miles north of Philadelphia. By the time hostilities ended a year later, Indians had killed more than four hundred redcoats and as many as two thousand colonists, captured hundreds, inflicted enormous amounts of property damage, and driven thousands of terrified colonists from their homes.[49]

Native people's explanations for this war cited the racism of the British and the Great Spirit's order for Indians to cleanse themselves of White influences. They asserted that Amherst's policies revealed, at minimum, that the British "did not look at them as brothers and friends." Far worse, they said, was that it "appears to them as if the English have a mind to cut them off the face of the earth." A Delaware who went by the name of John Armstrong explained that his people attacked Pennsylvania because "the white people covet the land and eat them out by inches and that they are doing the same here, which was against the will of God." Echoing Neolin, Armstrong "believed that God was angry with them [Indians]" for having previously failed to unite to roll back White settlement.[50]

One of the ironies of the Indians' racially fueled warfare is that their aims included capturing White people for adoption. By the mid-1760s, an estimated 15 percent of the more than ten thousand people living in Ohio Indian villages were White. On the surface, this pattern contradicted the principle that the Great Spirit made Indians and Whites separately for different ways of life. Yet that view does not account for the Indians' belief that ritual had the power to transform White people into Indians, just as it could turn Indian men from domestic neighbors of the village into ferocious warriors of the woods and back again. Indians put captives marked for adoption through a period of severe abuse, even torture, and the daily threat of execution, to break down their psychological and physical defenses and make them desperate and pliant. Then, step by step, the host society used healing, washing, dressing, decorating, feeding, and kind words to graduate captives from hated enemies standing on the precipice of death to beloved family and community members. In the final stage, the captive received the name of a recently deceased community member in the expectation that he or she would fulfill that person's role. The change was supposed to be so complete that former colonel James Smith remembered his Caughnawaga Mohawk captors instructing him that "every drop of White blood was washed out of your veins," just as a Shawnee told adoptee Simon Kenton that "you [are] no more a white man but an Indian and brother." From that point on, Smith and Kenton were full members of their host societies, with the right to marry and acquire political status—that is, if they behaved according to social expectations. Yet falling short of those standards sometimes led to beatings that would have been utterly unacceptable to anyone born into Native society, and a failed attempt at escape risked execution. In other words, Indigenous people widely believed that ritual had the power to turn Whites into Indians, while also recognizing its limits.[51]

Amherst's racist venom poured forth in letter after letter as news of Indian victories piled up on his desk. He demanded his subordinates to deal with Indian militants "not as a generous enemy, but as the vilest race of beings that ever infested the earth, and whose riddance from it must be esteemed a meritorious act for the good of mankind." Lest anyone misinterpret him, he added, "take no prisoners, but put to death all that fall into your hands." Opportunities to take and kill Indian prisoners were far and few between, however, given the remoteness of hostile Indian villages and the hit-and-run techniques of Native warriors. Instead, Amherst and his officers, Simeon Ecuyer and Henry Bouquet, schemed to infect them with smallpox by gifting blankets from patients in Fort Pitt's medical ward to diplomats from the Delawares. It is the only case of its kind on record during the colonial era, though that does not mean it was the sole attempt. Whether this wicked scheme succeeded is impossible to know, but the fact that smallpox broke out among the nearby Delawares, Shawnees, and Mingos shortly thereafter suggests that it did. There was no tactic too low to use against an enemy defined as "vermin."[52]

The problem for Moravian Indians (most of them Delawares, Shawnees, and Mohicans) living in and around Bethlehem, Pennsylvania, was that numerous colonists included them in that category, too. Their adoption of Christianity, and a pacifist form of it at that, did not matter, nor did the inescapable fact that their own communities had been attacked by enemy Indians. They pleaded "that they be not upbraided with the actions of other Indians, nor spitefully treated or threatened to [be] shot after, as some have already begun, they being under the government's protection as the white people." Instead, their frenzied colonial neighbors accused them of feigning allegiance while actually providing the warring Indians with weapons, intelligence, and sanctuary. Heckewelder recalled bitterly that frontier Whites considered Indians as "a race of beings which (in their opinion) had no claim to Christianity, and whom to destroy, root and branch, would not only be doing God a service, but also be the means of averting his wrath which they [frontier colonists] might otherwise incur by suffering them [Indians] to live, they [Indians] being the same as the Canaanites of old, an accursed race, who by God's command were to be destroyed." Here were both Indian and White militants justifying their violence against one another by claiming that God or the Great Spirit would punish his followers if they if they did not rid themselves of their enemies, particularly those who blurred the lines between peoples.[53]

Racial threats turned into action in the summer of 1763, when a band of White soldiers slaughtered a family of Moravian Indians a short distance outside Bethlehem, spurred on by a tavern keeper's offer of a gallon of rum to anyone "that should kill one of these black devils." Soon, other colonists joined the furor, with some of

"Baptism of Indians in America" [Moravian Church], from *Kurze, zuverläßige Nachricht Von der, unter dem Namen der Böhmisch-Mährischen Brüder bekanten, Kirche Unitas Fratum* (1757).

them demanding the extermination of all the Christian Indians. The Pennsylvania Assembly implored the public that "peaceable Indians" could be identified through their civilized dress, haircuts, and willingness to lay down their arms when challenged. Yet these words carried no weight beyond Philadelphia and its closest towns. The government's fecklessness in wartime had forfeited its legitimacy in the countryside. It could issue proclamations high and low, but, as local officials warned, "nobody would regard it." By October, even the governor had to admit that "it will not be long possible to restrain the ardor of the people for revenging the horrid cruelties daily committed on our inhabitants on all of that color, whether friends or foes, whenever they come across them. It is indeed enough to wear out the patience of a saint." With no good options, the Moravian Indians decided to flee the White mobs of the Lehigh Valley for the army barracks in Philadelphia, the only place where the government conceivably could protect them. Yet the threats made against them by White bystanders along the route, including in the city, must have made some of them fear that they were on a gallows march.[54]

Under similar threat, the Conestoga Indians waited too long. Since the early 1700s, this small community had lived on a reservation outside the Susquehanna town of Lancaster. Its people had a history of peace and quiet, but for months neighboring Whites had menaced these Indians, galvanized by the Presbyterian minister and militia leader John Elder, who preached, rifle at his side, that Indians were a cursed race of Canaanites who God's chosen people should wipe from the face of the earth. On December 14, 1763, the mob acted on these words. A band calling themselves the Paxton Boys, after the northernmost of Lancaster County's seventeen White communities, rode into the Indians' town at dawn, murdered the six people they found sleeping there, and burned their homes to the ground. When fourteen Conestogas who had been abroad at the time of the attack got word of what had happened, they fled for protection, not to other Indians, but to Lancaster's White sheriff. After all, the Contestogas were known, as the local colonist Rhonda Barber wrote in her journal, to be "much attached to the white people, calling their children after their favorite neighbors."[55]

The Paxton Boys severed those attachments once and for all on December 27 by breaking into the workhouse where the Conestogas had taken refuge and putting them all—men, women, and children—to the knife, scalping and otherwise mangling their bodies in the very same savage manner they attributed to enemy Indians. No one did anything to stop them, not the guardsmen, the sheriff, or a nearby detachment of Highland soldiers, and certainly not White civilians in a town of twenty-eight hundred people. In fact, when Governor John Penn offered a princely two-hundred-pound reward for information leading to the arrest of the ringleaders, he received no response. Perhaps the Paxton Boys had intimidated their neighbors into silence, but most officials viewed that silence as approval.[56]

Philadelphia's offer of sanctuary to the Moravian Indians in the face of the country people's determination to kill every Indian within reach nearly turned Pennsylvania into the site of another Bacon's Rebellion. In late January 1764, the Paxton Boys marched into Germantown, six miles north of the city, demanding the right to "inspect" Indians in the barracks or else they would force the issue. Some reports put the number of militants at fifteen hundred men, but the actual number was probably no more than three hundred. Panicked Quakers took to arms to defend the route into town despite their history of opposing war measures against Indians, as the mob was quick to criticize. Of greater concern to the rioters was the news that the British general Thomas Gage had dispatched three companies of redcoats to keep order. Thus, when Benjamin Franklin and a host of clergymen rode out to broker a compromise, the Paxton Boys were willing to bargain. In exchange for the publication of their grievances and the right to have their representatives identify any Moravian Indians implicated in the murder of Whites, they would disperse. They got the press they wanted, but could not single out any of the terrified Indians when they examined them.[57]

The ensuing pamphlet war between supporters and opponents of the Paxton Boys broadcast the mob's racial explanations for persecuting Indians. The Conestogas and Moravian Indians, Paxton writers contended, were not subjects of the English crown and therefore had no claim to the protections of its government. Rather, friend Indians were still "savages," "faithless and perfidious villains," and "butchers" who took advantage of their proximity to colonists "to distress them, and steal off without discovery." The Paxton Boys acknowledged that none of the allied Indians had ever been charged formally with any wrongdoing, but reasoned "it is hard matter to prove an Indian guilty, unless he was taken in the fact; for today they are painted red, tomorrow blue, and the next day any other color that they think will best prevent their being known." Thus, the safety of colonial settlements depended on assuming that all Indians were threats.[58]

The Paxton Boys also considered the Quakers to be enemies. Quakers showed more tenderness toward the "barbarians" than to "their distressed countrymen and fellow subjects." For instance, the slaughter of the Conestogas, which so horrified the Friends in Philadelphia, was, according to the Paxton Boys, "no more but what our people suffered on all occasions." The Paxton Boys' apologist Hugh Williamson went so far as to accuse that "very early in the war the Quakers persuaded the Indians that the proprietor and the traders had cheated them, and therefore they ought to scourge the white people who live on the frontiers. In other words, plunder, tomahawk, and burn them; and they faithfully adhered to the advice." One pamphlet suggested that the Quakers' love for Indians was "owing to the charms of their squaws," with a corresponding pornographic cartoon to illustrate the point. Other critics smeared the Quakers with bad poems, one of which read: "Go on good Christians, never spare / To give your Indians clothes to wear; / Send 'em good beef, and pork, and bread, / Guns, powder, flints, and store of lead, / To shoot your neighbors through the head." No one charged the Quakers outright with being "race traitors," but only because such a term did not yet exist. The Paxton Boys' march on Philadelphia warned that if Quakers continued to manage the Indian war through pacific measures, and protect Indian allies from the rage of the White mob, the country people would treat them like Indians. It was as if Nathaniel Bacon and his followers had risen again.[59]

The Paxton Boys' opponents tried to counter racist passion with reason that disaggregated "Indians" into different polities, friends and allies, Christians and pagans. They rejected that the Contestogas and Moravians "were heathens, and therefore should be cut off from the face of the earth." How could anyone "think

James Claypool, *The German Bleeds & Bears Ye Furs of Quaker Lords & Savage Curs*, 1764. Courtesy of the Library Company of Philadelphia.

This pro–Paxton Boys cartoon depicts a Quaker, Israel Pemberton, who led the effort to negotiate with Indians through "pacific measures," and an Indian (carrying a tomahawk and a bag bearing the initials of Pemberton) riding German and Scots-Irish frontiersmen across a landscape littered with murdered and scalped colonists. Benjamin Franklin stands at the left bearing a declaration against Pennsylvania's governor. An impasse between the Pennsylvania assembly and the governor over the taxation of proprietary lands was a key factor in the colony's failure to defend frontier areas against Delaware and Shawnee strikes.

it no offense to take away the life of a human creature who is of a different color or persuasion?" Benjamin Franklin, in his distinctively jocular style, asked:

> If an Indian injures me, does it follow that I may revenge that injury on all Indians? It is well known that Indians are of different tribes, nations, and languages, as well as the white people. In Europe, if the French, who are white people, should injure the Dutch, are they to revenge it on the English, because they too are white people? The only crime of these poor wretches seems to have been that they had a reddish brown skins, and black hair; and some people of that sort, it seems, had murdered some of our relations. If it be right to kill men for such a reason, then, should any man with a freckled face and red hair, kill a wife or child of mine, it would be right for me to revenge

it, by killing all the freckled red-haired men, women, and children I could afterwards anywhere meet with.

He added, as one last tweak to the hypocritical biblical fundamentalism of the Presbyterian Paxton Boys, that they ignored God's law "Thou shall do no murder; and justify their wickedness by the command given to Joshua to destroy the heathen."[60]

Colonial society was so premised on race that even Franklin could not help but invoke its false logic while arguing against it. He chastised the Paxton Boys that "we pretend to be Christians, and, from the superior light we enjoy, ought to exceed heathens, Turks, Saracens [Muslims], Moores, Negroes, and Indians in the knowledge of what is right." Instead, the Paxton Boys behaved "to the eternal disgrace of their country and color," prompting the question, "Do we come to America to learn and practice the manners of barbarians . . . Shall Whitemen and Christians act like a Pagan Negro?" When enlightened advocates of the Indians like Franklin took for granted that Christianity and reason were the innate qualities of White people, not darker-hued others, it was a sign of how hegemonic the idea of race had become.[61]

The Paxton Boys won the fight on the ground even if their opponents fared better in the war of words. The Moravian Indians finally felt safe to leave Philadelphia in the spring of 1764, thanking Pennsylvania's government for its protection when "we were in danger for our lives from the white people," yet there was no returning to their former lands and way of life. In the Susquehanna Valley, they found encroaching Whites to be so numerous and threatening that they quickly left to join their tribesmen in the Ohio country. It was a wise if heartbreaking choice. That same season, a colonist named David Owens, who had married a Delaware woman (and a former Moravian) after deserting a militia company, and who lived with her people on the Susquehanna for a spell, suddenly killed her and her kin, including children, and lifted five of their scalps for the bounty. Meanwhile, at Fort Pitt, a militiaman from Maryland, James Bow, killed and scalped a Shawnee hostage being held to guarantee the safe return of White captives. Not only did Bow receive no punishment, but also his commander showed off the scalp to local justices of the peace.[62]

What also drove the Delawares west was a flood of White migration that soon spread right across the Appalachians. Between 1760 and 1775, some forty thousand Scots, or about 3 percent of the entire population of Scotland, and fifty-five thousand Irish, or 2.3 percent of the total number of Irish, migrated to the British North

American colonies "for no other reason," one official remarked, "but because they hope to live better." Yet a better life for them meant misery for the Haudenosaunees, Delawares, Shawnees, and Cherokees whose lands they swarmed. Sir William Johnson bemoaned that these newcomers "seem regardless of the laws, and not only to perpetuate murders whenever opportunity offers, but think themselves at liberty to make settlements where they please." Johnson was writing in 1766, following reports of at least fifteen cases of Whites murdering Indians in the backcountry regions of Virginia, Pennsylvania, and New Jersey over the course of just six months, with far more to come.[63]

MAYHEM

Frontier colonists, or at least a critical mass of them, respected the authority of government only when it supported their aggression against Indians, not when it enforced restraint to prevent another war. Examples of this anarchy were everywhere. In March 1765, another Pennsylvania frontier mob, calling itself the Black Boys after the paint the members used to disguise their faces, intercepted and plundered a pack train of eighty-one horses carrying Indian trade goods to Pittsburgh, looted gunpowder from the storehouse of a local magistrate they suspected of supplying the Indians, and then engaged in months of firefights with British troops who tried to recover the merchandise and arrest the ringleaders. Eventually, authorities let the matter drop, though the Black Boys continued to harass anyone they suspected of trading with Indians. The trader George Croghan could only conclude that the "mob seems to rule."[64]

Just months later, a band of Virginians calling themselves the Augusta Boys waylaid a party of Cherokees passing through their Shenandoah Mountain county, killing five of them, despite the Indians' carrying an official pass. Authorities managed to arrest a couple of suspects, but the mob rescued one of them before he was jailed, and another spent only three nights behind bars before a hundred armed men broke down the door and spirited him away, declaring "that they would never suffer a man to be confined or brought to justice for killing of savages." From Pennsylvania, the Paxton Boys volunteered their assistance in case any officials dared to try. At least three other jailbreaks of Whites accused of killing Indians occurred in Virginia over the next few years. As Virginia lieutenant governor Francis Fauquier lamented to his Pennsylvania counterpart, John Penn, "I have found by experience, it is impossible to bring anybody to Justice for the Murder of an Indian, who takes shelter among our back[country] Inhabitants. It is among those People, looked on as a meritorious action, and they are sure of being Protected."[65]

Penn understood firsthand. When Cumberland County authorities arrested Frederick Stump and his servant, John Ironcutter, in early 1768 for a killing spree that claimed the lives of ten Indians (including three women, two girls, and a baby), a mob of up to eighty Whites sprung them from jail after learning that they were going to be transferred to distant Philadelphia for questioning and perhaps trial. English common law was on their side, for criminal cases were supposed to be tried in the county where they occurred. Yet the Indian-hating crowd had less interest in abstract legal principle than the practical fact that a local jury would guarantee that these killers faced little or no punishment. Fauquier observed that "no Jury from those parts . . . will convict a person of Murder for that offence, be it ever so atrocious." But a trial of Stump and Ironcutter in Philadelphia risked conviction and execution, which the mob rejected outright because "a number of White Men have been killed by the Indians since the Peace, and the Indians have not been brought to Justice." The prevalence of this attitude outside Philadelphia, and the inability of government to enforce its authority there, meant that brazen White murders of Indians continued to take place in Pennsylvania without prosecution for years. By the end of the Revolution, White Pennsylvanians had driven practically all Indians out of their state and their Quaker advocates out of government. Truly, William Penn's dream was dead.[66]

On the rare occasions that government managed to provide justice to Indians, it confronted the depth of Indian-hating among country Whites and the possibility of armed rebellion. These elements appeared in two separate cases in less than a year in which New Jersey authorities prosecuted White men for the murder of Native people. In the summer of 1766, a court in Burlington tried and executed James Arnen, age fifty-four, and James McKenzie, age nineteen, for the killing and probable rapes of two Christian Indian women, Hannah and Catherine, from the nearby Brotherton community. One of the victims was pregnant and near the time of delivery. By all accounts, the women's bodies "had marks of shocking torment which the most savage nations on earth could not have surpassed." McKenzie justified his crimes to the end, appealing "that he thought it a duty to extirpate the heathen." Six months later, special Court of Oyer and Terminer, appointed by Governor William Franklin to bypass the local Sussex County Court, convicted and executed Robert Seymour for the murder and robbery of an Oneida man, but only after an arrest that required a "great deal of trouble and management," in reference to a crowd breaking

Seymour out of jail before authorities managed to recapture him. His accomplice, David Ray, initially pled not guilty, but eventually confessed to his crime, claimed benefit of clergy, and received only a branding of his hand. Seymour held out to the last and "seemed to expect a rescue" even on the gallows, which Governor Franklin defended against by ordering twenty-five militiamen to guard the prisoner around the clock. Franklin knew all too well that large portions of the public, even in parts of New Jersey, thought that no White man should hang for murdering an Indian. When leaders like Franklin successfully pushed back against such bloodlust, they did so at the risk of provoking a rural White revolt.[67]

Yet doing nothing, as White officials and some civilians were acutely aware, was likely to spur another Indian war. In their councils with Sir William Johnson, Native people from throughout the East told him that the Stump affair "was considered by them as an introduction to something worse, which," Johnson editorialized, "their natural jealousy has long caused them to suspect." It was more than natural jealousy. One Indian speaker after another complained that Whites "murdered our people in Pennsylvania, Virginia, and all over the country . . . the road through the country is no longer safe. The Pennsylvanians and Virginians murder all those of our people they can meet, without any reason . . . You don't prevent this. You often tell us we don't restrain our people and that you do so with yours, but Brother, your words differ more from your actions than ours do." Seasoned Native leaders had no desire for another war, but warned they could not continue to restrain their young men when "the white people was settling their country" and killing them with impunity. Nativist calls for intertribal resistance arose once again, this time spreading as far south as the Cherokees and Creeks.[68]

Back-and-forth murders and raids plagued the entire trans-Appalachian region for the next decade before crystallizing in Virginia's 1774 campaign against the Shawnees, Delawares, and Mingos now known as Dunmore's War. Though Virginia's main purpose was to assert its claims to what is now West Virginia against the Indians and Pennsylvania, a string of gruesome killings had led to this moment. The precipitating act appears to have come in spring 1774, when a band of colonists killed eight Indians under the ruse of trade and friendship. The victims were the family of the late Shickellamy, an Oneida diplomat, who had spent his life working for peace, and of the Mingo leader Logan (Shickellamy's son). Some secondary accounts claimed, falsely, that the colonial attackers mutilated the body of one of their female victims by ripping a fetus from her womb and impaling it on a stake. What is true is that, in the war that followed, Indians and Whites alike targeted one another's pregnant women for atrocities that signaled genocidal intent. In turn, combatant Indian communities began inculcating their children with terror of the White people, warning those who misbehaved, "Hush! Cresap [one of the most notorious killers of Indians] will fetch you."[69]

The unfolding horrors gave Virginia governor Lord Dunmore the opening he needed for a war that everyone knew was coming and some say he orchestrated by encouraging his agents to murder Indians. The culmination saw Dunmore's army of twenty-four-hundred men overwhelm five hundred Shawnee, Mingo, and Delaware warriors in the Battle of Point Pleasant. Afterward, Shawnee chiefs signed a treaty ceding their claims to hunting lands in West Virginia and Kentucky in exchange for Dunmore's promise to keep Whites south of the Ohio River. Both parties began to violate the agreement as soon as it was signed. After all, even Virginia's official report of the campaign acknowledged that backcountry Whites would not respect treaties with Indians, "whom they consider as little removed from brute creation."[70]

DARK CLOUDS

Indians already knew as much. Eight years earlier, at the Fort Stanwix conference to negotiate a durable boundary between Indians and Whites, a Haudenosaunee speaker pronounced, "Daily experience teaches us that we can't have any great dependence on the white people and that they will forget their agreements for the sake of our lands." Clearly, Indians had discerned the lengthy pattern of White frontiersmen provoking armed conflicts that would force Indians to make additional cessions. The Delawares' explanation for White people's murderous land lust was "that the hair of [White people's] heads, their features, the various colors of their eyes, evince that they are not like themselves, Lenni Lenape, an Original People, a race of men that has existed unchanged from the beginning of time; but they are a mixed race, and therefore a troublesome one." By contrast, the Mohegan minister Samson Occom and a number of his followers thought the issue was less White people's grasping character than that Indians "are under a great curse from God." Ironically, this idea was consistent with the principles of militant Nativists like Neolin, who otherwise opposed Occom's Christianity and civilized living. Yet if God cursed Indians for their sins, they were not alone. Occom wondered pointedly, "Who is under the greatest curse, he that [inclines] to such hardness of heart, as to exercise the utmost cruelty upon their fellow creatures, or they that are thus tormented?"[71]

Indians from so many different backgrounds and circumstances searched for answers in the human body and the heavens because they seemed fated for a cataclysm beyond their control. The Delaware leader Killbuck spoke for Indians throughout the East when he warned Pennsylvania in 1771 that soon "it will be out of the Indians' power to govern their young men, for we assure you the black clouds begin to gather fast in this country, and if something is not soon done, those clouds will deprive us of seeing the sun." How right he was.[72]

CHAPTER 3

"Undistinguished Destruction"

White Americans like to remember their Revolution as the glorious birth of a nation based on the principles (if not necessarily the practice) of inalienable rights, democracy, economic opportunity, and the rule of law. Native people who lived through the event did not see it that way. Instead, they viewed the Revolution and the United States as vehicles for a race war in which Whites slaughtered Indigenous people to seize their land. How could they think otherwise? U.S. diplomats repeatedly told Indians that the new nation stood for "all the white inhabitants of this big island [America]" and that the country's president was "father and protector of all the white people." When the majority of Indians sided with Great Britain against the rebel colonies, those same White people responded by waging, in their own words, a war of extermination, characterized by their killing Native people indiscriminately and setting their country ablaze with a fury driven by revenge, race hatred, and land lust. They did not apply the same tactics to British soldiers and Loyalist civilians, cruel as they often were to them, because they considered these enemies to be fellow Whites, civilized people, and Christians. No wonder, then, that the Seneca leader Sayenqueraghta told the Wyandots in 1777 that White Americans "wish for nothing more, than to extirpate us from the earth, that they might possess our lands, the desire of attaining which we are convinced is the cause of the present war."[1]

Though Sayenqueraghta was mistaken about the cause of the Revolution, he was correct that the war and its settlement made Indian-hating, genocidal war against Indians, and the conquest of Indian land foundational to the United States. During an era of deep divisions among White Americans, the closest they came to consensus was the belief that, as White people, they were entitled to appropriate Indian territory and destroy anyone who resisted, including Indians who had sided *with them* during the Revolution. The nation had mortgaged its very future on this premise by recruiting Continental soldiers with land bounties and taking out massive loans from foreign creditors based on the assumption that eventually it would appropriate and sell practically the entire Indian domain east of the Mississippi River. When the federal government pursued this goal too cautiously in the interests of peace, economy, and reputation, White frontiersmen forced it to act by warring against Indians independently. The government then faced nothing but bad options. It could use the military against its own citizens to protect Indians, thus risking the loyalty of White voters. If it did nothing, it would lose its legitimacy by neglecting its basic duty to defend its own people against Indians. The final choice, which was the one it always took, was to do the bidding of the White mob. In fact, the conquest of Indians was the central activity of the federal government and several states and territories throughout the era of the early republic.

Native people responded in kind, first by allying in large numbers with the British during the Revolution, then by reviving the movement for intertribal resistance in the 1790s and 1810s. No less than their White American antagonists, the Natives conceived of their struggle as a clash of fundamentally different races, with their entire way of life and even survival at stake. Though hopelessly outnumbered, they fought with desperation and skill and earned their fair share of short-term victories.

These conflicts were part of a sixty years' race war stretching between the Seven Years' War (1754–63) and the War of 1812 (1811–15) for control of the eastern half of North America. During this generations-long conflict, both sides made "an undistinguished destruction of all ages, sexes and conditions," though White Americans, as, for example, in this quote from the Declaration of Independence, denounced only the Indians' barbarity and not their own. The horrors that Whites and Indians inflicted on one another produced lasting results, and not just in terms of thousands of lost lives and millions of acres of Indian land seized by Whites. The Revolution, then U.S.-Indian wars of the 1790s, and finally the War of 1812, consolidated mutually hostile White and Indian racial identities and made Whiteness fundamental to United States national identity. Indians faced a present and future indelibly shaped, no matter what they did, by a new nation premised on dispossessing and destroying them so White people could have their land.

A WAR BETWEEN WHITE BROTHERS

As the imperial crisis between Britain and its colonies turned into a revolutionary war in the mid-1770s, Indians throughout the East argued that they should be left out of it by virtue of race. The Mohegan Samson Occom counseled the Oneidas, "Use all your Influence, to your Brethren [the rest of the Haudenosaunees] ... not to intermeddle in these quarrels among the White People." The Oneidas agreed, telling the Americans in rebellion to "let us Indians be all of one mind, and live in peace with one another, and you white people settle your own disputes betwixt yourselves." The Oneidas easily prevailed on their western Iroquois confederates that neutrality was the best course because "the white people, particularly the Americans, are in nature treacherous and deceitful, have no true friendship for the Indians and are not to be depended upon for aid and protections—no sooner have they obtained victory but they turn about, fall upon the Indians."[2]

The problem was that neutrality was next to impossible. First and foremost, Indians wanted to maintain the flow of trade goods, and practically all of those items, including munitions, cloth, clothing, metal tools, cooking utensils, and liquor, came from Britain. Neutrality or even an alliance with the United States, which had little manufacturing, would gain them nothing. Indians also aimed to secure their lands, but on this issue the choice of sides was cloudier. True, Britain's 1763 Proclamation Line had banned White settlement west of the Appalachians, but that order was largely unenforceable without troops stationed down the entire length of the mountains. All the proclamation did, in effect, was to deny official recognition to private land titles based on purchases from Indians; only cessions conducted by crown agents were legal. Furthermore, it took only until 1768 for British officials to breach the line with the Treaties of Fort Stanwix and Hard Labor in which the Haudenosaunees and Cherokees, respectively, ceded most of what is now western Pennsylvania, West Virginia, and Kentucky. A surge of disorderly White migrants followed immediately. Yet at least British policy showed respect for Indian claims and protocols. American colonists, by comparison, wanted to return to the anarchic expansion that preceded the Proclamation Line. Therefore, when it came time to choose sides, most Indians leaned toward the British, all the while demanding greater protection of their lands once the rebellion was defeated.[3]

Indians viewed both Britons and Americans as Whites, as when the Mohawk Loyalist Joseph Brant referred to King George as "the head man of all nations of white people," but the clear colonial majority favoring the Revolution gradually led them to see the United States also as the government of "the White people." As early as 1775, the Delaware chief White Eyes told American officials that since "all the White people account themselves as one body," therefore, "when we look on you [the rebel colonies], we shall esteem you all [as] one people." The Cherokees likewise affirmed that they would recognize ambassadors from the Continental Congress as delegates of the "whole nation" because "you [the United States] are all of one color." The problem was what Indians thought it meant for the United States to be a White nation. A conference of Ohio Valley and Great Lakes tribes in May 1777 deliberated that "the white people have taken all our lands from us from time to time until this time, and that they will continue the same way." U.S. spokesmen denied the charge by proposing that White Americans and Native Americans were "the same people though of different complexions" because "the same island [America] is our common birthplace." Given White Americans' lengthy history of trying to engross that supposedly shared island, most Indians were skeptical.[4]

Convinced that the United States was gunning for their territory, Native people throughout the East revived the movement for intertribal unity that had proved so effective in Pontiac's War years earlier. The key moment came in late August 1776, when a deputation of Haudenosaunees, Ottawas, Shawnees, and Delawares from the north visited the Cherokee capital of Chota bearing a nine-foot-long purple wampum belt to represent the call to war. The Ottawas declared that unless Indians stopped fighting one another, their "common enemies," the White people, would continue to exploit their divisions until all was lost. A Shawnee speaker seconded this view, adding that as "the red people who were once masters of the whole country, hardly possessed ground enough to stand on … that it was plain there was an intention to extirpate them; and that he thought it was better to die like men than to dwindle away by inches." Cherokee warriors accepted the belt in hearty agreement while their cautious chiefs and elders, who had lived through the devastation of so many previous wars against the Whites, "sat down dejected and silent." They knew all too well that, in all likelihood, their people stood to lose no matter what they did.[5]

While Indigenous communities were rallying together as "red people," the British colonies were organizing a rebellion and nation around a White identity defined in great measure against Indians. Back in December 1773, the White participants in Boston's "Tea Party" protest had disguised themselves as Indians to signal that, like Native people, they had ancestral ties to America and a commitment to liberty. Yet once real Indians entered the picture, the White public's mood went from bold and boisterous to downright panicked. In August 1775, King George III declared the colonies to be in "open rebellion ... for the purpose of establishing an independent empire," and began hiring Hessian mercenaries for American operations, offering Virginia slaves freedom in exchange for British military service, and negotiating with Indian nations to attack exposed White settlements. The *Pennsylvania Evening Post* reported (truthfully or not) that the king's Northern superintendent for Indian affairs, Guy Johnson, then invited the Northern tribes to "FEAST ON A BOSTONIAN AND DRINK HIS BLOOD."[6]

Up to this point, Americans, especially in the Mid-Atlantic colonies, had resisted calls for independence because their dispute was with Parliament alone, not the crown. As long as they retained their allegiance to the throne, they remained loyal to Britain. The king's negotiations with soldiers of fortune, slaves, and "savages" to butcher his own people severed their fidelity once and for all. The colonies declared their independence from the crown in July 1776 by listing twenty-seven measures by which the king had driven them to this grave decision. The penultimate and most serious one was that "he has excited domestic insurrections [slave revolts] amongst us and has endeavoured to bring on the inhabitants of our frontiers the merciless savages, whose known rule of warfare is an undistinguished destruction of all ages and conditions." Generations of diverse colonists, who shared a White identity defined against Blacks and Indians, considered no act more defining of a tyrant than this one. For that reason, as the historian Robert Parkinson has shown, a crowd in Long Island represented its support for the Declaration of Independence by constructing an effigy of George III, painting its face black, adorning it with an Indian headdress, and then hanging and burning the figure. It foreshadowed the horrors of the war to come.[7]

REVOLTING

White Americans could not have been clearer about their intent to wipe out any Indian tribe that sided with the British. Colonel Elias Dayton of New Jersey threatened the Mohawks in May 1776 "that if they dared to take up the hatchet ... he would burn their upper and lower castles [villages] on the Mohawk river, would burn all their homes, destroy their towns, and cast the Mohawks with their wives and children off from the face of the earth." White military officers knew that Indians tended to avoid pitched battles and flee in advance of an invading army, but, as General John Armstrong of Pennsylvania explained, "their huts and cornfields must remain, the destruction whereof greatly affects their old men, their women, and their children."

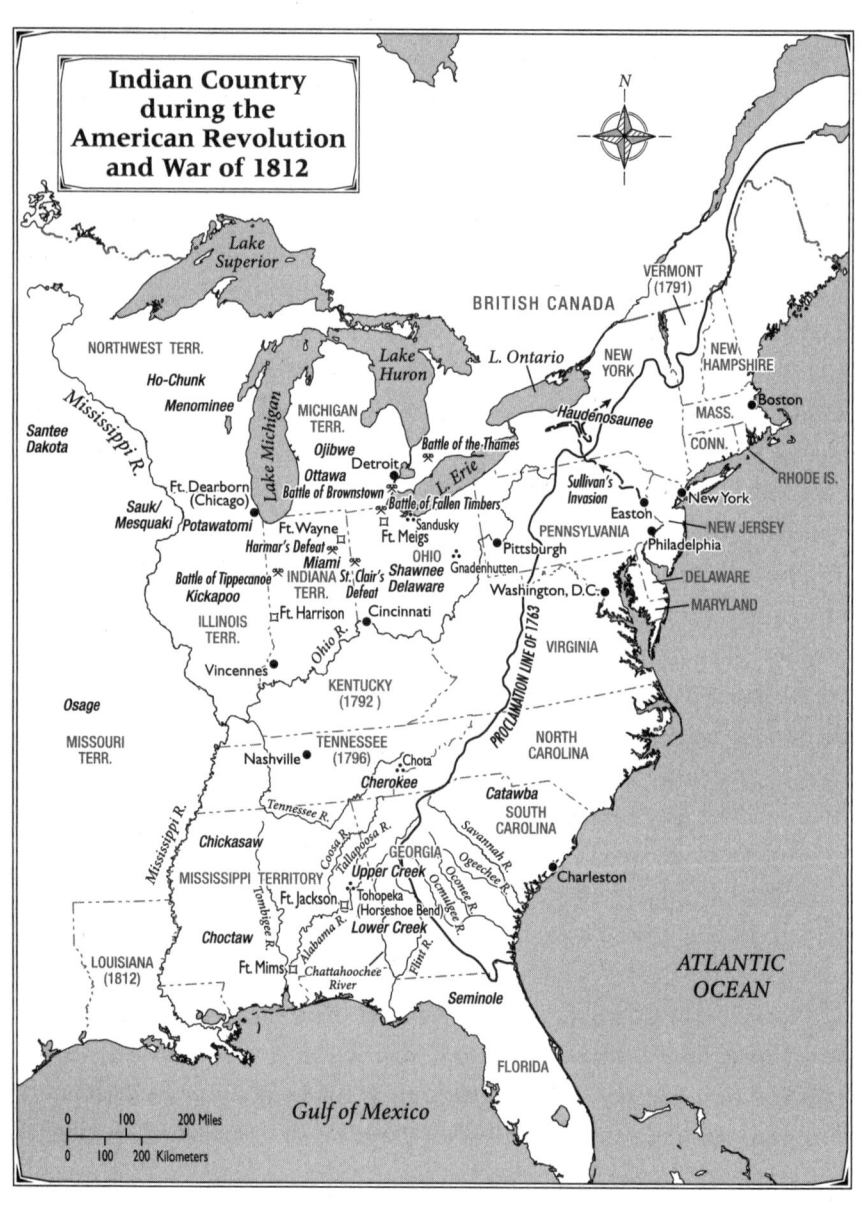

Delaware Indian leaders pleaded with their American counterparts to differentiate between Indian allies, neutrals, and enemies, even within a single tribe, just as they did with White people. "There are in several of your states people you call Tories," they reasoned, "but as that does not make those particular states your enemies, we hope you make a proper distinction between our nation and individuals who on account of their conduct have become outcasts from it." That was asking too much from a society that tended to see all Indians as threats, the elimination of them as opportunity, and "terror," as Dayton characterized it, as the only way to subdue them.[8]

Whites on the frontier were even less willing than their superiors to respect Indian distinctions. American colonel George Morgan was worried justifiably that Whites near Pittsburgh were eager "to massacre our known [Indian] friends at their hunting camps as well as messengers on business to me" because they were easier targets than the enemy. In November 1777, shortly after Morgan penned his words, Senecas journeying to a treaty conference at Fort Pitt came under fire by White settlers who rejected any notion of diplomacy with Indians. The attack left the Senecas "enraged at the white people, considering them as traitors, threatening them with revenge." That same month, the commander of Fort Randolph, in what is now West Virginia, responded to an enemy Indian killing of one of his soldiers by summarily executing the neutral Shawnee chief, Cornstalk, and four other Indian ambassadors. In February 1778, five hundred militia from Fort Pitt killed six Delawares camped on nearby Beaver Creek, including an old man, four women, and a boy, out of frustration at the strikes of other Indians. The Delaware chief White Eyes was a consistent advocate of peace, as his name suggested, but in November 1778 American militiamen murdered him, too, while he was leading them on an expedition into Indian territory. On and on it went. "If there is not a stop put to killing Indian friends," pleaded Captain Leonard Helm in 1779, "we must expect to have all foes." It was no coincidence that Indians responded affirmatively to British warnings "that it was the determination of the American people to kill and destroy the whole Indian race, be they friends or foes, and possess themselves of their country." The evidence was everywhere.[9]

Morgan attributed this wild violence to White people's "ardent desire for an Indian war, on account of the fine land those people possess," which was accurate in the broader scheme of things but minimized the role of race hatred generated by fear and vengeance. The Revolution was yet another spike in a twenty-year pattern of Indian raiding parties terrorizing all of New York west of the Hudson

River, Pennsylvania west of the Susquehanna, and the mountainous regions of Maryland, Virginia, the Carolinas, Georgia, and Kentucky. From his station at Fort Pitt, Colonel William Crawford felt the dread of an enemy who seemed capable of striking anywhere at any time and then retreating just as quickly. In April 1777, he reported that his neighborhood had recently suffered a "general eruption" of violence in which Indians killed and scalped one White American at Raccoon Creek, twenty-five miles distant; killed and scalped another man and burned a woman and four children at Machmore's plantation, forty-five miles down the Ohio; killed, scalped, and otherwise mangled a man in the western Virginia town of Wheeling; killed and scalped a man and a woman and captured three children at Dunhard's Creek; and "burned houses, killed cattle, hogs" everywhere they went. Crawford could have been describing practically anywhere in the western regions of the United States during the Revolution. The British officer Guy Johnson recorded that, in the year 1780 alone, sixty-three Indian war parties involving 2,400 men had fanned out from behind British lines against the northern frontier, claiming 170 dead, 211 prisoners, the destruction of 400 houses, barns, and mills, and the killing of hundreds of livestock. As these bloody totals accumulated year after year, so, too, did the rage of frontier Whites against Indians. This aspect of the Revolution was part of a cycle of bloodshed and dehumanization so long in duration that no one could remember its beginning or conceive of an end short of the other's elimination.[10]

The White targets of Indian attacks preferred to think of themselves as hapless victims of a savage aggressor, which is how future generation of White Americans recounted the Indian role in the Revolution, but that was not the Indians' perspective at all. Indigenous people were fighting for their very lives and lands against the White population's violent expansion. The Revolution was just another phase, if an especially furious one, in that lengthy struggle. No one understood those stakes better than the Cherokees. When the Revolution began, they remained haunted by the 1760–61 war in which the British Army kidnapped and murdered their chiefs, burned their settlements and crops to the ground, and left them starving. Fresher still were memories of how treaties like Fort Stanwix and Hard Labor in 1768, Lochaber in 1770, and Sycamore Shoals in 1775, had robbed them of tens of thousands of square miles of their ancient homelands and hunting grounds and attracted hordes of White invaders. The Revolution was an opportunity for the Cherokees to fight back. As their rising war leader, Dragging Canoe, explained, Cherokee warriors were eager to strike the Americans because "they were almost surrounded by the White People, that they had but a small spot of ground left for them to stand upon and that it seemed to be the intention of the White people to destroy them from being a people." Throughout the summer of 1776, Dragging Canoe and his men fulfilled their threat to make colonial settlements on their people's stolen lands "dark and bloody."[11]

As Cherokee elders had warned, the White response was severe. In the late summer and fall of 1776, some fifty-five hundred American troops forced their way into the Cherokees' Lower and Middle Towns and then the Overhill district (what is now the North Carolina / Georgia / South Carolina / Tennessee border region), driven by calls like that of South Carolina Chief Justice William Henry Drayton "that the nation be extirpated." By the time the campaign was over, the soldiers had laid waste to dozens of Cherokee towns, tens of thousands of acres of cornfields, and vast herds of livestock, and the people were starving once again. No one recorded the number of Cherokee dead, but the recollection of one White participant that he and his comrades "killed and destroyed as many of the Indians as we could get hold of" suggests that the Cherokees suffered an enormous loss of life even before the famine set in. Indeed, the troops took no prisoners because "the greater part... swore bloodily that if [Cherokee captives] were not sold as slaves on the spot, they would kill and scalp them immediately" for bounties that ran as high as seventy-five pounds.[12]

The following year, Cherokee leaders solicited peace by ceding another five million acres to Georgia, Virginia, South Carolina, and North Carolina, but they could not restrain their own warriors, and Whites refused to differentiate between the Cherokees who fought and those who held back. It did not matter to the White troops that Dragging Canoe's followers withdrew to separate towns in the south and west and even gave themselves a new name, Chickamaugas (or *Ani-Yunwiya*), meaning "real people," to distinguish themselves from the peace Cherokees, who they derided as "Virginians." Soon, real Virginians and many other White soldiers were at the Cherokees' threshold to revenge the Chickamaugas' depredations. In April 1779, Colonel Evan Shelby led Virginia militia in the destruction of eleven Chickamauga towns and some twenty thousand bushels of corn. The following year, American forces targeted the Overhill district, putting a thousand homes, another fifty thousand bushels of crops, and, reportedly, captive women and children to the torch. Then, in February 1781, Colonel John Sevier of Washington County, North Carolina (now Tennessee), led 150 men in the killing of fifteen Cherokees and the despoiling of fifteen of their Middle Towns in what is now the Georgia–North Carolina border area, only to return the next fall to ravage Chickamauga towns on the Coosa River. Cherokee country had indeed become a "dark and bloody ground," but the overwhelming majority of the victims were Cherokees. At the end of the Revolution,

Francis Parsons, *Cunne Shote, Cherokee Chief*, 1762. Wikimedia Commons.

Conocotocko (also Cunne Shote, Standing Turkey) was a Cherokee warrior and political leader throughout the era of the Seven Years' War and American Revolution, during which White Americans repeatedly waged total war against the Cherokee tribe.

their population stood at barely half its number in 1775. White Americans had meant what they said when they threatened the Cherokees' extirpation.[13]

Like the Cherokees, most of the Haudenosaunee tribes, including the Mohawks, Onondagas, Cayugas, Senecas, and many Tuscaroras, sided with Britain only to find themselves in a genocidal race war beyond their control. Beginning in early 1778, Haudenosaunee warriors outfitted at British Fort Niagara lashed exposed American settlements in the upper Susquehanna River Valley and eastern New York with near impunity. Americans considered the Mohawk Joseph Brant's squad to be the most vicious of the lot, partly because it included large numbers of poor White Loyalists who dressed and fought like their Indian compatriots. White revolutionaries branded these men as race traitors and threatened to execute them on the spot, particularly after their brutal November 1778 strike against Cherry Valley, New York. There, Brant's men (in defiance of Brant's orders) reportedly mutilated pregnant women, dashed the heads of infants against trees, and otherwise killed and butchered with grotesque creativity. Even a British partisan admitted that "the bloody scene is almost past description." White Americans hardly required a legitimate excuse to inflict equal cruelty on an enemy they dehumanized as savage, but now they had it.[14]

The goal of the 1779 U.S. counteroffensive against the Haudenosaunees led by Major General John Sullivan was, according to its architect, George Washington, to "extirpate them from the country." The first prong of the invasion, led by Colonel Goose Van Schaick, devastated the Onondagas' towns, burning fifty homes and food stores, slaughtering livestock, killing a handful of people, and capturing thirty-four.

Onondaga leaders remembered vividly that the troops also "put to death all the women and children, excepting some of the young women, whom they carried away for the use of their soldiers and were afterwards put to death in a more shameful manner," in a clear reference to rape.[15]

Even greater destruction accompanied the invasion's second phase, in which fifty-one hundred men marched from three directions into the heart of Iroquoia. On July 4, Sullivan's brigades passed a site on the Susquehanna where Haudenosaunee and Loyalist forces had destroyed White American settlements the previous year, inspiring the men to raise several patriotic toasts, including "civilization or death to all American savages." Once they reached Haudenosaunee territory, the goal of cashing in on state bounties, and returning the Indians' violence in kind, led some of the troops not only to scalp the Native people they killed, but also to search out their cemeteries, unearth the graves, and scalp the corpses. Yet bounty hunting cannot account for why the men skinned two dead Haudenosaunees "from the hips down, for boot legs, one pair for the Major, the other," recalled Lieutenant William Barton proudly, "for myself."[16]

Major Jeremiah Fogg of New Hampshire knew why. He recalled that when his company found a frail Haudenosaunee woman abandoned in her community's flight, "such is the enmity of our soldiery against the savages that they would have readily murdered this helpless, impotent wretch," that is, until their commander ordered them to halt. Instead, the troops apparently raped and certainly killed a young woman who emerged from hiding after seeing her elder spared. Then they turned to their primary mission of razing forty towns, burning 160,000 bushels of corn, and chopping down untold numbers of fruit trees. Every Indian they took prisoner, they killed on the spot. The Haudenosaunees could not help but notice that American forces did not treat British soldiers or Loyalists this way, "but we have no mercy to expect, if taken, as they will put us to death immediately, and will not even spare our women and children." Though Jabez Campfield of New Jersey, a surgeon in the Continental Army, found these barbarities to be "so cruel" that "it hurts my feelings ... however mean the Indians might be," he was decidedly in the minority. Major Fogg captured the spirit of the campaign when he mused, "had I any influence in the councils of America, I should not think it an affront to the Divine will, to lay some effectual plan, either to civilize, or totally extirpate the [Indian] race."[17]

Extirpation was the plan. Most of the Haudenosaunees who managed to escape the burning of their country spent the winter camped outside Fort Niagara suffering hunger, cold, disease, and death. In the years to come, they remembered this ordeal and who was ultimately responsible, by referring to George Washington by the name Conotocarious, meaning Town Destroyer.[18]

Nowhere did Indians return White people's violence in kind more than in Kentucky, a prime hunting ground for multiple tribes, into which thousands of Whites had been pouring since Daniel Boone blazed the trail through the Cumberland Gap in 1775. Native raids claimed the lives of at least 860 White Kentuckians during the Revolution, and drove all but 200 settlers back east over the mountains. This loss of life, while small in absolute numbers by the Revolution's standards, was the greatest by far relative to population for any White American region, with Kentucky suffering 70 war-related deaths for every 1,000 White people compared to just 10 for every 1,000 people in the thirteen original states. Desperate for protection, Jonathan Lloyd of Jefferson County appealed to Virginia governor Thomas Jefferson that everywhere he looked, "whole families are destroyed without regard to age or sex. Infants are torn from their mothers' arms and their brains dashed out against trees . . . not a week passes and some weeks scarcely a day without some of the distressed inhabitants feeling the fatal effects of the infernal rage and fury of those execrable hell hounds." Jefferson responded, as he was wont to do, by calling for the extermination of the perpetrators—or any Indians associated with them.[19]

The Virginian George Rogers Clark carried the same genocidal impulse deep into Indian country in his famous 1779 Illinois campaign. Fearing that the British post of Vincennes on the Wabash River was primed to become a center of supply and coordination for Indian raids, Clark led a small force on a rapid winter march that managed to surprise and take the enemy fort with little resistance. Clark immediately made an example of an Indian scouting party his men had managed to capture. According to British accounts, Clark had the prisoners dragged into the street before the fort "to be sacrificed" by tomahawk, though a flag of surrender was already raised. One of the Indian victims actually removed a hatchet left sticking out of his head "and gave it again into the hands of this executioner, who repeated the stroke a second and third time, after which the miserable being, not entirely deprived of life was dragged to the river and thrown in with the rope around his neck where he ended his life and tortures." Clark's explanation was that "to excel [Indians] in barbarity was and is the only way to make war upon . . . and gain a name among them." To this, he added, "for his part he would never spare Man woman or child of them on whom he could lay his hands."[20]

Clark got his chance the following year, when he led eight hundred Virginians into Shawnee territory, where they burned eight hundred acres of crops, scalped forty, and killed a female prisoner by "ripping up her belly and otherwise mangling her." Then, in 1782, Clark commanded the destruction of six more Shawnee towns and the killing of dozens of women and children. He was following orders from Virginia governor Thomas Jefferson to complete the Indians' "extermination, or their removal beyond the lakes or Illinois river." Every one of the Indian dead brought Clark's soldiers closer to capitalizing on the state's promise that they would enjoy three hundred acres each from the land they conquered. Not until 2021 did the University of Virginia finally remove its monument to Clark, replete with Indians in submissive pose. George Rogers Clark National Historical Park and Memorial remains in Vincennes, Indiana.[21]

Most White Americans did not experience this race war directly, but reading about it was nearly as effective at developing their hatred for Indians and their racial self-perception as civilized and innocent White people under siege. Congress knew as much when, in 1779, it directed Benjamin Franklin to commission anti-Indian illustrations for a nationalist children's schoolbook. One image was to depict "savages killing and scalping the frontier farmers and their families, women and children, English officers mixed with the savages and giving them orders and encouraging them." Another would show British officers receiving scalps from Indians, and George III signaling his approval. Suffice it to say, these coarse racial stereotypes

This former memorial to George Rogers Clark (since removed) in Charlottesville, Virginia, praises him as the "Conqueror of the Northwest." Note the cowering Indians in the foreground. Wikimedia Commons.

already filled the reading material of adults. Sensationalist newspaper accounts of the 1778 British-Indian attack on the Wyoming Valley led a Massachusetts delegate to the Continental Congress, James Lovell, to call for Indians to be "eradicated root and branch, as soon as we get a little relaxation from the war on the sea coasts." The strongest public outrage fixated on the mistaken killing, scalping, and supposed rape of a young Loyalist woman, Jane McCrea, by British-allied Indian warriors during the 1777 Saratoga campaign. No story was better suited to stoke White fury against Indians. Far away from the scene, New Jersey governor William Livingston vented his spleen over the McCrea murder with some prose that read, "I swear by George and by St. Paul, I will exterminate you all."[22]

EXTERMINATE THEM ALL

In a war that brooked no neutrality and in which White patriots tended to see all Indians as savage enemies, Moravian Delawares found themselves caught in the middle once again. As pacifists, they wanted nothing to do with this fight, but their new location on the Muskingum and Tuscarawas Rivers of Ohio placed them directly between American Pittsburgh to the east and British-Indian Detroit to the west. Reluctantly, they bowed to the demands of British-allied Delawares and Wyandots to relocate to Sandusky, on the south shore of Lake Erie, closer to Detroit, to prevent them from informing Americans about war parties on the march. Yet when famine struck during the late winter of 1782–83, 150 Moravians decided to return to their Ohio village of Gnadenhutten to gather seed corn they had left behind. It was a fateful decision. That spring, a Sandusky war party passed through Gnadenhutten with White American captives in tow, warning that a White militia from Pittsburgh was in hot pursuit, but the Moravians dismissed the danger, reasoning that everyone knew they posed no threat.

When the militiamen arrived, they willfully read all the signs of the Moravian Indians' commitment to living in peace with Whites as evidence of their treachery. They insisted that the Indians' branded horses, pewter utensils, teakettles, pots, cups, saucers, and tailored clothing could only be plunder from murdered Whites, traded to the Moravians by enemy warriors, rather than the products of the Moravians' hard work and civilized reformation. The missionary John Heckewelder thought these accusations were cynical, for the White troops understood that "when they killed the Indians, the country would be theirs; and the sooner this was done, the better!" They did, in fact, waste little time. After binding the Moravians, the militiamen dragged them one by one to be bludgeoned to death with a cooper's mallet, followed by scalping. As the Indians waited their turns, they calmed their panic by singing hymns in praise of the God they had adopted from the White people. But there was no divine intervention that night. The militia killed more than ninety people in cold blood, most of them women, children, and the elderly, all of them Christians, none of them enemies. Some of the victims were the offspring of the very Indians who had nearly met a similar fate at the hands of the Paxton Boys twenty years earlier. Two boys managed to escape, one by hiding under the floorboards where the killing was taking place, the other by surviving the wounds of his would-be execution and lying motionless under the mounting pile of bleeding dead bodies. Everyone else died horrifically.[23]

The militia's triumphant return to Pittsburgh sent the country people into "a fit of frenzy" that included murdering any local Indians they could find and threatening to include any White officer who tried to stop them. The first target was a band of peaceful Delaware refugees who had been living on Killbuck Island in the Ohio River, near Fort Pitt and under its protection. Once again, most of the victims were women and children, and two of the men had U.S. captain's commissions. Next, the mob turned against Fort Pitt's commanding officer, Colonel John Gibson, after he gave sanctuary to a handful of Delaware survivors. The armed crowd, as well as some soldiers with a "mutinous disposition," called for Gibson's scalp on the charge that he had "an attachment to Indians in general." In their eyes, as with so many White militants from across colonial history, one was either an Indian hater or an Indian lover, a White patriot or a race traitor. There was no in-between. No wonder that when General William Irvine took over for Gibson amid this havoc, he instructed his wife back East not to comment on the injustice of Gnadenhutten, for his safety and what little authority was left of his title. Colonel David Williamson, who had led the Gnadenhutten and Killbuck Island massacres, was later elected sheriff of Washington County, south of Pittsburgh. His role in this atrocity had become a qualification for office.[24]

Aware that prosecuting this affair ran the risk of a frontier rebellion, the state of Pennsylvania brought no charges against the Gnadenhutten killers despite the urging of the Continental Congress to investigate, and the Congress took no measures of its own. A century of hard experience had taught that local juries would not convict Whites for the murder of Indians, or, for that matter, for the range of alcohol-soaked fistfights, knife fights, gunfights, kidnappings, rapes, and horse thieving that poisoned day-to-day relations wherever Whites and Indians lived in close proximity.

The only thing that could have possibly brought an end to this mayhem would have been to institute military rule throughout the frontier, and then hope against hope that soldiers would respect law and order more than the crowd did. There was no appetite for such bold action among authorities, and not just because the national experiment was still insecure in every respect. Whatever differences would soon emerge between proponents of central power, like Alexander Hamilton and John Adams, and libertarians, like Jefferson and Madison, they all took for granted that democracy in the United States would mean government serving White interests. They would have found the notion of dispensing perfectly equal justice to Indians and African Americans to be noble but preposterous given the pervasiveness of racial bigotry in White society. They had no immediate answer for it. Eventually, their solution was to promote Indian civility and the development of White western regions in the expectation that these efforts would tame both populations. In the meantime, the question was less whether government would stand up to the genocidal campaigns of White frontiersmen against Indians, but whether it would stay out of the way or harness and direct that impulse.[25]

Irvine rationalized that "people who have had fathers, mothers, brothers, or children butchered, tortured, scalped by the savages reason very differently on the subject of killing the Moravians, to what people who live in the interior part of the country in perfect safety do." The same went for Indians who lost kin at Gnadenhutten. Their chance for revenge arrived a month later, when the same militia that had carried out the massacre went back on the hunt for Indians, this time against the Wyandots and Delawares of Sandusky. The troops advertised their genocidal intent by posting messages along the route that read "No quarter to be given to an Indian, whether man, woman, or child," and leaving effigies of Indians hanging upside down from trees. They were too confident for their own good. A multitribal force stalking the invaders from the woods waited patiently until the Whites inadvisably made camp in an open field ringed by dense forest, and then proceeded to pick them off from cover, killing forty, capturing five, and dispersing the rest in a panic. Their captives included Captain William Crawford, whom, according to John Heckewelder, the Indians subjected to elaborate torture while they "often mockingly asked, how he felt; and whether they did as well to him, as he had done to the believing [Moravian] Indians, they adding, 'we have to learn barbarities of you white people!'" In fact, Crawford had not participated in the Gnadenhutten massacre, though he clearly intended atrocities on his own march.[26]

There had always been Indians who suspected evangelists of playing a long game to soften up their charges for White exploitation, but now the Ohio tribes were certain, even going so far as to accuse that the Gnadenhutten killers had acted at the written invitation of White Moravian missionaries. As late as 1803, the Delaware chief Pakantschihiles (also known as Buckongahelas), now living on the White River of Indiana, rebuffed Moravian entreaties with the explanation that "we have not forgotten the murder of the Christian Indians in Gnadenhutten. The white teachers, your brethren, taught the same thing you are teaching here. They sought to attract the Indians to themselves, and after many had been so drawn to them, they called the white people to come and murder them. I know full well that the teachers were at fault." That same year, the Delawares evacuated their towns in a panic at the rumor that White Kentucky militia were on their way "with the purpose of carrying away captive the women and children and killing the men." They rejected the counsel of White Moravians that this was a false alarm, sneering "we do not want to make the same mistake they made in Gnadenhutten."[27]

In a seeming impossibility, White Indian-hating also deepened in the wake of Gnadenhutten. At best, White officials saw the killing of the Moravians and the torture of Crawford as equivalent, as when George Washington opined that "the cruelties committed on both sides" were "entirely repugnant to him." At worst, Whites fixated on the Indians' depredations and ignored their own to grow even more committed to Indian genocide. The year after Crawford's death, the magistrate Hugh Henry Brackenridge published the accounts of Sandusky veterans John Knight and John Slover, who had managed to escape Indian captivity after witnessing Crawford's terrible fate. They recounted every bit of it in graphic detail to make the point that only "animals, vulgarly called Indians" could be so cruel. Such was "the nature of an Indian," Brackenridge added, and therefore "an extirpation of them would be useful to the world, and honorable to those who can effect it." The victims of Gnadenhutten, in this view, deserved to die because even Christian Indians "retain the temper of their race." That was to say, they "are so degenerate from the life of man, so devoid of every sentiment of generosity, so prone to every vicious excess of passion, so faithless, and so incapable of all civilization, that it is dangerous to the good order of the world that they should live in it."[28]

Scandalized by this venomous bigotry, the Quaker Anthony Benezet of Philadelphia countered in his own publication that it was "blasphemy" to cast Indians as an inferior race "prone to every vice, and destitute of every virtue." No, they had the same "mental powers" as White people, however undeveloped. Furthermore, the Gnadenhutten massacre illustrated that White people could be every bit as savage as Indians. If Whites did not halt this talk of Indians being "naturally ferocious, treacherous, and ungrateful," Benezet warned, it would lead to a campaign for "the universal extirpation of Indians from the face of the earth."[29]

Yet that was precisely what Brackenridge and his neighbors wanted. Two years after Benezet's plea, a starving Delaware Indian with a broken leg stumbled into Pittsburgh and drew immediate suspicion that he had killed White locals during the Revolution. Though the war was over, the people demanded a show trial so they could "execute him according to the Indian manner, by torture and burning," citing the Sandusky Indians' treatment of Crawford. Remarkably, the hobbled Indian managed to escape. The White Long Knives, however, would always be close behind no matter how far he ran.[30]

SEARCHING FOR A PATH FORWARD

The Indian-White race war outlived the American Revolution because it had nothing to do with British sovereignty, American rights and independence, or any of the constitutional matters of concern to White people. Its issues were that White Americans sought to rob Indians of their land and autonomy, and Indians resisted. The looming question for peace-minded Whites and Indians alike was whether there was any way forward other than genocidal war.

Early signs pointed to no. The fighting in Indian country raged on even as the United States and Great Britain were negotiating peace in between the British defeat at the Battle of Yorktown in 1781 and the concluding Treaty of Paris in 1783. In fact, 1782 was one of the bloodiest years of the Revolution in Indian country, marked not only by Gnadenhutten and Sandusky, but also by Kentucky and Pennsylvania militia destroying several Shawnee towns, Seneca and British forces sacking the Pennsylvania community of Hannastown, Ohio Indians killing a hundred Kentuckians at Blue Licks, and Georgia and South Carolina militia torching Cherokee country yet again. The Treaty of Paris the following year made little difference. Not only did it ignore Native people entirely, but in addition the United States took it to mean that by defeating Great Britain it had also defeated Britain's Indian allies. "As we are the conquerors," declared U.S. commissioners to the stunned Six Nations, "we claim the lands and property of all the white people as well as the Indians who have left and fought against us." The republic tried to fulfill this swagger by coercing the Haudenosaunees to sign the 1784 Treaty of Fort Stanwix, surrendering western

Pennsylvania, and various Midwestern tribes to relinquish east and central Ohio in 1785's Treaty of Fort McIntosh. American officers threatened that if the Indians did not comply, they would face "the whole force" of the United States, including "the destruction of your women and children."[31]

Yet the treaties carried that exact same risk, given that they emboldened tens of thousands of White people to storm into the ceded areas and even beyond, spurring war. All British Canada could offer its former Indian allies, given its meager population of one hundred thousand compared to the United States' 2.5 million people, was refuge behind its lines or material support to those who remained in American territory. Seeing nothing but disaster ahead for his fellow Indians, the Mohegan Samson Occom wrote, "It seems to me at times that there is nothing but Wo, Wo, Wo written in every turn of the wheel of God's Providence against us. I am afraid we are devoted to destruction and misery."[32]

Even Indians who had allied with the United States during the Revolution, including Wampanoags, Stockbridge Mohicans, Narragansetts, Mohegans, Pequots, Montauketts, Oneidas, Tuscaroras, and Catawbas, faced a future of landlessness and discrimination within the republic. The fact that these Indians had endured casualties disproportionate to their numbers, and targeted abuse at the hands of the British and their Indian allies, meant nothing, because White Americans wanted their lands as well. Massachusetts uprooted the Stockbridges shortly after the war, and New York put such relentless pressure on the Oneidas, Brothertowns, and relocated Stockbridges that the majority of them left for Wisconsin in the 1820s. Most of the rest of the country's former Indian allies either scraped by on marginal reservations by piecing together wage work as mariners, soldiers, day laborers, peddlers, and servants, or else relocated to the "colored" neighborhoods of cities and port towns, where White people clumped them together with Blacks.[33]

Indian communities "behind the frontier" did not want this association because it did them no good. Doubtless some Native people were bigoted toward Blacks, given the prevalence of this attitude in American society. Others worried that an influx of Blacks into their communities would diminish their Native languages and common landholding traditions. At the same time, there were Indians with deep empathy for Blacks because of their shared abuse at White hands. Occom preached that the slave trade was "the most accursed and most devilish practice that ever was found among the children of men." Yet he also knew that if Indians intermixed with Blacks, it ran the risk that Whites would define the offspring of Afro-Indian relationships, and even entire Native communities, as "Negroes," and repeal what few special legal protections Indigenous people still possessed. Consequently, in 1756, Occom led a group of Montauketts, among whom he lived, in denying community rights to "all Mustees or Mulattoes that have Indian squaws to their mothers Natives of Montauk" and to any woman who partnered with a "Negro." Then on May 12, 1773, forty-four Mohegans headed by Occom agreed that any of their women who married "strangers" would have to leave the community and any children descended from "Negroes" would not be recognized as members of the tribe. Finally, in 1774, Occom helped negotiate a deal for the multitribal Christian Brothertown Indians to move from their homelands in southern New England and Long Island to Oneida country, which specified that the land "shall not be possessed by any persons, deemed of said tribes, who are descended from, or have intermixed with Negroes or Mulattoes." Other small Indian communities throughout the East took similar measures. These were desperate acts by people who knew that the existential threat posed to them by Whites would just become worse through any connection with Blacks.[34]

Though, on the surface, the United States' new Constitution permitted Indians to take advantage of republican citizenship, that was a false offer. Take, for instance, Article I, Section 2, which specifies that representation and direct taxation for the states will be apportioned by population, "determined by adding to the whole number of free Persons, including those bound to Service for a Term of Years, and excluding Indians not taxed, three fifths of all other Persons." This passage implies that because tax-paying Indians count toward state representation and taxes, therefore they are

Portrait of Captain Absalom F. Boston, by an anonymous artist of the Prior-Hamblin School, 1835. Courtesy of the Nantucket Historical Association, Gift of Sampson D. Pompey.

Absalom Boston was an Afro-Wampanoag mariner from Nantucket during an era of increased Black-Indian marriages. Native communities in which these relationships were prevalent struggled enormously to convince Whites to respect their status as Indians.

part of "the people." Precious few Natives, however, were interested in becoming "tax-paying Indians." That status would have required them to leave the tax-free common lands of the reservation and the governance of the tribal community. The tax-paying Indian would have to live among Whites, respect their laws, risk jail and confiscation of private property for unpaid debts and public dues, and face court proceedings run by possibly hostile and almost certainly prejudiced White judges and juries. And for what? Certainly not even-handed justice. But what of the vote, in the unlikely possibility that Indians were interested in choosing between White candidates? Only a few states (Massachusetts, New Hampshire, Vermont, and New York) theoretically permitted tax-paying Indians to cast ballots, and exercising that right would require an Indian to brave the dirty looks, insults, and possibly violence of Whites gathered at the polls. Clearly, U.S. citizenship held few attractions for Indians.[35]

White law did not even give Indians who had helped to win the nation's independence in the Revolution a formal role in defending it afterward. In 1792, the federal Congress passed a militia act that called on "each and every free able-bodied white male citizens of the respective states" to contribute to the common defense. Bearing arms in the Anglo-American tradition symbolized that the militiaman had a stake in the society and government he was defending. The republic did not recognize Indians as having such a claim, particularly given the militia's responsibility to fight Indians and suppress slave uprisings.[36]

With the enactment of the Constitution in 1789, the White public was less committed to the federal government's making citizens of Indians than forcing them from their land. As U.S. general Josiah Harmar anticipated shortly after the Constitution went into effect, "the wheels of government will now soon be put in motion that we may be enabled to extirpate these perfidious savages if they continue committing hostilities." To no small degree, the future of the country depended on it. If the central government failed to protect its western citizens, even as they goaded Indians to war, it ran the risk of them declaring their own independence, or throwing their loyalty to the bordering empires of Britain or Spain.[37]

George Washington's presidential administration wanted to pacify Indians as cheaply, peacefully, and reputably as possible, which required abandoning the fiction that the Treaty of Paris had given the United States title to all Indian land east of the Mississippi. Washington and his point man on Indian affairs, Secretary of War Henry Knox, believed that even if the government formally recognized the Indians' right to their lands, the Natives would "ever retreat as our settlements advance upon them, and they will be as ready to sell as we are to buy." The key was to have federal officials, not the states or land speculation companies, control the process to keep it orderly, just as Britain had attempted with the Proclamation Line of 1763. To that end, the Constitution invested the central government with the sole authority and ample financial and military resources to negotiate with Indian nations. Washington and Knox envisioned having federal appointees meet regularly with Indian leaders to secure land cessions from them in exchange for annuities (annual payments) of bullion, banknotes, or goods. Agents stationed in Indian country would help manage relations with neighboring Whites and the states and promote civilized reforms. If needed, soldiers would be placed along the borders between Indian and White territory to police trespass and murder. Government-run trade factories in Indian country would provide the Natives with steady access to the goods they wanted without the usual graft and liquor peddling. Finally, the federal government would offer moral encouragement and a small measure of financial support to Christian organizations to run schools among the tribes.[38]

The ultimate goal of this system was to ease Indians and their lands into White American society. Indians who had taken up plow agriculture by men would find they no longer needed their hunting grounds, thereby encouraging them to cede that excess territory to the United States. If those same Indians became Christian, received a formal education, and developed a taste for private landholding, they would desire White laws to protect their property and persons, thus encouraging them to leave their tribes and become American citizens. Washington, Knox, and other elites, such as John Adams, Thomas Jefferson, and Patrick Henry, also hoped that Christian, civilized Indians would intermarry with Whites as part of the process of White society absorbing detribalized Natives and their land, though none of these men volunteered their own kin for this public service. If it all worked according to plan, there would be no need for the kind of genocidal violence that had characterized the past half century and the accompanying dishonor to the United States. Acutely aware of the judgment of "future historians" and the international community, Washington and Knox desperately wanted to avoid this stain on the country's reputation, never mind their own.[39]

There was a strong dose of utopianism in this scheme, which its architects reluctantly acknowledged. The most significant obstacle to its realization was that revenge murders and horse stealing were endemic wherever Whites and Indians lived near each other. Worse still, frontier Whites obstructed any attempt to arrest and try, never mind punish, any of their own kind for such crimes, even as they held entire Indian communities responsible for the wrongdoing of their people. Seeing this pattern, Washington implored Congress that "unless the murdering of Indians can be restrained, by bringing the murderers to condign punishment, all the exertions of the government to prevent destructive retaliation by the Indians, will prove fruitless." Washington could pledge high and low "that his red children should be treated with the same humanity and justice as his white children," but, as Knox recognized, Indians considered such promises to be "mere delusions" in the absence of evidence to the contrary.[40]

They were mere delusions to the many White Americans who considered Indians incapable of civilizing in the first place. In 1792, the missionary Samuel Kirkland reported receiving a letter from an unnamed "gentleman" who admitted, "I cannot help being of the opinion that Indians never were intended to live in a state of civil society. There never was, I believe, an instance of an Indian forsaking his habits and savage manners, any more than a bear his ferocity." Yes, the author conceded, Indians could be herded into church and taught to mimic prayers, but they were "Indians still, and like a bear which you can muffle and lead out to dance at the sound of music, becomes a bear when his muffler is removed and the music ceases." Kirkland might very well have written this letter himself. Jaded after years of mostly fruitless evangelizing among the Oneidas, he wrestled constantly with the dark conclusion that "the improvement and civilization of the Indians" is "altogether unattainable and impracticable ... that there is a repugnancy in the very frame and constitution of their minds to intellectual improvement and the arts of civilized life." The only thing that restrained Kirkland from publicizing his opinion was fear that it would lend support to "the view of the politician to exterminate the whole race."[41]

The New England clergymen Jeremy Belknap and Jedidiah Morse did not doubt Indians' ability to reform, just the willingness of Whites and Indians alike to support the experiment. Most White people refused to extend basic respect even to a formally educated, Christian Indian because "to treat him as an equal would mortify their own pride, and degrade themselves in the view of their neighbors." Indians also treated such liminal figures as outcasts. Consequently, the civilized Native "is neither a white man nor an Indian; as he has no character with us, he has none with them." Congressman John Clopton of Virginia agreed that one of the primary obstacles to civilizing and absorbing Indians was the Indians' own "strong and marked enmity to the whites, which seems to have been transmitted by succession from generation to generation, and to have been interwoven, as it were, in their very constitution." Most Indians wanted independence from Whites, not assimilation by them.[42]

True enough, many Indians were as dubious as White racists of the new government's Indian policies because, as the Washington administration's Timothy Pickering recognized, "Indians have been so often deceived by White people that White Man is among many of them, but another name for Liar." The Mohawk leader Joseph Brant shared the widespread belief among Indians "that the white people under whatever pretense aim at their destruction . . . and seeing the sword in one hand supported by injustice and corruption, is it any wonder they suspect the sincerity of any proposals made to them on the other hand for so great a change as civilization must make, in whatever color it is represented?" Brant particularly distrusted President Washington, who, he charged, "speaks very smooth . . . and at the same time want[s] to ruin us." Some Indians returned to the Nativist argument that the spirits intended them to live as their ancestors once did, whereas "the Christian religion was not designed for Indians" and therefore destroyed the traits "of the genuine Indian." The Senecas, for instance, concluded that "learning would be of no service to us" after they watched the Mohawks, Oneidas, and Mohicans open schools and take up animal husbandry only to have White people then force them off the land. The Creek leader Cussetah Mico also opposed schooling because, as Belknap and Morse had heard from other Indians, he judged that formally educated Indians "turned out very worthless; became mischievous and troublesome, and involve the red and white people in difficulties."[43]

Even Indians who favored civilized reforms generally concurred that "we cannot take all the ways of the white people at once, but by degrees." Most progressive Indians rejected the long-term aim of the federal government and missionaries to have Indians divide their common lands into private property because they knew it would atomize and scatter their people. "Holding our lands in common, as we now do," explained the Senecas' Captain Pollard, "keeps us together," which was the goal for practically all Indians, Nativist or Christian, militant or pacifist. The question was how best to achieve that end, not how to become part of the United States.[44]

The most avid Indian proponents of Christian and civilized reforms, such as the Stockbridge Mohicans and Brothertowns, warned that Indians faced certain extinction if they did not adopt the White people's way of life. Both of these groups had adopted Christianity, plow agriculture, literacy, and even the English language, before White encroachment and persecution drove them out of their homelands. These Christian Indians made sense of their repeated displacements by syncretizing the New England Calvinists' belief in predestination with the Nativists' principle that the Great Spirit rewarded or punished entire races based on their adherence to his wishes. Their conclusion was that "God is angry with us Indians," not only for their own shortcomings but also for the sins of their ancestors. By contrast, they judged that White people "appear to be favorites of heaven and honorable in the sight of men." Dark as this vision was, the Stockbridge Mohicans offered a glimmer of light, venturing that "God will make a last trial with us ... to contrive for our own souls." By "our own souls," they meant the entire race of Indians, and the "trial" was their collective responsibility to accept and spread the gospels and civility. To that end, multiple figures from Brothertown and Stockbridge preached to the Oneidas and other Haudenosaunees in what is now New York, and eventually to Delawares in Indiana and Ho-Chunks and Menominees in what is now Wisconsin. The Mohican Hendrick Aupaumut went so far as to try to convince militant Nativists in the Ohio country "that our Great Creator made the Red people capable of performing such a work as well as the white people ... and that in case they should reject or neglect it, their country would be given to the whites who would till it."[45]

Christian Indians, never mind the Washington administration, were asking too much. Whereas Nativists urged obedience to the dictates of a familiar Great Spirit, the Christians were speaking for a foreign God whose White followers wanted to destroy them. As the Ottawa war chief Egushawa told a conference of Ohio country Indians, "many of these white people have an opinion, called religion, which they inculcate on the minds of their children, that they please God by exterminating us red men." For the meantime, such Indians could not see a path forward other than continuing to fight for their land, autonomy, and way of life.[46]

THE WAR WITH NO END

The United States would have to defeat the eastern tribes again before it could persuade a critical mass of them to agree to additional land cessions or a robust civilization program. While American officials were trying to convince Indians that their "white father" saw them as his "red children," Indian messengers were crisscrossing the entire East preaching "that we are one people of one color on this island, and ought to be of one mind." Joseph Brant of the Mohawks, Dragging Canoe of the Cherokees, Alexander McGillivray of the Creeks, and a long roster of other Native leaders met repeatedly in multitribal councils to forge a common front. Their program was to halt land sales, force White trespassers from Indian land guaranteed by treaty, and defend one another whenever the Americans attacked. From his post in Knoxville, Tennessee, at the geographic heart of this politicking, General William Blount worried that Indian men seeking "national honors," or the martial esteem so fundamental to their masculine status, would now "shed the blood of white people" only because "Indians will no longer kill Indians."[47]

Native people did not want war, just secure borders, but tens of thousands of White settlers poured across the Indians' negotiated bounds like the spring floods. As McGillivray framed it, White Americans believed "that they could seize with impunity every foot of territory belonging to the Red Natives of America and that it would be easy to exterminate them if necessary." Thus, the Creeks gave the governors of neighboring states derisive names such as "Always Asking for Land" and "Dirt King" and referred to Georgians as *Ecunnaunuxulgee*, meaning "people greedily grasping after the lands of the red people." The problem for White Dirt Kings was that the Creeks would not tolerate White encroachment west of the Oconee River of Georgia or anywhere in the Cumberland region of Tennessee. The Cherokees and Ohio Indians likewise announced an end to land sales and a determination to police their borders, which to White Americans amounted to declarations of war.[48]

Like Whites, Indians rallied their people for the expected clash by racially demonizing the enemy. The Creeks' federal agent, Benjamin Hawkins, noticed that Creek children ran away whenever Whites appeared, "because of the tales of the old people." Some Creeks even adopted the "singular custom" that "as soon as a white person has eaten any dish and left it, the remains are thrown away, and everything used by the guest immediately washed," to prevent pollution. Not coincidentally, the Creeks also began to "openly aver their intention to kill every white man they meet—adding that such is their orders." A Cherokee warrior by the name of White Mankiller doubtlessly would have approved.[49]

The federal government risked a rebellion of frontier Whites with its policy to leave the war against the Cherokees and Creeks to state and territorial governments and step in only when the parties were ready to negotiate. The people of Mero County, Tennessee, spoke for frustrated settlers throughout the contested zone when they declared that "to treat with the Creek Nation will never avail us anything until an army is sent into the heart of their country sufficient to extirpate their whole savage race." Between 1784 and 1788, Whites in the Watauga region of eastern Tennessee plotted to secede from North Carolina and form a new state called Franklin, partly because they wanted complete freedom to attack Indians and seize their land. When their effort failed, Franklin's leadership considered aligning with Spain, only for Cherokee attacks to drive them back into the American fold. Just a few years later, a band of Georgians, in defiance of the 1790 Treaty of New York, invaded Creek territory west of the Oconee River and declared themselves an independent "Trans-Oconee Republic," before state and federal troops dispersed them. Everyone knew that if Indian attacks continued, however provoked, and the federal government did nothing, it was only a matter of time before the next secessionist movement.[50]

Utter exhaustion, rather than any decisive tactical victory, ended this phase of Indian resistance. The Cherokees surrendered in 1794 after losing another two thousand dead (a sixth of their already diminished population), three quarters of their remaining land, and more than half of their towns. At the 1794 Treaty of Tellico Blockhouse to establish the peace, Chief Hanging Maw pledged that, henceforth, "I will kill my own people, if they kill white people." The war-weary Creeks followed two years later after Spanish Florida quit supplying them with munitions rather than hazard war with the United States. It spoke volumes about how profoundly the Creeks' options had narrowed that when their leaders sat down to the negotiating table, they asked the federal government to station White troops along their border with Georgia to protect them against other White people. They knew they would need it. The ink was barely dry on the Treaty of Colerain before Benjamin Hawkins was told by one of the Creeks' White neighbors, a woman named Ann Van Zandt, that "the doctrine in her neighborhood was, let us kill the Indians, bring on a war, and we shall get land."[51]

In effect, killing Indians for their land was the doctrine of the entire nation. Regardless of what Knox and Washington said in principle, the United States was determined to seize the Ohio country from Indians in practice. It telegraphed this goal not only in the Treaties of Paris, Fort Stanwix, and McIntosh, but also in the Northwest Ordinance of 1787, which established the rules for several territories in the Ohio country and Great Lakes, even though Indians had yet to cede that ground. In this, the federal government was following rather than leading the people. Roughly eighty thousand White Americans streamed into the Ohio country between 1775 and 1790, which rivaled the total population of Indians in the region. Though government officials decried the lawlessness of this expansion, a number of them had personal profits at stake in it. A who's who of the political and financial elite invested in land speculation enterprises like the Ohio Company, which lobbied and bribed officeholders for the right to sell the federal domain to White settlers.

The only differences about how this process should unfold was that elites wanted government to seize the Indians' territory, sell it to the land companies at a discount, and then permit those businesses to vend parcels to White settlers at a markup, whereas White squatters planned to seize the Indians' country themselves and then demand that government protect their claims. To Indians, there was no difference. As Shawnees and Cherokees warned, they "would scalp all whites that came within their limits."[52]

Washington and Knox dreaded the strain that a campaign for control of Ohio would put on the republic's empty treasury, but they could not deny the reality that an informal war already existed and therefore moved to take control of it. Pressured by newspapers like the *Maryland Journal* to "surprise [the Indians'] towns in all quarters, kill and burn without distinction," in 1790, Knox sent orders to Brigadier General Josiah Harmar "to extirpate, utterly, if possible, the said Banditti" along the Maumee and Wabash Rivers. Perhaps then, Knox hoped, Indians would realize that his plan for peace, land cessions, and civilization was less an offer than an ultimatum. The alternative was genocide.[53]

Utter extirpation turned out to be more difficult than Knox had anticipated. In the first campaign, a regional coalition of Shawnees, Miamis, Delawares, Ottawas, Wyandots, Mingos, Potawatomis, and others killed 183 of General Harmar's troops in just two days and drove the rest into retreat. Then, in September 1791, the allied tribes under the Miami chief Little Turtle and the Shawnee chief Blue Jacket repulsed General Arthur St. Clair's army of 2,300 men, killing 647 and wounding hundreds, in what stands as the greatest Indian victory over U.S. forces in history. Knox's nightmare was coming true, with five sixths of the federal operating budget going toward these disastrous ventures. The Indians' advice was that the federal government should take the money it was wasting trying to exterminate them and use it to have the army move White trespassers somewhere else.[54]

White Indian-hating came pouring forth as the Indians in resistance accumulated victories. In Cincinnati, six men placed an ad in the *Centennial* newspaper offering $136 (equivalent to $3,900 today) to the first person who brought in ten Indian scalps, and $117 ($3,350 today) to the next one. Settlers, soldiers, and military officers alike were heard to "swear that if they could catch one of the [Indians] out, they would kill them as soon as a deer." General Anthony Wayne's army of twenty-two hundred regular soldiers and fifteen hundred militia tried to make good on these sentiments. On August 20, 1794, Wayne's troops scattered the outnumbered allied Indians at Fallen Timbers, then vented their rage by scalping and mutilating the

Indigenous dead and unearthing Native graves to drive stakes through the corpses. Yet the army's real target was the noncombatant population. It spent the next three days torching the Natives' villages and immense cornfields along the Maumee and Auglaize Rivers. As designed, the Indians' will to sustain their resistance went up in flames, too. The following year, their chiefs signed the Treaty of Greenville, ceding most of what is now Ohio and part of Indiana.[55]

This result might seem inevitable, and perhaps it was. Despite the Indians' requests, the United States was not going to use its army to keep White intruders out of Indian territory. Yes, sometimes federal agents dispatched troops to force small numbers of White squatters from contested land, but not with any consistency. Whenever they tried, enraged locals threatened the prosecution of the officers and soldiers and mob violence. True, the federal government was so concerned with establishing its authority and a reputation for fair dealing that it reversed egregiously corrupt state treaties and returned land to Indians in the 1785 Treaty of Hopewell with the Cherokees, the 1790 Treaty of New York with the Creeks, and the 1794 Treaty of Canandaigua with the Haudenosaunees. But the United States simply did not have the will to force Whites from Indian land and keep them off. It would have been political suicide.[56]

That is not to say that the nation lacked the capacity to enforce the law among unruly frontier Whites. Consider that, in 1794, the same year as the Battle of Fallen Timbers, another American army, thirteen thousand men strong, marched to Pittsburgh to suppress a rebellion of White frontiersmen against a federal whiskey tax. In that case, the Washington administration's determination to project its authority and uphold social order trumped any concern that this action would produce a backlash from the voters. The sanctity of Indian borders guaranteed by Senate-ratified treaties, which under the U.S. Constitution are the "supreme law of the land," did not command the same defense. One reason was that the federal government had deep financial interests in acquiring and selling Indian territory and eventually collecting taxes on the economic activities of the Whites who settled on it. Another reason, certainly, is that most White Americans, including federal officers, thought the White American way of life based on private property, Christianity, and other "civilized" features was superior to the Indians' supposed savagery. Yet the main reason was that the republic was a White man's country with a White man's government. Any administration that dared to use federal force against Whites for the benefit of Indians could, at best, expect to be voted out of office quick. At worst, it would risk a domestic uprising.[57]

THE LAST CLASH OF WHITE NATIONALISM AND NATIVISM IN THE EAST

White Americans had every reason to believe that they possessed a stranglehold on the entire eastern half of the continent following their military victories over the Indians of the Ohio country and Southeast in the 1790s. The combined White and Black populations of Kentucky, Tennessee, and the Northwest Territory climbed from 250,000 to 380,000 people between 1796 and 1800, utterly eclipsing the Indians' numbers. By 1810, the number of Whites and Blacks between the Appalachians and the Mississippi exceeded that of Indians by a factor of about four to one. Amid this rush, Thomas Jefferson, who as president (1801–1809) characterized himself as "friend of all the red people" and "head of the white people of the sixteen fires," administered thirty-two treaties with a dozen different Indian tribes, securing title to an additional two hundred thousand square miles of land. Funneling payouts from these treaties through cooperative "treaty chiefs" or "annuity chiefs," like Black Hoof of the Shawnees, gave those leaders and their followers an interest in maintaining the peace and making additional land cessions. The usual tensions persisted, but Whites had grown so powerful and Native people so reduced that the prospect of another armed Indian resistance seemed unlikely.[58]

Native people confronting their total subjugation and dispossession responded once again by seeking spiritual favor through racial separation and purification. Most of the prophets of this message, like Handsome Lake of the Senecas, emphasized community reformation and renewal, not violent resistance, but the preaching of the Shawnee Tenskwatawa took his followers down the militant path. In Tenskwatawa's visions, the Great Spirit taught that Indians would return to their former glories only when they purged themselves of White influences—the poison of alcohol, first and foremost, but also store-bought clothing, tools, and eventually even guns. Indians were supposed to use only the Indian technologies the Great Spirit originally intended for them. Furthermore, they were to rebuff missionaries and, indeed, minimize contact with Whites altogether. Instead of permitting chiefs and their inner circle to live fat off annuities while others struggled, the people were to revive the old ethic of sharing. Tenskwatawa instructed them to pray to the Great Spirit several times a day and confess publicly whenever they violated his rules. Tribal identities were to be set aside in favor of Indian unity, with no land sales unless all the tribes unanimously agreed to them. Not least, the people needed to rid themselves of chiefs in the pocket of the federal government and of Christians, like other forms of White

George Catlin, *Ten-squat-a-way, The Open Door, Known as the Prophet, Brother of Tecumseh*, 1830. Courtesy of the Smithsonian American Art Museum, Gift of Mrs. Joseph Harrison Jr.

Tenskwatawa, the Shawnee Prophet, was the ideological inspiration behind Nativist militantism in the Midwest during the War of 1812.

pollution, by execution if necessary. When Indians completed these reforms, "a crab would turn over the land so that the white people are covered."⁵⁹

The first White people to confront the zeal of Tenskwatawa's followers were a small group of Moravian missionaries struggling to win an audience among the Delawares and Shawnees on the White River in Indiana. In July 1805, just two months after the prophet's first vision, a mob of Indians painted black burst into the Moravians' village and shot dead their best hog, followed by weeks of daily threats that if the missionaries did not leave and "take the Word of God to the white people," their lives were at risk. A terrified J. P. Kluge and Abraham Luckenbach pleaded for their superiors to recall them, exclaiming, "We are entirely surrounded by a people who simply cannot bear us because of our very color or because we are white people." The last straw came in March 1806, when Tenskwatawa visited White River to conduct a witch hunt against Indians who were too close to Whites. It involved the torture and execution by burning of Caritas or Anne Charity, an elderly Christian; Tetepachsit, a sometime liquor dealer; and Billy Patterson, a Christian with White ancestry. The missionaries feared they were next. Tenskwatawa's acolytes charged that the "white teachers" kept the witches' poison hidden in order "to put the Indians to death or make them sick if they would not do as they were told." When the Moravians wisely announced their intent to depart, their antagonists responded that that was fine; "none of us will come to hear your word, for you are white people and we are Indians. You are of another color than we, also another teaching; your teaching is good for white people but not for us."[60]

Tenskwatawa insisted that he did not seek war with the Whites, just the reform of Indians, but Indiana territorial governor William Henry Harrison had good reason to expect that a "race war" was brewing in which the Indians would receive the backing of British Canada. The prophet established his first headquarters at Greenville, site of the Ohio Indians' humiliating treaty of 1795, to signal that he viewed that cession and others as illegitimate. Then, in 1808, he relocated to a new, equally provocative location, Tippecanoe, on the Wabash River, which soon became known as Prophetstown. This site blocked the path of White expansion and was close to the tribes that constituted the heart of his movement, including Kickapoos, Sauks and Foxes, Ho-Chunks, Ojibwes, and Potawatomis. With as many as six thousand people, the population of Prophetstown was second only to New Orleans as the largest community west of the Appalachian Mountains. Meanwhile, reports streamed into Harrison's office of Tenskwatawa and his followers boasting that they wielded the power to "destroy the white people at any time" and "threatening that unless their lands are restored they will drive them back across the Ohio River." By appearances, they meant it.[61]

After annuity chiefs from several tribes agreed to the Treaty of Fort Wayne in 1809, yielding nearly thirty million acres in what are now Indiana and Illinois to the United States, the likelihood of a race war seemed greater than ever. Tenskwatawa's brother, the war leader, Tecumseh, told Harrison to his face that the chiefs had signed their own death warrants, and White people should not dare to enter the ceded territory. The treaty was invalid, he pronounced, because the land belonged to all Indians and the United States had pledged earlier not to seek any more of it. When Harrison countered that the United States treated Indians better than any other civilized nation would, an indignant Tecumseh unleashed a cascade of racial invective. There was no trusting Whites, he charged, citing as examples the Gnadenhutten massacre, the killing of Indians who flew the American flag, and even the crucifixion of Jesus. White people were so underhanded that they laced Indian trade goods with smallpox. It was all part of a grand design to reduce Indians to beggars, to the point that if "a poor Indian attempts to take a little bark from a tree, to cover him from the rain, up comes a white man and threatens to shoot him, claiming the tree as his own." Tecumseh did not threaten war directly, but Harrison could plainly see that it was just a matter of time. His view was only confirmed when, in 1811, Tecumseh made a long journey to the Southern tribes to preach the gospel of Indian unity and resistance.[62]

Tecumseh had good reason to expect a favorable reception in the South. Since at least 1803, the Creeks, Cherokees, Choctaws, and Chickasaws had held periodic counsels to oppose any land sales conducted without the unanimous consent of all four nations, though they always failed to reach a consensus on this motion. Cherokee and Creek warriors had a history of cooperating with Shawnees to drive Whites out of the contested parts of Kentucky and Tennessee. In a parallel to the Northern tribes' disputes over annuity chiefs and Christians, the Southern tribes faced growing discontent over the emergence of an elite faction, comprised disproportionately, though not entirely, of so-called "mixed-bloods" (people of Indian-White ancestry). This group eschewed traditional Indian economic activities in favor of Black slaveholding, cotton production, stock raising, innkeeping, storekeeping, and the management of toll roads and ferries. Such figures typically lived in square-framed houses, some of which rivaled those of White plantation elites, filled with the same furniture and accessories that one would expect to find in White homes, with locks on the doors to prevent theft. Their estates were surrounded by fences and plowed fields, which White people had long counted as two of the most important marks of civility. They encouraged missionary schools to spread literacy education, especially among their own children. Some of them spoke English only. The members of this acculturated class were full members of their tribes by right of matrilineal descent, but they did not live in the same manner as their neighbors. They seemed to be doing the White people's work for them by undermining Indian society from within.[63]

That resentment grew even deeper as the elites began to centralize the tribal governments they dominated. In the late 1790s Creek reformers, in consultation with their federal agent, Benjamin Hawkins, established a national council with a police force that would hold individuals responsible for crimes, just as Whites did, contrary to the traditions of clan revenge and town autonomy. They also passed a series of laws to protect their private property, encourage acquisitive values, and suppress behaviors like horse theft and murder that risked antagonizing Whites. In July 1803, the Creek police went so far as to execute two Indians and three Blacks and publicly whip twenty-four others for crimes as defined by the elites rather than Creek custom. The Cherokees followed a parallel path by outlawing clan revenge in 1797, forming a police force called the Lighthorse Guard in 1799, then creating a National Council with executive and judicial powers in 1809. With the Choctaws and Chickasaws adopting similar measures in the years to come, it seemed as if the governments of all the Southern tribes were just steps away from becoming indistinguishable from the adjoining White states.[64]

These reformists saw their agenda as a means not only to advance their personal wealth, though it was certainly that, but also to insulate the entire group from outside White pressure. Living like White people, they contended, was the only way for Indians to fend off White demands for more land and adjust to the decline of hunting grounds. The purpose was not to assimilate into White society, but to defend Indian autonomy. Yet Nativist critics saw these changes as the very manifestations of White encroachment, as the promotion of morally offensive White ways and values by leaders with White ancestry and loyalties masquerading as Indians. In protest, some traditional-minded Creeks left the tribal homeland for Florida, where they gradually became known as Seminoles. Back home, a series of prophets arose, propounding the familiar message of separate Indian and White creations and the need to purge White influences and recover the favor of the Great Spirit. "You yourselves can see that the white people are entirely different beings from us," one Cherokee vision went. "We are made from red clay; they out of white sand." Some Cherokees followed a prophet (whose name went unrecorded) who convinced them to burn all White clothing in anticipation of three-day period of darkness that would sweep away all the "wicked" Whites and Indians who lived like them. The tension throughout the southeastern tribes was palpable and combustible.[65]

Yet when Tecumseh called on the Southern tribes to join their Northern brethren against the Americans in the next expected war between Britain and United States, the answer was a resounding *no*. The Cherokees, especially, had already endured too much death and destruction at White hands to risk another defeat. They feared if they got involved "in the wars of the white people" again it meant "they would lose every foot of land." Dissident Creeks, however, took inspiration from Tecumseh and began gathering their forces.[66]

While Tecumseh was away preaching in the South, the great racial clash he anticipated was already unfolding in the North. On November 5, 1811, a day after President James Madison asked Congress to begin preparing for hostilities with Britain, Harrison took advantage of Tecumseh's absence to attack Prophetstown, in what is known today as the Battle of Tippecanoe. His men not only burned the community to the ground, but also dug up its graveyard to leave the Indians' corpses rotting aboveground. A coalition of Potawatomis, Kickapoos, and Ho-Chunks answered by raiding U.S. settlements and forts throughout Illinois, Indiana, and western Ohio, including the treacherous killing or capturing of ninety-five Americans evacuating Fort Dearborn (Chicago) under promise of quarter. White Americans countered with scorched-earth attacks on the Indians' towns. Tecumseh, the Shawnee prophet, and their followers subsequently withdrew behind British lines to regroup for a campaign to force Whites out of their country once and for all. In the meantime, however, they contributed to several British victories along the U.S.-Canadian border. Their mere presence was sometimes enough to put American troops to flight, for, as one British officer remarked, "it is inconceivable the horror and dread which they have of the Indians."[67]

United States culture had conditioned them to feel this way, and continued to do so with inflammatory accounts about Indians from the war zone. When the Reverend Benjamin Bell of New York preached on the "evil effects of war," he reflected how "sometimes, when the defenseless husband is gone to camp, the merciless savages break in at the dead of night, upon the defenseless mother and helpless children, kill and scalp them, plunder and burn the house, and escape the wilderness unrevenged." Captivity narratives, more than a dozen of which appeared in book-length form between 1812 and 1815, recounted Bell's scenario over and over, emphasizing that Indians were "inhuman creatures," "hideous animals," "vile monsters," and "hideous cannibals," who went so far as to take the scalps of fetuses cut out of their mothers' wombs. Newspapers performed their customary role, as when over two dozen of them reprinted Harrison's denunciation of war atrocities committed by Britain's Indian allies. Harrison cited a case from the shores of Lake Erie in which the Indians reportedly captured a woman "in an advanced state of pregnancy—she was immediately tomahawked, stripped naked, her womb ripped, and the child taken out!" The unmistakable message was that this war pit civilized White Americans against an irredeemably savage Indian enemy. The usual calls for a "war of extermination" echoed from every quarter.[68]

This demonization of Indians encouraged common soldiers and average citizens to treat Indians in ways to which they would never subject fellow Whites. Infamously, at the Battle of the Thames in Ontario on October 5, 1813, American forces skinned a corpse they believed was Tecumseh's to make razor straps. This was no isolated incident. A Pennsylvania officer serving during the war reported a conversation with a Captain Ballard of Kentucky who "said he had twenty [Indian] scalps at home, and that he would raise fifty scalps before he would die." Colonel John Ketchem's own reminiscences of the War of 1812 included killing and scalping an Indian during his first month in the field, then bringing the grisly trophy home to show his parents, who "thought I had done about right."[69]

The power of Indian-hating even infected parts of the home front where there was no risk of Indian attack. Stoneham, Massachusetts, was hundreds of miles away

William Charles, *A Scene on the Frontiers, as Practiced by the Humane British and Their Worthy Allies!*, 1812. Courtesy of the Library of Congress.

American propaganda during the War of 1812 commonly linked the British to Indian scalping and other atrocities, real and imagined.

from the fighting in a state that widely opposed the war. Nevertheless, in 1813, four White men killed a local Indian man and injured his wife by shooting them full of nails, not lead pellets, from a shotgun, in order to inflict maximum pain. The night before the murder, the killers were heard proclaiming, "The Devil take the Indians, or damn the Indians," just as the country's wartime rhetoric encouraged. The jury came back with a verdict of guilty, but only after the judge implored it that Indians were entitled to the same justice as everyone else. Even then, he felt the need to lecture the killers before sentencing, and, through them, the public, that Indians were not "wild beasts or vermin, to be hunted and destroyed."[70]

Creeks who took up arms up against their tribe's progressives following Tecumseh's visit also saw themselves as engaged in a race war. The final spark came in the spring of 1813, after the National Council, led by plantation grandees William McIntosh and Big Warrior, administered the execution and flogging of several Creek men for crimes against Whites. "We mean to kill off all our red people that spill the blood of our white friends," explained the council chiefs to the agent Hawkins. Creek prophets Josiah Francis and Cusseta Harjo invoked the principles of Tenskwatawa to contend that now the council chiefs deserved to die, and if Whites tried to intervene the Great Spirit would cause an earthquake to prevent them. Nativist warriors quickly answered the summons. Calling themselves the Red Sticks after their traditional painted war clubs, they executed four chiefs in the town of Coosa, another five in the town of Okfuskee, and then attacked the progressive town of Tuckabatchee, headquarters of the National Council. This was civil war.[71]

White authorities preferred to stay out of it, given the demands of the war in the North, but the Red Sticks pushed too far in September 1813 when they struck Fort Mims on the lower Alabama River, which sheltered an array of progressive Creeks, White settlers, and Black slaves. The warriors slaughtered some 250 people in short order, sorting out racial enemies from those with whom they had no quarrel. One of the survivors, an unnamed Black man, reported that during the carnage, "an Indian, seeing him in the corner, said, come out, the Master of Breath has ordered us not to kill any but white people and half breeds." In fact, the Red Sticks also spared some "half breed" noncombatants. Another witness confirmed that the Red Sticks "put all the white people to death in the fort" but "made prisoners only of some half-breed women and children." The Red Sticks' own ranks included many such mixed-bloods, including Josiah Francis. Yet when Creeks of mixed background acted like an advance guard of the White people, the Red Sticks rejected their claims to be Creek and Indian. The political problem was that this violent purge of mixed-blood Creeks necessarily claimed the lives of White Americans, too, given the closeness of their ties.[72]

After Fort Mims, it was time to test Hawkins's warning to the Red Sticks months earlier that "war with the white people will be your ruin." The disastrous lot of the Red Sticks was that those White people included the Indian-hating militia of Tennessee, led by the Indian-hating Tennessee general Andrew Jackson. "Brave Tennesseans!" beckoned Jackson in his call for volunteers. "Your frontier is threatened with invasion by the savage foe! Already do they advance toward your frontier with scalping knives unsheathed to butcher your wives, your children, and your helpless babes. Time is not to be lost." White men responded enthusiastically, pledging to "exterminate the Creek nation." To that end, Jackson's troops, reinforced by Georgia militia and even warriors from the Creeks, Cherokees, and Choctaws, devastated one Red Stick town after another in the fall and early winter of 1813–14, before trapping and slaughtering eight hundred Red Sticks at Tohopeka, or Horseshoe Bend, on March, 27, 1814. Overall, the Red Sticks suffered the loss of more than eighteen hundred warriors, or 40 percent of the Creeks' able-bodied men, and several hundred women and children; forty-eight towns destroyed, twelve abandoned, and eighty-two hundred people left homeless and starving. The *Salem Gazette* of North Carolina broke the news with the celebratory headline EXTERMINATING THE INDIANS.[73]

WHITE REPUBLIC, WHITE LAND

The Red Sticks had preached from the beginning that "if the red people would unite, nothing could withstand them." Instead, portions of the Upper Creeks and Cherokees had contributed to Jackson's army as a warning to Nativists and a show of solidarity with Whites. Jackson's troops did not return this goodwill as they marched through Cherokee country against the Creeks. Instead, they shot down livestock for sport, plundered and burned houses, and looted cornfields, like conquerors. In a letter to President Madison seeking damages, Cherokee leaders remonstrated that the soldiers' "prejudice" was "founded only on the differences in shades of complexion." The same went for their purported ally, Jackson, who the federal government appointed to impose new land cessions on the Southern Indians, as if they bore responsibility for the Red Sticks. During his six-year term, Jackson cajoled the Creeks, Cherokees, Choctaws, and Chickasaws to relinquish a fifth of Georgia, half of what is now Mississippi, and most of what is now Alabama: in all, about fifty million acres. The alternative, he threatened, was for the federal government to withdraw all its protections and leave them to deal on their own with circling frontier Whites.[74]

The Southern Indians' cessions alone disprove the old adage that the War of 1812 ended with a mere return to the prewar status quo. That interpretation is true only as it relates to the state of affairs between the United States and Britain, but it studiously ignores White Americans' victories at Indian expense. The 1815 Treaty of Ghent ending the War of 1812, like the Treaty of Paris before it, did not include Indians at the negotiating table. Nevertheless, a British minister involved in the proceedings observed that his American counterparts were utterly contemptuous of Indian rights, "thereby menacing the final extinction of those nations." True enough, though Article 9 of the treaty obligated the United States to return all lands it had seized from its Indian enemies since the year 1811, the young republic not only ignored this provision entirely, but also forced Britain's former Indigenous allies to surrender additional territory. For instance, federal officials bullied the Potawatomis into ceding practically all of their eighteen million acres of land in twenty-eight treaties between 1816 and 1833. These former hosts of Prophetstown, like the rest of the Indians east of the Mississippi, could no longer resist the United States without Britain's diplomatic and military support. The end of the war meant that such aid was over, once and for all.[75]

This dramatic shift in the balance of power emboldened White Americans to revise the nation's approach to Indian affairs established during the Washington administration. Whereas the earlier goal had been to negotiate with Indians to live like Whites on less land as steps toward their assimilation, now some Americans, like Secretary of War William Crawford, anticipated "the extermination or expulsion of the aboriginal inhabitants of the country to more distant and less hospitable regions." Crawford's successor, John C. Calhoun of South Carolina, went so far as to contend that the United States should no longer treat Indians as "independent nations," but instead "our views of their interest, and not their own, ought to govern them." The Indians' interest, in Calhoun's self-serving estimation, was remarkably similar to the Whites', for he warned them that if they did not divide their land, live like Whites, and sell their excess territory, "you will find you have to emigrate, or become extinct as a people."[76]

Calhoun represented an early stage of what would become a long tradition in which White Americans insisted that Indian death and dispossession was the result of natural forces or God's will rather than White American aggression. Indians knew better. Between 1800 and 1820, Whites had seized from them some six hundred thousand square miles, leading to the migration of more than two million Whites west of the Appalachian Mountains, the construction of roads and canals linking White western agricultural settlements to urban hubs and ports in the east, and the addition of six western states to the union. The nation's line of frontier military posts now stretched north to the headwaters of the Mississippi River, and had begun to creep up the Missouri. There was no end in sight. All the Seneca leader Red Jacket could think to do was plead "that wicked white men may not devour us at once ... lest God who has appeared so strong in building up white men and pulling down Indians, should turn his hand and visit our white brother for their sins..."[77]

For generations, Whites had told Indians that the way to survive White dominance was to civilize, which was the approach favored by most Eastern Indians now that Whites had defeated the Nativists decisively. The major problem was that White people's faith in that solution was dwindling once again. Already, at the start of the War of 1812, the popular *Niles Weekly Register* of Baltimore had pronounced that it "looks forward to the moment when all the southern Indians shall be pushed across the Mississippi..." In other words, rather than exterminating Indians, White people would remove them from their homelands into the far distance, where they would no longer represent a threat or obstacle.[78]

By the end of the war, there was a new, even more sinister version of this idea. It posited that such removal was not only to the benefit of White people, but also good for Indians because it distanced them from the vices of White society, to which they were supposedly so prone, and allowed them to civilize at their own pace without the threat of immediate displacement. No one found this model more appealing than Andrew Jackson, whose political career was ascendant after his exploits during the War of 1812. "Humanity requires that something should be done for them," he wrote of the Southern Indians while serving as a commissioner to wrest their land from them, or else they "must dwindle to nothing." Such humane sentiments barely cloaked the Indian-hating of generations of White Americans born of the horrors of a sixty years' war stretching from the Seven Years' War through the War of 1812. The Indian haters wanted Native people dead or gone, not as civilized neighbors living on even dramatically diminished portions of their ancestral homelands. And soon the Indian haters would have their choice of president, none other than Jackson, who would grant their wish to be done with Native people once and for all.[79]

CHAPTER 4

Whitewash

Indian Removal was criticized in its own time as a human rights disaster and is remembered as such today. After all, this policy of the United States to force Native people from the East to Federal Indian Territory in what is now Oklahoma and Kansas resulted in enormous losses of life and inestimable heartbreak. Yet Removal's proponents insisted that they were saving Indians, not damning them. Their contention was that Indians plunged into physical and moral decline toward extinction when exposed to superior White civilization. Since White expansion was as certain as the Indians' withering from it, the most humane thing Whites could do was relocate the Indians somewhere out of harm's way. Then, at least, the Indians would have time and space to try to become fully civilized and Christian so they could merge with American society whenever it overran them again. In essence, the circular rationale of Removal was that if Indians stayed in the East, they would disappear, so they had to disappear from the East.[1]

American historical memory has taken over the work of disappearance from there. Though practically any discussion of Removal acknowledges the misery of the Cherokees on the Trail of Tears, generations of Americans have viewed this episode primarily as a crisis of United States federalism. From this perspective, the most consequential legacy of Indian Removal is President Andrew Jackson's refusal to enforce the Supreme Court's rulings that the state of Georgia's unilateral assertion of jurisdiction over the Cherokees and their lands was unconstitutional. It is a story about how a populist president altered the checks and balances between branches of the national government and the federal relationship between Washington, D.C., and the states. It willfully ignores that Removal was fundamentally a national land grab rationalized through White supremacy and Indian-hating that affected a much wider array of Indigenous peoples than just the Cherokees.[2]

Indians and their White advocates who opposed Removal understood this fact all too well. They answered the cant of Removal with counterarguments that Native people were just as capable of civilized living (which was to say, the White way of living) as Whites, that many of them had already achieved this standard, and, therefore, that they were not fated to extinction. Rather, Indians throughout the East were on the rise and would continue that ascent if White people would only respect their sovereign rights to land and self-governance. Indian decline was not a matter of God's will or nature, but purely of White behavior driven by morally bankrupt values and politics. Indians in resistance convinced millions of White Americans that they were right, but it was not enough to defeat Removal. Racial ideologues were endlessly capable of ignoring or dismissing evidence that confounded their preferred beliefs.

Removal involved the nation's most prominent politicians covering the crass, land-driven Indian-hating and White supremacy of the mob with a humanitarian veneer and institutional legitimacy. When such ideas emanated from the White House, Congress, statehouses, and their media outlets, and became translated into policy, they acquired unprecedented power. Now it was not just isolated individuals or frenzied crowds acting out race, it was an entire government and society. This is the civics lesson of Removal that generations of Americans have whitewashed from our histories.

EXTINCTION AND ITS OPPONENTS

Though the United States had failed to exterminate its Indigenous enemies during the War of 1812, close as it came with the Creeks, the resulting White nationalism and Indian-hating did produce a wave of cultural productions that anticipated the Indians' extinction. A man of letters named James Hall observed in 1835, after years spent living in Pittsburgh and Illinois, that a child raised "on the frontier" learned "to hate an Indian, because he always hears him spoken of as an enemy. From the cradle, he listens continually to horrid tales of savage violence, and becomes familiar with narratives of aboriginal cunning and ferocity." One did not need to grow up on the frontier or have an interest in Indian land to be influenced by such accounts. The Maryland-born Superintendent for Indian Affairs Thomas McKenney, addressing an audience in New York City, asked rhetorically, "Which of us has not listened with sensations of horror to the nursery stories that are told of the Indian and his cruelties?" Even the Pequot writer William Apess developed a terror of Indians as a child servant of White families in New England, "occasioned by the many stories I had heard of their cruelty toward the whites." The moral of such tales was that the Indians' barbarities justified their destruction.³

School lessons propagated the same crude message. The racial conditioning began in the earliest grades with a common alphabet song that went, "I is for Indian, He is going to slay." Next came the popular McGuffey's Readers, which introduced young people to heroic frontier settlers enduring merciless raids and captivity at Indian hands. Another national textbook, *Lights of Education*, acknowledged some value in the study of Indian customs, but only as "an authentic memorial of a people, whose manners will be totally changed before their race is exterminated." Even Native boys enrolled at the Choctaw Academy boarding school in Kentucky were taught that Indians "will never become enlightened or civilized; and in the course of half a century, they will be extirpated." Anyone taking this reading seriously would have to question the point of educating Indians in the first place.⁴

As adults, White Americans continued to consume memoirs, histories, captivity narratives, and fictional literature propagating the idea that Indians deserved annihilation for their savagery. Consider some of the titles that appeared in the wake of the War of 1812: *Narrative of the Tragical Death of Mr. Darius Barber . . . Inhumanely*

Indians Attacking White Settlers, from Samuel Augustus Mitchell, *Mitchell's Primary Geography, An Easy Introduction to the Study of Geography* (Philadelphia: Thomas, Cowperthwait, 1846).

Images and descriptions of Indian savagery were common in American schoolbooks throughout the nineteenth and twentieth centuries.

Butchered by the Indians (1818); *A Narrative of the Sufferings of Massy Harbison from Indian Barbarity . . . with an Infant at Her Breast* (1825); and *Indian Anecdotes and Barbarities: Being a Description of Their Customs and Deeds of Cruelty . . . All Illustrating the General Traits of Indian Character* (1837). Whereas in the late seventeenth century the point of captivity narratives had been to teach about the redemptive power of faith under trials and tribulation, by the early nineteenth century this genre had become a vehicle of White nationalist propaganda. Reaching general audiences through cheap formats like broadsides, almanacs, and newspapers, these accounts told of innocent White people bravely defending hearth, home, and civilization itself from bloodthirsty Indian aggressors. "Such monsters of barbarity," pronounced the captivity narrative of Mary Smith, "ought certainly to be excluded from all the privileges of human nature, and hunted down as wild beasts, without pity or cessation." Extermination or forced removal of the Indians were the only solutions these writings proposed. They no longer supported "the folly of attempting to civilize the savage."[5]

This view encouraged White Americans to lionize White "Indian killers" of the past and present. Indian-killing exploits during the War of 1812 helped launch the political careers of no less than Presidents Andrew Jackson, William Henry Harrison (Old Tippecanoe), and Zachary Taylor, Vice President Richard Mentor Johnson, four U.S. senators, numerous congressmen, and three state governors of Kentucky. Meanwhile, schoolbooks and the popular press began to feature swashbuckling histories of Indian-killing "pioneers" such as Benjamin Church of King Philip's War, Robert Rogers of the Seven Years' War, and Daniel Boone of Revolutionary Kentucky, who adopted Indian war tactics to defeat Indians for civilization. White Americans' sense of themselves as a race and nation was beginning to involve not only the slaughter of Indians and seizure of their land, but also the romanticizing of it as well.[6]

Tom Quick the Indian Slayer did not run for high office, but if he had, his semi-fictional life story might very well have convinced White Americans to name him emperor. White settlers on the upper Delaware River told of how Quick, after witnessing Lenape warriors scalp his father during the Seven Years' War, dedicated his life to the killing of Indians using the skills of tracking, ambush, and sharpshooting he had learned from Native playmates in childhood. "The young and the old, the weak and the strong of the hated race, appeared to be equally the objects of his vengeance," his neighbors recalled. Quick's justification for killing of Indian children was that "if their lives were spared, [they would] become as bad as their parents," just as "nits make lice." The story went that Quick, after a lifetime of hunting Indians like wild animals, died of smallpox, despondent that he had fallen just short of a hundred kills. Yet when his Indian adversaries unearthed and dismembered his body for their own revenge, they contracted the deadly disease themselves, thereby allowing Quick to reach his goal posthumously. In the nineteenth century, Milford, Pennsylvania, took such pride in this psychopath that it erected a monument to him (destroyed in recent times by vandals) and still has an inn bearing his name.[7]

If, in the short term, the passions of war led White Americans to demonize Indians and glorify their killers, in the long term, the defeat of large-scale Indian resistance in the East inspired nostalgia for Native people and lament over their demise, at least among coastal literati. James Fenimore Cooper's Leatherstocking Tales, published between 1827 and 1841, epitomize this movement. They tell the adventures of Nathaniel (Natty) Bumppo, a White man, like Quick, who has been raised by Indians in the ways of the woods. Whereas those skills empower Bumppo to survive the dangers of the colonial frontier, his Indian compatriots recede with the forest toward their ultimate disappearance. Though Cooper and his literary peers such as Washington Irving, Nathaniel Hawthorne, and Henry David Thoreau denounced the injustices of White American conquest, they attributed the Natives' supposedly inevitable extinction to the law of nature and history that civilization should expand at the expense of savagery. In Cooper's writing, all the tragic Indians can do is to take solace that Bumppo will carry on some of their traditions. All White readers can do is to lament the vanishing race and honor its noble virtues like independence, rootedness, and connection to nature. These characteristics are unable to save the Indians, but they offer comfort to civilized people experiencing the alienation of a mobile, rapidly industrializing society.[8]

The combination of romanticism about Indians, resignation about their supposed extinction, and moral critique of Western modern life infused American arts and letters from the early to mid-nineteenth century. Plays, poems, novels, paintings, ethnographies, and histories poured forth to celebrate Indian leaders like "Metamora" (or King Philip) and Logan, who made tragic last stands against White expansion, only to melt away like snow, which was one of the most common metaphors in the genre for the Indians' demise. Even Tecumseh, who within recent memory had been White America's prime example of bloodthirsty savagery, suddenly became a folk hero for his lost cause, evident in the middle name of U.S. general William T. Sherman. Sentiment for the disappearing Indian also inspired the painter George Catlin's journey up the Mississippi and Missouri River Valleys during the 1830s to capture the likenesses of Indigenous people before they were gone. Dividing his subjects into "corrupted" and "uncorrupted" categories, he estimated that 1.4 million out of 2 million Natives were already debased and on the cusp of oblivion. Published town and county histories in New England (one for nearly every municipality) routinely featured a chapter about the neighborhood's last Indian, even when Natives were still very much around. Statues of Indians beckoned customers into tobacco shops, household weathervanes featured Indian bowmen, and Indian figureheads graced the bows of whaling ships carrying Native American names. Practically overnight, Native people had turned from murderous threats to domestic symbols of the natural world, independent spirit, and White American pride. Yet these seemingly opposite views of Indians shared a basic assumption: They both considered the disappearance of Indians to be inevitable because of the divinely ordained rise of White civilization.[9]

The centrality of these images to White national identity was evident in the Indian-themed artwork decorating the United States Capitol. A series of reliefs in the Capitol Rotunda depicted Indians passively handing over their country to White people, as in scenes of Pocahontas saving John Smith, the Wampanoags greeting the Pilgrims, and the Delawares conferencing with William Penn. The history of warfare between Whites and Indians was memorialized, too, in a relief of Daniel Boone engaged in hand-to-hand combat with a tomahawk-wielding Indian warrior while another Indian lies dead at their feet, and later in a statue entitled "The Rescue" in which an oversized frontiersman seizes hold of a Native attacker just before he can hatchet a defenseless White woman and child. Here, in one of the most prominent spaces in the country, were multiple images of Indians as both noble and bloodthirsty savages, endlessly malleable to the needs of White society. The through line was that the contest for America (or at least the eastern half of it) was over, the Indians' resistance, savage though it was, had been noble in its principles if not its practices, Whites had triumphed, Indians had lost, and the struggle had produced a great nation. In their munificence, White people could now safely grieve the extinction of Native people this progress had required.[10]

White science offered intellectual support for these views, in a departure from two hundred years of race theory. Throughout the seventeenth and eighteenth centuries, White thinkers struggled to explain the origins and meanings of the racial categories that were coming to define the colonial world. James Adair, the South Carolina deerskin trader and intellectual who published his influential *History of the American Indians* in 1775, typified the resulting eclecticism of race science during this early period. He attributed the complexion of Indians to a combination of the

Horatio Greenough, *The Rescue*, from Glenn Brown, *History of the United States Capitol* (Washington, D.C.: Government Printing Office, 1903).

Images of Native Americans can be found throughout the United States Capitol. Typically, they portray Indians as either peacefully welcoming White people to take over their country, or, as in this statue, savagely resisting progress. American Indians protested *The Rescue*, generation after generation, before it was finally removed in 1958, after 105 years of standing by the Capitol's east facade.

"corpus mucosum or gluish web" beneath their skin, exposure to the elements, and application of bear's oil, grease, and pigment to their bodies. At the same time, he claimed to have seen Indians give birth to White babies who only later grew copper-toned, and White captives gradually assume the skin shade of their captors. He even posited that people's imagination during sexual intercourse could determine the color of their offspring. Such notions were consistent with the principle of most elites that culture and complexion were fluid, that people could change physically and behaviorally depending on a range of circumstances.[11]

In the early nineteenth century, however, science began to confirm and reinforce White folk wisdom that Indians were hopeless savages fated to disappear before White civilization. The notion of separate creations, or polygenesis, so roundly rejected by Adair and most of his contemporaries, became more widely (though far from universally) accepted in intellectual circles. Other scholars, such as Samuel George Morton of Philadelphia, trailblazed the racial junk science of phrenology, the study of the bumps, craters, angles, and volume of human skulls. Its predetermined conclusion was that Whites were a superior race characterized by inventiveness and strength, Blacks were inferior by virtue of inherent docility and ignorance, and Indians were born barbarians. The White American dispossession and killing of Indians became just nature running its course.[12]

Rigor is not a feature of racial ideology, given that the real world repeatedly contradicts its supposed rules. Thus, Cooper could write *The Last of the Mohicans* about the Seven Years' War even though the actual Stockbridge Mohicans had once lived near his boyhood home of Cooperstown and, in 1826, the year of the book's publication, were building anew in Wisconsin, including establishing the territory's first public schoolhouse and sawmill. John Augustus Stone used the subtitle *Last of the Wampanoags* for his 1829 play, *Metamora*, without regard to the Wampanoags of southeastern Massachusetts, who spoke and wrote in fluent English, ran their own Protestant churches, and practiced animal husbandry and plow agriculture, even as they maintained their distinctive communal customs on their tiny reservations. Most of all, the White nationalist insistence that Indians faced "imminent extinction" because they were incapable of adapting to White civilization obviated the tens of thousands of Native people, particularly in the Southeast, who were not only civilizing according to White standards, but also growing in population. Determined to both survive and thrive, those people would not remain invisible for long.[13]

REFORM AS RESISTANCE

While White intellectuals and the public were consigning Indians to extinction, the federal government and missionary societies were encouraging Native people to adopt civility and Christianity and eventually become American citizens. In 1796, the Washington administration appointed former North Carolina senator Benjamin Hawkins as its representative to the Creek Nation, with oversight of an agency boasting an instructor for spinning and weaving, a schoolmaster, a model farm to exhibit White agricultural ways, and a store that purchased Indian farm products at above-market rates. Christian missionaries followed quickly on Hawkins's heels, with Moravians, Congregationalists, Presbyterians, and Baptists opening several stations and schools among each of the major Southern tribes, and itinerant Methodist preachers evangelizing even the remotest Indian neighborhoods. To the north, Quakers preached the virtues of civilization among the Senecas of New York and the Shawnees, Delawares, Wyandots, and Miamis of the Midwest. The federal government's Bureau of Indian Affairs, created in 1824 by Secretary of War John C. Calhoun, would oversee and fund these activities. Influential elements in White society clearly desired Indians to become civilized and Christian, even if White settlers generally wanted Indians dead and gone.[14]

This campaign would have amounted to nothing if Indians had not been interested in making a change. They grasped that they no longer had the military capacity to resist White expansion, and that the onslaught of White people in the absence of that threat made it impossible to preserve their traditional way of life in total. As the

Benjamin Hawkins and the Creek Indians, artist unknown, ca. 1805. Courtesy of the Smithsonian American Art Museum.

This painting depicts Hawkins on his plantation on the Flint River in Georgia instructing Creek men how to use a plow as part of a wider Indian transition to intensive market agriculture, as encouraged by the federal government.

Choctaw leader Mushulatubbee conceded, "We cannot expect to live any longer by hunting. Our game is gone." The question facing Indians was not whether to reform, but how.[15]

There was a fundamental difference between Indian and White proponents of civility. White reformers imagined that the Indians' progress would lead them to abandon communal living in favor of private property, dissolve their tribal governments, and become U.S. citizens, but most Indians did not share that goal. They hoped their civilized reforms would convince White people to respect their territory and autonomy. An unidentified Cherokee man explained that his people were determined to "attend to business, to make themselves good houses and farms, and attend well to the raising of cattle" because "if we pursue this course, we shall be firmly established and those who ask of us our land will be discouraged. This is the way the whites have done . . ." Put another way, if Indians adopted some of the ways of White people, it might prevent complete dispossession *and* assimilation by them. Civilized Indians could remain independent Indians—together, on their own land, under their own governance.[16]

The results were beginning to show well before Removal. A census of the Cherokees in 1825 counted 31 gristmills, 14 sawmills, 6 powder mills, 18 ferries, 19 schools, 62 blacksmith shops, 2 tanning yards, 762 looms, 2,486 spinning wheels, 172 wagons, 2,923 plows, 7,628 horses, 22,405 cattle, 46,732 pigs, 2,566 sheep—and 1,038 slaves. The Creeks, Choctaws, and Chickasaws boasted similar numbers, with the Choctaws in 1828 averaging 2.07 head of cattle per person compared to the state of Mississippi's average of 1.8 per person in 1840. Whereas earlier generations from these tribes had traded deerskins, beaver pelts, and Indigenous slaves to Whites, modern Indians sold livestock on the hoof, meat, tallow, cotton, rice, tobacco, indigo, corn, and timber to markets as distant as New Orleans, Mobile, and Pensacola. Women's labor at spinning, weaving, and sewing permitted them to clothe their people with garments from their own hands, sometimes made of wool and cotton from their own farms. Nearly everyone lived in a square-framed house or log cabin outfitted with furniture "not inferior to that of new settlers in our country," as one missionary judged. This description also fit Northern tribes like the Senecas of New York and Shawnees, Delawares, Miamis, and Potawatomis of the Ohio country, who saw civilized reforms as a means to make do with less land and lay claims to their remaining territory in ways Whites might respect. The signs of change were everywhere.[17]

Yet the extent of economic reform was uneven, most noticeably among men. In Indian tradition, the role of men was to take life in hunting and warfare for the good of the people, whereas women produced and nourished life through childbirth, childcare, horticulture, and cooking. The U.S. agent Return J. Meigs wrote in 1808 that most Cherokee men found the idea of farming "painful" and "dishonorable," especially when their roles as hunters and warriors were in eclipse. As such, an 1809 census of the Cherokees' Overhill Towns found only forty plows, a heavy implement handled by men, among its 3,649 people. It would take another fifteen years before most Cherokee families had adopted this equipment out of grudging recognition that poverty and hunger were more intolerable than emasculation. Likewise, though Indian men widely raised livestock to address the decline of deer, and used horses for travel, some of them simply refused to reorient their lives around the care of these animals. Rather than fencing in pasture, constructing barns, and storing up hay, they released their cattle and hogs to fend for themselves, including during the winter, and then hunted them like game when it was time for slaughter. This was animal

Dennis Cusick "Son of the Chief," *Female School*, ca. 1821. Museum purchase with funds provided by The Gund Collection of Western Art 2015.17.1. Courtesy of the Eiteljorg Museum of American Indians and Western Art, Indianapolis, Indiana.

Schools like this one were fundamental to the United States campaign to assimilate Indians, and to the Indian effort to parlay civilized reforms into a defense of their sovereign independence, in the decades preceding Removal. Dennis Cusick, who captured this scene, was a Tuscarora artist.

husbandry without the husbanding. Elite Indians avoided fieldwork by assigning it to Black male slaves. These people were adapting to the civilization model, but at their own pace, in their own ways, and generally not wholesale.[18]

Whereas most Native families took up civilized economic activities to one degree or another, the majority approached formal education and Christianity ambivalently, if at all, partly because of racial beliefs. Some Indians continued to insist that the Great Spirit intended these things for Whites only. Others saw literacy and English language skills as useful for political and commercial leaders who dealt with Whites "so that the white man cannot cheat us," but unnecessary for everyday people. There was widespread resentment of White teachers because of their condescension toward full-blood Indians and favoritism toward light-complexioned, English-speaking ones. More than a few Native people also distrusted school instructors as having "an object to form a large settlement of white people and get possession of their land." For all of these reasons and more, the Cherokees sent only 882 children to school between 1817 and 1833, most of them irregularly. The few who did attend were told by their parents to heed only language and literacy lessons, but not religious ones, because their concerns were this world rather than the next. Despite all the efforts of White missionaries and educators, as few as 5 percent of Cherokees identified as Christian on the eve of Removal.[19]

The advance in literacy among the Cherokees was less the result of Whites teaching in English than of a brilliant Chickamauga Cherokee named Sequoyah, or George Guess, who invented an eighty-five-character syllabary for his people's own language. By all counts, this syllabary captured the sounds of the Cherokee language more accurately than the Roman alphabet, and was remarkably easy to learn. Some eyewitnesses claimed that after Sequoyah presented his work to the Cherokee National Council in 1821, a majority of the tribe learned the system within a matter of months. Cherokee oral tradition taught that at the time of Creation, the Great Spirit had offered the first Indian literacy in the form of a paper with writing on it, but the first White man snatched the paper away and claimed the gift for his own people. Sequoyah's syllabary finally enabled the Cherokees to recover this blessing, and it filled the nation with pride.[20]

Civilized reforms contributed to overlapping class and racial divisions in Native society, particularly when it came to slavery. Of the 16,542 people in the Cherokee Nation in 1835, less than a fifth had White ancestors, as opposed to 75 percent of Cherokee slaveholders, who comprised just 7.4 percent of the overall Cherokee population. People of Indian-White backgrounds were even more overrepresented among Cherokees with the largest slaveholdings. They included Charles Hicks, Samuel Riley, and John McDonald, each of whom owned more than ten slaves, and James Vann, who claimed more than a hundred on a plantation rivaling that of the richest White southerners. As the Cherokee leader John Ridge explained in 1826, "the African slaves are generally mostly held by half breeds and full Indians of distinguished talents." The same was true among the Creeks, Choctaws, and Chickasaws. In other words, whereas a small percentage of the people, disproportionately of Indian-White ancestry, had a direct interest in slaveholding, the overwhelming majority of tribal members tended "little farms" and lived in one-room cabins without bound labor.[21]

Despite their small numbers, wealthy, slaveholding Indians with White ancestry dominated the National Councils of the Cherokees, Creeks, Choctaws, and

Chickasaws. Not coincidentally, these governments spent a disproportionate amount of attention and resources promoting slaveholders' interests. During the 1820s, the Cherokees and Creeks passed comprehensive slave codes modeled on neighboring White states that restricted Black movement, economic activity, and social gatherings, and imposed extra-harsh penalties on Blacks found guilty of crimes. In earlier times, Indians in these tribes had been at liberty to marry Blacks of whatever status and pass on property to their Afro-Indian children, but now those activities were illegal. The Creek National Council went so far as to declare that romantic relationships with Blacks were "a disgrace to our nation." To be sure, White observers often criticized the Creeks and other Indians as lackadaisical slaveholders because they sometimes permitted their slaves to be "idle" or work independently as long as they surrendered a share of what they produced. Nevertheless, there were always some slaves among the Southeastern tribes who toiled under conditions just as oppressive as one would find among Whites in Georgia and Alabama. In laws and sometimes in practice, Southeastern Indian society increasingly resembled those anti-Black police states.[22]

The Seminoles took an entirely different approach to slavery. Their numbers included a substantial number of Red Stick Creeks who fled to Florida precisely because they did not want to live in a stratified society headed by the plantation elite. Generally, the Seminoles did not use Black slaves as labor for market production or evidence of civilized living. Instead, they permitted their "slaves," a number of whom were fugitives from Whites, to live independently in their own towns as long as they paid tribute and provided military service. Some Seminoles openly married Blacks and consulted with them in politics. This topsy-turvy arrangement made Southern White planters fear that the Seminoles were turning Florida into a revolutionary Haiti in waiting, particularly after Nat Turner's uprising of 1831 in Virginia gave them a stark reminder about the threat of slave revolt.[23]

Indian leaders hoped to use select civilized reforms to defend their people's sovereignty, but Whites from across the political spectrum gave them no chance of even surviving short of thorough reformation and incorporation into the United States. The New England–based Board of Commissions for Foreign Missions promoted Indian education out of the conviction that "the Indian tribes must... be progressively civilized, or successfully perish." William Henry Harrison agreed that the government's civilization policy was "the only one which will save them from utter extirpation," though he could not conceive of Indian men yielding unless "by absolute necessity." That time of necessity had already arrived, according to Secretary of War Calhoun in 1820, nine years before he became Andrew Jackson's first vice president. "They must be brought gradually under our authority and laws," he told Congress, "or they will insensibly waste away in vice and misery ... A system less vigorous may protract, but cannot arrest their fate."[24]

Many White Americans would not grant Indians even this narrow option, contending that any effort on the Indians' behalf was futile. Yale College president Timothy Dwight judged that an Indian man unable to hunt or make war became "rather a moving vegetable than a rational being," who "lounges, saunters, gets drunk, eats when he can find food, and lies down to sleep under the nearest fence." Similar beliefs led Massachusetts politician Edward Everett to encourage the federal government to cease its promotion of civility. "Leave him [the Indian] to the operation of his character and habits," Everett opined. "Do not resist the order of providence which is carrying him away, and when he is gone, a civilized man will step into his place." Rural Whites with designs on the Stockbridge Mohicans' remaining land in New York urged the state to rescind its laws safeguarding the tribe because it was "a fact of such notoriety as not to need confirmation, that Indians will not to any considerable extent become agriculturalists. They have an aversion to labor, and will sooner starve than work." According to the New York poet and journalist William Cullen Bryant, this belief was shared by "the great mass of the community" of White Americans. The power of that majority opinion made it unlikely that the federal government would restrain White aggression against Indians no matter how civilized they had become.[25]

THE REMOVAL ARGUMENT BEFORE REMOVAL

The main impetus to the Indians' reforms was the imminent threat of their displacement, including in the North, amid the crush of White expansion. By the early nineteenth century, Pennsylvania had already forced nearly all Indians out of its boundaries, other than isolated families and individuals. In this, it joined states like New Hampshire, Vermont, New Jersey, Delaware, and Maryland in having atomized Native communities so thoroughly that it was easy for Whites to believe that there were no Indians left at all. The other New England states, in addition to Virginia and North Carolina, had Indian populations numbering only in the hundreds or low thousands of people, divided mostly between remote town-sized reservations and "colored" neighborhoods in ports and cities. New York was the only Northern state that still had a substantial Indian population, despite the relocation of most of the

Mohawks, Cayugas, and some Senecas to British Canada during the Revolutionary era, but it did not intend to remain that way. It subjected the remaining Oniedas, Brothertowns, Stockbridge Mohicans, Onondagas, and Senecas to relentless pressure to cede their lands, driving many of them off to Wisconsin and restricting the rest to marginal reservations that Whites still eyed greedily. As early as 1811, Governor DeWitt Clinton presaged that "the minister of destruction is hovering over" the Indians of New York "and before the passing away of the present generation, not a single Iroquois will be seen in the state." A similar danger loomed over Native people in the Midwest—including Shawnees, Delawares, Miamis, Potawatomis, Ottawas, Ojibwes, and Wyandots—whom American officials confined to small reserves while White hordes turned their once vast homelands into a checkered landscape of cleared fields and fences. With Ohio claiming nearly one million White Americans by 1830, Indiana some 338,000, Illinois another 155,000, and Michigan 31,000, Indians were in no position to prevent Whites from appropriating the meager lands they still retained, regardless of treaty promises.[26]

The White campaign to convince Indians in the East to move west of the Mississippi began well before the presidency of Andrew Jackson. No sooner had Thomas Jefferson completed the Louisiana Purchase in 1803 than he began scheming to convince Indians who did not want to civilize and accept American law to swap their lands for federal tracts west of the Mississippi River. To that end, in 1809, the U.S. agent Return J. Meigs bribed his way to a secret treaty with the chiefs of the Cherokee Lower Towns (the former Chickamauga settlements on the Tennessee River) to convince their followers to uproot and cede 1,250 acres per migrant in exchange for equivalent lands in the West and government funding of their migration. Meigs predicted that this deal would net the United States an immediate 2.5 million acres and weaken the Cherokees so severely that soon the holdouts would cave as well. Fortunately, the rest of the Cherokees caught wind of the deal and managed to persuade the Madison administration to scrap it. Yet their intervention could not prevent over a thousand Cherokees from relocating to the West at their own expense to seek better hunting and escape White encroachment and the hostility of their countrymen for having entertained this machination in the first place. They could no longer tolerate life near White America, never mind in it.[27]

The fallout from this debacle continued long after the migrants' exit, because the Southern states had expected a complete removal of the Cherokees under Meigs's terms and therefore encouraged land-hungry Whites to flood the tribe's territory. "These intruders are always well armed," exclaimed Meigs, "some of them shrewd and desperate characters, having nothing to lose and hold barbarous sentiments toward the Indians . . . nothing but force can prevent their violation of Indian rights." The issue finally came to a head in treaties of 1817 and 1819 in which U.S. commissioner Andrew Jackson cajoled the Cherokees into releasing seven hundred thousand acres in North Carolina, eight hundred thousand acres in Georgia, eight hundred thousand acres in Alabama, and over a million acres in Tennessee—3.8 million acres in all. In exchange, the federal government would compensate three thousand tribal members displaced by the Meigs scheme for their improvements and guarantee them and the Cherokees already in the West equivalent lands in Arkansas. For the meantime, the other ten thousand or so other Cherokees could stay back East on their remaining territory.[28]

These treaties contained little-known precedents for Indian private property holding and U.S. citizenship that would come into play during Jacksonian Indian Removal and again in the Indian Allotment Act (or Dawes Act) of 1887 that dismantled federal Indian reservations. Under the terms, several hundred Cherokees who did not want to vacate the ceded lands would receive individual grants of 640 acres each. Most of the recipients of these grants, 311 in all, were prohibited from selling these lands during their lifetimes, based on the premise that they were too unfamiliar with private property, American law, and the English language to act in their own best interests. When their next of kin inherited these allotments, however, they would hold them on the exact same terms that Whites owned their land, with all of the opportunities and risks that entailed, and become U.S. citizens subject to state law. Another 31 grantees, most of whom were either mixed-blood Cherokees judged civilized enough to compete in White society or married couples of White men and Cherokee women, became private-property holders and citizens immediately. These arrangements amounted to a small-scale test of whether the federal government's civilization program was realistic. As it turned out, it was not. No sooner had the Cherokees received their private grants and citizenship than local Whites and the states used threats, violence, and fraud to dispossess them almost entirely. Though this plundering occurred in plain sight and Indians protested it vigorously, federal officials did practically nothing about it.[29]

The Cherokee crisis was no isolated incident; the U.S. government relentlessly pressured *all* the Southeastern tribes to cede and vacate their lands. In 1820, Jackson and his fellow commissioners warned that if all the Choctaws did not leave for the West straightaway, except "those who wish to stay and cultivate their earth," President Monroe would be furious and "the Choctaw nation must dwindle to nothing." The Choctaws were willing to take that chance, surrendering half their land at the subsequent Treaty of Doak's Stand, but steadfastly refusing to abandon the rest of their territory. They even threatened to execute any of their people who dared to tell U.S. officials otherwise. Undeterred, in 1824, the Monroe administration considered a voluntary removal program based on a report from Secretary Calhoun that Indians living in the neighborhood of Whites faced imminent extinction. Their only long-term hope, Calhoun proposed, was to pursue the slow process of civilizing somewhere else. The following year, Mississippi governor Gerard Brandon demanded the immediate expulsion of Choctaws and Chickasaws, though he relented when his bluster failed to sway federal authorities. John Quincy Adams's administration tried to offer the states half a loaf with a proposed bill to encourage Indians to move West as individuals rather than as entire nations, and eventually combine the migrants under a single Indian-run territorial government. The measure failed, but only because congressmen said they lacked sufficient information about the degree to which the affected Indians had become civilized and were open to the plan. Year by year, the White drumbeat to force Eastern Indians to move west of the Mississippi was growing louder.[30]

No state pounded out this message harder than Georgia, to the point of threatening unilateral violence if the Creeks and Cherokees did not vacate. In 1802, Georgia had released its western land claims to the United States in exchange for the federal government's promise to extinguish all Indian titles within the state as soon as it could be done "peaceably . . . on reasonable terms." As time wore on with scanty results, Georgia abandoned peace, reason, and patience in favor of impunity. In 1823 and again in 1826, it demanded the national government to fulfill its obligation or relinquish the responsibility. Federal agents actually managed to intimidate the Creeks into ceding their remaining lands in Georgia (while retaining other territory in Alabama) in the 1826 Treaty of Cusseta, but only after nullifying the blatantly corrupt 1825 Treaty of Indian Springs, which would have terminated practically the entire Creek domain. The Creeks, like the Cherokees, had escaped an early removal, but only by a hair's breadth.[31]

Most Indians were just as insistent on staying put as White southerners were to displace them. The Creeks assassinated three of the signatories of the Treaty of Indian Springs, including Chief William McIntosh, who helped orchestrate the deal, and threatened to execute anyone who dared to desert the nation. Roughly three thousand of McIntosh's supporters, facing their own retributive beatings and destruction of property, decamped anyway for a tract west of the Mississippi reserved to them under the previous agreement. Their explanation was that life would be better at a distance from White land sharks, liquor dealers, and horse thieves. Seeing the need to close ranks, the Southern tribes, one after another, declared that henceforth they would make no more cessions, never mind withdraw. The Cherokee "Beloved Woman" (a woman of respect and influence) Nancy Ward led the matrons of her community in denouncing Removal as "highly oppressive, cruel and unjust," and akin to "destroying your mothers." After all, the people had inhabited their country "from time immemorial."[32]

Their resolve meant nothing to Southern states drunk with the profits of cotton and the power of their multiplying populations. The invention of the cotton gin in 1793 so quickly elevated cotton into the great American cash crop that by 1820 it accounted for more than half the value of American agricultural exports. Mississippi and Alabama, which were admitted to the Union in 1817 and 1819, respectively, saw their total collective populations increase more than tenfold between 1810 and 1830, from 40,000 to 445,000. Georgia's population doubled from 251,407 to 516,823 during that same time frame. The White people of these places were unwilling to leave Indians, whom they considered inferior, in possession of millions of acres, which they insisted were underused. Georgia declared in 1827 that "the Indians are tenants at [Georgia's] will, and [Georgia] may at any time, determine that tenancy by taking possession of the premises." Therefore, "if the United States will not redeem her pledged honor, and if the Indians continued to turn a deaf ear to the voice of reason and friendship, we now solemnly warn them of the consequences. The lands in question *belong* to Georgia. She *must* and she *will* have them."[33]

Portrait of William McIntosh, attributed to Nathan and Joseph Negus, 1821. Courtesy of the Alabama Department of Archives and History.

Whites rarely justified Removal solely on the basis of coveting Indian land, but instead turned their power play into a racial morality play. In 1830, Lewis Cass, the governor of Michigan Territory, published a widely read essay in the *North American Review* in which he predicted that Indians would degenerate into landless drunkards and go extinct if Whites enveloped them before they became civilized. "A barbarous people," he proclaimed, "depending for subsistence upon the scanty and precarious supplies furnished by the chase, cannot live in contact with a civilized community." Cass's opinions, for all the weight they carried, merely reflected already well-established ideas. Six years earlier, Georgia's congressional delegation had urged the Cherokees "that there is no alternative between their removal beyond the limits of the state of Georgia and their extinction." Yes, echoed Senator William Hendricks of Indiana in 1826, Indians "surrounded by the increasing settlements of Georgia, Alabama, and Florida, must finally become extinct. They cannot, and will not, adopt for their subsistence agricultural pursuits, and their country is too limited for them to live by the chase." If Indians would not consent to Removal, Whites should coerce them, "for their preservation." This was cynical racial dogma masquerading as reason. Native people throughout the East *were* embracing White standards of civility, as was plain to anyone open to seeing it. The news circulated in speech and print in every sector of White American society. The real issue was the number of White Americans whose ideology and interests made them blind to the obvious truth, or willing to lie about it bald-facedly.[34]

Georgia governor George Troup rejected the possibility that Indians could remain in their homelands even if they did take up private property, accept state jurisdiction, and become American citizens. "If such a scheme were practicable at all"—and he did not grant that it was—"the utmost of rights and privileges which public opinion would concede to Indians would fix them in a middle station between the negro and the white man; and that, as long as they survived this degradation, without the possibility of attaining the elevation of the latter, they would gradually sink to the condition of the former." Removal, he concluded, was the only viable alternative to Indian extinction. Troup actually had some basis for his argument about the intractability of White prejudice given White southerners' flagrant dispossession of the Cherokee allottees back in 1819 despite the Indians supposedly enjoying equal protection under the law. There was no reason to think another attempt would go any differently.[35]

Beyond the disgraceful example of how Whites had exploited the Cherokee allottees, everyone had heard about the public uproar in Cornwall, Connecticut, in the mid-1820s when two Cherokee boys, John Ridge and Elias Boudinot (future editor of the *Cherokee Phoenix*), attending a boarding school for "heathens," became engaged to White girls in the neighborhood. The backlash among local Whites grew so heated that a crowd burned the couples in effigy and published denunciations that the marriages would "make our daughters become nursing mothers to a race of mulattoes." To exorcise that specter, the school had to close. If this was the case in New England, which provided more encouragement for Indian civility than any other region, what hope was there of the White people of Georgia treating Indians any better? The only way for Indians to be spared such persecution, Removal proponents contended, was through Removal. The argument was fully developed before the presidency of Andrew Jackson.[36]

It did not bode well for Indians that White elites also widely supported the removal of free Blacks, though not to the West. The year 1816 saw the founding of the American Colonization Society (ACS) and its colony of Liberia to encourage the migration of liberated African Americans "back" to Africa, even though practically none of them had ever been there. The movement boasted such luminaries as Kentucky senator Henry Clay, New England statesman Daniel Webster, and Supreme Court Justice Bushrod Washington, and drew support from Presidents Jefferson, Madison, and Monroe. The ACS's grand ambition, in fact, was to convince Whites to end slavery by disproving the widespread belief that Blacks were innately inferior and incapable of civility, and therefore better kept in bondage. However, it also believed that the struggles of freed people in the North due to entrenched White racism had reinforced the prejudice of slaveholders and their defenders that Blacks lacked the ability to care for themselves. The society's answer was to send Black colonists to Liberia, where they could rise as far as their talents would take them. Once the settlers proved their ability to live nobly as Christian, civilized people, and Whites saw that liberated Blacks had somewhere else to go besides the United States, slaveholders and the American public would be more likely to support emancipation. The society ignored that the overwhelming majority of African Americans rejected colonization as denying them their American birthright because of White people's shortcomings. In the end, less than ten thousand freed people ever consented to go in the forty years before the Civil War. Here were some of the most racially enlightened and politically powerful members of American society concluding once again that the solution to White bigotry and oppression was to force the victims of it to relocate somewhere far away in order to prove themselves. The parallels to the Removal debate spoke to the depths of White racism and the height of the challenges facing Indians who wanted to remain in their homelands.[37]

SOVEREIGN INDEPENDENT INDIAN REPUBLICS OR DOMESTIC DEPENDENT NATIONS?

Andrew Jackson was the clear front-runner for the presidency in 1828, and there was little doubt that he would throw his weight behind Removal. After all, he had a record of brutalizing Native people as a military officer and bullying them as a U.S. treaty commissioner. Furthermore, Jackson trumpeted his belief that the United States had grown so powerful and Indians so insignificant that it was "absurd" for the republic to continue to negotiate with them as sovereign nations. His position was that the United States should dictate whatever it claimed was good for them—and for its White citizens.[38]

Indians made their case to remain in the East with governmental reforms, public relations campaigns, and lawsuits that built on their advances in civility. In 1827 the Cherokees took the revolutionary step of adopting a new, written frame of government modeled on the U.S. Constitution in which they declared themselves to be "sovereign and independent" within boundaries "solemnly guaranteed and reserved forever to the Cherokee Nation by the treaties concluded with the United States." The following year, they founded a newspaper, the *Cherokee Phoenix*, to serve as the government mouthpiece, with most of the articles in English and a few columns per issue in the Cherokee language. The *Phoenix*'s indefatigable editor, Elias Boudinot (or Galagina, "The Buck"), designed the paper for two audiences, Cherokee and White. It would keep Cherokees informed about the politics of Removal while encouraging progressive reforms consistent with Cherokee values. White readers, including ministers, missionaries, politicians, and newspaper editors, would see a civilizing people desperately defending their autonomy and ancient homeland from the assaults of greedy, dishonest, and even godless brutes.[39]

It had been bad enough for land-hungry Whites that Indians had been laying physical claims to the land through their civilized economic reforms, but now they were erecting written legislative barriers using the language of the United States' founding documents. A startled President John Quincy Adams put it frankly: "When we have had the rare good fortune of teaching them the arts of civilization and the doctrines of Christianity, we have unexpectedly found them forming in the midst of ourselves, communities claiming to be independent of ours and rivals of sovereignty within the territories of our Union." The Cherokees were alerting Whites that educated Indians might be able to fight back within the same American system that so often victimized them.[40]

Georgia's aggressive response signaled that nothing short of federal force could stop it. Its legislature declared that an independent Cherokee nation within the state was an affront to Georgia's sovereignty, and that the state's laws were supreme everywhere within its borders, including Cherokee country. As such, Georgia would extinguish the Cherokees' title whenever and however it pleased, and the time was coming soon. Unfortunately, the Cherokees had to look for protection to Andrew Jackson, who made clear from the beginning of his presidency that he would grant them nothing of the sort. In fact, he was eager for Georgia to do its dirty work as a step toward coercing Indians everywhere to "consent" to Removal after his bill authorizing it squeaked through Congress in May 1830.[41]

The Southern states' campaign to harass Indians from their lands began in earnest from the very moment of Jackson's election, a year and a half before passage of the bill. Their tactics included nullifying all the powers and prohibiting the meetings of the Cherokee, Choctaw, and Chickasaw National Councils, and extending state law over all Indians and Indian land. Georgia, soon to be followed by most of the other Southern states, also prohibited Indians from testifying in court or filing suit against any White man, even though Indians were subject to the courts' authority. The Cherokees had not yet ceded their remaining territory, but that did not stop Georgia from having state surveyors chart and divide it into

Andrew Jackson as the Great Father, unknown artist, 1835. Courtesy of the William L. Clements Library, University of Michigan Library Digital Collections.

This cartoon captures the hypocrisy of Jackson claiming that Removal was a humanitarian policy to save Indians rather than a White land grab.

plots for distribution to Whites in a lottery. In theory, Georgia was amenable to the Cherokees staying on small private tracts of land as detribalized individuals, but everyone knew that neighboring Whites would not allow them to remain for long.[42]

In fact, Georgia would not allow them to retain anything. When Whites discovered in 1828 that Cherokee country contained gold deposits (which the Indians had known for a century), the state banned any Indians from mining it even as hundreds of Whites flooded in to strike it rich. These miners, encouraged and sometimes joined by authorities, plundered, beat, raped, and murdered Cherokees with impunity. In December 1830, Georgia went so far as to hang a Cherokee named Corn Tassel on the charge of killing another Cherokee in Cherokee territory while the state's jurisdiction over the case was being litigated. "The popular cry is—exterminate the savages," one Georgia resident observed. Clearly, there was nothing voluntary about the Removal process, despite Jackson's claims.[43]

Against this ominous backdrop, the Cherokees enlisted former federal attorney general William Wirt to craft an appeal to the U.S. Supreme Court for help. At the very least, the Cherokees hoped, "If we are to be removed . . . we wish to leave in the records of [U.S.] tribunals, for future generations to read, when we are gone, ample testimony that she acted justly or unjustly." Yet the contagion of race permeated that institution, too. The court, under Chief Justice John Marshall, had already rejected the full sovereignty of Indian nations in *Johnson v. McIntosh* (1823) based on what has since been called the Doctrine of Discovery. This theory held that, during the colonial era, Christian, European nations gained the title to those parts of America they "discovered" before rival nations of similar civilized status, even if Indians were already living there. As Marshall phrased it, "civilized nations" all agreed that the inferior "character and religion" of "fierce savages, whose occupation was war," meant that "the superior genius of Europe might claim an ascendancy" over them. Europeans' claims to ascendancy became real once they conquered the Indians, which transformed the Natives into "mere occupants" of their own territory. Henceforth, the Indians could not transfer their land to anyone they wished, just to the supreme colonial power. As the successor to Great Britain, the United States now possessed that supreme status, and, under U.S. law, Indigenous people were not "citizens" but simply "inhabitants," viewed by the federal and state governments "as an inferior race of people." Marshall admitted that this line of reasoning amounted to might makes right, but excused himself that "conquest gives a title which the courts of the conqueror cannot deny." With this, the justices legitimized centuries' worth of European cultural and religious chauvinism that, in its American context, had morphed into White supremacy.[44]

Rejecting the discovery doctrine, the Cherokees argued in *Cherokee Nation v. Georgia* (1831) that they were "a foreign state, not owing allegiance to the United States, nor to any State of this union, nor to any prince, potentate or State, other than their own." If the court had upheld this principle, the implications would have extended beyond Georgia's aggression to deal a severe blow to the overarching justification for Removal. Instead, the justices decided that the Cherokees were not a foreign state under Article III of the U.S. Constitution and therefore had no standing to bring suit.[45]

Yet the court's judgment that Indian polities like the Cherokee Nation were not fully sovereign foreign states did not mean that they were entirely without rights. They were "domestic dependent nations," in Marshall's nebulous phrase, subject to the Unites States' restraint on their diplomacy with other foreign powers and to its governance of their affairs with American citizens, even as they retained authority to govern their own people and lands. In the long term, this judgment was a theoretical half victory for the Cherokees and other Indian nations, for it established that they had some measure of sovereignty in American jurisprudence. Today, that principle is the bedrock for Indian law in the United States. But, in the short term, which was the Cherokees' priority, the court's finding that the tribe had no standing had the disastrous effect of giving Georgia and the other states license to terrorize Indians into acquiescing to Removal.

It probably would not have mattered even if the court had found in the Cherokees' favor. The following year, the court considered *Worcester v. Georgia* over the question of whether Georgia could arrest a missionary to the Cherokees, Samuel Austin Worcester, for refusing to take a loyalty oath to the state (though the real reason was that the state blamed White missionaries for stoking the Cherokees' resistance). The court's decision, building on its earlier reasoning in *Cherokee Nation v. Georgia*, was that "the Cherokee nation . . . is a distinct community occupying its own territory in which the laws of Georgia can have no force. The whole intercourse between the United States and this nation, is, by our constitution and laws, vested in the government of the United States." Yet this legal victory for the Cherokees had no teeth because Georgia ignored the ruling and President Jackson would not enforce it. His response was that if the Cherokees or other Indians wanted relief from their merciless persecution by local Whites and the states, they would have to find it in the West. With this, the sole alternative left for Native people was to try to delay the implementation of Removal until a new government opposed to it took control. Jackson's reelection and then his succession by his vice president, Martin Van Buren, meant that day did not come soon enough.[46]

THE GREAT RACE DEBATE

As the Supreme Court cases reflected, Jackson's Indian Removal Bill of 1830 hastened an already vigorous national debate over race and Indian policy. This legislation empowered the federal government to obtain Indian lands in the East, compensate the Indians for improvements they would leave behind, assign them new lands west of the Mississippi, and cover the costs of relocating them. The questions of whether this proposal was wise and just pivoted on the natures of Indian and White peoples and the racial character of the United States. Though the most famous exchanges in this fight took place between White elites in the halls of Congress and before the Supreme Court, Native people were full participants. Often, their appeals were so stirring that, to paraphrase the Cherokee women, it was as if they were defending their own mother.

Indians rejected that they were destined for extinction if they did not relocate. Rather, the problem, including the burden to change, rested with White people. The *Cherokee Phoenix* asserted that the causes of Indian extermination "did not exist in the Indians themselves, nor the will of heaven, nor simply in the intercourse of Indians with civilized men, but they were precisely such causes as are now attempted by the state of Georgia—by infringing upon their rights—by disorganizing them, and circumscribing their limits." As evidence of this abuse, the paper featured the account of a Pennsylvania man who, during his travels through Tennessee, was astonished to hear one White resident after another say that "he would murder every Indian who passed his house." The author could only hope that this opinion was limited to "the lowest class," but Indians had every reason to wonder if there were enough righteous people left in the country "to protect them from violence and robbery."[47]

Under the Constitution, Senate-ratified treaties were the supreme law of the land, which should have been sufficient for the Indians to fend off encroachment by the states. "The treaties are plain and the terms reasonable," pointed out an excerpt from the *New York Observer* in the *Phoenix*, "but the Indians are weak, and their white neighbors will be lawless. The way to please these white neighbors is, therefore, to burn the treaties, and call the Indians our dear children, and deal with them precisely as if no treaties had ever been made." The *Phoenix* had it right when it predicted that "if the public opinion is not for the Indians, we must fall in spite of laws and treaties, for the signs of the times convince us that laws and treaties form no barrier to the cupidity of our white brethren." It was blatant hypocrisy for the United States to expect Indians to be bound by treaties while it was not.[48]

Native people charged that the Southern states had it backward when they insisted that Indian sovereignty was a violation of *their* rights. "The country which you now possess, and that which we now remain on," explained the Creeks, "was by the Great Spirit originally given to his red children." The Cherokee National Council stressed that Indian people "are not foreigners, but original inhabitants of America, and that they now inhabit and stand on the soil of their own territory ... the states by which they are now surrounded have been created out of lands which were once theirs, and that they cannot recognize the sovereignty of any state within the limit of their territory." In this, the council was echoing a petition it had received from Cherokee women that "the land was given to us by the Great Spirit above as our common right, to raise our children upon, and to make support for our rising generations." Georgia might employ the age-old imperial argument that the Indians' title to the land was no better than that of forest animals, but, the *Phoenix* retorted, "the Indian claims his land upon a better right than the white man has to monopolize this same land, and with republican tyranny to expel its original occupants." Native people's sovereignty was "inherited from the author of our existence, which we have always exercised, and have never surrendered." The Indians' view, in short, was that they were sovereign by virtue of being Indigenous, not by might or political process. No other group of Americans could make such a claim.[49]

Indians and their White advocates also called out the Jacksonian lie that Native people, in their "inferiority," had "neither the intelligence, the industry, the moral habits, nor the desire of improvement which are essential to any favorable change in their condition" and therefore had to yield to a "superior race." This argument, the *Phoenix* advised its Cherokee readers, was no more than a pretext to make it "perfectly right to rob you of your property." In fact, declared the Chickasaws, "industry is spreading amongst us, population is increasing; we hope soon to arrive at that state of improvement that is so much desired by our father the President." In case there was any doubt, the *Phoenix* ran one article after another about communities throughout Indian country, including the Northeast and Midwest, pursuing civilized reforms successfully. "Indians are capable of improvement!" it pronounced.[50]

John Ridge took this message directly to the White public, giving a speech in Philadelphia in 1832 in which he appealed, "You asked us to throw off the hunter and warrior state. We did so—you asked us to form a republican government: We did so—adopting your own as a model. You asked us to cultivate the earth, and learn the mechanic arts: We did so. You asked us to learn to read: We did so. You asked us to cast away our idols, and worship your God: We did so." His plea was for the United States to allow the experiment to continue. If it did, predicted the Cherokee National Council, "the day would arrive when a distinction between their race and the American family would be imperceptible," and it would no longer make sense for Whites to say, "Do what you will and an Indian will still be an Indian." The *Phoenix* advised the United States to take the projected costs of Removal and instead dedicate those funds to Native people's advancement. Then everyone would know whether White people's "desire to possess the Indian's land is paramount to a desire to see him established on the soil as a civilized man." If such a good-faith effort failed, Indians would submit to Removal voluntarily.[51]

Indians disproved every pro-Removal explanation for why life in the West would be better for them. Rather than promoting civility, Removal would actually force a rapidly civilizing people from the neighborhood of other civilized people and deposit them among Plains tribes they considered savage and hostile. The Choctaw leader Peter Pitchlynn could not fathom how proximity to the Western Indians was supposed to promote civility among his kind. "You never saw such a people in your life," he exclaimed. "Their manners and action[s] are wild in the extreme." Furthermore, how would moving West ease the pressure of Whites for long? For decades, bands of Cherokees, Creeks, Delawares, and Shawnees had fled to Arkansas and Missouri only to have Whites follow them there and demand the Indians' to relocate again. Likewise, Whites had driven the Christian, civilized Brothertowns and Stockbridges from New England to New York, then to Indiana, and then to two locations in Wisconsin in the space of barely fifty years, just as they had previously forced the Delawares from the banks of their namesake river to the Ohio country and then to the Mississippi. Clearly, one displacement would just lead to another. The Cherokee leader John Ross observed that "a State has already been created on the boundary of the retreat set apart for the exile of the Indians—the State of Arkansas; another State, and an independent one—a new republic, made up of the old foes of the Indians—Texas, is rising on another boundary; and who shall say how soon these, and other new bordering states, may become as uneasy from the Indian neighborhood as the old ones are now?" The Oneida chief Daniel Bread added that "wherever we go, whites go also, and to get away from them is impossible." The *Phoenix* claimed that ancient Cherokee seers had prophesized the entire Removal crisis, including

John Ross, a Cherokee Chief, from Thomas L. McKenney and James Hall, *History of the Indian Tribes of North America*, 3 vols. (Philadelphia, 1837–44). Courtesy of the National Portrait Gallery, Smithsonian Institution, Gift of Betty A. and Lloyd G. Schermer.

that after relocating "you will find no resting place there, for your elder brother [the United States] will drive you from one place to another until you get to the western waters." Better to take their chances where they were in the ancient homeland.[52]

Some of the most charged racial debates of Removal centered on whether the Indians' civilized reforms were attributable to Indians at all or just to people the Jacksonians slurred as "half-breeds." "The aboriginal people are as ignorant, thoughtless, and improvident as formerly," charged Georgia governor George Gilmer in a common refrain, whereas the "polished gentlemen" who led the tribes' opposition to Removal and attracted so much praise from New England missionaries "are not Indians, but the children of white men." This criticism propagated a view, which remains common to this very day, that Indian tribal nations are racial entities rather than political units. According to this thinking, only "full-bloods" can claim to be authentic Indians and, by extension, authentic Cherokees, Creeks, or some other tribal designation. People of mixed descent lose this authenticity to the extent that they are mixed, regardless of how their tribal nation views them or how they define themselves. Given the inevitability that neighboring peoples will produce children together, eventually, the tribal nation can no longer make a legitimate claim to land and jurisdiction on the basis of Indian identity. During the Removal era, the Jacksonians' views functioned to undermine the identity claims of mixed Indians, particularly leaders with educations that enabled them to parry Whites in their own political arenas.[53]

The Cherokee, Creek, Choctaw, and Chickasaw people reckoned clan membership matrilineally and therefore considered the children of any women in the nation to be full members of the group, at least when the non-Indian parent was White rather than Black. "They are our blood," the Creek leader Abihka Tusta Mico explained, "and we will provide for them." This custom remained in place despite the efforts by some Indian planters to introduce the patrilineal traditions of Whites. *Probably* (though the documentary record for this era is largely silent on the point), they also judged mixed-bloods by whether they spoke the people's language, abided by their customs, participated in their ceremonies, and looked out for their neighbors. Neither complexion nor any other physical feature appears to have had anything to do with it. Even on the question of Black ancestry and belonging, it is unclear how deeply anyone outside of the slaveholding elite actually cared. These matters were too subtle and situational for Indians to debate them publicly with White people. More to the point, it would not have mattered anyway.[54]

The *Phoenix* acknowledged that mixed-bloods, as Whites defined them, comprised a disproportionate number of the most civilized Indians, but with the caveat that a number of full-bloods also fit that description while a number of mixed-bloods fell short. In other words, there was no direct correlation between mixed-bloodedness and civility or full-bloodedness and primitiveness. The *Phoenix* also produced hard numbers to disprove the Jacksonians' criticism that all of the Indians' leaders were more or less White. Yes, according to the calculations of blood quantum, the Cherokees' principal chief, John Ross, was just one-eighth Cherokee and the second principal chief, Major George Lowery, was one-half. Yet, overall, two thirds of the officers in government were full-bloods. The Cherokees' opposition to Removal was not a case of fake Indians seizing control to betray the interests of their authentic Indian relatives. The overwhelming majority of Indians of every background did not want to uproot.[55]

Of all the arguments against Jackson's plan, the one that resonated most with the White public was that Removal was a moral travesty because it violated the country's treaty obligations to respect the Indians' boundaries and promote their Christianity and civility in order to welcome them as citizens in due time. Not just Indians, but White Northern evangelicals levied this charge in print and speech and in church and Congress, with special emphasis on the Cherokees because they saw them as having fulfilled their part of the bargain to reform. White women also got involved after the activist Harriet Beecher Stowe called on them to come to the assistance of the "helpless race." One anti-Removal petition to Congress from the ladies of Pittsburgh contained 670 signatures and clearly struck a chord with Senator Theodore Frelinghuysen of New Jersey. He expressed his opposition to Removal in a six-hour, three-day-long speech in which he demanded, "Do the obligations of justice change with the color of skin? Is it one of the prerogatives of the white man, that he may disregard the dictates of moral principles, when an Indian shall be considered?"[56]

Indians made the most powerful case that Removal violated not only American law and reason but also basic morality as well. The Cherokee Margaret Ann Scott lamented in a letter published in the *Missionary Herald* that "white people seem to aim at our destruction," contrary to their self-serving profession that they wanted only to save Indians from extinction. Creek headmen concurred, writing directly to President Jackson that Removal meant "nothing better than the final extinction of our race." Jacksonians could pretend that they knew what was best for Indians better than Indians themselves, but Indians saw right through the charade. As the *Phoenix* put it, "There is not a man within our limits so ignorant as not to know that he has a right to live on the land of his fathers, in possession of his immemorial privileges, and that this right has been acknowledged and guaranteed by the United States." When John Ridge reflected on how the "cruel policy" of Andrew Jackson and the state of Georgia had encouraged "the wicked and profligate to exercise their inhuman ferocity on the now defenseless Cherokees and Creeks," he had to wonder: "Who are now the savage people? Who heathen? And who are the pagans?"[57]

WHO ARE NOW THE SAVAGE PEOPLE?

Though the dominant images of Removal are of aggressive federal troops rounding up passive Cherokees and putting them to the march, in fact a sizable portion of Native people futilely took up arms to resist, turning Removal into a series of race wars. The first was in the Midwest, where a band of Sauk Indians under the leadership of Black Hawk refused federal demands to remain west of the Mississippi in Iowa and no longer return to their people's spring and summer territory in Illinois. After years of mounting tension, in May 1832, jittery militiamen fired on Black Hawk as he approached them to parley, sparking months of running battles. The local *Galenian* newspaper urged the government to "carry on a war of extermination until there shall be no Indian (with his scalp on) left in the northern part of Illinois," adding that its readers were "ready to exterminate the whole race of the hostile Indians." This was no exaggeration. Over the course of the fifteen-week campaign, Black Hawk's men killed some seventy White settlers and soldiers but lost approximately five hundred of their own people, many of them at the Battle of Bad Axe after getting trapped by American forces while trying to escape west across the Mississippi. The defeated Sauks had no

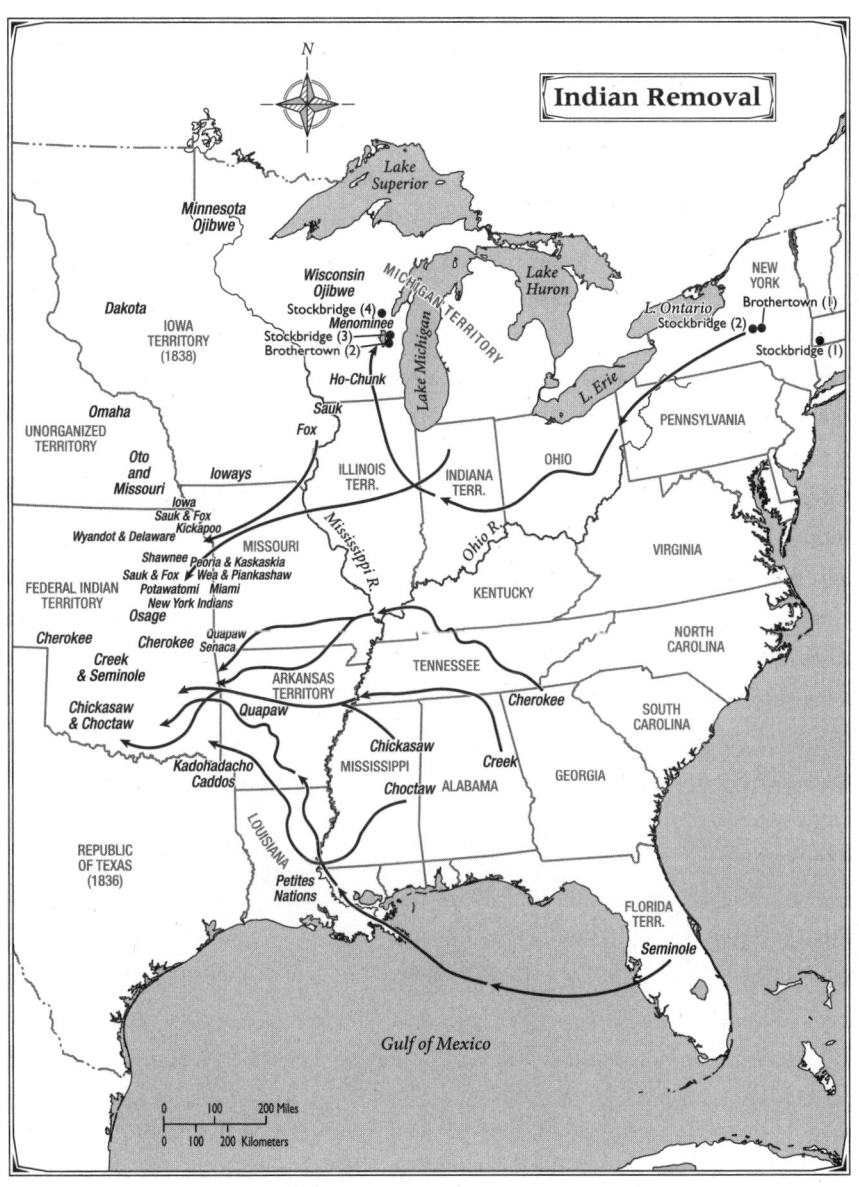

choice but to return to Iowa, only to have the federal government force them from that land, too, just a few years later.[58]

The Seminoles put up an even stiffer fight and nearly succeeded. They rejected the fraudulent 1832 Treaty of Payne's Landing, which required them to leave Florida within three years, despite their unwillingness to go, and to hand over all Black Seminoles deemed fugitive slaves by White authorities. When a U.S. military force arrived in 1835 to put them to the march, the Seminoles did not wait for Whites to fire the first shot. During the first few days of hostilities Seminoles killed 107 of the 110 U.S. troops plus their federal agent and a handful of chiefs who had cooperated with the Americans. Then they took refuge in Florida's swamps and hammocks, emerging only to raid White farms and ambush detachments of soldiers. This strategy to bog down the Americans until they gave up out of frustration nearly worked. A strong showing by the Whig Party in Congress in 1838 briefly opened negotiations to permit the Seminoles to remain in Florida, so war weary was the United States. Instead, the fighting continued for another four years, until the army had managed to force some four thousand Seminoles to relocate. It killed a thousand Seminoles in the process.[59]

This war was the clearest indication of White America's determination to implement Removal no matter what. Fighting the Seminoles cost the United States fifteen hundred U.S. troops and between thirty and forty million dollars, about twice the average annual federal budget during the first seven years of the Jackson

Attack of the Seminoles on the block house, 1837. Courtesy of the Library of Congress.

administration. To put these numbers in perspective, for every four Seminoles deported, the United States killed one person, lost three soldiers, and spent thirty-two thousand dollars. In today's money, that would be equivalent to about $8.5 million for every deportee. The financial and political strain of this war was so great that the federal government eventually dropped its insistence on the return of Black Seminoles to slavery and conceded to their joining their Indian compatriots in the West in the hope that this decision would weaken Seminole resistance. Remarkably, five hundred Seminoles held out and managed to remain in their Florida homeland. Their descendants, as the Seminole and Miccosukee tribes, are there still.[60]

The Creek removal degenerated into war, too. The Creek Indians' deal with the U.S. government, the 1832 Treaty of Cusseta (or Washington), ceded all of the tribe's five million acres to the Americans, out of which the head of each Indian family would receive a 320-acre allotment that he could either keep and manage himself or sell and migrate West. No sooner did numerous families agree to such terms than land speculators began hiring corrupt Indians to pose as the owners and sell fraudulent claims to these tracts, after which the speculator would transfer the claim to a White settler who would drive the actual titleholders off the land. Whites seized 1,970,234 of 2,142,720 acres of guaranteed Creek land through such schemes, forcing some thirty-five hundred Creeks westward before the rest of their tribe. Desperate, starving, and furious, in spring 1836 Creek warriors boasting that they could "whip the white people" ambushed a mail coach and killed five Americans, followed by an estimated three thousand Creeks raiding White plantations on the road between Columbus, Georgia, and Tuskegee, Alabama. They even seized the town of Roanoke, Georgia, on the Chattahoochee River. White land speculators celebrated this uprising as opportunity, because now they could "kill all the Indians off, and that would close the matter." True enough, U.S. troops subdued this revolt throughout the summer, putting eight hundred warriors in chains, then shipping them and their families, three thousand in number, by steamboats down the Alabama River, west along the north shore of the Gulf of Mexico to New Orleans, then up the Mississippi River to the Cache River, where they began a 275-mile overland march. Only some 2,300 arrived in the West still breathing, all of them in "total destitution." Fourteen thousand more Creeks would follow over the next year, interspersed with mop-up operations in which White militia hunted Creeks in hiding "like wild beasts," killing hundreds and raping numerous Creek women along the way. As armed guards drove the Creeks onward, in rushed the craniologist Josiah C. Nott to collect skulls from the tribe's dead for science experiments that justified the racial order that had created

Basil Hall, *Chiefs of the Creek Nation and a Georgia Squatter*, from Basil Hall, *Forty Etchings: From Sketches Made with the Camera Lucida, in North America, in 1827 and 1828* (London: Simpkin & Marshall, and Moon, Boys & Graves, 1829).

this nightmare in the first place. No wonder the Creek chief Menawa declared that "when I cross the great river, my desire is that I may never again see the face of a white man!"[61]

U.S. agents managed to intimidate Choctaw chiefs into signing the Treaty of Dancing Rabbit Creek in 1830, authorizing Removal, but most Choctaws remained determined to stay. Much to the surprise of American authorities, some five thousand Choctaws, or about a quarter of the tribe, decided to accept allotments in Mississippi, totaling some three million acres, and make a go of it among the Whites. Yet federal officers refused to file these claims based on the empty excuse that "designing men" had manipulated Choctaw opinion. With no legal protection, Choctaws who claimed citizenship found their land and livestock easy prey to the unscrupulous White land jobbers and squatters overrunning their country. "The White men is stealing our horses, cattle, and hogs, and whipping some of the Indians for claiming their [own] property," protested John Pitchlynn, himself a White man who had long lived among the Choctaws, married one of their women, and produced many children with her. "The longer I stay, the worse I despise white people." This episode proved once again that most White Americans were unwilling to grant peace and citizenship even to Indians who consented to pursue civilized lives under White law. Ultimately, most of the Choctaws joined their relatives in Indian Territory, though several hundred retreated into the pine barrens and cedar swamps of Mississippi to form the core of a Choctaw community that remains in the state to this day.[62]

The only place Indians successfully became citizens was Wisconsin, where the several hundred Brothertown Indians and Stockbridge Mohicans took the option (which they called "becoming White") rather than relocate yet again, this time to Kansas. Like their Southern counterparts, they knew all too well that life west of the Mississippi would be at best a temporary respite. Some of them were confident that their status as civilized Christians equipped them to compete in White society despite the obstacles of White race prejudice. Their people generally spoke and wrote English, they governed their own churches, and they ran sawmills, gristmills, farms, and logging operations. Three Brothertowns would go on to serve in the Wisconsin legislature. Yet many of these Indians came to regret the transition to citizenship as White creditors, the taxman, and hucksters zeroed in on their allotments. Three years into the experiment, most of the Stockbridges petitioned to return their citizenship and revert to the legal status of Indians. "They have all of their lives been called *Indians*," appealed the Stockbridges to Congress, and "it is their desire so to continue," emphasizing "that their natures and their dispositions can no more be changed, than their skins be made white and transparent."[63]

The Stockbridges' period of indeterminacy had the fortunate effect of outlasting the Removal policy, thus allowing them to remain in Wisconsin, though they had to leave their original Fox River lands and relocate to a new reservation far to the north in Menominee territory. Most of the Brothertowns managed to stay in Wisconsin, too, but not as a consolidated community. The combination of White predation and the usual atomizing effects of private landownership eventually scattered their people until only a small core was left in their base territory along Lake Winnebago. Such was the gift of citizenship in a state with a seal containing the Latin saying, "Civilization Replaces Barbarism," and depicting an Indian hunter retreating westward pursued by a White man guiding his plow.[64]

The Cherokees' nonviolent resistance to Removal produced only greater oppression. Georgia's lottery distribution of their lands emboldened masses of armed Whites to force the Indians from their very homes, to the point that by 1835 there were more White people in Cherokee country than Cherokees. Georgia twice arrested the *Cherokee Phoenix* editor Elias Boudinot on trumped-up charges of libel, though it subsequently dropped them due to the lack of evidence. Boudinot wondered in print, "Would a white man have been treated as I have been ... in this free country, where the liberty of the press is solemnly guaranteed?" When Boudinot finally resigned, the state also arrested his successor, Elijah Hicks, after he dared to report the attempted rape of a Cherokee woman by White sheriff David Duke and chastised the courts for dismissing the case because it depended on Indian testimony. Eventually, Georgia just shut down the paper altogether. Even the Cherokees' White missionaries suffered from this oppression. Georgia sentenced Elizur Butler and Samuel Austin Worcester to four years of hard labor for their rejection of the state's authority over them in Cherokee country, the fateful case that led to *Worcester v. Georgia*. White evangelicals throughout the country howled in protest that the tyranny of Jackson and Georgia toward Indians was now afflicting White Christians, but none of it mattered. As a Georgian under the pseudonym Socrates wrote, "Let them whine; but let us be white people still."[65]

Seeing no other options, several leading Cherokees calling themselves the Treaty Party, including Major Ridge, John Ridge, and Boudinot, gave up the fight. They admitted "that our people cannot exist amidst a white population, subject to laws which they have no hand in making, and which they do not understand." Before resigning from his editorship because he could no longer support the National Council's opposition to Removal, Boudinot published one last column explaining his change of heart. "Think for a moment my countrymen," he appealed, "the danger to be apprehended from an overwhelming white population, a population overcharged with high notions of color, dignity, and greatness—at once overbearing and impudent to those whom, in their sovereign pleasure, they consider as their inferiors. Thus should we, our sons and daughters, be slaves indeed." That is, unless they headed West, terrible as that choice was, too. Leaders of the Treaty Party, despite representing a tiny minority of the Cherokee public, committed the entire nation to Removal

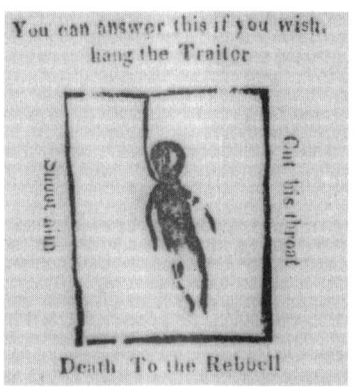

A threatening image sent to the editor of the *Cherokee Phoenix*, Elias Boudinot, depicting a hanging man with the sayings "Death To the Rebbell," "Shoot him," and "Cut his throat," from *Cherokee Phoenix* 4, no. 7, August 13, 1831, p. 3, col. 2.

in the Treaty of New Echota on December 29, 1835, conscious that they might be signing their death warrants at the hands of their own people, as indeed they were. Roughly two thousand Cherokees immediately headed West. Yet the majority, led by John Ross, their elected chief, stood their ground, denouncing the Treaty Party as traitors and their Removal agreement as a fraud. Not surprisingly, on the date earmarked for the rest of the Cherokees to begin their migration, only 250 of them assembled at the government agency.[66]

Subsequent events have become known as the Trail of Tears. In the face of the unwilling Cherokees, U.S. general Winfield Scott ordered seven thousand soldiers to round up the dissidents at bayonet point. Without warning, detachments of troops showed up at Cherokee homes and forced the inhabitants out without time to gather their possessions. No sooner was this done than White Georgians waiting in the wings rushed in to loot the Indians' property. One empathetic soldier observed that "well-furnished houses were left prey to plunderers, who, like hungry wolves... rifle the houses, and strip the helpless, unoffending owners, of all they have on earth." The soldiers kept five thousand Cherokees confined in stockades for a month until guards were available to march them West, even as malnutrition and dysentery took their toll. Then the misery really began.[67]

Robert Lindneux, *The Trail of Tears*, 1942. Courtesy of the Woolaroc Museum, Bartlesville, Oklahoma.

AN ACCOUNTING

Americans are widely taught that the Trail of Tears resulted in the deaths of thousands of Cherokee migrants (some five thousand out of twenty-three thousand), and that the United States was responsible because it forced the people from their homes. That is but a glimpse of the whole picture. The Cherokees did not die simply because the walk was long and hard. Their suffering was also the result of poor governmental planning and rampant corruption and incompetence by contractors supposed to supply the migrants with food, clothing, and medical care along the way. They died because the soldiers kept them marching even when they needed to stop. They died because they were heartbroken and terrified. And the Cherokees were far from alone in their travails. The calculations of the historian Jeffrey Ostler are that Removal cost the Choctaws 2,500 dead out of a population of 21,000; the Chickasaws 150 dead out of 4,000; the Creeks between 5,000 and 7,000 dead out of 24,000; and the Seminoles between 900 and 2,000 dead out of perhaps 6,000. Ostler's best estimate is that of the 88,000 Indians in total forced from their homelands by the United States, between 12,000 and 17,000 (between 14 and 19 percent) perished during their ordeals.[68]

Even those sobering numbers are too low. They do not include the Black Hawk War, in which the United States killed hundreds of Sauks. They do not count the Indians who committed suicide back East in their homelands before soldiers could force them West. Not to be overlooked, the great dying continued in Indian Territory after the migrants' arrival, due to disease, malnutrition, and attacks by Plains Indians. Between 1842 and 1860, removed Chickasaws lost 15 percent of their population, the Creeks nearly 25 percent, the Cherokees 20 percent, the Potawatomis 25 percent, and the Sauks and Foxes (or Mesquakies) a shocking 80 percent.[69]

Ostler emphasizes that these deaths cannot be dismissed as unintended, accidental, or unanticipated. Removal took place over the course of more than fifteen years, and it did not take long for American authorities to confront that every forced migration and resettlement produced fatalities that would have been completely unacceptable if the victims had been White. Yet the United States stuck with the process, all the while repeating the claptrap that it was in the best interests of Native people. But what was it really for?[70]

The actual purpose was to enable White people to seize Indian land. According to the historian Claudio Saunt, the federal government spent about $75 million on Indian Removal, equivalent today to about a trillion dollars, or $12.5 million for each deportee. In return for that $75 million spent, the federal government took in $80 million by selling the Indian land it expropriated. Of course, it got far more than that in the end. In 1850, those lands produced some 160 million pounds of ginned cotton (16 percent of the entire cotton crop in the United States) and 6 percent of the nation's overall agricultural output. Slavery and the value of Southern White estates expanded in turn. There were also increased profits for the Northern financial industries that sold insurance and issued loans to slaveholding interests. Northern cloth factories got cheaper cotton, and new markets to which to sell slave clothing. In the Midwest, the expulsion of Indians opened vast tracts of territory for White people to farm, log, mill, and otherwise develop. The heightened economic activity increased government revenues. In other words, Removal made good financial sense.[71]

Though not for Indians. By Saunt's count, Removal cost the Chickasaws between $7 million and $10 million in the lost value of their land and property, or, in today's dollars, between $117,000 and $1 million per Chickasaw family. The Choctaws lost at least $10 million and the Creeks $8 million. Today, the descendants of these people live with the consequences of White people's theft of this wealth, just as assuredly as the descendants of the White people who took, sold, and planted (or had slaves plant) Indian land have profited from it through the generations.[72]

Those figures document race at work. Race is a tool used by human beings to achieve their material, political, and cultural ends. The majority view among Whites that they were chosen by God to spread Christianity and civility, and that Indians were savages by nature or culture, was the justification for this massive plunder of wealth and destruction of human life. Whites would use similar racial arguments to justify filling the Indians' stolen land with Black slaves to toil for their profit. Not all White Americans shared these beliefs, but there were not enough of them, or at least not enough of them willing to fight for their principles, to make a difference.

What precious little restraint the federal government had been able to impose before 1828 on the exploitation of Indians by state governments and local Whites was swept away by the election of Andrew Jackson and his political allies. American memory has celebrated Jackson as an iconic president for a rapidly democratizing country, crystallized by the image of everyday people crowding into the White House to celebrate his first inauguration. Generations of White Americans have been less willing to grapple with his role as the populist leader of a White nationalist movement hostile to the very presence of Indians. Everyday Euro-Americans who conceived of themselves as a White political community had consistently advocated for the elimination of Indians since the seventeenth century. The goals were to seize the Indians' land and stamp out Indian resistance. When that bottom-up democratic impulse received sanction from the government, and especially when government adopted it as policy, it spelled disaster for Native people, enormous profits for Whites, and greater misery for enslaved Blacks. This sordid episode was not restricted to the South, nor was it the sole creation of Andrew Jackson. It was a national political movement premised on a national culture of land lust and White supremacy.

Removal did not completely clear the Eastern United States of Indians. Small communities of Native people remained scattered across nearly every state, making do on marginal lands and trying to remain as inconspicuous as possible. But Removal came close to achieving its goal of whitewashing the country of Indians, and the White racial imagination took it from there. It made the Indians who remained invisible as Indians by insisting that their intermarriages with White and Black outsiders diminished their claims to Indian identity. By this reckoning, the first mixed generation became half-bloods, the next one quarter-bloods, and then—poof!—they were gone forever, and with them, their claims to the land. This was a catch-22 if there ever was one, for these tiny communities in the East could not survive as Indian places if their people did not seek outside partners. When strangers moved into Native communities and adhered to local custom, Indians saw them as having married in, rather than the Indian partner as having married out, and considered their children to be full members. White Americans would not grant them that option.

Whites insisted that mixed Indians were diminished Indians with weaker claims to protection than previous generations of full-bloods. This was not just a matter of Whites adhering to their invented racial rule that Blackness always defined a person of White and Black ancestry, which allowed them to expand the servile Black labor pool and limit access to White privileges. When it came to mixed Indians, custom led White Americans to assume reflexively that Whiteness trumped Indianness, bleaching each mixed generation until it became entirely White. The instrumentality of this thinking was that it gave White people claim to Indian land, as the Jacksonians illustrated in their denial that mixed Indian leaders opposed to Removal were actual Indians. Self-identifying Native people remaining in the East had to navigate these racial conventions constantly, especially if they had diverse origins.

The racial logic of Removal evolved seamlessly into the White American conquest ideology of Manifest Destiny. Though the term "Manifest Destiny" was not coined until 1845, amid the U.S. war with Mexico, its principles that the United States was chosen by God to spread democratic civilization, and lesser people had no choice but to make way, were minor variations on White rationales for forcing Indians west. Those justifications included that Indians diminished through contact with White civilization, that White people had the right and even duty to seize uncultivated Indian land and put it to use, and that whatever losses Indians suffered in their dispossession were in the service of progress. Since its inception, the ideology of Manifest Destiny has become a staple of triumphalist American history education and culture, including with contemporary White Americans who contend that the United States is "exceptional" as God's model to the rest of the world. This way of thinking deliberately whitewashes White supremacy and the genocide of Native people from United States history.[73]

The Pequot writer William Apess had his own story to tell about Removal and American history. During the 1830s, he went on a writing blitz and speaking tour to educate the people of Massachusetts, who were overwhelmingly opposed to Jackson's policy, that they, too, had Indians in their backyard who they treated as second-class citizens. Apess was quite unlike any of the Indians White people encountered in the novels of James Fenimore Cooper. He was formally educated despite a childhood spent in servitude, and deeply read in American history. His military service in the War of 1812 and travels up and down the Eastern Seaboard afterward gave him a broad view of American society, while his training as a Methodist preacher provided him with a thorough knowledge of the Bible and Christian moral principles. Most of all, his tribulations as an Indian child in White New England, his social networking in the community of Northeastern abolitionists, and then his ministry to the Mashpee Wampanoags on Cape Cod filled him with rage toward American racial injustice.

He fashioned some of his critiques to appeal to White New Englanders' anti-Jackson politics. His audiences must have nodded in approval as he asked them to imagine Americans' response if a foreign army marched into the United States to subdue and remove *its* people. "How quick would they fly to arms," he observed, "gather in multitudes around the tree of liberty, and contend for their rights with the last drop of their blood." But when Indians like the Sauks and Seminoles did the same thing, "what a hue and cry is instantly raised . . . for the purpose of driving them from their country and taking possession thereof." If this was not wrong, nothing was, Apess and his listeners could readily agree.[74]

But what of themselves? Apess charged that throughout New England, and not just back in the mists of time but in the here and now, White people subjected Indians to "murder by inches" by exploiting them for land and labor, even as they insisted that there were no real Indians left. President Jackson had even justified his Removal policy by claiming that "the fate of the Mohegan, the Narragansett, and the Delaware is fast overtaking the Choctaw, the Cherokee, and the Creek," failing to notice that none of these tribes was extinct, and the Mohegans and Narragansetts remained on portions of their ancestral homelands in Connecticut and Rhode Island, respectively. No one bothered to correct Jackson because even White New Englanders generally assumed that these groups no longer existed, so pervasive was the myth of Indian disappearance.[75]

Apess was there to proclaim that the White supremacy and anti-Indian racism behind Jackson's Indian Removal policy pervaded American society, even in the enlightened social circles of Boston. Apess knew full well that most Whites had been "bred to look upon Indians with dislike and detestation." In fact, he had "often been told seriously, by sober persons, that his fellows were a link between the whites and the brute creation, an inferior race of men to whom the Almighty had less regard than to their neighbors who he had driven from their possession to make room for a race more favored." Apess knew White people from all walks of life, including those who styled themselves humanitarians. It was his opinion that this prejudice was found "in every white man, from the oldest to the youngest."[76]

Apess accused self-proclaimed Christians who subscribed to such beliefs of hypocrisy and even blasphemy. "If black or red skins or any other skin of color is disgraceful to God," he observed, "it appears that he has disgraced himself a great deal—for he has made fifteen colored people to one white and placed them here upon this earth." Then he turned the screw:

> Assemble all nations together in your imagination, and then let the whites be seated among them . . . Now suppose these skins were put together, and each skin had its national crimes written upon it—which skin do you think would have the greatest? I will ask one question more. Can you charge the Indians with robbing a nation almost of their whole continent, and murdering their women and children, and then depriving the remainder of their lawful rights, that nature and God require them to have? And to cap the climax, rob another nation to till their grounds and welter out their days under the lash with hunger and fatigue under the scorching rays of a burning sun? I should look at all the skins, and I know that when I cast my eye upon that white skin, and if I saw those crimes written upon it, I should enter my protest against it immediately and cleave to that which is more honorable. And I can tell you that I am satisfied with the manner of my creation, full—whether others are or not.

Apess was saying aloud what White Americans, throughout the entire nation, had invented elaborate racial arguments to avoid. They were not innately superior to anyone else. They were not even true to the Christian faith they claimed as bodily inheritance. They constructed the ideas that they were White and superior, that Native Americans were destined to extinction, and that people descended from Africans were Blacks fit only for servitude, in order to justify killing Indigenous people and taking their land, and subjugating African Americans and taking their labor. With figures like Apess, John Ridge, Elias Boudinot, and Nancy Ward to shock their consciences, no wonder so many White Americans wanted Indians to disappear.[77]

CHAPTER 5

"Exterminate Them!"

In July 1865, less than two years after locally recruited United States soldiers had massacred at least 150 peaceful Cheyennes and Arapahos at Sand Creek on the Colorado Plains, Senator James R. Doolittle of Wisconsin had the temerity to stand before a capacity crowd in a Denver theater and argue that Americans had a responsibility to address the "Indian problem" more humanely. He did not even get the chance to finish his remarks before the outraged audience began to shout him off the stage. "Exterminate them! Exterminate them!" they hollered, "almost loud enough to raise the roof of the Opera House." Paralyzing attacks by Indians against stagecoaches, ranches, and overland travelers, magnified by sensationalist newspaper coverage, had whipped up the White people of this gold-rush city and its hinterlands into a frenzy of terror and rage. Every story raised the passions to new heights, particularly when it featured Indian warriors braining helpless infants, raping White women and girls, dragging away captives to a future as slaves and concubines, and leaving behind the desecrated corpses of their innocent victims. White Coloradans, as Doolittle discovered the hard way, had no interest in the plaintive appeals of bleeding-heart Eastern do-gooders that Whites had wronged Indians at least as much as Indians had wronged them. They were even less willing to hear that Christian principles demanded a national effort to bring Indians to civility with as little bloodshed as possible. No, the crowd's only solution was to "Exterminate them!" and thus end the futile attempt to sort out which Indians were actual threats. As the Cheyennes and Arapahos had already learned, these people meant what they said.[1]

Though the leaders of the two tribes had pledged in the Treaties of Fort Laramie (1851) and Fort Atkinson (1853) not to abuse Americans who passed through their territory, that was before an 1858 gold strike in the Rockies attracted a rush of tens of thousands of rugged White fortune seekers intending to stay. Almost overnight, they transformed the sea of grass approaching the mountains into a capitalist machine that siphoned off every profitable resource, whether above or below the ground. There were fewer places for the bison or the Indians' horses to graze and water once the White people's vast herds of livestock arrived, and still less as their cart paths, railroad tracks, and telegraph lines began spiderwebbing across the landscape. Though Whites remained vulnerable to Indian attack in isolated settings, their populated market towns like Denver were impregnable, and their expanding network of military posts threatened a prompt response to depredations. Growing numbers of Cheyennes and Arapahos, pinched with hunger and simmering with resentment, were beginning to see that if they did not fight back now, Whites would drive them out altogether. The Indians "arrogantly declare that the land belongs exclusively to them," warned firsthand reports from White traders and federal agents. "They intend to regain and to hold it, if they have to destroy every white man, woman, and child to accomplish their purpose."[2]

The United States' answer was reservations. American policymakers unanimously agreed that the Plains Indians' nomadic hunting life was unsustainable because White expansion, as the manifestation of God's will, could not and should not be contained. Leaving Indians to manage this crisis by their own devices would mean their raiding White people's settlements for plunder and revenge, followed by White campaigns to exterminate the culprits or any other Indians within reach. The best option for everyone, therefore, was for Indians to cede most or all of their land and relocate to designated tribal territories where federal troops could keep them in and Whites out. In these restricted but protected zones, Indians would survive for the meantime on government handouts and what little hunting remained. In the long term, though, the government demanded that Indians begin living like White people. Indian men would have to swap wide-ranging hunting, raiding, and trading on horseback in bands of friends and relatives for the monotony of farming and ranching fenced-in plots of private property. Women would tend to the home, children, and garden by themselves, whereas before they had shared the work of running the camp, processing bison meat and hides, and gathering wood and wild foods with female kin and other tribeswomen. Children, rather than shadow adults to learn their responsibilities and otherwise play and train in the camp and surrounding country, would attend school daily for academic instruction by rote and cultural reprogramming by former enemies. The freedom, variety, beauty, community, and, yes, danger, of the nomadic horse life would all be gone, replaced with drudgery, routine, loneliness, and subjugation to White authority.

The United States offered no other choice but extermination. Increasingly, the military treated all Indians who remained outside the reservations as hostiles, killing their women, children, and elders, and destroying their horse herds and lodges. Put another way, if Indians would not submit entirely to White American rule, White Americans threatened to wipe them all from the face of the earth. In many frontier regions, the White settlers who arrived ahead of the army did not even grant Indians the alternative of reservation life. They intended only to annihilate them or, failing that, drive them away by any means necessary and thus appropriate their land and eliminate the threat they posed. The scale of this indiscriminate violence, and the explicit dehumanization of the Indian victims by White perpetrators, can only be characterized as genocidal. To be White in the context of the euphemistic "winning of the West" was to claim and exercise the power of life and death over Indians.

The Cheyenne chief Black Kettle did not want this fight. During a visit to Washington, D.C., in 1863, he had witnessed firsthand the awesome population and resources of the United States and heard directly from President Abraham Lincoln about the country's plans for Indian people. Black Kettle knew that the Whites' advantages, even just on the central Plains, had already grown so formidable that it was no longer a real possibility for Indians to take back their country through force, though some dreamers still clung to the hope. The question was whether complying with the Americans' demands would offer any relief. The United States had repeatedly failed to deliver annuities it owed to the Cheyennes for the vast tracts of land they had already ceded. When the food and goods did arrive, they were of such poor quality and in such small amounts that they served more as an insult than a lifeline. These conditions forced even those Indians inclined to cooperate with the Americans to go back onto the Plains to hunt, and, too often, also to steal White people's cattle and sheep, if only to get something to eat. Ranchers and farmers who suffered these losses, and the murders that often accompanied them, did not see such Indians as compliant friends, but instead as part of an undifferentiated savage threat.

The real danger to White interests came from a group of Cheyenne militants known as the Dog Soldiers. They would hear nothing of reservations, farming, schools, or treaties. As far as they were concerned, Maheo, the All Being, had willed them to live as horse-mounted hunter-warriors and guided them from the Great

Camp Weld Council, unknown photographer, 1864.
Courtesy of the Denver Public Library.

The Cheyennes under Black Kettle (middle seat, middle row here) tried repeatedly to keep peace with White Coloradoans, as in this conference, only to be massacred by troops led by Colonel John M. Chivington at Sand Creek.

Lakes onto the Plains to fulfill this destiny. The "White man's road," as Natives called it, seemed to lead nowhere but hunger and emasculation. As the Cheyennes' federal agent and kinsman, William Bent, wrote in 1859, "a smoldering passion agitates these people, perpetually fomented by the failure of food [and] the encroachment of the white population . . . a desperate war of starvation and extinction is therefore imminent and inevitable, unless prompt measures should prevent it."[3]

White frustration reached its peak in the summer of 1864, following the public display of the corpses of the White Hungate family, who the Arapahos, close allies of the Cheyennes, had killed and scalped. The time had come, according to the *Daily Rocky Mountain News*, "to fight [the Indians] in their own way. A few months of active extermination against the red devils will bring quiet, and nothing else will." To that end, Colorado territorial governor John Evans ordered all Indians to report to designated military posts or else be considered hostiles. Then, he recruited local men to form the U.S. Third Volunteer Regiment to hunt down any renegades. Their commander was Colonel John M. Chivington, a Methodist minister who despised Indians hardly less than the Devil himself and believed that exterminating them was God's work.[4]

Most Cheyennes and Arapahos favored compliance over resistance. Throughout the fall, moderate chiefs such as Black Kettle, White Antelope, Yellow Wolf, Ochinee, Left Hand, and Little Raven led their followers to the U.S. army post of Fort Lyon, 180 miles southeast of Denver, even as the Dog Soldiers continued their marauding. Black Kettle's band of 120 lodges camped on the banks of nearby Sand Creek, cautiously secure in the promise that they were under U.S. protection. In fact, they were sitting ducks.

Chivington, eager to claim some victory before his men's one-hundred-day commissions expired, ordered the Third Regiment to march on November 14, not against the Dog Soldiers on the Smoky Hill River, which would have been dangerous and time-consuming, but against the unsuspecting and vulnerable Indian peace factions. Several subordinate officers from Fort Lyon objected that these Indians posed no threat, only for Chivington to snap back, "Damn any man who is in sympathy with an Indian!" A soft target was a prime one, in his view. Before leading seven hundred troops out into the cold night of November 28, Chivington told them, "Now boys, I shan't say who you shall kill, but remember our murdered women and children."[5]

The colonel got just what he wanted. Arriving undetected at the Indians' camp, Chivington's soldiers "just went at it pell-mell," as the Indians' agent Samuel G. Colley characterized it, even though Black Kettle flew a large U.S. flag that President Lincoln had personally gifted to him. John J. Smith, a White man who was living with the Cheyennes at Sand Creek, having fathered a son among them, remembered of that horrifying morning that "all manner of depredations were inflicted on their [the Indians'] persons; they were scalped, their brains knocked out; the [White] men used their knives, ripped open women, clubbed little children, knocked them in the head with their guns, beat their brains out, mutilated their bodies in every sense of the word." By the time the slaughter ended, between 150 and 230 Indians lay dead, most of them women and children, to all of whom the United States had pledged its protection. Black Kettle was among the few who lived to see another day; he also managed to save his wife, despite the soldiers having shot her nine times.[6]

Denver gave a heroes' welcome to the returning troops as they paraded dozens of scalps, other bodily trophies, and plunder through the streets. To the cheering throngs, this massacre was another victory of White civilization over savage "redskins." Chivington whipped up the crowd by boasting that he had ordered his men to "kill and scalp all, little and big," based on the time-worn genocidal argument "that nits make lice." Hardly any White people publicly denounced

Howling Wolf, *At the Sand Creek Massacre*, 1874–75.
Courtesy of the Picture Art Collection/Alamy.

Howling Wolf was a Cheyenne survivor of the horrors that day.

the atrocity committed in their name, even if they rued it privately, because, as Colley explained, "it is almost as much as a man's life is worth to speak friendly of an Indian." This was no exaggeration. Shortly after Captain Silas Soule testified to military investigators about the crimes he had witnessed at Sand Creek, he was assassinated in the streets of Denver by Charles W. Squier, a veteran of the Second Colorado Cavalry. There was widespread suspicion that Chivington had ordered this murder, but any chance of linking him to the crime was lost when Squier escaped from jail and disappeared. Regardless of Chivingston's role, the message had been sent. The mob's principle of "Exterminate them!" now determined acceptance in the local White community.[7]

The Civil War temporarily distracted Americans in the East from the Sand Creek Massacre, but once they took notice, they were outraged and ashamed, hence Doolittle's inquiry. In October 1865, federal authorities even issued a formal apology to Black Kettle and his fellow Cheyennes and Arapahos for the country's "gross and wanton outrages" against them, and promised reparations that included thirty years of annuities. Bigoted frontier provincials and the occasional rogue commander might favor the Indians' eradication, but the self-anointed civilized portion of American society sought the Natives' peaceful assimilation through Christianity and civility and favored the application of only measured force when they resisted. This had been the aim of cosmopolitan elements in White America since the beginning of colonization.[8]

They were lying to themselves. In fact, whenever Indians rejected subjugation without conditions, which is to say, when they refused to endure starvation and White depredations on the reservations despite U.S. promises to feed and protect them, large portions of the White public, including high-ranking politicians and military brass, immediately demanded and pursued Indian extermination. U.S. General William T. Sherman, who was in charge of clearing the Central Plains of Indians, judged that the Natives "must be exterminated, for they cannot and will not settle down, and our people will force us to do it." His strategy, as with the U.S. Army throughout the West, was to storm the Indians' winter camps, shoot everything that moved, including the Natives' mounts, and set their lodges and the contents ablaze so anyone left would be unable to survive outside the reservation agency.[9]

All Indians were at risk, regardless of their politics, as Black Kettle would have to rediscover with fatal consequences. Though the chief continued to do practically whatever U.S. authorities instructed, including cede additional land and move his followers to a part of Indian Territory reserved for Native people who had signed peace treaties, ongoing hostilities between Whites and the Dog Soldiers constantly threatened to engulf his people. That was especially the case when they went out to hunt and sometimes plunder because the United States did not provide enough food on the reservation. Unfortunately for them, the general assigned to hunt them down was none other than George Armstrong Custer, whose Seventh Cavalry was known for scorning Indians as "redskins" and "red niggers" and killing them with impunity. On November 27, 1868, Custer's bluecoats marched through the snow to attack Black Kettle's unwary village on the Washita River, in what is now western Oklahoma. After mowing down somewhere between a few dozen and 150 people and destroying nearly all the people's horses and property, they retreated from a fierce counterattack by using captive women and children as human shields. Left behind was the dead body of Black Kettle, who had been a consistent advocate of peace.[10]

The wars for the West taught the Cheyennes and many other Indians that there was no life worth living based on negotiated terms with White Americans. Whites asserted the right, as the supposedly superior race, to dictate to Indians without limits, granting them no self-determination other than complete surrender. Even the Eastern Christian humanitarians who now touted themselves as Friends of the

The Seventh U.S. Cavalry Charging into Black Kettle's Village at Daylight, November 27, 1868, Harper's Weekly, December 19, 1868.

Indian approved of forcing Indians onto reservations without freedom to choose how to own and manage what was left of their own land, govern themselves, defend their communities, raise their children, worship, marry, travel, and sometimes even eat. The only alternative presented by White society was total destruction. Indians faced with these choices sometimes concluded that all White Americans favored extermination and disagreed only over the means.

Native people throughout the West, like their Eastern counterparts in earlier times, employed racial arguments to try to meet this existential threat. Their most common initial response was to call for tribes to unite as Indians in resistance against their common White enemy. At other times, they tried to convince American authorities to respect their way of life by contending that the Creator had endowed Indians and Whites with fundamentally different characteristics from each other. The failure of these attempts does not negate their importance. The fact is that Indians did not submit passively, though in certain times and places White people utterly overwhelmed them. Equally to the point, many Indians maintained the spirit of resistance even under the most oppressive conditions. Their perseverance during what the Ojibwe writer David Treuer has aptly characterized as an apocalypse was more than an inspiring example of human resilience under unimaginable adversity, though it was certainly that. It was also a sacrifice so that future generations of Indians might someday thrive again.[11]

THE RACIAL ROOTS OF MANIFEST DESTINY

White Americans in the mid-nineteenth century saw ample evidence for their contention that God destined them to possess the continent and spread their way of life. Their population had grown from 5.3 million people in 1800 to 17 million in 1840 to over 38 million in 1870. Meanwhile, the United States had followed up the Louisiana Purchase of 1803 with the annexation of Florida in 1819, the annexation of Texas in 1845, the seizure of the American Southwest and California from Mexico in 1846, and an 1846 agreement with Britain that placed the future states of Washington and Oregon within the national domain. White Americans had spread all the way from the Mississippi River to the Pacific Ocean and were in the process of overrunning the spaces in between, aided by the transportation advances of military roads, turnpikes, canals, steamboats, and, ultimately, railroads. Lucrative trade crisscrossed these routes. Livestock, agricultural produce, and precious minerals passed from the continental interior to riverine market towns and ultimately to industrial and export centers on the Atlantic coast. Manufactured goods traveled in reverse. The American military tended to lag behind the spread of the White population, but eventually it caught up to aid in the subjugation, dispossession, and extermination of Native people. As far as most White commentators were concerned, this expansion was progress that should continue unimpeded whatever the cost to savages. National greatness and civilization, by God's very will, required sacrificing Indians.[12]

This ideology pervaded the federal government's Bureau of Indian Affairs, which managed the growing number of Indian reservations, distributed annuities, and advised other federal branches on policies affecting Native people. Commissioner Luke Lea, who served in the 1850s, spoke for a broad swath of White Americans when he contended that human history was one long chronicle of conflict between savage and civilized societies in which the latter always triumphed. He expounded that "when civilization and barbarism are brought in such relation that they cannot coexist together, it is right that the superiority of the former should be asserted and the latter compelled to give way." That was doubly true when the barbarians were racial inferiors, as Lea considered Indians to be because he judged their savagery to be innate. He explained that, to the extent that "the red man" had suffered injury at White hands in the great civilizational contest, it was "the inevitable consequence of his own perverse and vicious nature." Such thinking led Thomas Twiss of the Indian Department's Upper Platte Agency to conclude that nothing could or should be done to halt the mass of White emigrants overrunning Indian country. "It is beyond human power to retard or control it," he ventured, "nor would it be wise to do so, even were it possible... the savage, the wild hunter tribes, must give way to the white man" because Whites made more efficient use of the land. "It cannot be," added Richard M. Smith, U.S. Indian agent of Michigan, "that Almighty God ever intended that this great country... should be and always remain the mere hunting ground for savages." According to these perspectives, White people's decimation of Indians was not a matter of choice, but divine fate in the cause of human advancement. Such ideas were ubiquitous in White American society, removing guilt for the human cost of expansion and thereby driving it forward.[13]

The only alternatives this vision afforded to Indians was to vanish or merge with the superior race and civilization, but not to persist as tribes. The *New York Tribune* editor Horace Greeley proclaimed in an 1860 essay entitled "Lo! The Poor Indian," that Native Americans belonged to "the very lowest and rudest ages of human existence." Therefore, "these people must die out—there is no help for them. God has given the earth to those who will subdue and cultivate it, and it is vain to struggle against his righteous decree." Many White Americans, particularly those living in direct contact with Native people in the West, favored hastening this supposedly natural decline in the interests of their own security and profits. As the Indian agent B. C. Whiting observed in California, the settlers' "first and perhaps most popular plan... is to wage indiscriminate war upon all the dark races, including the Indians, and wipe them out of existence as speedily as possible, and then attempt to justify it upon the exploded doctrine that 'might makes right.'" Yet even self-identifying enlightened Americans, who favored civilizing and Christianizing Indians rather than destroying them, expected that this transformation would lead to the Natives' absorption by White society, thereby eliminating their tribal territories, polities, and cultures. "They must seek to change entirely their customs and habits," insisted the missionary Stephen R. Riggs in 1846. "If they would continue to exist all, it must be as individuals and not as a nation." According to this view, Indians, unlike Whites, had no right to chart their own futures. The only way for them to avoid the supposedly natural fate of extinction to which so many Whites consigned them was to abandon their distinctiveness and try to become White culturally, politically, and, through intermarriage and the production of children with Whites, even physically. Such was the guiding principle of the Indian Department well into the twentieth century. The national benefit for the United States was that the entire Indian domain would be thrown open to the market.[14]

Two images of Manifest Destiny. Top: Fanny Palmer, *Across the Continent*, 1868. Bottom: George Gast, *American Progress*, 1873.

In Palmer's painting, Indians are cut off from the progress of civilization by the train tracks and enveloped by exhaust as a locomotive speeds past them. In *American Progress*, the forces of White civilization, led by the angelic Columbia (school book and telegraph wire in hand), inexorably overtake Indians and the bison in retreat.

Though the department charged its officers with advancing this assimilationist vision, many of them shared the popular view that the mission was futile because the intellect of Indians was "little above that of a dumb brute," and their character was marked by "apathy, brutality, fondness for activity without labor, ingrained perfidy, shameless mendacity, [and] mere animal existence." Such views allowed White officials, soldiers, and everyday ranchers and farmers to force Indians from their lands and reduce them to destitution while keeping a clear conscience. The reason skeptical members of the Indian Office cooperated with official policy was that the only conceivable alternative was extermination, which was "too monstrous to deserve a moment's consideration." After all, the international community and posterity would be watching.[15]

GENOCIDE

Unrestrained violence by Whites against Indians revealed the weakness of the U.S. commitment to assimilation, including, remarkably, in the Kansas portion of Federal Indian Territory, which was supposed to be a secure place for removed Indians to become civilized. Between 1854 and 1860, a mere twenty years after the federal government began forcing Indians from throughout the Midwest into Kansas, more than a hundred thousand Whites inundated the area, heedless of the Natives' claims. The partisan battle between these Whites over the future of slavery has dominated the historical memory of 1850s Kansas. Almost completely overlooked is that both sides favored dispossessing the Indians, driven by their shared sense of White supremacy, Indian-hating, and disdain for government attempts to protect Native people.[16]

White assaults on the Kansas Indians' property and lives were widespread and unrelenting. Armed settlers completely unsettled the Delawares, Shawnees, Miamis, and New York Indians (a mix of mostly Senecas, Oneidas, Brothertowns, and Stockbridges), poaching their timber, plundering their cattle and horses, and sometimes driving them at gunpoint from their own houses. When federal Indian agents protested, the trespassers set upon them, too, with deadly results in at least one case. A number of officers, seeing the futility of trying to swim against the tide, decided instead to go with the flow by cooperating in the fleecing of Indians under their protection. Nearby U.S. troops did nothing to halt the bedlam until President Franklin Pierce finally ordered them to remove the intruders, and even then "to go very slow." They went so slow that by 1860 the New York Indian Reserve contained

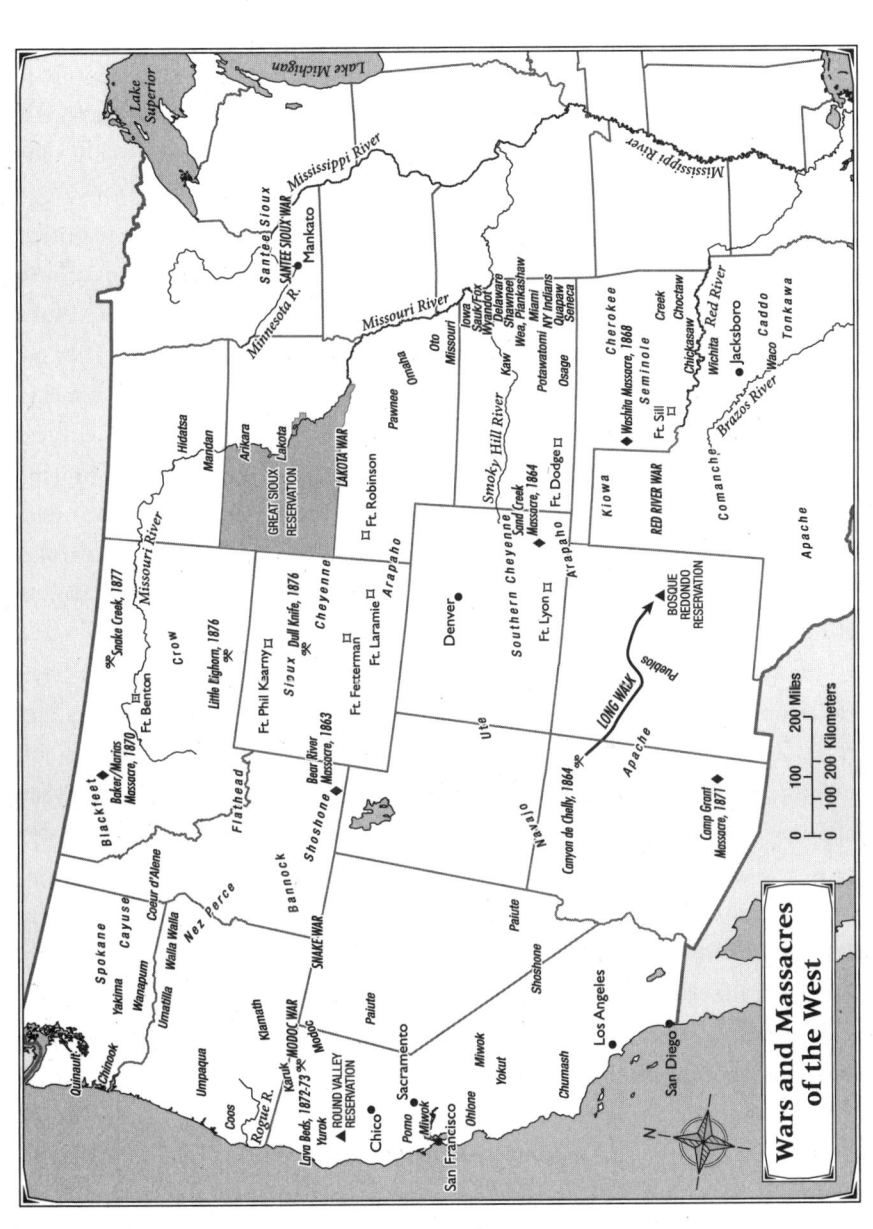

2,202 White squatters compared to just 50 Indians. The only solution offered by Indian commissioner J. W. Denver was for the Indians to redouble their striving toward civility, even though they already boasted farms, livestock, churches, schools, and mills. His rationale was that if their reservations remained communal property with surplus land, "it will be impossible, when surrounded by a dense white population, to protect them from constant disturbance, intrusion, and spoliation by those on whom the obligations of law and justice rest but lightly."[17]

Lightly, indeed. Kansas Whites did not lack a sense of law and justice in general, but rather refused to extend it to Indians. They saw civilized society as an exclusive compact that kept Whites from unfairly abusing one another, but granted them liberty to exploit supposed racial others. Indians, regardless of whether they had submitted themselves to U.S. authority and become Christian and civilized, including having adopted private property, rested outside that understanding by virtue of race. As one agent put it, Indians in Kansas were "surrounded in most cases by white settlers who too often act upon the principle that an Indian has no rights that a white man is bound to respect... [The Indians'] stock are stolen, their fences broken down, their timber destroyed, their young men plied with whiskey, their women debauched," leaving them "discouraged beyond endurance."[18]

One source of discouragement was that Indians in Kansas retained a "vivid recollection of the reassurances made to them at the time of their removal, that their present locations should be their permanent homes, and that the white race should never interfere with them or their possessions." Like so many times before, the White definition of "never" turned out to be pliable. The inaugural address of Kansas governor R. J. Walker in 1857 anticipated the "extinguishment" of all Indian reservations in the territory, and two years later the First District Court ruled that there were no laws to stop Whites from stealing timber from Indian reserves. Ultimately, White harassment drove almost all the Indians in Kansas to Oklahoma, leaving, by 1875, only a handful of Kaws, Kickapoos, Sauks and Foxes, and Potawatomis. Bleeding Kansas had bled the place White.[19]

White supremacist violence against Indians also reigned just south of Indian Territory in Texas, morphing into an outright genocide that lasted for decades and spread across the West. In effect, this campaign consisted of two phases. The first involved White settlers forcibly displacing a diverse array of farming Indians from the river valleys in the east. This Native population included small bands of Cherokees, Delawares, Shawnees, Creeks, and Chickasaws who had moved into Texas after earlier stops in Arkansas and Indian Territory. Local tribes included the

Pisehedwin, a Potawatomi, and others in front of his Kansas farm home, unknown photographer, 1877. Courtesy of the National Archives and Records Administration.

A farmstead of the sort that Whites drove scores of Indians from in 1850s Kansas. Courtesy of National Archives.

Wichitas, Caddos, and Apaches. Though these groups were well-armed by virtue of their participation in the fur trade, and, in the case of the Eastern bands, federal annuities, ultimately they had to retreat in the face of the White population's overwhelming numbers. The second, longer-lasting phase took place on the Texas Plains and pit Whites against horse-mounted Comanches and Kiowas, whose plundering of livestock and raids against encroaching settlements drove Whites into a murderous rage. White Texans easily outnumbered these equestrian groups, too, but the Natives' exquisite horsemanship and related ability to strike quickly and retreat made them formidable enemies. Formidable, that is, until White Texans were through killing every one of them they could.

White Texans made genocide against Indians their goal from the start. As early as the 1820s, when White newcomers to Texas still lived under the rule of Mexico, ranger companies organized by Stephen Austin undertook what they called "Indian hunting" expeditions against the Tonkawas and Wacos of the Brazos River, the Karankawas of the Gulf Coast, and the Wichitas of the Red River. The Whites killed and burned indiscriminately and went "chasing squaws," which meant capturing women and girls to rape and hold as sex slaves. Indian survivors retreated farther up the rivers or deeper into Mexico. This period also witnessed fifteen years of mutual raids between White Texans and the various removed Indians from the East that ultimately pushed those Natives north into the Oklahoma portion of Federal Indian Territory.[20]

During Texas's independence, from 1836 to 1845, after which it finally joined the United States, the Lone Star Republic continued to follow an explicit policy of "exterminating" all Indians within its borders. President Mirabeau Lamar declared in his inaugural address that Texas would wage "an exterminating war upon their warriors, which will admit of no compromise and have no termination except in their total extinction." This "exterminating war" involved paramilitaries searching the countryside for vulnerable Indian villages, annihilating or enslaving the inhabitants, seizing the horses, and putting everything else to the torch. Native deaths, particularly among the farming tribes, ran into the thousands. Despite some humanitarian opposition from Texas founding father Sam Houston, Lamar spoke for the majority of Whites when he proclaimed that "the proper policy to be pursued toward the barbarian race is absolute expulsion from the country," because Whites and Indians "cannot dwell in harmony together. Nature forbids it!" Following Comanche and Kiowa counterstrikes in 1840 in which they destroyed the coastal town of Linnville and rustled some two thousand mules and horses, the *Austin City Gazette* joined the call for "a war of extermination," echoing Texas secretary of war Branch T. Archer's reasoning "that humanity to them [Indians] would be cruelty to ourselves."[21]

Texas newspapers contributed mightily to the devaluation of Indian life that justified such violence. The U.S. Indian agent Robert S. Neighbors denounced local publishers for agitating the public with graphic accounts of Indian depredations that were not only exaggerated, but also oftentimes entirely fictional. Examples abounded, most glaringly in the aptly named *White Man* newspaper published out of Jacksboro by John Baylor, a rancher, former ranger, and up-and-coming politician. The ulterior motive of this propaganda, Neighbors perceived, was to heighten pressure for the government to fund ranger companies often under the command of the men who had circulated these falsehoods in the first place. Propagandists knew that if they could secure salaries and weapons for local men and gain personal reputations as Indian fighters, it might lead to military promotions and elected office, as was the case for Baylor himself.[22]

The federal government eventually joined in this genocide. During the 1840s, Washington, D.C., contributed pay and supplied equipment to Texas ranger units in lieu of the army's presence, even though the paramilitaries' exploits were public knowledge. When federal troops finally arrived on the scene, including a whopping 3,294 soldiers in 1853, they employed the same indiscriminate tactics. The government's sole, half-hearted alternative was to commission two lightly guarded reservations on the upper Brazos in West Texas and hope for the best. The strategy backfired, however, because White Texans interpreted the reservations as license to clear Indians from the rest of the state, then turned their guns against the reservations as well. Baylor was at the forefront of this agitation, publishing a manifesto on behalf of his Jacksboro Rangers that "we regard the killing of Indians of whatever tribe to be morally right and that we will resist to the last extremity the infliction of any legal punishment on the perpetrators." "Whatever tribe" included the reservation Indians, most of them Caddos, Anadarkos, Wacos, and Tonkawas. The Jacksboro Rangers, claiming to act "in the name of mothers whose daughters have been violated by the 'reserve Indians' and robbed of that virtue that God alone can give," displayed their bravado by killing an eighty-year-old woman from the reservation, scalping her husband, and then fleeing after a shootout with the Indians and the arrival of federal troops. Afterward, these vigilantes had the gall to petition Congress for reimbursement of their expenses in the name of "frontier defense." As in so many previous times and places in America, White citizens of the frontier attacked governmental authority when it made even the slightest effort to protect Indians against White persecution. Shortly after Agent Neighbors returned to Texas from escorting the besieged reservation Indians out of the state, he was shot dead in the back by Baylor follower Edward Cornett, who despised Indians at least partly because his wife had run off with a Caddo man. Cornett did not just want Indians gone, he wanted anyone who advocated for them dead and gone, too.[23]

Concluding the obvious, that "Indians are no longer safe in either [lives or property] in Texas," authorities ordered all remaining Natives to move north into Federal Indian Territory and then declared any Indians still left to be hostile. It was now federal and state policy, as Elias Rector, the Southern superintendent of Indian affairs, phrased it, for Whites in Texas to hunt Indians "like wild animals." The Red River War of 1874–75, in which federal troops and state rangers squared off against Comanches, Cheyennes, Kiowas, Kiowa-Apaches, and Arapahos in the Panhandle region, is the best-known chapter in the struggle for control of Texas, but it was merely the conclusion of a decades-long genocide. When the starving, war-weary, and disease-ridden Indian survivors finally surrendered, Texas was indisputably a White man's country except for tiny, isolated Indian communities like that of the Alabama-Coushatta people of the Big Thicket, north of Houston. Countless bodies were left strewn along the way.[24]

The genocide of Indians in California and Oregon was even more ferocious. In these places, the rush of Whites chasing gold and cheap land was unparalleled. California's population of Whites (including small numbers of Mexicans, Chinese, and Chileans) spiked from some 14,000 in 1848 to 223,856 in 1852. Oregon attracted far fewer migrants, but by 1850 it boasted over 13,000 White Americans and by 1860 more than 60,000, which eclipsed the Native population. Furthermore, whereas these Whites were armed with long-range rifles, pistols, and other sophisticated weaponry, most of the local Indians had only bows, arrows, spears, and clubs, and, in the case of coastal bands, no horses. Indians also faced the disadvantage of simultaneously coping with epidemic and venereal diseases introduced by the newcomers, and malnutrition caused by the Whites' devastation of the ecosystem. Natives along the California coast and Central Valley had dealt with the Spanish and their associated ills since 1769, including Catholic missions where lethal diseases, forced labor, and sexual exploitation were rife. Yet the Spanish colonial presence had always been slight, never exceeding 3,500 people. Oregon Indians were even more isolated historically, engaging only periodically with shipboard merchants and sometimes with mountain men, but never with White settlers. This challenge was unprecedented and proved catastrophic.[25]

The White miners and ranchers who overran California had no use for Indians other than as servile labor and sex slaves. They were utterly indifferent to how their sluicing and use of mercury destroyed the streams that Indians relied on for fish, or how their grazing of livestock cut off Indians from their other staple of acorns and drove away wild game. For countless generations, these resources had contributed to California hosting arguably the largest and most linguistically diverse Indian population in North America, estimated at upward of three hundred thousand on the eve of colonization. Native people were so numerous despite their lack of horticulture because they had an intimate generational knowledge of what could be hunted, fished, and gathered, and when. Their religious ceremonies, they believed, sustained this richness. Now, Indians began to starve wherever White people and their cattle appeared, that is, unless they poached on the newcomers' herds, which invariably spurred White calls for extermination. With every passing year, Indians in growing parts of California faced the impossible choice between slowly starving to death or killing the livestock that infested their ancestral lands and risking massacre by Whites.[26]

White Californians hardly needed the excuse. During their journey west, they had consumed stories by word of mouth and print reporting that bloodthirsty

Indians lurked everywhere, just waiting for a chance to lift their scalps, which merely built on the devilish depictions of Indians that circulated in Eastern media. Never mind that, on average, only three overland travelers out of two thousand lost their lives to Indians, that White migrants killed more Indians than Indians did them, or, according to multiple authorities, that along the cross-country trails "the most atrocious cases of murder and rapine charged to the account of the Indians have in reality been committed by white men wearing the disguise of Indians." Whites arrived in California already convinced that the area's Indians were "about the lowest specimens of humanity upon the earth," as related by the minister Horace Bushnell. They scorned local Indians as "Diggers," in reference to their root gathering and in obvious allusion to the common White epithet for Blacks. They hardly ever referred to Native women as anything but "squaws." The point was to dehumanize Indigenous people in order to ease White consciences as they dispossessed, enslaved, sexually assaulted, and slaughtered them.[27]

Already by 1850 the Indian agent Adam Johnston, stationed in the Sacramento and San Joaquin Valleys, was sounding the alarm that White ruffians all across the California countryside would "shoot down Indians wherever they meet them," and, for that matter, go searching for Indians in the mountains when they could not find them in the valleys. The following year, a "border war"—really a human hunt by Whites against Indians—erupted throughout the gold mining country. As told by the Indian agent G. W. Barbour, it featured "reckless and vicious white men . . . traveling over the country in bands or parties, murdering and robbing those who happen to be so unfortunate as to fall into their power." In the Round Valley north of San Francisco, local Whites, led by the livestock manager H. L. Hall, went about "killing all the Indians they could find in the mountains." One source "heard Mr. Hall say that he did not want any man to go with him to hunt Indians, who would not kill all he could find, because a knit would make a louse." A participant in Hall's campaigns against the Yukis recounted matter-of-factly that "we would kill, on an average, fifty or sixty Indians on a trip . . . frequently we would have to turn out two or three times a week." Another estimated, "for every beef [cow] that has been killed by them ten or fifteen Indians have been killed." By the time Hall and his men were done, they had effectively "depopulated a country, which," an army officer judged, "but a short time since swarmed with Indians."[28]

White Indian-hunters took women and children as slaves when they did not kill them outright. The gold rush was barely a decade old before a federal agent noticed that the Round Valley Indians "have very few children—most of them doubtless

John Ross Browne, *Protecting the Settlers, Harper's New Monthly Magazine*, August 1861.

Whites did not hide their genocide of California Indians. They wrote and spoke about it openly and illustrated it in newspapers and magazines. This image depicts settlers massacring the Yukis at Round Valley.

having been stolen and sold." The *Humboldt Times* reported that child captives were selling publicly for between $50 and $250 each. The enslavement and scattering of Indian children practically guaranteed that these captives would grow up without learning their people's languages and customs or identifying with their tribes, never mind enjoying the comfort and protection of kith and kin. The same went for women and girls captured and sex-trafficked by self-proclaimed White "squaw men." The *Maysville Appeal* admitted in 1861, "It is notorious that there are parties in the Northern counties of this state whose sole occupation is to steal young children and squaws from the poor Diggers, who inhabit the mountains." The account continued that these kidnappers would sell their victims "at handsome prices to the settlers, who... willingly pay fifty or sixty dollars for a young Digger to cook and wait upon them, or a hundred dollars for a likely young girl." By one count, Whites forced some ten thousand California Indians, including between three and five thousand children, into servitude between 1850 and 1863. Other estimates double these numbers.[29]

As in Texas, the state government not only did little to combat this genocide, but also actively promoted it. California's first civilian governor, Peter Burnett, went so far as to declare in his inaugural address "that a war of extermination will continue to be waged... until the Indian race becomes extinct." In September 1859, Governor John B. Weller hired Walter Jarboe to captain a volunteer militia force charged with forcing the Yukis onto a reservation or killing them if they resisted, not despite but because of Jarboe's well-earned reputation as a murderous Indian-hater. Jarboe's men subsequently committed nine widely reported massacres against Indians, including twenty-five Indians killed in late September, twenty in October, thirty on December 9, and another thirty on December 13. "However cruel it may be," Jarboe explained to Weller, "nothing short of extermination will suffice to rid the Country of them [the Yukis]." Neither the governor nor the legislature did anything to stop him, but instead voted funds and arms for the slaughter.[30]

The same went for the federal government, which partially reimbursed California for its military spending in full awareness of the atrocities it was perpetrating. Simultaneous efforts to establish Indian reservations under federal protection went nowhere. Though U.S. commissioners negotiated eighteen treaties that would have set aside approximately 7 percent of California as federal Indian reservation lands, in 1852 the U.S. Senate refused to ratify. California senator and future governor Weller had lobbied successfully for that outcome by contending that "the fate of the Indian is irrevocably sealed ... Humanity may forbid, but the *interest* of the white man demands their extinction." Yet, in the face of criticism from the Eastern public and President Millard Fillmore, the federal Congress eventually authorized five tiny military reservations to offer the Indians some measure of sanctuary. The experiment failed miserably. The legal status of these places was so ambiguous that army officers judged they had "no right to ... exclude the Whites from entering and occupying the reserves, or even prevent their taking from them Indians, squaws and children." In 1862, Whites went so far as to kill forty-five Wailacki Indians who were on their way to the Round Valley reservation. Their justification was that "that they had done so to prevent [the Wailackis] from stealing their cattle." California Natives were still at the mercy of the state's White populace, which had none.[31]

Local Whites reveled in the racial dominance that this genocide represented. The *Yreka Mountain Herald*, published in the northern gold-mining region, called for the deaths of every last Modoc, Shasta, Karuk, Hupa, Chimariko, Wintu, and Nomlaki within range. "Extermination is no longer even a question of time," it declared in 1853; "the time has already arrived, the work has been commenced, and let the first white man who says treaty or peace be regarded as a traitor and coward." Five years later, the White residents of Humboldt County, on the northern coast, put their money where their mouths were by approving a local tax "to prosecute the Indian war to extermination." The sentiment was so widespread that in 1861 the *San Francisco Bulletin* featured a local man "who boasted of having killed 60 infants with his own hatchet at the different slaughter grounds." Indians no longer posed any conceivable threat in 1865, but the *Chico Weekly Courant* was still demanding "nothing but extermination" on the grounds that Natives were "of no benefit to themselves or mankind ...

If necessary, let there be a crusade, and every man that can carry and shoot a gun[,] turn out and hunt the red devils to their holes and bury them, leaving not a root or branch of them remaining."[32]

This rooting out extended beyond human hunts and enslavement. The *Daily Alta California* wrote in 1853 that Whites in the northern part of the state were so incensed by Indian cattle raids that they were "ready to knife them, shoot them, or inoculate [infect] them with smallpox—all of which have been done," as additional sources confirmed. There are also multiple documented cases of White settlers trying to finish off already starving Indians by leaving out sugar and meat laced with strychnine, a poison typically used for killing wolves. In Los Angeles and other well-established communities from the Spanish era, White American newcomers systematically reduced former mission Indians to bondage. The law permitted Whites to purchase any Indian who had been sentenced to jail for debt, loitering, or criminal behavior, all liberally defined. To take advantage, Whites openly enticed Indians to drink, then set the law on them. This pattern, too, made Indian family and community life difficult and even impossible. It also produced random abuse and murder. White masters of Indian servants and slaves, according to the *Sacramento Union*, "use them as they please[,] beat them with clubs, and shoot them down like dogs, and no one to say, 'Why do you do so?'" Indians were in constant peril of Whites blaming them for other people's crimes, as in 1863 in Chico, where settlers hanged five Indians on the baseless charge of stealing horses. When two White children turned up murdered following this execution, the locals seized upon two other Indians, whom "they tied two up to a tree, and shot and scalped them [with] no proof against them whatever," according to a federal agent. As had been the case in the East during the colonial era, there was no accountability because it was impossible to convince a White court or jury to hold White people responsible for any crimes they committed against Indians. State law would not even permit Indian eyewitness testimony against Whites. "The only wonder is that any [Indians] remain," mused one agent in 1872.[33]

The scale of this killing and exploitation extended, certainly, from the White people's massive advantage in population and technology and the profits to be gained from California's mines and grazing lands. Yet it was also profoundly shaped by a White American culture that for generations had conditioned its people to dehumanize Indians as bloodthirsty savages and bestialize them as wolves while simultaneously upholding White people as God's agents of progress. Such thinking assured Whites that they were superior, civilized, and in the right even as they murdered, raped, scalped, enslaved, and plundered Indians with abandon, and doubly so when White authority figures lent their support. There is no other way to explain the multiple accounts of Whites who literally shot down Indians for sport, as in the case of a settler near Clear Lake, who sicced his dogs on two elderly Indians, killing a woman, and said that he did it merely "for fun," because, after all, "they were only Diggers."[34]

Genocidal principles like these, often cloaked in the lofty rhetoric of Manifest Destiny, contributed to White Americans' killings of somewhere between 9,492 and 16,094 California Indians from 1846 to 1873, according to the careful calculations of the historian Benjamin Madley. Yet the toll Whites took on the Indian population was far greater than even these sobering numbers indicate. Indian displacement and enslavement at White hands led to malnutrition, psychic stress, beatings, and venereal diseases, which, in turn, left Indians even more vulnerable to epidemics like smallpox than they would have been otherwise. Consequently, California's overall Indian population plunged from some 150,000 to just 30,000 between 1846 and 1870. Some groups disappeared altogether. Others barely hung on, like the Yukis, whose numbers fell 90 percent to just a few hundred people. White contemporaries were able to characterize this tragedy as progress only by convincing themselves that they were chosen and the Indians were damned.[35]

Charles Christian Nahl, *A Road Scene in California*, 1856.
Courtesy of Science History Images/Alamy.

A White guard drives forward a band of Indians, including women and children, to either a reservation or slavery, while gold miners flood into their land.

California Indians did not see it that way, damning Whites for their brutality rather than accepting extinction as their own fate. When Luther E. Sleigh toured the Indian villages around San Diego in 1873, Native people at every stop protested White Americans' heartless exploitation of them, adding "that they [Indians] ought to be allowed to remain where their forefathers have lived for long." Hundreds of miles to the north, a Modoc from the California-Oregon border shared a similar lament, that though "we have lived here in peace, we cannot get along with the white people. They come along and kill my people for nothing. Not only my men, but they kill our wives and children. They will hunt us like we hunt the deer and antelope." No wonder, then, that as early as 1851 the federal agent O. M. Wozencraft concluded that Indians throughout California had "little confidence in the white man. Their intercourse has been well calculated to make them skeptical as to his goodness and fidelity. I find it very difficult to remove or correct this impression of theirs; they are slow to believe any good is intended them." How right they were.[36]

The genocidal mayhem of Oregon and Washington Territories was barely distinguishable from that of California. Whites settled wherever they wanted, regardless of the Indian presence, a presumption shaped by the Oregon Donation Act, which granted every White adult in the territory 320 acres for free after four years of residence and cultivation. Federal officials tried to head off conflict by negotiating nineteen treaties that would have relocated all the territory's Indians to reservations east of the mountains, but the Indians refused to move. They explained that "their fathers had lived and were buried in this country; that it was their native land, and that they wished to be buried by the graves of their ancestors." White settlers did not want them to possess any land at all. Fighting began almost immediately following an influx of miners to the Rogue River Valley of southern Oregon, just north of the California border in the territory of the Shasta, Coquille, Tutuni, Taltushtuntude, and Dakubetede peoples. As in California, Oregon miners beat, raped, and murdered these Indians wantonly. When a miner was found murdered in Jacksonville in 1853, presumed by Whites to have occurred at Native hands, genocidal rage came pouring forth. A meeting of local citizens passed a resolution to pursue "the Extermination of the Indian race," then publicly hanged an Indian boy of perhaps ten years old, "not," according to a local lawyer, "for any alleged crime, but for the purpose of exterminating the Indian race." Self-named squads of "Squaw Hunters" and "Exterminators" fanned out through the river valleys and thickly forested hills to kill any and all Indians on sight.[37]

Stretching on for two years, this was a war in which Whites were the aggressors and showed themselves "to be as barbarous and cruel as the Indians," according to the Indian commissioner George Manypenny. Oregon's federal Indian agent warned his superiors in 1854 that there were "reckless and evil-disposed whites roaming through the country," seeking "to carry out their favorite scheme of annihilating those Indians. These miscreants, regardless of age or sex, assail and slaughter these poor, weak, and defenseless Indians with impunity, as there are no means in the hands of the agents to prevent those outrages, or bring the perpetrators to justice." The outrages of these squads included killing twenty-three Chetco Indians and torching their village when the Natives refused to cease operating a river ferry that cut into the business of a White rival. The ringleader was arrested but subsequently released, demonstrating once again, in the words of Oregon's superintendent of Indians, Joel Palmer, that "no act of a white man against an Indian, however atrocious, can be followed by a conviction." No wonder that the chief of the Coquille Indians threatened "that he meant to kill all the white men he could; that he was determined to drive the white men out of his country." The only alternative was abject submission and even extermination.[38]

When a gold strike on the upper Columbia River brought a cascade of Whites and the usual attendant abuses into Washington Territory, the Indians there fought back, too, starting with the Yakamas, then extending to the Cayuses, Walla Wallas, Palouses, Coeur d'Alenes, Spokanes, and Umatillas, in what both sides came to see as race war. White civilian troops, whom one missionary described as "without discipline, order, and similar to madmen," attacked Indians at random on the assumption that they plotted a general uprising. It became a self-fulfilling prophecy. As Joel Palmer understood things, "the avowed determination of the [White] people to exterminate the Indian race, regardless as to whether they were innocent or guilty... has had a powerful influence in inducing these tribes to join the warlike bands" because they took it "as evidence of the necessity for all to unite in war against us." Like Native people across the continent over the previous two hundred years, Indians in the Pacific Northwest were coming to see themselves as sharing a common cause and identity by virtue of their collective exploitation by self-identified Whites. The Indians in arms finally moved onto reservations after Colonel George Wright marched six hundred troops to the Spokane River in August 1858, killed about a hundred warriors, and then hanged another sixteen as an example. Nevertheless, the successes of the Native coalition during the war and the government's willingness to feed them rather than continue to fight them "tended," according to their agent, "to produce the impression in their minds that they have the ability to contend successfully against the entire white race."[39]

Any such impression had worn off on the vastly outnumbered Modocs of the Oregon-California border region by 1873, yet they continued to fight rather than concede to White authority. Since the 1850s, White militias had subjected the Modocs to relentless murders, sexual violence, and plundering, which, combined with epidemic disease, reduced their population from between 1,000 and 2,000 people to just 250. Reluctantly, most of them had relocated to the Klamath Reservation in the hopes of escaping this violence and receiving something to eat, but by 1871 the degradation and starvation there led a band of them to return to their homeland along the Lost River. The cavalry's brute attempt to force the Modocs to return instead chased them into a nearly impenetrable series of lava beds near Tule Lake. Desperate and determined, the Indians managed with just fifty or so fighters to hold out for five months against a White army that began with four hundred soldiers and eventually reached nearly a thousand.[40]

Repeated negotiations to end the standoff failed each time because the Americans' terms were unconditional White supremacy and Indian subordination. The Modocs' leader, Kientpoos (or Captain Jack), said that he was willing to surrender but wanted the "same law for white and Indian. Want Indian same as white man," including the right to "go to store, buy what I want." That is not what the government had come

William Simpson, *The Modoc Indians in the Lava Bed*, London Illustrated News, 1873. Wikimedia Commons.

to offer. The agent Elijah Steele lectured Kientpoos that, right or wrong, Whites simply would not tolerate the Modocs' presence outside the reservation, and whereas Whites were too numerous to control, the Modocs could be moved easily. He warned that "if you do not agree to this, you will stay here and be killed." The Americans also demanded the surrender of any Modocs who had killed White people. "Who will try them," wondered Kientpoos, "white men or Indians?" "White men, of course," answered Commissioner Alfred Meacham, to which Kientpoos followed up, "Then will you give up the men who killed the Indian women and children on Lost River, to be tried by the Modocs?" "No," replied an incredulous Meacham, "because the Modoc law is dead; the white man's law rules the country now." "Oh yes, I see," parried Kientpoos, as if setting up Meacham the whole time. "The white man's laws are good for the white man, but they are made so as to leave the Indian out."[41]

When the Modocs treacherously killed American peace commissioners as part of an ill-conceived plan to break the soldiers' will, instead they provoked White cries for their immediate annihilation. The *Daily Alta California* explained that "we regard the red men of California, Oregon, Nevada, and most of those of Arizona, as entirely irreclaimable, savage to the backbone, designed to misery, brutal savagism, and extermination." White forces did not go quite that far, but they came close. After driving the Modocs from the lava beds, soldiers hunted down the survivors and then imprisoned them at Fort Klamath in preparation for a mass hanging. They wound up disappointed. Before the executions took place, concerned Eastern citizens, especially the philanthropic Indian Aid Association of Philadelphia, a Quaker charity that raised donations for distribution to Native tribes, intervened and managed to get the number of killings reduced to four. Then officials sent the remaining 153 Modocs to confinement far away at Quapaw Agency in Oklahoma, where only fifty of them were still left by 1899. Even then, authorities would not allow them to return to Oregon until 1909. As for the men who were hanged, including Kientpoos, officials had their heads severed and shipped to the Army Medical Museum and then the Smithsonian Institution in Washington, D.C., to serve as symbols and scientific evidence of Indian inferiority, White supremacy, and the inevitable march of American progress.[42]

EXTERMINATION AS PACIFICATION

Whereas White citizen militias largely carried out the campaigns to exterminate Indians in Texas, California, and Oregon, the U.S. Army, albeit sometimes comprised of volunteer companies, was the impetus in most other parts of the West. Policy-wise, the military considered extermination as a means rather than a goal. The logic was that, except under rare circumstances, Indian warriors refused to face U.S. soldiers on the battlefield, but instead struck fast and then retreated to their home populations. Engaging them was especially difficult when they were on horseback, as was the case for the vast majority of Native people on the Plains and the Columbia Plateau. Yet the Indians' civilian camps were far more vulnerable, particularly in winter, when they sheltered in forested river bottoms below the frozen Plains. The point of these attacks was less to wipe out the Indians than force them to move onto reservations and stay there. The effect, however, was a region-wide pattern of U.S. troops massacring Indians. Combined with the devastation of epidemic disease and White Americans' decimation of the bison, the result was a catastrophic loss of Indian life. As Whites and Indians sought to make sense of it all, they both turned to race.

For Indians, there was no escape from White swarming. Between 1840 and 1860, some three hundred thousand Americans traveled overland to the Far West, including fifty-three thousand to Oregon, two hundred thousand to California, and forty-three thousand to Utah. Then the discovery of gold in the Colorado Rockies in 1858 promoted a rush of one hundred thousand to that region, soon to be followed by twenty thousand migrants to Idaho by 1862, and thirty thousand to Montana by 1864. The overwhelming majority of these voyagers were unattached men in youth and middle age, described by one commentator as a "shiftless, lazy, lousy, scurvy, profane, insane, and idiotic herd of rapscallions, nincompoops, and ninnies." New territorial governments followed in their wake, including Dakota, Colorado, and Nevada in 1861, Idaho and Arizona in 1863, and Montana in 1864. The Native American population simply could not compete with these masses. Consider the meager populations of even the most powerful tribes in the West: The Comanches stood at just some twenty thousand in the 1830s, and had dropped to no more than five thousand by 1870 and fifteen hundred by 1875. The Blackfeet plummeted from a height of as many as forty-five thousand in the early 1830s to as few as nine thousand in the 1850s, with far more losses to come. The Lakota population actually grew during most of this era, but even at its peak in the 1850s it stood at a mere twenty-five thousand. The Navajos claimed only fifteen thousand people in 1870. Most other tribes were but a fraction of these groups. Almost overnight, Indians had become a slim minority in their own country.[43]

Indigenous people would have been unable to withstand this tempest under the best of circumstances, never mind as they suffered catastrophic losses due to the epidemic diseases that accompanied Whites and their destruction of the Natives' livelihoods. As many as half of Plains Indians died in a smallpox epidemic in 1779–81. Smallpox struck again in 1801–2, nearly wiping out the farming Mandans, Hidatsas, and Arikaras of the Missouri River Valley. Smallpox again devastated the Comanches in 1816, the Sioux in 1819, the Pawnees in the early 1830s, and the Mandans in 1837, who were still struggling to recover from previous epidemics. By the time the 1837 outbreak subsided, there were only 138 Mandans left. Over the next three years, smallpox once again decimated the Assiniboines, Blackfeet, Arikaras, Crows, and Pawnees, sweeping away sometimes a quarter and as much as two thirds of the people. This tragic pattern only grew worse with the opening of the Oregon Trail and the traffic of settlers to the gold fields of California and the Rockies. The relentless attack of strange plagues left Indians just a skeleton of what they had been within recent memory.[44]

The Natives knew White people were to blame, even if they were unsure how. The Kiowas told a story about how their cultural hero, Saynday, once saw a man dressed all in black and riding a black horse approaching from the east. This stranger's face was cratered with scars. He introduced himself as "Smallpox" and announced, "I am one with the white men—they are my people as the Kiowas are yours. Sometimes I travel ahead of them, and sometimes I lurk behind. But I am always their companion and you will find me in their camps and in their houses." Other Indians told more or less the same story. "You cannot remove the impression from among them but that the diseases—cholera, smallpox, and measles—were first introduced among them by the whites passing through their country," wrote the agent Alfred J. Vaughan from among the Arikaras, Mandans, and Hidatsas, and of course they were right. One Arikara man, crazed with mourning after losing his entire family to smallpox, killed a White fur trader in revenge after a Pawnee told him "the disease was brought in the country by the whites on purpose to destroy the Indians." The Nez Perce of Idaho imagined that the barrage of disease was punishment from the spirits for the people's adoption of White ways. They observed that Indians who held true to their customs "are more healthy and stout than those who work their farms and live in houses. They will all die off if they continue to live as the whites." Meanwhile, Whites, like the missionary Gustavus Hines of Oregon, continued the long tradition of interpreting such Indian die-offs as "the hand of Providence ... removing them to give place to a people more worthy of this beautiful and fertile country." No wonder Indians suspected that Whites infected them with disease deliberately.[45]

Hostilities were already building to a pitch when the Civil War suddenly altered the playing field by withdrawing federal troops back to the east of the

Mississippi River even as unruly White migrants continued to spread throughout the West. Arizona and New Mexico quickly degenerated into a cycle of murderous raids between White adventurers and ranchers, on the one hand, and Apaches and Navajos, on the other. Both sides lost untold numbers of cattle, horses, mules, and sheep to plunderers, thousands of people to captivity and enslavement, and many more dead. In June 1861, the Apache resistance, according to Thomas Cruse of the Sixth U.S. Cavalry, was drawing inspiration from the teachings of an unidentified "medicine man who said that he could bring back the spirits of their forefathers if the whites would only get out of the country." White popular opinion, for its part, was "[in] favor of an utter extermination of the ruthless savages," as captured in an 1864 editorial of the *Arizona Miner* calling on the people "to exterminate nearly if not the whole race of savages . . . and the sooner this is accomplished the better for the whole country."[46]

Federal troops took this policy halfway. Between 1862 and 1864, U.S. brigadier general James Carleton launched what he called a "war of extermination" against the Apaches and Navajos that included capturing the Mimbreño Apache leader, Mangas Coloradas, under a flag of truce, killing him while in custody, then severing his head, boiling it, and shipping it to scientists in New York. Apaches retaliated in kind with brutal raids that drove most of the miners out of the Mimbres Mountains in southwestern New Mexico. Meanwhile, Brigadier General Kit Carson led volunteers in a scorched-earth campaign against the Navajos that managed to win their surrender after his breach of their stronghold of Canyon de Chelly reduced them to starvation. The U.S. terms led to the notorious Long Walk. In fifty-three separate marches, the army drove more than eight thousand Navajos and several hundred Mescalero Apaches three-hundred-plus miles from the beauty and richness of their ancestral territory eastward to the arid, featureless, insect-infested reservation of Bosque Redondo, on the Pecos River. The number who died along the way is unknown. Navajos remember Bosque Redondo as *Hwéeldi*, the place of suffering. The government confined them there for four years, forcing them to raise crops in the sand and drink putrid water before finally permitting them to return home, chastened. General Carleton's explanation for this cruelty was that Indians needed to learn that "it was their destiny, as it had been that of their brethren, tribe after tribe, away back toward the setting sun, to give way to the inevitable progress of our race."[47]

More than thirteen hundred miles away, back east toward the rising sun, the Santee Sioux of the Minnesota River Valley were resisting that supposed destiny. In 1837 they had ceded enormous portions of their territory to the United States in

Navajo Indian captives under guard, Fort Sumner, New Mexico, ca. 1864–68. Photograph by the United States Army Signal Corps. Courtesy of the Palace of the Governors Photo Archives [NMHM/DCA], 028534.

exchange for an ever-shrinking reservation and unkept promises of annuities. All the while, tens of thousands of White migrants teemed into Minnesota, forcing the Santees to absorb still more losses. A small portion of the tribe responded by experimenting with civilized reforms and Christianity, but most of the rest derided them as "farmer Indians" and "cut-hairs" and, according to their agent W. J. Cullen, threatened "the entire annihilation of all who assumed the white man's customs and garments." The Santees' mood was already combustible when their corrupt agent dismissed their pleas to relieve their starvation by telling them to "eat grass." Their response was war.[48]

The Santee chief Big Eagle gave numerous explanations for this decision, all of them bristling with resentment over the White people's cultural and racial chauvinism. One was that "the whites were always trying to make the Indians give up their life and live like white men—go to farming, work hard and do as they did—and the Indians did not know how to do that, and did not want to anyway. It seemed too sudden to make such a change. If the Indians tried to make the whites live like them, the whites would have resisted, and it was the same with many Indians." Worse still, the Santees had become hotly divided between "a white man's party," favoring compliance with the Americans' demands, "and an Indian party," which rejected capitulation. In day-to-day interactions, "many of the whites seemed to say by their manner when they saw an Indian, 'I am much better than you,' and the Indians did not like this." Furthermore, "some of the white men abused the Indian women in a certain way and disgraced them, and surely there was no excuse for that." Given this background, when the Santees took up arms, the call rang out, "Kill the whites and kill all these cut-hairs who will not join us."⁴⁹

White Minnesotans answered with their own racial fury as reports streamed in of the Santees' nailing White children to fences and trees, raping women, and mutilating the dead in the course of killing more than six hundred White civilians and dozens of soldiers and creating forty thousand terrified refugees. Newspaper after newspaper called for A WAR OF EXTERMINATION AGAINST THE SIOUX SAVAGE, with the *Manketo Independent* demanding, "Minnesota must be either be a Christian land or a savage hunting ground . . . the two races can never live peacefully and prosperously together again." Governor Alexander Ramsey likewise proclaimed that the Santees "must be exterminated," and General John Pope pledged "utterly to exterminate the Sioux if I have the power to do so . . . they are to be treated as maniacs or wild beasts."⁵⁰

These champions of genocide very nearly got their wish. Following the Santees' bloody defeat, White crowds assaulted Indian prisoners of war as the military marched them to internment camps, then lurked outside the gates threatening to overrun the guards and put all the Natives to the knife. Authorities feared an outright revolt if troops had to fire on White civilians to keep order. It took the condemnation of 303 Santees to death after a series of show trials (most lasting only a minute or two) to quiet the bloodlust of the mob. The *St. Croix Monitor* celebrated the news of the prisoners' sentences by writing, "Panthers and rattlesnakes are in the same manner a law unto themselves, but who for this reason will spare them? The Indian's refusal to be civilized, forces upon us the hard alternative of exterminating him."⁵¹

President Abraham Lincoln, under pressure from Christian lobbyists to show mercy, ruled that the proceedings against the Santees had been unfair, and therefore extended clemency to all but thirty-nine of them, but this reprieve did not stop what was still the largest mass execution in United States history. Afterward, grave robbers scooped up the remains, just as they had done with the Santee war dead, to sell to collectors and scientists. William Mayo, founder of the Mayo Clinic, acquired the body of Marpiya Okinajin (He Who Stands in the Clouds, or Cut-Nose), which he dissected in front of an audience before displaying the shellacked bones in his office. The skeleton of Little Crow, one of the Santees' most prominent leaders, went on display in the Minnesota Historical Society and remained there until 1919 as a representation of the triumph of White civilization over savagery.⁵²

The hangings were not enough to satisfy the people of St. Paul, who demanded the removal of all the remaining Sioux bands, Santee or otherwise, even though only the Santees had taken up arms. "The Indian's nature can no more be trusted than

Execution of the Thirty-Eight Sioux Indians at Manketo, Minnesota, December 26, 1862, 1883.

the wolf's," they wrote. "Tame him, cultivate him, strive to Christianize him as you will, and the sight of blood will in an instant call out the savage, wolfish, devilish instincts of the race." On this point, the government was willing to comply in full. It removed the innocent Wokpoeton and Sisseton Sioux to miserable reservations in North and South Dakota. As for the surviving Santees, authorities restricted them to Crow Creek, South Dakota, where at one point starvation and disease were killing three to four people a day until there were only five hundred of the original thirteen hundred people left.[53]

Barely a year after the Santees' executions, in southern Idaho, a volunteer unit in the U.S. Army perpetrated what historians believe to have been the nation's largest ever massacre of Indians. For a decade, the equestrian Shoshones, Bannocks, and Northern Paiutes of the mountainous Utah-Idaho-Wyoming border region had violently defended their homeland from overland migrants and encroachment by Mormon settlements around the Great Salt Lake, but Whites saw their actions as little more than bloodthirsty savagery. Overall, the Indians' attacks claimed as many as four hundred victims during this period, including twenty in the 1854 Ward Party Massacre, and twenty-two in the 1862 Utter Massacre. The army's efforts to subdue these raiders only made things worse, for when Major Edward McGarry marched out to revenge the Utter Massacre, his forces killed twenty-four Indian men (unidentified by tribe) who probably had been uninvolved. Afterward, Native people warned that if Americans were going to hold Indians collectively responsible for violence against Whites, then "the Indians would combine and drive the white men from the country." They waited too long. In the bitter cold of January 1863, Colonel Patrick Connor, at the head of the Third California Volunteers, marched against the winter village of Shoshone chief Bear Hunter along the banks of the Bear River. Descending from three sides on the unsuspecting camp, the soldiers killed approximately three hundred people over two hours, including some ninety women and children, a portion of whom died trying to escape through the river's freezing waters. By all accounts, the American forces put wounded prisoners to the sword and raped female captives one after another before slaying them, too.[54]

As in Colorado after Sand Creek, local Whites roared in approval, particularly given that this slaughter contributed to the Indians surrendering to reservations. In the years that followed, settlers continued to organize "Indian hunting" expeditions funded by scalp bounties to keep the Natives restricted to those zones and punish them for ongoing plundering of White livestock and homesteads. After one of these crews killed sixteen Boise Shoshones in 1866, the *Idaho Statesman* declared, "We long to see this vile race exterminated."[55]

This vile sentiment had been echoing for decades throughout White society in the vast American West, building on centuries of precedent from the United States' Eastern core. These were not empty words or unfulfilled wishes. They routinely galvanized a wide range of White Americans, including vigilantes, rangers, U.S. army volunteers, regular U.S. troops, U.S. generals, and state and federal policymakers to hunt down and kill Indians of all ages and sexes, rape and enslave women and children, and destroy the survivors' means to sustain themselves outside of reservations. Carrying out this strategy required an ideology that simultaneously dehumanized Indians as *savages, barbarians, wolves, nits, lice, diggers, redskins, red niggers, red devils, squaws,* and *rattlesnakes*, while elevating Whites as carriers of civilization, Christianity, and progress. In other words, Whites designed this racial ideology to justify murderous conquest. Indians responded in kind with their own horrific violence and racial ideologies that cast White people as evil and called on Indigenous people to make common cause as Indians. However repugnant many of the Natives' own actions might have been, they were overwhelmingly defensive in nature. After all, the West was suffering an invasion of self-proclaimed White people that not only put the Indian way of life at risk, but also threatened to wipe out Indians entirely. And it was far from over.

UNCIVIL WAR

Indians factored into United States racial history during this era not only in the context of the genocidal war for the West, but the struggle over slavery's future that was at the heart of the Civil War. By mid-century, slaveholding planters among the Cherokees, Choctaws, Creeks, and Chickasaws, removed by the United States from the East to Federal Indian Territory, were reasserting their will in the public affairs of their tribes. As they had back East, Indian planters used their control of tribal government to pass laws that forbade slaves to own property, established slave patrols, prohibited slaves from carrying weapons or accessing literacy education, and banished manumitted Blacks from tribal territory. They took advantage of their tribes' communal traditions, which allowed families to use as much land as they wanted, to engross territory for slave-based cotton production and cattle ranching. Furthermore, they continued their efforts to "civilize" their people with compulsory public schooling and advanced educational academies. Though slaveholders were still a minority, they were well on their way toward refashioning their tribes on the model of the White cotton South. Yet they faced stiff resistance. Traditionalists among the Cherokees responded by forming the Keetoowah Society to promote the people's ancestral language and cultural principles, discourage Indian-White race mixing, campaign against slavery, and politically outmaneuver the grandees. Among the Seminoles, an antislavery faction operated a north-to-south underground railroad of sorts that spirited Blacks away from bondage in Indian Territory to freedom in Mexico. From a close-up view, these Native societies were as divided over slavery as White America.[56]

The strain of the Civil War split these rifts wide open. All the so-called Five Civilized Tribes signed treaties of alliance with the Confederacy out of defensive considerations, as they were surrounded by Southern states, and it was in their own interest to protect "property in negro slaves," as the Cherokees put it. Thousands of their men went on to serve in the Confederate ranks. Yet while the Choctaws and Chickasaws remained mostly united behind the Southern cause, the Cherokees, Creeks, and Seminoles degenerated into their own civil strife. Roughly three thousand Unionists from each of those tribes, in addition to numerous Black Seminoles, fled north into Kansas to escape abuse at the hands of their Confederate kin. Their fighting men joined the blue-coated Kansas Indian Home Guard, and their political leaders denounced their people's respective treaties with the South and pledged to end slavery as soon as peace was restored. In the meantime, the hostile factions raided each other mercilessly, as well as participated alongside White forces in a series of major battles in Indian Territory. By the time the smoke cleared, the country was in ruins. During the war, the Cherokee population plunged from twenty-one thousand to fifteen thousand people, seven thousand people were homeless, a third of married women were widowed and a quarter of children orphaned, and some three hundred thousand head of cattle had been looted. The number of Seminoles declined by a third. Like much of the South, large portions of Indian Territory and innumerable lives were destroyed.[57]

In the aftermath, the federal government imposed a peace settlement on the Five Civilized Tribes that was far more ambitious and punitive than the terms placed on the White South. Not only did it require the abolition of slavery, but also, in the cases of the Cherokees, Creeks, and Seminoles, it effectively forced the Indians to grant Black freedmen full tribal citizenship, including the right to vote, *and land*—forty acres to each freedman, albeit without a mule. Seminole leaders protested that this settlement "is presented to us so suddenly that it shocks the lesson we have learned for long years from the white man as to the negro's inferiority." The Chickasaws and Choctaws retained the right not to incorporate the freedmen and instead have the United States remove them somewhere else, but when the Chickasaws exercised this option, the federal government refused to fulfill its part of the bargain. Peace also came at the cost of tribes' ceding millions of acres of territory that the United States had formerly pledged to them forever, largely to make room for the removal of other tribes from throughout the West, and for railroad rights of way. Many Northern Republicans fantasized about imposing parallel measures on the Confederate states, but the vision went unrealized because the White South, even in the wake of its failed rebellion, retained more power and respect in the United States than any Indian tribes. Indeed, the Reconstruction measures in Indian country represented more than just the reshaping of a defeated slave society. They telegraphed Washington, D.C.'s authoritarianism for Indians throughout the country—that is, once it managed to force them onto reservations.[58]

RESERVATION OR EXTERMINATION

Though the Union victory in the Civil War ended Black slavery and dramatically expanded Black citizenship, it reinvigorated the policy of confining Indians to reservations under threat of extermination and the underlying conjoined ideologies of White supremacy and Indian inferiority. White Republicans in the North who controlled the government, particularly the party's wing of evangelicals, saw an opportunity to reinvent the nation along the uniform principles of Christianity, private enterprise, personal striving, public education, and racial uplift (as they understood it) of Blacks and Indians. Their view was that the barbarity perpetrated by the Southern White "Slave Power" had been broken, and soon so would the barbarity of Indian life. White southerners, Black freedmen, and Indians all needed to be reformed—"reconstructed"—at their enlightened direction and then integrated into the nation to rise or fall as individuals according to their abilities. The race of an individual would not matter in this context because everyone would be culturally homogenous and protected under the law. Black freedmen hoped this program would enable them to acquire the skills and government protection they needed to survive and even thrive in American society. Their aspiration was to enjoy all of the rights and responsibilities of their fellow White Americans. For Native people, though, to live this way would amount to defeat. Assimilation represented not equality or opportunity, but foreign rule. Unfortunately, White authorities were uninterested in whether the Natives approved or not. In fact, they did not see Indigenous people in their supposedly savage state as capable of judging what was best for themselves. Indians were to do as Whites told them, or Whites would eradicate them.

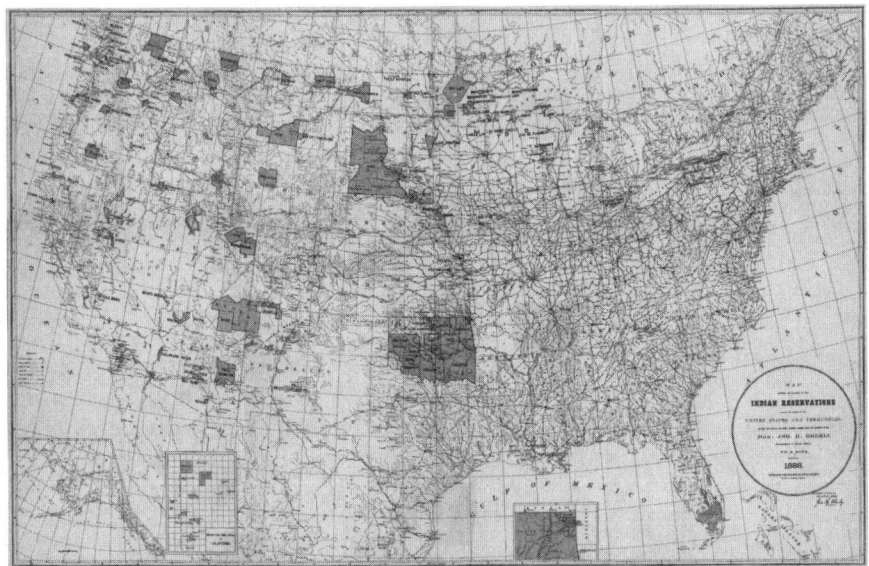

Paul Thomas Brodie and Hiram Price, *Map Showing Indian Reservations Within the Limits of the United States*, 1883. Courtesy of the Library of Congress Geography and Map Division.

The reservation system, to which the nation committed itself in full after the war, was a half step between the Indians' extermination and full integration. It was plain to see that allowing Indian-White relations to take their course would just result in back-and-forth depredations and, ultimately, the Indians' destruction at White hands. Indians in the grip of American expansion could not even feed themselves without raiding White-owned livestock. The bison was already in steep decline before the Civil War due to a combination of Indian overhunting and habitat loss related to White settlement. In the fifteen years after the war, Whites purposefully hunted the species to near extinction to profit from its skins, eliminate the risk bison herds posed to railroad traffic, and, not least of all, starve Indians onto the reservations. U.S. general Philip Sheridan thought White bison hunters deserved medals of honor for having done more "to settle the vexed Indian question than the entire regular army has done in the last thirty years." By "settle," he meant confining Indians to reservations where their dependence on the government for food and protection would make them passive and pliable. Then White agents could teach them how to become individualized farmers and tradesmen. As the Sioux agent Thomas J. Galbraith put it in 1863, the goal of the reservation system was, "in short, make white men of them, and have them adopt the habits and customs of white men." Following this transition, Indians would enter the mainstream of American society as citizens, whereupon tribal identity would no longer represent membership in a polity with a homeland and distinct culture, but just ethnicity. Indians as tribes would disappear even as Indians as individuals would survive—that is, if they rose to the challenges of civilized life.[59]

The rough political consensus in favor of reservations masked that White science and society continued to debate whether Indians were even capable of making this

Frederic Remington, *Twilight of the Indian*, 1897, from *Drawings by Frederic Remington* (New York: R. H. Russell, 1897).

A drawing that captures the goals of U.S. assimilation policy as well as tensions surrounding it, as evident in the cabin and teepee standing side by side.

change. Phrenologists determined from the size and shape of Indian skulls that Indians were "untamable" (which was to say, incapable of becoming civilized) and fated to extinction. For instance, Josiah C. Nott and George R. Gliddon wrote in their *Types of Mankind* (1854) "that it is clear as the sun and noon-day that in a few generations more the last of these Red men will be numbered and dead." Yet, by the last quarter of the nineteenth century, practitioners of the new field of ethnology, such as Lewis Henry Morgan, John Wesley Powell, and Alice Fletcher, were arguing that Indians did indeed have the capacity to advance through the proposed stages of human evolution and reach some measure of civility. The questions were how long it would take and how thorough the transformation would be. The influence of ethnological theory on policy is impossible to determine, but clearly it had some effect. One can see its influence on Secretary of the Interior Orville H. Browning's contention that the Indian "cannot immediately be transformed from the hunter to the farmer or mechanic . . . He should be gradually won from the chase to a pastoral life, and under its influences he will ultimately acquire a taste for agricultural pursuits. The first step in the process of improvement is to localize the Indians." Browning represented a well-to-do element of White American society that liked to imagine itself as more enlightened, humane, and cultivated than the ignorant bigots who exterminated Indians throughout the West. After all, they believed in the Indians' aptitude for change and worked to make it happen. Yet such progressives also held firmly to a vision of White supremacy in which they claimed the right to demand Indians to adhere to the White way of life, or else.[60]

Native people generally shared White Americans' sense of impending doom for them, but overwhelmingly attributed the blame to White people rather than to some abstract Manifest Destiny or Indian inferiority. Lewis Downing, a Cherokee chief and Baptist minister, lamented in 1870, "Today, the Cherokees, and the whole Indian race are in distress and danger. Powerless we lie in the hands of the United States [that] can bring the might of forty millions of people, and untold wealth, power, and skill to crush us in our weakness . . . The vortex of ruin, which has swallowed hundreds of Indian nations, now yawns for us." In Washington Territory, a Tulalip Indian known to Whites as Napoleon presented American authorities with a bundle of sticks representing the number of his people killed by Whites over the course of the year. Then he criticized that "nothing has been done by the government to punish the wicked white men who killed my people . . . the whites now scare all the Indians, and we look now wondering when all the Indians will be killed." The Crow medicine woman Pretty Shield recalled that when she was growing up on the Plains, "nobody believed, even then, that the white man could kill all the buffalo," even as this tragedy was unfolding before their very eyes. When they finally awakened to the species' imminent extinction, the Crows rationalized that it was because "the buffalo will not return to the same place again where he may have scented the white man." Decades later, as an elder living on the reservation, Pretty Shield perceived the awful truth of what had happened. She resisted the urge to "let myself hate the white man, because I knew that this would only make things worse for me. But he changed everything for us . . ." Sitting Bull, the famed Lakota warrior and religious seeker, reportedly said that there was "not a true Indian but who hated a white man . . . They regard us as a body of false and cruel invaders of their country."[61]

Native people commonly opposed reservations not only because they despised White values and White people, but also because they shared the historic Nativist view that the Great Spirit had created "Indians" or "red people" separate from "Whites" to follow a distinct way of life. The most vocal proponent of this view was the Oglala Lakota chief Red Cloud, who told White agents, and even the president himself, that "the white man can work if he wants to, but the Great Spirit did not make us to work." "My face is red; yours is white," he declared on another occasion. "The Great Spirit has made you to read and write, but not me." The same message echoed throughout the Native American West, with many Indians scoffing that the notion of becoming farmers "is wholly absurd and impossible of realization." Some Indian spokesmen went to far as to claim "that to adopt the habits of the whites will be certain to cause their annihilation as a people." Others simply rejected the White way of life as repulsive. The Apache Gianatah observed that White people were full of work and worry. "Now, we call that slavery. You are slaves from the time you begin to talk until you die, but we are free as the air . . . we will not be slaves." Sitting Bull agreed that the White way life was "slavery," adding, "I would rather die an Indian than live a white man."[62]

Despite such English-language accounts of Indians denouncing "Whites," not all or even most Indians in the West referred to the Americans as White people in their own languages. The Crows called them *mastacheeda*, "yellow eyes"; the Lakotas *wasicun*, "long knives"; the Cheyennes *veho*, "spider" (connoting trickery); the Kiowas *bedalpago*, "hairy mouths"; the Comanches *huuyɨkkwi?*, "lumberman" (referring to log cabins); the Nez Perce *soyápo*, "crowned ones" (referring to hats); and the Shoshones, Paiutes, and Bannocks *taivo*, "sun men/easterners." The Arapahos were rare in calling them *nihanatayeche*, "white skinned." Yet such terminology hardly matters when it comes to determining whether Indians thought in terms of race. They all agreed that the Great Spirit had made Native people fundamentally different from these "yellow eyes" and "hairy mouths," and that they should remain that way.[63]

In the early 1870s, a Wanapum Indian prophet named Smohalla, like Neolin and Tenskwatawa of earlier times, drew on these principles to articulate a Nativist vision that attracted thousands of followers in his Columbia River Valley homeland and beyond. He taught, according to reports, "that a new god is coming to [the Indians'] rescue; that all the Indians who have died heretofore, and who shall die hereafter, are to be resurrected, that as they will then be very numerous and powerful, they will be able to conquer the whites, recover their lands, and live as free and unrestrained as their fathers lived in olden times. Their model of a man is an Indian. They aspire to be Indians and nothing else." Smohalla contended that being a true Indian meant a rejection of precisely those things that White authorities advocated for Indian survival. "No one has any respect for these book Indians," he explained. "My young men shall never work. Men who work cannot dream and wisdom comes to us in dreams." Smohalla believed that Indians were meant for "natural work" like hunting, fishing, and gathering that did not desecrate the environment. "We simply take the gifts that are freely offered," he preached. "We no more harm the earth than would an infant's fingers harm its mother's breast. But the white man tears up large tracts of land, runs deep ditches, cuts down forests, and changes the whole face of the earth. You know very well this is not right . . . But the white men are so greedy they do not consider these things." Smohalla insisted that he was no militant, at least when questioned by Whites, claiming that he did not call on Indians to take up arms but rather to adhere to prayer, ritual, and reform. Changing the world rested with the Great Spirit alone, who, at his own discretion, would drive away all the people who had not obeyed his laws, leaving only true followers. But Smohalla's adherents were more forthcoming about the prophet's teaching that Whites and any Indians who followed their directives "are not to be included in the benefits of the resurrection, but are to be turned over with all that the white man's civilization has put upon the present surface of the land." In an era in which Indians were losing everything they valued, this vision offered some promise for the future, a future free of White people. It would not be the last of its kind.[64]

A minority of Indians conceded that their way of life was at an end and that moving to reservations and following the "White man's road" might be the best way forward, but they maintained that this arrangement would require as many concessions from White people as from them. Klamath chiefs in California told

Chief Smohalla, Called the Prophet of Columbia River, with His Priests Inside Wood Lodge, from James Mooney, *The Ghost-Dance Religion and the Sioux Outbreak of 1890: Fourteenth Annual Report of the Bureau of Ethnology to the Secretary of the Smithsonian Institution, 1892–93, Part 2* (Washington, D.C.: Government Printing Office, 1896).

their agents that Indians saw no point in laboring on the reservation like Whites if Whites were just going to steal everything they produced or accumulated. Likewise, if American authorities were going to prohibit Indians on reservations from defending themselves against Whites, then they had to own the responsibility. The Seneca Ely S. Parker, the military secretary to General Ulysses S. Grant, agreed, writing that nothing would go further to persuade Indians to surrender to reservations and their reforms "than the realization of the benefits of an impartial dispensation of justice among themselves and between them and the whites." What that meant, General George R. Crook gathered after twenty-five years of conversations with Indians across the West, was that "the government needed to protect [the Indian] in life and property. Keep white thieves from plundering him, let him see that peace means progress, that he has a market for every pound of beef and every hide and every sack of grain." Government also had to fulfill its pledge to provide Indians with food, clothing, and shelter until they adjusted to the reservation setting. "If you want us to be like the whites," a council of Grand Ronde Indians in Oregon put it plainly in 1871, "give us what we need." Few Indians trusted Whites to do these things as long as they treated Native people "like dogs and rats" and openly advocated for their slaughter.[65]

"TO SAVE THEMSELVES FROM EXTERMINATION"

The military phase of the U.S. effort to subdue the Western Indians continued well into the 1870s and, in the Southwest, into the 1880s, filled with White calls and campaigns for the Natives' destruction. Between 1866 and 1872, in what is sometimes remembered as the "Snake War," U.S. Army troops and volunteer forces pursued the Shoshones, Paiutes, and Bannocks throughout the border region of California, Oregon, Nevada, Utah, and Idaho, killing hundreds in an effort to get them to "beg for peace." When the Natives finally surrendered, they found themselves at the mercy of Whites, who, one agent admitted, "favor their extermination" and for whom "a suspicion against an Indian is tantamount to his death warrant."[66]

U.S. cavalrymen also terrorized the Cheyennes and Lakotas throughout the winter of 1876–77, punctuated by a strike on November 25, 1876, against the camp of chiefs Dull Knife and Little Wolf in the Bighorn Mountains of Wyoming. The troops killed forty Cheyennes on the spot, then abandoned the survivors without supplies to brave temperatures that plummeted to thirty degrees below zero. Eleven babies froze to death. The next spring, the famed Lakota warrior Crazy Horse led most of the remaining holdouts into the agencies of the Great Sioux Reservation, where they relinquished twelve thousand horses and guns, pledged themselves to peace, and hoped without evidence that, finally, the killing would stop and the people would have something to eat. Sitting Bull and his followers, who had fled north to Canada rather than suffer this fate, grudgingly followed five years later under pressure from red-coated Mounties and the pangs of empty bellies.[67]

Even Indians at peace with the Americans were at risk. On January 23, 1870, in Montana, U.S. forces under Major Eugene M. Baker attacked a camp of Piikani Blackfeet Indians led by the cooperative chief Heavy Runner, instead of the original target, the village of Mountain Chief. In short order, they mowed down 173 people, slaughtered 500 horses, and fed the people's tepees and food stores to the flames. Then Baker's men rode away, abandoning the 140 survivors, many of them in the throes of smallpox, in subzero weather. "Oh, how cruel, how terribly cruel are the white men," one of the women was heard to wail. The following year, far to the south in Arizona, a combined force of White Americans, Mexicans, and Tohono O'odham Indians fell upon unsuspecting Pinal and Aravaipa Apaches on the U.S. reservation of Camp Grant, killing 150, as punishment for raids of murder and plunder that were almost certainly attributable to other bands. It took six months of pressure before federal authorities finally brought charges against the ringleaders, and then just nineteen minutes for a local jury to find them innocent. The people of nearby Grant County, New Mexico, responded to this massacre by resolving, like their counterparts in Arizona, that they would recover stock plundered by the Apaches by whatever means necessary, "even if it be at the sacrifice of every man, woman, and child in the tribe." The same went for the army. It spent the winter of 1872–73 hunting down every group of independent Apaches it could find, killing some two hundred people. Official military publications rationalized that the Apaches were "bloodthirsty, cruel, cowardly, treacherous, incapable of gratitude or any other generous emotion," and possessed of "all the ferocity of the most savage wild beast." When Geronimo led the last Apache breakout from the reservation system in 1885, Arizona counties offered civilian rangers scalp bounties that ran from $250 to $500 each, or $8,126 to $16,252 in today's money, in what might have been the last public rewards of their kind after more than two hundred years of the practice.[68]

Native people, impelled by their own racial ideologies, fought back with every resource they could muster, but to no avail. Plains Indians held numerous intertribal councils to discuss whether to "confederate for defense against the white people," as inside sources reported. The grand alliance never materialized, but, on the northern Plains, the allied Sioux, Northern Cheyennes, and Arapahos won far more victories over U.S. forces than their meager populations and resources should have permitted, most famously in their annihilation of 226 troops of General Custer's Seventh Cavalry at the Little Bighorn on June 25–26, 1876. Even Indians who kept the peace praised the Sioux "as fighting for the rights of the whole red race, and to save themselves from extermination." On the southern Plains, Comanches, Kiowas, and Southern Cheyennes banded together against the U.S. cavalry and Texas rangers, culminating in the Red River War. But most groups were out to save themselves first, which sometimes meant assisting the Americans in the conquest of other tribes. As the Crow chief Plenty Coups explained, his people made this hard choice "not because we loved the white man, who was already crowding other tribes into our country, or because we hated the Sioux, Cheyenne, and Arapaho, but because we plainly saw that this course was the only one which might save our beautiful country for us."[69]

In 1877, the Nez Perce under Chief Joseph attempted to find a third way by making a run for the Canadian border. Inspired by Smohalla's teachings, Chief Joseph's followers resisted moving onto the reservation and living like "White men Indians." "I do not believe that the Great Spirit Chief gave one kind of men the right to tell another kind of men what they must do," Chief Joseph explained to the "great white chiefs." When the United States gave the final order for the remaining Nez Perce to comply or else, a group of their young men responded by killing four White settlers, followed by a battle with U.S. cavalry and local militia that augured a wider war. In a desperate attempt to escape, eight hundred Nez Perce fled over the towering Bitterroot Mountains to the Montana Plains in the hopes of either linking up with the Sioux or crossing into Canada, land of the "Great White Mother" (Queen Victoria). U.S. soldiers in pursuit would not grant them those options, killing eighty-nine, mostly noncombatants, on August 9, 1877, along the Big Hole River, then capturing the rest on September 30 on Snake Creek, less than forty miles short of the border. Later, Chief Joseph said his people could have escaped "if we had left our wounded, old women, and children behind. We were unwilling to do this. We had never heard of a wounded Indian recovering while in the hands of white men." The United States sent the survivors, like the Modocs, to Federal Indian Territory to waste away until 1885, when they finally received permission to return home.[70]

This genocidal conduct by the United States Army, volunteer forces, and White citizens was open knowledge and, in some circles, at least, a source of shame. General George R. Crook, who fought against Indians in multiple theaters, shared in published remarks that the hardest part of his job was "to be forced to kill the Indians when they are clearly in the right . . . when these Indians see their wives and children starving and their last source of supplies cut off, they go to war. And then we are sent out there to kill them." The public did not need to take Crook's word for it. This era saw a procession of Indian leaders from defeated tribes make East Coast speaking tours under the sponsorship of Christian humanitarians in which they confronted White Americans with their avarice, cruelty, and hypocrisy, but also their responsibility to protect and sustain subjugated Native people. Among them was none other than Chief Joseph. Two years after his surrender, he spoke to an audience at Lincoln Hall in Washington, D.C., in which he remarked, "Some of you people think an Indian is like a wild animal. I think this is a great mistake . . . I believe much trouble and blood would be saved if we opened our hearts more . . . Whenever the white man treats the Indian as they treat each other, then we will have no more wars."[71]

He would never see the day, in no small part because of the designs of men like the former abolitionist and self-proclaimed Friend of the Indian Wendell Phillips. In June 1871, when the U.S. extermination campaign was as its height, Phillips shared the stage at Boston's Tremont Temple with the chiefs Little Raven of the Arapahos, Stone Calf of the Cheyennes, and Buffalo Good of the Wichitas, who were there to make the same plea as Chief Joseph years later. Phillips agreed with his Indian counterparts that the United States offended God and man alike in its decimation of Indigenous people, but he did not share their immediate goals of convincing Whites to grant them autonomy, self-governance, and justice as *they* understood it. No, that would just re-create the same bloody results they were protesting. But how could they know better? Phillips patronized the chiefs to their faces (knowing they probably understood little English) as "rude tenants of the forest, men with few ideas, scanty traditions, [and] rude arts." By contrast, Phillips considered men of his kind to possess the kind of sophisticated grasp of the world that could solve the vexing "Indian problem." Preaching to the converted, he waxed:

> Ladies and gentlemen ... the extremes of the earth meet on this platform tonight. Here we are the fruit of two or three thousand years of civilization. All that art and letters and religion could do for us we have inherited. We harness the steam; we send the lightning on errands; we subjugate nature. More than that, we have learned the omnipotence, the absolute omnipotence of order. We know what patient, persevering effort, generation after generation, marrying the ages together, can accomplish. We are educated by a thousand years into the consciousness of the sacredness of law. These are very great powers.

Then he shared the profound answer to the Indian problem to which these great powers would be put: to "make the law"—by which he meant, U.S. law—"as potent on the prairies as it is in State Street" in Boston.[72]

Phillips did not specify *who* would carry the law to the West and how, perhaps because his audience already agreed that refined and enlightened White Christians like themselves should direct Indian policy and the reservations. In fact, they had recently prevailed on President Ulysses S. Grant and Congress to appoint humanitarian churchmen rather than political hacks to Indian agencies and oversight boards, and to let them open schools and churches on the reservations. The White House euphemistically called this program its "Peace Policy." For the first time in U.S. history, Christian reformers from the Northeast's White middle and upper classes had a realistic chance to seize control of Indian affairs from frontier roughnecks and military officers. Even though the main goals of the U.S. wars against Indians had been to seize their land and crush their resistance, now there was an additional purpose. The philanthropic class of U.S. society would cordon off the Indians from the worst sort of White people and instruct them how to live and think. Only when

Indians made significant progress on this front, which the reformers presumed would take only a generation or two, would the government release them from their confinement.[73]

Phillips also skipped another critical detail, probably the one of greatest concern to the Indians onstage, which was what would happen if they did not comply. After all, Native people still viewed life as individualized American citizens, even with equality under the law, not as a gift but as colonial conquest. It would have been out of tenor with the occasion for Phillips to admit that, when it came to this matter, the people of Boston and Denver had more in common than they liked to admit. The fact was that they shared a commitment to White supremacy, Indian subordination, and even the Indians' elimination, though they differed on how to define the latter goal. White Friends of the Indian wanted to eradicate Indian tribes as political and cultural entities not through mass murder but through forced civility, in the interest of preserving Indians as individual citizens. What also went unsaid among denunciations of the military by Phillips and his reform-minded colleagues was that their agenda also relied on the Indians' violent suppression, for precious few Indians would submit to it voluntarily.

Thus, in 1871, the same Congress that legislated for the Peace Policy also voted to end the practice of the government of conducting diplomacy with Indians through treaties, in recognition of their status as sovereign nations. Henceforth, it would make policy for them unilaterally. The principle at work, as expressed by General Sherman, was that, henceforth, "all Indians must be made to know that when the government commands, they must obey, and until that state of mind is reached, through persuasion or fear, we cannot hope for peace." Put more bluntly, Indians could either get with the program or risk slaughter at White hands, as had been the operative logic of U.S. Indian policy for decades. Indians who survived the killing and the reform would be left to wonder whether this was more of a Devil's bargain than God's will.[74]

CHAPTER 6

"A Race of Tenants"

The United States designed its reservation policy not just to prevent hostilities between Indians and White settlers, but to teach Indians how to live like their conquerors so they could join American society. Yet, as far as the Indians on the Southern Cheyenne and Arapaho reservation in western Oklahoma could tell, the only advantage this new system offered was a slow, miserable death rather than a quick, violent one. Malaria, measles, and dysentery struck the people in rapid succession, preying on victims already weakened by malnutrition and despair. White authorities demanded that the Natives farm, but the land was too arid to till and most of the people had no interest anyway. Some Indians engaged in cattle and horse ranching, which was more viable than agriculture on the southern Plains and compatible with their previous way of life, only to confront plundering raids by White outlaws. These marauders operated with near impunity, emboldened by the passive response of White authorities and Indians' inability to take matters into their own hands without risking another massacre. Meanwhile, shipments of food pledged by the federal government in exchange for peace were repeatedly late, scanty, and of poor quality. Even then, the agent used the people's dependence on these rations as leverage, such as attempting to bypass the people's chiefs and thereby diminish their power by distributing shares to each family directly. When Native parents refused to send their children to the reservation school, they got nothing to eat. One official judged that there was little chance of the Cheyennes rebelling unless they were "starved into it," but that was precisely what was happening. Reservation life at this stage meant little more than the people wasting away, diseased, starving, and depressed, until half of them had perished within the span of a year.[1]

A band of Northern Cheyennes, who had moved onto the reservation in 1877 after a brutal defeat by the U.S. Army, concluded after less than a year that they would rather take the chance of facing the bluecoats again than endure this torment any longer. Chiefs Dull Knife and Little Wolf led 350 of their followers in a "breakout" in hopes of returning to their homeland in the Powder River Valley of Wyoming and Montana, three hundred miles away. But they never made it there. After fending off pursuing troops and killing some forty White settlers along the way, the fugitives split into two bands. Dull Knife's group eventually surrendered at the Lakota agency of Fort Robinson, but refused to return to the Southern Cheyenne reservation voluntarily. To break their will, authorities imprisoned them for days in bone-chilling temperatures without food or water, only for them to escape once again. American soldiers shot down fifty of the runaways during their flight and dozens more in the dragnet that followed. Ultimately, the public backlash against this brutality led the federal government to permit the survivors (including Little Wolf's band, which surrendered a year later) to remain up North, but there were not many of them left. White authorities intended the carnage to serve as a warning to other Indians not to dare attempt their own dashes for freedom.[2]

Though White reformers, called Friends of the Indian, considered themselves enlightened humanitarians for attempting to civilize Indians and assimilate them into American society, their system of reservations and boarding schools relied on the ongoing threat of massacre and starvation. The assimilationists did not give Indians the option to say yes or no. The only choice they presented was "extermination or civilization," as Secretary of the Interior Carl Schurz put it. When Indians like the Northern Cheyennes tried to flee the reservations, White military forces hunted them down. If they stayed on the reservations but rejected White ways or withheld their children from schools, their agents cut off their rations to starve them into submission. When that tactic failed, reservation police rounded up the children and delivered them to the schools under guard. Once they were there, White authorities subjected the children to White supremacist cultural reprogramming reinforced by corporal punishment. Malnutrition, disease, and physical and sexual abuse were common in these places. The point of this mistreatment was to destroy Indians as groups.[3]

If we adopt the perspective of the Friends of the Indian, we lose sight that they shared a basic White supremacy with the violent racists who called for the Indians' annihilation. Both parties, after all, aimed to subjugate Native people to White authority, dispossess them of their land, and shatter their societies and cultures. Furthermore, even though assimilationists wanted to preserve and absorb detribalized individuals who had adopted White ways rather than killing them, their policies resulted in terrible losses of Indian life and the deprivation of those who survived. Indeed, no sooner were the reservations in operation than the Friends successfully lobbied for passage of the Dawes Act of 1887 and the Curtis Act of 1898 to divide and distribute reservation lands among Indians as private property tracts and sell the "surplus" to Whites. The result was a massive loss of Indian territory, in what the historian Angie Debo characterized as an "orgy of exploitation," and a corresponding spike in Indian poverty, homelessness, and death. The White campaign to corral, civilize, and atomize Indians, and in the process appropriate the rest of their lands, was nearly as destructive as earlier efforts to exterminate them, as was plain to anyone willing to see it or just to listen to the Indians themselves. This program was White supremacy under a different name.[4]

Often, the unintended effect was to promote Indian identity. Both the reservations and boarding schools turned the Natives' maintenance of heretofore taken-for-granted customs into acts of racial defiance and gave people from different tribes a common set of grievances as Indians against Whites. The boarding schools brought together children from diverse tribal backgrounds on the premise that they were all Indians, drowned them with the message that White civilization was superior to Indian savagery, and gave them a common language, English, and experience through which to bond. In later years, formally educated Indians would create national intertribal political organizations to advance their shared interests. In these ways and more, the assimilation era had the contradictory effects of simultaneously weakening and strengthening Indian identity and resistance to White dominance, and dispossessing Indians from their lands and cultures while inadvertently giving them tools to defend what remained.

"THE ORDEAL OF ACCLIMATION"

The fiction that reservations were about the assimilation of Indians and the reality that they were a brute expression of White supremacy and its degradation of Indians was on stark display in the poverty and despair that afflicted Native people across 102 reservations west of the Mississippi River. In 1875, the Arapaho agent accused his reservation contractor of "criminal neglect" for delivering "entirely inadequate" food and goods, and even then only irregularly, leaving the people "hungry and ill-humored." This dysfunction occurred not only in the critical first years of the reservations, when the system was still a work in progress, but also sometimes long afterward due to widespread corruption among Indian agents and their commercial contacts. The resulting malnutrition and even starvation was bad enough. Worse still were the diseases that afflicted the people in their weakened conditions. Influenza, measles, and whooping cough knifed through the Lakota reservations between 1888 and 1890, while at the same time the government announced a 20 to 25 percent cut in the peoples' beef ration. Starvation forced women in numerous reservation communities into prostitution, which produced such an alarming rise in venereal diseases like syphilis that one agent feared it would complete the work of extermination. Meanwhile, a great many men turned to the bottle in response to White authorities' prohibiting nearly everything that defined male achievement in Native societies, including hunting, warfare, diplomacy, long-distance trade, plural marriage, ceremony, and especially the protection of loved ones. The Blackfeet of Montana lost an estimated 25 percent of their people to alcohol-fueled fights and accidents and overdrinking between 1867 and 1873. The cumulative effect of disease, malnutrition, depression, and alcohol abuse and its associated violence and accidents led the Crow population to decline by 31 percent during the 1890s, with half of the dead under the age of twenty. At the Lakotas' Standing Rock Agency, the death rate during these years was fifty per one thousand people, almost three times higher than the national average of the United States. Reformers and policymakers might have intended the reservation as a protected site for Indians to learn a new way of life, but in practice it was a new place to suffer extermination from forces introduced by White America. As the Lakota holy man Black Elk described the nightmare, "our power is gone and we are dying."[5]

Incursions by neighboring Whites and the widespread indifference of White authorities left Indians to question if the point of the reservations in the first place had been to kill them off. By 1871, White hunters, cattlemen, and gold seekers had already overrun the Crow reservation in Montana, shooting down the Indians' horses to make room for their own cows and sheep. Likewise, the Southern Cheyennes' "fine herd of cattle" had completely "disappeared" by 1891, with most of it "taken by the whites," according to General Nelson Miles, and rest consumed by the Indians in their hunger. Feckless federal agents throughout the reservation system complained futilely that they lacked sufficient resources to do anything about this mayhem, though apathy was an equally important factor. The White plunderers, in turn, viewed the "neglect of the government to assist the supremacy of law . . . as a tacit approval of criminal acts," at least as far as one Osage agent could tell. Indians had a similar view. The brazenness of White horse thieves led the Southern Cheyennes and Arapahos to disparage White law as "a complete farce, an absolute nullity." Yet there was little they could do without risking a disproportionately violent White response, which drove home the disparity of White power and Indian degradation during the reservation era. "If any white community were preyed upon as these Indians," Captain J. M. Lee remarked "such community would take matters in its own hands and make short work of the miscreants."[6]

These outrages were more than just isolated crimes of opportunity. The perpetrators shared a view of themselves as belonging to a superior White race entitled to exploit an inferior, Indian one, which was so pathetic that it could not defend itself. They also believed that the government's job was to represent their interests no matter what the cost to Native people or the country's integrity. This ideology was so widespread that in 1869 and again in 1879 a network of dissolute Whites stretching across Kansas, Missouri, Arkansas, and Texas plotted to swarm Federal Indian Territory and seize the Natives' lands. Their rallying cry was "Settlers' Rights" and "Land for the Landless." President Rutherford B. Hayes made a rare show of force the second time around by calling out federal troops to block the invasion routes and issuing a proclamation denouncing the scheme. Yet there was no national will to offer armed protection to Indians everywhere they lived, whatever injustices they faced. Without it, attacks by White bandits and land sharks continued to plague reservations throughout the country.[7]

While the federal government ignored all but the most extreme abuses by Whites against Indians, it aggressively expanded its criminal jurisdiction over Natives on the reservations on the premise of instituting civilized rule. In 1878, Congress authorized the creation of Indian police forces, and five years later it created a system of reservation courts with Indian judges. Punishments for polygamy, bride price, shamanism, and ceremony included reduced rations, fines, and even hard labor, though sometimes it proved difficult to convince Indian officials to enforce the law. Yet the 1883 Supreme Court case of *Ex parte Crow Dog* revealed that the most significant protections of White justice did not extend to the reservations. The court's ruling overturned the conviction of a Brulé Lakota named Crow Dog for the murder of Spotted Tail, a corrupt, womanizing chief on the Rosebud Reservation, on the basis that the United States did not have the legal right to prosecute murder cases between Indians on reservation lands. Congress answered in 1885 with the

Major Crimes Act, which made U.S. law supreme on reservations in cases of Indian-Indian murder, manslaughter, rape, assault with an intent to kill, arson, burglary, and larceny. It was upheld in 1886 in *United States v. Kagama*. The Major Crimes Act was yet another expression of White Americans' determination to reduce Indians to complete submission while claiming to civilize them, even as lawless Whites ravaged the reservations with hardly any official reaction.[8]

Native people cited these conditions to charge that the reservation system was a White design to grind them into dust. Sitting Bull chastised White authorities, "I do not consider that they [Indians] should be treated like beasts ... It is your own doing that I am here. You sent me here, and advised me to live as you do, and it is not right for me to live in poverty." The Yankton Sioux chief Palaneapape (The Man Who Was Struck by the Ree) also accused Whites of treating his "starving" people as if they were animals, for "when we receive anything from the white man it is given as you would throw it to a hog." "Our grandfather [the president] at Washington," however, "promised that we should be raised up." The Crow medicine woman Pretty Shield, from her vantage as an elder in the early twentieth century, bitterly recalled how at the start of reservation life "the white men began to fence the plains so that we could not travel; and anyhow there was now little good in traveling, nothing to travel for. We began to stay in one place, and to grow lazy and sicker all the time." Black Elk attributed this misery to the Americans' program to "make us be like *Wasichus* [White people]," which, as far as he was concerned, meant turning boys into girls. "The *Wasichus* have put us in these squares," he continued, in reference to homesteads and farming plots. "We are prisoners of war while we are waiting here."[9]

Only rarely did Indians respond with violence, which speaks volumes about the White intimidation behind the reservation system. One isolated example took place among the Crows in 1887, when a charismatic warrior named Sword Bearer led a horse-stealing raid against the Piikani Blackfeet in defiance of the reservation agent, Henry E. Williamson. Sword Bearer's men flaunted their insubordination with a triumphant return, riding through the agency with celebratory gunfire, shooting up the buildings, threatening Williamson and his staff, and challenging nearby soldiers. Though no one was killed in this fray, U.S. officials feared it was the beginning of a general uprising, particularly when they learned that Sword Bearer had reached out to the Northern Cheyennes and even Sitting Bull for support. U.S. troops poured into the Crow reservation to snuff out this challenge, followed by a pitched battle that cost the lives of one U.S. soldier and as many as half a dozen Crows. Afterward, most of the rebels surrendered, and a Crow police officer shot an unsuspecting Sword

Clarence Grant Morledge, *Ration Day at the Commissary*, Pine Ridge Reservation, South Dakota, 1890. Courtesy of the Nebraska State Historical Society.

Bearer dead. Authorities then arrested and shipped off eight of the ringleaders to prison at Fort Snelling, Minnesota. In death, Sword Bearer became a Crow hero, but no one ever again followed his example of taking up arms against the United States. Maintaining White authority on the reservations depended on such overwhelming displays of force against any Indian resistance.[10]

Peaceful protest was also of limited value, as revealed by the famous legal case of the Ponca chief Standing Bear, which is otherwise known as a landmark in establishing Indian dignity in American jurisprudence. In 1879, Standing Bear fled his people's reservation in Indian Territory in a quest to bury his son back in the tribe's Nebraska homeland and escape the misery of confinement. Arrested and imprisoned after a six-hundred-mile journey, Standing Bear brought a habeas corpus suit in federal district court challenging the right of the government to restrict his movement. Obviously, it would have done Standing Bear no good to argue in a White courtroom that the Great Spirit had made his people separately from Whites in order to live in their own ways on their own land. Instead, he held out his hand to the judge and appealed, "That hand is not the color of yours, but if I prick it, the blood will flow, and I shall feel pain. The blood is the same color as yours. God made me, and I am a man." Duly moved, the court ruled that "an Indian is 'a person' within the meaning of the laws of the United States," and set Standing Bear and his people free to return to their ancestral territory if they wished. Yet, for all the outpouring of humanitarian sympathy surrounding this case, in the immediate term it did nothing to ease the oppression experienced by Indians on other reservations, including restrictions on their mobility. For every White evangelical reformer who viewed Standing Bear's case as an argument for U.S. society to extend basic liberties to Indians, there was another citizen sharing the bigotry expressed in a letter to the *New York Tribune*, which asked "what rights the Poncas or any other Indians have or are entitled to? What right have they to be in the country anyhow? They are nothing but barbarians . . . the land they occupy is unprofitable, and I for one cannot see why any white man who is a voter and desires the land should not make a claim to it, and if necessary, get help from the government to obtain it." Worse still, White Friends of the Indian who rallied around Standing Bear against such hate began to propose that the answer to the Indians' exploitation was to redouble the efforts to civilize them, eventually dispense with reservations altogether, and make Indians into U.S. citizens. Within short time, the reformers imagined, there would be no more tribal governments, and most Indians would disappear into the White American masses, culturally and even biologically.[11]

The strictures of the reservations required Native people to adopt subtle means to assert their cultural values and autonomy. Across the reservation system, the people ignored their agents and continued to live in extended-family villages instead of on individual farming plots. Tepees stood alongside frame houses, which themselves were decorated with pictographs invoking earlier, better times. Traditional-minded Crows and Nez Perces gravitated toward the Catholic Church because it had a much greater tolerance for customs like curing rituals, gambling, and long hair than the strict assimilationist Protestant denominations. Indians learned that they could perform their traditions in the open if they made them part of the celebration of White American holidays like the Fourth of July, Washington's birthday, and Christmas. At other times of the year, they just went about their business indoors. It was enough to make the agent of Lower Brulé Agency exclaim that "among the people of this tribe, communal interest in property, polygamy, heathen worship, and other barbarous customs prevails almost as generally as when they lived on the buffalo and had no home."[12]

Plains Indians also devised ways to invoke those halcyon days when they still lived off the buffalo. On one reservation after another, they prevailed on their agents to dole out beef rations "on the hoof," which meant releasing live animals from a corral so men on horseback could chase and kill the beasts like the bison of old. Their wives and children would then butcher the animals on the spot and perform the customary ritual of drinking some of the blood and consuming the liver raw. Agents considered this practice to be a "disgrace to our civilization" that served to "perpetuate in a savage breast all the cruel and wicked propensities of his nature," but feared that prohibiting it would rile the reservations. It took years of debate before Washington, D.C., finally ordered the distribution of packaged beef without exception.[13]

Even when Indians did take up domestic livestock, they did so in their own distinctive manner, not like Whites. The government provided Indians with cattle in the expectation that they would learn to treat the animals like investments, which was to say, with an eye toward increasing their numbers and quality for eventual sale. But Indians were just as likely to gamble away the beasts in ritual games of chance, present them to neighbors in ceremonial giveaways, or donate them to community feasts. It was all part of a widely held Indian value system that put a higher value on sociability and generosity to others than hoarding wealth, which Indians had come to associate with White people.[14]

Ironically, Indians made one of their most overt challenges to the reservations' civilizing agenda through the Wild West Shows, created by a White man, Buffalo Bill (William F.) Cody, for White audiences. Cody, a military veteran of the Plains Wars, brought the violent drama of this experience to the safety of the stage in cities and towns where White conquest was already a settled fact. Cody told a reassuring, if largely fictional, story that White "pioneers" were not the aggressors in the wars for the West. They fought valiantly only to defend themselves against savage Indians, who attacked for no apparent reason other than bloodlust. But barbarism could not arrest the divinely ordained spread of White American civilization. The pioneers had triumphed and now the United States stretched from sea to shining sea. To capture this epic as spectacularly as possible, Cody wanted real Indian performers, especially Indians who could handle a horse, rifle, and scalping knife. Starting with thirty-six Pawnees in 1883, Cody soon employed up to a hundred Natives, including Sitting Bull. The show was a smash, marked by an 1885 tour of forty North American cities that drew over a million people, annual runs in western European capitals, and headliner status at the 1893 World Columbian Exposition in Chicago. Cody's Indian hires not only earned between twenty-five and ninety dollars a month (the latter amounting to two thirds of the salary of a reservation agent) and got to travel to exotic places, but also enjoyed the opportunity to play cherished roles otherwise prohibited on the reservation, albeit as Indian imitations of White stereotypes of Indians.[15]

Buffalo Bill's Wild West and Congress of Rough Riders of the World: A Congress of American Indians [. . .], 1899. Courtesy of the Library of Congress Prints and Photographs Division.

White reformers hated how Cody's depiction of Indians as savages undermined their argument about the Indians' capacity for civilization and diverted actual Indians from the path of improvement. More infuriating still, Indians from the Wild West Shows sometimes returned home to tell their tribesmen that White society was not as impressive as the agents of progress had led them to believe. Sitting Bull's tales of the East included that "white men loved their whores more than their wives," half of the people had no respect for the president of the United States, and the "soul of a white man" was "odored with whiskey." The reformers' indignation was no match for the Wild West Shows' attractiveness to Indians, not least of all because of a basic principle articulated by a Sioux performer named Black Heart that the Indian should be able "to work at any place and earn money" just as "[the] white man got privilege to do." Apparently, Indians did require Whites to teach them to labor for their own benefit. All they needed was opportunity and evidence that White society would permit them to enjoy what they earned.[16]

KILL THE INDIAN, SAVE THE MAN

Pervasive Indian opposition to White domination strengthened a belief among reformers that the most effective way to transform Native people was to remove their children to boarding schools. There, at least, Whites could habituate the students to civilization without the interference of parents, kin, and community. The results would be lasting because Indians raised in the schools would not know any other way. Additionally, these institutions would teach them to despise their own heritage. As early as 1873, the majority of employees in the federal Indian Office were said to favor this approach to Indian assimilation. Short of outright violent extermination, it was the most despotic attempt White Americans would ever make to subordinate Native people, all in the name of humanity and progress.[17]

The White movement for boarding schools began, tellingly, with the incarceration of Indian prisoners of war. The United States followed its victories over the tribes of the southern Plains and Southwest by sending the most recalcitrant warriors to prison in Fort Marion, far away in the humid, coastal setting of St. Augustine, Florida. The captives included dozens of Cheyennes, Kiowas, Comanches, Arapahos, Caddos, and eventually hundreds of Chiricahua Apaches. The officer in charge, Richard H. Pratt, witnessing the prisoners' dispiritedness, conceived that their isolation under White authority was an ideal opportunity to teach them the English language and civilized habits while keeping them busy. To that end, he had the prisoners' hair cut short in the fashion of White people, dressed them in military uniforms, and for three years put them through a daily regimen of marching and rifle drills, academic classes, and work assignments. He also publicized the Indians' remarkable progress by inviting White tourists to witness their exercises and permitting the inmates to visit St. Augustine's downtown. Pratt the promoter sometimes won over Pratt the cultural purist. One of the ways he lured Whites to the spectacle of Fort Marion was by having the Indians exhibit traditional dances. These shows gave the performers a chance to learn one another's customs and then bring that knowledge home. Such exchanges were but a foreshadowing of the pan-Indian identity that would emerge from the boarding schools.[18]

There was so little White commitment to treating civilized Indians as equals that the only institution of higher education willing to enroll the Fort Marion students after their release was the segregated Black Hampton Agricultural and Industrial School in Virginia. Its leader, General Samuel Chapman Armstrong, an abolitionist and former missionary, thought that "both races need similar methods" because both of them were "a thousand years behind us [Whites] in moral and mental development." Pratt delivered seventeen Indians to Hampton in 1878 and forty-nine the next year. "Now I am a white man—I think," wrote one of the Kiowa students to Pratt on the eve of his matriculation. Hampton was but the first and most dedicated of a number of Black institutions, including Howard University in Washington, D.C.,

St. Augustine, Florida: Fort Marion and Indian prisoners, unknown photographer, 1875. Courtesy of Yale University Library.

and Lincoln Institute outside Philadelphia, to enroll Indian students in the late nineteenth century. Hampton continued to accept Indigenous students until 1923, when Congress finally pulled funding for the program in order to keep Indians, whom White authorities wanted to assimilate in order to appropriate their land, from Blacks, whom they wished to segregate in order to continue appropriating their labor.[19]

The Hampton experiment had barely begun before Pratt began lobbying for a strictly Indian school under his direction, partly because he worried that the Indians' affiliation with Blacks would diminish their accomplishments in the eyes of a bigoted White public. In 1879, his efforts gave birth to the Carlisle Industrial School in central Pennsylvania. Eventually, it enrolled as many as a thousand students in a given year, and during its history included children from every reservation agency in the country. It did not, however, accept Indians with Black ancestry from Eastern tribes, including a group of youths from the Shinnecocks of Long Island whom Pratt sent home just four days after their arrival at Carlisle because they exhibited, in his judgment, "too much of the Negro."[20]

Carlisle's express goals were to sever the students' ties to their home communities' languages, customs, beliefs, and rituals, and replace them with White people's ways in order to give them a fighting chance to succeed in mainstream American life. As Pratt decreed to an assembly of pupils, "We put aside Indian thoughts, and Indian ways, Indian dress and Indian speech. We DON'T want to hold onto anything INDIAN." The school's motto was "To civilize the Indian, place him in the midst of civilization; to keep him civilized, make him stay." Nowadays, the public associates Carlisle with another Pratt slogan, "Kill the Indian, save the man," which was a play on the genocidal maxim "The only good Indian is a dead one." Pratt meant that for individual Indians to have any hope of survival, they had to abandon their savage tribal ways and plunge headlong into the victorious culture of White progress. Pratt documented and publicized this transformation by commissioning photographs of the students in their traditional dress and hairstyles as soon they arrived at Carlisle, then another picture of them years later in civilized appearance, replete with front lighting and powder to lighten their complexions. He also took more than three hundred of his students to march in the 1892 Columbian quadricentennial parades in New York and Chicago carrying U.S. flags and banners that read INTO CIVILIZATION AND CITIZENSHIP.[21]

Convinced that Pratt was right, in 1883 Congress authorized four new off-reservation boarding schools: in Chilocco, Oklahoma; Genoa, Nebraska; Albuquerque, New Mexico; and Lawrence, Kansas. Twenty more would follow over the next two decades until, by 1900, these institutions boasted 17,708 students.

These "Before and After" photographs depict, from left to right, Wounded Yellow Robe (Sicangu Lakota / Rosebud Sioux), Henry Standing Bear (Oglala Lakota), and Chauncey Yellow Robe (Sicangu Lakota / Rosebud Sioux) in 1883, when they first entered Carlisle, and 1886, after three years of assimilationist conditioning. Courtesy of the Carlisle Indian School Digital Resource Center and the Cumberland County Historical Society.

Contrary to public memory, only a handful of these schools were church-run, unlike in Canada, which had its own boarding school system run primarily by religious orders. Beginning in 1896, Congress cut appropriations for church schools by 20 percent every year until 1900, when it eliminated funding entirely. The reason was not any aversion to Christianity, for Christian teachings permeated even federal schools. Rather, the point was to avoid the appearance of government favoring of any one religious denomination over another. From that point forward, the vast majority of Indian pupils attended institutions managed by the Bureau of Indian Affairs. Though most of these schools were located west of the Mississippi or in the Great Lakes states, either on or relatively close to the reservations from which they drew their students, their model was faraway Carlisle.[22]

This method of forcibly assimilating Indian children in isolation from their people was a new, if long-considered, approach to national Indian reform, distinct from the government's policies toward other American minorities. During the Reconstruction era, the federal government devoted enormous resources to educating African American youth and preparing freedmen for the responsibilities and duties of citizenship, but it made no attempt to seize the people's children from them as part of that agenda. Nor did the government force the children of America's Irish, Jewish, and southern European immigrants into boarding schools, even though the same class of reformers who styled themselves Friends of the Indian disparaged such people as deficient in practically every aspect of their lives. The government treated Indians differently partly because they were conquered, dependent, small in population, divided into hundreds of communities, and wedded to their land, which made it difficult for them to resist when authorities took their children away. Additionally, the reform of Indians seemed to require extreme coercive measures because they, unlike African Americans and most immigrants, opposed being culturally assimilated into the United States, particularly when it came to schooling, Christianity, and private property. They had neither entered the United States willingly, as in the case of immigrants, nor asked to participate in the country as equals, as in the case of African Americans. Instead, the country had imposed its authority on them. Now the question was what to do with them. White racial ideology, whether colloquial or scientific, posited that Indian savagery was innate and therefore Indians were doomed. The boarding schools, like the reservations, aimed to test and hopefully disprove that theory by forcing Indians to change, whether they wanted this "gift" or not.[23]

Yet the boarding schools, in their actual operation, were about Whites in power conditioning Indians to be subordinate rather than assimilating them into the mainstream. When reservation police conducted their roundups, "the children were almost out of their wits with fright," according to an account from the Mescalero Apache reservation. The writer Luther Standing Bear remembered that, when he was a boy traveling from South Dakota to Carlisle on the train, itself a terrifying foreign technology, Whites along the route "acted so wild at seeing us. They tried to give the war-whoop and mimic the Indian and in other ways got us all wrought up and excited and we did not like this sort of treatment." Arrival at school brought no relief, for the introduction involved White authorities strapping each child into a barber's chair for a stark haircut, which Indians associated with mourning. Next came a delousing bath and change into strange, ill-fitting, and coarse clothing, identical to everyone else's of the same sex; that meant military-style uniforms for the boys and drab dresses for the girls, which turned decorative ribbons into a coveted item in the students' underground economy. Each child also received a new Anglophone name, yet another sign of replacing a former, savage identity with a new, civilized one. The harsh first day ended with a meal of unfamiliar food, and then bedtime in an open dormitory filled with strangers whose only commonality was sharing a complexion darker than that of the White adults who already domineered over them.[24]

Standing Bear, like probably all students, grasped the symbolism of the haircutting ritual, never mind the rest of the orientation. "The fact is," he wrote, "that we were to be transformed, and short hair being the mark of gentility with the white man, he put upon us the mark." Henceforth, he was supposed to be "an imitation of a white man." As S. M. Cowan, the former superintendent of the Fort Mohave Boarding School, admitted, he ordered the children's hair cut "not because of any objection to the long hair itself, but merely because long hair was a symbol of savagery." The message was that the rest of the students' savagery, like their hair, would be severed and fall to the ground in due time.[25]

A new daily routine of racial conditioning began the next morning. A bugle announced dawn wake-up, followed by roll calls, marches, rifle drills, flag bearing, class sessions, set meals, work details, and study, signaled by the chime of the bell, practically every day, week in and week out. Everyone was to speak English only, and no one was to engage in dancing, play, or other frivolity without the school administrators' permission. Work assignments involved a range of gender-specific tasks on a model that was already becoming outdated in the rapidly industrializing American economy and ill-suited to the underdeveloped contexts of most reservations. Despite the schools' goal of assimilating Indians, the fact was that practically no White

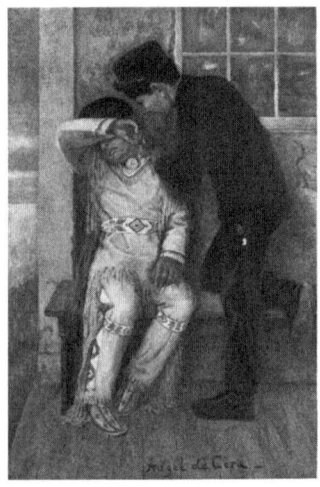

Angel De Cora, frontispiece of *The Middle Five: Indian Boys at School* by Francis La Flesche (Boston: Small, Maynard, 1909). Courtesy of Heard Museum, Phoenix, Arizona, and J. Andrew Darling.

A Ho-Chunk artist's depiction of the heartbreak suffered by new arrivals to the boarding schools, and the comfort provided by other students.

people other than prisoners and soldiers lived under such oppressive conditions as the Native students.[26]

White society so devalued Native life that authorities knowingly created conditions in the boarding schools that left the children hungry, weak, and diseased. In practically every school, the food was monotonous and of meager nutritional value, and in some times and places it fell far short of the students' bodily needs. Not surprisingly, given the malnutrition, psychological stress, and crowded conditions, diseases such as tuberculosis, measles, pneumonia, mumps, and influenza ravaged the pupils. A congressional study in 1912 found that nearly 30 percent of Indian schoolchildren suffered from trachoma, a bacterial eye infection that, left untreated, can lead to blindness. Combating the disease was as simple as providing clean hand towels and isolating the sick. Yet the schools did not bother. Another congressional report sixteen years later shared the startling finding that Indian children in boarding schools were six times as likely to perish underage as the rest of the children in America. A hundred Carlisle students died during the institution's first decade, causing such embarrassment that Pratt began sending ailing children back home to reduce the official rate. To the students' loved ones, these losses still counted.[27]

Abuse in the schools was as omnipresent as disease. When the children broke the rules, as children were prone to do, administrators punished them corporally with a severity that was practically unknown in Native society and increasingly rare in White schools and households. It included strapping, confinement in jail cells, and heavy labor such as floor scrubbing and breaking rocks with sledgehammers.

Students were subject to random beatings, sexual assaults, and public humiliation from administrators, teachers, and other pupils, as, for example, when an instructor threw a boy across the room for speaking his language, breaking his collarbone. One former Carlisle student recalled living in constant "terror" of sexual predation by a male teacher. More recent testimony from survivors of Catholic boarding schools detail a widespread pattern of molestation and rape by priests and nuns alike, who silenced the children by threatening that they would go to hell or be prohibited from ever returning home if they ever told. There was no recourse. Instead, the victims were left to carry the shame and nightmares for the rest of their lives.[28]

To the extent that the boarding schools prepared Indian students for American life, it was a subordinate role. English-language reading and writing and math were necessary for practically anyone in the United States, but that does not explain the schools' emphasis on history and civics lessons that trumpeted the superiority of White American civilization and denigrated the supposed inferior savagery of Indian life. Essays from Indian students at Hampton include statements such as "The Caucasian is the strongest in the world. The semi-civilized have their own civilization, but not like the white race," or "The white people they are civilized; they have everything... The red people they big savages; they don't know nothing." These were the takeaways from a curriculum that celebrated the Whites' "discovery" of America and the introduction of Christian civilization to a savage land each Columbus Day, or that used the Thanksgiving holiday as an opportunity to mythologize that Indians had welcomed the Pilgrim "fathers" to their land and then disappeared so White people could establish religious freedom and democracy. The point was to make Indian students ashamed of their backgrounds and shift their allegiance to their conquerors.[29]

Indian subordination also permeated Pratt's "outing system," in which students lived with White host families as farmhands or servants or took wage work nearby. Typically, these arrangements lasted only a summer, but for older students they sometimes ran a year or longer. The principle was that this experience would give the students firsthand experience with civilized White households and communities, but that also meant suffering degradation as racial outsiders and menial laborers and being subject to yet more abuse of every sort. When Luther Standing Bear arrived in Philadelphia from Carlisle to work in the famous Wanamaker department store, he struggled to find a White landlord who would rent an apartment to an Indian. One of Standing Bear's co-workers at Wanamaker's, fellow Sioux and classmate Clarence Three Stars, quit his job almost immediately, explaining that "as I go behind

Francis Benjamin Johnston, *Young Students Standing in Classroom*, 1901. Courtesy of the Carlisle Indian School Digital Resource Center and the Cumberland County Historical Society.

the counters the clerks all call me 'Indian' and I don't like it; it makes me nervous." Similar testimony led the superintendent of Indian schools, Daniel Dorchester, to reject the outing system for other boarding schools. He concluded that "with too many [White people] the common idea is that the Indian is a creature to be cheated, debauched, and kicked out of decent society. Young Indians from the schools cannot be safely located among such people." The Carlisle Industrial School had to create its own cemetery because local Whites did not want Indians buried alongside them.[30]

SAVE THE INDIAN AND THE MAN

There was no reason for Indian parents to trust White schools with their children. They had witnessed White Americans massacre their people while calling for their extermination, force them into confinement and poverty on the reservations, engross nearly all of their territory, and destroy the very natural world Indians considered sacred. Now Whites were coming for the Native young, claiming to want to save them. It took the government's raw power to pry the children loose. For all the innumerable ways that the United States exhibited its principles of White supremacy and Indian inferiority during the assimilation era, there was nothing quite like this, except, perhaps, the boarding schools themselves.

The children's parents and tribes resisted in every way they could conceive. The Southern Cheyenne leader Little Chief protested that "the Spirit above did not intend for our children to read and write—he gave the white people the desire to read, write, farm, and to live as white people live." A federal agent countered that the destruction of the bison meant young Indians needed to learn how to live without hunting, to which the Cheyennes answered "that they do not desire to live after the buffalo shall become extinct." They proposed that if the government wanted students, maybe it should look for them among the Arapahos. One unidentified Kiowa father halted a school recruiter at his front door, pointed to his son, and proclaimed, "Take that axe and knock him on the head. I will gladly bury him. I would rather you do that than take him to school." The Crows refused to hand over their sons and daughters to the reservation school until the agent threatened to suspend the distribution of all annuities, including desperately needed food. Grudgingly, they capitulated, but then the parents set up camp right outside the school grounds, leading the director to erect a tall board fence to keep them separated from their own children. Mescalero Apaches would usher their young people into the mountains whenever the agent started rounding up students, and if his police managed to catch some of them, adults would offer up orphans and the disabled in their stead. Shoshones and Bannocks on the Fort Hall Reservation in Idaho took up arms against school recruitment in 1897 until the arrival of federal troops made them think better of it. Even then, the government's coercion barely worked. By the end of the nineteenth century, school attendance among the Southern Cheyennes and Arapahos remained sporadic at best, with 250 of 833 children receiving no formal education at all, and only 15 percent receiving more than a few years of primary school. The Lakota reservations in South Dakota produced similar numbers. Nationwide, no more than half of Indian children were enrolled in day or boarding schools.[31]

A minority of Indian parents believed schooling was necessary to prepare their children for a new, challenging way of life under White dominance, though not with the aim of eliminating all vestiges of the children's cultural inheritance. Their express intent was to use the White people's education to strengthen tribal communities. The Shawnee Thomas Wildcat Alford, a great-grandson of Tecumseh, remembered that when he was a boy, "there was a feeling among our people that some of our young men should be educated so that they could read and write and understand what was written in the treaties and old documents in our possession." The tribe sent him to Hampton Institute on that errand, but counseled that he "should not accept the white man's religion." Alford also recalled that his father's generation "had such a bitter hatred against the white race, or rather against those things that the white race represented ... generally, the Indian hated the thought of civilization." The Santee Sioux Charles Eastman's father admonished him before he left for school: "Remember, my boy, it is the same as if I sent you on your first warpath. I shall expect you to conquer," while the Lakota Luther Standing Bear's father advised him "that fighting would not get the Indian anywhere, and that the only recourse was to learn the white man's ways of doing things, get the same education, and thus be in a condition to stand up for his rights." Still other parents, mired in poverty with only heart-wrenching choices before them, saw boarding school as a way to provide for at least one child's basic needs while easing the financial burden on the rest of the household. Demand for a spot at Carlisle was sufficiently robust that one of the returned Fort Marion prisoners, a Cheyenne named Antelope, tried to sneak his son aboard a train to Pennsylvania. In the broader scheme of things, however, none of these decisions were genuinely voluntarily. They took place in the context of Indian people suffering food insecurity, material dependence on a foreign and often hostile society, with no clear sense of direction for the near or distant future. Resistance and compliance were both acts of desperation to enable the people to survive White domination.[32]

Students in the boarding schools took their own measures to maintain some shred of autonomy and dignity, and in so doing contributed to a meaningful Indian identity among their peers. Most of this defiance was imperceptible to authorities, taking place in the mind or in the shadows, but occasional glimpses of it surface in the historical record. It is evident in a poem by Navajo students that went, "I do not believe you / The things you say, / Maybe I will not tell you / That is my way." The Black educator and activist Booker T. Washington recounted that when he visited a Hampton Institute classroom, the White teacher invited one Black and one Indian pupil to identify any special contribution that the other race had made to "civilization." The Indian cited African American patience, musical talent, and desire to learn. The Black scholar acknowledged Indian courage, honor, and racial pride. Then the teacher asked the entire class "in what respects the white race was superior." They sat there refusing to answer, even after the teacher repeated the question. Their silence spoke volumes.[33]

Students were more openly resentful when White authorities were absent. Students at the Chilocco school in Indian Territory would insult one another with the slur *stahitkey*, or "White man," and *stalustey*, or "Black man," with the obvious implication that the target was not a genuine Indian. In that same institution in

1912, students somehow managed to avoid the administration's editorial controls and slip an article into the school newspaper that asserted, "This race [Indians] is very suspicious of the white man, for they have long learned that the white man has only made agreements with their people to break them. This race, if it only had the power, would wipe the white man off the earth." Alumni leveled criticisms with even greater abandon. Once Thomas Wildcat Alford was free of Hampton, he derided White civilization as "nothing more or less than a multiplication of man's needs and wants." Zitkala-Ša (Gertrude Simmons Bonnin) denounced her former boarding school, the Indiana Manual Labor Institute, as a cruel and dehumanizing cog in the "iron routine of the civilizing machine" based on nothing more than "superstitious ideas." She prodded White readers "to question whether real life or long-lasting death lies beneath the semblance of civilization." Luther Standing Bear, drawing on his English-language literacy education at Carlisle, castigated "Whites" as "devils" for their destruction of the bison, indiscriminate slaughter of Indians, and reduction of the survivors to destitution. "These people cared nothing for us," he seethed, "and it meant nothing to them to take our lives... This was the beginning of our hatred for the white people."[34]

Widespread student hatred of the boarding schools, combined with an abiding longing for home, made running away a constant temptation. Students felt the heartache of often going years without a visit to their families while having their letters, their sole means of communication, censored by school administrators to prevent them from sharing how miserable they were. Meanwhile, parents complained endlessly that they had no idea about how their children were actually doing or when they would see them again. Faced with these obstacles, some students decided to take matters into their own hands. The high fences, gates, and guards designed to keep them locked in only heightened the determination of some of them to break out. A handful of others decided just to burn the place down. In 1897, two Carlisle girls, the Menominee Elizabeth Flanders and the Sioux Fannie Eaglehorn, twice tried to set their dormitory on fire, once by stuffing a pillowcase full of paper and then lighting it in a closet full of dresses while everyone else was at chapel. Someone extinguished the blaze before it raged out of control, but this would not be the last case of arson in an Indian boarding school because student resentment continued to smolder.[35]

Students also foiled the schools' agenda by actively cultivating an Indian identity that had been foreign to most of them as youngsters back home but became salient when they were grouped together in an institution that pronounced its intent to destroy their common heritage. Native schoolgirls at Carlisle, for instance, learned quilting from neighboring Whites of German heritage, then turned it into an expression of Native artistry for which Indian women today are widely renowned. Likewise, the famed Carlisle football team achieved a greater purpose than Pratt's intent of proving that Indians could compete with Whites if given a fair chance. Instead, the players developed an enhanced sense of being Indian and, for that matter, of the opponents' and their fans' identity as White. Newspaper accounts of Carlisle games trafficked endlessly in the motifs of frontier warfare, such as referring to the competitors scalping, massacring, or tomahawking each other and making last stands. Carlisle players became "the Redskins" and their White rivals "the Palefaces." The Carlisle boys, as the saying goes, took this ball and ran with it. Their coach, Pop Warner, sensed that the players conceived of their games less as school versus school than as "the Indian versus the White Man," adding "if there was one team that the Indians liked to beat more than any other, that team was the Army." Their roster received a massive boost in 1907–8 and then again in 1911–12 with the inclusion of Sauk-Fox Jim Thorpe, a future Olympic champion, player in both Major League Baseball and the National Football League, and arguably the greatest American male athlete ever. Native people throughout the country took enormous pride as Indians in their offsprings' accomplishments on the gridiron. In 1926, the oil-rich Osage tribe raised $185,000 for a football stadium at the Haskell Institute boarding school in Kansas. The opening of this building drew representatives from seventy-five tribes and involved a giant pan-Indian powwow. Clearly, the schools were failing to "kill the Indian." Better put, Indian students and their communities were scratching to survive.[36]

THE TORMENT OF BEING IN BETWEEN

Despite such formidable resistance, the schools' relentless messaging sometimes succeeded at making some of the students ashamed of their Indian backgrounds. The agent Albert H. Kneale, who spent thirty years in the Indian service stationed among half a dozen different tribes, wrote of having seen Native schoolgirls "dressed in the latest creations" return home after absences of years. "When they first cast eyes upon their parents," he could not forget, they "stared in abject horror, then as the truth dawned upon them, burst into tears." Likewise, he continued, "I have seen parents glance fleetingly on these visions of civilized loneliness, then turn away in disgust returning to their homes, leaving the children to shift for themselves." This was no exaggeration. Sun Elk, from Taos pueblo, told that after years at Carlisle, he and some of his classmates began to internalize the messages "that Indian ways were bad" and "we must get civilized . . . to be like the white man." He reflected contritely of those days, "We all wore white man's clothes and ate white man's food and went to white man's churches and spoke white man's talk. And so after a while we also began to say Indians were bad. We laughed at our own people and their blankets and cooking pots and sacred societies and dances." The chiefs found him so arrogant and unmoored that they declared, "He is not one of us." Sun Elk then became a sojourner through White towns, in search of work and somewhere to belong.[37]

Identity crises of this sort were common among boarding school alumni. As a mature man, Luther Standing Bear shuddered to recall how he and some of his schoolmates visiting home had refused to shake hands with their unrefined tribesmen, and at how pleased he had been as a young adult when his first child was born with a light complexion. Sometimes, the disdain was mutual. Jason Betzinez returned to the Apache reservation from Carlisle to find, "If you minded your own business and tried to live in the white man's way, then the Indians branded you as being some kind of outcast who no longer loved his own people." A Hidatsa named Buffalo Bird Woman complained that schoolgirls developed loose sexual morals, "for they now learned English ways." The tension and resentment between Indians who had attended the boarding schools and those who remained home, and the overlapping strains between young and old, progressives and traditionalists, became defining features of reservation life throughout Indian country. Colonialism had always worked to turn Indigenous people against one another.[38]

Prideful or not, boarding school alumni had few opportunities to make a living on the reservation using the skills they had acquired, which contributed to a growing White stereotype of Indians as lazy dependents on government handouts. If formally educated Indians were lucky, they obtained employment in the Indian service or reservation schools. For everyone else, good jobs were in short supply. U.S. Army veteran William H. Powell recalled visiting the Great Sioux Reservation and meeting several young Indian men dressed in white men's clothes hanging around aimlessly. They explained that they were formally educated, but still could not find work. "What is there to do out here?" they asked. "Nobody will give an Indian anything to do out here."[39]

Nearby White communities offered only marginally better prospects, not because of low demand for workers, but race prejudice. Powell's contacts complained, "We can't go into the cities and compete with white men for labor, because they have been brought up in white men's ways, while we have had no such advantages, and they look upon us as nothing but Indians." Thomas Wildcat Alford grew discouraged after graduating from Hampton Institute because "although I was a pretty good workman at several different kinds of labor, no one seemed to want to hire an Indian when there were white men to do the work." The problem was so pervasive that another Hampton graduate, Harry Hand, founded a newspaper, the *Crow Creek Chief*, on the Crow reservation precisely to answer local Whites "who think that the Indians count for nothing."[40]

Despite the innumerable abuses the boarding schools inflicted on Native children and their people, a portion of adult alumni concluded that the experience did more to prepare them for modern American life than they ever could have hoped for on the reservation. Some of them even looked back on their school days nostalgically. They appreciated that the schools provided regular, if often poor, food and shelter at a time when too many reservation families lacked both. Schoolchildren made cherished friends and often enjoyed their extracurricular activities. A number of them fell in love. As adults, alumni occasionally granted that Indian existence under U.S. rule was, in fact, shaped by a choice between assimilation or extinction and that the hard life afforded by the schools was infinitely better than the gradual death of the reservation. They recognized that their ability to speak and write English, perform mathematical calculations, and adhere to the discipline and hierarchy of the modern workplace was critical to whatever successes they had earned. To them, boarding school had been the best of several bad options in a world of pervasive racial injustice.[41]

The boarding schools, like the reservations, were supposed to transform Native America into civilized White producers in the space of a generation or less, but as the years wore on with disappointing results, self-identifying Friends of the Indian began to lose confidence. Some of them returned to the old racial explanation that Indians were incapable of civilized living after all. Others criticized that schools were bound to fail if graduates returned to underdeveloped reservations where Indian customs still prevailed. The most enlightened observers blamed the poison of White prejudice and the cruelty of trying to break up families and make children abhor their parents. The only consensus was that it was time again for a seismic shift in policy. On that point, Indians agreed.[42]

GHOST DANCING

In the late 1880s, at the very same moment that the boarding schools were claiming ever more Indian children, White agents and military officers throughout the West voiced increasing concern, even alarm, about a new religious ritual spreading across the reservations. Its prophet was a Paiute named Wovoka (Jack Wilson) who preached from his home in Nevada's Mason Valley that if the people swore off alcohol, lived in peace, and performed a circular dance and accompanying chants while wearing "ghost shirts," they could restore the old Indian world. The spirits of their ancestors would spring back to life, the bison would cover the Plains again, and, not least of all, Whites would disappear. Like so many other pan-Indian movements over the centuries, including revivals in the Great Basin and Pacific Northwest within Wovoka's lifetime, this resort to the spirits reflected Native people's desperation for health, hope, and a positive sense of Indian identity in a time of upheaval and denigration by Whites. It also resembled some of its predecessors in resulting in a White massacre of Indians.

A racial binary of Indians versus Whites stood at the center of Wovoka's worldview. Whenever Whites questioned Wovoka, he assured them of his belief that "the whites and Indians" could become "one people" if Whites followed his teachings. Yet he made little effort to recruit them. Instead, he preached that "the Indian redeemer" would obliterate Whites and their profane civilization as part of the sacred revival of Native America. Many of Wovoka's adherents, especially among the Lakotas, fixated on this part of his message, eagerly anticipating when "a hurricane with thunder and lightning will come to destroy the whites alone." Whereas the reservations and boarding schools intended to "kill the Indian and save the man," the Great Spirit's justice would kill the Whites and save the Indians.[43]

Arapaho Ghost Dance, unknown artist, 1981, based on a photograph by James Mooney. Courtesy of Corbis Historical/Getty Images.

Ironically, Wovoka's message spread through Indian country through his disciples' inter-reservation travel by train and written correspondence using literacy and English-language education acquired through day and boarding schools. Close to sixteen hundred Indians from thirty-four different tribes scattered across the West and Indian Territory visited Wovoka on the Walker River, often arriving by the same rail lines that had contributed to the ruin of the Indian world. Some of these travelers had learned about Wovoka through English-language letters written by other Indians or read about him in newspapers, including a number published on their own reservations. Reading, writing, and a shared imperial language were equipping Native people to express a newfound sense of Indian identity and confront the pressures of White dominance that had exposed them to those skills in the first place.[44]

A prime example comes from a formally educated Indian named John Daylight (Masse-Hadjo), who responded to a mocking depiction of the Ghost Dance in the *Chicago Tribune* with his own biting letter to the editor. Writing from his home on the Quapaw agency in Indian Territory, he charged White Americans with crass hypocrisy for their combination of Christianity and violent racism:

> You say, "if the United States army would kill a thousand or so of the dancing Indians there would be no more trouble." I judge by the above language that you are a "Christian" and are disposed to do all in your power to advance the cause of Christ. You are doubtless a worshipper of the white man's Savior, but are unwilling that the Indians should have a "Messiah" of their own. The Indians have never taken kindly to the Christian religion as preached and practiced by the whites. Do you know why this is the case? Because the Good Father has given us a better religion—a religion that is all good and no bad, a religion that is adapted to our wants... The code of morals as practiced by the white race will not compare with the morals of the Indians... If our Messiah does come, we shall not try to force you into our belief. We will never burn innocent women at the stake or pull men to pieces with horses because they refuse to join our ghost dances... You are anxious to get hold of our Messiah so you can put him in irons. This you may do—in fact, you may crucify him as you did the other one, but you cannot convert the Indians to the Christian religion until you contaminate them with the blood of the white man.

Whatever the shortcomings of the boarding schools' education, clearly it equipped some of its students to speak cutting truth to power.[45]

The Ghost Dance swept through Indian country, from its center in the Great Basin into the Pacific Northwest and eastward onto the Plains as far as the Southern Cheyenne and Arapaho reservation in Indian Territory. Only among the Lakotas, however, did the U.S. military attempt to subdue the dancers at gunpoint. General Nelson Miles, in charge of this campaign, feared that the Lakota believers intended "to hasten the coming of the messiah" by helping to "remove the whites and thereby show their faith by their works." He was additionally concerned that if he left the Lakotas unchecked, other Indians might follow their example, whereupon the American West was "liable to be overrun by a hungry, wild, mad horde of savages." Skeptics accused Miles of exaggerating this threat in order to give him an excuse to suppress it, the better to enhance his political résumé for a presidential run. Miles, however, was not alone. A number of White officials worried that the Lakotas, above all tribes, would revolt against the reservation regime. Not only had this nation of warriors sustained a decades-long resistance to the United States, but also even after surrendering they had frustrated their reservation agents at every turn. Tensions were especially high following the 1889 Sioux Agreement, in which the United States engrossed another 9,274,668 acres of Lakota land and divided the Great Sioux Reservation into six separate agencies. Dreading that war was at hand, neighboring White settlers in the *Black Hills Daily Times* called for the army to exterminate the Ghost Dancers preemptively. The Lakotas had not so much as fired a shot or even issued a threat. Their offense was merely refusing to heed their agent's orders to halt their ceremony and tend to their livelihoods.[46]

The U.S. overreaction produced one of its most infamous massacres of Indians in a long history. By December 1890, the U.S. Army had dispatched as many as seven thousand troops to subjugate the four to five thousand Ghost Dancers among the Lakotas, none of whom appear to have been plotting an armed uprising, most of whom were women and children. This show of force succeeded at driving most of the disciples from their ceremonial camps back into the agencies, but some thirteen hundred people held out. Insistent on bringing them in as well, the agent James McLaughlin's first move was to arrest Sitting Bull, on the premise that he would be the leader if any revolt occurred. Reservation police shot him dead in the process, which only heightened the authorities' worries about an insurrection. Their concerns centered on a band of Miniconjou Lakotas led by the chief Big Foot, though by December 27 those Indians were on their way to surrender to the agency, too. Unfortunately, it was left to the U.S. Seventh Calvary, Custer's old command, to escort them the rest of the way. Pausing at Wounded Knee Creek, twenty miles from their destination, the soldiers positioned artillery guns on the hills ringing the Indians' camp, then, on the morning of December 29, went tent to tent and person to person searching for weapons. The Miniconjous, fearful of what the soldiers might do to them once they were disarmed, began to panic. During a struggle over a rifle, a shot rang out, whereupon the soldiers started firing indiscriminately. In the chaos, they slaughtered about three hundred out of the four hundred members of Big Foot's band. Later, a burial party found dozens of bodies bloody and frozen well outside the boundaries of the camp, many of them women and children who had been running away or huddled together in terror. "All this," wrote the Santee Sioux doctor Charles Eastman, who witnessed the aftermath firsthand, "was a severe ordeal for one who had so lately put all his faith in the Christian love and lofty ideas of the white man." Twenty members of the Seventh Cavalry received Congressional Medals of Honor for their roles in the atrocity. Modern efforts to revoke these awards have repeatedly failed.[47]

American history lessons often treat Wounded Knee as the last battle of the Plains wars, but there is growing recognition that this was no battle and had nothing to do with war in the military sense. It was simply a massacre. More than that, it was a display of the murderous lengths to which White authorities would go to keep Indians subordinate even under abject conditions. The Ghost Dance, even among the Lakotas, was a peaceful protest against the degradation of the reservation system and all the misery that led up to it. Tellingly, the movement included not only staunch traditionalists but also a number of boarding school alumni. They included Plenty Horses, a Lakota graduate of Carlisle and resident of the Pine Ridge reservation, who killed an army officer in a rage after learning about the carnage at Wounded Keee. He explained at his trial: "I am an Indian. Five years I attended Carlisle and was educated in the ways of the white man . . . I was lonely. I shot the lieutenant so I might make a place for myself among my people. Now I am one of them." The court set Plenty Horses free on the basis that he had committed this act in a state of war, which served as much to excuse the soldiers as it did him. What bound the formally educated Plenty Horses to the dead at Wounded Knee, writes the historian Gregory E. Smoak, is that all of them "rejected the demand that they abandon their separate identity and dissolve into a sea of English-speaking, petty capitalist farmers." They did not want that world or any of the White efforts to force them into it. One of the Ghost Dancers reflected, "I suppose the authorities did think they were crazy—but they weren't. They were only terribly unhappy." Or, as Black Elk explained, "I thought

John C. H. Grabill, *Tasunka, Ota (alias Plenty Horse[s]), the slayer of Lieut. Casey, near Pine Ridge, S.D.*, 1891. Courtesy of the Library of Congress Prints and Photographs Division.

maybe it was only despair that made people believe [in the Ghost Dance], just as a man who is starving may dream of plenty, of everything good to eat."[48]

Before the massacre, fair-minded observers had judged that the Ghost Dance movement would collapse of its own weight when the Indian new world failed to materialize. White authorities just needed to keep back and allow the process to take its course. The Lakota agent and the Seventh Cavalry refused because they subscribed to the principle that they, as civilized White Americans with official powers, were to command, and the Indians, as savages, were to obey. If the Natives resisted, the result in 1890 was to be the same as at any point in the recent American past, or, for that matter, future: extermination. White newspapers throughout South Dakota cheered the news of Wounded Knee as evidence that the U.S. government had finally realized that the only answer to the "Indian problem" was to "wipe them from the face of the earth."[49]

Yet Indians across the West, including the Lakotas, kept on Ghost Dancing. It was as if every life stuffed out in the massacre merely strengthened the survivors' determination to continue in honor of the dead. Among the Kiowas, the Ghost Dance became fused with officially sanctioned annual celebrations of the Fourth of July and Christmas, like so many other traditional Indian rituals. God "gave the book to the white people," one of the Kiowas' ceremonial leaders explained, "but he gave to the Indians the dance road." Even the White program of herding Indians onto reservations, forcing Indian children to boarding schools, and subduing resistance with mass killings could not crush this faith.[50]

"GOD DAMN A POTATO!"

The United States' promises to Indians had always been cheap, but its decision to begin dismantling the reservations with the Dawes Act of 1887 and the Curtis Act of 1898, so soon after telling Indians that they would possess these places forever, was a particularly harsh betrayal. The reservations, of course, were supposed to be the Indians' pittance for having ceded hundreds of millions of acres of territory after wars that cost them untold numbers of lives. For all the debasement of the reservation regime, at least it gave the people somewhere they could call their own, with a measure of safety against White militias. The Dawes and Curtis Acts not only threatened but also promised to sweep away these limited protections based on the fantasy that Indians would enjoy equal protection under the law once they became private-property-holding citizens of White America. But the fact was that many Whites throughout the United States simply would not extend Indians justice or dignity under any circumstances.

Legislation to allot and privatize the reservations enabled White people to fleece Indians of their territory while lying to themselves that they were benefiting the Natives with civility and citizenship. The Dawes Act authorized the division of Indian lands into tracts of 160 acres or less and the allotment of those parcels among Native individuals. There would be a twenty-five-year restriction on the allottee's selling the tract to provide time for him or her to learn how to manage land as private property. Once that interim period elapsed, each Indian would receive a fee patent lifting all restrictions on alienation, mortgages, and leases. From then on, the titleholder would be responsible for property taxes and run the risk of having the parcel confiscated for debt, like White landowners. Furthermore, he or she would become an American citizen. In 1906, the Burke Act amended Dawes with the provision that if the government judged an allottee to have become civilized before the end of the twenty-five-year wait, he or she could be granted unrestricted ownership and citizenship early. As for the remaining undivided lands of the reservation, the government would purchase this "surplus" from the tribe and keep most of the proceeds in an interest-bearing account to fund its civilization programs, including the boarding schools. It was a strange species of cruelty to force people to fund the kidnapping and cultural reprogramming of their own children. As if to twist the knife further, the government's plan was to sell the Indians' surplus territory to White homesteaders. The idea was that, by the time Indians became private-property-holding citizens, they would be enveloped by White society and ready to join it. There was no consideration of whether White society would permit them to do so.⁵¹

The Five Civilized Tribes (Cherokees, Creeks, Choctaws, Chickasaws, and Seminoles) of Federal Indian Territory successfully lobbied to remain exempt from the Dawes legislation, only to wind up eleven years later with the Curtis Act. This measure stood out from Dawes in allowing Indians to hold their allotments in "fee simple" from the start rather than in government trust and permitting the allottees to incorporate themselves into towns. These features gave Native people the ability, and incentivized them, to create municipalities run by Indians that partially filled the vacuum created by Curtis's other distinguishing feature, its immediate abolishment of tribal government. This silver lining has contributed to Indians remaining a political force in Oklahoma to the present day. Yet the Curtis Act had the same devastating effect as Dawes: allowing Whites to cheat Native people out of most of their land.⁵²

Allotment had been in the works for years as White reformers concluded that the reservations were failing to turn Indians into civilized yeomen, and White economic interests concluded that Indians should not retain any profitable resources whatsoever. By 1876, the commissioner of Indian affairs was already questioning "whether any high degree of civilization is possible without individual ownership of land," reflective of ethnological teachings on human evolution. Over the next several years, the self-proclaimed Friends of the Indian, gathering at their annual conference on Lake Mohonk, in the upper Hudson River Valley, turned this principle into a mantra. In one of the conference series' more memorable speeches, Merrill E. Gates, the president of Amherst College, declared that "we must make the Indian more intelligently selfish before we can make him unselfishly intelligent. We need to awaken in him wants . . . Discontent with the teepee and the starving rations of the Indian camp in winter is needed to get the Indian out of the blanket and into trousers, and trousers with a pocket in them, and in a pocket that aches to be filled with dollars!"⁵³

Massachusetts senator Henry Dawes, whose surname became synonymous with allotment, sensed little ache of this sort when he visited the Cherokees in 1885. One Cherokee officer boasted to him "that there was not a family in that whole [Cherokee] Nation that had not a home of its own. There was not a pauper in that Nation, and the Nation did not owe a dollar. It built its own capitol . . . and it built its own schools and hospitals." But Dawes was unimpressed by the shared security afforded by the Cherokees' communal principles. "They have gone as far as they can go," he judged, "because they own their land in common." Consistent with the ideology of his Republican Party, Dawes wanted to see individual striving for wealth to create a rising economic sea that lifted all boats. Practically every commissioner of Indian affairs from the late nineteenth through the early twentieth centuries agreed wholeheartedly with him, as did the vast majority of organizations created by Friends of the Indian, including the Indian Rights Association and the National Indian Association.[54]

If there was any Indian who reformers had in mind when crafting this legislation, it was Kansas Senator Charles Curtis, a mixed-blood member of the Kaw tribe who would later go on to become vice president of the United States in the administration of Herbert Hoover. Curtis was the child of Orren Arms Curtis, a United States soldier, and Julie Gonville, a half-blood Kaw, who died in 1863 when Curtis was just three years old. For the next ten years, Curtis lived with his mother's family near the Kaw reservation and attended the tribe's Quaker-run day school, but in his early teens his grandmother advised him to leave and "make something of himself." Following her counsel, Curtis gained wealth and reputation first as a successful horse jockey, then by studying law and becoming an attorney, and finally by selling his portion of the Kaws' "half-breed tract" to permit the founding of the town of Eugene, right across from Topeka on the Union Pacific Railroad. The United States government had created fifty such distinct "half-breed tracts" for mixed-ancestry Indians between 1800 and 1871 in the context of negotiating land cessions and reservations for those people's tribes; usually the terms prohibited the residents from selling their lands during a probationary period, at the conclusion of which they could alienate their allotments the same as Whites. The operating principle was that the White blood of "half-breeds" made them inherently better equipped to function in civilized society than their "full-blood" relatives, particularly when it came to managing private property. Biology, in other words, stood proxy for culture.[55]

Curtis seemed to prove the point. By middle age, he had risen to become the Kansas Republicans' most formidable candidate for office, on the strength of his advocacy for courts and public schools in Indian country and a loosening of restrictions of corporate leases of Indian land. His belief, shared by most of his White Republican colleagues, was that any man, regardless of background, should have the opportunity to rise or fall in the capitalist economy on his own merits. That vision included Native people, whom Curtis and the Republicans wanted to transform into just another ethnic group in the American melting pot rather than domestic dependent nations with their own cultural practices, territory, and sovereignty. The 1898 allotment legislation for Federal Indian Territory carries the name of Curtis because he was the one who sponsored it. Republican Friends of the Indian were convinced

G. V. Buck, portrait of Charles Curtis, 1908.
Courtesy of Everett Collection Historical/Alamy.

that if Indians became civilized private-property holders, there was no telling how many Charles Curtises they might produce.[56]

At the same time, some reformers claimed that they favored allotment to protect full-blood Indians from crafty mixed-bloods like Curtis, whom they accused of using their formal educations and cultural knowledge of White society to hoard putatively common Indian resources. Those subscribing to this view assumed that Indian blood corresponded to ignorance of the market, whereas White blood transmitted ambition and cunning. They cited as an example the Creeks, among whom just sixty-one people, mostly mixed-blood cattle ranchers, controlled some 1,107,251 acres, or one third of the entire tribal domain. The reformers' answer to such problems was identical to their solution for persistent Indian savagery and White encroachment: distribution of the commons as private property so full-blooded Indians would have the means and motivation to protect themselves before the law.[57]

Just a handful of White people saw through this ideology and denounced the Dawes and Curtis Acts as plundering operations that would drive Indians into destitution, which had always been the effect of Whites' forcing the division and privatization of the Indian domain. Citing that pattern, a House minority report in 1880 charged that the point of allotment was "not to help the Indian, or solve the Indian problem, or provide a method for getting out of our Indian troubles, so much as it is to provide a method for getting at the valuable Indian lands and opening them up to white settlement . . . Nothing can be surer than the eventual extermination of the Indian under the operation of this bill . . . If this were done in the name of Greed, it would be bad enough; but to do it in the name of Humanity, and under the cloak of an ardent desire to protect the Indian's welfare by making him like ourselves, whether he will or not, is infinitely worse." Senator Henry M. Teller of Colorado predicted that, under Dawes, "in thirty years thereafter there will not be an Indian on the continent, or there will be very few at least, that will have any land." He thought the legislation should be entitled "A bill to despoil the Indians, and to make them vagabonds on the face of the earth." Nobody in Congress could claim that he had not been warned.[58]

With few exceptions, Indians also pleaded that allotment would prove disastrous. The Creeks knew firsthand that "those [Indians] holding their lands in common have, as a general rule, retained their numerical strength better than those who have held them as individuals by separate titles." Their fear was that allotment would "throw the whole of our domain in a few years into the hands of a few persons." The Senecas agreed that their "condition of independence and prosperity is largely due to the system by which the lands are owned in common, controlled by the national councils, and are permanently inalienable." The Five Civilized Tribes issued a joint protest calling attention to the cases of the Shawnees, Potawatomis, and Kickapoos in Kansas, all of whom received allotments even before Dawes, with the proviso that they could not sell their divided lands for twenty years. Encroaching Whites seized practically everything before five years had passed. The fact that such tribes, and others before them like the Omahas of Nebraska and the Brothertowns of Wisconsin, had petitioned for allotment precisely to avoid dispossession made these failed experiments all the more poignant. Well-informed Indians also knew that the Indigenous people of Hawaii had lost most of their lands to White foreigners, the majority of them Americans, after privatizing their territory in the 1840s in a futile attempt to guard against colonial dispossession. In this light, the Oglala chief Hollow Horn Bear warned that allotment "is only another trick of the whites to take our land away from us." A Cherokee writing in the *Indian Chieftain* concurred that it was "the graspings of this American people after wealth," rather than a desire to promote Indian assimilation, that was the source of White opposition to "our present land tenure system." No wonder, then, that when an American commissioner tried to convince the old chief Washakie of the Shoshones that his people would live better if they divided their lands and cultivated their own particular vegetable gardens, he shot back, "God damn a potato!"[59]

Indians opposed allotment in practically every reservation setting, often unanimously. Each community had traditionalists who refused to accept their allotment assignments no matter how much pressure the agent brought to bear.

They continued to live together in extended-family camps, leaving private tracts to lie uninhabited and fallow. One dissenter, an elderly Ute named Red Cap, "became very angry" when pressed to take up his allotment. "You say this little land is mine!" he proclaimed in disbelief. "You do not know what you are talking about." Waving his arms over his head in a circular motion, he asserted, "Everything is mine. This whole land is mine. You look down and see everywhere the tracks of white men, but under these tracks are my tracks and the tracks of my people." Another aged man on the Rosebud Sioux reservation responded to the appearance of allotment agents by donning his breechclout, picking up his rifle, and chasing them off until the police intervened. Yakamas in Washington State yanked out the stakes marking allotment bounds, while Arapahos in Wyoming stampeded their horses through the federal surveyors' camp. Resisters among the Cherokees, made up disproportionately of full-bloods, revived the Keetoowah Society, or Nighthawks, committed to the preservation of tribal customs, including communal landholdings. A portion of the group withdrew into the Collison Hills to remain undetected and undisturbed. The Nez Perces eventually bowed to White pressure to divide their lands, but even then they tended to select allotments in canyon bottomlands with prime fishing, near the grave sites of their ancestors, or on spots where they had grown up, with no regard to agricultural potential. This was cautious resistance in the shape of calculated conformity, whereas in the pre-reservation days it might have taken the form of an armed uprising.[60]

Among the Creeks, resistance turned into a minor rebellion. Traditionalists led by Chitto Harjo formed a dissident "Snake" party, established an independent government, and began corporally punishing tribal members who accepted allotments or rented land to Whites. It took federal troops making mass arrests in 1900–1901 and indicting 253 people for conspiracy and assault and battery to suppress this movement. Yet authorities could not stop the Snakes from continuing to live separately in their own way, claiming to be the authentic Creek Nation and banding together with "irreconcilables" among the Cherokees, Chickasaws, and Choctaws as the Four Mothers Society. Finally, in 1909, local White militias, unnerved by the presence of armed Indians and the growing numbers of mostly unaffiliated Blacks who clustered around the Snakes' ceremonial Hickory Grounds, violently broke up the movement, driving a wounded Chitto Harjo into hiding among Choctaw compatriots and the rest of his followers underground. Everywhere one turned, Indians were refusing United States' supposed gift of private land and citizenship, knowing that it was yet another scheme to strip them of their territory and remaining autonomy.[61]

CALCULATING

The challenge of determining of who would be counted as a tribal member entitled to a full allotment was considerable to judge from figures compiled by the 1910 census. It reported that 93,423 people, or 37.8 percent of the total Indian population, were "mixed-blood," including 43,937 people who were considered "more than half White" and 4,048 who had some degree of "Negro" ancestry. In Oklahoma, which boasted the largest Native population of any state, 74,825 Indians, or 62.6 percent, were reported in the 1910 census as being of mixed descent. Though few Indian groups west of Oklahoma had appreciable numbers of community members with Black ancestry, most of them had at least some and often many people with White progenitors as a legacy of the fur trade. These patterns led the educator Samuel Chapman Armstrong to quip that "by the admixture" of blood, "we shall ultimately have ... an Indian problem without Indians." For the meantime, the problem was how to reduce such complexity to bureaucratic categories of identity.[62]

Dawes allotment commissioners determined the eligibility of someone of mixed ancestry based on dominant White American notions of Indian "blood" (or degrees of racial "purity") as identity. In the compilation of tribal rolls (or member lists) for the assignment of lands, officers listed anyone who was clearly of Indian background and considered a tribal member in the "Citizens by Blood" category, alongside an identifying blood quantum. The other two categories for people affiliated with the tribes were "Citizens by Marriage" (pertaining to Whites and Indians from other tribes) and "Freedmen" (pertaining to Blacks). Such people would also receive allotments, but in lesser amounts, and would not be subject to the full range of restrictions on selling the tracts that applied to Indians, based on the assumption that their racial makeup equipped them to navigate the civilized marketplace.[63]

Yet race, as the commissioners understood it, did not fit neatly with the intricate reality of many tribal societies, particularly the Five Civilized Tribes, which originated in the Southeast and had been in contact with Whites and Blacks for centuries. As one White census taker remarked in 1890, "a serious difficulty was met in the answer to 'Are you an Indian?'" because "a person white in color and features is frequently an Indian, being so by remote degree of blood or by adoption." Furthermore, "Negroes are frequently met who speak nothing but Indian languages, and are Indians by tribal law and custom." Indians of mixed descent who did not meet the commissioners' expectations of how Native people should look had to prove their Indian bona fides by documenting their presence on previous tribal

Dawes Enrollment Card, with blood quanta for enrollees in the "Blood" column, sixth from the left. Courtesy of the National Archives and Records Administration.

rolls and testifying or having witnesses attest whether they could speak the people's Indian language, whether they lived in the manner of other Indians, and who their ancestors were.[64]

The commissioners were unlikely to categorize any mixed person with visible Black ancestry—hair texture, not just complexion or facial features, mattered a great deal in this respect—as either a citizen by blood or a citizen by marriage because of the widespread White American notion that Blackness eclipsed other heritages in a person of complex ancestry. Today that concept is known as the "one-drop rule" or "hypodescent." It did not matter if the person in question spoke only an Indian language or belonged to the tribe according to its reckonings, though few people with such backgrounds were tribal members in the first place because most of them descended from relationships between Indian men and Black women and the tribes were matrilineal. The issue for the commissioners was that, in White American racial logic, Blackness trumped all, or, put more accurately, polluted everything it touched. The commissioners did not and most probably could not explain why they thought this way, having been conditioned to do so since birth based on standards set well before their time. The function of these rules in White society was to limit the number of White-Black people who could claim the privileges of White identity; in the previous era of slavery, such calculations also had the effect of expanding the pool of Blacks who labored for Whites. In the context of Indian allotment, the effect was to keep Afro-Indians off tribal rolls.[65]

Indians had varying beliefs about whether and to what degree "blood" mattered to belonging. Even before allotment, cultural conservatives among the White Earth Ojibwes of Minnesota had widely referred to themselves as "real Indians" and sometimes as "full-bloods" and to those with White ancestry as "mixed-bloods." The Ojibwe word for mixed-blood, *wiisaakodewikwe* (female) or *wiisaakodewinini* (male), means "half-burned man or woman," like a burned piece of wood, charred on one side, light on the other. Many Cherokees, and undoubtedly Indians from other tribes, also reflexively considered full-bloods to be cultural standard bearers in terms of speaking the people's language and adhering to traditions. Yet even Indian schoolchildren could see the faultiness of too strictly associating mixed-bloods with civility and full-bloods with savagery. The *Indian School Journal* out of Chilocco quoted the Choctaw Gabe E. Parker "that there are hundreds of full bloods who are just as competent to manage their affairs as the most competent of those less than half blood, and that there are hundreds of half bloods and less who are no more competent than the incompetents of the full-blood class." Such reasoning was hard to find among the Cherokees and Creeks, whose widespread prejudice against Blacks obstructed their tribal governments from compiling their own citizenship lists ahead of the Dawes Commission. Indians were just as divided as Whites about the relationship between race and tribe, which meant that the issue would have to be settled politically with significant White involvement.[66]

Blood quantum policy and practice during the allotment era had the unintended but nevertheless damaging effect of obstructing Indians from repossessing their land

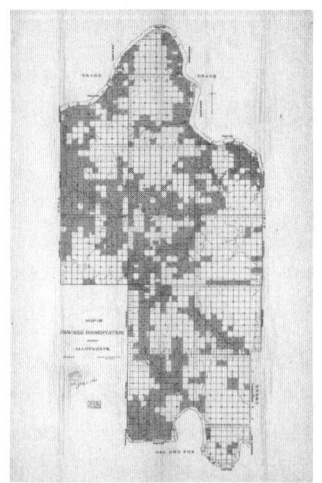

Hudson-Kimberly Publishing Company, cartographer, *Map of Pawnee Reservation showing allotments*, Oklahoma, 1893. Courtesy of the Library of Congress.

during the "Indian New Deal" of the 1930s and '40s. As this book will discuss later, the administration of Franklin Delano Roosevelt reversed the federal government's long-standing goal of eliminating tribal governments and territories. Instead, it aimed to reconstitute reservations by consolidating unsold allotments and surplus under government trust. It could not easily recover land that had never been allotted to mixed-bloods and freedmen in the first place, or that people in those categories had already sold off or been swindled out of before the twenty-five-year waiting period for full-bloods had expired. Clearly, creating this dilemma had not been the purpose of legislators from the allotment era. The express point of the Dawes and Curtis Acts was to privatize the land of *all* Indians of whatever blood quantum, eliminate all laws giving Indians special status, and make citizens of *all* Indians, eventually. The assumption was that the government would no longer need an Indian policy by the early to mid-twentieth century.

The Dawes and Curtis Acts, just as their critics had warned, functioned as a giant White land grab that left tens of thousands of Indians destitute. There had been 155,632,312 acres of Indian land in 1881. By 1900, just 77,865,373 remained, and by 1934 that amount had been further reduced to 48 million acres. Two thirds of Indians were left either completely landless or so land poor that they could not earn a subsistence. Indians became minorities on their own reservations, nowhere more so than in Federal Indian Territory, where, by 1907, when Oklahoma became a state, the number of Whites stood at 538,500, compared to 80,000 African Americans and just 61,000 Indians. Superintendent of Indian Affairs Charles H. Burke, surveying the wreckage in 1923, lamented that "a race of landlords, through their own inexperience and lack of appreciation for thrift, or through the farsighted activities and often cunning of their fellows, have been transformed into a race of tenants..."[67]

In a seeming impossibility, Indian life in White America had become more miserable than ever, out of both White aggression and White indifference. After thirty thousand Whites rushed in to claim portions of the Southern Cheyenne and Arapaho reservation, they did everything they could to harry the Indians off the rest of their territory. Newly formed White counties began to impose taxes on the Natives and impound their personal property when they refused or were unable to pay, even though Indians were legally exempt from county and state taxes as long as they lived on reservation land. White citizens followed with their own plundering of Indian property. The new order of things, one White resident half joked, was "buy a pony and steal four." Thieves also targeted the farming implements and even fence wood Indians were supposed to use to follow the civilized life. The Indians turned to the

Top: *One Minute before the Start, Sept. 16th, 1893*. Above: *Chilloco Reserve Sept. 16th, 1893*.

This "land run" was one of several such events in which Whites raced one another to stake first claim to former Indian reservation land opened to the market. Almost overnight, Indians became a minority in Federal Indian Territory.

agent to protect them, but he was too overwhelmed and intimidated by local Whites to be effective. Sometimes he was even in cahoots with them. When asked to explain, Whites complained that the government had given "the very best land to the Indians" and "how useless the effort was to benefit them" because "they are bound to die out."[68]

Whites in and around the Southern Cheyenne and Arapaho reservation grew so shameless that they murdered Indians in cold blood in broad daylight with no consequences. For instance, on November 20, 1893, a Texas cowboy named Tom O'Hara followed a Cheyenne named Wolf Hair out of town, then shot him dead without provocation. A U.S. attorney indicted O'Hara for first-degree murder, only for an all-White jury to find him innocent. Even a local newspaper had to admit that the proceedings were a "farce." Another travesty of justice occurred less than two years later when a lynch mob seized a Cheyenne named Red Lodge from the sheriff, who had taken him to a baseball game under custody because the county lacked a jail. The crowd beat and stabbed him within an inch of his life for the suspected rape of a White woman. As it turned out, another man was guilty of the crime. To the perpetrators, it hardly mattered. One White resident bragged that he and his neighbors would "like no better fun than the job of killing those damned Indians," and a White cattleman was overheard remarking: "I wish they were all dead."[69]

Such widespread persecution during the so-called assimilation era discouraged Indians from the pursuit of civilized living, to the extent that they were committed to it in the first place. In 1900, seven out of eight Southern Cheyenne and Arapaho families still lived in tepees. At most 18 percent were growing any crops. The agent and police were supposed to be in charge, but traditional chiefs and warrior societies continued to run things away from the agency headquarters, where Indians actually lived.[70]

If Indians made a living from their land, mostly it was in the form of collecting rent from Whites, which defeated the professed goal of the Dawes and Curtis Acts to promote Indian self-support and assimilation. Government policy stated that the only Indians permitted to lease their lands were widows, orphans, the disabled, the elderly, and those who had inherited allotments too small or remote to be of use to them. In practice, the Indian Office approved nearly every lease application submitted. Consequently, by 1898, the Poncas cultivated only 1,500 acres themselves while leasing 30,000 acres. The Pawnees likewise tended just 1,443 acres and rented out 36,784. These arrangements had the benefit of producing much-needed income for Native people in poverty, and provided the opportunity for wage work in the enterprises of White lessees, but they also turned the Dawes and Curtis Acts into mechanisms that reduced Indians to greater dependency on Whites. The Bureau of Indian Affairs reported in 1938 that only one-seventh of the Indian population earned its own living.[71]

Worse still, abuse and corruption were legion in the business of leasing Indian land and declaring competency. Native people complained endlessly that their agents leased or sold allotments without their permission, failed to disburse the proceeds to them, and gave White friends and relatives favorable deals, particularly when the agents were in charge of managing the interests of Indian minors. White lessees commonly refused to pay their rents, fearing neither the agents nor the courts. On the Ojibwe White Earth reservation, the agent colluded with lumber companies to allot the best woodlands to mixed-bloods and Indians he judged to be compliant, declared them "competent," then prevailed on the allottees to sell the tracts immediately. By 1909, a full 90 percent of this land had been mortgaged or sold and stripped of timber, thereby robbing the people of their primary sustainable resource. Meanwhile, private-property claims and ecological damage cut them off from their traditional mixed economy of fishing, wild rice harvesting, hunting, and maple sugaring. Utterly impoverished, most of the Ojibwes were reduced to squatting on deforested tracts at the edge of lakes that had belonged to them since time immemorial, but no longer. It was the same story practically everywhere in Indian country.[72]

The allotment acts and their supporting legislation had not turned Indians into White people. Instead, these measures became another example of how Whites in America exploited Indians with impunity while claiming to act in their benefit, reducing them to destitution, and then blaming them for the results based on their supposed racial characteristics. Montana congressman Charles Hartman spoke for a wide cross section of White society when he attributed the failures of the reservations and allotment to Native people's innate qualities, charging, "We have given these big buck Indians, any of them physically equal to four white men, this subsistence year after year... The result has been that fully 90 percent of them are loafers today. Not a single one of them desires to do any manual labor... they remain wards, sponges, and leeches upon the United States government." To be White, from this vantage, was to be a self-sufficient, contributing member of society, the very opposite of the lazy and dependent Indian. Indians had a different view of things. The Seneca Ely S. Parker, who served as commissioner of Indian affairs between 1869 and 1871, denounced the allotment and citizenship program from the beginning as an extension of the age-old White American principle of "might makes right," bound to produce "a sure, certain death to the poor Indians." He, like Native people across the country, not only knew but also experienced daily that White Americans no longer feared them, but instead either despised them as hopeless or ignored them altogether. Indians had gone from masters of the continent to a race of tenants. They had become victims of the nation of which they were now a part.[73]

And they had indeed become a part of it, not only in terms of living within its bounds and under its authority, but also as citizens. For Indians, however, this citizenship was not a gift of opportunity, legal equity, and dignity, as White Americans thought of it, but an imposition leading to greater injustice, segregation, landlessness, and destitution. Throughout the mid- to late nineteenth century, the federal government had granted citizenship piecemeal to Indian communities that requested it, such as the Brothertowns, Stockbridges, Ho-Chunks, and Potawatomis, as long as they allotted their lands and accepted White law. Increasingly, however, White authorities did not give Indians a chance to say yes or no. Beginning in the late 1860s, the New England states forced small groups like the Wampanoags, Narragansetts, Mohegans, and Pequots to divide their remaining common lands, then pronounced them to be full-fledged citizens. One of the states' arguments was that these Indians were too racially mixed, particularly with Blacks, to warrant keeping their legal Indian status any longer. In 1881, the U.S. Senate voted 29–12 against making all Indians citizens immediately, but, as allotment progressed, the federal government gradually made citizens out of select portions of Native America, regardless of their wishes. In 1901, it declared all Indians in Federal Indian Territory to be citizens, including those who refused allotments. Then, in 1919, the federal government extended citizenship to Indians who had served in the armed forces in World War I. By the time President Calvin Coolidge signed the Indian Citizenship Act into law in 1924, making U.S. citizens of all the nation's Indigenous people, 175,000 of the country's 300,000 Indians already held such status.[74]

Many of them had passed through an anachronistic ritual instituted by the Indian Office when issuing fee patents (or private-property rights) that dripped with racial stereotypes. It involved a male Indian stepping out from a tepee and shooting off an arrow to signify that he was leaving the Indian way of life. Next, he would put his hands on a plow to represent the transition to the farming life of White people. Finally, he pledged an oath to the United States and received a badge with an American eagle and a red, white, and blue ribbon. This rite captured the highest ideals of the Friends of the Indian, really an article of faith, that the White way of life constituted the pinnacle of human progress, Indians were capable of reaching this standard, and Whites had the right and the duty to force them to do so if they would not comply of their own accord. Friends of the Indian acknowledged that some Natives would fail miserably, probably at a higher rate than White people, but others would become respectable, contributing members of American society.[75]

The greatest deterrent to this vision was not Native people's disdain for White living, however significant it was. Rather, the main barrier was the refusal of White people in practically every Indian neighborhood to give them a fighting chance, and the unwillingness of the federal government, based on the interests of the White general public, to provide Indians with adequate protection and resources. Convincing Indians of the value of civilized living required real equality under the law. Without it, the system of reservations, boarding schools, allotments, fee patents, and citizenship amounted to a sprawling White plunder of Indian land and systematic abuse of Indian communities and families. This result had not been the intent of the Friends of the Indian when they designed the assimilation program—quite the contrary. However, they willfully ignored the fact that exploiting Indians was the exact design of a great many powerful White interests at the local level, including land speculators, cattle companies, timber companies, railroad companies, mining companies, and even small-scale ranchers and farmers. The driving motivation of such elements was profit, which they justified with the belief that God chose White people to enjoy the riches of America and damned Indians to destitution and extinction. Over the next century, the great challenge confronting Indians was to prove to the rest of American society but especially to themselves that this thinking was nothing more than colonial ideology and that defeating it was the only way to restore Indian sovereignty and hope.

CHAPTER 7

Visions in an Age of Systematic Racism

By 1918, Native Americans were supposed to be well on their way toward civility and incorporation into United States society, at least as far as White policymakers were concerned. Yet that same year a subcommittee of the House of Representatives' Committee on Indian Affairs conducted a lengthy hearing on a new, distinctly Indian cultural phenomenon that suggested that the assimilationist agenda was off track. All across Indian country, Native people were ingesting a psychoactive drug called peyote, made from the dried button of a cactus, during a nightlong ritual dedicated to Jesus. The legislators wanted to know whether peyote should be classified with other dangerous illegal narcotics like cocaine and heroin. Given that Indians were the users, the answer to that question hinged on not only the drug's physiological effects, but also its influence on Native people's integration into the White mainstream. The committee's proceedings would further reveal that a witness's position often extended from his or her sense of self as a full-blood Indian, mixed-blood Indian, or White, and views about the nature of those identities.

The rise of peyotism was swift and unexpected. Though there is petroglyphic evidence of peyote use in Mexico dating back forty-two hundred years, its consumption within what is now the United States had been limited always to groups such as the Lipan Apaches who lived close to the peyote cactus's growing zone along Texas's southern border. Then, in the late nineteenth century, peyote spread lightning quick throughout Indian country. Part of it had to do with the newfound ease of distribution afforded by trucks, railroads, and mail service. The main driver was demand, however, cultivated by prophets or "roadmen" such as the Comanche Quanah Parker, the Caddo-Wichita-Delaware John Wilson, and the Delaware Elk Hair. They taught that peyote was the Indian path to Jesus and, as such, a cure for drunkenness, sickness, moral degeneracy, and lethargy. Some practitioners contended that peyote was the very physical and spiritual manifestation of Jesus Christ. God meant it as a special gift to Indians, just as He had bestowed the Bible on White people. Indians needed this gift desperately, because under White American dominance their lives were shaped indelibly by systematic racism, meaning a vast range of both institutional and informal degradation based on their status as Indians. This new peyote religion was a way for Indians to take pride in themselves despite the misery of their oppression.[1]

The tiny population of Indians with university backgrounds and professional careers generally opposed peyote as an obstacle to progress that exploited their people's vulnerabilities. Of them, the most outspoken was Gertrude Simmons Bonnin, a Yankton Sioux musician, author, and activist who had studied at Indiana's Manual Labor Institute, Earlham College, and the New England Conservatory of Music. Her disapproval of peyote was not some manifestation of her having been brainwashed by White institutions to reject anything associated with Indians. Sometimes she went by her Lakota name, Zitkala-Ša, and in 1902 she published a provocatively titled essay, "Why I Am a Pagan," in the *Atlantic Monthly*. As secretary for the pro-integration Society of American Indians (SAI), she denounced the reservation system and the Bureau of Indian Affairs for keeping Indians subordinate rather than preparing them for independence in White America. In her mind, peyote only made things worse. It was "undermining the uplift work of the churches and our benevolent Government," she argued. It allowed drug pushers and faux spiritualists to fulfill their "unscrupulous greed" at the expense of "the ignorance and superstition of a people" and thus led to "race suicide."[2]

Zitkala-Ša, or Gertrude Simmons Bonnin, unknown photographer, frontispiece of *American Indian Stories* (Washington, D.C.: Hayworth Publishing House, 1921). Courtesy of Science History Images/Alamy.

Charles Eastman, a Santee physician, essayist, historian, and activist, shared Bonnin's views. Eastman's guiding principle was that Indian traditions could and should enrich modern American society, but peyote, he maintained, "is not an Indian idea nor is it an Indian practice." Having witnessed firsthand the bloody aftermath of the Wounded Knee Massacre, Eastman worried that peyotism was akin to the "ghost dance craze," which had precipitated that disaster. Additionally, peyote tended to attract and degrade Indian country's best and brightest, the boarding school alumni, who should have been leading the march to civility. Peyote appealed mostly to "those who are opposed to the white man's religion, claiming that there is something hypocritical in the white man's religion, and that something ought to be developed for the Indians that is superior to the white man's religion." Eastman and Bonnin's overarching concern was that peyote meant continued segregation and destitution, not integration and enhanced opportunity.[3]

The testimony of White Friends of the Indian echoed the same points with additional histrionics. These witnesses imagined that peyote caused hallucinations and even insanity, despite Indian users' insistence that typically it produced no visual effects and at most just enhanced color schemes. S. M. Brosius of the Indian Rights Fund of Philadelphia had never seen peyote or anyone under its influence, but he was certain that it was worse than gambling and liquor, a grave danger to pregnant women, a discouragement to Indians seeking proper medical treatment, and a gateway to divorce and lust. The missionary Mary W. Roe submitted that peyotism tempted a young Native man fresh from boarding school because it seemed like a traditional Indian practice, onto which he could layer what he had "superficially learned" from Whites. The result mocked Christianity and civility by infusing them with barbarism, which so infuriated Adelbert Leech, superintendent of the Yankton Sioux reservation, that he exclaimed, "If anything could be said in favor of [peyote's] use, it would be that it would probably result in the extermination of those who use it."[4]

Most of the Indians who appeared before Congress testified that peyote actually promoted Christianity and civility, but in a manner special to Indians. They agreed almost to a person, whether they were peyotists or not, that peyote cured or at least combated the scourge of Indian alcohol abuse as well as other physical ills resistant to White medicine. The Omaha ethnologist Francis La Flesche submitted, for that reason alone, that peyote should remain available to Indians. Some peyotists also wanted the committee to understand *why* peyote was so effective. Jock Bull Bear, an Arapaho alumnus of the Carlisle school, explained that peyote allowed Indians to commune with "Almighty God," which was why he and so many other users "are living uprightly under the United States flag, and helping to improve the conditions of our Indian race, to make them better Christians, and to live the real civilized life." A group of Osage peyotists, in a letter to the committee, added that "we are living more peaceable, honorable, and Christlike" because God had given "red men" peyote just as he had placed them in America.[5]

The meeting received a jolt of controversy when James Mooney, a White scholar in the Smithsonian Institution's Bureau of Ethnology, took the stand to support the Indians who claimed that peyotism was a legitimate religion and a source of medicine. Mooney was part of a burgeoning trend in the still young field of ethnology that rejected the proposition that Indian cultures were inferior stages on a human evolutionary scale. Instead, this new approach viewed Indian traditions as worthy of understanding on their own terms as expressions of human diversity. From this perspective, all human cultural differences were value-neutral rather than hierarchically ranked, and certainly did not derive from biological differences. Novel and broad-minded as this position was, it rested on the old presumption that Indian cultures had remained basically static until the arrival of White civilization, whereupon they plunged into decline toward disappearance. The ethnographer's job was to document whatever was left of ancient Native life before that fateful moment. Mooney himself had conducted extensive research on peyotism (and got himself kicked off the Kiowa reservation by its federal agent in the process) as a follow-up to his pathbreaking research on the Ghost Dance, the Sun Dance, and Cherokee folklore. He was, by most White people's lights, an expert on Indians.[6]

Mooney's fellow witness Richard H. Pratt did not grant him this honor. Pratt, the founder of the Carlisle school, despised Mooney and his fellow ethnologists for

James Mooney 1861–1921, unknown photographer, 1901. Courtesy of the Smithsonian Institution Libraries, Gift from the library of John C. Ewers.

convincing the federal Indian Office to be more tolerant of Native cultural practices on the reservations and even in the boarding schools. Now, at the hearing, Pratt had to suffer not only former Carlisle students like Bull Bear and the Kiowa Lone Wolf touting the virtues of peyote, but also Mooney's defense of them. Pratt used his time on the stand to accuse ethnologists of deliberately stalling Indians' progress in the interest of collecting research data when they should have been instructing them, "My brother, you can become a citizen of the United States; you can become civilized, and you can become thoroughly useful in the United States." Mooney, for his part, chided Pratt that perhaps for once he should check his facts before he spoke. As their quarrel grew hot, the hearing's chairman broke in, "This is not throwing very much light on the subject of peyote."[7]

Mooney's testimony also ignited the heated politics of Indian identity. Whereas Pratt and other assimilationists praised Bonnin and Eastman as "intelligent Indians" who had "come forward in a very few years to a fair position and knowledge of our life," Mooney saw Bonnin as a fraud. Her self-presentation as Indian was a hodgepodge of what ethnologists considered separate cultural elements and therefore, in Mooney's estimation, it was inauthentic. Mooney criticized that her dress was from some "southern tribe," her belt was that of a Navajo man, and the fan she carried, with no sense of irony, was "a peyote man's fan, carried only by men, usually in the peyote ceremony." Mooney would grant only that Bonnin was "someone who claims to be a Sioux woman, in Indian costume," with a stress on *claims*. His point was that the assimilationists' star Indian witness did not even know how to be a proper Indian.[8]

The Southern Arapaho Cleaver Warden agreed with Mooney not only on the basis of Bonnin's cultural presentation but also on her insufficient Indian "blood." A Carlisle alumnus, farmer, and dedicated peyotist, Warden advised Congress to learn about the drug from genuine Indian practitioners, "not half breeds who do not know a bit of their ancestors and kindred. A true Indian is one who helps for a race, and not that secretary of the Society of American Indians." "Half-breed," of course, was a historic slur of Indians of mixed Indian-White ancestry as ambiguous, incomplete, and untrustworthy, neither fish nor fowl. Warden did not speak from the position of a reservation traditionalist. After seven years at Carlisle, he had worked for a year as a scout at Fort Reno, two years as a stagecoach driver, four years as a store clerk, and another four years at Chicago's Field Museum, one of the leading institutions of Indian ethnography. He had visited Washington, D.C., several times on tribal business and consulted with the American Museum of Natural History in New York.

He was formally educated, "neat" in appearance, and owned property that included a three-room house, barn, and shed. Unlike Bonnin, however, he had returned home and stayed there to apply his education for the benefit of his people. He also claimed cultural authority over her by virtue of his being a full-blood, which Indians and Whites both commonly associated with Indian authenticity. Not least of all, Warden was a peyotist, which, as far as he and other believers was concerned, was the future of Indian religion and peoplehood.[9]

Peyotists then did not and today still do not see their religion as universal, but as an Indian faith. The Ho-Chunk peyote leader Albert Hensley testified before Congress in 1908 that peyote "was given exclusively to the Indians and God never intended that White men should understand it." It would continue to spread "til every Indian in the boundaries of our great country has learned the truth, and knows God and God intends they should know him." Emerging at a time when reservations, boarding schools, and pervasive White discrimination were wearing down Indians body and soul, peyotism offered sanctified hope, direction, and self-esteem as Indians. It also critiqued the pervasive greed and loneliness of White society even as it encouraged values that would permit Indians to live fulfilling lives under White rule. Though peyotists on the Northern Plains twice flirted with messianism in the 1940s, in which they presaged Jesus's return as an Indian child and the coming of a great wind that would sweep away the Whites and assimilated Indians, that fervor was short-lived. For most of its history, peyotism has advanced a quieter, practical message that the Creator wants Indians to care for one another, tend to their marriages and families, work hard, remain sober, and otherwise live uprightly confident in who they are. There has long been a saying among peyotists that "the peyote religion is the only thing left to us Indians."[10]

Peyote ritual is unmistakably an Indian religion. Worshippers meet in a tepee instead of a rectangular-framed building. They often arrive at the ceremony in distinctive Indian clothing adorned with colorful artwork that has become known as the "peyote style." Peyote ritual generally takes place in English, but individual prayers often go up in tribal languages. Participants gather around an altar and central fire in a circle and sit "in the Indian way," as they put it, "close to Mother Earth," because they are too poor to worship in comfort like Whites. Ingesting peyote leads some of them to throw up in what they understand as a purge of sickness and bad feelings, as in the Nativist ceremonies of previous centuries. Praying, singing, and doctoring go together, which has been Indian tradition since time out of mind. Paraphernalia

James Mooney, *Peyote Ceremony*, Kiowa-Comanche Reservation, Oklahoma, 1892.
Courtesy of National Anthropological Archives.

include a drum with a buckskin head, gourd rattle, eagle-wing whistle, cluster of sage, cedar incense, feathers, tobacco, corn husks, and a staff, all of which would have been recognizable to the ancestors. The evening-long ceremony ends with a breakfast of parched corn, fruit, and meat, understood as Indigenous foods meant for Indigenous constitutions. The only significant way peyote ceremony differs from most Indian rituals is its lack of dancing.[11]

Devotees see no contradiction in their insistence that peyotism is an Indian form of Christianity. Some of them say that Whites rejected Jesus by murdering him, so now Jesus tends to rejected Indians. They commonly assert that the spirit embodied in peyote is Jesus himself or the Holy Ghost. They teach and follow the Ten Commandments and the Golden Rule. Their rituals are full of Christian symbolism. Sometimes, they paint Jesus's face on a peyote button placed on their central altar alongside the Bible. The poles supporting the tepee stand for Jesus and his disciples. Crosses adorn a ritual staff with feathers representing the twelve apostles, and worshippers in prayer make the sign of the cross. Blowing the eagle-bone whistle "is to announce the birth of Christ to the world," and a drink of water at midnight marks the time when Jesus was born. A fan of eagle feathers is used to sprinkle water on the worshippers, like baptism. As peyotists sum it up, "The White man who knows how to read, learns God's way from the Bible. The Indian, who does know how to read, learns God's way through peyote."[12]

Peyotists, reportedly at Mooney's urging, incorporated their various congregations as the Native American Church immediately following the 1918 congressional hearings to protect their faith under the First Amendment from government persecution. Though they did not act fast enough to stop the House of Representatives from voting to outlaw peyote, they did prevail on Oklahoma's senators to defeat the bill in the upper chamber. That victory, plus incorporation, has helped to prevent any future federal laws against peyote, despite occasional efforts by the Indian Office to suppress it and largely ineffective bans at the state level. By 1925, there were an estimated 13,345 peyotists. Today, there are some three hundred thousand from seventy or so tribes. The late anthropologist Omer C. Stewart went so far as to propose that "except the powwow, [peyotism] is the most pan-Indian institution in America." Unable to halt the movement, in the 1950s and '60s even states that otherwise criminalized peyote began to make exceptions for members of the Native American Church. Finally, in 1994 Congress responded to a 1990 Supreme Court decision upholding Oregon's refusal to permit a religious exemption for peyote by passing the Religious Freedom Act, which gave full protection to the sacramental use of peyote by Indians. It remains the law of the land.[13]

Peyote might not cause hallucinations, but, clearly, peyotists in the early twentieth century had an alternative vision for the future of Indians than White and Indian assimilationists, White ethnographers, or even Indian traditionalists for whom peyote was an unwelcome innovation. Peyotism provided them with a framework not just to retain but positively express cherished Indian values and practices despite the endless injuries and indignities to which White Americans subjected them. Furthermore, though the peyotists disagreed with fellow Indians Bonnin and Eastman about the value of peyote, they all shared the principle that being Indian and modern was not a contradiction, contrary to what the vast majority of Whites believed. The question was what Indian modernity would mean in practice given the narrow range of White opinion on that issue. Practically the entirety of White officialdom, ranging from Pratt to Mooney, took for granted that Indians could not survive for long in the contemporary world as tribal nations, only as individuals, though they differed on how quickly that disappearance would and should occur. Other White Americans, of every rank, continued to assert that Indians as groups and as individuals were damned to extinction while Whites were chosen to thrive. Indian racial politics in the twentieth century involved expanding the possibilities to include modern Indian futures, cultural distinctiveness, and even self-determination as tribes on their own territory, in what amounted to a fundamental challenge to Indian and White identities alike.

BEING INDIAN IN WHITE AMERICA

One of the main appeals of peyotism for Indians was that it countered their relentless racial subordination and denigration by White Americans, even those without designs on Indian land. The reservations and boarding schools continued to operate on the old White supremacist ideal that Indians must become civilized and assimilated, but enthusiasm for that agenda had weakened in the face of Indian opposition and persistent misgivings among Whites that most Indians simply were not up to the task. Even Francis Leupp, chief administrator of the Bureau of Indian Affairs in the early 1900s, favored replacing Indian education in the arts and sciences with simple, practical skills like basic math, reading a newspaper, and writing a letter. He explained in *The Indian and His Problem* (1910) that "nature has drawn her lines of race, which it is folly for us to try to obliterate along with the artificial barriers we throw down in the cause of civil equality. The man whom she has made an Indian, let us try to make a better Indian, instead of struggling vainly to convert him into a Caucasian." He was not suggesting that Whites should leave Indians alone, just that they should not expect too much from them.[14]

Some Whites resolved that the question hardly mattered anymore because, as Superintendent W. S. Campbell of the Pipestone Indian School in Minnesota framed it, "In another generation the Indian, as such, will have passed away ... He is rapidly assimilating American ideas and in another generation it will be impossible to distinguish him from the white man." The thirteenth U.S. census of 1910 revealed that just under half of all Indians in the country were of mixed White ancestry, which, according to the *Denver News*, meant that "but a few more than half of the so-called Indians in the United States are real Indians." Given that mixed ancestry usually led to accelerated termination of one's protected legal status as Indian, the long-anticipated day of Indian extinction seemed to be near.[15]

Textbook authors and educators taught schoolchildren across the country that Indians were savage, if sometimes noble, and fated to disappear, whereas Whites were civilized, Christian, and therefore blessed by God to expand and thrive. Most Indians were not buying it. The Seneca Arthur C. Parker declared in 1915 that "no race of men has been more unjustly misrepresented by popular historians than the American Indian. Branded as an ignorant savage, treacherous, cruel and immoral in his innocent nature, the Indian has received little justice from the ordinary historian." Sherman Coolidge, an Arapaho Episcopalian minister and Parker's colleague in the SAI, added that "in our early school days, the Indian was defined as a savage ... He was a fierce, ferocious, cruel, crafty, treacherous, bloodthirsty, red devil! Exterminate him! Exterminate him! Again, he has been described as a dirty, lazy, shiftless loafer, beggar, and drunkard." Even school songs propagated this view. Floyd O'Neil, a White man educated on the Uintah and Ouray reservation in Utah in the 1930s, remembered being required, along with his Indian classmates, to sing a hymn that went: "Let the Indian, let the Negro, let the rude barbarian see / That divine and glorious conquest / Once obtained on Calvary." He also recalled the Indian students' stubborn refusal to say these words, which "incensed" the teacher. The point of such exercises was less to degrade Indians than to tout Whites and, by extension, the United States. When the anthropologist Franz Boas conducted a study in the 1930s about how race was taught in American high schools, his team found that 32 of 166 textbooks in history, geography, and civics contained explicit arguments for White superiority, with one pronouncing that "civilization has been developed and history has been made chiefly by the white race." Indians factored only as an inferior counterpoint destined to vanish before that civilization, like the primeval forest or bison.[16]

Virtually all Americans grew up with these racial lessons, so it is no wonder that Indians commonly suffered discrimination and degradation by Whites. Secretary of the Interior Franklin Knight Lane recognized that "there is a large and unscrupulous class of citizens whose view of the Indian problem is simply that the Indians are a race doomed to early extinction and that in the meantime they may be made the natural prey of every knave and land shark who is shrewd enough to exploit and rob them." The mistreatment was even more widespread and varied than Lane acknowledged. Ben Stonecool, a Pitt River Indian of California, complained to the BIA that local Whites "won't let us eat in hotel or sleep in rooming house," and that, even when Indians managed to get served, Whites "bring food out in [a] dishpan like they [were] going to feed [a] dog or hog." Indians everywhere complained about merchants charging them more than Whites, and of White employers refusing them jobs for which they were qualified on the excuse, "We hire Americans only. We don't employ dark races." Whites routinely slurred Indians as "redskins," which, the Chilocco Indian Boarding School newspaper stressed, is "harsh and unkind." Many Whites, as Arthur C. Parker objected, questioned Indians to their faces as to whether they were "half-breeds" or "ignorant fullbloods." Practically every Indian who played on a majority White sports team carried the nickname "Chief," as in the case of Major League Baseball pitcher Charles "Chief" Bender (Ojibwe), who won over two hundred games with four different teams in the 1900s and 1910s. Bender pleaded with the press corps, "I do not want my name to be presented to the public as an

Indian, but as a pitcher," though in vain. The sports pages regularly identified him and other Native athletes as "the Indian," usually accompanied by racial clichés that he had scalped, tomahawked, massacred, or ambushed the batters he faced, or been on the receiving end of such treatment. Meanwhile, opposing teams and their fans taunted Indigenous players with war whoops and racial epithets.[17]

White systematic racism toward Indians was more than just a matter of insults, misrepresentations, or vicious racial theories: It was policies and practices that hobbled Native people's ability to feed, house, and clothe themselves and their loved ones; wrecked their health; landed them in prison; and, for far too many, deflated their sense of self-worth. Practically every measure of Indian well-being in the twentieth century signaled a crisis. More than half of Indians in 1928 had incomes of less than $200 a year, at a time when the average per capita income for working Americans stood at $1,362. Five years later, a government report found that 49 percent of Indians on allotted reservations were landless. Reports from the Blackfeet reservation in northern Montana in 1921 were that Native veterans of World War I were literally "dying by the roadside" from hunger, and others reduced to eating prairie dogs and skunks because "their hunting grounds have been pre-empted and their land filched." Clearly, the policies of reservations, allotment, and forced assimilation had been abject disasters.[18]

Yet officials continued to blame Indians themselves. In 1917, E. B. Linnen of the Department of the Interior had the nerve to lecture a Lakota audience at Pine Ridge that "white men are not so favored as you Indians. They were not given the land as were you ... You Indians have not had to pay for your lands ... You do not have to pay taxes on your land and there is no reason why you should not be able to prosper and support yourselves and your families if you will but try, if you will but work." He neglected that Whites had usurped the Indians' best lands and often continued to poach on what few resources the Natives had left, that the graft of federal agents robbed Native people of incalculable wealth owed to them by treaty right, and that there were practically no jobs on the reservations.[19]

Linnen also overlooked how hard it was for Indians to care for themselves when they were in such poor health, though it was no secret. The Indian Office's own statistics showed that, in 1918, 46 percent of Indians nationwide were infected with trachoma and 36 percent with tuberculosis. A staggering 27 percent of Native children died before age three. The 1918–19 global influenza epidemic made this horrific situation even worse by carrying off 2 percent of the Native population, a mortality rate four times greater than that of urban Whites. The only good news was that the Native population was growing again, albeit slowly, after reaching its nadir of 237,196 in 1900.[20]

Assimilation policy was premised on the idea that private property, hard work, and formal education would equip Indians to participate in White society, but the vast majority of Indians were not receiving quality educations, in large part because too many White educators considered them unworthy of it. Indians who attended federal boarding schools or majority-White public schools faced constant racial scorn from White teachers and students in addition to the insulting themes of White supremacy and Indian inferiority in the curriculum. Harriette Shelton of the Tulalip tribe of Washington state recalled of her school days during the 1910s that one staff member regularly criticized Native students in front of everyone with the slight, "Isn't that just like an Indian?" This was no isolated incident. Lily J. Neal, the first woman to serve on the Navajo Tribal Council, complained that Whites, ranging from schoolchildren to schoolteachers and administrators to everyday people, casually treated Indians as "backward, noncooperative, dumb, and illiterate." The Indian Office attempted to make federal schools more welcoming by including some lessons in Native American history and art, but these reforms could not offset the racism that pervaded American educational institutions, crushing students' will to learn, confidence in their abilities, and faith in society.[21]

Indians put up their own resistance to formal education shaped by their racial attitudes toward Whites and Blacks. After numerous Hopis suffered arrest and imprisonment rather than send their children to boarding schools, their leader, Yukeoma, petitioned President William Howard Taft, "We don't want schools and school teachers. We want to be let alone to live as we wish ... without the white man always there to tell us what we must do." School, from this perspective, was just another form of White domination, as indeed it was. In the Southeast, where the federal government left Indians to the public education system, many Native people refused to abide by the Jim Crow prohibition of them from White schools and relegation of them to so-called Colored institutions with Blacks. The Pamunkeys of Virginia and Lumbees of North Carolina managed to secure state funding for their own "Indian" schools, but most other tribal communities had to live with the Black schools or do without. The Mississippi Choctaws, among several Southern tribes, chose the latter, fearing with good reason that otherwise Whites would recategorize and treat them even worse, as Blacks.[22]

The justice system joined the reservations and schools in propagating White supremacy and Indian inferiority. During the 1920s, the Osages of Oklahoma suffered at least twenty murders perpetrated by a gang that included White guardians, lawyers, and lawmen in pursuit of the tribe's incredible oil wealth. It took three years to indict the ringleader of this operation, rancher William Hale, and just eighteen years to parole him. As an investigation by the American Indian Defense Association concluded, Indians throughout Oklahoma were "being, and have been, shamelessly and openly robbed in a scientific manner" because they were "virtually at the mercy of groups that include county judges, guardians, attorneys, bankers, merchants ... all regarding the Indians' estates as legitimate game." The problem of the justice system's serving as a weapon for White interests and a shield against White accountability, however, was not limited to Oklahoma. It was everywhere.[23]

A 1928 investigation of U.S. Indian policy and the state of Indian country conducted by the Brookings Institution, known as the Meriam Report, revealed that destitution and injustice were pervasive, systematic, and steeped in racism. Nowhere was this argument more poignant than in the report's discussion of conditions at the boarding schools. It found White policymakers and administrators to blame for schools' disgraceful record of leaving students malnourished, overworked, and riddled with diseases, never mind undereducated. Such needless suffering led the investigators to charge that White Americans needed to reform their attitudes toward Indians before they could formulate wise and humane polices for them. "To lift a people up and look down on them at the same time is not possible," the authors emphasized. "Nor can one without respect for a people and faith in their future inspire them to self-respect and faith in themselves." It did not occur to the investigators to recommend allowing Indians to govern and educate themselves on land protected from White encroachment, so ingrained was paternalism and cultural chauvinism even among the most empathetic Whites.[24]

The Meriam Report's vision of an Indian policy shaped by greater resources, humanity, and intelligence simply could not compete with popular culture's demeaning imagery of Indigenous people, particularly in the movies. During the first half of the twentieth century, Americans across the social spectrum went to the movies, on average, once a week or more. Given that more than a hundred "Indian" movies appeared each year (including two hundred in 1911 alone) in the early years of Hollywood, and remained prominent until after World War II, audiences were exposed to an endless succession of Indian stereotypes. The most popular Indian genre was the western, a drama set, as the name would suggest, in the mid-to-late-nineteenth-century West during its so-called frontier stage, when Indians and the land were still wild. The hero is a White male gunslinger who, as a loner, drifts between White and Indian societies without belonging fully to either one. Ultimately, though, his brave exploits advance the cause of Manifest Destiny for White people to tame and possess the continent. John Wayne's classic roles in *Stagecoach* (1939) and *The Searchers* (1959) are some of the best-known examples of this figure. Indians, by contrast, are "hostiles," who violently oppose White progress, sometimes nobly and even justifiably, most times savagely, always futilely. Nearly all Indians in the westerns adhere to a generic Plains type characterized by elaborate feathered headdresses, horses, and tepees. With the introduction of sound to the movies in the late 1920s, Indians tend to grunt and war-whoop rather than talk, except when giving elaborate, metaphorical speeches about their impending demise. They enter the frame to the standard musical theme of tom-tom beats and a horn arrangement supposed to resemble Native chanting. They exit their final scene by fading into the distance while the White protagonists march triumphantly into the future. For decades, these typified Indians and Whites existed in counterpoint on silver screens across America and in American minds.[25]

On the rare occasions that Indian films ventured beyond the wars for the West, usually it was to explore the plight of semi-civilized Indians trapped between two worlds. Such figures are shunned by their natal communities because they have become dandified snobs while away in boarding school or the city. They are also rejected by Whites because they are Indians. The inability of even these educated Indians to adapt to the modern world makes them prone to backslide into savagery, get themselves murdered, and even take their own lives. The moral of the story is that Indians are so hopelessly primitive that they must make way for Whites. The contrast with the White heroes of the westerns, whose familiarity with both settlers and Indians enables them to contribute to the triumph of White civilization, could not have been starker.[26]

These storylines exhibit a surprising tendency to use Indian-White romances for narrative tension, only for dramatic circumstances to break up the pair and return them to their respective racial communities, as nature supposedly intended. When films like D. W. Griffith's *Call of the Wild* (1908) toy with passion between an Indian man and a White woman, this split always occurs before the relationship is consummated. Sex and reproduction between a White man and a Native woman was more easily broached, as in *The Squaw Man* (1914) or *The Red Woman* (1917), as part of the historical association of those relationships with White conquest. Yet even those fictional pairings almost always end in disaster, even death, to signal that such unions are wrong. Filmmakers propagated the same message by depicting "mixed-bloods" as conniving villains, loyal to no one but themselves. It would have been unthinkable for Hollywood to produce similar scripts involving White and Black lovers because crossing the White-Black divide was utterly taboo, even illegal. Likewise, it would have made no sense to feature "mulatto" characters in "trapped between two worlds" plots because American racial logic considered people of complex Black ancestry to be just Black. Movie scripts followed the White social and political agenda of keeping Whites and Blacks segregated and encouraging Indian assimilation, futile as it might have seemed. Any potential White outrage at depictions of White-Indian passion, however unfulfilled, was lessened by the fact that most Indian leads were not played by Indian actors but instead by Whites in redface.[27]

Indians understood the power this new medium was having in shaping the public's image of them as a race of primitive relics who were disappearing if not already disappeared. As early as 1911, a delegation of thirty Ojibwes from Minnesota visited Washington, D.C., to urge federal lawmakers to combat the "grossly libelous" depictions of Indians in the movies. They were particularly offended by *Curse of the Redman*, in which a civilized, formally educated Apache football star gives into "the call of the wild" in the form of drunken murder after suffering rejection by both White society and his own tribe. A man called Red Eagle wrote to the film industry newsletter *Motion Picture World* to protest that Hollywood productions caricatured the Indian as a "yelling, paint bedaubed creature, reeking of barbarism and possessing little or no intelligence." Whites might claim harmless fun, but Red Eagle warned that they were "instilling an antagonistic germ in the mind of the young American

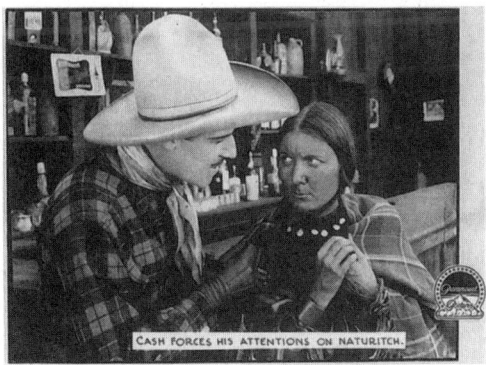

A moment from the film *The Squaw Man*, one of several Hollywood productions that broached the subject of sexual relationships between Whites and Indians, particularly White men and Native women. Courtesy of LMPC/Getty Images.

against the American Indian that, if continued, may cause bitterness." The message was clearly lost on one White defender of Hollywood, who answered with a mocking letter to the editor in the same broken English that Westerns portrayed Indians as speaking: "This show heap bad. Heap big lie. Pictures show Injun men bad men and do heap bad thing all time." The fight continued into the 1930s, as the star athlete turned actor Jim Thorpe helped found an Indian Actors Association to lobby for a federal film code that would require filmmakers to hire Indians for all Indian parts. The effort failed, but even if successful its likely result (in addition to more jobs for Indians) would have been Native people playing roles that reinforced rather than challenged White stereotypes of Indians. After all, the studios' bottom line depended on meeting the expectations of White audiences.[28]

The problem was that American culture as a whole, not just the movies, trafficked in stereotypes of primitive Indians, sometimes noble, sometimes savage. Take commercial advertisements, for example. Now that real Indians were defeated, subjugated, and invisible to most of the White public, ads could use their caricatured likeness to convey quintessential Americanness, nature, purity, authenticity, and nostalgia for simpler times. All manner of companies used Indians in their promotions. This list included manufacturers of tobacco, corn, motor oil, firearms, bubble gum, butter, motorcycles, honey, soda pop, fruit, and liquor. Actual Indians might have been relegated to the margins, but images of Indians were everywhere.[29]

Equally ubiquitous was the White use of clichéd Indian imagery for sports monikers. Examples from baseball's professional ranks included the Boston Braves (named 1912) and Cleveland Indians (1914); in football there were the Akron Indians (1908) and Washington Redskins (1937); hockey had the Chicago Blackhawks (1926). Among the mascots of higher education were the Indians of the College of William and Mary (1916), Dartmouth College (ca. 1920), and Stanford University (1930), the Redskins of Miami University (1928), and the Redmen of the University of Massachusetts (1948). Indian themes at high schools were more common still. The reason was that the White public wanted to imagine their sports teams as being imbued with warrior spirit and connection to place. Furthermore, fans delighted in war whooping, dressing up in feathers and face paint, and making tomahawk gestures as if they were Indigenous people defending their ground against the opposing squad. It did not matter what actual Indians thought of White people caricaturing them because they were supposed to be extinct, thoroughly assimilated, or at least easily ignored. Such misrepresentations contributed to American society's distorted measures of Indian authenticity.[30]

Squaw Beans

Land O' Lakes Butter. Courtesy of Richard Levine/Alamy.

Big Chief root beer stand. Courtesy of Bettmann/Getty Images.

Silent Chief Gasoline

Native people in the East who wanted public recognition as Indians had little choice but to play up to the stereotype. When peoples like the Wampanoags of Massachusetts, Narragansetts of Rhode Island, or Pamunkeys, Mattaponis, and Chickahominies of Virginia appeared in public for civic ceremonies, almost invariably they donned Plains-style costumes. To have worn their people's traditional dress, never mind street clothes, would have risked White people's dismissing them as imposters, thereby undermining their ongoing struggles to have their respective state governments honor their Indigenous rights. When the Wampanoags held a tribal powwow in 1928, their insignia made the connection plainly: It featured an Indian in a Plains-style headdress with the saying, "I Still Live."[31]

Some Indians profited by exploiting White people's image of them as a primal antidote for the alienation of modern life. The early twentieth century witnessed a spike in White Americans' appreciation for Indigenous arts—a movement known as "primitivism"—with a corresponding market for Indian pottery, blankets, baskets, needlework, and painting. Subsequently, tourist dollars became essential to the economies of many impoverished reservation communities. Painters such as Fred Kabotie (Hopi), Tonita Peña (San Idelfonso Pueblo), Carl Sweezy (Arapaho), and a group known as the Kiowa Six (consisting of Spencer Asah, James Auchiah, Jack Hokeah, Stephen Mopope, Monroe Tsatoke, and Lois Smoky) took their depictions of tribal

Four full-blooded Indians of the Wampanoag nation who gathered for the three-day powwow of their tribes as Mashpee, 1929.

From left to right: Chief Standing Rock of the Herring Pond tribe; Chief Red Shell of the Wampanoags; Chief Small Bear of the Mashpee tribe; and Chief High Eagle, medicine man of the Wampanoags. Courtesy of the Boston Herald-Traveler Photo Morgue, Boston Public Library.

ceremony to some of the most prestigious museums and galleries in the western world. Such opportunities were precious, regardless of how they encouraged Whites to view Indians as relics.[32]

Yet the relentless destitution and degradation that Indians suffered because of Whites took an enormous psychological toll on their individual and collective sense of self-worth. In 1912, the Oneida orator, organizer, and activist Laura Cornelius Kellogg proposed that among Native America's greatest challenges was "our growing disbelief in ourselves due to our having been misrepresented so long, and in defining everything to the white man's opinions of us," and she was far from alone. Indians in Los Angeles told the Meriam Committee that "feeling Indian" meant lacking the confidence to engage in even routine interactions in White society. As one of them explained, "I never got away from being Indian until I made the first payment in buying my home. Before then, I never could approach a white man and put out my hand and say, 'How do you do!'" How could it be otherwise? Another anonymous source admitted that "there was a time when I just didn't want to be Indian ... the forces out there were much greater than I; the movies portraying us as savages. When you are laughed at, you become inferior." Indian political activism in the twentieth century would always involve combating this internalized sense of inferiority amid the seemingly impossible struggle to end White racial oppression.[33]

RACE PROGRESS

Shortly after a group of progressive Indians formed the Society of American Indians, in 1911, they began publishing a magazine with a masthead announcing, "A Journal of Race Progress." Comprised of formally educated and professionally accomplished Native men and women, most of whom had spent their formative years away from reservations, they advocated for Indians to get out from under the control of the Bureau of Indian Affairs and into mainstream American society, confident that they could compete and contribute. Their own lives testified to the possibility. The founders included Thomas L. Sloan, an Omaha lawyer; Charles E. Dagenett, a high-ranking Peoria officer in the BIA; Laura Cornelius Kellogg; the Seneca archaeologist Arthur C. Parker; the Lakota political leader Henry Standing Bear (the younger brother of Luther); the Santee physician Charles Eastman; and the Yavapai-Apache physician Carlos Montezuma. Though these figures saw no future in the segregation and bureaucratic controls of the reservation, they believed that Indian values and practices had a great deal to offer the modern world if only Indians would join it and Whites would give them a chance. Their society aimed to promote this vision by holding an annual conference, lobbying, publishing, and advocating. Not least of all, this class of bourgeois Indians wanted to hold themselves up as examples of self-made "modern Indians" to Indian country and the rest of the world. "The Indian race is not vanishing but changing," proclaimed Montezuma. "He must stand on his own two feet."[34]

The SAI favored assimilation, but with caveats. Most of its members agreed that allotment, individualization, and integration was the best and only course for Native people. The key was to end the stifling range of federal controls over Indian lives, because, as Parker put it, "the reservation Indian has his heart strangled by the fears that beset him. He does not know what will happen next. He knows that something is being done to him, and perhaps for him, but having little or no part in its initiation, his interest may be only a morbid one ... It is appallingly true that the majority of reservation Indians do not even know what their rights are or where or how to turn in case of difficulty." The SAI agreed with White Protestant reformers and anthropologists that though Indians and Whites were separate races, the only

Cover page of the Society of American Indians' journal, *American Indian Magazine*, volume 6, no. 4 (Winter 1919).

significant difference between them was that Indians lagged on the evolutionary scale. The key was to encourage them to try to catch up, and convince Whites to help rather than treating them as incompetent wards. "The future of the Indians is with the white race," Eastman believed, "and in a civilization derived from the old world."[35]

Note that Eastman said "with the white race," not "in the white race." The SAI did not want or expect Indians to vanish through assimilation, but instead to retain a sense of tribal and racial identity even as they adhered to White standards. The organization took two notable steps toward these goals. The first was convincing the states of New York, Connecticut, Wisconsin, Illinois, Nebraska, and Washington to hold an annual "American Indian Day" celebrating Indigenous culture and achievements. The practice did not last long or spread very far—indeed, a number of progressive Indians soured on it quickly because organizers so often presented Indians in stereotypical fashion for the entertainment of White crowds—but it was a step toward the current national recognition of Native American Heritage Month each November. Far more consequential was the Indian Citizenship Act, or Snyder Act, of 1924, which granted U.S. citizenship to all Native people regardless of whether they had taken up allotments or met the government's standard of civilized competence. To be sure, some groups, such as the Haudenosaunees and several Pueblo communities, denounced the measure as a violation of their autonomy and a Trojan horse for taxation, while Luther Standing Bear disparaged it as "the greatest hoax" ever perpetrated on Native America. But most SAI members considered citizenship to be a watershed because, as Gertrude Bonnin imagined, "only when the Indian wields his vote effectively, will the system be reformed."[36]

Usually, Indians in the SAI were cautious about criticizing White supremacy, lest they risk alienating their supporters among the Friends of the Indian, but sometimes they could not suppress their frustration. At the organization's inaugural meeting in 1911, Emma D. Johnson, a Potawatomi teacher from Oklahoma, disputed the Arapaho minister Sherman Coolidge that most White people believed in the Indian capacity to become Christian, civilized, and moral. "I regret very much," she countered, "that the majority of the Caucasian race of the United States do not recognize the ability of the Indian to compete with the white race. So many people seem to think that the Indian is an animal, that he is incapable of thinking." Four years later, Arthur C. Parker suggested that Whites should stop blaming the Indians' intractability for their lack of civilizational progress and instead look in the mirror. In his view, White mistreatment of the Indian was the main cause because it included having "(1) Made him a man without a country; (2) Usurped his responsibility and right of acting; (3) Demeaned his manhood; (4) Destroyed his ideals; (5) Broken faith with him; (6) Humiliated his spirit; (7) Refused to listen to his petitions." In another piece, Parker lambasted an article from the journal *American Medicine*, which claimed that "a physique evolved from savage life is somehow unfit to live in civilization." No, Parker answered. The real issue was the White supremacist view "that the blonde Aryan or white man is the destined ruler of the world. A closer analysis would show that the theorists of this school are, as a rule, self-admiring egotists, whose emotional nature is to say the least erratic."[37]

Eastman and Parker believed that the best way to counter White race prejudice was to show American society how much Indian cultures had to offer civilization. To this end, Eastman helped to found the Boy Scouts of America and Campfire Girls and established several summer camps through which to teach Indian outdoor skills like archery, woodworking, and gardening. He also opened thirty-two Native American chapters of the Young Men's Christian Association (YMCA) and wrote about Indian history and folklore for the general public. He and Parker envisioned that Indians, through such efforts, could help Whites who had grown "sick of themselves" to replace "commercial greed" with connection to the natural world and their fellow human beings. By the same token, Indians would benefit by adopting the mindset, "I am not a red man only, I am an American in the truest sense, and a brother man to all human kind." Everyone stood to learn that "all civilization does not lie in the ways of the white race—far from it."[38]

Though the SAI dissolved in the early 1920s over disagreements about peyotism and the pace of dismantling federal oversight, the organization signaled the beginning of a new era of progressive Native American activism. Rejecting the strategy of "kill the Indian, save the man," the SAI encouraged Native people to be simultaneously Indian, Christian, and civilized, and to consider themselves as citizens of their tribes, the United States, and the world. Contemporaneous with the SAI were regional intertribal groups such as the Black Hills Convention, the Alaska Native Brotherhood and Sisterhood, and the Northwestern Federation of American Indians, which fought for their members' treaty rights. Other Indians turned to international politics. In 1919, Gertrude Bonnin had unsuccessfully tried to gain entrance to the Paris Peace Conference, held by the victorious allies in World War I, in order to press for Native American citizenship. Four years later, a delegation of Arapahos from Wyoming ventured to Paris to ask the League of Nations to intervene in the United States' oppression of them. Domestically and on the world stage, progressive Indians intended to thwart predictions of their imminent extinction and assert their people's nationhood. Their ambition resembled that of the reforming Cherokees and Creeks in the 1820s before Removal.³⁹

Indian participation in World War I contributed to these muscular assertions of rights, as well as to the United States' decision to extend citizenship to all Native people. Approximately twelve thousand Indians served in the armed forces during the war, including nearly all eligible boarding school students. Unlike Black servicemen, whom the military put in segregated units, Indians fought alongside Whites as a reflection of the nation's assimilationist goals for them. For a great many Indians, this experience was their greatest exposure ever to White people, the English language, and the skills required in an industrial economy. It also put them in grave danger, to a greater degree than their White counterparts. The White stereotype of Indians, as voiced in the *New York Times*, that "it was in their nature to fight," and that their lives were of lesser value, encouraged officers to assign them to the most perilous duties. The result was that 5 percent of Indian soldiers in World War I died in uniform compared to just 1 percent of Whites. Their disproportionate sacrifice convinced enough Whites of their abilities and worthiness for Congress to grant citizenship to Indian veterans in 1919. A blanket Indian Citizenship Act followed in 1924, though not until after World War II did states like New Mexico, Arizona, and Alaska permit Native people to vote. In the decades that followed, Indian activists would use that platform to press for the same "right to self-determination" for which President Woodrow Wilson advocated for all nations in the postwar era.⁴⁰

INDIAN BLOOD AND THE NEW DEAL

If the purpose of assimilation policies and citizenship was to make Indians disappear, and the goal of the SAI was for Indians to modernize without losing their tribal identities and values, then the aim of the federal government under the New Deal was to revive Indian tribes on reservation land. John Collier, the commissioner of Indian affairs under President Franklin Delano Roosevelt from 1933 to 1945, was that rare bureaucrat who not only recognized that the country's assimilation policy was devastating Native people but also cared enough to try to do something about it. Collier's goal fit neatly with the Roosevelt administration's New Deal agenda to apply government programs to the United States' sinking economy and runaway unemployment during the Great Depression. Collier also shared with many New Dealers an abiding concern with how modern industrial society isolated and dispirited the people. Where he stood out was in his conviction that traditional Indian societies had answers to these problems. While living in New Mexico during the 1920s advocating for the rights of Indigenous communities, Collier had formed the belief that the Pueblos, and, by extension, all Indians, possessed "the fundamental secret of human life" in being tight-knit, communal, deeply connected to the natural world, and culturally rich. He rode this certainty to the commissionership, from which he advocated ending forced assimilation, encouraging Indigenous cultural expression, and giving Indians the resources to ease their way into mainstream American life at their own pace. If he had his way, the government's sink-or-swim approach to Indian assimilation would be over.[41]

The result was the Indian Reorganization Act (IRA) of 1934, known colloquially as the Indian New Deal, which represented the first time in United States history that the government used its power to slow Indian assimilation and reverse Indian land loss. Under its provisions, allotment would come to a halt and the government would attempt to return previously divided and alienated lands to protected trust status on Indian reservations. Agents would no longer suppress traditional Indian religious rituals or other cultural expressions. The government would favor schools on the reservations, and those institutions (formally, at least) were to permit bilingualism and even teach Indian arts and history. Tribes were urged, but not required, to adopt constitutions with democratic governments. Tribes that took this option would exercise greater authority over their own affairs and become eligible for certain government aid programs. At the same time, the New Deal's Civilian Conservation Corps would provide vocational training for Indians as carpenters, mechanics, engineers, surveyors, and more, while putting them to work at improving conditions on the reservations, a program that served eighty-five thousand Native people between 1939 and 1942. The point of this legislation, to be clear, was not to establish permanent Indian homelands under tribal leadership. Rather, as Collier stressed to his conservative critics, it meant to continue encouraging Indian assimilation, but at a more measured and humane pace.[42]

The Indian New Deal invigorated discussion about what it meant and should mean to be Indian and White in the United States. None other than FDR contended that Collier's program was the Indians' last, best hope to prevent "the extinction of the race." The Metís–Salish-Kootenai author and BIA official D'Arcy McNickle touted the IRA as "a training school in self-government and economic self-management." It was a signal that White society, or at least the federal government, was finally ready to respect Native people and their cultures. Furthermore, freezing allotment, as the Blackfeet man Rides at the Door put it, meant that "I can always hold that property intact so that no white man can take it away from me." To be Indian would no longer entail the constant risk and reality of landlessness at White hands. The significance of these reforms was captured in an incident on the Rosebud Sioux reservation, in which the federal agent forwarded the BIA a request from Bert Kills Close to Lodge to hold a dance. The answer, "no," was usually a formality, but Collier telegrammed back that if the people wanted to hold dances, that was their business. According to Benjamin Reifel, one of the reservation's residents, upon receipt of Collier's message, "Bert sat there, stroked his braids, looked off in the distance, and he said in Lakota, 'Well, I'll be damned.' "[43]

Quite a number of Indians, however, feared that the IRA would damn them by reversing their hard-won efforts to adopt private property and White civilizational standards and sentencing them to return to primitivism. Equally alarming, the BIA would retain control over fiscal matters and Indian schools instead of promoting full Indian self-governance. As the *Muskogee Daily Phoenix* commented, Collier seemed to want the Indian to "[throw] off the mantle of civility he has assumed ... and revert to the supervised barbarian." A number of Collier's Indian opponents, including former SAI president Thomas L. Sloan, formed the American Indian Federation, which denounced the IRA as a "red" Communist front that would send civilizing Indians "back to the blanket." This group would eventually undermine its reputation by forging close ties with German-American supporters of Nazism. Other Native

John Collier with Blackfoot chiefs in Rapid City, South Dakota, 1934, to discuss the Howard-Wheeler Act (later known as the Indian Reorganization Act). Courtesy of Bettmann/Getty Images.

critics, particularly the Pueblos and Haudenosaunees, were less concerned with the IRA's undermining assimilation than the IRA's foisting on them a democratic majority-rule form of government that clashed with their consensus-based political customs. The Navajos had such an abiding distrust of the federal government, and of Collier in particular after a devastating forced livestock reduction program, that they rejected the IRA as a stalking horse for more draconian measures. The cumulative effect was that, though 181 tribes adopted tribal constitutions under the IRA within two years of its passage, another 78 rejected it.[44]

The goal of the IRA might have been to preserve Indians, but it instituted a definition of "Indian" based on blood quantum—the measure of ancestry in halves, quarters, and eighths—that functioned to deny the tribal identities of many people with mixed backgrounds. The IRA defined as Indian anyone from a federally recognized tribe, meaning a tribe for whom the federal government acknowledged a trust responsibility and with whom it had a political relationship. That matter was straightforward. The murky question was whether Indians from unrecognized tribes, like the small bands of the East and Pacific Northwest, qualified for the act. In their cases, the IRA stated it would also consider as Indian "all other persons of one-half or more Indian blood." Collier considered most unrecognized Indian communities to be mere "folk groups," not actual tribes, because their people were largely acculturated and mixed. If such people, or portions of them, wanted to take advantage of the IRA, first they had to establish that their members were at least half Indian.[45]

Here, it is useful to consider how White society defined mixed Whites and Blacks differently from mixed-blood Indians on the basis of White society's assumptions of different functions for those racial groups. In the United States, Whiteness conveyed privilege. White society did not recognize mixed Whites as White because they did not want the children of people of color to make claims on White power, wealth, and status. Instead, mixed Whites, whether they were of Black or Indian ancestry, belonged to the racial group of the parent with the lower rank. Mixed Blacks might be called "mulatto" in some circumstances, but generally, society and the law categorized them simply as Black. The initial purpose of this custom had been to make Black ancestry of any degree the basis of a person's enslavement, the better to enlarge the slave-labor pool for Whites and warn Whites not to cross the color line lest their progeny suffer degradation. In the post-emancipation era, its function was to expand the population of low-wage laborers and maintain the exclusivity of White privilege. Similar functional considerations dictated White society's categorization of Indians with complex ancestry. Whites never called such people "half-Whites" or just "Whites," because those terms would have commanded dignity and justice, which Whites were reluctant to grant Indians despite the official goal of assimilation. Nor were mixed Indians just "Indians," because Whites wanted Indians to disappear to free up land for Whites. Labeling Indians with complex ancestry as mixed-bloods or half-breeds and measuring their claims to Indian-ness by diminishing fractions achieved this end. Montana senator Burton K. Wheeler, chairman of the Senate Committee on Indian Affairs, made the point plainly when he argued against Collier's initial proposal to set the IRA's blood-quantum minimum at one quarter. "What we are trying to do," Wheeler protested, "is get rid of the Indian problem rather than add to it." As far as the senator was concerned, quarter-bloods were "no more Indians than you or I, perhaps, I mean they are white people essentially." Collier conceded and raised the minimum to one half.[46]

Fact-finding missions to determine whether an unrecognized Indian tribe, or portions of it, qualified for the IRA revealed the inherent flaws of race science and the impossibility of reducing the social and political ties of Indian tribes to blood. In the case of the Lumbees of North Carolina, written documentation was insufficient to prove the blood quantum of several individuals, so Collier's office sent ethnologists to scrutinize 206 applicants' faces, teeth, skin, and hair for supposedly "Indian" characteristics and take testimony about their ancestry and cultural lives. This process led to such absurdities as assigning different blood quanta to siblings of the same parents. A mere twenty-two Lumbees passed the test, only for Collier's office to refuse to grant even them federal recognition as a tribe and reservation land. Blood quantum carried and continues to carry an air of scientific authority, but it is little more than a tool of domination and subordination, like race itself.[47]

Yet, to this day, blood-quantum standards used by the Dawes Allotment Commissioners and then the IRA determine Indian eligibility for certain federal programs (though the minimum has been reduced to one quarter in most instances). One factor in the federal government's continued reliance on blood quantum is the lack of better alternatives. It seems impossible to create another definition of "Indian" that is consistent, fair, and widely accepted, even among Indians. Standards of tribal belonging are too diverse and contested to serve as a general guide. At the same time, there was and is no escaping that, in some bureaucratic contexts, blood quantum has reduced tribal identity to the fiction of race.[48]

Federally recognized tribes, which had the authority to define tribal membership however they chose under the IRA, increasingly relied on blood quantum, too. One reason was their own genealogical traditions, which conferred elite status on certain lineages and privileged full-bloods as culture bearers. Yet another was that tribes under the IRA were becoming organizations that managed access to economic resources. This function was a significant change from the earlier tradition of tribes operating as political groups whose members cooperated for defense, diplomacy, and subsistence based on shared kinship, language, ritual, and residency. In the era of the IRA, tribes determined who was entitled to the people's shrinking land base and payouts from the sale or rent of natural resources. Established tribal members thus had a direct financial stake in limiting their ranks in order to maximize individual shares. Blood quantum was a means toward that end. Of the tribes that adopted new constitutions under the IRA, 44 percent of them defined that membership on the basis of either Indian or tribal blood quantum (usually of one half or more), whereas most of the remaining 56 percent required residency on the reservation or lineal descent from a tribal member on an official historic membership roll.[49]

By encouraging a blood quantum standard for membership, the IRA exacerbated rivalries between full- and mixed-bloods. For instance, Amos Red Owl, a full-blood spokesman from Pine Ridge, wrote to Collier complaining that the mixed-bloods on his reservation "are white people, essentially, they are no more Indian than you ... [There] should be some separate provision excluding [them] from the benefits of the Act. They make too much trouble on the reservation." A number of Pine Ridge mixed-bloods, for their part, wanted to prohibit full-blood or "ration Indians" from serving in tribal government on the basis that they could not represent "non ration, progressive, intelligent members of the Oglala Sioux Tribe in matters of vital importance." The mixed-bloods charged that full-bloods were nothing more than "peyote users, those who receive pensions and those who receive rations. They are afoot, do not own stock, and are not earning a living." One should not read these labels too literally. In most settings, "full-blood" could refer to someone of mixed ancestry who behaved traditionally, while a "mixed-blood" could be a full-blood who acted like Whites. Yet the Indian assumption behind these markers was that race, culture, and politics typically went hand in hand. The struggle between blood factions for control of tribal membership and resources has been a recurrent theme in Native American life ever since.[50]

The equally widespread countervailing principle in Indian country was and is that a person's membership in a tribe depends on a combination of kinship, culture, and residency. Felix Cohen, a pathbreaking scholar of Indian law during Collier's era, used the occasion of a failed purge of mixed-bloods by full-bloods on the Tongue River Cheyenne Reservation to venture, incorrectly, that blood rivalries were diminishing as a factor in tribal belonging. "The general trend of the tribal enactments on membership," he wrote, "is away from the older notion that rights of the tribal membership run with Indian blood... Instead, it is recognition that membership in a tribe is a political relationship rather than a social attribute." As a matter of legal principle, however, Cohen was onto something: today U.S. Indian law defines tribes as political entities, not as racial groups, even though, again, some government offices continue to use blood quantum to determine Indian eligibility for services. Yet Cohen did not foresee how stubborn blood quantum thinking would remain among Indians and Whites alike. The two modes of identity existed, and continue to exist, in tension.[51]

The point of the IRA was not to make tribes and reservations permanent or sustain the racial category of Indian in American life, but those have been its unintended legacies. The IRA slowed the destructive forces that seemed poised to wipe out tribal existence altogether, and established a modern precedent for tribes to engage in government-to-government relationships with Washington, D.C. The late historian Wilcomb Washburn had it right when, in 1983, he reflected on the IRA: "The alternative to involving tribes in the context of the American political system was not that they would remain independent nation-states. It was that they would be extinguished entirely. I do not think there would be a single Indian tribe in existence today if it had not been for John Collier and the Indian Reorganization Act." One might go so far as to contend that the IRA was an emergency anti-genocide measure. By tying a person's Indian identity to eligibility for public benefits, the IRA also set the stage for ongoing fights over whether "Indian" was a racial classification, political status, cultural marker, or some combination thereof. Those debates continue to this day. Yet, before they became truly relevant, tribal society first had to endure a new government threat to its very survival as part of a conservative backlash to FDR's New Deal.[52]

TERMINATION

The shorthand for the policy, Termination, said it all. In 1953, Republicans reclaimed full control of Congress and the presidency for the first time in over twenty years. Their agenda included abandoning Collier's reforms and returning with newfound vigor to the old program of removing Indians from federal trust by allotting and privatizing their territory, dissolving tribal governments, and placing Native individuals under the laws of their respective states. Back in 1946, Congress had established the Indian Claims Commission to consider tribal complaints that the United States had not lived up to its treaty obligations and pay monetary damages when those charges proved true; it was supposed to finish its work in ten years but wound up continuing until 1978. Whereas supporters of the Indian New Deal had seen this commission as overdue justice, conservatives wanted it to serve as a final settlement toward ending the special legal status of Indians, and their existence as tribes, once and for all. The Republican Party's long-awaited control of government was their chance.

Termination was also a conservative reaction to a generation of democratic-socialist policy and the emergence of the Cold War. For small-government conservatives, the size of the Bureau of Indian Affairs and the control it exercised over Native people's lives was a crystallization of their fears of what America would become for everyone if the New Deal continued apace. That concern went double for the BIA's toleration of Indian customs under Collier's direction. Conservatives blamed the poverty and dispiritedness of reservations on the Indian ethic of sharing, which, in turn, they interpreted as evidence about the dangers of Communism. They argued that the United States could hardly be expected to counter the Soviet Union and China on the world stage when it ran a Communist enterprise for Indians domestically. Some Americans were aware, and embarrassed, that the Soviets charged the United States with hypocrisy for proclaiming itself to be a champion of human rights while relegating Indians and African Americans to segregation, poverty, and second-class citizenship. The answer for many legislators was to end the Indians' peculiar status and accelerate their assimilation, even as a number of those same lawmakers continued to support Black segregation. Lending support to this argument was the military service of some twenty-five thousand Indians during World War II, and another twenty-five hundred during the Korean War, which conservatives read as a signal that Native Americans were ready to join American society as full and equal members without government direction and protection.[53]

Indians were divided over the policy and its meanings for being Indian in White America. Quite a number of Indian veterans favored Termination on the principle, "I was good enough to fight for my country. I am good enough to own property and support my family." Assimilated mixed-bloods, especially, wanted the personal profits that would accrue from the liquidation of the tribal domain. Nevertheless, a clear majority of Indians opposed Termination both out of commitment to their own communities and because they could not trust White Americans to treat them with dignity. The lasting impression of military service for some veterans had been of White troops taunting them as "Chief" or "Geronimo," and of returning home to find that bankers still refused to lend them money even on guaranteed GI Bill loans, employers still denied them work, and landlords still rejected their lease applications. Better to deal with the inefficiencies of the BIA, or, better yet, fix its problems and those of the reservations. To that end, the Blackfeet called for a domestic version of the Marshall Plan for Indian country instead of Termination, because if the nation could afford to rebuild Germany and Japan, surely it could help transform the reservations into thriving homelands for semiautonomous Native peoples. Other Indians agreed. "We are doing our best to win the war to be free from danger as much as the white man," explained Lewis Naranjo of Santa Clara Pueblo. Equally to the point, "We are fighting with Uncle Sam's army to defend the right of our people to live our own life in our own way," not, as White terminationists envisioned, to disappear into the American melting pot. The National Congress of American Indians, founded in 1944 to lobby the government for the collective interests of its member tribes, had by 1960 adopted the platform "Self-Determination—Not Termination."[54]

Termination's main proponent, Utah senator Arthur Watkins, spurned any Indian opposition to the policy as a cynical ploy for "representation without taxation" at the expense of Whites. When Billy P. Salgado of the Cahuilla Band of Indians of California reminded Watkins that Native people's freedom from state taxes was part of the deal that had secured White Americans a continent's worth of land, Watkins shot back with a revisionist history combining Manifest Destiny and the White man's burden: "You have not given up everything and this country nothing," he railed. "We have developed civilization. You have a wonderful country out there in California that was not worth very much until the white people took it over and started to develop it, and you are getting the advantage of that ... Really, you have to pay something." Assistant Secretary of the Interior Orme Lewis was equally dismissive of the argument that Termination would decimate the Indians' cultural life because he believed that assimilation was to their economic benefit. He snapped, "I have utterly no patience with those who think more about Indian culture than they do about Indians. The world is made up of people who overrun others, as a result of which we have great nations. America is an outstanding example of that ... The culture will live as it deserves to."[55]

Indians had a right to be skeptical that Termination had anything to do with their welfare. Though Congress claimed that it would terminate only those tribes poised to integrate, in fact its decisions appear to have been made based on political calculations, as evidenced by its termination of the Utah Paiutes, from Watkins's own state, even though they were among the poorest and least formally educated Indians in the country. Congress said Termination would be voluntary, but it lied to tribes about the terms and bullied them by threatening that they would not receive the awards from successful suits against the government unless they complied. Most of all, Congress either fooled itself into believing that the White public was willing to treat Native people fairly, or simply did not care.

The results were plain: in 109 cases of Termination during the 1950s and early 1960s, nearly every Native community suffered greater destitution than ever before. The loss of a minimum of 1,790,649 acres between 1953 and 1957 does not come close to telling the tale. Termination left the Menominees of Wisconsin with no doctors, dentists, or hospitals; it ruined a tribal lumber mill that had provided jobs and sustainable logging; it required them to send their children to the Shawano County schools, where the discriminatory environment produced high rates of failure, suspensions, and expulsion; and it made them dependent on local police, who offered the Indians little protection but plenty of abuse. By 1965, the Wisconsin Legislature could no longer ignore that the Menominees were "as demoralized as any poverty-stricken people anywhere." The same went for the Klamaths of Oregon, whose median age of death had plunged to 46 by 1961 and 39.5 by 1971, largely because of a spike in alcohol abuse as they tried to numb the misery unleashed by Termination. "The devastation was incredible," recalled Keith Pike of Guidiville Rancheria in Talmage, California, whose people simultaneously lost 95 percent of their land and sank into despair. Worst of all, according to the accounts of Native people who suffered Termination, was being told repeatedly by Whites and fellow Indians alike that they were no longer real Indians. Some people from terminated tribes feared that they were losing their Indian identity as their communities atomized and ceased their rituals. All the while, as Coquille Tribal Council Chairman Wilfred C. Wasson put it, "Employers, teachers, and government officials still treated us like Indians," which, in the words of the Klamath Gerald Skelton, meant "being treated as a lesser person by the white folks ... White people expected the worst of us."[56]

Even as White society expected the worst of Indians, it continued to advance policies to force Native people into the general population, part of a pitiless continuum that stretched back to reservation civilization programs, boarding schools, and allotment. In 1953, Public Law 280 extended state jurisdiction over select tribes in California, Minnesota, Nebraska, Oregon, and Wisconsin (Alaska was added in 1959), and allowed other states to petition to do the same, leading to its extension to Arizona, Florida, Idaho, Iowa, Montana, Nevada, North Dakota, South Dakota, Utah, and Washington. As with Termination, the results were destructive, contributing to a spike in the violent crime rate among Indians that was twice the national average, and among some tribes ten times the national average. Meanwhile, the federal government enticed and pressured Indians to the cities with promises of jobs, education, material comfort, and ample support, a policy known as Relocation. It contributed to some 160,000 Indians leaving their reservations between 1950 and 1970, and to a dire prediction by the NCAI that "relocation ... will probably exterminate Indian tribes even more surely than the termination legislation."[57]

Urban life revealed the gulf between the government's vision of Indian assimilation and the reality of pervasive White discrimination toward Indians. Indians reported that most landlords were unwilling to lease to them, and those who would offered only slum dwellings at exorbitant rates. Indians pooled their meager

A recruitment poster for the Relocation program, in this case, to Denver, Colorado. Courtesy of National Archives and Records Administration, College Park, Maryland. Photo no. 75-N-REL-1G-1.

resources, sometimes with utter strangers from other tribes, to make the rent in places where they had to sleep in shifts to account for the limited floor space. Even then, a Minneapolis business owner complained, "Put them in a newly painted place and in a month it is wrecked. Rent to one and you have twenty living there. They live like pigs." When Indians did find reasonably decent housing, neighboring Whites often tried to drive them out. In 1960, the Ho-Chunk Bearskin family managed to rent a flat in Chicago's Humboldt neighborhood, which was 99 percent White, only to return home on their first evening in residence to find their windows broken and a note that read: "You Mexicans, get out of here. This is only the beginning. No kidding." It was signed "the Whites." "It's tough to have to take such treatment," Fredeline Bearskin admitted. "We belong to this country." The Indian unemployment rate in the cities was twice that of urban Whites, largely because of negative White stereotypes of Native people. The Ojibwe Ignatia Broker recalled one Minneapolis businessman telling her, "I'm sorry, but we don't hire Indians because they only last the two weeks till payday, then they quit." Yet the supposed propensity of Indians to leave their jobs could not explain why some hospitals denied Indian patients, or why some restaurants refused to serve Indian customers. The reason had nothing to do with Indians. It was White supremacy.[58]

A new urban Indian identity, as well as a White image of urban Indians recycled from old stereotypes, emerged from this wreck. In New York, Minneapolis, Chicago, Los Angeles, and Seattle, diverse Native people banded together under a shared "Indian" identity to form mutual assistance organizations, social clubs, sports leagues, dance groups, churches, bars, powwows, and newsletters. They perceived that they held something in common aside from their discrimination at White hands. "We are a sharing people," observed Broker; "our tribal traits are still within us." The support of this new urban community allowed some city Indians to beat the odds and secure gainful employment, schooling for their children, and stable housing. Though some of them grew distant from their natal reservations, most maintained their ties through regular visiting, sharing what little wealth they had with those in need back home, moving back and forth between city and reservation as circumstances warranted, and providing a place to stay for Indians who were new to town. A great many others were less fortunate, sinking into despair, substance abuse, and sometimes chronic unemployment, homelessness, and criminality. In places like Seattle and Minneapolis, these were the urban Indians on whom Whites focused their attention, which served to reinforce the racial stereotype of Indians as incapable of adjusting to modernity.[59]

The modern governmental campaign to destroy tribal life extended beyond Termination and Relocation to include seizing Indian children from their families, not, as in previous generations, for boarding school, but for foster care and adoption, overwhelmingly to White families. The economic rationale for this program was that it would allow states to offset some of the costs of assuming the administration of Indians from the federal government by shifting the burden to private couples. The intent was also to act in the best interests of the children, but the reasons cited by authorities to separate children from their kin and tribal communities sometimes had nothing to do with clear abuse or abject neglect. Too often, such decisions rested on White cultural judgments about whether an Indian household was normal. For instance, White social workers might cite the parents' reliance on care provided by older children, extended family, or neighbors, taking no heed of the Indian custom of raising children within a wide network of family and friends. Officials also removed children on the bases of dilapidated housing, poor school attendance, and other relatively minor issues rarely applied to Whites. Practically no one in charge raised the possibilities of offering greater support to Indian families or prioritizing keeping Native children with their own kind because the stereotype was that Indians were pathological, damaged, unsuitable, and irresponsible. Conversely, social workers favored Whites because they assumed them to be more civilized and, for that matter, more reliably Christian. State agencies worked in close concert with church groups, particularly the Church of Latter-Day Saints and the Catholic Church among several denominations to place Indian children with Whites from the sponsoring faith. As to why the White families wanted Indian children, one reason was that there was a dearth of White babies available for adoption, and White couples generally would not accept Black children. Indian babies were the default. These couples also genuinely believed they were doing good to innocents in need.[60]

The damage this program caused should be remembered as a national scandal fueled by White supremacy. According to the calculations of the historian Margaret Jacobs, during this era Indian children were twenty-two times more likely to be put in foster care and nineteen times more likely to be adopted out than other American children. She adds, "When boarding school placements are factored in, some states were separating Indian children from their families at 74 times the rate for non-Indian children. This meant that in most Indian communities, 25 to 35 percent of all Indian children were living apart from their families." The trauma permeated Native society. The historian Ned Blackhawk relates that "in one study, nearly half of the [Indian] participants indicated that their adoptive family abused them, and of these, 70 percent reported sexual abuse." Many adoptees and foster children grew up alienated with high levels of substance abuse, incarceration, and depression. Their biological parents and family members often blamed themselves, leading to shame and similar destructive results. Native people were correct when they linked the theft of their children to the Termination and Relocation policies. It was part of a systematic effort by White society and part of a long history to eliminate them as tribes and reduce them as individuals to utter subordination.[61]

POISON

The country's environmental assault on Indian lands and bodies should remove any doubt that such policies extended from a White American tradition of viewing Indians as inferior and disposable. The trend effectively began in World War II, when the government appropriated a million acres of tribal land for use as bombing and gunnery ranges, often leaving behind unexploded ordnance. After the war, Indians bore a disproportionate brunt of the country's exploding demand for energy amid rapid urban and suburban growth in the West. In the course of the government's building the Garrison Dam in North Dakota, the Fort Randall Dam in South Dakota, the Yellowtail Dam in Montana, and the Kinzua Dam in Pennsylvania, it seized hundreds of thousands of acres of Indian land, displaced hundreds of families, and cut off access to sacred sites. The series of postwar dams that transformed the wild Columbia and Snake Rivers into tamed back-to-back reservoirs devastated the salmon runs on which Indigenous people of the Pacific Northwest had relied since ancient times, even though treaty rights guaranteed their access to the fish. The National Congress of American Indians cited the Oahe Dam, which robbed the Cheyenne River and Standing Rock Sioux reservations of 309,584 acres, to observe that Indians were being impacted disproportionately by projects that primarily benefited White people in faraway places. "It is hard to believe that it is strictly a coincidence," the NCAI observed wryly. "Can it be because Indians are thought to be a weak people, impotent politically, and that therefore the Army Engineers will encounter less resistance to the taking of fertile lands? Or is it the ugly fact of racism expressing itself in that old attitude we run into, even among Senators of the United States, that Indians really have no right to own property which could, in their opinion, be put to better use by someone else?" The questions were meant to be rhetorical because the answers were obvious.[62]

The juggernaut of U.S. energy production robbed Indians not only of land but also of their health, too. Energy companies contracted with the Department of the Interior to extract coal, oil, gas, and uranium from reservations throughout the West belonging to the Navajos, Hopis, Mescalero and Jicarilla Apaches, Northern and Southern Utes, Crows, and Northern Cheyennes. These corporations showed little concern for how those activities would poison tribal land, water, and air, and damage the health of Indigenous mine workers. Zinc and lead mining on the Quapaw Reservation in Oklahoma left behind fourteen thousand abandoned mine shafts, seventy million tons of lead-laced tailing, thirty-six tons of toxic sand and sludge, and so much toxic water at the Tar Creek site that in 1983 the government gave it Superfund status and advised people to leave the area. The Four Corners Generating Station in Navajo country emitted eighty thousand tons of contaminants per year, much of it deposited in an enormous toxic lake near the San Juan River on which the Navajos depended for water. Such examples abound. The fact is that 532 of 1,322 Superfund sites existed on Indian land as of 2014.[63]

The environmental assault on Indian country inflicted ill health and early death on Native peoples, sometimes out of willful negligence, sometimes deliberately. Uranium mining, including the wind-drift of its "yellow dirt," the poisoning of water supplies, and the use of its radioactive refuse as building materials for homes, explains the alarming rates of cancer, miscarriages, birth defects, and allergies for generations of Navajos, Eastern Shoshones, Northern Arapahos, and Oglala Lakotas. The Yakamas of Washington State have suffered similar effects from forty years of radioactive pollution in the Columbia River caused by the Hanford Nuclear Site. One study likened their exposure "to levels of radiation similar to that of the Chernobyl nuclear accident."[64]

These were not accidents. Scientists and medical experts had warned of the results and the projects proceeded anyway. Cleanup has been slowed by blame-shifting, an unwillingness to allocate funds, a basic lack of urgency, and the sheer vastness of the problem. When the United States began to conduct nuclear tests, more than six hundred took place in Shoshone territory. Radiation exposure and ash fallout from the Trinity Site in New Mexico reached two Apache tribes, several Navajo communities, and nineteen Pueblo groups, but not until 2014 did the government begin to study the effects. Clearly the U.S. Geological Survey knew what it was doing in 1962 when it removed fifteen tons of radioactive waste it had deposited in Shoshone territory in Nevada and buried it in Inuit territory near Point Hope, Alaska, to observe how it would impact caribou, lichen (both of which the Inuit ate), and humans.

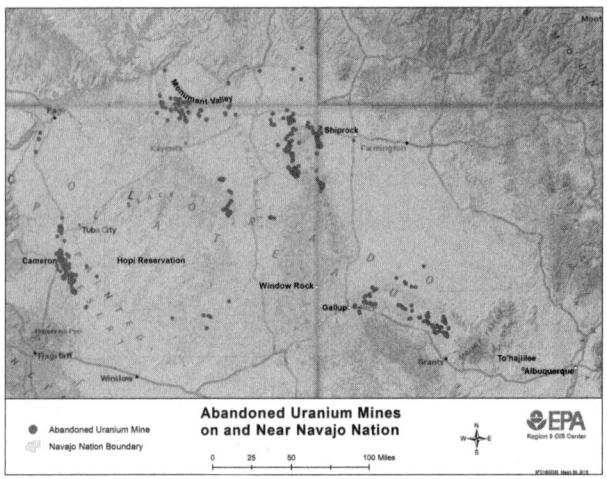

Environmental Protection Agency map, *Abandoned Uranium Mines on and Near Navajo Nation*, 2016.

Thirty years later, when University of Alaska researchers uncovered this secret experiment through a Freedom of Information Act request, the site still contained one thousand times the legal level of radiation. Nobody had told the Inuits, to whom doctors had attributed their alarming rates of cancer to cigarette smoking.[65]

The moral excuse for the widespread misery caused by Termination, Relocation, and Indian foster care and adoption was that, in the long run, Indians would benefit from assimilation into White society, whether they wanted it or not. Considering those programs alongside the nation's decades-long environmental assault on Indian country reveals the thinness of that veneer. The government and energy companies would not have willingly poisoned Indian people if they had prioritized improving Native lives. As the Environmental Protection Agency has reluctantly acknowledged in more recent ties, the most important interests accounting for these patterns of environmental damage were profits for White investors, national security for a country with a White supermajority, and ample White access to cheap energy. White power brokers were willing to sicken, disable, and even kill Indians to achieve these goals, just as they were willing to shatter Indian families and communities and throw them into greater destitution when the reward was the appropriation of Native people's remaining lands. Though Indians had long since become American citizens, clearly that citizenship was of a second-class sort.[66]

ELIMINATION

White Americans' systematic racism toward Indians meant that the overwhelming majority of Native people were "incredibly poor" during the mid- to late twentieth century, according to the federal government's own reckoning. This era saw Indian landholding reach an all-time low of 50.5 million acres. Off-reservation unemployment stood at 50 percent in 1960. On reservations, it sometimes ran as high as 90 percent. The median income for an Indian family at mid-century was just $870, compared to $3,750 for non-Indians. Tens of thousands of Natives lived in dilapidated housing without running water or electricity. Benjamin Reifel, a Rosebud Sioux, remembered being raised amid "the most sickening poverty that one could imagine."[67]

Desperate economic conditions, combined with environmental hazards, led to desperately poor health and social outcomes. In 1940, Indian life expectancy lagged 13.2 years behind that of Whites and 2.1 years behind that of Blacks. Twenty years later, Indians still died, on average, 8.9 years before Whites and 1.9 years before Blacks. To the extent that these numbers improved over the decades, it was largely because growing numbers of White-appearing people identified as Indians. Practically every other measure of ill-being was also shockingly high for Indians during this era: infant mortality ranged two to five times above the national average; rates of suicide, homicide, incarceration, domestic abuse, sexual abuse, substance abuse, tuberculosis, diabetes, cirrhosis of the liver, and even periodontal disease were staggering. It was as if White society either wanted Indians dead, or simply could not have cared less.[68]

Education did not offer most Indians a way out. Nearly 60 percent of Indians dropped out of high school at a time when two thirds of them were in public schools, not federal or religious boarding and day schools. The majority of Indians who remained in school performed far worse than their peers. Only 18 percent of Indian high school graduates went on to college, compared to 50 percent of Americans nationally, and only 3 percent of them finished college, compared to 32 percent nationally. The report of a 1969 Senate investigation headed by Ted Kennedy of Massachusetts was aptly titled *Indian Education: A National Tragedy, a National Challenge*. It reached the obvious conclusion that the country had "not offered Indian children—either in years past or today—an educational opportunity anywhere near equal to that offered the great bulk of American children."[69]

Nor did Indians receive the same justice as the great bulk of White Americans. Crime data from 1960 showed that the Native American arrest rate was three times that of African Americans and eight times that of White Americans, driven largely by alcohol-related offenses for which White people might get off with a mere warning or a night of sobering up in jail. Too often, police treated the Indians they encountered as racial inferiors to be violently subordinated. Abuse at the hands of non-Indian police was especially prevalent on or near the several Sioux reservations near South Dakota's southern border with Nebraska, as would remain the case up to recent times. Indians who testified to a Senate investigation "accused sheriffs, deputies, and towns marshals of clubbing, kicking, dragging, and shooting men and women prisoners." Though authorities overpoliced Indians when it came to subjugating them, they underpoliced Indians when it came to protecting them. Indians in South Dakota, and undoubtedly elsewhere, were reluctant to contact the police even when they were in danger because, as often as not, the officers gave the caller "brutal beatings" for bothering them. No wonder that *Talking Leaf*, an Indian newspaper out of Los Angeles, contended in an article entitled "Discrimination Anyone?" that South Dakota had two systems of justice, one for Whites and another for Indians.[70]

A 1947 report by the President's Committee on Civil Rights acknowledged that Indians faced "public prejudice and discrimination" throughout the country, particularly in border towns near reservations, where White civilians openly insulted them as "bucks, squaws, and blankets" and denied them "access to all but the most unsanitary and undesirable eating, lodging, and restroom facilities." The mayor of Chamberlain, South Dakota, just east of the Rosebud reservation, said point-blank to federal officials in 1954, "We have no interest of making an Indian comfortable around here." If the commission had looked hard enough, it would have found similar patterns in any one of a number of cities and rural counties in which a critical mass of Indians resided. In 1951, a White cemetery in Sioux City, Iowa, refused to permit the burial of a Ho-Chunk man, John Rice, who had been shot dead while serving in the military in the Korean War. An outraged President Harry Truman had Rice buried in Arlington Cemetery and his family flown in for the funeral at government expense, but the gesture was woefully insufficient to meet the larger problem. That same decade saw such outrages as two White men receiving just three months in jail after killing a fifteen-year old Indian girl by throwing her out of a moving car, and a White police officer receiving no jail time after shooting a Sioux war veteran in the back. Reports by congressional committees and civil rights commissions on the issue of White discrimination against Indians have appeared practically every decade to the present day, with few signs of improvement.[71]

Something had to change, and Indians would have to be the ones to change it.

RED POWER

In retrospect, the Osage Clyde Warrior's mere two-line campaign speech to become president of the Southwest Regional Indian Youth Council in 1960 signaled a new era of Indian politics and self-identity. Standing before an assembly of young Native activists, he held out his arms and proclaimed: "This is all I have to offer. The sewage of Europe does not flow through these veins." There was more to his theatrics than appealing to widespread Indian resentment toward Whites or even mixed-bloods. His larger point had to do with Indians' self-conception. If they were going to improve their lives, they had to value their lives. They had to take pride in who they were, brandish it, and fight. Their blood connected them to one another and their ancestors and gave them a distinct place within the United States.[72]

Warrior and other formally educated Indians who would create the National Indian Youth Council (NIYC) in 1961 envisioned a new, assertive politics for Native people built on that foundation of self-esteem. Policy-wise, the goals were to end Termination and establish that tribes on protected reservations were a permanent feature of American life. "We are not going to disappear," NIYC founder Melvin Thom decreed. But just surviving would mean little without a thoroughly new attitude among Native people. Warrior called on Indians to conquer the "poverty of spirit" that White subjugation had inflicted on them and build the confidence that they could and should exercise self-determination. Furthermore, self-determination needed to focus on recovering and embracing Indian values without shame. Like the Nativist movements of old, it was about purging colonial influences and pursuing an authentic Indianness. Societal respect would come only with self-respect. Later, Warrior and Thom called this vision Red Power, echoing the era's Black Power movement for African American rights and dignity.[73]

The NIYC's tenets helped energize Indian activism throughout the 1960s. Tribes in the Pacific Northwest and Great Lakes exercised their treaty rights in violation of state laws by fishing for salmon without licenses; Mohawks in New York boycotted public education until White municipalities gave them a say in school board elections; Mohawks also blockaded the International Bridge between the United States and Canada to protest the two nations' refusing them the right of free passage guaranteed by the Jay Treaty of 1794; Navajos and Hopis in the Southwest and Alaska Natives demonstrated against oil and gas developers' despoiling of their sacred lands; and the list went on and on. A growing roster of Native newspapers, such as *Akwesasne Notes* from Haudenosaunee country and *Wassaja* and the *Indian Historian* out of San Francisco, kept readers informed of this agitation and the layered reasons for it. They chronicled, without using the term, the prevalence of systematic racism in Native people's lives. Everywhere, it seemed, Indigenous people were at a breaking point.[74]

The National Congress of American Indians, led by the Standing Rock Sioux intellectual, Vine Deloria Jr., charted an Indian future based on the U.S. constitutional principle that Senate-ratified treaties are the "supreme law of the land" rather than on a special Indian racial status. Boasting experience in the marines, degrees in theology and law, and membership in a prominent Sioux family, Deloria brought credentials, pedigree, and biting intellect and wit to the presidency of the NCAI. His strategy, pursued in conjunction with the Native American Rights Fund led by the Pawnee John Echohawk, was for Indians to focus their rights claims on their status as tribal polities under White people's own law. At the same time, he was unflinching about castigating White supremacy as the root of Native people's problems. In his provocatively titled 1969 book, *Custer Died for Your Sins*, he wrote that the problem of race in America was not a matter of misunderstanding between groups, as had become the euphemism during the post–World War II era. Rather, "it involves the white man himself. He must examine his past. He must face the problems he has created within himself and within others. The white man must no longer project his fears and insecurities onto other groups, races, and countries. Before the white man can relate to others, he must forego the pleasure of defining them." The same went for the White people's widespread mischaracterization of Native politics. Deloria answered White charges that Red Power was a Communist front by explaining, "Red Power means we want power over our own lives. We do not wish to threaten anyone. We are only half a million Indians. We do not wish power over anyone. We simply want the power, the political and economic power, to run our own lives in our own way. It frightens people, I know, to talk of Red Power, but we don't want to frighten them. We want to shock them into realizing how powerless the Indians have been. We feel that if we don't get that power—now—we may not be around much longer."[75]

Indian activists found a good-faith partner for their visions in President Lyndon Johnson as part of his larger agenda to address Black civil rights and societal poverty.

Clyde Warrior (left) and Vine Deloria Jr. (right), leaders of the Red Power movement. Courtesy of the Oklahoma Historical Society; Courtesy of *Denver Post*/Getty Images.

His administration signaled a new approach to Indian affairs as early as 1964, when it funneled millions of dollars in Office of Economic Opportunity programs through tribal governments rather than the BIA. For the first time, Washington, D.C., was leaving it up to Indians to receive, disburse, and track monies for their own welfare. The results included the establishment of Navajo Community College, with a curriculum that taught Navajo culture and a policy of prioritizing the hiring of Native staff. It was the beginning of an efflorescence of tribal educational institutions. Johnson also set a precedent, followed to this day, of presidents appointing Indians to the position of Commissioner of Indian Affairs and its successor office, Assistant Secretary of Indian Affairs. Then, in 1968, Johnson made explicit the principle behind these actions. In a special message to Congress "on the Problems of the American Indian," Johnson proposed "a new goal for our Indian programs: A goal that ends the old debate about 'termination' of Indian programs and stresses self-determination; a goal that erases old attitudes of paternalism and promotes partnership self-help." He pledged massive aid to help Indians achieve the same standard of living as other Americans, though that assistance would fall short of its intended mark. The following month, Johnson signed the Indian Civil Rights Act, which committed the federal government to protect Native people's liberties the same as all other Americans. The nation's pledge to preserve Indian people as distinct tribal groups with real political influence was a rejection of more than just the policy of Termination, but literally the entire history of U.S.-Indian affairs. The irony was that Deloria's deemphasis of Indians as a racial group in favor of Indians as tribes with particular legal rights worked partly because it took place in the context of a wider national movement against racial inequality and injustice.[76]

Young, radical Indian activists, particularly those from the cities, saw these reforms as too little, too late. Growing up in urban environments, they had suffered degradation from Whites throughout their lives, but no one seemed to care, certainly not White officials, and not even most Indian advocacy organizations because of their focus on the reservations. Tired of it all, in November 1969, a group of Indian college students calling themselves the Tribes of All Nations, soon to be joined by Indians from all across the country, occupied the abandoned federal prison on Alcatraz Island in San Francisco. A small group of stalwarts would remain there until June 1971. Though the occupation failed to achieve its original demands to secure the transfer of the island to Indian possession, citing the 1868 Fort Laramie Treaty, and public funding for an Indian cultural center there, in its first several months it succeeded spectacularly at drawing unprecedented media attention to the wider struggles of modern Native America.[77]

Equally important, Native people throughout the country took heed, and it filled them with confidence. The future Cherokee chairwoman Wilma Mankiller, who visited Alcatraz several times during the occupation, explained, "I'd never heard anyone actually tell the world that we needed somebody to pay attention to our treaty rights, that our people had given up an entire continent, and many lives, in return for basic services like health care and education, but nobody was honoring those agreements. For the first time, people were saying things I felt but hadn't known how to articulate. It was very liberating." Or, as other Indians put it, finally "somebody is doing something"; "we got back our worth, our pride, our dignity, our humanity." The Oglala Sioux college senior Merri Pat Cuney was amazed to see that the Alcatraz occupiers "weren't ashamed of anything."[78]

That same bold spirit of race pride galvanized the American Indian Movement (AIM), which during the early 1970s captivated the nation and inspired Indian country with a series of chaotic marches and occupations. The organization formed in Minneapolis, largely to combat police brutality. Yet, under the leadership of firebrands Clyde Bellecourt (White Earth Ojibwe), Dennis Banks (Leech Lake Ojibwe), and Russell Means (Oglala Lakota), AIM soon adopted a confrontational style of political theater in which its members showed up in numbers to take over places of symbolic significance, while its leaders mugged before the cameras and microphones in Plains-warrior dress to make demands and declare principles. The pattern began when AIM crashed the first National Day of Mourning Protest held by the United Tribes of New England in Plymouth, Massachusetts, on Thanksgiving morning, 1970. Unsatisfied with the hosts' wearisome speeches, AIM led a charge on a replica of the Mayflower, painted Plymouth Rock red, and disrupted a dinner hosted by the Plimoth Plantation museum with war whoops and assaults on the roasted turkeys. In November the following year, hundreds of AIM members rolled into Washington, D.C., calling themselves the Trail of Broken Treaties, and occupied and vandalized the Bureau of Indian Affairs for several days. AIM confronted injustice at the local level, too. In February 1972, it led fourteen hundred Indians from eighty different tribes into the town of Gordon, Nebraska, to protest the suspected murder of Raymond Yellow Thunder, who had been found dead after a night in which four White men beat him in front of a bar, stripped him of his clothes, drove him around town stuffed into a car trunk, and then made him dance bloodied and intoxicated at an American Legion Post. AIM's show of strength forced town officials to agree to a human rights commission and the suspension of an abusive police officer, and the state and federal governments to investigate Yellow Thunder's death. As one anonymous Lakota woman warned, "Yellow Thunder wasn't the first of us to be mistreated, but he'd better be the last."[79]

AIM simultaneously reached the pinnacle of its influence and laid the seeds for its downfall the following year when it took over the town of Wounded Knee, South Dakota, where the U.S. Seventh Cavalry had massacred some three hundred Miniconjou Lakotas in 1890. The site itself was an offense to Native people, like so many other patriotic tourist attractions across the United States. Local billboards called on tourists to VISIT THE MASS GRAVE, while a nearby gift shop sold postcards picturing the frozen corpses of Indians slaughtered by American troops. But what galvanized the occupation was the federal government's support for the flagrantly corrupt, abusive, and mostly mixed-blood government of the Pine Ridge Reservation under tribal chairman Dick Wilson. AIM's response was a armed takeover of Wounded Knee, which, as it turned out, would last seventy-one days and involve a face-off with federal marshals and FBI agents armed to the teeth. Knowing that the government desperately did not want any headlines of "The Second Massacre at Wounded Knee," not with a reported 93 percent of the country following the story, the protestors held out against the odds. All the while, they broadcast to America, "This is our last gasp as a sovereign people . . . because nobody is recognizing the Indian people as human beings." The images of desperate Native people standing up to federal bullies were remarkably effective publicity, but, in effect, Wounded

Knee was AIM's last moment in the spotlight. After one of their members was killed and others wounded in a shootout with the feds, the hungry occupiers surrendered the site without achieving any of their demands. In the years that followed, the FBI and Department of Justice hunted down AIM's leaders and prosecuted them into submission.[80]

A century of Indian activism, combined with day-to-day Indian resistance, charted a future of Indians in America as viable tribal nations exercising a measure of sovereignty and consisting of people who could be proud of who they were, even in a country that continued to be dominated by White people. AIM's radicalism made the demands of other Indian activists, like the NCAI, seem much more reasonable, contributing to a string of policy victories over the next thirty years that would bring genuine Indian self-determination closer to reality and improve the quality of life throughout Indian country. For the first time in American history, the country's White leadership acted around a consensus that Indians as tribes were a permanent and distinct part of the United States, entitled to practice their cultures and religions on their own lands within unprecedently broad limits. There would be no more official talk or action premised on Indian assimilation, disappearance, or extermination. This was more than just a new way of White people viewing Indians. It was a new way for White people, or at least some of them, to view themselves. White identity could include being tolerant, restrained, and empathetic in relation

American Indian Movement occupation of Wounded Knee.
Courtesy of Bettmann/Getty Images.

to Indians. Whites could also imagine their country as multicultural rather than culturally homogeneous.

The other legacy was the change in how Indians understood themselves, which is poignantly captured in a 1971 editorial in *Akwesasne Notes* entitled "Self Hate." The anonymous author related a youthful struggle of trying to hide his or her Indian ancestry from White friends and neighbors, including cheering for the cowboys who killed Indians on TV and in the movies, and joining Whites when they ridiculed Native people who appeared visibly as Indians in public. This person had been ashamed to be Indian because "I saw around me on the reservation—too much drinking, child neglect, apathy. I called that being Indian. I took all the hatred I felt for white people and directed it to my own people, and myself... After all, Indians are the people other people kill. After all, Indians are the savages, the heathens, the scalpers." The era of Indian activism revealed that self-hatred was only self-oppression, and now the author had a new vision of what it meant to be Indian. "Brothers and sisters, hiding in your white disguises," the writer beckoned, "join us. Fight for the liberation of your people. The drunken, lazy ones you know are not accidents, nor are they true to Indian values. America has created them. Free yourself, free your people."[81]

It would prove easier in theory than in practice.

CHAPTER 8

Choosing

In retrospect, one of the clearest signs that Native American activism was having the desired effect was getting conservative Republican president Richard Nixon to join with his liberal Democrat predecessor, Lyndon Johnson, in supporting the movement's basic principle, tribal sovereignty. For all the progress made during Johnson's presidency, it was under Nixon that the federal government committed wholeheartedly to this framework. White officialdom was finally ready to abandon the country's goal, ever since its inception, of eliminating Native tribes and forcing individual Indians to adhere to the White way of life. Now, instead, it would actively defend Native people's lands and self-determination in governance, culture, and economy. A special message by Nixon to Congress delivered on June 4, 1970, charted this new course for his administration and, effectively, for future ones as well. This was a new era in American racial history

Nixon began by getting the past and present right, which also showed that Red Power advocates had been getting their points across. "The first Americans—the Indians—are the most deprived minority group in the nation" was his attention-grabbing opening statement. "On virtually every scale of measurement—employment, income, education, health—the condition of Indian people ranks at the bottom." More remarkable still was his acknowledgment that the primary reason for the devastation of Indian country was "injustice" in the forms of "the white man's frequent aggression, broken agreements, intermittent remorse and prolonged failure." Nixon's most important contention, however, was about how to fix this problem. He did not propose yet more top-down government programs, or the opposite solution of cutting off Indians from government support and protection and just wishing them luck. Rather, he declared that "both as a matter of justice and of enlightened social policy, we must begin to act on the basis of what the Indians themselves have long been telling us. The time has come to break decisively with the past and to create the conditions for a new era in which the Indian future is determined by Indian acts and Indian decisions." It was stunning to have such broad-minded principles being spoken by a White conservative, whose politics otherwise aimed at national cultural uniformity.[1]

One of the achievements in Native American political thinking and activism during the 1960s had been to establish the legal foundation, and advance the moral argument, that tribal sovereignty was a matter of constitutionality, and to downplay questions of race. This strategy, most closely associated with the work of Vine Deloria Jr. and the National Congress of American Indians, asserted that tribal polities existed before the creation of the United States and historically engaged with the United States on a government-to-government basis. When negotiating treaties with the United States, Indian tribes had retained whatever inherent sovereign powers they did not explicitly relinquish in the agreements. Thus, the special "rights" of Indians were not gifts from the United States, but belonged to them by virtue of being Indigenous. Likewise, U.S. obligations to provide Indians with protection, health care, and education, and protect their territory, were not charity, but the provisions of Senate-ratified treaties, which, again, under the U.S. Constitution are the supreme law of the land. U.S. violations of those terms over the years did not negate the treaties' ongoing constitutional legal authority. The focus of Native politics, therefore, was to convince the federal government to fulfill those treaties according to the understanding of the Indian party at the time of signing, and to redress the country's repeated failure to do so. This political approach did not require Native leaders to invoke arguments about how Indian and White peoples had separate creations, innate qualities, or unique destinies. It did not hinge on convincing Whites of the history of White exploitation of Native people or their moral responsibility to answer for it. It did not involve settlement of the debate over whether Indians were capable or incapable of civility or worthy of public welfare. Rather, it zeroed in on the execution of treaties under White Americans' own law.

This argument convinced Nixon that the government had erred, as in its Termination policy, in assuming that its "special relationship" with tribes was "an act of generosity toward a disadvantaged people and that it can therefore discontinue this responsibility on a unilateral basis whenever it sees fit." Instead, the special relationship was a "solemn obligation." As long as the United States kept the Indian land it had acquired in treaties, its commitments to the tribes remained. Nixon saw that "to terminate this relationship would be no more appropriate than to terminate the citizenship rights of any American." He also recognized that Termination had produced terrible practical results. Calling Termination a "morally and legally unacceptable" policy, Nixon called on Congress to renounce it once and for all.[2]

Following the lead of Indian activists, Nixon endorsed a whole new approach to Indian affairs in which federal government's top-down "paternalism" toward Indians would be replaced by a "complementary" government-to-government relationship between Washington and the tribes in which Indians would exercise maximum choice. Tribal officials would have the authority to take over any federally funded program they wished, even in the face of opposition from the government agency that previously administered it. In turn, their desperate communities would reap the benefits of the jobs accompanying those administrative duties and escape the indifference of the BIA. Nixon pledged a massive influx of funds for tribal loan guarantees, entrepreneurial seed money, education, health, and independent legal counsel. He also made a potent gesture by restoring to Taos Pueblo its sacred Blue Lake, which the federal government had seized during Theodore Roosevelt's administration for inclusion in a national forest. It was a sign that the government might be ready to show greater respect for Native culture alongside its newfound commitment to tribal self-determination.

Nixon's embrace of some of the key goals of Red Power activists is especially striking in contrast to his "Southern strategy" to exploit White racial resentment toward Blacks following the end of racial segregation laws, passage of the Civil Rights Act, and the rise of the Black Power movement. Part of it had to do with the strategic differences between Native American and African American activism. Indian rights claims focused on fulfilling preexisting law, whereas Black rights claims largely required changing it. More important still were differences in White racial attitudes toward the two populations. White Americans might have been generally surprised at the notion that Indian tribes claimed sovereign rights, and even that modern Indians existed at all, but few of them took offense at those principles because, by the late 1960s, the stakes seemed so low, at least for the present. The fact was that every major Indian reservation was located in the vast West, far from White population centers. Therefore, whatever sovereign rights Native people exercised had no discernible impact on the vast majority of Americans. Even Whites living near or, in some cases, on reservations could scarcely imagine Indian tribes asserting treaty rights and

Oliver F. Atkins, *President Nixon Meets with Taos Pueblo Leaders*, July 8, 1970. Courtesy of Richard M. Nixon Presidential Library and Museum / National Archives and Records Administration.

launching entrepreneurial initiatives that would impinge on them, given how low most of Indian country had fallen.

The same could not be said for Blacks. African Americans numbered 22.6 million people in 1970, compared to less than 800,000 Indians. African Americans were highly visible in practically all of the country's cities and throughout the South. Whereas the recognition of Native American self-determination required nothing of most White people, the Black rights agenda depended on convincing Whites that Blacks were worthy of dignity and justice in schools, on the street, in places of business, and in the public square. Red Power activism tended to focus on remote if symbolically important locations like contested fishing places, Alcatraz, abandoned military bases, and Wounded Knee. Cases like AIM's takeover of the BIA in the heart of Washington, D.C., were rare and fleeting. By contrast, African American militancy, most commonly associated with the Black Panthers, occurred right in the middle of major American cities. Furthermore, the White public widely associated Black Power with riots that engulfed a number of U.S. cities during the mid- to late 1960s, whereas the more inflammatory tactics of AIM had not yet occurred when Nixon delivered his message on Indian affairs. The greatest factor was that White Americans had already achieved the main purpose of their racial denigration of Indians—the appropriation of nearly all of their land; keeping

African Americans subordinated in a low-wage, low-status class required ongoing daily effort.

Vine Deloria Jr. had long maintained that Indians should keep their distance from the Black civil rights movement, and certainly from Black Power proponents. For one, he did not want the public to think of Indians as just some "other" minority riding the coattails of Black activists, because that would obscure Native people's special political status. Though Indians certainly wanted justice and equality outside the reservations, just like African Americans and every other minority group, sovereignty was their main agenda and particular to them. As Deloria wrote in 1971, "the most important aspect of the story of the red man is his stubborn refusal to give up his tribal identity and become simply another American. While the years have shown a partial assimilation of other groups, only the red man has stood firm, resisting all efforts to merge him with the groups that surround him." Whatever this declaration lacked in nuance, such as its failure to acknowledge generations of Indian assimilationists, it made up for in capturing the determination of Indians to have their resilient tribal nations play a central role in the future of the people. Additionally, Deloria judged that Black activism since the passage of the 1964 Civil Rights Act had grown both hopelessly ambitious and unclear about its goals, whereas establishing the legal foundation for Indian sovereignty had to be deliberate and slow. Not least of all, he worried about Indians getting stained by White people's animus toward Blacks, which, among the general population, if not in White communities near reservations, eclipsed any lingering enmity toward Natives. Nixon's support for Indian self-determination showed that it was possible to win the support of politicians otherwise opposed or indifferent to Black equality and justice. Indeed, such figures could point to their votes for seemingly unimpactful Indian rights as evidence that they were not racists.[3]

There were many Indians critical of the careful moderation of Deloria and the NCAI. Clyde Warrior, Mel Thom (Paiute), and Hank Adams (Assiniboine), among many members in the National Indian Youth Council, were vocal supporters of Black civil rights, particularly Martin Luther King Jr.'s Poor People's Campaign, both out of commitment to universal justice and recognition that Indians would benefit if White Americans treated everyone better. Doubtless they also appreciated that Black civil rights spokesmen such as King and James Baldwin were among the few non–Native Americans who publicly acknowledged the historic U.S. treatment of Indians as a genocide. Young Red Power activists also tended to dismiss signs of progress, like Nixon's Indian policy principles, as insultingly insufficient. AIM's direct-action militantism took place *after* Nixon's special message, because its members did not trust the pledges of the president or anyone else in power in the United States. They wanted not platitudes but immediate, substantive change. They also advanced a bold, confrontational racial worldview. Their aim was to inculcate Indians with pride based on the premise of a distinct Indian racial character. Additionally, they directly condemned White supremacy and sometimes even White people's supposedly innate racial qualities. These ideas were so powerful that Deloria himself invoked them on occasion, contrary to his own advice.[4]

It was a major achievement to bring Johnson, Nixon, and other White power brokers around to Indian self-determination, but convincing the White American public that tribes were political entities, not racial ones, was a much greater challenge. Most Americans had never been taught how to conceive of Native people as members of modern society, never mind as tribal nations with distinct constitutionally protected rights. Acceding to Native demands for sovereignty was one thing when it was a theoretical matter applicable to distant tribes. There would be much more resistance once tribes, particularly small bands in the heart of White America, began to assert their interests against White ones. The White backlash would involve questioning the racial identities and cultural authenticity of such groups. The era of self-determination was new, but old ways of racial thinking and acting died hard.

The same was true for Native people. Indian leaders at the national level were asking tribes to break with their own traditions and define themselves in the public arena as polities, not racial groups. Today, Indian scholars and activists have taken this position a step further to argue that tribes should reject blood quantum—the conflation of blood and identity—as a standard for tribal citizenship because it is nothing more than a racist colonial imposition designed to make Indians disappear. Yet Indians since time out of mind have thought of clans and tribes fundamentally as blood groups. Since the colonial era, they have also conceived of Indian identity in terms of blood. Furthermore, some modern Indians see the association of blood and belonging as useful for limiting the number of tribal citizens when finite economic benefits are at stake. Race was and is always partly instrumental, for Indians as well as Whites.

SOVEREIGNTY

The symbolic and economic advantages of tribal affiliation and Indigenous identity have increased since Nixon's speech, sometimes dramatically. In the 1971 Alaska Native Claims Settlement Act, the federal government addressed the historic wrong of White Americans' appropriation of Alaska Native land and fishing places without treaties, reservations, or compensation by transferring $962.5 million and forty-four million acres (or 12 percent of the land in Alaska) to several newly created Native corporations in exchange for the release of all other Indigenous claims. It was the largest Native settlement in U.S. history. Then, in quick sequence, the Indian Education Act (1972), Indian Financing Act (1974), Indian Self-Determination and Education Assistance Act (1975), and Indian Health Care Improvement Act (1976) transferred enormous power from the federal government to the tribes and funneled far more resources than ever before into tribal communities. The government was even willing to recognize and extend trust status to tribes it had already terminated or never recognized in the first place. The 1973 Menominee Restoration Act, spearheaded by the tireless lobbying of the Menominee tribal member Ada Deer, began the process of reversing earlier congressional Termination decisions and reconstituting previously extinguished reservations. In another remarkable break with history, the American Indian Religious Freedom Act (1978) established that "it shall be the policy of the United States to protect and preserve for American Indians their inherent right of freedom to believe, express, and exercise the traditional religions of the American Indian, Eskimo, Aleut, and Native Hawaiians, including but not limited to access to sites, use and possession of sacred objects, and the freedom to worship through ceremonials and traditional rites." For generations, Indigenous people had risked fines, arrest, imprisonment, and even massacre for practicing their religions. No more.[5]

U.S. courts, which had long stood as sites of grievous injustice to Native peoples based on racial double standards, began upholding Indian treaty rights. In 1974, U.S. District Judge George Boldt ruled in the case of *U.S. et al. v. State of Washington et al.*, after years of litigation, that Congress had not annulled the historic treaties of Washington State tribes. Therefore, the tribes still had the right to fish "in common" with other citizens at the tribes' "usual and accustomed places" and take half of the state's harvestable salmon. In 1983, the U.S. Court of Appeals for the Seventh Circuit issued a similar ruling that Wisconsin Ojibwes could still legally fish, hunt, and gather in areas they had otherwise ceded based on the terms of their treaties. It was one thing to acknowledge Indian sovereign rights over land and people on reservations, but quite another for U.S. courts to uphold those rights *off reservations*. Native people's increased leverage in the legal arena led the federal government in 2009 to settle a class-action case over its mismanagement of Indian trust fund accounts, following an adverse court ruling and two contempt of court charges against secretaries of the interior. The deal involved a $1.4 billion payout to three hundred thousand

Native Americans fishing from Nisqually River, 1966. One of many "fish-in" protests in the Pacific Northwest during the mid-to-late 1960s. Courtesy of Bettmann/Getty Images.

or so plaintiffs, a $2 billion Trust Land Consolidation Grant, which by 2016 had returned an estimated 1.7 million acres to reservations, and an Indian Scholarship Fund of up to $60 million—this from the same government that had been pursuing Termination just a generation earlier.[6]

Soon, the roster of federally recognized tribes eligible to benefit from these reforms would include small bands that heretofore had dealt solely with state governments. In 1976, the Penobscots, Passamaquoddies, and Maliseets of Maine sued for the return of all lands taken from them by state authorities since 1790, the date of the first Federal Trade and Intercourse Act, which had vested the power to conduct land treaties with Indians solely in the federal government. Neither Maine (which separated from Massachusetts in 1819) nor most of the original thirteen states had ever abided by this act. This suit threw into question the ownership of roughly two thirds of Maine, a crisis that grew so urgent that President Jimmy Carter intervened directly. His mediation produced an out-of-court settlement in which the tribes received $81.5 million and three hundred thousand acres taken into trust as reservations. Shortly after, so many other Native communities began to file similar claims that the government established an intensive application process for them to seek federal recognition outside the courts. As of this writing, eighteen groups have acquired federal recognition through this means, including the Shinnecocks of New York; the Mohegans of Connecticut; the Aquinnah Wampanoags and Mashpee Wampanoags of Massachusetts; the Narragansetts of Rhode Island; the Pamunkeys of Virginia; the Poarch Band Creeks of Alabama; the Choctaws of Louisiana; the Match-E-Be-Nash-She-Wish Band of Potawatomis, Huron-Potawatomis, and Grand Traverse Band of Ottawas and Chippewas of Michigan; the Cowlitz, Snoqualmie, Samish, and

Jamestown Callam tribes of Washington State; the Death Valley Timbisha Shoshone Band of California; and the San Juan Southern Paiutes of Arizona. The government has also denied recognition to thirty-four tribes through this process. Occasionally, Congress has addressed a tribe's failed application by extending federal recognition on its own, as in the cases of the Mashantucket Pequots of Connecticut in 1983, and the Chickahominy, Eastern Chickahominy, Upper Mattaponi, Rappahannock, Monacan, and Nansemond tribes of Virginia in 2018. Meanwhile, twenty-one states have extended their own recognition (which carries far fewer benefits) to another 116 tribes. These developments signal that White legislators no longer believe that tribes are relics and Indians are destined to extinction, or that being White is license to accelerate that supposed fate. To the contrary, the federal recognition process has led to Indian visibility all along the Atlantic seaboard, where the White public had long assumed that Indians had disappeared.[7]

Federally recognized tribes have benefited economically in this new legal environment in ways scarcely imagined by previous generations. A secure land base, combined with access to federal grants, has allowed them to pursue an astonishing range of entrepreneurial activities, including aquaculture, golf resorts, restaurants, hotels, green energy, telecommunications, craftwork, mining, fireworks sales, and far, far more. A recent government estimate is that there are now over 341,064 Native-owned businesses employing some 215,000 Indigenous people. Gaming is part of this picture. Actions by the courts and Congress have recognized that "tribes have exclusive right over gambling on their reservations except when it is banned by federal law or when a state prohibits an entire class of gaming." The National Indian Gaming Association reports that, as of 2024, there are over 250 tribes engaged in gaming with more than 500 operations supporting 1.2 million jobs. Gross revenue in 2022 was $40.9 billion, though more than half of tribal gaming operations take in less than $25 million annually. Poverty continues to plague too many reservation communities, but it has grown far more difficult to presume that to be Indian is to be destitute.[8]

Many tribal communities now have the means to devote resources to cultural revitalization, in a marked departure from the assimilationist pressures of previous generations. Tribes increasingly run their own schools, including programs for young children to learn their people's language. Examples range from the Pueblo of Isleta in New Mexico to the Mashpee Wampanoags of Massachusetts. In many cases, high school dropout rates have plummeted, and graduation rates have risen. Following the dramatic expansion of tribal colleges, the number of Indians in higher education, including graduate school, has skyrocketed. Furthermore, the number of courses

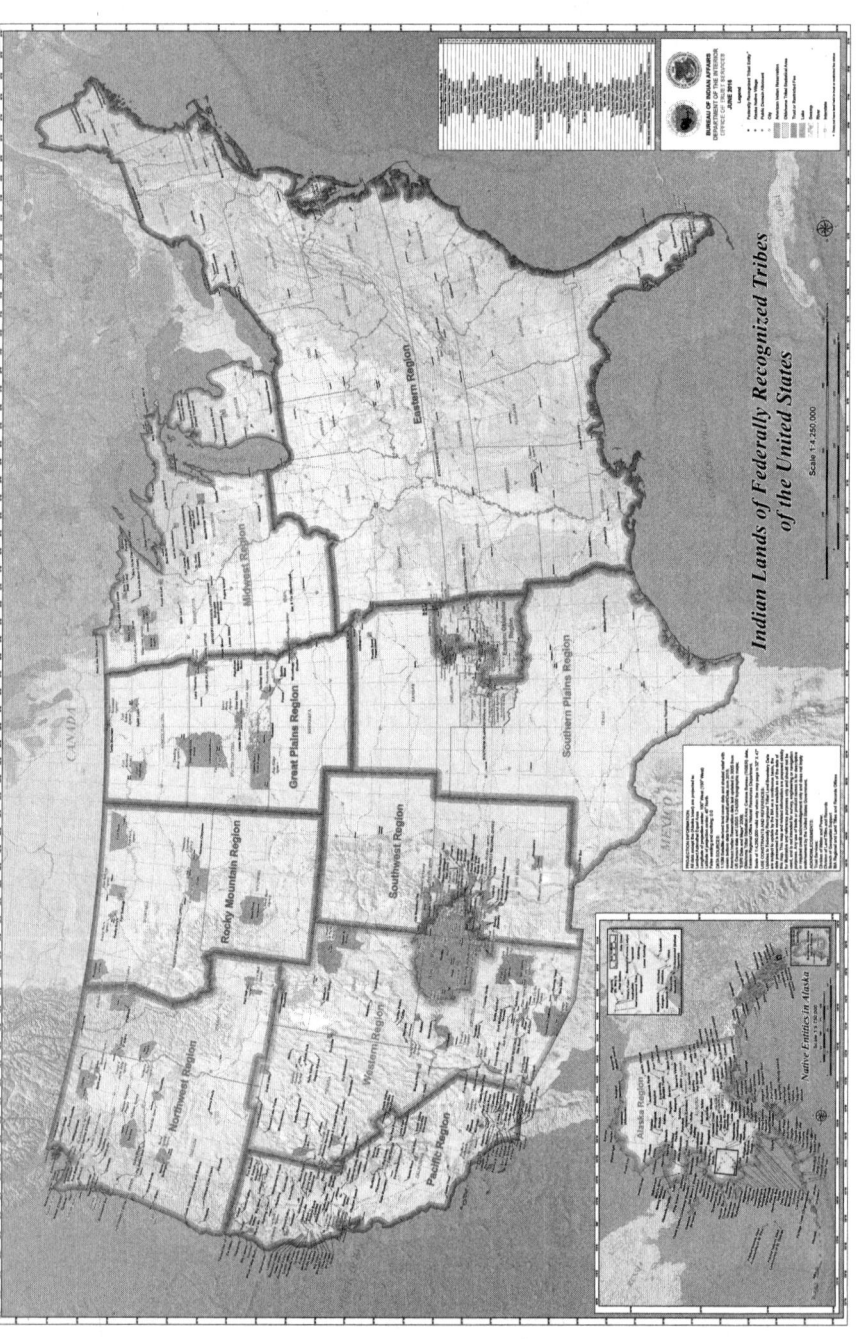

2016 Bureau of Indian Affairs Map of Indian Lands of Federally Recognized Tribes, 2019. U.S. Bureau of Indian Affairs.

they can take on Indian-related issues, with Indian instructors and texts by Indian authors, has expanded dramatically, headed by the rise of Native American Studies programs at institutions such as the University of Minnesota, the University of New Mexico, the University of Oklahoma, UCLA, and Dartmouth College. Throughout the country, there are Indian people practicing their ancestral tongues, reviving culinary and craft traditions, learning and in turn teaching tribal songs and dances, and reconnecting with the land. Tribal museums, where Indian peoples get to tell their own stories, have proliferated, highlighted by such examples as the Mashantucket Pequot Museum in Connecticut and the Ziibiwing Center of Anishinabe Culture & Lifeways, run by the Saginaw Chippewa tribe in Michigan. Tribes have built low-cost housing to permit those in need to live on the reservation or return to the reservation. They have gone out searching for tribal members once fostered or adopted out who want to come home and reintegrate. Some groups, such as the Navajos, have prioritized reform and healing over prison by eliminating jail time and fines for certain offenses while requiring peacemaking sessions. Taken together, these developments signal a nationwide Indian revival pushing back against a long history of genocide, forced assimilation, and economic destitution.[9]

Bison herd at a natural watering hole on ranchlands managed by the Mandan, Hidatsa, and Arikara Nation, on the Fort Berthold Indian Reservation, North Dakota. Courtesy of Danita Delimont/Alamy.

Indian people are also demanding dignity for themselves and their ancestors by recovering the remains of their dead. The desecration of Indian graves and collection and sometimes display of Indian remains by White museums ranks among the most hurtful racist injuries suffered by Indigenous people. After more than a century of Native lobbying to outlaw this practice, in 1990 Congress finally passed the Native American Graves Protection and Repatriation Act (NAGPRA), requiring all museums that receive federal funds to follow a process of returning Indigenous human remains and objects of cultural patrimony to their original tribal communities. The last push for this law accompanied congressional approval for the creation of the Native-run National Museum of the American Indian as part of the Smithsonian Institution. As the Cheyenne-Muscogee activist Suzan Shown Harjo explains, "We couldn't build a dream of a museum out of the nightmares of the stuff that were the reason for repatriation. You had to have them both." This undertaking has been enormous and slow, partly because of foot-dragging and underfunding by some museums, but also because of its breathtaking scale. At the time of the law's passage, American museums held between three hundred thousand and six hundred thousand Indian skeletal remains, more than the total Native American population in the early twentieth century. At the time of this writing, more than thirty years after passage of NAGPRA, Harvard University's museums still hold the remains of seven thousand Native people, and the Smithsonian museums some fifteen thousand. The scandal of this delay is that the museums not only violate the spirit of the law but also insult Native beliefs about the sacredness of the dead and their belongings. Indian ceremonies accompanying repatriation are full of emotion, reflecting that an unimaginable ordeal is finally coming to an end, sometimes after an extraordinarily long time. Only recently, the Wampanoags recovered and reburied the remains of none other than Massasoit, their leader who allied with the Pilgrims of Plymouth colony back in 1621. His grave in Warren, Rhode Island, had been ransacked along with forty-two others back in 1851. Generations later, in 2017, his tribesmen and women returned him to his original resting place with prayers in a revived Wampanoag language once assumed to be dead.[10]

The Indian Child Welfare Act (ICWA) of 1978, the product of intensive Indian lobbying, addresses yet another racial crime committed by White America against Native people, the large-scale state-directed fostering and adoption of Native children by White families. This legislation gives tribal courts authority over most welfare cases involving Indian children, including those living off reservation. It provides due-process guarantees to Indian families threatened with child removal, including requiring the highest standards of proof for abuse or neglect. Perhaps most important, it assigns ranked preference for placement of Indian children, beginning with extended family, then with their tribe, then with other Indians. Notably, it directs increased support for Indian families in need to sustain, not destroy, them. A long list of Native women activists, such as the social workers Evelyn Blanchard (Laguna/Yaqui) and Goldie Denny (Quinnault), made a desperate push for this law combined with a careful constitutional strategy by the Native American Rights Fund. They contended that the ICWA's favoring of Indian families in welfare cases involving Indian children was not a matter of racial preference, which would have been illegal, but rather of the survival and sovereignty of tribal polities. Put another way, their concern was less that Native children grow up "Indian," but as members of their ancestral tribal communities. Once again, Indians presented their tribes as domestic-dependent nations under U.S. law rather than as racial groups.[11]

While Indians in the U.S. legal arena were focusing their rights claims narrowly on their status as polities rather than as a race, they participated in an international movement to establish global Indigenous rights. In the mid-1970s, AIM and the activist newspaper *Akwesasne Notes* took inspiration from Third World decolonization movements to expand their cause to the shared challenges of Indigenous people around the globe. Their efforts quickly began to bear fruit, with the United Nations sponsoring a series of conferences around the themes of racism, racial discrimination, Apartheid, and decolonization, and forming a Working Group on Indigenous Peoples. In 2007, the United Nations passed its Declaration on the Rights of Indigenous Peoples, which asserts that human rights for Indigenous peoples has to account for them as groups, not just as individuals. This position was a far cry from the long tradition of global leaders dismissing Indigenous people as primitives or savages. Four years later, President Barack Obama, at the Second White House Tribal Nations Summit—which itself was a remarkable new development—endorsed the declaration and called for the maintenance of Native American cultures, languages, and identities, fulfillment of treaty obligations by the federal and state governments, the end of discrimination against Native people, and the rights of tribes to be involved in any decision-making process that would affect them. The new Indigenous internationalism meant that the world would be watching ever more closely in case the United States failed to live up to these pledges.[12]

The emerging consensus that Indigenous people worldwide and at home were entitled to particular rights and basic human dignity was reflected in American popular culture, most noticeably in movies and television. Already in the 1960s and '70s, widespread American disillusionment related to the Vietnam War and racial discrimination, combined with Native activism, led Hollywood to abandon the savage stereotypes that had characterized generations of filmmaking. To be sure, the new movie Indians were also stereotypes. Instead of being bloodthirsty savages, now they were romantic savages who lived in an Eden—akin to a pacifist, environmentalist, hippie commune—until the Fall came in the form of White people. Such caricatures appeared across a span of time stretching from Arthur Penn's *Little Big Man* (1970) to Kevin Costner's *Dances with Wolves* (1990). Yet this was also the beginning of a period in which Indian characters began to appear in three-dimensional form. The appearance of *House Made of Dawn* in 1972, based on the Kiowa author N. Scott Momaday's 1968 Pulitzer Prize–winning novel of the same name, was an early start to the trend. It addresses the trauma experienced by Indian veterans who returned home to systematic oppression and presents Native tradition as a source of strength and wisdom instead of a primitive weight to be dropped. In the years that followed, equally sophisticated films about Indians appeared, increasingly with Indian writers and producers in addition to actors. The 1998 landmark *Smoke Signals*, based on a screenplay by the Spokane author Sherman Alexie, features two young friends and their families on the Coeur d'Alene reservation in Idaho struggling with parental alcoholism, domestic abuse, poverty, and the pervasive degradation of colonialism, but also finding belonging in each other and their shared history. Recent years have seen an upsurge in Native television productions, including *Reservation Dogs*, *Rutherford Falls*, and *Dark Winds*, and innumerable documentaries. Native actors and actresses have landed leading roles in feature films such as *Prey* (2022), *Killers of the Flower Moon* (2023), and more. Sometimes, they even speak Native languages with English subtitles. The agenda of classic Hollywood's Indian activists to provide creative and professional opportunities for their kind, and thereby to circulate more realistic and positive portrayals of Native people, has finally materialized.[13]

Even the Indian sports mascots long cherished by White fans and resented by many Natives have begun to fade. Activists gradually convinced fans, host cities, and advertisers to oppose these caricatures, leading colleges and even professional sports teams to replace them. The pressure campaign included an NCAI poster counterposing the Cleveland Indians' denigrating "Chief Wahoo" logo with equivalent images from fictional teams such as the "New York Jews" and "San Francisco Chinamen." Other opponents of the mascots produced video clips of actual Native people confronting fans of the Washington Redskins. By 2021, both teams had resigned their Native-themed mascots, with the Cleveland baseball club becoming the Guardians and the Washington football team becoming the Commanders. Other organizations,

National Congress of American Indians, Indian mascot protest, 2001.

such as the Kansas City Chiefs, Atlanta Braves, and Chicago Blackhawks, and college teams like the Florida State University Seminoles, continue to hold out, citing tradition, an intention to honor Indians, and the support of at least some Native people. It seems only a matter of time before they buckle, too.[14]

OLD WAYS DIE HARD

For all the progress achieved by Native people over the past sixty years, certain ingrained patterns of systematic racism have persisted in American society, putting Indian country's recent political gains under threat. President Ronald Reagan's agenda of social spending cuts during the 1980s disproportionately impacted Indian tribes, as encouraged by Secretary of the Interior James Watt, who considered reservations as embodiments of the failures of socialism. Reservation unemployment during Reagan's administration skyrocketed from 40 percent to nearly 80 percent. His successors have since abandoned his draconian policies, and under Presidents Barack Obama and especially Joe Biden, funding for Indian country reached unprecedented levels. Nevertheless, the Reagan presidency was a cautionary tale that a conservative political wave always carries the risk of a return to the Termination era, or worse.[15]

Indeed, less than a decade after President Johnson's declaration that a new era in U.S.-Indian relations was underway, a new, unimaginable crime targeting Native people came to light: the systematic sterilization of Indian women in Indian Health Service hospitals and among its contractors during the early to mid-1970s and perhaps far earlier. Over three thousand women of childbearing age had been sterilized at four IHS hospitals between 1973 and 1976, usually without proper consent. In some cases, hospital staff had threatened the patients that unless they signed an authorization form, their welfare payments would end or social services would come for their children. Some of the women said they had no knowledge in advance that the hospital was going to sterilize them. Two girls sterilized in Montana were just sixteen. White doctors were taking it upon themselves to decide that these women, who were overwhelmingly poor, unmarried, young, and sometimes mothers already, should no longer reproduce. An independent study by the Choctaw-Cherokee Constance Redbird Pinkerman-Uri, the first Native American woman to hold both law and medical degrees, broke the story. Combined with political pressure from the newly formed advocacy group Women of All Red Nations, an official government inquiry ensued. The investigation limited its scope to just four of the IHS's twelve service areas and downplayed the testimony of Native victims in favor of hospital staff. Even so, its findings were horrific. It exposed that physicians in these institutions sterilized at least a quarter of women of childbearing age who passed through their operating rooms. The problem might very well have been much broader in scope than just the hospitals under scrutiny and the result of racial bias rather than miscommunication and faulty paperwork procedures, contrary to what the investigators concluded. It also might have been occurring for several decades. Susie Yellowtail testified that when she was a registered Crow nurse way back in the 1920s, she saw doctors in Crow Hospital sterilize women without their consent frequently. It even happened to her, with the White doctor saying afterward, "Three is all you want and three is all you're going to get." As a number of scholars and activists had argued, this dark practice belongs in the catalog of actions that constituted the White American genocide against Indians.[16]

Meanwhile, Native women experience sexual assault and murder at rates so horrifying that it would produce a national outcry if the White population suffered similarly. A 2011 report by the NCAI concluded that violence against Native women had reached "epidemic proportions," in response to findings that 34 percent of Native women were raped during their lifetimes and 39 percent were victims of domestic violence. Another report, by the Centers for Disease Control and Prevention, found that 49 percent of Native women had been victims of sexual violence. In some communities, it was no longer a question of whether a girl or woman would be raped, but when. The overwhelming majority of perpetrators of this violence have been non-Native men, usually White, for reasons ranging from racial animus, to predators exploiting the weak police presence on reservations, to the anarchic drinking and

Women of All Red Nations logo. Wikimedia Commons.

drug environments of "man camps" in mining and fracking enterprises in and around reservations. The problem is especially prevalent where states still have criminal jurisdictions over reservations, for in such contexts crime often goes uninvestigated and unprosecuted.[17]

The violence American society inflicts on Native women has finally begun to garner public attention. In 2007, Amnesty International issued a report entitled *Maze of Injustice: The Failure to Protect Indigenous Women from Sexual Violence in the U.S.A.*, which spurred two major pieces of federal legislation in 2013: the Tribal Law and Order Act and the Violence Against Women Act Reauthorization, giving tribes the authority, in some circumstances, to sentence a convicted rapist to jail for a maximum of three to nine years and a fine of up to five thousand dollars. Even then, since 2016, some six thousand Indian and Alaska Native women and girls have gone missing, with less than 1 percent of these cases reported to federal authorities. The damage done is staggering. The Muscogee lawyer Sarah Deer puts it starkly:

> Imagine living in a world in which almost every woman you know has been raped. Now imagine living in a world in which four generations of women and their ancestors have been raped. Now imagine that not a single rapist has been prosecuted for these crimes. That dynamic is a reality for many native women—and thus for some survivors, it can be difficult to separate the more immediate experience of their assault from the larger experience that their people have endured through a history of forced removal, displacement, and destruction.

One reason it is so difficult to make that separation is that American colonialism has always involved Whites exploiting Indians through sexual violence. The trauma stretches on and on.[18]

In the border towns near reservations, from the northern Plains to the desert Southwest, Indians continue to face high rates of discrimination and violent abuse from White citizens and even the police. The most glaring example is the racial terror of so-called Indian rolling—a euphemism for outright assault—in places like Gallup and Farmington, New Mexico. Both of these places, like so many border towns, are filled with liquor stores and bars catering to Indians from dry reservations. Generations of pleading by tribal leaders for these businesses to stop preying on their people's addictions have run aground on the preeminent American value of free enterprise. Thus, the public spaces of these municipalities are often populated by Indians passed out or in stupors. "Indian rolling" involves gangs of White youths beating up these vulnerable targets. This horrific practice has evolved over the course of generations into something of a White rite of passage. The activist newspaper *Akwesasne Notes* denounced it as far back as 1970 in articles that characterized Farmington as the "Selma of the West," in reference to the notorious Alabama town where White troopers and deputized citizens brutalized peaceful civil rights marchers in 1965. The torture and murder of three Navajos by three White teenagers in Farmington in 1974 (the bodies were beaten and burned beyond recognition) was just the most extreme example of a much larger trend. More recently, the Brulé scholar Nick Estes has likened Indian rolling to lynching. It is an apt characterization.[19]

Just as lynching upheld the greater system of Jim Crow, Indian rolling is the violent edge of a range of discrimination and abuse that Indians face in border towns, which are premised on exploiting Indians. As one civil rights commission after another has concluded, housing in these places is almost totally segregated by race. Border town hospitals have a history of providing subpar treatment to Indians in need and even of accommodating White patients who do not want to share a room with Indians. Police brutality is ubiquitous, involving beatings, verbal abuse, and the wicked practice of taking drunk Indians into custody and then abandoning them miles away. All the while, the economic life of these places involves taking advantage of Indian vulnerabilities. Beyond the liquor peddlers, there are check cashing and payday lending stores, auto dealers, and pawnshops that charge extortionate interest rates to Indians who lack regular bank accounts. When Indians enter respectable stores to shop, too often the proprietors treat them as if they are there to steal. Employers, including public entities, have been found by the Department of

Justice and Civil Rights Commissions to discriminate against Indians in recruitment, hiring, assignment, and promotion. Indians report White citizens taunting them frequently—"Go back to the reservation." "How much beer have you had today?" "What are you going to steal?" "Prairie nigger." "Timber nigger." "Indian whore"—and physically accosting them. Until recent years, businesses sometimes posted signs reading NO DOGS OR INDIANS. Such treatment is so common, particularly in border towns but also in many other parts of the United States, that in a study based on interviews with three hundred Native people, the majority of them shared that they or someone close to them had been the victim of some sort of hate crime. They widely testified to feeling vulnerable anywhere off the reservation.[20]

When political disputes inflame the passions, the racial abuse gets worse. In the 1980s, the effort of Ojibwes in Wisconsin to exercise fishing and hunting rights based on treaties from 1837 and 1842 led to White outbursts of racism that the public normally did not associate with the Midwest, but that Indians knew all too well. Several White rights groups formed, such as the euphemistic Equal Rights for Everyone, based on a principle expressed in the *Milwaukee Journal* that the courts had "handed American Indians rights far superior to those of all other American citizens." *Time* magazine went so far as to publish an essay with the loaded question "Should We Give the U.S. Back to the Indians?" as if this were the actual issue. Ojibwes often went to their cars to find the tires slashed and the windshields broken. A brewing company began producing "Treaty Beer," with the proceeds directed to the effort to thwart the Natives' campaign. Bumper stickers appeared on White cars reading "Save a Walleye, Spear an Indian," "Spear a Squaw," "Red Niggers," and "How do you starve an Indian? Put his food stamps under his work boots." Indian fishermen faced attacks in which Whites shot at them, threw pipe bombs, and tried to capsize their boats. Indian parents had to withdraw their children from predominantly White schools out of concern for their safety. Donald Fixico, a Creek-Fox-Sauk-Shawnee professor at the University of Wisconsin–Milwaukee, who had nothing to do with this affair, even received an anonymous phone call threatening to kill his wife. The environment was so combustible that the American Civil Liberties Union and then a U.S. Civil Rights Commission got involved. One member of the latter group said he was "appalled at the rampant racism he found in Northern Wisconsin." But it was not just northern Wisconsin. Whites have responded similarly throughout the country wherever and whenever Indians have asserted their jurisdiction over fractionalized lands and highways on their reservations, tried to open a gaming operation, sought federal recognition, exercised hunting and fishing

White protests against Ojibwe fishing rights.
Courtesy of the Great Lakes Indian Fish and Wildlife Commission.

rights, or virtually any act of sovereignty that their neighbors fear comes at the expense of Whites.[21]

Among the most common tactics of Whites who oppose the Indian exercise of sovereignty has been to question the Indians' authenticity based on stereotypes. When the Mashpee Wampanoags sued the Cape Cod town of Mashpee in the 1970s for the return of tribal lands, the community did not yet have federal recognition and the application process for acquiring that status was not yet in place. Therefore, it had to establish its legal standing by proving in court that it was an actual Indian tribe before it could litigate for its territory. Taking place in 1979, the proceedings were a remarkable demonstration of White people's struggle to understand how a largely acculturated, mixed-race community could present itself as Indian and a tribe. For their part, Mashpee Wampanoags were forced to explain publicly for the first time how they conceived of themselves as Wampanoag and Indian. In one exchange, the judge asked a teenage Wampanoag girl how she knew she was an Indian and she answered, "My mother told me." In other testimony, Wampanoags recounted their people's custom of dropping Wampanoag words and phrases into otherwise English conversations, even though none of them could speak the language fluently; occasions on which people wore regalia; the annual herring run; the tradition of placing a rock or stick on a pile where a historic event occurred; elders teaching splint basket making, quill work, herbal remedies, and fishing techniques; powwows with other Indians; preference for marriage with other Indians; and how everyone knew of Mashpee as an "Indian town."

There were two main problems for the Mashpee Wampanoags: First, ever since Massachusetts officially dissolved their tribe in 1869, their community had effectively become a municipality, meaning that they lacked evidence of a distinct and ongoing *tribal* political organization; second, they did not fit stereotypes of Indians propagated by the movies and other popular culture. That is to say, these residents of Cape Cod did not ride horses, live in tepees, wear feathered headdresses, hunt buffalo, or attack stagecoaches. Here were modern-looking people who spoke English, had regular jobs, drove cars, and shopped at the supermarket, many of whom were of complex ancestry, claiming to be Indians. It did not make common sense to Whites raised in America's racial culture. Consequently, the all-White jury found that though the group had been a tribe at certain points in its history, at others it had not, and therefore it could not meet the standard required to file the suit for land. It took another thirty years for the Mashpee Wampanoags finally to gain federal recognition through the formal application process and begin reconstituting some of their tribal territory.[22]

The public's questioning of the authenticity of Indian tribes tends to target bands like the Mashpee Wampanoags that are small, of mixed heritage, and heavily acculturated, particularly when they pursue gambling enterprises. Part of the issue is that American society, including quite a number of Indians, have come to associate poverty with Indianness so closely as to assume that they must go together. By this reckoning, the pursuit of wealth is a White, or at least non-Indian, characteristic. If the Indians display African American ancestry, as is often the case in the East, skeptics often accuse that the so-called Natives are just Black fortune-seekers, based on the old American standard that Black ancestry trumps all other racial backgrounds. When the Mashantucket Pequots gained federal recognition in 1983 and then opened the enormously profitable Foxwood casino, the law student Jeff Benedict responded with a book-length exposé, *Without Reservation*, denouncing them as racial frauds. The real estate mogul (and future U.S. president) Donald Trump, whose Atlantic City casino business was threatened by Indian gaming in the Northeast, made the same argument in testimony before the Senate in 1993. He complained, "When you go up to Connecticut and look—now [the Pequots] don't look like real Indians to me; and they don't look like real Indians to other Indians." Not just the Pequots but practically every newly reorganized tribe had their racial identities questioned in public. When the Golden Hill Pagussetts applied for federal recognition, the *Hartford Courant*, Connecticut's biggest newspaper, published a cartoon depicting tribal members with African American features and names like "Chief Go Sioux Me" and "Nike Hide Tanner." During that same period, White politicians in Louisiana attempted to thwart the revitalized Tunicas and Choctaws from exercising their sovereignty, including gaming, by exploiting the local view of them as "Redbones" (a local term meaning Blacks with just a smattering of Indian heritage) and framing their Indigenous rights as an affirmative action program.[23]

The public is almost equally unaccepting of upstart Indian tribes with mixed White backgrounds, because Whiteness also eclipses Indianness in defining a person's or group's identity in American racial culture. Debate over the gaming operations and land claims of the reemerged Chumash of California has included accusations that they are nothing more than White and Hispanic poseurs chasing riches. By these measures, to be an Indian tribe entitled to sovereign rights requires the group to have remained unmixed with any other race over the course of hundreds of years, accept poverty, and look and act like Indians in Hollywood westerns. Given the impossibility of any tribe meeting these standards, the only other option is to disappear. These age-old racial ideas remain predominant, even in the age of Indian self-determination.[24]

RACE AND NATION

Debates about Indian authenticity centered on blood purity also take place among Native people, partly for reasons as instrumental as those that shape White racial ideology, but also out of tradition. The new modern context for these questions might be conceptualized as a transition from tribal membership to tribal citizenship. Customarily, being a member of a tribe meant being related to others in the group while remaining present and engaged. Sometimes, to be sure, tribes adopted outsiders, but only rarely in significant numbers. The overwhelming majority of their people consisted of blood kin, which, in effect, made the tribe an extended cousinage. In modern times, tribal membership, as a bureaucratic matter, has had less to do with active participation in the group than a qualification to profit from the tribe's economic resources and government programs and vote in its elections. This change has coincided with the argument of Native activists and the agreement of the federal government, including the Supreme Court in 1974's *Morton v. Mancari*, that American Indian tribes are not racial groups but nations, or sovereign polities, comprised of citizens. There are countervailing pressures on tribes to extend citizenship to all those who have biological, cultural, and political allegiance to the community, while guarding against extending citizenship to anyone who does not possess those qualities. It is the power of tribes, as sovereign entities, to set their own citizenship standards without interference from the United States, a right that the Supreme Court upheld in 1978's *Santa Clara Pueblo v. Martinez*. By and large, they have settled on two methods. One is descent from someone who appeared on a tribal census, or base roll, taken in the late nineteenth or early twentieth century. The other is blood quantum.[25]

Blood quantum is the most common means of determining eligibility for tribal citizenship and, as such, a major source of controversy in Indian country. Roughly 70 percent of tribal constitutions contain a blood quantum provision. Sometimes, that standard is a tribal blood quantum, say a quarter. In such a case, someone would qualify by descending from one full-blood grandparent, or two half-blood grandparents, or one half-blood parent and another outsider parent, or two quarter-blood parents. A tribal blood quantum standard means that a person could be a full-blood Indian and still not qualify if most of that ancestry came from other tribes. A majority of tribal nations using blood quantum, however, require minimum levels of *Indian* blood rather than *tribal* blood, which permits citizens to have multiple tribal backgrounds. Even the Native American (peyote) Church has an Indian blood quantum minimum of a quarter for membership. Indians are the only group in the United States that, officially, at least, place such emphasis on blood quantum.[26]

Just as blood quantum divides ancestry into fractions, so, too, does it sometimes divide communities. As in the case of base roll membership, proving blood quantum depends on an ancestor's having gone through the bureaucratic process to document his or her background. Yet many Indians during the period in which that paperwork was being generated were either absent from the reservation where the recording took place, unwilling to participate in the process out of revulsion for it, or mistakenly categorized by White administrators. Such people are sometimes referred to in Indian country as "outalucks," and there are a great many of them—nearly half the people who identified as Indian on the 1980 and 1990 U.S. censuses are not tribally enrolled. Yet some of them used to be. A recent study by David E. Wilkins and Shelly

PARENTS																
	N.I.	1/16	1/8	3/16	1/4	5/16	3/8	7/16	1/2	9/16	5/8	11/16	3/4	13/16	7/8	15/16	4/4
1/16	1/32	1/16	3/32	1/8	5/32	3/16	7/32	1/4	9/32	5/16	11/32	3/8	13/32	7/16	15/32	1/2	17/32
1/8	1/16	3/32	1/8	5/32	3/16	7/32	1/4	9/32	5/16	11/32	3/8	13/32	7/16	15/32	1/2	17/32	9/16
3/16	3/32	1/8	5/32	3/16	7/32	1/4	9/32	5/16	11/32	3/8	13/32	7/16	15/32	1/2	17/32	9/16	19/32
1/4	1/8	5/32	3/16	7/32	1/4	9/32	5/16	11/32	3/8	13/32	7/16	15/32	1/2	17/32	9/16	19/32	5/8
5/16	5/32	3/16	7/32	1/4	9/32	5/16	11/32	3/8	13/32	7/16	15/32	1/2	17/32	9/16	19/32	5/8	21/32
3/8	3/16	7/32	1/4	9/32	5/16	11/32	3/8	13/32	7/16	15/32	1/2	17/32	9/16	19/32	5/8	21/32	11/16
7/16	7/32	1/4	9/32	5/16	11/32	3/8	13/32	7/16	15/32	1/2	17/32	9/16	19/32	5/8	21/32	11/16	23/32
1/2	1/4	9/32	5/16	11/32	3/8	13/32	7/16	15/32	1/2	17/32	9/16	19/32	5/8	21/32	11/16	23/32	3/4
9/16	9/32	5/16	11/32	3/8	13/32	7/16	15/32	1/2	17/32	9/16	19/32	5/8	21/32	11/16	23/32	3/4	25/32
5/8	5/16	11/32	3/8	13/32	7/16	15/32	1/2	17/32	9/16	19/32	5/8	21/32	11/16	23/32	3/4	25/32	13/16
11/16	11/32	3/8	13/32	7/16	15/32	1/2	17/32	9/16	19/32	5/8	21/32	11/16	23/32	3/4	25/32	13/16	27/32
3/4	3/8	13/32	7/16	15/32	1/2	17/32	9/16	19/32	5/8	21/32	11/16	23/32	3/4	25/32	13/16	27/32	7/8
13/16	13/32	7/16	15/32	1/2	17/32	9/16	19/32	5/8	21/32	11/16	23/32	3/4	25/32	13/16	27/32	7/8	29/32
7/8	7/16	15/32	1/2	17/32	9/16	19/32	5/8	21/32	11/16	23/32	3/4	25/32	16/16	27/32	7/8	29/32	15/16
15/16	15/32	1/2	17/32	9/16	19/32	5/8	21/32	11/16	23/32	3/4	25/32	13/16	27/32	7/8	29/32	15/16	31/32
4/4	1/2	17/32	9/16	19/32	5/8	21/32	11/16	23/32	3/4	25/32	13/16	27/32	7/8	29/32	15/16	31/32	4/4
1/32	1/64	3/64	5/64	7/64	9/64	11/64	13/64	15/64	17/64	19/64	21/64	23/64	25/64	27/64	29/64	31/64	33/64
3/32	3/64	5/64	7/64	9/64	11/64	13/64	15/64	17/64	19/64	21/64	23/64	25/64	27/64	29/64	31/64	33/64	35/64
5/32	5/64	7/64	9/64	11/64	13/64	15/64	17/64	19/64	21/64	23/64	25/64	27/64	29/64	31/64	33/64	35/64	37/64
7/32	7/64	9/64	11/64	13/64	15/64	17/64	19/64	21/64	23/64	25/64	27/64	29/64	31/64	33/64	35/64	37/64	39/64
9/32	9/64	11/64	13/64	15/64	17/64	19/64	21/64	23/64	25/64	27/64	29/64	31/64	33/64	35/64	37/64	39/64	41/64
11/32	11/64	13/64	15/64	17/64	19/64	21/64	23/64	25/64	27/64	29/64	31/64	33/64	35/64	37/64	39/64	41/64	43/64
13/32	13/64	15/64	17/64	19/64	21/64	23/64	25/64	27/64	29/64	31/64	33/64	35/64	37/64	39/64	41/64	43/64	45/64
15/32	15/64	17/64	19/64	21/64	23/64	25/64	27/64	29/64	31/64	33/64	35/64	37/64	39/64	41/64	43/64	45/64	47/64
17/32	17/64	19/64	21/64	23/64	25/64	27/64	29/64	31/64	33/64	35/64	37/64	39/64	41/64	43/64	45/64	47/64	49/64
19/32	19/64	21/64	23/64	25/64	27/64	29/64	31/64	33/64	35/64	37/64	39/64	41/64	43/64	45/64	47/64	49/64	51/64
21/32	21/64	23/64	25/64	27/64	29/64	31/64	33/64	35/64	37/64	39/64	41/64	43/64	45/64	47/64	49/64	51/64	53/64
23/32	23/64	25/64	27/64	29/64	31/64	33/64	35/64	37/64	39/64	41/64	43/64	45/64	47/64	49/64	51/64	53/64	55/64
25/32	25/64	27/64	29/64	31/64	33/64	35/64	37/64	39/64	41/64	43/64	45/64	47/64	49/64	51/64	53/64	55/64	57/64
27/32	27/64	29/64	31/64	33/64	35/64	37/64	39/64	41/64	43/64	45/64	47/64	49/64	51/64	53/64	55/64	57/64	59/64
29/32	29/64	31/64	33/64	35/64	37/64	39/64	41/64	43/64	45/64	47/64	49/64	51/64	53/64	55/64	57/64	59/64	61/64
31/32	31/64	33/64	35/64	37/64	39/64	41/64	43/64	45/64	47/64	49/64	51/64	53/64	55/64	57/64	59/64	61/64	63/64

Bureau of Indian Affairs blood quantum chart. By matching the blood quanta of parents in the vertical column and horizontal row, one can determine the blood quantum of any of their children. For instance, the child of a 1/8 mother (from the vertical column) and a 3/16 father (from the horizontal row) will be 5/32.

Hulse Wilkins finds that, as of 2016, as many as eighty tribes, disproportionately in California, have acted to disenroll or banish members. Insufficient blood quantum is among the most common explanations given. The desires to consolidate access to gaming revenues and purge political opponents are usually the instrumental reasons.[27]

Tensions over the stunning growth and diversity of the Indian population has also galvanized the blood-quantum debate. By the standards of the U.S. Census, the Native American population has risen exponentially over the past sixty years, from 551,700 in 1960 to 9.6 million in 2020. The primary cause has not been an increase in births over deaths, but of individuals who previously categorized themselves in some other way newly identifying as Indian now that the stigma of that association has ebbed and the rewards have begun to flow. Large numbers of these so-called race shifters have sought to become formal members—citizens—of the tribes from whom they claim ancestry, thereby challenging the tribes to judge their merits. Tribes have weighed a number of factors in setting the qualifications for new citizens, including customary definitions of belonging, acceptable forms of evidence for identity claims, the effect of more citizens on tribal resources, the ways the broader American public will view the new citizens, and justice for both the applicants and the tribe. Considerations of blood factor in all these respects.[28]

Full-bloods often see themselves as keepers of tribal traditions and setters of the pace of change. As characterized in 1962 by Frell M. Owl, a member of the Eastern Band of Cherokee Indians who had worked in the BIA for thirty years, they are generally "jealous [protective] of full-blood status, often wary of the intentions of the government personnel, scornful of mixed-bloods," who they sometimes deride as "White Indians." These attitudes extend from a view, expressed by the Kiowa author N. Scott Momaday, that there is a deep-seated mystical relationship between Indigenous people and their ancestors that he likens to "memory in the blood," or a "racial memory that leaps across the generations." He is not alone. The anthropologist Circe Sturm, who has worked extensively with the Oklahoma Cherokees, writes that practically every Cherokee with whom she has spoken about the matter contends that "Cherokee blood is a literal, shared substance that binds them to one another and to every other Cherokee on the planet." The assumption is that a high quantum of Cherokee blood corresponds to Cherokee traditionalism and commitment to the group. The United Keetoowah Band of Cherokee Indians, a separate entity from the much larger Cherokee Nation of Oklahoma, prides itself in requiring a one-quarter blood quantum rather than descent from a base roll out of the belief that this standard preserves its status as a tribe of "real Indians." As the historian Malinda Lowery writes, her people, the Lumbees, regularly invoke "good blood," "bad blood," "her blood," and so forth, in conversation. She continues, "The idea behind those offhand remarks is that blood transmits certain qualities of behavior, power, and authority." It is "a way to distinguish between qualities the speaker wants in an insider and qualities one rejects or reserves for outsiders."[29]

Blood thinking encompasses racial identity as well as tribal identity. In a survey of Indian college students, the respondents reported Native peers constantly asking, "What percent are you?" and conflating degrees of full-bloodedness with cultural authenticity and the right to speak on Indian issues. One Wichita-Seneca man in his fifties says that from the time of his youth until today, he has witnessed community leaders remove light-skinned Indians from powwow dances on the premise that they do not belong. The reckoning of Indian identity by fractions is unquestionably a White invention, but blood consciousness was and is very much part of Native American cultures.[30]

Blood consciousness and the bureaucratic importance of blood quantum have profound effects on young people seeking marriage partners. The Native Studies academic Adrienne Keene writes that though she belongs to the Cherokee Tribe of Oklahoma, which does not have blood quantum citizenship, she worries what her children will look like if the father is not an Indian with a high blood quantum. She confesses, "I get crap constantly for the way I look and not being 'Native' enough—even when the work I do is completely for Native communities and all about giving back. I think I've cried more tears in graduate school over identity politics than anything else." The Tonawanda Seneca Leslie Logan remembers her grandparents teaching her that "when it came to dating and mating... there is only one option: Native." She followed their direction and nowadays provides the same guidance to her children, which she sees as among her most important roles. She cannot forget how her father married a White woman and produced her light-skinned half sister, whose experience on the reservation involved getting "spit on, teased, poked, and prodded for being a 'half-breed.'" At sixteen, this sister left the reservation "because she was *hoyno'oh*; because she did not belong." It was a cautionary tale about the danger of "mating ourselves out of Seneca existence as we know it." And not just tribal existence. Though elders usually prefer partners from the same tribe, the greater pressure is to marry Indian. This expectation, according to one study, "seems premised on the notion that race is in fact a biological essence," and that "maintaining the 'race' is at least as important as maintaining the 'culture.'" Indian people's lived experiences often teach that blood carries culture and that Indians need Indian-looking people to represent the group if they are going to convince Whites to respect their sovereignty.[31]

The many Indian critics of blood quantum citizenship charge that Indians will define themselves out of existence by this standard, given the inevitably of continued intermarriage with non-Indians, never mind members of other tribes. For instance, among the Senecas, who have been in contact with Europeans for four hundred years, a 2011 tribal study found that the group's aggregate blood quantum was at most one quarter. Thus, writes Logan, "at current and sustained out-mating rates, the diminishment of Seneca blood is moving like an out-of-control race car speeding downhill with the brakes cut." The result will be, at best, de facto termination, but Suzan Shown Harjo warns that it also risks a revival of de jure termination when "some clever neo-terminationist" manages "to unravel the Indian political status doctrine [that Indian tribes are polities, not racial groups] by using the fixation on and fiction of tribal blood." Blood quantum, she declares, is just "internalized oppression."[32]

Indians who favor blood quantum definitions of belonging contend that if tribes shift en masse to citizenship based on descent from an ancestor on a base roll, they will become like the Oklahoma Cherokees, commonly known as the Whitest of tribes. As Sturm reported about that tribal nation back in 2002, "the degree of Cherokee blood among citizens ranges from full-blood to 1/2048 . . . According to the Cherokee Nation's Department of Registration, 21 percent of that tribe has 1/4 or more degree of Cherokee blood . . . Twenty-nine percent has 1/4 to 1/16 degree of Cherokee blood . . . And 21 percent has between 1/16 and 1/64 . . . That leaves 29 percent . . . somewhere between 1/16 and 1/2048." To some Native people, one cannot be considered a real Indian with such slight Indian ancestry.[33]

A number of tribes have experimented with alternatives to both blood quantum and base roll citizenship. The Northern Cheyennes have waived a half-blood quantum minimum requirement for individuals who live on the reservation. The Swinomish of Washington State also stress participation in the community, while the Tohono O'odham extend citizenship to all children of parents living on the reservation. Doubtless tribes in the future will experiment with a variety of other arrangements rather than define themselves out of existence through a blood quantum requirement to belong. Whatever course they choose, it will be full of debate, dissent, inconsistencies, and unexpected consequences, like the entire history of race.[34]

RACE MATTERS

Against this background, we are in a better position to understand three recent episodes of public controversy in Indian country related to questions of blood: debates over the enrollment of the descendants of freedmen (or former slaves); Massachusetts senator Elizabeth Warren's claim to be Cherokee; and the larger phenomenon of pretendians—people fraudulently claiming to be Indian. All of these issues hinge on the question of what documentable tribal or Indian blood means to citizenship in modern Indian tribal nations. The answers reveal the ongoing power and instrumentality of racial ideology in Indian country and the United States in general.

Between 1979 and 2007, four out of the so-called Five Civilized Tribes of Oklahoma—Cherokees, Creeks, Choctaws, and Seminoles—removed the descendants of freedmen (former slaves of those tribal nations) from tribal citizenship, contrary to the terms of peace imposed on them by the United States after the Civil War. These actions sparked outcry, litigation, and rare public attention to the racial dynamics of Indian country, particularly when it comes to Blacks. The first move came in 1979, when the Creeks expelled anyone who did not descend from the

"Indians by Blood" rolls compiled by the Dawes Commissions in the late nineteenth and early twentieth centuries. The Choctaws and Cherokees followed in 1983, as did the Seminoles in 2000. The tribes had barely tolerated the freedmen since the war. Though most freedmen took up land within the tribes' borders following emancipation, usually it was in segregated townships at a remove from the main Indian communities. Freedmen formally possessed the rights to vote and hold office, but Indians sometimes obstructed them. With the passage of the Dawes and Curtis Acts, the freedmen received allotments of tribal land and had their names recorded on a Freedmen's Roll, separate from the Indians by Blood roll. The Indians by Blood roll specified the blood quanta for each individual. The Freedmen's Roll did not, though sometimes it mentioned whether an individual claimed some Indian ancestry. That discrepancy would prove consequential in recent times.[35]

Modern tribal purges of freedmen descendants are based on new tribal constitutions requiring documented tribal blood, sometimes of a minimum quantum, based on the Dawes Rolls. These constitutions do not target freedmen descendants specifically, but they were clearly drawn with freedmen descendants in mind because such people usually cannot produce written proof of Indian ancestry. Even if they could, the pattern of Indian-Black racial segregation during the twentieth century usually would mean that most of them would fall short of some tribes' blood quantum minimum. The defense of these measures rests on two principles: (1) that the tribes, as sovereign nations, have the right to define citizenship any way they want, and (2) that they have always, when left to their own choosing, defined group belonging through ancestry, or blood. Freedmen descendants and many scholars maintain that the Dawes commissioners ignored the Indian ancestry of many freedmen based purely on racial ideology, but tribal leaders dismiss such arguments as mere conjecture and sour grapes and consider any such cases to be mere accidents of history. Furthermore, they forecast that if they begin to accept claims of tribal blood without accompanying documentation, they will be overrun by impostors. They point out that they do not, as a rule, exclude people with Black ancestry. These tribes have a number of tribal members with Black backgrounds, but all of those people have written proof of Indian ancestry. The excluded freedmen descendants do not. As far as tribal spokespeople are concerned, that is the crux of the matter.[36]

Freedmen organizations see anti-Black racism, profiteering, and legal double standards at work. They submit that some of them have more Indian ancestry than the Indians fighting to deny their tribal citizenship. They cite historic and contemporary patterns of Indians using anti-Black slurs. They note that the efforts to deny their citizenship coincide with the self-determination era's rise of tribal gaming, increased federal grant money for tribal services, and, in the case of the Seminoles, a fifty-six-million-dollar compensation for land in Florida illegally seized by the United States in the nineteenth century. Purging freedmen descendants, they charge, is a cynical ploy to increase per capita payouts to the tribal citizens who are left. Not least of all, they note the hypocrisy of tribes claiming the powers of sovereign nations based on the sanctity of treaties with the United States, while in the next breath denying the tribal citizenship of freedmen descendants in violation of those same treaties. Take these opposing arguments together, and the result, writes Philip Deloria, "is akin to an optical allusion: look at the situation one way, and you see Native people affirming the significance of their ancestry, look at it another way, and you see anti-Black racism."[37]

Anti-Black racism certainly is at play, the only question is to what degree. Not only did these tribes hold Black slaves before the Civil War, premised on theories of Black inferiority, but in addition, in the century that followed the pressures for Indians to distance themselves from Blacks actually mounted. Oklahoma's founding constitution in 1907 recognized two legal races, White and Black, and placed Indians in the White category. This framework, combined with the Five Tribes' ongoing pattern of intermarriage with Whites, gave these Indians a direct stake in the Jim Crow system. The danger of association with Blacks became even more apparent in the 1920s due to developments in Virginia, where Walter Ashby Plecker of the Bureau of Vital Statistics led a eugenicist crusade to prove that all the Indians in the state had Black ancestry and therefore should be categorized as Black, not Indian. He contended that failure to do otherwise would somehow lead Whites to let down their guard and reproduce with Indians who were actually Blacks, thereby polluting White bloodlines. The result was Virginia's 1924 "Act to Preserve Racial Integrity," which codified the so-called one-drop rule in which any degree of Black ancestry defines a person as Black. It stipulated that mispresenting one's racial ancestry was punishable with up to a year in prison. It was this kind of thinking that led Mildred Loving, litigant in the famous 1967 *Loving v. Virginia* Supreme Court case that struck down bans on interracial marriage, to be categorized as Black even though she often identified primarily as an Indian of the Rappahannock tribe. The same anti-Black, White supremacist forces at work in Virginia were prevalent in Oklahoma, as Indians were all too aware. If they wanted to preserve their claims to Indian identity and Indian rights, it was incumbent on them to keep their distance from Blacks, whatever prejudices they might or might not have had toward them.[38]

The Cherokees, Seminoles, and Choctaws have relented in the face of adverse publicity, federal and tribal court rulings in favor of the freedmen descendants, and threats from the BIA and the Congressional Black Caucus to cut the tribes' funding. Nevertheless, the Seminoles consider freedmen descendants only as "members," not citizens, without the right to certain tribal services and monies. For its part, the Muscogee (Creek) Supreme Court finally ruled in 2025 in favor that nation's freedmen. There is no question that a majority of tribal citizens, left to their own devices, would not include freedmen descendants among their ranks, as popular referendums of the issue have demonstrated. Yet it is too simplistic to attribute this pattern solely or even mostly to anti-Black racism instead of a widely held Native American belief in the centrality of blood to group belonging. The power of that idea is evident in other controversies of blood unrelated to the freedmen descendants.

The Cherokees' public rejection of Massachusetts senator Elizabeth Warren's claim to be Cherokee is a case in point. During Warren's initial Senate run in 2012, the campaign of her opponent, Republican Scott Brown, revealed that Warren had occasionally identified as "Indian" in personnel surveys when she was a law professor at the University of Pennsylvania and Harvard. Contrary to the assertions of Warren's detractors, there was no evidence that she used this claim to secure a hiring preference. Warren's explanation was that her family had always understood her mother to have Cherokee ancestry. Republican president Donald Trump, a frequent target of Warren's criticism, insulted her repeatedly as Pocahontas and Fauxcahontas, including during a 2017 visit to the White House by a delegation of Navajo war veterans, which Trump delivered while posing the visitors in front of a portrait of President Andrew Jackson, the force behind Indian Removal. The issue of Warren's ancestry arose again when she continued to tell this story as an early front-runner for the Democratic Party's nomination for president in 2020 (in which she ultimately lost out to Joe Biden), as in a speech to the National Congress of American Indians. She even took a DNA test in an attempt to prove her claims, which showed that she did indeed have slight Indian background. This time, however, the most powerful blowback came from Native people, including the Cherokees.

The thrust of their criticism was that remote Indian ancestry is not the same thing as tribal citizenship, nor was living as a phenotypically White person outside of a tribal setting the same thing as living visibly as an Indian in American society. An open letter to Warren by two hundred citizens of the Cherokee Nation of Oklahoma, United Keetoowah Band of Cherokee Indians, and Eastern Band of Cherokee Indians of North Carolina, explained:

> While the average American thinks of Native Americans as a racial category, we are actually political groups. Our rights are based on citizenship in sovereign Nations and those Nations' treaty relationship to the United States. But that hasn't stopped opponents to tribes from arguing that laws defending Native rights treat us differently based on race and therefore should be declared unconstitutional. If they win, it could be the end of tribes as we know them. By publicly equating race and biology with Native identity, your DNA test promoted the exact same logic the Right is currently using to try and destroy Native rights.

Warren's DNA test could prove that she had a distant progenitor from some Indigenous person in North or South America, but it could not specify tribal descent, and it certainly meant nothing in terms of her formal affiliation with a tribal nation. To the tribes, the controversy was "more than an annoyance; it represents the most public debate about our identity in a generation. In a country where Indigenous people are mostly invisible, what Americans conclude from this debate will impact Native rights for years to come."[39]

A variety of scholars and journalists took it from there. The Mohawk professor Kim TallBear chastised Warren as a White person using a shallow genetic claim to Indian identity in place of Native people's emphasis on "lived social relations" as the main standard of belonging. Warren seemed to want whatever advantage she would derive for having a diverse background without having shared the individual or group struggles of people who lived outwardly as Indians. The Sappony journalist Nick Martin noted that Warren "is not Native because she is not, and has never been, a Native American to anyone else, especially not Native peoples." He continued, "I am not Native because of my blood. I am Native because I belong to a tribe . . . a tribe is not a group of people gathered together because they are of the same race. It is a collective, a nation of citizens bonded by ancestral and historical commonalities, the likes of which no other group has on this land." The historian Gregory Smithers warned that ignorance of this principle carries real danger, as illustrated by oral arguments for a 2013 Supreme Court case over protections for Native American children in foster care and adoption cases. In the proceedings, Chief Justice John Roberts wondered, seemingly unaware of his own institution's precedent of defining Indians as a political group, if "one drop" of Native American blood gave Indigenous people "all these extraordinary rights." Warren eventually conceded "that DNA does not determine tribal citizenship," and apologized for any harm she had done. Lost in the hand wringing was how many tribes themselves use blood quantum as a criterion for citizenship, contrary to the emphasis of Warren's critics.[40]

One factor in the forceful Native reaction to the Warren controversy was that it coincided with a spike in people with little to no Native ancestry or actual relationships with tribal communities claiming to be Indian and even organizing into tribes seeking official recognition. Colloquially, critics refer to these newfound Indians as "pretendians" or "race shifters." Indian pretenders have existed throughout the entirety of United States history, but it is only during the era of self-determination that they have surfaced in such considerable numbers and, unable to produce the evidence to secure tribal citizenship, attempted to form their own communities. The scale of this phenomenon is best measured by the anthropologist Circe Sturm's finding that at least thirty-six states have an entity claiming to be a Cherokee tribe; California, Texas, and Ohio each have as many as thirteen such "Cherokee" groups. There are dozens of unrecognized, self-declared tribes that have appropriated other Indian identities. These are not just innocent clubs of no consequence. In Vermont, four bands calling themselves Abenaki managed to secure state recognition through an implausibly lax process and then win competitive grants that could have gone to legitimate tribes. Recently, the Canadian scholar Darryl Leroux has argued in a peer-reviewed study, with the moral support of the historically established and formally recognized Odanak Abenakis of Quebec, that the Vermont "Abenakis" are phonies with little to no documentable Native ancestry or tribal ties. Their case has raised questions about the standards applied in other state recognition cases across the country. Pretendians have also been discovered throughout academia. Back in 1933, Congress actually considered a bill to prohibit White people from posing as Indians, in response to the number of charlatans who were appearing at public events, like National Indian Day celebrations. The *Chicago Defender*, a Black newspaper, quipped in response, "Isn't this a hot one? We've heard of persons passing for white for definite advantages, but for the life of us we fail to see what advantage there is in passing for an American Indian." The editors would have been stunned to see just how extensive this phenomenon has become in modern times.[41]

The reasons speak to the improved status of Indian peoples in contemporary U.S. society and changes in the values of White America. To be Indian today, particularly outside of border towns, no longer carries the stigma it once did. Instead, the exoticism of belonging to the first people is sometimes a source of prestige. It can also bring economic reward, depending on the tribe. The most obvious financial benefit comes from gaining citizenship in a federally recognized tribe with significant revenues and services. That many otherwise White-appearing people have successfully taken this course is reflected in the 1,000 percent increase in the population of the Cherokee Nation between 1970 and 2000. Membership in a state-recognized tribe does not include the same benefits as citizenship in a federally recognized tribe, but it can provide access to grants intended for Indians that provide some jobs and services. It also allows the members to claim the advantage of Indian identity in hiring by organizations that want to achieve greater diversity. Contributing to the spate of Indian pretenders in academia is that, for the past several decades, higher education has been so desperate to diversify its faculty and staff that it has treated identity as a credential. College and university administrators are usually ignorant that the federal government is much more rigorous than states in the process of vetting tribes for recognition, and that federally recognized tribes are much more rigorous than state ones in reviewing applications for citizenship. Few human resources officers seem to ask an applicant who claims to be Indian for an official tribal identification card or even a federally issued Certificate of Blood, even though the federal government uses the latter, for example, to determine eligibility for the Indian Health Service. Impersonators have taken advantage to land tenure-track jobs, book awards, grants, and even leadership positions in scholarly organizations.[42]

Yet Sturm has found that the most common element in inventing an Indian identity is a person's desperate need for community and spirituality paired with "a painful sense of hidden history, the notion that at one point in time, often long ago, an authentic racial self had to be denied and obscured from public view to protect an Indian person from social discrimination and the force of law." The authentic Indian self, from this perspective, can emerge now that the danger has passed. Such people acknowledge that they lack documentation for their identity claim, but argue that they carry this knowledge in the blood. Curiously, the same Indians who reject the tribal identities of race-shifters on the basis of their lack of documentation often think similarly to them in terms of blood.[43]

REFLECTIONS

For some Native people, the phenomenon of White people trying to reinvent themselves as Indian is further evidence for an argument they have been making for centuries: that White civilization is spiritually empty and morally bankrupt in its individualized quest for material riches and will lead only to destruction. As we have explored, the oldest manifestations of this vision were Nativist movements that appeared periodically between at least the mid-1700s and as late as the 1940s, in which prophets augured that the Great Spirit would wipe America clean of Whites and return it to Indians who adhered to proper Indian ways. Since World War II, theories of how this upheaval would occur have focused on the seeming destiny of Western nations to obliterate one another with nuclear weapons, or, more recently, to make the world uninhabitable through man-made global warming. These prognostications contend that Native people blessed with spiritual favor will survive just as they always have, while Whites perish. Over the past thirty years, this author has encountered numerous Native people, from various walks of life, voicing this idea. Growing up, the Ute tribe's Francis McKinley heard it, too. He recalled his father saying, "You know, we always think that white people are superior because they have more things, can read and write better, and are more aggressive. They seem to have more freedom than we have. So, we think they are better people, but they are not. They are stupid and ignorant like we are sometimes. Do you think a smart man would go and destroy everything he touches? Do you think a smart man would try to accumulate a lot of things that he is not going to use, and that he cannot take with him when he dies? That is stupidity." Whereas Whites are killing themselves, they have failed to finish off the Indians. Native people have persevered through generations of genocide, dispossession, and degradation. Here they are still, facing the future rather than fading into oblivion.[44]

Tribes all across the country are showing that modern futures do, in fact, belong to them as sovereign nations. What these futures will be depends in no small part on how Native people define themselves to themselves and the wider public. In the near term, that project will require grappling with the tensions, born of a long history, between "Indian" as a racial category and tribes as polities. It will also require non-Indians, above all Whites, to confront the tension between the reality of modern Indians and a centuries-old national ideology that Indians disappeared by God's will so the country could become a great Christian civilization. The power of race depends on people's taking for granted that ideas, practices, and symbols premised on race are natural or, as the saying goes, just the way it is. Race loses its power to justify oppression, hate, and indifference toward others, and to get people to internalize a sense of inferiority, powerlessness, and hopelessness, when we illuminate how and why it functioned in the past and continues to operate in the present. There is enormous work ahead.

EPILOGUE

Transitions

If the proposed National American Indian Memorial in New York Harbor insulted Native people with its falsehoods that their ancestors had welcomed colonization and that they were on the cusp of extinction, Mount Rushmore, begun in the 1920s and completed in 1941, was an even greater offense. On a rock face in the Black Hills, the most sacred land of Lakotas, stolen from them by the United States in violation of its own treaties, loomed the giant carved visages of four American presidents central to the conquest of Indian country: George Washington, the "Town Destroyer," who authorized one extermination campaign after another against Indians during his generalship and presidency; Thomas Jefferson, who as governor of Virginia directed his state militia to exterminate the Shawnees, and as president schemed to use government trade posts to drive Indians into debt and then demand them to cede land as payment; Abraham Lincoln, who administered the largest mass execution in United States history with the hanging of thirty-nine Santee Sioux in 1862; and Theodore Roosevelt, whose presidency witnessed the height of Indian boarding schools and allotment of the reservations, and whose scholarly writings included a denunciation of Indians in the following terms: "I don't go so far as to think that the only good Indian is the dead Indian, but I believe nine out of every ten are, and I shouldn't like to inquire too closely into the case of the tenth. The most vicious cowboy has more moral principle than the average Indian." Mount Rushmore, like practically all presidential memorials, sidestepped whether these presidents were great because of or despite their roles in the genocide of Indians. Either way, Lakotas living near Mount Rushmore on some of the country's most impoverished reservations, never mind Native people who visit the site as tourists, have to suffer the indignity of their White conquerors rubbing the victory in their faces from heights that by morality and law still should belong to Indians.[1]

Henry Standing Bear, an Oglala Lakota leader and founding member of the Society of American Indians, refused to allow this provocation to go unanswered. In 1940, he reached out to Korczak Ziolkowski, a Boston-born Polish American sculptor who had briefly worked on Mount Rushmore, and recruited him to create an equally grand Black Hills carving of the Lakota war hero Crazy Horse. The site would be Thunderhead Mountain, just ten miles southwest of Mount Rushmore as the crow flies. As Standing Bear explained in one of his letters, "My Fellow Chiefs and I would like the White Man to know the Red Man had great heroes, too." Together, Standing Bear and Ziolkowski planned to depict Crazy Horse in the round, 640 feet long and 560 feet high, astride his mount, pointing toward the very countryside the United States had seized from the Lakotas. The scene harkened back to a legendary and perhaps apocryphal exchange in which a White man taunted Crazy Horse after his surrender, "Where are your lands now, Crazy Horse?," to which Crazy Horse responded by gesturing toward the distance and declaring, "My lands are where my dead lie buried."[2]

The model for the Crazy Horse Memorial (foreground) and the progress of the project (background) as of 2022. Courtesy of Getty Images.

The massive project became an obsession for Ziolkowski and, since his death in 1982, for his family as well, right up to the present day. Beginning shortly after World War II, the sculpture has inched forward year after year. Ziolkowski and his heirs have refused any government funding (citing that the United States cannot be trusted, given its pattern of violations of Indian treaties) and thus have not been able to rely on much labor other than their own. As of this writing, only Crazy Horse's face and hand are complete; the rest of the features remain encased in stone. Yet the effort proceeds, inspired by Standing Bear's plea and the recognition that this monument has become practically and symbolically even more important today than at its inception. Its visitor center contains a Native-curated museum with Native docents and vendors, and sometimes hosts Lakota cultural events. The ultimate vision is for the monument to anchor a campus that will include the museum on a grander scale and a medical training center for Native people. If Mount Rushmore, like the National American Indian Memorial, represented White America's Manifest Destiny and Native America's defeat and disappearance, the Crazy Horse Monument was and is about resistance, resiliency, and a modern future.[3]

That goes double for another grand monument to Native America, the Smithsonian Institution's National Museum of the American Indian (NMAI), which opened in 2004 in Washington, D.C. Originating in the stunning collection of Indian artifacts assembled by the New York investment banker George Gustav Heye in the early twentieth century, NMAI overturned the long White American tradition, of which Heye was a part, in which non-Indians, whether by virtue of wealth or academic pedigree, practically monopolized the public telling of the history of Indigenous peoples. At its worst, the historic arrogance of White "experts" on Indians involved grave robbing, the display of Indian bodily remains, and the exploitation of Indian poverty to acquire sacred objects normally off limits to outsiders. The impetus for creating NMAI, in fact, had been public outrage at the realization that the collections of so many of the nation's leading institutions contained Indian skeletal remains. Even at their best, White-run museums routinely portrayed Native Americans in ways that actual Indians found offensive and judged incorrect. NMAI, with Indigenous leadership that included its director, W. Richard West (Cheyenne), his special assistant Gerald McMaster (Plains Cree/Siksika), and a board of trustees containing a who's who from Indian country, aimed to break with that sorry record. Its mission was to create a museum in which Native people could see their lives represented accurately and respectfully, and where they felt at home.[4]

The National Museum of the American Indian, Washington, D.C. Courtesy of Library of Congress, Prints & Photographs Division, photograph by Carol M. Highsmith.

The keys to it all were the museum's collaboration with contemporary Indigenous communities and a focus on the present and future instead of on the horrors of the previous four hundred years. Visitors often enter NMAI expecting to see exhibits about what they think they already know—great chiefs, last stands, lost cultures. But NMAI is neither a history nor an anthropology museum. The focus is on the diversity of contemporary Native communities throughout the Americas, the variety of modern Indian experiences, and the enduring aesthetics and values of Indigenous people as told through their art, stories, and day-to-day lives. Indeed, until recently, NMAI exhibits have paid scant attention to change over time. The subtle message is: We are here, we have always been here, we will always be here. The museum's distinctive architecture makes the very point. It resembles a sandstone canyon, sediment built upon sediment like human generations, that endures forever even as it is endlessly shaped by the elements.[5]

As a regular visitor to NMAI from its opening to this very day, I have always thought of this institution as an expression of what engaged Native intellectuals think the general public needs to know about Indian country, but also of the political limits of conveying such a perspective. The Smithsonian, and, by extension, NMAI, is a unique private-public institution which receives a significant amount of its funding from Congress. Furthermore, NMAI it is located at the head of the National Mall directly across the street from the Capitol, which means that it is highly visible to lawmakers. Not surprisingly, then, NMAI has taken a cautious approach to the subjects at the heart of this book: race and genocide in the historic U.S.-Indian relationship.

Go through the current exhibits at NMAI, and you will see ample evidence that White Americans perpetrated a genocide against Indians, but only once will you encounter the term. For years, the only exhibit to gesture toward this charged subject was a display of historic firearms dating from across five centuries, while in the background video and audio of a raging storm set the tone. The message, of course, was that, for Native people, colonialism has been like an unrelenting hurricane sweeping almost everything away and leaving whatever was left in ruin. Who could disagree? Yet there was little mention of the specific events that constituted this storm or a discussion of what we should call them in their totality. Such hesitancy has drawn sharp criticism from several critics, above all Native ones. The National Congress of American Indians, for instance, passed a resolution in 2013 calling for a space within NMAI to create a National American Indian Holocaust Museum. Nowadays, NMAI is much more direct about difficult history. There are exhibits on Indian Removal, treaty-making and treaty violations, the Plains Wars, the horrors of gold-rush California, boarding schools, and Termination. Yet the sole time this history receives the label "genocide" is well into a video installation, and even then, it is couched in qualifications. The film recounts the terrible history of Removal, then notes the catastrophic population losses of Native people in the centuries leading up to 1900, after which the Native activist and intellectual Suzan Shown Harjo appears and asks: "Wasn't that genocide? We don't make the case that there was genocide. We know there was, yet here we are." It takes a patient visitor to discover this profound statement, even as the rest of NMAI's historical exhibits provide support for it.[6]

When it comes to the subject of race, NMAI also has taken an indirect approach. A current exhibit on images of Indians in American popular culture helps non-Native visitors understand the disjunction between the diverse images of modern-day

Indians that appear throughout the museum and the racial expectations about Indians with which most of them have been raised. A giant gallery is filled floor to ceiling with a century of advertisements, consumer products, magazine covers, cartoons, and more that reduce Indians to crude racial and cultural stereotypes: True American Straight Bourbon Whiskey, Squaw Sifted Peas, Land O Lakes Butter, Savage Arms, Indian Head Corn Meal, Calumet Baking Powder, Cher's record album *Half-Breed*, a White Victoria's Secret underwear model in a headdress, and dozens of images of feathered Indians with hook noses and tomahawks. Like American society itself, everywhere the visitor looks there are damaging misrepresentations of Indians in the service of consumer society. It is a brilliant way of helping visitors recognize their own prejudices and some of the sources for those views without blaming them individually for it.

A greater challenge is to help non-Native visitors understand the racial appearances of modern Indians depicted in the museum's exhibits. Though the word "race" appears sparingly in NMAI, practically every exhibit implicitly argues against the principles of Indian primitiveness and imminent disappearance so evident in the proposed National American Indian Memorial and countless White American productions about Indians before and since. Instead, visitors pass through exhibit after exhibit demonstrating that Native America is diverse, resilient, endlessly creative, distinct, proud, grounded, cosmopolitan, important, very much still here, and bounding toward the future. When the museum first opened, it contained an exhibit, "Our Lives," which included a gallery of headshots of modern Native Americans. The photographic subjects' diverse skin tones, hair colors and textures, eye colors, facial features, dress, and jewelry were a bold if indirect statement that Indigenous people nowadays often defy racial expectations because of centuries of contact with other peoples and the forces of the world. I recall my (then) young grade-school daughter pointing to one picture after another asking, "Is he an Indian? Is she an Indian?" The repeated answer, "Yes," was precisely the point. On the opposite side of the gallery was a pointed, if short, exhibit on the historic ways the United States government and anthropologists have defined Indian identity, including through blood quantum, usually in disregard of how Native communities define themselves or attempt to define themselves.

NMAI's emphasis on the diversity of Indian country has been simultaneously pathbreaking and prudent. In 2009, a twenty-panel exhibit titled "IndiVisible: African–Native American Lives in the Americas," broached the subject of Afro-Indians and the history that produced them, even though this issue is often divisive in Native communities and confounding to non-Natives who have been conditioned to think that Black ancestry defines a person entirely as Black and that Indian identity always recedes through mixing with others. The equally common assumption in America that race issues always have to do with being Black probably softened the public reception of this exhibit. The museum has been less bold about the more widespread phenomenon of White-Indian mixing and the difficulty for individuals who appear phenotypically White to convince society of their Native identity. To be sure, representations of such people appear throughout NMAI exhibits, but the museum does not give visitors the conceptual tools to recognize such people as Indians. It is as if the museum assumes that much of the American public, never mind the Congress, will respond hostilely to a federal institution's applying a critical lens to Whiteness in U.S. society, particularly in connection to White people's historical efforts to kill Indians, take Indian land, and make the remaining Indians disappear.[7]

For now, the subject of race at NMAI, particularly when it involves Whiteness, remains understated while omnipresent. Recently, I was struck by the museum's display of the endlessly ironic, often hilarious, and always poignant drawings of the Oglala Lakota artist Dwayne Wilcox. Wilcox chooses as his canvas the same kind of ledger paper on which many Plains Indian men in the early reservation period drew cherished scenes from the free-ranging days of bison hunting and warfare that had once shaped their lives. But Wilcox has no interest in nostalgic lament. Instead, he reverses customary scenes of White people treating Native people and their lifeways as curiosities in favor of depicting Indians subjecting Whites to the same gaze: In one such example, Natives in traditional dress take pictures of a stereotypical family of White tourists, while in another Indians in feathered headdresses and buckskin photograph a White couple doing one of their people's customary dances, the tango. At other times, Wilcox challenges stereotypes merely by depicting modern Native people, in all their variety, engaged in their people's customs, as when he draws people lined up for the opening dance of an intertribal powwow. Some of them are phenotypically recognizable Indians in regalia, others are Indians in T-shirts and baseball hats, and one is a balding White man with eyeglasses and a ponytail. The message is simultaneously illuminating and sidesplitting, but only if you know how to read it.

In NMAI's early days, the curator Paul Chaat Smith (Comanche) reflected that the organization had a precious opportunity "because the country's decided, in the mysterious ways nations decide such matters, that it's time, at last, to speak about the hard things, the painful things, the unspeakable things." In practice, the museum has been more conservative than this statement projected. When it comes to the "hard things" of race (particularly the relation of Whiteness to Indianness) and genocide, visitors are left largely to reach their own conclusions, if the questions occur to them at all. It is difficult for this writer to imagine that anyone unfamiliar with or adverse to such controversial topics would apply what they had seen to reconsider their previous understandings. Yet, for all the criticism NMAI has received for its risk avoidance, perhaps it is time to congratulate its leaders for their farsighted prudence. It is as if they knew from their own people's history that the White majority's sufferance of Indian sovereignty, including the right and opportunity for an Indian museum to interpret American history and society with Native people at the center, was fragile and likely temporary.[8]

As anyone who has lived in the United States for the past decade knows, we live in a time of transition. People of color are gradually rising to power and challenging a host of old assumptions about who has the right to rule and how government and society should or should not address historic inequities. Mixed marriages and children of diverse backgrounds are visible and accepted to a degree that would have caused riots among Whites of past generations. Monuments and building names honoring White supremacists, slaveholders, and Indian killers are coming down, and school curriculums are being revised to feature the full spectrum of Americans and their historical experiences, warts and all. The resurgence of Native Americans, many of whom have complex ancestry themselves, is part of this moment. Meanwhile, a portion of the White population is reacting to these developments with authoritarianism, conspiracy theories, insurrection, book bans, and limits on the teaching of historical subjects that make them uncomfortable. As tribes continue to assert their sovereignty in ways that their White neighbors and corporate interests oppose, there will be backlashes based on claims that they are not real Indians, just impostors seeking unfair advantage. It has already happened in some places, as we have traced.

There is a real risk of this issue becoming partisan. For more than fifty years, there has been a consensus in the upper ranks of American government that Indian tribes should exercise the maximum amount of sovereignty possible within the limits of the domestic-dependent nation framework, including the right to decide their membership any way they choose. On the surface, that principal remains intact, as evidenced by Democrats and Republicans alike regularly expressing their commitment to the government-to-government relationship between the United States and the tribes. Yet current right-wing politics threatens to dissolve this principle. Barack Obama's presidential administration, building on the example of Bill Clinton's 1994 summit with 322 tribal leaders, inaugurated the annual White House Tribal Nations Conference to enhance dialogue between the federal and tribal governments. Donald Trump scrapped the practice during his first term, only to have Joe Biden revive it during his. The first Trump administration also withdrew recognition (and the trust land that accompanied it) from the Mashpee Wampanoags, apparently in response to lobbying from the gaming industry and as an attempt to inflict a political injury on one of his rivals, Massachusetts senator Elizabeth Warren, who championed the tribe. That decision has since been overturned, but it was a stark warning that Trumpian politics might include a new era of federal assaults on Native rights. Recall that Trump, before he was in office, had publicly opposed federal recognition of various Connecticut tribes that threatened to become competitors to his gaming interests, on the basis that they "don't look like Indians to me." Trump's reelection in 2024 runs the serious risk of the Republican Party using the power of government to revive and expand the pattern of dispensing with tribal recognition and sovereign powers to benefit favored industries based on unashamedly vulgar denials of Indian racial authenticity.

This time, however, the main targets likely will not be small tribes in the East, but tribes with rich natural resources in the West. The Trump movement, and the Republican Party more generally, prioritizes allowing energy companies to extract American coal, oil, natural gas, and minerals to the fullest, including stripping away federal obstacles based on environmental concerns. Tribes that want to thwart this goal (to be clear, some support it) currently can defend themselves through the authority of tribal sovereignty and federal trust status. Yet those arrangements exist only at the sufferance of the American government; Congress can, and has several times throughout history, unilaterally discarded treaties and other agreements with tribal nations. The political risk should be evident to anyone who has followed the Trump movement's tactics. The danger to the health and well-being of the tribes should be apparent to anyone who has read this book.[9]

It would be naïve to assume that the principle of Indian sovereignty, developed in the 1960s and '70s and rarely discussed outside Indian or policymaking circles since, will continue to hold under the strain of these crosswinds if left undefended. American society's acceptance of this framework has been passive and uninformed. I submit that if Indians are going to protect and enhance their recent gains, Native American history, including the history of Indians in American race-making, and the status of tribal nations in the United States, needs to be taught accurately and unflinchingly across the country. The good news is that the scholarship on Indian history is now abundant, much of it is rigorous and rational, there is a thirst for this material among students and the general public, and there are growing numbers of

Indigenous scholars writing and teaching it. The bad news is that the reactionary portion of the White public not only does not want it, but also sees it as a threat to the country's future. Some Indians (a seeming minority, in my view) also have trepidation about promoting Indian history at the national level if that means acceding to non-Indians teaching it in a manner with which they might disagree or take offense. What unites White cultural conservatives with Indians who consider Indian history to be theirs alone to tell is the notion that historical scholarship should serve present-day agendas. Again, anyone who has read this book should appreciate what a threat that approach poses to truth and a pluralistic democracy, including, I would submit, to Native American sovereignty.

The greatest challenge will be convincing the public to be critical and historically informed about White identity. A sizable portion of White Americans respond defensively and even militantly to the very notion of studying White identity formation and the historic manifestations of White supremacy. They charge that the exercise is unpatriotic and undermines the country's foundation. To an extent, they are right, insofar as White supremacy has been a defining force in American history from its beginning, as Native American history reveals in spades.

Taking Indians seriously in the history of American race-making reinforces the view that White supremacy, including the genocide of Indigenous people, has been a central feature of the United States from its beginning, with elements that persist right up to this day. This history also reveals the Native determination to survive as sovereign tribal communities within the United States.

The concept of race has united the various aims of White Americans toward Indians across the centuries. Sometimes the goal was **extermination**, as in the many episodes of White mob violence and militia and military campaigns to conquer Indian land and crush Indian resistance. The sterilization of Indian women and girls was also exterminationist in the pursuit of reducing the burden of poor Indian households on public services. At other times, Whites sought Indian **subordination** to White authority through military actions, slavery, Removal, reservations, the Major Crimes Act, and Public Law 280. Once Whites had subordinated Indians, their primary object was the Indians' **assimilation** through Christian missions, civilization campaigns, reservations again, boarding schools, allotment, citizenship, and foster care and adoption. Each of the aforementioned objectives rested on a three-part racial premise: (1) **White superiority**, whether defined in terms of biology, civilization, or both; (2) **White supremacy**, including the right of White people to dominate Indians; and (3) **Indian inferiority**, again, whether defined in terms of biology, civilization, or both. Racial ideologies and the destructive actions they justified have morphed and continued with each new generation partly because of this country's long-standing failure to teach and learn this history. Some states today actively suppress such knowledge. Too often, this damage is perpetrated by people who mean well but cannot see the full implications of what they do because they were not taught American racial history or Native American history and they will not listen to Indians or anyone else who challenges their views.

Honest, evidence-based, resolute historical perspective is necessary to combat White supremacy in the present and future and defend the gains Indian country has secured in the past fifty years. This book has chronicled a great deal of repetition in how race has factored into White Americans' exploitation of Native people across the centuries. Those cycles are bound to continue unless we learn to identify them by name, cite their precedents, and predict their results based on history.

This history is full of hard truths, ranging from the prevalence of extermination campaigns by Whites against Indians premised on those racial identities to the assimilationist horrors repeatedly unleashed by self-proclaimed Friends of the Indian who were certain they were doing right. The pattern of past actors across the political spectrum contributing to a structural genocide of Native America based on a shared commitment to White supremacy and Indian subjugation is a national cautionary tale.

The history related in this book also teaches something more uplifting. Native people are still here, largely because they have fought, protested, and made incredible adaptations under the most adverse circumstances. They have been part of this country from the beginning. Like African Americans, they have repeatedly challenged this nation to consider how its enlightened principles should pertain to them, too. Perhaps most important, they have consistently argued for their distinctiveness as sovereign tribal nations by virtue of being here first and having a government-to-government relationship with the United States. Historically, they have framed these arguments and actions in racial terms, both because of their own and White Americans' beliefs about race.

It is up to all of us to determine whether our public debates about the behavior and character of the United States and the status of Native communities will continue along these lines. It will take reason, humanitarian commitment, and historical perspective to free ourselves from the grip of race. When we see how humans have invented and revised race throughout history in pursuit of worldly goals, we confront our collective power to rid our society of this false and destructive concept.

ACKNOWLEDGMENTS

I wrote half of this book while in isolation during the COVID pandemic, and the other half while teaching in person, which required me to lean heavily on the staff and resources of George Washington University's Gelman Library. My thanks to everyone at Gelman who assisted me in obtaining access to digital collections of primary sources, interlibrary loans, and various other odds and ends.

I have inflicted drafts and related underdeveloped ideas on several undergraduate and graduate seminars of my course Native American Racial History. The students who gave me constructive feedback are too numerous to list here, but I wish to thank by name a handful who made a significant difference on the final version: Alleson Herron, Olivia Gower, Christoper Carpenter, Sofija Juodaitis, Patrick Pedersen, Julia Swanson, Christopher Canty, and David Kongstvedt. Herron also served an invaluable role as a research assistant into Native American boarding school newspapers. A special shout-out to doctoral student Jonathan (J.J.) Nattrass for serving as a trusted sounding board and proofreader throughout the late stages.

Professional friends and colleagues have also made this a better book. The George Washington University Department of History's works-in-progress colloquium was an incubator for drafts of the introduction and chapters four and five. My old friend and department chair Denver Brunsman and GW graduate students Matthew Goetz and Joshua Irvin provided enormously helpful responses at a "draft dinner" focused on chapters one through four. My longtime informal peer reviewer and chum, Michael Oberg of SUNY Geneseo, and up-and-comer Peter Olsen-Harbich of the McNeil Center for Early American Studies, provided gracious critical readings of chapter drafts and then the entire manuscript. Richard Boles of Oklahoma State University, a friend and former doctoral student of mine, greatly improved the early chapters at a critical stage. I am fortunate to have such committed, generous, and wise people in my corner.

Numerous institutions assisted me in obtaining the illustrations for this book, as acknowledged in the image credits. I am particularly grateful to the Great Lakes Indian Fish & Wildlife Commission for going above and beyond.

Special thanks to my literary agent, Lisa Adams, of the Garamond Agency, for expert guidance in matters great and small from the first inkling of a proposal to the actual publication. I am additionally appreciative of the professionalism of the entire operation of Bloomsbury Publishing, led by my editor, Anton Mueller, who sharpened my thinking considerably, managing and copy editors extraordinaire Barbara Darko and Greg Villepique, and editorial assistant Sage Gilbert.

The historical profession lost some of its leading lights, and I lost too many cherished mentors, during the writing of this book. I never would have conceived of this project, or approached it in the way I did, without the sage, humane examples and counsel of the late Neal Salisbury, Alden Vaughan, Richard Dunn, Gary Nash, and especially my graduate advisors John Murrin and James Axtell. I am grateful and humbled for having had the opportunity to learn from their scholarship and examples.

My family, as ever, was a beacon during the writing of this book. My gratitude to my parents, Richard and Julia Silverman, and my daughters, Aquinnah and Bela Silverman, for checking in and sometimes helping me to check out.

My greatest thanks go to my wife, the historian Julie A. Fisher, for spending the last five years helping me to develop my ideas and polish my prose in real time. Her influence is all over these pages. She might have felt more damned than chosen as I cut my way through the weeds, and as she proofread my every word and concept, but it has been my lucky fate to have her along for this journey, and so many others. I dedicate this book to her.

ABBREVIATIONS

ARCIA. Annual Report of the Commissioner of Indian Affairs (Washington, D.C., by year).

ASP. American State Papers, 38 vols. (Washington, D.C., 1832–61).

DHSM. James Phinney Baxter, ed., *Documentary History of the State of Maine*, 19 vols. (Portland, ME, 1889–1916).

Doolittle Report. Condition of the Indian Tribes: Report of the Joint Special Committee Appointed Under Joint Resolution of March 3, 1865, with an Appendix. Senate Report No. 156. 39th Congress, 2nd Session (Washington, D.C., 1867).

DRCHNY. E. B. O'Callaghan, ed., *Documents Relative to the Colonial History of the State of New York*, 15 vols. (Albany, NY, 1853–87).

EAID. Alden T. Vaughan, gen. ed., *Early American Indian Documents: Treaties and Laws, 1607–1789*. University Publications of America. City and year of publication vary by volume.

Eyewitnesses to the Indian Wars. Peter Cozzens, ed., *Eyewitnesses to the Indian Wars, 1865–1890*, 5 vols. (Mechanicsburg, PA, 2001–5).
 Vol. 1: *The Struggle for Apacheria* (2001).
 Vol 2: *The Wars for the Pacific Northwest* (2002).
 Vol. 3: *Conquering the Southern Plains* (2003).
 Vol. 4: *The Long War for the Northern Plains* (2004).
 Vol. 5: *The Army and the Indian* (2005).

Iroquois Indians. Francis Jennings, William N. Fenton, and Mary A. Druke, eds., *Iroquois Indians: A Documentary History*, 50 microfilm reels.

Johnson Papers. Papers of Sir William Johnson, 14 vols. (Albany, NY, 1921–65).

Meriam Report. *The Problem of Indian Administration. Report of a Survey Made at the Request of Honorable Hubert Work, Secretary of the Interior, and Submitted to Him, February 21, 1928* (Baltimore, MD, 1928).

MHS. Massachusetts Historical Society, Boston.

Peyote Hearings. Peyote: Hearings Before a Subcommittee of the Committee on Indian Affairs of the House of Representatives on H.R. 2614 (Washington, D.C., 1918).

SPG. *America in Records from Colonial Missionaries, 1635–1928, Society for the Propagation of the Gospel in Foreign Parts, Records*, British Online Archives.

TPUS. Clarence Edwin Carter et al., eds., *Territorial Papers of the United States*, 28 vols. (Washington, D.C., 1934–75).

Wheelock Papers. The Papers of Eleazar Wheelock, Together with the Early Archives of Hanover, New Hampshire, Through the year 1779, 16 reels (Hanover, NH, 1971).

WMQ. William and Mary Quarterly, 3rd series.

NOTES

INTRODUCTION: A MEMORIAL BY THE CHOSEN TO THE DAMNED

1. Alan Trachtenberg, *Shades of Hiawatha: Staging Indians, Making Americans, 1880–1930* (New York: Hill and Wang, 2004), 81; Luther Standing Bear, *My People the Sioux*, ed. E. A. Brinninstool (1928; Lincoln: University of Nebraska Press, 2006), 178, 183–84.

2. Trachtenberg, *Shades of Hiawatha*, 253; Russel Lawrence Barsh, "An American Heart of Darkness: The 1913 Expedition for American Indian Citizenship," *Great Plains Quarterly* 13, no. 2 (Spring 1993): 92–93; Richard Lindstrom, "'Not from the Land Side, but from the Flag Side': Native American Responses to the Wanamaker Expedition of 1913," *Journal of Social History* 30, no. 1 (Fall 1996): 210–11.

3. Joseph K. Dixon, *The Vanishing Race: The Last Great Indian Council; A Record in Picture and Story of the Last Great Indian Council, Participated in by Eminent Indian Chiefs from Nearly Every Indian Reservation in the United States with the Story of Their Lives* (Garden City, NY: Doubleday, 1913), 4 ("yield"), 214.

4. Dixon, *Vanishing Race*, 5, 77, 103–4.

5. Barsh, "American Heart of Darkness," 96–97. On the Improved Order of Red Men, see Philip J. Deloria, *Playing Indian* (New Haven, CT: Yale University Press, 1998), 62–68.

6. Lucy Maddox, *Citizen Indians: Native American Intellectuals, Race, and Reform* (Ithaca, NY: Cornell University Press, 2005), 35 ("hope"), 37 ("original Americans"); Barsh, "American Heart of Darkness," 96 ("war weaponry").

7. Paul Scolari, "Indian Warriors and Pioneer Mothers: American Identity and the Closing of the Frontier in Public Monuments, 1890–1930" (PhD diss., University of Pittsburgh, 2005), 37.

8. Barsh, "American Heart of Darkness," 96; Richard Slotkin, *Gunfighter Nation: The Myth of the Frontier in Twentieth-Century America* (New York: Atheneum, 1992); Richard White and Patricia Nelson Limerick, *The Frontier in American Culture*, ed. James R. Grossman (Berkeley: University of California Press, 1994).

9. *Ceremonies Attending the Official Inauguration of the National American Indian Memorial at Fort Wadsworth, Harbor of New York, February 22, 1913* (n.p.), 6, babel.hathitrust.org/cgi/pt?id=loc.ark:/13960/t7mp5d08x&seq=1 (last accessed May 9, 2025); "Indians See Taft Handle the Spade," *New York Times*, Feb. 23, 1913, p. 15.

10. *Ceremonies*, 8–9.

11. *Ceremonies*, 3.

12. "Visting Chiefs Go on a Sightseeing Trip," *New York Times*, Feb. 24, 1913, p. 16. On such visits, see Herman J. Viola, *Diplomats in Buckskin: A History of Indian Delegations in Washington City* (Washington, D.C.: Smithsonian Institution Press, 1981); and C. Joseph Genetin-Pilawa, "The Indians' Capital City: Diplomatic Visits, Place, and Two-Worlds Discourse in Nineteenth-Century Washington, D.C.," in *Beyond Two Worlds: Critical Conversations on Language and Power in Native America*, ed. James Joseph Buss and Genetin-Pilawa (Albany: State University of New York Press, 2014), 117–36.

13. "Council of Eleven Tribes; Office of Indian Affairs," Record Group 75, Box Records of the Bureau of Indian Affairs, Central Classified Files, 1907–39, General Service, 48386-1939-042 to 37717-1913-044, Box No. 165, Folder 24222, National Archives of the United States, Washington, D.C.

14. Hazel W. Hertzberg, *The Search for an American Indian Identity: Modern Pan-Indian Movements* (Syracuse, NY: Syracuse University Press, 1971); Maddox, *Citizen Indians*, 45 ("irony"), 49 ("not yet"); Thomas Constantine Maroukis, *We Are Not a Vanishing People: The Society of American Indians, 1911–1923* (Tucson: University of Arizona Press, 2021).

15. Maddox, *Citizen Indians*, 41 ("justice"); Barsh, "American Heart of Darkness," 105 ("destiny"); Lindstrom, "'Not from the Land Side'"; Dixon to R. Wanamaker, Jan. 16, 1916, Record Group 75, Box Records of the Bureau of Indian Affairs, Central Classified Files, 1907–39, General Service, 48386-1939-042 to 37717-1913-044, Box No. 165, Folder 37717, National Archives of the United States, Washington, D.C. (Lincoln).

16. Lindstrom, "'Not from the Land Side,'" 216 ("bothering").

17. Trachtenberg, *Shades of Hiawatha*, 272 (Osages), 274 (Kickapoos); Charles W. Buchanan to James McLaughlin, Aug. 26, 1913 ("pageantry"), and Memo to Mr. Wanamaker, July 18, 1913 ("Mexican flag"), Record Group 75, Box Records of the Bureau of Indian Affairs, Central Classified Files, 1907–39, General Service, 48386-1939-042 to 37717-1913-044, Box No. 165, Folder 37717, National Archives of the United States, Washington, D.C.

18. Lindstrom, "'Not from the Land Side,'" 221–22 (Chilocco); Parker to Cato Sells, Jan. 2, 1914, Record Group 75, Box Records of the Bureau of Indian Affairs, Central Classified Files, 1907–39, General Service, 48386-1939-042 to 37717-1913-044, Box No. 165, Folder 37717, National Archives of the United States, Washington, D.C.

19. E. Shwortzlander to Commissioner of Indian Affairs, Sept. 24, 1913, Record Group 75, Box Records of the Bureau of Indian Affairs, Central Classified Files, 1907–39, General Service, 48386-1939-042 to 37717-1913-044, Box No. 165, Folder 37717, National Archives of the United States, Washington, D.C. On the history of such ideas in No Shirt's region, see James Mooney, *The Ghost-Dance Religion and the Sioux Outbreak of 1890* (1896; Norman: University of Oklahoma Press, 1991).

20. Barsh, "American Heart of Darkness," 108–11.

21. Patrick Wolfe, "Land, Labor, and Difference: Elementary Structures of Race," *American Historical Review* 106, no. 3 (June 2001): 866–905; Wolfe, "Settler Colonialism and the Elimination of the Native," *Journal of Genocide Research* 8, no. 4 (Dec. 2006): 387–409. For a cogent example of this criticism, see Adam Kirsch, *On Settler Colonialism: Ideology, Violence, and Justice* (New York: W. W. Norton, 2024).

22. Michael A. McConnell and A. Dirk Moses, "Raphael Lemkin as a Historian of Genocide in the Americas," *Journal of Genocide Research* 4, no. 4 (Dec. 2004): 501–29. I am grateful to James Rice for this reference.

23. Donald J. Trump, "Restoring America's Fighting Force," Jan. 20, 2025, whitehouse.gov/presidential-actions/2025/01/restoring-americas-fighting-force (last accessed Feb. 2, 2025).

24. Making the case for "structural genocide" is Wolfe, "Settler Colonialism and the Elimination of the Native." For specific instances, see Brendan C. Lindsay, *Murder State: California's Native American Genocide, 1846–1873* (Lincoln: University of Nebraska Press, 2012); Benjamin Madley, *An American Genocide: The United States and the California Indian Catastrophe, 1846–1873* (New Haven, CT: Yale University Press, 2016); Robert Aquinas McNally, *The Modoc War: A Story of Genocide at the*

Dawn of America's Gilded Age (Lincoln: University of Nebraska Press, 2017); and the essays in *Colonial Genocide in Indigenous North America*, ed. Andrew Woolford et al. (Durham, NC: Duke University Press, 2014). For a more general application of the term to American history, see Jeffrey Ostler, *Surviving Genocide: Native Nations and the United States from the American Revolution to Bleeding Kansas* (New Haven, CT: Yale University Press, 2019); and, with qualifications, Benjamin Madley, "Reexamining the American Genocide Debate: Meaning, Historiography, and New Methods," *American Historical Review* 120, no. 1 (Feb. 2015): 98–139. Taking issue with use of the term are Alex Alvarez, *Native America and the Question of Genocide* (Lanham, MD: Rowman and Littlefield, 2014); Gary Clayton Anderson, "Native Peoples of the American West: Genocide or Ethnic Cleansing?" *Western Historical Quarterly* 47, no. 4 (Nov. 2016): 407–33; and, with qualifications, Margaret Jacobs, "Genocide or Ethnic Cleansing: Are These Our Only Choices?" *Western Historical Quarterly* 47, no. 4 (Nov. 2016): 444–48.

25. Karen E. Fields and Barbara J. Fields, *Racecraft: The Soul of Inequality in American Life* (New York: Verso, 2014), 4–5.

26. Fields and Fields, *Racecraft*, 17. I have also been particularly influenced by George M. Frederickson, "The Concept of Racism in Historical Discourse," in his *Racism: A Short History* (Princeton, NJ: Princeton University Press, 2003), 151–70; Michael Omi and Howard Winart, *Racial Formation in the United States, from the 1960s to the 1990s*, 2nd ed. (New York: Routledge, 1994); Ann Laura Stoler, "Racial Histories and Their Regimes of Truth," *Political Power and Social Theory* 11 (1997): 183–206; and Wolfe, "Land, Labor, and Difference."

27. For an exploration of hegemony at work, see Jean Comaroff and John L. Comaroff, *Of Revelation and Revolution*, vol. 1: *Christianity, Colonialism, and Consciousness in South Africa* (Chicago: University of Chicago Press, 1991).

28. "Historical Population Change Data (1910–1920)," United States Census Bureau, Apr. 26, 2021, census.gov/data/tables/time-series/dec/popchange-data-text.html.

29. On disease, see David S. Jones, "Virgin Soils Revisited," *WMQ* 60, no. 4 (Oct. 2003): 703–42; Paul Kelton, *Epidemics and Enslavement: Biological Catastrophe in the Native Southeast, 1492–1715* (Lincoln: University of Nebraska Press, 2007); Tai S. Edwards and Paul Kelton, "Germs, Genocides, and America's Indigenous Peoples," *Journal of American History* 107, no. 1 (June 2020): 52–76; and Elizabeth A. Fenn, "Biological Warfare in Eighteenth-Century America: Beyond Jeffery Amherst," *Journal of American History* 86, no. 4 (Mar. 2000): 1552–80. On English colonists' interpretations of the disproportionate impact of epidemics on Indians,

see Joyce E. Chaplin, *Subject Matter: Technology, the Body, and Science on the Anglo-American Frontier, 1500–1676* (Cambridge, MA: Harvard University Press, 2001). On intertribal warfare, see David J. Silverman, *Thundersticks: Firearms and the Violent Transformation of Native America* (Cambridge, MA: Harvard University Press, 2016).

30. Classics along these lines include Winthrop D. Jordan, *White over Black: American Attitudes Toward the Negro, 1550–1812* (Chapel Hill: University of North Carolina Press for the Institute of Early American History and Culture, 1968); David Brion Davis, *The Problem of Slavery in Western Culture* (Ithaca, NY: Cornell University Press, 1967); and George Frederickson, *The Black Image in the White Mind: The Debate on Afro-American Character and Destiny, 1817–1914* (New York: Harper and Row, 1971). Among the most important early works addressing Native Americans, see Robert F. Berkhofer Jr., *The White Man's Indian: Images of the American Indian from Columbus to the Present* (New York: Alfred A. Knopf, 1978); Richard Slotkin, *Regeneration Through Violence: The Mythology of the American Frontier* (Middletown, CT: Wesleyan University Press, 1973); Richard Drinnon, *Facing West: The Metaphysics of Indian-Hating and Empire-Building* (Minneapolis: University of Minnesota Press, 1980); Reginald Horsman, *Race and Manifest Destiny: The Origins of American Racial Anglo-Saxonism* (Cambridge, MA: Harvard University Press, 1981); Brian W. Dippie, *The Vanishing American: White Attitudes and U.S. Indian Policy* (Middletown, CT: Wesleyan University Press, 1982); Francis Paul Prucha, *The Great Father: The United States Government and the American Indians*, 2 vols. (Lincoln: University of Nebraska Press, 1984); and Frederick E. Hoxie, *A Final Promise: The Campaign to Assimilate the Indians, 1880–1920* (Lincoln: University of Nebraska Press, 1984).

31. Scholars of colonial Virginia have led this shift. See Kathleen Brown, *Good Wives, Nasty Wenches, and Anxious Patriarchs: Gender, Race, and Power in Colonial Virginia* (Chapel Hill: University of North Carolina Press for the Institute of Early American History and Culture, 1991); Anthony Parent, *Foul Means: The Formation of a Slave Society in Virginia, 1660–1740* (Chapel Hill: University of North Carolina Press for the Omohundro Institute of Early American History and Culture, 2003); Rebecca Anne Goetz, *The Baptism of Early Virginia: How Christianity Created Race* (Baltimore: Johns Hopkins University Press, 2012); and Ethan A. Schmidt, *The Divided Dominion: Social Conflict and Indian Hatred in Early Virginia* (Boulder: University Press of Colorado, 2015). For similar examples from other regions, see Thelma Foote, *Black and White Manhattan: The History of Racial Formation in Colonial New York City* (New York: Oxford University Press, 2004); John

Wood Sweet, *Bodies Politic: Negotiating Race in the American North, 1730–1830* (Philadelphia: University of Pennsylvania Press, 2006); and Jennifer M. Spear, *Race, Sex, and Social Order in Early New Orleans* (Baltimore: Johns Hopkins University Press, 2009).

32. Alexander Saxton, *The Rise and Fall of the White Republic: Class Politics and Mass Culture in Nineteenth-Century America* (New York: Verso, 1990); David R. Roediger, *The Wages of Whiteness: Race and the Making of the American Working Class* (New York: Verso, 1991); Ruth Frankenberg, *White Women, Race Matters: The Social Construction of Whiteness* (Minneapolis: University of Minnesota Press, 1993); Noel Ignatiev, *How the Irish Became White* (New York: Routledge, 1995); Matthew Frye Jacobson, *Whiteness of a Different Color: European Immigrants and the Alchemy of Race* (Cambridge, MA: Harvard University Press, 1998); Mia Bay, *The White Image in the Black Mind: African-American Ideas About White People, 1830–1925* (New York: Oxford University Press, 2000); Nell Irvin Painter, *The History of White People* (New York: W. W. Norton, 2010).

33. Jill Lepore, *The Name of War: King Philip's War and the Origins of American Identity* (New York: Alfred A. Knopf, 1998); Peter Silver, *Our Savage Neighbors: How Indian War Transformed Early America* (New York: W. W. Norton, 2008); Gregory Evans Dowd, *A Spirited Resistance: The North American Indian Struggle for Unity, 1745–1815* (Baltimore: Johns Hopkins University Press, 1992); Nancy Shoemaker, *A Strange Likeness: Becoming Red and White in Eighteenth-Century North America* (New York: Oxford University Press, 2004); Alfred A. Cave, *Prophets of the Great Spirit: Native American Revitalization Movements in Eastern North America* (Lincoln: University of Nebraska Press, 2006); David J. Silverman, *Red Brethren: The Brothertown and Stockbridge Indians and the Problem of Race in Early America* (Ithaca, NY: Cornell University Press, 2010).

34. Nancy Isenberg, *White Trash: The 400-Year Untold History of Class in America* (New York: Viking, 2016); Tyler Stovall, *White Freedom: The Racial History of an Idea* (Princeton, NJ: Princeton University Press, 2021); Jefferson Cowie, *Freedom's Dominion: A Saga of White Resistance to Federal Power* (New York: Basic Books, 2022); Steven Hahn, *Illiberal America: A History* (New York: W. W. Norton, 2024); Richard Slotkin, *A Great Disorder: National Myth and the Battle for America* (Cambridge, MA: Harvard University Press, 2024).

35. Dean Moses, "Indigenous People's Day Celebration on Randall's Island Recognizes Holiday's Importance and Cultural Impact," *AMNY Newsletter*, Oct. 14, 2024, amny.com/entertainment/arts-entertainment

/indigenous-peoples-day-randalls-island-2024/ (last accessed Feb. 13, 2025); James Ford, "NYC Hosts One of the Region's Biggest Indigenous People's Day Events," PIX11, Oct. 14, 2024, pix11.com/news/nyc-hosts-one-of-the-regions-biggest-indigenous-peoples-day-events/ (last accessed Feb. 13, 2025).

36. Maria Caspani, "U.S. Parades, Protests Mark Columbus Day, Now Also Indigenous Peoples' Day," Reuters, Oct. 11, 2021, reuters.com/world/us/us-parades-protests-mark-columbus-day-now-also-indigenous-peoples-day-2021-10-11 (last accessed Feb. 13, 2025); Zachary Small, "Nearly 500 Protesters Stage Anti-Columbus Day History Tour at New York Museums," *Art Newspaper*, Oct. 15, 2019, theartnewspaper.com/2019/10/15/nearly-500-protesters-stage-anti-columbus-day-history-tour-at-new-york-museums (last accessed Feb. 13, 2025); Kathleen Foody and Wilson Ring, "Columbus Day vs. Indigenous Peoples Day Tension and Controversy," Fox 5, Oct. 21, 2021, fox5ny.com/news/columbus-day-vs-indigenous-peoples-day (last accessed Feb. 13, 2025); tiktok.com/@stephaniekeith17/video/7426945435886996779 (last accessed Feb. 13, 2025).

37. "Native American New Yorkers Grow in Number, Latest Census Shows," *The City*, Oct. 10, 2021, thecity.nyc/2021/10/10/native-american-new-yorkers-grow-numbers (last accessed Feb. 13, 2025); John A. Strong, *We're Still Here: The Algonquian Peoples of Long Island Today* (Interlaken, NY: Heart of the Lakes Publishing, 1998); Audra Simpson, *Mohawk Interruptus: Political Life Across the Borders of Settler States* (Durham, NC: Duke University Press, 2016); George C. Shattuck, *The Oneida Land Claims: A Legal History* (Syracuse, NY: Syracuse University Press, 1991); Michael Leroy Oberg, *The Central Fire: The Rise, Fall, and Rise Again of the Onondaga Nation* (New Haven, CT: Yale University Press, forthcoming); Laurence M. Hauptman, *In the Shadow of Kinzua: The Seneca Nation of Indians Since World War II* (Syracuse, NY: Syracuse University Press, 2016).

CHAPTER 1: LOSS OF FAITH

1. The First Charter of Virginia; Apr. 10, 1606, Avalon Project, avalon.law.yale.edu/17th_century/va01.asp (last accessed Oct. 30, 2024); The Charter of Massachusetts Bay: 1629, Avalon Project, avalon.law.yale.edu/17th_century/mass03.asp (last accessed Oct. 10, 2025).

2. Frederick Gleach, *Powhatan's World and Colonial Virginia: A Conflict of Cultures* (Lincoln: University of Nebraska Press, 1997), 117–22; Franklin B. Hough, ed., *Narrative of the Causes Which Led to Philip's Indian War, of 1675 and 1676* (Albany, NY: J. Munsell, 1858), 12 ("great man").

3. The following section draws on a vast literature, including Anthony Pagden, *The Fall of Natural Man*, rev. ed. (Cambridge, UK: Cambridge University Press, 1986); Pagden, *Lords of All the World: Ideologies of Empire in Spain, Britain, and France, c. 1500–c. 1800* (New Haven, CT: Yale University Press, 1995); Karen Ordahl Kupperman, *Indians and English: Facing Off in Early America* (Ithaca, NY: Cornell University Press, 2000); Colin Kidd, *The Forging of Races: Race and Scripture in the Protestant Atlantic World, 1600–2000* (Cambridge, UK: Cambridge University Press, 2006); Robert F. Berkhofer Jr., *The White Man's Indian: Images of the American Indian from Columbus to the Present* (New York: Alfred A. Knopf, 1978), 3–31; and James Axtell, *The Invasion Within: The Contest of Cultures in Colonial North America* (New York: Oxford University Press, 1985).

4. Robin Blackburn, "The Old World Background to European Colonial Slavery," *WMQ* 54, no. 1 (Jan. 1997): 65–102; James H. Sweet, "The Iberian Roots of American Racist Thought," *WMQ* 54, no. 1 (Jan. 1997): 143–66.

5. William Bradford, *Of Plymouth Plantation*, ed. Samuel Eliot Morison (New York: Alfred A. Knopf, 1979), 26.

6. Kupperman, *Indians and English*.

7. John Winthrop to Sir National Rich, May 22, 1634, *Winthrop Papers*, vol. 3, ed. Allyn Bailey Forbes (Boston: Massachusetts Historical Society, 1943), 171–72; Thomas Morton, *The New English Canaan*, ed. Charles Francis Adams Jr. (Boston: Prince Society, 1883), 134. See also Bradford, *Of Plymouth Plantation*, 260, 271. On English interpretations of epidemics, see David S. Jones, *Rationalizing Epidemics: Meanings and Uses of American Indian Mortality Since 1600* (Cambridge, MA: Harvard University Press, 2004); Christobal Silva, *Miraculous Plagues: An Epidemiology of Early New England Narrative* (New York: Oxford University Press, 2011); and Joyce E. Chaplin, *Subject Matter: Technology, the Body, and Science on the Anglo-American Frontier, 1500–1676* (Cambridge, MA: Harvard University Press, 2001).

8. James Axtell, *Beyond 1492: Encounters in Colonial North America* (New York: Oxford University Press, 1992), 8 ("bearded"); Michael P. Clark, ed., *The Eliot Tracts: With Letters from John Eliot to Thomas Throwgood and Richard Baxter* (Westport, CT: Praeger, 2003), 119.

9. Roger Williams, *A Key into the Language of America*, eds. John J. Teunissen and Evelyn J. Hinz (1643; Detroit: Wayne State University Press, 1973), 85, 121, 133; James Axtell, *After Columbus: Essays in the Ethnohistory of Colonial North America* (New York: Oxford University Press, 1988), 136.

10. Christien Le Clerq, *New Relation of Gaspesia*, trans. and ed. William Ganong (1691; Toronto: Champlain Society, 1910), 103–6 ("five or six"); Michel de Montaigne, *Essays by Montaigne*, 2nd ed. (London: Alex Murray and Son, 1869), 150 ("set fire"); Gabriel Sagard, *The Long Journey to the Country of the Hurons*, 2 vols. (1632; Toronto: Champlain Society, 2013), 89 ("charity"). On imprisonment, see Ian K. Steele, "Shawnee Origins of Their Seven Years' War," *Ethnohistory* 53, no. 4 (Fall 2006): 657–87. Generally, see Axtell, *After Columbus*, 125–43; and James Axtell, ed., *The Indian Peoples of Eastern America: A Documentary History of the Sexes* (New York: Oxford University Press, 1981).

11. Williams, *Key into the Language of America*, 85; Clark, *Eliot Tracts*, 95.

12. Reuben Gold Thwaites, ed., *The Jesuit Relations and Allied Documents*, 73 vols. (Cleveland: Burrows Bros., 1896–1901), 3:121.

13. Williams, *Key into the Language of America*, 85 ("clothes"), 189 ("deny not"); Alexander Long, "A Small Postscript on the ways and maners of the Nashon of Indians called Charikees [1725]," *Southern Indian Studies* 21 (Oct. 1969): 8, 12, 18, 28; Karen Ordahl Kupperman, *Pocahontas and the English Boys: Caught Between Cultures in Colonial Virginia* (New York: New York University Press, 2019); Alden T. Vaughan and Daniel K. Richter, "Crossing the Cultural Divide: Indians and New Englanders, 1605–1763," *Proceedings of the American Antiquarian Society* 90, pt. 1 (Apr. 1980): 23–99; James Axtell, "The White Indians of Colonial America," *WMQ* 32, no. 1 (Jan. 1975): 55–88; Evan Haefeli and Kevin M. Sweeney, *Captors and Captives: The 1704 French and Indian Raid on Deerfield* (Amherst: University of Massachusetts Press, 2003).

14. Jerald T. Milanich, *Laboring in the Fields of the Lord: Spanish Missions and Southeastern Indians* (Washington, D.C.: Smithsonian Institution Press, 1999); Robert Galgano, *Feast of Souls: Indians and Spaniards in the Seventeenth-Century Missions of Florida and New Mexico* (Albuquerque: University of New Mexico Press, 2005); Axtell, *Invasion Within*; Allan Greer, *Mohawk Saint: Catherine Tekakwitha and the Jesuits* (New York: Oxford University Press, 2005); Tracy Leavelle, *The Catholic Calumet: Colonial Conversions in French and Indian North America* (Philadelphia: University of Pennsylvania Press, 2012); Robert Michael Morrissey, *Empire by Collaboration: Indians, Colonists, and Governments in Colonial Illinois Country* (Philadelphia: University of Pennsylvania Press, 2015); Jean François Lozier, *Flesh Reborn: The Saint Lawrence Mission Settlements Through the Seventeenth Century* (Montreal: McGill-Queen's University Press, 2018).

15. Michael Leroy Oberg, *Dominion and Civility: English Imperialism and Native America, 1585–1685* (Ithaca, NY: Cornell University Press, 1999), 66 ("reasonable"); Ethan A. Schmidt, *The Divided Dominion: Social Conflict and Indian Hatred in Early Virginia* (Boulder: University Press of Colorado, 2015), 75 ("scarce").

16. On the Pequot War, see Arthur A. Cave, *The Pequot War* (Amherst: University of Massachusetts Press, 1996). On Native missionaries and ministers and the praying towns, see Daniel Gookin, "Historical Collections of the Indians in New England," *Collections* (Massachusetts Historical Society) 1st ser., vol. 1 (1792): 180–201, 205; Richard W. Cogley, *John Eliot's Mission to the Indians Before King Philip's War* (Cambridge, MA: Harvard University Press, 1999); Clark, *Eliot Tracts*, 124 ("forty"); and Edward E. Andrews, *Native Apostles: Black and Indian Missionaries in the British Atlantic World* (Cambridge, MA: Harvard University Press, 2013), 21–86.

17. *EAID*, vol. 17, *New England and Middle Atlantic Laws*, vol. eds. Alden T. Vaughan and Deborah Rosen (Bethesda, MD, 2004), 105–6 ("brought"). On possibly the only example of an Indian who took up the offer of Massachusetts, see Jenny Hale Pulsipher, *Swindler Sachem: The American Indian Who Sold His Birthright, Dropped Out of Harvard, and Conned the King of England* (New Haven, CT: Yale University Press, 2018). On the lack of intermarriage, see David D. Smits, "'Abominable Mixture': Toward the Repudiation of Anglo-Indian Intermarriage in Seventeenth-Century Virginia," *Virginia Magazine of History and Biography* 95, no. 2 (Apr. 1987): 157–92; and Smits, "'We Are Not to Grow Wild': Seventeenth-Century New England's Repudiation of Anglo-Indian Intermarriage," *American Indian Culture and Research Journal* 11, no. 4 (1987): 1–32.

18. James Brooks, *Captives and Cousins: Slavery, Kinship, and Community in the Southwest Borderlands* (Chapel Hill: University of North Carolina Press for the Omohundro Institute of Early American History and Culture, 2002); Ramón A. Gutiérrez, *When Jesus Came, the Corn Mothers Went Away: Marriage, Sex, and Power in New Mexico, 1500–1846* (Stanford, CA: Stanford University Press, 1991); Paul Conrad, *The Apache Diaspora: Four Centuries of Displacement and Survival* (Philadelphia: University of Pennsylvania Press, 2021).

19. Susan Sleeper-Smith, *Indian Women and French Men: Rethinking Cultural Encounter in the Western Great Lakes* (Amherst: University of Massachusetts Press, 2001); Gilles Havard, *Empire et métissages. Indiens et Français dans le Pays d'en Haut, 1660–1715*, 2nd ed. (Quebec: Septentrion, 2017); Sophie White, *Wild Frenchmen and Frenchified Indians: Material Culture and Race in Colonial Louisiana* (Philadelphia: University of Pennsylvania Press, 2012); Kathleen DuVal, "Indian Intermarriage and Métissage

in Colonial Louisiana," *WMQ* 65, no. 2 (Apr. 2008): 267–304; Guillaume Aubert, "'The Blood of France': Race and Purity of Blood in the French Atlantic World," *WMQ* 61, no. 3 (July 2004): 456, n. 37 (marriage numbers).

20. J. Frederick Fausz, "The Powhatan Uprising of 1622: A Historical Study of Ethnocentrism and Cultural Conflict" (PhD diss., College of William and Mary, 1977).

21. *EAID*, vol. 4, *Virginia Treaties, 1607–1722*, vol. ed. W. Stitt Robinson (Frederick, MD, 1983), 31–40 ("remorse," "miscreants," "viperous," "creatures"); Michael Guasco, *Slaves and Englishmen: Human Bondage in the Early Modern Atlantic World* (Philadelphia: University of Pennsylvania Press, 2014), 184–85 ("Cham"); Berkhofer, *White Man's Indian*, 20–21 ("vermin"). For more on the Curse of Cham, see Kidd, *Forging of Races*; and Alden T. Vaughan, *Roots of American Racism: Essays on the Colonial Experience* (New York: Oxford University Press, 1995), 136–75.

22. Schmidt, *Divided Dominion*, chs. 3 and 5.

23. Warren M. Billings, ed., *The Old Dominion in the Seventeenth Century: A Documentary History of Virginia, 1606–1689* (Chapel Hill: University of North Carolina Press for the Institute of Early American History and Culture, 1975), 226–29 ("lawful" on 226, "rashness" and "scandal" on 228).

24. *Papers and Biography of Lion Gardiner, 1599–1663*, ed. Curtiss C. Gardiner (St. Louis: Levison and Blythe Stationary, 1883), 29–30; Michael Leroy Oberg, "'We Are All Sachems from East to West': A New Look at Miantonomi's Campaign of Resistance," *New England Quarterly* 77, no. 4 (Sept. 2004): 478–99.

25. *Records of the Colony of Rhode Island and Providence Plantations in New England*, ed. John R. Bartlett, 10 vols. (Providence, RI: A. Crawford Greene, 1856–65), 2:408; Hough, *Narrative of the Causes*, 9 ("good to be killed"). On opponents of Miantonomo, see, for instance, Michael Leroy Oberg, *Uncas: First of the Mohegans* (Ithaca, NY: Cornell University Press, 2003), 87–109. On the war scares, see Julie A. Fisher and David J. Silverman, *Ninigret, Sachem of the Niantics and Narragansetts: Diplomacy, War, and the Balance of Power in Seventeenth-Century New England and Indian Country* (Ithaca, NY: Cornell University Press, 2014), 54–86.

26. This paragraph and those that immediately follow draw on Douglas Edward Leach, *Flintlock and Tomahawk: New England in King Philip's War* (New York: Macmillan, 1958), 4–5, 8; Richard Melvoin, *New England Outpost: War and Society in Colonial Deerfield* (New York: W. W. Norton, 1989), 41–47, 97–107; Jenny Hale Pulsipher, "Massacre at Hurtleberry Hill: Christian Indians and English Authority in Metacom's

War," *WMQ* 53, no. 3 (July 1996), 459–86; Christopher J. Bilodeau, "Creating an Indian Enemy in the Borderlands: King Philip's War in Maine, 1675–1678," *Maine History* 47, no. 1 (Jan. 2013): 11–41.

27. Daniel Gookin, "An Historical Account of the Doings and Sufferings of the Christian Indians in New England in the Years 1675, 1676, 1677," *Transactions and Collections of the American Antiquarian Society* 2 (1836): 450; Thomas Walley to John Cotton Jr., Nov. 18, 1675, Curwen Papers, Box 1, Folder 3, American Antiquarian Society, Worcester, MA ("rash"); Jenny Hale Pulsipher, *Subjects unto the Same King: Indians, English, and the Contest for Authority in Colonial New England* (Philadelphia: University of Pennsylvania Press, 2005), 135–59; Margaret Ellen Newell, *Brethren by Nature: New England Indians, Colonists, and the Origins of American Slavery* (Ithaca, NY: Cornell University Press, 2015), 131–58; Nathaniel B. Shurtleff, ed., *Records of the Governor and Company of the Massachusetts Bay in New England*, 6 vols. (Boston: William White, 1854), 5:64 ("innocent"); Shurtleff and David Pulsifer, eds., *Records of the Colony of New Plymouth*, 12 vols. (Boston: William White, 1855), 5:183.

28. Gookin, "Historical Account," 437, 450, 454; Cotton Mather, *Triumphs of the Reformed Religion in America* (Boston, 1691), 43.

29. Benjamin Batten to Sir Thomas Allen, June 9–July 6, 1675, CO 1/34, no. 108, *Colonial State Papers Online*, about.proquest.com/en/products-services/Colonial_State_Paper/ (last accessed May 9, 2025); Benjamin Church, *Entertaining Passages Relating to King Philip's War*, ed. Martyn Dexter (1716; Boston: J. K. Wiggin, 1865), 45–46; Pulsipher, "Massacre at Hurtleberry Hill"; Jill Lepore, *The Name of War: King Philip's War and the Origins of American Identity* (New York: Alfred A. Knopf, 1998), 178–84.

30. Lepore, *Name of War*, 131–36 ("apostatized" on 133); *The Sovereignty and Goodness of God, by Mary Rowlandson, with Related Documents*, 2nd ed., ed. Neal Salisbury (1682; Boston: Bedford/St. Martin's, 2018), 137; Colin G. Calloway, "Rhode Island Renegade: The Enigma of Joshua Tefft," *Rhode Island History* 43, no. 4 (Nov. 1984): 136–45.

31. Petition of the Pequot Indians, Groton, Sept. 22, 1725, Talcott Papers, *Collections of the Connecticut Historical Society*, vol. 4 (Hartford: Connecticut Historical Society, 1829), 320 ("see plainly"); Letter of John Thomas, June 12, 1709, SPG, A Ser., vol. 5; Roger Williams to John Winthrop Jr., May 28, 1664, *The Correspondence of Roger Williams*, ed. Glenn La Fantasie, 2 vols. (Hanover, NH: University Press of New England, 1988), 528 ("God land"). On later Christian movements, see

Linford D. Fisher, *The Indian Great Awakening: Religion and the Shaping of Native Cultures in Early America* (New York: Oxford University Press, 2012). On New England Indian communities after King Philip's War, see Daniel R. Mandell, *Behind the Frontier: Indians in Eighteenth-Century Eastern Massachusetts* (Lincoln: University of Nebraska Press, 1996).

32. Shurtleff, *Massachusetts Bay Records*, 5:58–63 ("strange fashions"); Slotkin and Folsom, *So Dreadful a Judgment*, 143–44. On the lineage of Manifest Destiny, see Reginald Horsman, *Race and Manifest Destiny: The Origins of American Racial Anglo-Saxonism* (Cambridge, MA: Harvard University Press, 1981); Richard Slotkin, *Regeneration Through Violence: The Mythology of the American Frontier* (Middletown, CT: Wesleyan University Press, 1973); and Richard Drinnon, *Facing West: The Metaphysics of Indian-Hating and Empire-Building* (Minneapolis: University of Minnesota Press, 1980).

33. James D. Rice, *Tales from a Revolution: Bacon's Rebellion and the Transformation of Early America* (New York: Oxford University Press, 2013), 16.

34. Charles Andrews, ed., *Narratives of the Insurrections, 1675–1690* (New York: Charles Scribner's Sons, 1915), 20 ("no man"), 49–50 ("devised"); Matthew Kruer, "Bloody Minds and Peoples Undone: Emotion, Family, and Political Order in the Susquehannock-Virginia War," *WMQ* 74, no. 3 (July 2017): 412, 416; Rice, *Tales from a Revolution*, 13, 35.

35. Andrews, *Narratives of the Insurrections*, 63 ("apt to receive"); "The Virginians' plea for opposing the Indians without the Governor's order" (June ?, 1676), CO 1/37, no. 14, *Colonial State Papers Online*, about.proquest.com/en/products-services/Colonial_State_Paper/ (last accessed May 9, 2025).

36. Schmidt, *Divided Dominion*, 4, 164; *Samuel Wiseman's Book of Record: The Official Account of Bacon's Rebellion in Virginia, 1676–1677*, ed. Michael Leroy Oberg (Lanham, MD: Lexington Books, 2005), 145 ("giddy"), 148 ("ruder"); Edmund S. Morgan, *American Slavery, American Freedom: The Ordeal of Colonial Virginia* (New York: W. W. Norton, 1975), 250–70.

37. *Wiseman's Book of Record*, 182 ("look upon"); Rice, *Tales from a Revolution*, 44 ("common cry"); Andrews, *Narratives of the Insurrections*, 109 ("greatly cheered"); Kruer, "Bloody Minds," 428.

38. Andrews, *Narratives of the Insurrections*, 21; Rice, *Tales from a Revolution*, 67 ("innocent") and passim; Morgan, *American Slavery, American Freedom*, 250–70;

Wilcomb Washburn, *The Governor and the Rebel: A History of Bacon's Rebellion in Virginia* (Chapel Hill: University of North Carolina Press, 1957).

39. Andrews, *Narratives of the Insurrections*, 112 ("impossible"), 113 ("vulgar").

40. *Wiseman's Book of Record*, 89 ("inconsiderate"), 241 ("immediate"); Declaration of Col. Herbert Jeffreys, Governor of Virginia, Apr. 27, 1677, CO 1/40, no. 53, CO 5/1355, pp. 145–49, *Colonial State Papers Online*; *EAID*, vol. 6, *Maryland Treaties, 1632–1775*, vol. ed. W. Stitt Robinson (Frederick, MD, 1987), 90 ("not one"); Lord Culpepper to the Lords of Trade and Plantations, Dec. 12, 1681, CO 1/47, no. 105 ("bandits"); Rice, *Tales from a Revolution*, 124, 137–51; Matthew Kruer, *Time of Anarchy: Indigenous Power and the Crisis of Colonialism in Early America* (Cambridge, MA: Harvard University Press, 2022), 113–44; Rebecca Anne Goetz, "The Nanziatticos and the Violence of the Archive: Land and Native Enslavement in Colonial Virginia," *Journal of Southern History* 85, no. 1 (Feb. 2019): 33–60.

41. On the Pueblo Revolt, see Andrew L. Knaut, *The Pueblo Revolt of 1680: Conquest and Resistance in Seventeenth-Century New Mexico* (Norman: University of Oklahoma Press, 1995); Gutiérrez, *When Jesus Came, the Corn Mothers Went Away*, 95–142; David J. Weber, *The Spanish Frontier in North America* (New Haven, CT: Yale University Press, 1992), 122–46; Colin G. Calloway, *One Vast Winter Count: The Native American West Before Lewis and Clark* (Lincoln: University of Nebraska Press, 2003), 165–95; and Andrés Reséndez, *The Other Slavery: The Uncovered Story of Indian Enslavement in America* (Boston: Houghton Mifflin Harcourt, 2016), 149–71. On the wars between New France and the Haudenosaunees, see José António Brandão, *"Your Fyre Shall Burn No More": Iroquois Policy Towards New France and Its Native Allies to 1701* (Lincoln: University of Nebraska Press, 1997); and Peter Moogk, *La Nouvelle France: The Making of French Canada; A Cultural History* (East Lansing: Michigan State University Press, 2000), 17–52.

42. Owen Stanwood, *The Empire Reformed: English America in the Age of the Glorious Revolution* (Philadelphia: University of Pennsylvania Press, 2011), 67 ("vagrant"); Emerson Woods Baker II, "New Evidence on the French Involvement in King Philip's War," *Maine Historical Society Quarterly* 28, no. 2 (Sept. 1988): 85–91; Bilodeau, "Creating an Indian Enemy"; William Hand Browne et al., eds., *Archives of Maryland*, 72 vols. (Baltimore, 1883–), 5:134–52; James D. Rice, "Bacon's Rebellion in Indian Country," *Journal of American History* 101, no. 3 (Dec. 2014): 745–47.

43. *DHSM*, 4:446–51, 5:35, 40; Andrews, *Narratives of the Insurrections*, 197–99 ("foolish" on 197), 247–48, 255–56; *The Andros Tracts*, ed. W. H. Whitmore, 3 vols. (Boston: Prince Society, 1868–74), 1:30–31, 102–26.

44. Roger Heaman, *An Additional Brief Narrative, of a Late Bloody Design against the Protestants in Ann Arundel County, and Severn in Maryland* (London, 1655), 2; Clayton Colman Hall, ed., *Narratives of Early Maryland, 1633–1684* (New York: Barnes and Noble, 1910), 236, 242; Axtell, *After Columbus*, 73–85; John Kugler, *English and Catholic: The Lords Baltimore in the Seventeenth Century* (Baltimore: Johns Hopkins University Press, 2004); Russell R. Menard, "Maryland's 'Time of Troubles': Sources of Political Disorder in Early St. Mary's," *Maryland Historical Magazine* 76, no. 2 (Summer 1981): 124–40; *Archives of Maryland*, 8:74–75, 78–79, 82, 83–84, 86, 93, 94; Stanwood, *Empire Reformed*, 62–64 ("cut off" on 64), 107–8; Michael G. Hall et al., eds., *The Glorious Revolution in America* (New York: W. W. Norton, 1964), 144, 174, 178; Rice, "Bacon's Rebellion," 748.

45. Mary Beth Norton, *In the Devil's Snare: The Salem Witchcraft Crisis of 1692* (New York: Alfred A. Knopf, 2002); John M. Murrin, "Coming to Terms with the Salem Witch Trials," *Proceedings of the American Antiquarian Society* 110, no. 2 (Oct. 2000): 309–47.

46. On Le Jau, see the introduction to Frank J. Klingberg, ed., *The Carolina Chronicle of Dr. Francis Le Jau, 1706–1717* (Berkeley: University of California Press, 1956). On South Carolina society, see Peter H. Wood, *Black Majority: Negroes in Colonial South Carolina from 1670 Through the Stono Rebellion*, rev. ed. (New York: W. W. Norton, 1996). On the Indian slave trade, see Alan Gallay, *The Indian Slave Trade: The Rise of the English Empire in the American South, 1670–1717* (New Haven, CT: Yale University Press, 2002). On the Settlement Indians, see James H. Merrell, *The Indians' New World: Catawbas and Their Neighbors from European Contact Through the Era of Removal* (Chapel Hill: University of North Carolina Press for the Institute of Early American History and Culture, 1989), 99–101, 106–9. On surrounding tribes, see Eric E. Bowne, *The Westo Indians: Slave Traders of the Early Colonial South* (Tuscaloosa: University of Alabama Press, 2005); Steven C. Hahn, *The Invention of the Creek Nation, 1670–1763* (Lincoln: University of Nebraska Press, 2004); Thomas E. Hatley, *The Dividing Paths: Cherokees and South Carolinians Through the Era of Revolution* (New York: Oxford University Press, 1993); Steven J. Oatis, *A Colonial Complex: South Carolina's Frontiers in the Era of the Yamasee War, 1680–1730* (Lincoln: University of Nebraska Press, 2004); and William L. Ramsey, *The Yamasee War: A Study of Culture, Economy, and Conflict in the Colonial South* (Lincoln: University of Nebraska Press, 2008).

47. Jack P. Greene, "Colonial South Carolina and the Caribbean Connection," *South Carolina Historical Magazine* 88, no. 4 (Oct. 1987): 192–210; Richard S. Dunn, *Sugar and Slaves: The Rise of the Planter Class in the English West Indies* (New York:

W. W. Norton, 1972); Simon P. Newman, *A New World of Labor: The Development of Plantation Slavery in the British Atlantic* (Philadelphia: University of Pennsylvania Press, 2013); Vaughan, *Roots of American Racism*, 55–81.

48. Edward B. Rugemer, "The Development of Mastery and Race in the Comprehensive Slave Codes of the Greater Caribbean During the Seventeenth Century," *WMQ* 70, no. 3 (July 2013): 447; William Waller Hening, ed., *The Statutes at Large; Being a Collection of All the Laws of Virginia* (New York: R. & W. & G. Bartow, 1823), 3:86–88; *EAID*, vol. 17, *New England and Mid-Atlantic Laws*, 177; *Minutes of the Provincial Council of Pennsylvania*, 10 vols. (Philadelphia: J. Severns, 1852), 3:605–7.

49. On the evolution of the Barbados slave regime and its racial ideology, see Rugemer, "Development of Mastery and Race"; and Newman, *New World of Labor*. On Godwyn, see Vaughan, *Roots of American Racism*, 55–81; and Katharine Gerbner, *Christian Slavery: Conversion and Race in the Protestant Atlantic World* (Philadelphia: University of Pennsylvania Press, 2018). On such moral debates generally, see Guasco, *Slaves and Englishmen*; and Linford D. Fisher, "'Dangerous Designes': The 1676 Barbados Act to Prohibit New England Indian Slave Importation," *WMQ* 71, no. 1 (Jan. 2014): 99–124.

50. Gerbner, *Christian Slavery*, 102–5; William Dunn, Charles Town, to the Secretary, Apr. 21, 1707, SPG, A Ser., vol. 3, item XCIX ("after their slaves"); A. Leon Higginbotham, *In the Matter of Color: Race and the American Legal Process; The Colonial Period* (New York: Oxford University Press, 1978), 200; Le Jau to the Secretary, Feb. 18, 1708/09, SPG, A Ser., vol. 4, item XCVI ("many masters"); Le Jau to the Secretary, Feb. 10, 1708/09, SPG, A Ser., vol. 4, item CI ("praying posture").

51. A. S. Salley, ed., *Records in the British Record Office Relating to South Carolina, 1663–1693*, 2 vols. (Atlanta: Foote and Davies, 1928–29), 1:258 ("covetousness"). On Indian slavery in other colonies, see Newell, *Brethren by Nature*; Christina Snyder, *Slavery in Indian Country: The Changing Face of Captivity in Early America* (Cambridge, MA: Harvard University Press, 2010); Brett Rushforth, *Bonds of Alliance: Indigenous and Atlantic Slaveries in New France* (Chapel Hill: University of North Carolina Press for the Omohundro Institute of Early American History and Culture, 2012); and Reséndez, *Other Slavery*.

52. Susan Juster, *Sacred Violence in Early America* (Philadelphia: University of Pennsylvania Press, 2016); Thomas Nairne to Dr. Marston, Aug. 20, 1705, SPG, A Ser., vol. 2, item CLVI, insert ("kniving"); Le Jau to the Society, Apr. 20, 1708, SPG,

A Ser., vol. 4, item LXIV; Le Jau to the Society, Aug. 5, 1709, SPG, A Ser., book 5, item 48 ("many grown"); Le Jau to the Society, Feb. 19, 1709/10, SPG, A Ser., book 5, item 82.

53. Alexander S. Salley, Jr., ed., *Narratives of Early Carolina, 1650–1708* (New York: Charles Scribner's Sons, 1911), 300 ("profess'd").

54. Committee of the Assembly of Carolina to Messrs. Boone and Beresford, Dec. 5, 1716, CO 5/1293, pp. 42–52, *Colonial State Papers Online*.

55. David La Vere, *The Tuscarora War: Indians, Colonists, and the Fight for the Carolina Colonies* (Chapel Hill: University of North Carolina Press, 2013); Ramsey, *The Yamasee War*; Le Jau to the Secretary, May 10, 1715, SPG, vol. 10, pp. 112, 114 ("crying sins"); Le Jau to the Secretary, Aug. 30, 1712, SPG, A Ser., vol. 7 ("destroy").

56. Thomas Hassell to the Secretary, SPG, A Ser., vol. 10, p. 97 ("cruel"). Governor Hunter to the Council of Trade and Plantations, June 23, 1712, CO 5/1050, nos. 51 i–v, CO 5/1123, pp. 30–48; Council of Trade and Plantations to Earl of Dartmouth, Aug. 27, 1712, CO 5/1123, pp. 57, 58; Abel Kettleby and other planters, Carolina, to the Council of Trade and Plantations, July 18, 1715, CO 5/1264, no. 150, CO 5/1292, pp. 445–54; South Carolina to Joseph Boone, June 8, 1717, CO 5/1265, no. 79; Extracts of several letters from Carolina, Aug. 19, 1718, CO 5/1265, no. 107; Committee of the Assembly of Carolina to Mr. Boone, Mar. 8, 1718, CO 5/1265, no. 99; Nathaniel Osborne to the Sec., SPG, A Ser., vol. 10, pp. 99–100 ("destroy"); William Tredwell Bull to the Secretary, n.d., SPG, A Ser., vol. 11, p. 61 ("addicted"); Capt. Dennis to the Sec., May 28, 1715, SPG, vol. 12, p. 102; Gideon Johnston to the Sec., Dec. 19, 1715, SPG, A Ser., vol. 11, pp. 102–3 ("military men").

57. On the transition, see Oatis, *Colonial Complex*, 171; Wood, *Black Majority*; Ramsey, *Yamasee War*, esp. 171–72. On the evolving transatlantic trade in African slaves, see David Eltis, *The Rise of African Slavery in the Americas* (New York: Cambridge University Press, 2000); and Peter C. Mancall et al., "Slave Prices and the South Carolina Economy, 1722–1800," *Journal of Economic History* 61, no. 3 (Sep. 2001): 616–39. Guasco, *Slaves and Englishmen*, 187 ("two words"); Ramsey, *Yamasee War*, 166 ("mustee"). See the annual census reports filed by SPG ministers in South Carolina, e.g., Census of St. George's Parish, SC, 1725, SPG, A Ser., vol. 19, p. 104; and Guasco, *Slaves and Englishmen*, 185–87.

58. Guasco, *Slaves and Englishmen*, 187 ("two words"); Ramsey, *Yamasee War*, 166 ("mustee").

59. For one such case, see Steven C. Hahn, *The Life and Times of Mary Musgrove* (Gainesville: University Press of Florida, 2012).

60. John Lawson, *A New Voyage to Carolina; containing the exact description and natural history of that country* (London, 1709), 185. Generally on so-called mixed-race relationships, see A. B. Wilkinson, *Blurring the Lines of Race and Freedom: Mulattoes and Mixed Bloods in English Colonial America* (Chapel Hill: University of North Carolina Press, 2020); Thomas N. Ingersoll, *To Intermix with Our White Brothers: Indian Mixed Bloods in the United States from Earliest Times to the Indian Removals* (Albuquerque: University of New Mexico Press, 2005); Andrew K. Frank, *Creeks and Southerners: Biculturalism on the Early American Frontier* (Lincoln: University of Nebraska Press, 2005); Theda Perdue, *"Mixed Blood" Indians: Racial Construction in the Early South* (Athens: University of Georgia Press, 2003); and Kirsten Fisher, *Suspect Relations: Sex, Race, and Resistance in Colonial North Carolina* (Ithaca, NY: Cornell University Press, 2004), 65–97 (see esp. 73). On the children of Indian-European relationships, see Gideon Johnston to Jonathan Chamberlain, May 28, 1712, SPG, A Ser., vol. 7, p. 424; Nathaniel Osborne to the Secretary, Mar. 1, 1714/15, A Ser., vol. 10, p. 93; William Tredwell Bull to the Secretary, Jan. 20, 1714–15, SPG A Ser., vol. 10, p. 90; and Parochialis, enclosed in Merry's letter of Nov. 3, 1722, SPG, A Ser., vol. 6., p. 133.

61. On Indians returning runaway slaves, see Council of Trade and Plantations to Duke of Newcastle, Dept. Sept. 30, 1730, CO 5/4, no. 46, CO 5/401, pp. 2–3; William Bull to the Commissioners of Trade and Plantations, Oct. 5, 1739, CO 5/367, pp. 114–15d; Gov. Burnet to Board of Trade, 1721, CO 5/1053; Gov. Robert Johnson to Council of Trade and Plantations, Dec. 15, 1732, CO 5/364, pp. 162–65, 167–68 ("maxim"); Gov. George Burnington to Mr. Popple, Nov. 2, 1732, CO 5/294, pp. 114–15; *DRCHNY*, 5:635, 639; *EAID*, vol. 6, *Maryland Treaties, 1632–1775*, 259; *EAID*, vol. 1, *Pennsylvania and Delaware Treaties, 1629–1737*, vol. ed. Donald H. Kent (Washington, D.C., 1979), 262; *EAID*, vol. 5, *Virginia Treaties, 1723–1775*, vol. ed. W. Stitt Robinson (Frederick, MD, 1983), 290; and Richard Ludham to the Secretary, 1725, SPG, A Ser., vol. 19, pp. 66–67 ("check").

62. *EAID*, vol. 17, *New England and Mid-Atlantic Laws*, 178 ("malicious"), 326–27, 739; *Records of the Colony of Rhode Island*, 4:193. On the Hallet murders: William Urquhart to the Secretary, Feb. 4, 1707/08, SPG, A Ser., vol. 3, item CLXXVI; *Boston Evening Post*, no. 199, Feb. 2–9, 1707/08. On the New York slave revolt, see Jennifer Playstead, "'By Reason of their Colour': Public Executions and the Racializing of New York City," 28 (seminar paper in possession of the author, 2017); Robert Hunter to Council of Trade and Plantations, June 23, 1712, CO 5/1050,

nos. 51, 51 i–v, 5/1123, pp. 30–48; Council of Trade and Plantations to Early of Dartmouth, Aug. 27, 1712, CO 5/1123, pp. 57, 58; John Sharpe to the Secretary, SPG, A Ser., vol. 7, p. 214, item 33; and Elias Neu to the Secretary, Oct. 15, 1712, SPG, A Ser., vol. 7, item 39, p. 226.

63. Douglas Edward Leach, *Arms for Empire: A Military History of the British Colonies in North America, 1607–1763* (New York: Macmillan, 1973); Verner W. Crane, *The Southern Frontier, 1670–1732* (Durham, NC: Duke University Press, 1928); Ian K. Steele, *Warpaths: Invasions of North America* (New York: Oxford University Press, 1994); Charles E. Clark, *The Eastern Frontier: The Settlement of Northern New England, 1610–1763* (New York: Alfred A. Knopf, 1970); Haefeli and Sweeney, *Captors and Captives*.

64. James Axtell and William C. Sturtevant, "The Unkindest Cut, or Who Invented Scalping," *WMQ* 37, no. 3 (July 1980): 451–72; Richard J. Chacon and David H. Dye, eds., *The Taking and Displaying of Human Body Parts as Trophies by Amerindians* (New York: Springer, 2007).

65. James Axtell, "Scalping: The Ethnohistory of a Moral Question," in *The European and the Indian: Essays in the Ethnohistory of Colonial North America* (New York: Oxford University Press, 1981), 219, 223–24, 225–26, 231–32, 234 ("deal exactly"), 235 ("unchristian"); Andrew Lipman, "'A meanes to knitt them together': The Exchange of Body Parts in the Pequot War," *WMQ* 65, no. 1 (Jan. 2008): 3–28; Margaret Haig Roosevelt Sewell Ball, "Grim Commerce: Scalps, Bounties, and the Transformation of Trophy-Taking in the Early American Northeast, 1450–1770" (PhD diss., University of Colorado, 2013), 74, 77, 83, 106, 148–49. On Massachusetts scalp bounties, see Steven C. Eames, *Rustic Warriors: Warfare and the Provincial Soldier on the New England Frontier, 1689–1748* (New York: New York University Press, 2011); *DHSM*, 9:4, 7, 22, 25; Guy Chet, *Conquering the American Wilderness: The Triumph of European Warfare in the Colonial Northeast* (Amherst: University of Massachusetts Press, 2003), 90–91; Mairin Odle, *Under the Skin: Tattoos, Scalps, and the Contested Language of Bodies in Early America* (Philadelphia: University of Pennsylvania Press, 2023), 68–90; and Minutes of Council in Assembly of Massachusetts Bay, Dec. 1, 1703, CO 5/789, pp. 896–900.

66. On Norridgewok, see Gov. Drummer to Gov. Vaudreuil, Jan. 19, 1724, and Col. T. Westbrook to Lt. Gov. Drummer, Aug. 18, 1724, *DHSM*, 10:178, 215; John Grenier, *The First Way of War: American War Making on the Frontier, 1607–1814* (New York: Cambridge University Press, 2005), 49–50; and Juster, *Sacred Violence*, 115. On Lovewell, see Thomas Symmes, *Lovewell Lamented. Or, A sermon occasion'd by the*

fall of the brave Capt. John Lovewell (Boston, 1725); Ball, "Grim Commerce," 101–2, 105; Grenier, *First Way of War*, 50–52; and Odle, *Under the Skin*, 87–90.

67. Jay Atkinson, *Massacre on the Merrimack: Hannah Duston's Captivity and Revenge in Colonial America* (Lanham, MD: Lyons Press, 2015); Barbara Cutter, "The Female Indian Killer Memorialized: Hannah Duston and the Nineteenth-Century Feminization of American Violence," *Journal of Women's History* 20, no. 2 (Summer 2008): 10–33; Odle, *Under the Skin*, 68–69. On wage rates, see Daniel Vickers, *Farmers and Fishermen: Two Centuries of Work in Essex County, Massachusetts, 1630–1830* (Chapel Hill: University of North Carolina Press for the Omohundro Institute of Early American History and Culture, 1994), 248.

68. Ball, "Grim Commerce," 109; *Proposals to Prevent Scalping* (New York, 1755) ("What must strangers think?").

69. On French scalp returns see Ball, "Grim Commerce," 89–91, 113, 117–18; Grenier, *First Way of War*, 65; *DHSM*, 9:259 ("barbarous"); Anastasia M. Griffin, "Georg Friedrici's *Scalping and Similar Warfare Customs in America*, with a critical introduction" (master's thesis, University of Colorado, 2008), 79 (1746 New York bounty); Grenier, *First Way of War*, 128 ("barbarous custom"), 140 ("Canadians"); and Thomas Peotto, "Dark Mimesis: A Cultural History of the Scalping Paradigm" (PhD diss., University of British Columbia, 2018), 243.

70. Colin G. Calloway, ed., *North Country Captives: Selected Narratives of Indian Captivity from Vermont and New Hampshire* (Hanover, NH: University Press of New England, 1992), 219 ("kennels," "habitations"); Alden T. Vaughan and Edward W. Clark, *Puritans Among the Indians: Accounts of Captivity and Redemption, 1676–1724* (Cambridge, MA: Harvard University Press, 1986), 141, 143, 174 ("heathen"), 176 ("cruel and bloodthirsty"); Vaughn and Richter, "Crossing the Cultural Divide." Generally, see Kathryn Zabelle Derounian-Stodola and James Arthur Levernier, *The Indian Captivity Narrative, 1550–1900* (New York: Maxwell Macmillan Intl., 1993); and Pauline Turner Strong, *Captive Selves, Captivating Others: The Politics and Poetics of Colonial American Captivity Narratives* (Boulder: University Press of Colorado, 1999).

71. *Boston News-Letter*, no. 1025, Sept. 12–19, 1723. The full range of citations is available from the author on request.

72. For the Pittomee story, see *Boston News-Letter*, no. 155, Nov. 8–15, 1733, and no. 1566, Jan. 24–Feb. 7, 1734. The full range of citations to runaway ads and stories about Settlement Indians is available from the author on request.

73. John Talbot to the Secretary, Oct. 28, 1714, SPG, A Ser., vol. 9, p. 169 ("bad as the Indians"); James Honyman to the Secretary, May 15, 1718, SPG, A Ser., vol. 13, p. 504 ("rude and void"); Vestry of Queen Anne's Creek to General Nicholson, Mar. 2, 1713/14, SPG, A Ser., vol. 10, p. 68 ("danger").

74. *Livingston Indian Records*, p. 115, in *Iroquois Indians*, reel 3 ("one skin"). On the second scare, see *DRCHNY*, 2:11–13, in *Iroquois Indians*, reel 3 ("wage war"). See also reel 5, *Account of a Treaty between NY governor Fletcher and the Five Nations* (Albany, NY, 1694), p. 7; and reel 6, *Councils involving the Five Nations*, Sept. 14, 1698. On the 1700 scare, see Earl of Bellomont, *The Calendar of State Papers, Colonial: North America and the West Indies 1574–1739*, vol. 18 (Apr. 20, 1700) in the following files: CO 5/861, nos. 31, 31, pp. i-xvii, CO 5/909, pp. 33–45, CO 5/1043, No. 25, CO 5/1117, pp. 252–62 ("general insurrection"). On subsequent charges of English-French plotting, see Cadwallader Colden Papers, May 8, 1711, New York Historical Society, in *Iroquois Indians*, reel 7 ("English and French"); and *EAID*, vol. 1, *Pennsylvania and Delaware Treaties, 1629–1737*, 375–76 ("white men").

75. *DRCHNY*, 5:372–76, 382–89; John Sharpe to the Secretary, June 23, 1712, SPG, A Ser., vol. 7, p. 214, item 33; *EAID*, vol. 20, *New England Treaties, North and West, 1650–1776*, vol. ed. Daniel R. Mandell (Bethesda, MD, 2003), 519 ("league," "destroy ourselves"); *EAID*, vol. 2, *Pennsylvania Treaties, 1737–1756*, vol. ed. Donald H. Kent (Frederick, MD, 1984), p. 143 ("be more careful"); Report of Speech of Mohicans to Mohawks, Moravian Archives, B 323, F 8, item 2, in *Iroquois Indians*, reel 12 ("determine their disputes"); Cadwallader Colden Papers, vol. 50, pp. 128–34, in *Iroquois Indians*, reel 8 ("enslave themselves").

76. On New York during this period, see Cathy D. Matson, *Merchants and Empire: Trading in Colonial New York* (Baltimore: Johns Hopkins University Press, 1998); Joyce Goodfriend, *Before the Melting Pot: Society and Culture in Colonial New York City, 1664–1730* (Princeton, NJ: Princeton University Press, 1992); Thomas Elliot Norton, *The Fur Trade in Colonial New York, 1686–1776* (Madison: University of Wisconsin Press, 1974); and Serena R. Zabin, *Dangerous Economies: Status and Commerce in Imperial New York* (Philadelphia: University of Pennsylvania Press, 2011). On the SPG, see William B. Hart, *"For the Good of Their Souls": Performing Christianity in Eighteenth-Century Mohawk Country* (Amherst: University of Massachusetts Press, 2020).

77. Andrews to the Secretary, Sept. 7, 1713, SPG, A Ser., vol. 8, p. 184 ("hopes"); Andrews to the Secretary, Oct. 1, 1717, SPG, A Ser., vol. 12, p. 332 ("addicted"). See also Thomas

Barclay to the Secretary, Sept. 26, 1710, SPG, A Ser., book 5, item 176; Jon Sharpe to the Secretary, June 23, 1712, SPG, A Ser., vol. 7, item 33, p. 214; Andrews to the Secretary, May 25, 1714, SPG, A Ser., vol. 9, p. 124; Andrews to the Sec., Mar. 9, 1712/13, SPG, A Ser., vol. 7, p. 147 ("slothful"); and Andrews to the Secretary, July 12, 1715, SPG, A Ser., vol. 10, pp. 187–88 ("hearty").

78. Daniel K. Richter, *The Ordeal of the Longhouse: The Peoples of the Iroquois League in the Era of European Colonization* (Chapel Hill: University of North Carolina Press for the Institute of Early American History and Culture, 1992), 105–32; Ashhurst to the Secretary, June 30, 1703, SPG, A Ser., item XCII ("great prejudices"); Thoroughgood Moore to the Secretary, Nov. 13, 1705, SPG, A Ser., vol. 2, item CXXII ("hated Christianity").

79. Andrews to the Secretary, Sept. 7, 1713, SPG, A Ser., vol. 8 ("make war"); Andrews to the Secretary, Oct. 17, 1715, SPG, A Ser., vol. 11, p. 268 ("cut them"); Andrews to the Secretary, April 23, 1717, SPG, A Ser., vol. 12. See also Andrew to the Secretary, July 2, 1719, SPG, A Ser., vol. 13, p. 466; Andrews to the Secretary, July 12, 1715, SPG, A Ser., vol. 10 (baptism); and Andrews to the Secretary, Apr. 23, 1717, SPG, A Ser., vol. 12 ("all occasions").

80. Andrews to the Secretary, May 25, 1714, SPG, A Ser., vol. 9, p. 123 ("useless"); Andrews to the Secretary, Oct. 1, 1717, SPG, A Ser., vol. 12, p. 328 ("denying").

81. Andrews to the Secretary, Apr. 20, 1716, A Series, vol. 11, p. 318 ("poor"); Andrews to the Secretary, Apr. 20, 1716, A Ser., vol. 11, p. 325 ("smell"); Andrews to the Secretary, Apr. 17, 1718, A Ser., vol. 13, pp. 319 ("heathens"), 324 ("inhumane").

CHAPTER 2: RACE WARS

1. For population figures, see Jack P. Greene, *Pursuits of Happiness: The Social Development of the Early Modern British Colonies and the Formation of American Culture* (Chapel Hill: University of North Carolina Press, 1988), 178–79; and Colin G. Calloway, *The Scratch of a Pen: 1763 and the Transformation of North America* (New York: Oxford University Press, 2006), 24–25. In the lengthy literature on this era, see Fred Anderson, *Crucible of War: The Seven Years' War and the Fate of Empire in British North America, 1754–1766* (New York: Vintage, 1991); Richard White, *The Middle Ground: Indians, Empires, and Republics in the Great Lakes Region, 1650–1815* (New York: Cambridge University Press, 1991); Michael N. McConnell, *A Country Between: The Upper Ohio Valley and Its Peoples, 1724–1774* (Lincoln: University of Nebraska Press, 1992); Eric Hinderaker, *Elusive Empires: Constructing Colonialism*

in the Ohio Valley, 1673–1800 (Ithaca, NY: Cornell University Press, 1997); Patrick Griffin, *American Leviathan: Empire, Nation, and Revolutionary Frontier* (New York: Hill and Wang, 2007); and Colin G. Calloway, *The Indian World of George Washington: The First President, the First Americans, and the Birth of a Nation* (New York: Oxford University Press, 2018).

2. *The Journals of Samuel Kirkland: 18th-Century Missionary to the Iroquois, Government Agent, Father of Hamilton College*, ed. Walter Pilkington (Clinton, NY: Hamilton College, 1980), 23–24 ("condition"), 37–38; *The Life of the Rev. David Brainerd, Missionary to the Indians*, ed. Jonathan Edwards (London: Burton and Smith, 1818), 442 ("not the same").

3. *EAID*, vol. 6, *Maryland Treaties, 1632–1775*, vol. ed. W. Stitt Robinson (Frederick, MD, 1987), 231.

4. Samson Occom, "Autobiographical Narrative, 2nd draft," Sept. 17, 1768, in *The Collected Writings of Samson Occom, Mohegan: Leadership and Literature in Eighteenth-Century Native America*, ed. Joanna Brooks (New York: Oxford University Press, 2006), 58 ("because I am an Indian"); Joseph Johnson, Speech to Kanoarohare, Jan. 20, 1774, in *To Do Good to My Indian Brethren: The Writings of Joseph Johnson, 1751–1776*, ed. Laura J. Murray (Amherst: University of Massachusetts Press, 1998), 206.

5. *Johnson Papers*, 12:374.

6. *Johnson Papers*, 7:726, 11:165–66 ("design"); Griffin, *American Leviathan*, 91 ("advanced").

7. *Declaration of the distressed and bleeding Frontier Inhabitants* (Philadelphia, 1764), 8 ("dangerous"); Thomas Barton and John Ewing, *The Conduct of the Paxton Men Impartially Represented* (Philadelphia, 1764), 17 ("serpent").

8. Stephen Warren, *The Worlds the Shawnees Made: Migration and Violence in Early America* (Chapel Hill: University of North Carolina Press, 2014); Sami Lakomäki, *Gathering Together: The Shawnee People Through Diaspora and Nationhood, 1600–1870* (New Haven, CT: Yale University Press, 2014); Laurence M. Hauptman, "Refugee Havens: The Iroquois Villages of the Eighteenth Century," in *American Indian Environments*, ed. Christopher Vecsey and Robert W. Venables (Syracuse, NY: Syracuse University Press, 1980), 128–39.

9. Jane T. Merritt, *At the Crossroads: Indians and Empire on a Mid-Atlantic Frontier* (Chapel Hill: University of North Carolina Press for the Omohundro Institute of Early American History and Culture, 2003), 124 ("nothing to do").

10. *EAID*, vol. 20, *New England Treaties, North and West, 1650–1776*, vol. ed. Daniel R. Mandell (Bethesda, MD, 2003), 586–87 ("were but small"); *EAID*, vol. 10, *New York and New Jersey Treaties, 1754–1775*, vol. ed. Barbara Graymont (Bethesda, MD, 2001), 275 ("weak and few"); *EAID*, vol. 1, *Pennsylvania and Delaware Treaties, 1629–1737*, vol. ed. Donald H. Kent (Washington, D.C., 1979), 206 ("dogs"). Population figure in Greene, *Pursuits of Happiness*, 178–79.

11. John Heckewelder, *History, Manners, and Customs of the Indian Nations Who Once Occupied Pennsylvania and the Neighboring States* (1818; Philadelphia: Historical Society of Pennsylvania, 1876), 189 ("wonder"); Samuel G. Drake, ed., *Tragedies of the Wilderness; or, True and Authentic Narratives of Captives* (Boston, 1842), 227; William M. Beauchamp, ed., *Moravian Journals Relating to Central New York, 1745–1766* (Syracuse, NY: Dehler Press, 1916), 9; *Adair's History of the American Indians*, ed. Samuel Cole Williams (1775; New York: Promontory Press, 1930), 1 ("meanly"), 34–35 ("contempt," "nothings," "accursed"), 140 ("fowls," "swine eater"), 242 ("ugly").

12. *EAID*, vol. 2, *Pennsylvania Treaties, 1737–1756*, vol. ed. Donald H. Kent (Frederick, MD, 1984), 244 ("evil spirits"); Beauchamp, *Moravian Journals*, 92; "Journal of James Kenny," *Pennsylvania Magazine of History and Biography* 37, no. 1 (1913): 19 ("hurt").

13. Pennsylvania Provincial Minutes, May 20, 1723, vol. G, pp. 1–11, in *Iroquois Indians*, reel 9 ("half"); Answer of the Indian Chiefs of the Cherokee Nation to the Proprietors . . . , Sept. 9, 1730, CO 5/4, no. 46, CO 5/401, pp. 2–3 ("red").

14. Ives Goddard and Kathleen Bragdon, eds., *Native Writings in Massachusett*, 2 vols. (Philadelphia: American Philosophical Society, 1988), 1:364–65; Massachusetts Archives Series, 32:632, Massachusetts State Archives, Boston; Nancy Shoemaker, "How Indians Got to Be Red," *American Historical Review* 102, no. 3 (June 1997): 625–44; *EAID*, vol. 11, *Georgia Treaties, 1733–1763*, vol. ed. John T. Juricek (Frederick, MD, 1989), 290 ("red people"); George Milne, *Natchez Country: Indians, Colonists, and the Landscapes of Race in French Louisiana* (Athens: University of Georgia Press, 2015), 165–71.

15. *EAID*, vol. 11, *Georgia Treaties, 1733–1763*, 46 ("White man"); Goddard and Bragdon, *Native Writings*, 1:451 ("*wompessue*"); Heckewelder, *History, Manners, and Customs*, 143 ("*Wapside Lenape*").

16. Milne, *Natchez Country*, 168. See also Alexander Long, "A Small Postscript on the ways and maners of the Nashon of Indians called Charikees [1725]," *Southern Indian Studies* 21 (Oct. 1969): 8, 12, 18, 28.

17. Roger Williams, *A Key into the Language of America*, ed. John J. Teunissen and Evelyn J. Hinz (1643; Detroit: Wayne State University Press, 1973), 132–33 ("coal black"); Goddard and Bragdon, *Native Writings*, 1:451 ("Legroo"); *DRCHNY*, 4:997 ("no courage"); Shoemaker, "How Indians Got to Be Red," 638–39 (origin stories); Long, "Small Postcript," 13 (origin story); Hugh Jones, *The Present State of Virginia from Whence Is Inferred a Short View of Maryland and North Carolina*, ed. Richard L. Morton (Chapel Hill: University of North Carolina Press, 1956), 50 ("hate"); William B. Hart, "Black 'Go-Betweens' and the Mutability of 'Race,' Status, and Identity on New York's Pre-Revolutionary Frontier," in *Contact Points: American Frontiers from the Mohawk Valley to the Mississippi, 1750–1830*, ed. Andrew R. L. Cayton and Fredrika J. Teute (Chapel Hill: University of North Carolina Press for the Omohundro Institute of Early American History and Culture, 1998), 88–113.

18. *Life of the Rev. David Brainerd*, 360 ("my design"); John Heckewelder, *A Narrative of the Missions of the United Brethren Among the Delaware and Mohegan Indians* (1820; New York: Arno Press, 1971), 22–23 ("debauched"); Samuel Hopkins, *Historical Memoirs, Relating to the Housatunnuk Indians* (Boston, 1753), 165–66 ("destroy"). Generally on the Moravian missions and their struggles, see Rachel Wheeler, *To Live upon Hope: Mohicans and Missionaries in the Eighteenth-Century Northeast* (Ithaca, NY: Cornell University Press, 2008); and Linford D. Fisher, "'I believe they are Papists!': Natives, Moravians, and the Politics of Conversion in Eighteenth-Century Connecticut," *New England Quarterly* 81, no. 3 (Sept. 2008): 410–37.

19. *Life of the Rev. David Brainerd*, 210–11, 439–40; Eleazar Wheelock, *A Plain and Faithful Narrative of the Original Design, Rise, Progress and the Present State of the Indian Charity-School at Lebanon, in Connecticut* (Boston, 1763), 16 ("deep-seeded"); Eleazar Wheelock to Gideon Hawley (copied Andrew Oliver), June 10, 1761, *Wheelock Papers*, 761360.2 ("unwilling").

20. *Johnson Papers*, 7:597–99.

21. Hawley to Eleazar Wheelock, Feb. 10, 1763, *Wheelock Papers*, 763160.1.

22. "Book of a journal after my mission in the Country of the Six Nations," Jan. 27 to May 31, 1754, Gideon Hawley Journal and Letters, 4 vols., vol. 1, Congregational Library, Boston ("sensible"); Wheelock to George Whitefield, Nov. 25, 1761, *Wheelock Papers*, 761625.1 ("right way").

23. David Crosby to Eleazar Wheelock, Nov. 4, 1767, *Wheelock Papers*, 767604.1 ("powder and ball"); Alan Taylor, *The Divided Ground: Indians, Settlers, and the*

Northern Borderland of the American Revolution (New York: Alfred A. Knopf, 2006), 51 ("cursed").

24. Alfred A. Cave, *Prophets of the Great Spirit: Native American Revitalization Movements in Eastern North America* (Lincoln: University of Nebraska Press, 2006), 11 ("indolent"); John Sergeant, *A Letter from the Revd Mr. Sergeant of Stockbridge, to Dr. Colman of Boston* (Boston, 1743), 6 ("difficult"); *Writings of Samson Occom*, 68, 69, 70, 73; *Writings of Joseph Johnson*, 69.

25. Linford D. Fisher, *The Indian Great Awakening: Religion and the Shaping of Native Cultures in Early America* (New York: Oxford University Press, 2012), 112 ("dispossess"); *Diary of David McClure . . . 1740–1820*, ed. Franklin B. Dexter (New York: Knickerbocker Press, 1899), 190 ("get to Heaven"). For descriptions of the Narragansett congregation, see Joseph Fish to Eleazar Wheelock, July 30, 1766, *Wheelock Papers*, 766430; and Edward Deake to Wheelock, Apr. 25, 1767, *Wheelock Papers*, 767275.1.

26. For two such seventeenth-century cases, see Alden T. Vaughn, *Roots of American Racism: Essays on the Colonial Experience* (New York: Oxford University Press, 1995), 200–212; and Jenny Hale Pulsipher, "Massacre at Hurtleberry Hill: Christian Indians and English Authority in Metacom's War," *WMQ* 53, no. 3 (July 1996): 459–86.

27. *DHSM*, 23:343 ("spirit"), 344, 345–56.

28. *DHSM*, 23:343, 344, 350.

29. *DHSM*, 23:325, 327, 329–30 ("revenge"), 332–35; David L. Ghere and Alvin H. Morrison, "Searching for Justice on the Maine Frontier: Legal Concepts, Treaties, and the 1749 Wiscasset Incident," *American Indian Quarterly* 25, no. 3 (Summer 2001): 100–101.

30. David L. Ghere and Alvin H. Morrison, "Sanctions for Slaughter: Peacetime Violence on the Maine Frontier, 1749–1772," in *Papers of the Twenty-Seventh Algonquian Conference*, ed. David H. Pentland (Winnipeg: University of Manitoba Press, 1996), 111–15; *DHSM*, 14:30. On wage rates, see Daniel Vickers, *Farmers and Fishermen: Two Centuries of Work in Essex County, Massachusetts, 1630–1830* (Chapel Hill: University of North Carolina Press for the Omohundro Institute of Early American History and Culture, 1994), 248.

31. Ian K. Steele, *Setting All the Captives Free: Capture, Adjustment, and Recollection in Allegheny Country* (Montreal: McGill-Queen's University Press, 2013);

A. B. Wilkinson, *Blurring the Lines of Race and Freedom: Mulattoes and Mixed Bloods in English Colonial America* (Chapel Hill: University of North Carolina Press, 2020), 154 ("tincture").

32. *Boston News-Letter*, no. 2947, Dec. 25, 1760 ("hell hounds"). This letter also appeared in the *New-York Gazette*, Dec. 15, 1760; and *New-York Mercury*, Dec. 15, 1760. On newspapers, see Troy Bickham, " 'I shall tear off their scalps, and make cups of their skulls': American Indians in the Eighteenth-Century British Press," in *Native Americans and Anglo-American Culture, 1750–1850: The Indian Atlantic*, ed. Tim Fulford and Kevin Hutchings (New York: Cambridge University Press, 2009), 56–73.

33. John Grenier, *The First Way of War: American War Making on the Frontier, 1607–1814* (New York: Cambridge University Press, 2005), 115; *DHSM*, 12:89 ("suddenly"), 13: 341–45 ("contemptible").

34. Grenier, *First Way of War*, 124 ("as bad"); Israel Williams to ?, 1754, 71-D66, Israel Williams Papers, MHS ("threatening"); *EAID*, vol. 20, *New England Treaties, North and West, 1650–1776*, 591, 596; Committee appointed to hear Captain Konkapot and some other Stockbridge Indians, Apr. 1755, Williams Papers, MHS ("vile"); *DRCHNY*, 7:960 ("extirpate").

35. *Adair's History of the American Indians*, 259–61; Daniel J. Tortora, *Carolina in Crisis: Cherokees, Colonists, and Slaves in the American Southeast, 1756–1763* (Chapel Hill: University of North Carolina Press, 2015), 76 ("unpardonable"), 94 ("kill all").

36. John Oliphant, *Peace and War on the Anglo-Cherokee Frontier, 1756–1763* (Baton Rouge: Louisiana State University Press, 2001); Anderson, *Crucible of War*, 457–71; Jeff W. Dennis, *Patriots and Indians: Shaping Identity in Eighteenth-Century South Carolina* (Columbia: University of South Carolina Press, 2017), 35–38; Grenier, *First Way of War*, 143; *EAID*, vol. 5, *Virginia Treaties, 1723–1775*, vol. ed. W. Stitt Robinson (Frederick, MD, 1983), 124 ("cut them off").

37. Generally, see Amy C. Schutt, *Peoples of the River Valleys: The Odyssey of the Delaware Indians* (Philadelphia: University of Pennsylvania Press, 2007); Robert S. Grumet, *The Munsee Indians: A History* (Norman: University of Oklahoma Press, 2009); James H. Merrell, *Into the American Woods: Negotiators on the Pennsylvania Frontier* (New York: W. W. Norton, 1999); and Jean R. Soderlund, *Lenape Country: Delaware Valley Society Before William Penn* (Philadelphia: University of Pennsylvania Press, 2016). On population, see Thomas J. Sugrue, "The Peopling and Depeopling of Early Pennsylvania: Indians and Colonists, 1680–1720," *Pennsylvania History* 116, no. 1 (Jan. 1992): 3–31.

38. Merritt, *At the Crossroads*, 177; David L. Preston, *The Texture of Contact: European and Indian Settler Communities on the Frontier* (Lincoln: University of Nebraska Press, 2009), 130 ("daily"). Generally, see Peter Silver, *Our Savage Neighbors: How Indian War Transformed Early America* (New York: W. W. Norton, 2008); and Kevin Kenny, *Peaceable Kingdom Lost: The Paxton Boys and the Destruction of William Penn's Holy Experiment* (New York: Oxford University Press, 2009). For how Pennsylvania and its Indian allies tried to handle murder before this era, see Nicole Eustace, *Covered with Night: A Story of Murder and Indigenous Justice in Early America* (New York: Liveright, 2021).

39. James Axtell, *The European and the Indian: Essays in the Ethnohistory of Colonial North America* (New York: Oxford University Press, 1981), 226 ("reward"); "Journal of James Kenny," 7; *EAID*, vol. 2, *Pennsylvania Treaties, 1737–1756*, 26–27.

40. Axtell, *European and the Indian*, 226; Kenny, *Peaceable Kingdom Lost*, 78–79, 81–82, 84 ("pacific measures"); *Several conferences between some of the principal people amongst the Quakers in Pennsylvania, and the deputies from the Six Indian Nations* (Newcastle upon Tyne, 1756), 11 ("inexpressibly cruel"); *EAID*, vol. 3, *Pennsylvania Treaties, 1756–1775*, vol. ed. Alison Duncan Hirsch (Bethesda, MD, 2004), 243 ("four dead").

41. *EAID*, vol. 3, *Pennsylvania Treaties, 1756–1775*, 23 ("not secure"), 68 ("great many"); Preston, *Texture of Contact*, 276 ("unbrotherlike," "extirpation"); Griffin, *American Leviathan*, 69 ("disgusted").

42. The key studies are Gregory Evans Dowd, *A Spirited Resistance: The North American Indian Struggle for Unity, 1745–1815* (Baltimore: Johns Hopkins University Press, 1992); Cave, *Prophets of the Great Spirit*; Joel W. Martin, *Sacred Revolt: The Muskogees' Struggle for a New World* (Boston: Beacon Press, 1991); R. David Edmunds, *The Shawnee Prophet* (Lincoln: University of Nebraska Press, 1983); and Anthony F. C. Wallace, *The Death and Rebirth of the Seneca* (New York: Random House, 1969).

43. *EAID*, vol. 2, *Pennsylvania Treaties, 1737–1756*, 84 ("ancestors"), 96 ("colors"), 262, 309 ("Both you"); Preston, *Texture of Contact*, 158; *Johnson Papers*, 3:210–11, 10:505–9.

44. Cave, *Prophets of the Great Spirit*, 15 ("seer"), 16 ("making beasts"); Merritt, *At the Crossroads*, 90 ("brown and white"); Dowd, *Spirited Resistance*, 30; Beauchamp, *Moravian Journals*, 199–200; Robert S. Grumet, ed., *Journey on the Forbidden Path: Chronicles of a Diplomatic Mission to the Allegheny Country, March–September, 1760* (Philadelphia: American Philosophical Society, 1999), 73; Merrell, *Into the American Woods*, 278 ("I am not").

45. *EAID*, vol. 2, *Pennsylvania Treaties, 1737–1756*, 262 ("fear"). The rest of this discussion draws from "Journal of James Kenny," pt. 2, *Pennsylvania Magazine of History and Biography* 37, no. 2 (1913): 188; and "Journal or History of a Conspiracy by the Indians," *Collections of the Michigan Pioneer and Historical Society* 8 (1886): 270–71.

46. "Journal of James Kenny," pt. 2, 172 ("feasts"), 175 ("Imposter," "no White people"); Heckewelder, *History, Manners, and Customs*, 292–93.

47. "Journal of James Kenny," pt. 2, 171–72; Heckewelder, *History, Manners, and Customs*, 292–93 ("Great Spirit"); Archibald Loudon, ed., *A Selection, of Some of the Most Interesting Narratives, of Outrages, Committed by the Indians, in Their Wars, with the White People*, 2 vols. (Carlisle, PA: A. Loudon, 1808–11), 1:273 ("drive"); "Journal or History of a Conspiracy by the Indians," 299–301, 317–18, 324–27; Gregory Evans Dowd, "The French King Wakes Up in Detroit: 'Pontiac's War' in Rumor and History," *Ethnohistory* 37, no. 3 (Summer 1990): 254–78.

48. Amherst to Bouquet, June 6, 1763 ("fully convinced"), *Amherst Papers*, microfilm. Generally, see Anderson, *Crucible of War*; and Calloway, *Scratch of a Pen*.

49. Anderson, *Crucible of War*, 552; Gregory Evans Dowd, *War Under Heaven: Pontiac, the Indian Nations, and the British Empire* (Baltimore: Johns Hopkins University Press, 2002); Howard H. Peckham, *Pontiac and the Indian Uprising* (1947; Detroit: Wayne State University Press, 1994); Richard Middleton, *Pontiac's War: Its Causes, Course, and Consequences* (New York: Routledge, 2007).

50. McConnell, *Country Between*, 162–63 ("brothers"); "George Croghan's Journal, 1759–1763," ed. Nicholas Wainwright, *Pennsylvania Magazine of History and Biography* 71 (1947): 410 ("cut them off"); Henry Gladwin to Sir Jeffery Amherst, Apr. 20, 1763, p. 59 of "Extracts of Letters, etc, regarding some bad dispositions of the Indians in the Western Department," *Amherst Papers*, microfilm; *New-York Gazette*, Oct. 31, 1762, p. 2; "Journal of James Kenny," pt. 2, 193 ("covet").

51. Daniel K. Richter, "War and Culture: The Iroquois Experience," *WMQ* 40, no. 4 (Oct. 1983): 528–59; Dowd, *Spirited Resistance*, 13–14; White, *Middle Ground*, 326–27, 393 ("no more"); Andrew K. Frank, *Creeks and Southerners: Biculturalism on the Early American Frontier* (Lincoln: University of Nebraska Press, 2005), 55; Loudon, *Selection of the Some of the Most Interesting Narratives*, 1:130 ("every drop").

52. Instructions to Capt. Lt. Gardiner, Aug. 10, 1763, CO 5/63, pp. 220–21, *Amherst Papers*, microfilm ("no prisoners"); Amherst to Bouquet, June 29, 1763, *The Papers of Col. Henry Bouquet, Series 21634*, ed. Sylvester K. Stevens and Donald H. Kent (Harrisburg: Pennsylvania Historical Commission, 1940), 204; Elizabeth A. Fenn,

"Biological Warfare in Eighteenth-Century America: Beyond Jeffery Amherst," *Journal of American History* 86, no. 4 (Mar. 2000): 155280; Kenny, *Peaceable Kingdom Lost*, 121 ("vermin").

53. *EAID*, vol. 3, *Pennsylvania Treaties, 1756–1775*, 665 ("upbraided"); Heckewelder, *Narrative of the Missions*, 42–43 ("race of beings").

54. Heckewelder, *History, Manners, and Customs*, 332–36 ("black devils" on 332); Heckewelder, *Narrative of the Missions*, 70–77; *EAID*, vol. 3, *Pennsylvania Treaties, 1756–1775*, 665; Alicia Lengvarsky, "Women and Intercultural Cooperation: Moravian, Delaware, Mahican Women and the Negotiating Space, 1741–1763" (master's thesis, Ohio State University, 2009), 31 ("regard it"); James Hamilton to Timothy Horsfield, Oct. 10, 1763, Horsfield Papers, American Philosophical Society, Philadelphia ("not be long"); Kenny, *Peaceable Kingdom Lost*, 133–34.

55. Preston, *Texture of Contact*, 129 ("much attached").

56. Kenny, *Peaceable Kingdom Lost*, 29, 34–35, 144–45.

57. Heckewelder, *Narrative of the Missions*, 82–85; General Thomas Gage to Lord Halifax, May 12, 1764, in *The Correspondence of General Thomas Gage with the Secretaries of State, 1763–1775*, ed. Clarence Edwin Carter (New Haven, CT: Yale University Press, 1931), 26; Kenny, *Peaceable Kingdom Lost*, 148–51; Griffin, *American Leviathan*, 48.

58. John Smolenski, "Murder on the Margins: The Paxton Massacre and the Remaking of Sovereignty in Colonial Pennsylvania," *Journal of Early Modern History* 19, no. 6 (2015): 513–38; *An Address to the Rev. Dr. Alison* (Philadelphia, 1765), 1 ("savages," "distress"); Barton and Ewing, *Conduct of the Paxton Men*, 8 ("faithless"); David James Dove, *The Quaker Unmask'd*, 2nd ed. (Philadelphia, 1764), 4, 12 ("hard matter").

59. *Address to the Rev. Dr. Alison*, 3 ("no more"); Barton and Ewing, *Conduct of the Paxton Men*, 30 ("distressed"); Hugh Williamson, *The plain dealer . . . Number III* (Philadelphia, 1764), 11 ("very early"); *Quaker Unmask'd*, 8 ("charms"); John Shebbeare, *A letter, from Batista Angeloni* (Philadelphia [?], 1764), 7 ("Go on").

60. *Address to the Rev. Dr. Alison*, 30 ("heathens"); Benjamin Franklin, *A Narrative of the Late Massacres* (Philadelphia, 1764), 13.

61. Franklin, *Narrative of the Late Massacres*, 9 ("disgrace"), 14 ("pretend"), 25 ("barbarians"), 26–27 ("Pagan"). See also [Andrew Stewart?], *A Dialogue* (Philadelphia, 1764), 8–9.

62. *EAID*, vol. 3, *Pennsylvania Treaties, 1756–1775*, 674–75 ("danger"); Rachel Wheeler and Thomas Hahn-Bruckart, "On an Eighteenth-Century Trail of Tears: The Travel Diary of Johann Jacob Schmick of the Moravian Indian Congregation's Journey to the Susquehanna, 1765," *Journal of Moravian History* 15, no. 1 (Sept. 2015): 44–88; Narrative of Robert Robison, in Loudon, *Selection, of the Some of the Most Interesting Narratives*, 2:166; Griffin, *American Leviathan*, 70–71 (Bow); McConnell, *Country Between*, 209; Merritt, *At the Crossroads*, 299.

63. Bernard Bailyn, *The Peopling of British North America: An Introduction* (New York: Alfred A. Knopf, 1986); Bailyn, *Voyagers to the West: A Passage in the Peopling of America on the Eve of the Revolution* (New York: Alfred A. Knopf, 1986) ("live better" on 30); *DRCHNY*, 7:836–37 ("regardless"); *EAID*, vol. 10, *New York and New Jersey Treaties, 1754–1775*, 517.

64. Patrick Spero, *Frontier Rebels: The Fight for Independence in the American West, 1765–1776* (New York: W. W. Norton, 2018); Dowd, *War Under Heaven*, 203–12; Croghan to Johnson, April 18, 1766, *Johnson Papers*, 5:182 ("mob").

65. *EAID*, vol. 5, *Virginia Treaties, 1723–1775*, 315–18 ("suffer" on 315); Jay Donis, "'No man shall suffer for the murder of a Savage': The Augusta Boys and the Virginia and Pennsylvania Frontiers," *Pennsylvania History* 86, no. 1 (Winter 2019): 38–66 ("impossible" on 49); Jeffrey Ostler, *Surviving Genocide: Native Nations and the United States from the American Revolution to Bleeding Kansas* (New Haven, CT: Yale University Press, 2019), 45 (Paxton Boys).

66. Donis, "'No man,'" 52, 56 ("White Men"); White, *Middle Ground*, 344–51, esp. 349–50. On the legalities of this case, see G. S. Rowe, "The Frederick Stump Affair, 1768, and Its Challenge to Legal Historians of Early Pennsylvania," *Pennsylvania History* 49, no. 4 (Oct. 1982): 259–88; and Alden T. Vaughan, "Frontier Banditti and the Indians: The Paxton Boys' Legacy, 1763–1775," *Pennsylvania History* 5, no. 1 (Jan. 1984): 12–13. Generally, see Silver, *Our Savage Neighbors*; Spero, *Frontier Rebels*; Kenny, *Peaceable Kingdom Lost*; Merrell, *Into the American Woods*; Merritt, *At the Crossroads*; and Preston, *Texture of Contact*.

67. On Arnen and McKenzie, see *New Jersey Archives*, 1st series, 42 vols. (Newark, NJ, 1880–1949), 25:183–85 ("duty" on 185); and *Massachusetts Gazette*, no. 3282, Aug. 28, 1766 ("marks"). On Seymour and Ray, see *New Jersey Archives*, 9:575–76, 25:265–67, 271–72 ("seemed"); *Massachusetts Gazette*, no. 3304, Jan. 29, 1767; Robert M. Owens, *Killing Over Land: Murder and Diplomacy on the Early American Frontier* (Norman: University of Oklahoma Press, 2024), 15–16.

68. Johnson to John Penn, Mar. 16, 1768, *Johnson Papers*, 12:431, 467–68 ("something worse"), 13:189; *DRCHNY*, 7:837 ("white people"), 8:46–47 ("murdered"); George Croghan to Sir William Johnson, Oct. 18, 1767, in *Trade and Politics, 1767–1769*, ed. Clarence Walworth Alvord and Clarence Edwin Carter (Springfield: Trustees of the Illinois State Historical Library, 1921), 89; *EAID*, vol. 5, *Virginia Treaties, 1723–1775*, 351.

69. Loudon, *Selection of the Some of the Most Interesting Narratives*, 2:201 ("Hush!"); Calloway, *Indian World of George Washington*, 207–8; Griffin, *American Leviathan*, 109–10, 115; White, *Middle Ground*, 357–62; Robert G. Parkinson, *Heart of American Darkness: Bewilderment and Horror on the Early Frontier* (New York: W. W. Norton, 2024).

70. Reuben Gold Thwaites and Louise Phelps Kellogg, eds., *Documentary History of Dunmore's War, 1775* (Madison: State Historical Society of Wisconsin, 1905), 371 ("brute"); McConnell, *Country Between*, 273–74; Woody Holton, "The Ohio Indians and the Coming of the American Revolution in Virginia," *Journal of Southern History* 60, no. 3 (Aug. 1994): 453–78.

71. *Writings of Samson Occom*, 59 ("curse"), 104 ("poor Indians"); Proceedings of Fort Stanwix, Oct. 22–Nov. 6, 1768, Etting Manuscript Collection, Historical Society of Pennsylvania, case 30, item 25, p. 21, in *Iroquois Indians*, reel 29 ("Daily experience"); Heckewelder, *History, Manners, and Customs*, 187, 332–36; *Writings of Samson Occom*, 59 ("curse").

72. *EAID*, vol. 3, *Pennsylvania Treaties, 1756–1775*, 754.

CHAPTER 3: "UNDISTINGUISHED DESTRUCTION"

1. *EAID*, vol. 18, *Revolution and Confederation*, vol. ed. Colin G. Calloway (Bethesda, MD, 1994), 128 ("white inhabitants"); *ASP, Indian Affairs*, 1:31 ("father"); Wayne E. Lee, *Barbarians and Brothers: Anglo-American Warfare, 1500–1865* (New York: Oxford University Press, 2011), 171–231; Holger Hoock, *Scars of Independence: America's Violent Birth* (New York: Crown Publishing, 2017); David L. Preston, *The Texture of Contact: European and Indian Settler Communities on the Frontier* (Lincoln: University of Nebraska Press, 2009), 287–88 ("extirpate").

2. *The Collected Writings of Samson Occom, Mohegan: Leadership and Literature in Eighteenth-Century Native America*, ed. Joanna Brooks (New York: Oxford University Press, 2006), 111–12 ("Influence"); Oneidas to the New England Provinces, Jun. 19, 1775, in *To Do Good to My Indian Brethren: The Writings of Joseph*

Johnson, 1751–1776, ed. Laura J. Murray (Amherst: University of Massachusetts Press, 1998), 263 ("one mind"); Kirkland to Philip Schuyler, Mar. 11, 1776, Kirkland Papers, 64b, Hamilton College Special Collections ("white people").

3. On the Proclamation Line, see Woody Holton, *Forced Founders: Indians, Debtors, Slaves, and the Making of the American Revolution in Virginia* (Chapel Hill: University of North Carolina Press for the Omohundro Institute of Early American History and Culture, 1999), 3–36; and Jack Sosin, *Whitehall and the Wilderness: The Middle West in British Colonial Policy, 1760–1775* (Lincoln: University of Nebraska Press, 1965). On subsequent murders and risk of war, see CO 5/90 019; CO 5/90 064; CO 5/74 Pt. 1 045; CO 5/75 Pt. 2 002; CO 5/75 Pt. 2 032; Richard White, *The Middle Ground: Indians, Empires, and Republics in the Great Lakes Region, 1650–1815* (New York: Cambridge University Press, 1991), 343–51; and Patrick Griffin, *American Leviathan: Empire, Nation, and Revolutionary Frontier* (New York: Hill and Wang, 2007), 72–94. On Indian debates about choosing sides, see Colin G. Calloway, *The American Revolution in Indian Country: Crisis and Diversity in Native American Communities* (New York: Cambridge University Press, 1995), 26–64.

4. Thomas S. Abler, ed., *Chainbreaker: The Revolutionary War Memories of Governor Blacksnake, as Told to Benjamin Williams* (Lincoln: University of Nebraska Press, 1989), 79 ("head man"), 127; *EAID*, vol. 18, *Revolution and Confederation*, 15 ("same island"), 98 ("one people"), 117, 193 ("one color"); Hendrick Aupaumut, "A Short Narration of My Journey to the Western Country, May 1777," Papers of the Continental Congress, *Iroquois Indians*, reel 33; Council at Pittsburgh, Oct. 15–Nov. 6, 1776, binder: Mohican, 1776–1819, Ethnohistory Archive, Indiana University, Bloomington ("same people").

5. *EAID*, vol. 18, *Revolution and Confederation*, 214.

6. Philip J. Deloria, *Playing Indian* (New Haven, CT: Yale University Press, 1998), 10–37; *By the King, a Proclamation for suppressing Rebellion and Sedition* (Aug. 23, 1775), masshist.org/database/viewer.php?item_id=818&mode=large&img_step=1&&pid=2 (last accessed June 30, 2022); Robert G. Parkinson, *The Common Cause: Creating Race and Nation in the American Revolution* (Chapel Hill: University of North Carolina Press for the Omohundro Institute of History and Culture, 2016), 181 ("BLOOD").

7. Robert G. Parkinson, "Twenty-Seven Reasons for Independence," in *Declaring Independence: The Origin and Influence of America's Founding Document*, ed. Christian Y. Dupont and Peter S. Onuf (Charlottesville: University of Virginia Library, 2008), 11–18; Parkinson, *Common Cause*, 258.

8. *Citizen Soldier: The Revolutionary War Journal of Joseph Bloomfield*, ed. Mark E. Lender and James Kirby Martin (Newark: New Jersey Historical Society, 1982), 50–51 ("hatchet"); Samuel Hazard et al., eds., *Pennsylvania Archives*, 1st ser. (Philadelphia: Joseph Severns, 1853), vol. 6, p. 614 ("huts"); Deputies of the Delaware Nation to the United States in Congress, May 29, 1779, Daniel Brodhead Papers, 1H91, Wisconsin Historical Society, Madison ("several").

9. John Heckewelder, *A Narrative of the Missions of the United Brethren Among the Delaware and Mohegan Indians* (1820; New York: Arno Press, 1971), 159 ("enraged"), 170–71 ("determination"); Gregory Evans Dowd, *A Spirited Resistance: The North American Indian Struggle for Unity, 1745–1815* (Baltimore: Johns Hopkins University Press, 1992), 75–80 ("massacre" on 75); White, *Middle Ground*, 384–85; Calloway, *American Revolution in Indian Country*, 37, 39; Helm to Clark, May 9, 1779, in *George Rogers Clark Papers, 1771–1781*, ed. James Alton James (Springfield: Trustees of the Illinois State Historical Library, 1912), 317 ("not a stop"). See also *EAID*, vol. 18, *Revolution and Confederation*, 188.

10. Dowd, *Spirited Resistance*, 75 ("ardent"); *The Washington-Crawford Letters. Being the Correspondence Between George Washington and William Crawford, from 1767 to 1781*, ed. Consul W. Butterfield (Cincinnati: R. Clarke 1877), 65; Preston, *Texture of Contact*, 287–88.

11. Colin G. Calloway, *Pen and Ink Witchcraft: Treaties and Treaty Making in American Indian History* (New York: Oxford University Press, 2013), 81, 90, 91, 104; Calloway, *American Revolution in Indian Country*, 190 ("dark"), 191 ("surrounded").

12. Jeff W. Dennis, *Patriots and Indians: Shaping Identity in Eighteenth-Century South Carolina* (Columbia: University of South Carolina Press, 2017), 72 ("extirpated"), 84; John Grenier, *The First Way of War: American War Making on the Frontier, 1607–1814* (New York: Cambridge University Press, 2005), 152–53; Parkinson, *Common Cause*, 271, 275–76 ("killed"); Calloway, *American Revolution in Indian Country*, 48 ("swore").

13. Calloway, *American Revolution in Indian Country*, 49–50, 199, 201 ("real"); Grenier, *First Way of War*, 152–53, 160.

14. Max M. Mintz, *Seeds of Empire: The American Revolutionary Conquest of the Iroquois* (New York: New York University Press, 1999), 46–50, 72–74; Joseph T. Glatthaar and James Kirby Martin, *Forgotten Allies: The Oneida Indians and the American Revolution* (New York: Hill and Wang, 2006), 221–22, 230–31; Alan Taylor, *The Divided Ground: Indians, Settlers, and the Northern Borderland of the American Revolution* (New York: Alfred A. Knopf, 2006), 91, 93; Barbara Graymont, *The Iroquois in the American Revolution* (Syracuse, NY: Syracuse University Press, 1972), 165–66, 183–90 ("bloody" on 90).

15. Colin G. Calloway, *The Indian World of George Washington: The First President, the First Americans, and the Birth of the Nation* (New York: Oxford University Press, 2018), 248–49 ("put to death"), 250; Mintz, *Seeds of Empire*, 75–146; Joseph R. Fisher, *A Well-Executed Failure: The Sullivan Campaign Against the Iroquois, July–September 1779* (Columbia: University of South Carolina Press, 1997); Lee, *Barbarians and Brothers*, 209–31.

16. *Journals of the Military Expedition of Major General John Sullivan Against the Six Nations of Indians in 1779*, ed. Frederick Cook (Auburn, NY: Knapp, Peck, and Thomson, 1887), 8 ("hips"), 26, 64 ("civilization or death"), 168–69, 182, 244; Grenier, *First Way of War*, 167.

17. *Journals of the Military Expedition*, 44 ("hurts"), 98 ("influence"), 100 ("enmity"), 164; Lee, *Barbarians and Brothers*, 228 ("no mercy"); Calloway, *Indian World of George Washington*, 253.

18. Graymont, *Iroquois in the American Revolution*, 192–222; Calloway, *American Revolution in Indian Country*, 129–57; Calloway, *Indian World of George Washington*, 69–70, 244–59; "Conotocarious," *Digital Encyclopedia of George Washington*, mountvernon.org/library/digitalhistory/digital-encyclopedia/article/conotocarious (last accessed June 30, 2022). On Haudenosaunees associating the name with the 1779 campaign, see *Pennsylvania Archives*, 2nd ser., vol. 4 (Harrisburg, PA: Clarence M. Busch, 1800), 528.

19. John Mack Faragher, *Daniel Boone: The Life and Legend of an American Pioneer* (New York: Holt, 1992), 130, 144; *Clark Papers*, 530 ("whole"); Calloway, *American Revolution in Indian Country*, 172.

20. *Clark Papers*, 298 ("excel"); White, *Middle Ground*, 368 ("never spare"), 376–77.

21. Grenier, *First Way of War*, 159, 162; White, *Middle Ground*, 388 ("ripping"); *Clark Papers*, 37; Jeffrey Ostler, *Surviving Genocide: Native Nations and the United States from the American Revolution to Bleeding Kansas* (New Haven, CT: Yale University Press, 2019), 64 ("extermination"); "UVA and the History of Race: The George Rogers Clark Statue and Native Americans," *UVA Today*, July 27, 2020, news.virginia.edu/content/uva-and-history-race-george-rogers-clark-statue-and-native-americans (last accessed Aug. 1, 2024); "Photos: Removal of the George Rogers Clark Statue," *UVA Today*, July 12, 2021, news.virginia.edu/content/photos-removal-george-rogers-clark-statue (last accessed Aug. 1, 2024).

22. Parkinson, *Common Cause*, 340–49 ("swear" on 344), 401–2 ("savages"), 416 ("eradicated"); *Journals of a Military Expedition*, 248; Taylor, *Divided Ground*, 93.

23. Peter Silver, *Our Savage Neighbors: How Indian War Transformed Early America* (New York: W. W. Norton, 2008), 265–74; Heckewelder, *Narrative of the Missions*, 317–18 ("killed"); *Diary of David Zeisberger: A Moravian Missionary Among the Indians of Ohio*, ed. Eugene F. Bliss, 2 vols. (Cincinnati: Robert Clarke 1885), 1:82–83, 85.

24. Alan Taylor, *American Revolutions: A Continental History, 1750–1804* (New York: W. W. Norton, 2016), 261; *Washington-Irvine Correspondence: The Official Letters Which Passed Between Washington and Brig.-Gen. William Irvine and Between Irvine and Others Concerning Military Affairs in the West from 1781 to 1783*, ed. Consul W. Butterfield (Madison, WI: D. Atwood, 1882), 99–103 ("fit" on 99, "attachment" on 103), 343–44 ("mutinous"); Silver, *Our Savage Neighbors*, 278.

25. Jonathan D. Sassi, "Religion, Race, and the Founders," in *Faith and the Founders of the American Republic*, ed. Daniel L. Dreisbach and Mark David Hall (New York: Oxford University Press, 2014), 174–200; Nicholas Guyatt, *Bind Us Apart: How Enlightened Americans Invented Racial Segregation* (New York: Basic Books, 2016), 17–114.

26. *Washington-Irvine Correspondence*, 343–44 ("people"), 373; Heckewelder, *Narrative of the Missions*, 341–42 ("no quarter," "mockingly"); *Diary of David Zeisberger*, 133.

27. *Diary of David Zeisberger*, 115, 296, 409; Lawrence H. Gipson, *The Moravian Indian Mission on the White River: Diaries and Letters, May 5, 1799, to November 12, 1806*, ed. Lawrence H. Gipson, trans. Harry E. Stocker et al. (Indianapolis: Indiana Historical Bureau, 1938), 249 ("purpose"), 256 ("not forgotten"), 439, 453, 509.

28. David Andrew Nichols, *Red Gentlemen and White Savages: Indians, Federalists, and the Search for Order on the American Frontier* (Charlottesville: University of Virginia Press, 2008), 3 ("repugnant"); Hugh Henry Brackenridge, *Narratives of a Late Expedition Against the Indians* (Philadelphia: Francis Bailey, 1783), unnumbered ("extirpation"), 37 ("temper"), 82 ("animals"). On Brackenridge's publication, see James M. Greene, *The Soldier's Two Bodies: Military Sacrifice and Popular Sovereignty in Revolutionary War Veteran Narratives* (Baton Rouge: Louisiana State University Press, 2019).

29. Anthony Benezet, *Some Observations on the Situation, Disposition, and Character of the Indian Nations of This Continent* (Philadelphia: Joseph Crukshank, 1784), 8 ("mental"), 35 ("blasphemy," "extirpation").

30. Archibald Loudon, ed., *A Selection of the Some of the Most Interesting Narratives, of Outrages, Committed by the Indians, in Their Wars, with the White People*, 2 vols. (Carlisle, PA: A. Loudon, 1808), 1:56 ("execute him").

31. Nichols, *Red Gentlemen*, 2; *EAID*, vol. 18, *Revolution and Confederation*, 284 ("conquerors"), 324 ("whole force"), 347 ("destruction"); Reginald Horsman, *Expansion and American Indian Policy, 1783–1812* (East Lansing: Michigan State University Press, 1967), 19–21.

32. Horeman, *Expansion and American Indian Policy*, 19–21; Nichols, *Red Gentlemen*, 58; Taylor, *Divided Ground*, 119; *Writings of Samson Occom*, 121 ("seems").

33. Calloway, *American Revolution in Indian Country*, 85–107; Glatthaar and Martin, *Forgotten Allies*; James H. Merrell, *The Indians' New World: Catawbas and Their Neighbors from European Contact Through the Era of Removal* (Chapel Hill: University of North Carolina Press for the Institute of Early American History and Culture, 1989), 215–22; Captain Johann Ewald, *Diary of the American War: A Hessian Journal*, ed. and trans. Joseph P. Tustin (New Haven, CT: Yale University Press, 1979), 145; Parkinson, *Common Cause*, 21–22, 25, 377–80; Laurence M. Hauptman, *Conspiracy of Interests: Iroquois Dispossession and the Rise of New York State* (Syracuse, NY: Syracuse University Press, 1999), 27–100; David J. Silverman, *Red Brethren: The Brothertown and Stockbridge Indians and the Problem of Race in Early America* (Ithaca, NY: Cornell University Press, 2010), 125–48; Daniel R. Mandell, *Tribe, Race, History: Native Americans in Southern New England, 1780–1880* (Baltimore: Johns Hopkins University Press, 2008); Mikaëla M. Adams, *Who Belongs? Race, Resources, and Tribal Citizenship in the Native South* (New York: Oxford University Press, 2016), 61–85; Warren Eugene Milteer Jr., *Beyond Slavery's Shadow: Free People of Color in the South* (Chapel Hill: University of North Carolina Press, 2021).

34. *Writings of Samson Occom*, 218 ("devilish"); "Agreement Respecting Strange Indians Living at Montauk, 1754," typescript, Indian Deeds of Montauk, accession no. F129.E13 I53 1900Z, Brooklyn Historical Society, Brooklyn, NY; William Samuel Johnson Papers, vol. 3, Docs. 72–73, Connecticut Historical Society, Hartford; *Johnson Papers*, 13:683–84. Generally on Afro-Indian relationships, see Daniel R. Mandell, "Shifting Boundaries of Race and Ethnicity: Indian-Black Intermarriage in Southern New England, 1760–1880," *Journal of American History* 85, no. 2 (Sept. 1998): 466–501.

35. Gregory Ablavksy, "'With the Indian Tribes': Race, Citizenship, and Original Constitutional Meaning," *Stanford Law Review* 70, no. 4 (Apr. 2018): 1025–76, esp. 1054–61; Alexander Keyssar, *The Right to Vote: The Contested History of Democracy in the United States* (New York: Basic Books, 2000), 59; Deborah A. Rosen, *American Indians and State Law: Sovereignty, Race, and Citizenship, 1790–1880* (Lincoln: University of Nebraska Press, 2007), 116–17.

36. Matthew Frye Jacobson, *Whiteness of a Different Color: European Immigrants and the Alchemy of Race* (Cambridge, MA: Harvard University Press, 1998), 25–26; Saul Cornell, *"A Well Regulated Militia": The Founding Fathers and the Origins of Gun Control* (New York: Oxford University Press, 2006).

37. Ostler, *Surviving Genocide*, 98 ("wheels"); Alan Taylor, "'To Man Their Rights': The Frontier Revolution," in *The Transforming Hand of Revolution: Reconsidering the American Revolution as a Social Movement*, ed. Ronald Hoffman (Charlottesville: University of Virginia Press for the United States Capitol Historical Society, 1995), 231–57.

38. George Washington to James Duane, Sept. 7, 1783, in *The Writings of George Washington from the Original Manuscript Sources, 1745–1799*, ed. John C. Fitzpatrick, 39 vols. (Washington, D.C.: United States Government Printing Office, 1931), 27:133 ("retreat"); Francis Paul Prucha, *The Great Father: The United States Government and the American Indians*, 2 vols. (Lincoln: University of Nebraska Press, 1984), 35–60; Gregory Ablavsky, "The Savage Constitution," *Duke Law Journal* 63, no. 5 (Feb. 2014): 999–1089; Emilie Connolly, "Fiduciary Colonialism: Annuities and Native Dispossession in the Early United States," *American Historical Review* 127, no. 1 (Mar. 2022): 223–53.

39. Guyatt, *Bind Us Apart*, 122; Henry Knox, Report on Indian Affairs, Dec. 29, 1794, *Papers of George Washington Digital Edition*, 80 vols. (Charlottesville: University of Virginia Press, Rotunda, 2008) ("future").

40. In the *Papers of George Washington*: Report of Henry Knox, Dec. 27, 1790; Timothy Pickering to Washington, Dec. 4, 1790; Heckewelder, *Narrative of the Missions*, 396; *ASP, Indian Affairs*, 1:43 ("children"), 70, 203, 205, 256, 430 ("delusions"), 496, 618.

41. Letter from a Gentleman, Aug. 8, 1792, Kirkland Papers, F151a, Hamilton College Special Collections ("bear"); Kirkland Journals, entry for May 20, 1791, Society for the Propagation of the Gospel in North America, Records, Box 1, Folder 3, MHS.

42. Noble E. Cunningham Jr., ed., *Circular Letters of Congressmen to Their Constituents, 1789–1829*, 3 vols. (Chapel Hill: University of North Carolina Press, 1978), 34; Jeremy Belknap and Jedidiah Morse, "Report of a Committee . . . Who Visited the Oneida and Mohekunuh Indians in 1796," Massachusetts Historical Society, *Collections*, 1st ser., vol. 5 (1978), 21 ("neither"), 29–30 ("mortify").

43. Pickering to George Washington, Mar. 21, 1792, *Papers of George Washington* ("White Man"); "Good Peter's Narrative, April 1792," Pickering Papers, vol. 60, MHS; Brant to Samuel Kirkland, Mar. 8, 1794, Pickering Papers, vol. 61, MHS ("pretense");

Nichols, *Red Gentlemen*, 146 ("smooth"); *The Journals of Samuel Kirkland: 18th-Century Missionary to the Iroquois, Government Agent, Father of Hamilton College*, ed. Walter Pilkington (Clinton, NY: Hamilton College, 1980), 177, 266 ("genuine"); *The Collected Speeches of Sagoyewatha, or Red Jacket*, ed. Granville Ganter (Syracuse, NY: Syracuse University Press, 2006), 104 ("learning"); *ASP, Indian Affairs*, 1:602 ("worthless").

44. *Collected Speeches of Sagoyewatha, or Red Jacket*, 24 ("degrees"); Daniel H. Usner Jr., "Iroquois Livelihood and Jeffersonian Agrarianism: Reaching Behind the Model and Metaphors," in *Native Americans and the Early Republic*, ed. Frederick E. Hoxie et al. (Charlottesville: University of Virginia Press for the United States Capitol Society, 1999), 220 ("common").

45. *Journals of Samuel Kirkland*, 167 ("angry"); Kirkland to James Bowdoin, Mar. 10, 1784, Kirkland Papers, Folder 85c, Hamilton College Special Collections; David J. Silverman, "The Curse of God: An Idea and Its Origins Among the Indians of New York's Revolutionary Frontier," *WMQ* 66, no. 33 (July 2009): 495–534; Silverman, "To Become a Chosen People: The Missionary Work and Missionary Spirit of the Brotherton and Stockbridge Indians, 1775–1835," in *Native Americans, Christianity, and the Reshaping of the American Religious Landscape*, ed. Joel W. Martin and Mark A. Nicholas (Chapel Hill: University of North Carolina Press, 2010), 250–75; Hendrick Aupaumut to Henry Dearborn, May 21, 1805, Ethnohistory Archive, Mohican Binder, 1776–1819, Indiana University, Bloomington ("Great Creator").

46. Ostler, *Surviving Genocide*, 377 ("called religion").

47. *ASP, Indian Affairs*, 1:264, 324 ("one people"), 325 ("national honors"), 465, 477, 481.

48. John Walton Caughey, *McGillivray of the Creeks* (Norman: University of Oklahoma Press, 1938), 244 ("seize"); *The Collected Works of Benjamin Hawkins, 1796–1810*, ed. H. Thomas Foster II (Tuscaloosa: University of Alabama Press, 2003), 9s (*Ecunnaunuxulgee*), 9s–10s ("Asking for Land," "Dirt King").

49. For accounts of this violence, see *ASP, Indian Affairs*, 1:56, 280, 398, 414, 423, 615; *TPUS*, 4:179, 198, 271, 320; Grenier, *First Way of War*, 172–80; James P. Pate, "The Chickamauga: A Forgotten Segment of Indian Resistance on the Southern Frontier" (PhD diss., University of Mississippi, 1969), 194, 248; Joshua S. Haynes, *Patrolling the Border: Theft and Violence on the Creek-Georgia Frontier, 1770–1796* (Baton Rouge: Louisiana State University Press, 2019), 130, 144; Calloway, *American Revolution in Indian Country*, 211–12; *Collected Works of Benjamin Hawkins*, 23, 36s–37s ("singular" on 36s); and *TPUS*, 4:177 ("openly"), 179, 271.

50. Grenier, *First Way of War*, 190; *TPUS*, 4:282; *ASP, Indian Affairs*, 1:472; Citizens of Mero County, NC, to President and Congress, Nov. 30, 1789, *Papers of George Washington*; Kevin T. Barksdale, *The Lost State of Franklin: America's First Secession* (Lexington: University Press of Kentucky, 2019), 15–16, 56, 62–63, 92, 100–117; Haynes, *Patrolling the Border*, 180–84.

51. Pate, "Chickamauga," 248; Calloway, *American Revolution in Indian Country*, 211–12; *ASP, Indian Affairs*, 1:538 ("kill"); Haynes, *Patrolling the Border*, 188–99; Leonard J. Sadosky, *Revolutionary Negotiations: Indians, Empires, and Diplomats in the Founding of America* (Charlottesville: University of Virginia Press, 2010), 165–75; *Collected Works of Benjamin Hawkins*, 102 ("doctrine").

52. Peter Onuf, *Statehood and Union: A History of the Northwest Ordinance* (Bloomington: Indiana University Press, 1987); Calloway, *American Revolution in Indian Country*, 174; White, *Middle Ground*, 418; Calloway, *The Victory with No Name: The American Defeat of the First American Army* (New York: Oxford University Press, 2015), 35–60; Taylor, "'To Man Their Rights'"; Nichols, *Red Gentlemen*, 38 ("scalp").

53. Samantha Seeley, *Race, Removal, and the Right to Remain: Migration and the Making of the United States* (Chapel Hill: University of North Carolina Press for the Omohundro Institute of Early American History and Culture, 2021), 93 ("surprise"); Grenier, *First Way of War*, 195 ("extirpate"). On Harmar's raids, see *TPUS*, 2:360, 363; *ASP, Indian Affairs*, 1:60, 88–90, 121–22; and Griffin, *American Leviathan*, 194.

54. Calloway, *Victory with No Name*, 64–67, 115–28; Wiley Sword, *President Washington's Indian War: The Struggle for the Old Northwest* (Norman: University of Oklahoma Press, 1985), 96–119, 160–95; Thomas P. Slaughter, *The Whiskey Rebellion: Frontier Epilogue to the American Revolution* (New York: Oxford University Press, 1986), 94; *ASP, Indian Affairs*, 1:354.

55. Robert M. Owens, *Mr. Jefferson's Hammer: William Henry Harrison and the Origins of American Indian Policy* (Norman: University of Oklahoma Press, 2007), 33; Griffin, *American Leviathan*, 248–49 ("swear"); Adam Jortner, *The Gods of Prophetstown: The Battle of Tippecanoe and the Holy War for the American Frontier* (New York: Oxford University Press, 2011), 68; *ASP, Indian Affairs*, 1:490; Calloway, *Victory with No Name*, 149–52; Susan Sleeper-Smith, *Indigenous Prosperity and American Conquest: Indian Women of the Ohio River Valley, 1690–1792* (Chapel Hill: University of North Carolina Press for the Omohundro Institute of Early American History and Culture, 2018), esp. 312–14.

56. Calloway, *Indian World of George Washington*, 304–5, 368; Calloway, *Pen and Ink Witchcraft*, 103–5, 107, 110–11; Michael Leroy Oberg, *Peacemakers: The Iroquois, The United States, and the Treaty of Canandaigua, 1794* (New York: Oxford University Press, 2016).

57. Slaughter, *Whiskey Rebellion*.

58. Nichols, *Red Gentlemen*, 161; Calloway, *Victory with No Name*, 153; Alfred A. Cave, *Prophets of the Great Spirit: Native American Revitalization Movements in Eastern North America* (Lincoln: University of Nebraska Press, 2006), 113; *Collected Works of Benjamin Hawkins*, 397 ("friend," "head"); Anthony F. C. Wallace, *Jefferson and the Indians: The Tragic Fate of the First Americans* (Cambridge, MA: Harvard University Press, 1999), 239; Dowd, *Spirited Resistance*, 116–22; Owens, *Mr. Jefferson's Hammer*, 31–32; R. David Edmunds, *Tecumseh and the Quest for Indian Leadership* (Boston: Pearson Longman, 1984), 89.

59. Anthony F. C. Wallace, *The Death and Rebirth of the Seneca* (New York: Random House, 1969), 239–302; Cave, *Prophets of the Great Spirit*, 8, 183–84; Douglas Winiarski, "Revisioning the Shawnee Prophet: Revitalization Movements, Religious Studies, and the Ontological Turn," *Early American Studies* 22, no. 2 (Spring 2024): 305–50; Dowd, *Spirited Resistance*, 116–47; Edmunds, *Tecumseh*, 75–79; Jortner, *Gods of Prophetstown*, 58, 97–98, 100; Gipson, *Moravian Indian Mission on the White River*, 392 ("crab").

60. Gipson, *Moravian Indian Mission on the White River*, 364 ("take the Word"), 368, 371, 417 ("white teachers"), 419 ("good"), 539 ("surrounded"); Owens, *Mr. Jefferson's Hammer*, 123–25.

61. *Messages and Letters of William Henry Harrison*, ed. Logan Esarey, 2 vols. (Indianapolis: Indiana Historical Collections, 1922), 1:261 ("threatening"), 277 ("race war"), 292, 300; *ASP, Indian Affairs*, 1:798–801; Edmunds, *Tecumseh*, 110; White, *Middle Ground*, 511; R. David Edmunds, "Black Hoof and the Loyal Shawnees," in *Native Americans and the Early Republic*, Hoxie et al., 163–64; Jortner, *Gods of Prophetstown*, 145; Hendrick Aupaumut to John Sergeant, Jan. 3, 1809, Brothertown Indian Collection, Box 39, Folder 4, New England Historic Genealogical Society, Boston ("destroy").

62. Dowd, *Spirited Resistance*, 139–40; *Messages and Letters of William Henry Harrison*, 1:354 ("poor"), 465–67.

63. Joel W. Martin, *Sacred Revolt: The Muskogees' Struggle for a New World* (Boston: Beacon Press, 1991), 103, 118; Claudio Saunt, *A New Order of Things: Property, Power,*

and the Transformation of the Creek Indians, 1733–1816 (New York: Cambridge University Press, 1999), 164–85; Theda Perdue, *Slavery and the Evolution of Cherokee Society, 1540–1866* (Knoxville: University of Tennessee Press, 1979), 50–69; Theda Perdue, *Cherokee Women: Gender and Culture Change, 1700–1835* (Lincoln: University of Nebraska Press, 1998), 115–34.

64. Saunt, *New Order of Things*, 179–80; Michael D. Green, *The Politics of Indian Removal: Creek Government and Society in Crisis* (Lincoln: University of Nebraska Press, 1982), 33–38; William G. McLoughlin, *Cherokee Renascence in the New Republic* (Princeton, NJ: Princeton University Press, 1986), 157–58; James Taylor Carson, *Searching for the Bright Path: The Mississippi Choctaws from Prehistory to Removal* (Lincoln: University of Nebraska Press, 1999), 76.

65. Saunt, *New Order of Things*, 233–48; Dowd, *Spirited Resistance*, 148–66, 174 ("wicked"), 178; William G. McLoughlin, *Cherokees and Missionaries, 1789–1839* (New Haven, CT: Yale University Press, 1984), 82–101 ("red clay" on 87).

66. ASP, *Indian Affairs*, 1:809 ("wars"); Edmunds, *Tecumseh*, 148–53; Dowd, *Spirited Resistance*, 154–57.

67. Alan Taylor, *The Civil War of 1812: American Citizens, British Subjects, Irish Rebels, and Indian Allies* (New York: Alfred A. Knopf, 2010), 127, 153, 164–65, 189, 203–14, 222 ("horror"); Cave, *Prophets of the Great Spirit*, 122; Owens, *Mr. Jefferson's Hammer*, 222–23; Edmunds, "Loyal Shawnees," 176; Ann Durkin Keating, *Rising Up from Indian Country: The Battle of Fort Dearborn and the Birth of Chicago* (Chicago: University of Chicago Press, 2012), 1–2, 98, 174–75; Carl Benn, *The Iroquois in the War of 1812* (Toronto: University of Toronto Press, 1998), 50.

68. Nicole Eustace, *1812: War and the Passions of Patriotism* (Philadelphia: University of Pennsylvania Press, 2012), 69 ("sometimes"), 118–20 ("advanced" on 119), 121, 125 ("inhuman," "hideous"), 126 ("vile," "merciless"); Kathryn Zabelle Derounian-Stodola and James Arthur Levernier, *The Indian Captivity Narrative, 1550–1900* (New York: Maxwell Macmillan Intl., 1993), 31; Taylor, *Civil War of 1812*, 205–6, 213, 255; *Messages and Letters of William Henry Harrison*, 2:41 ("extermination"); Robert M. Owens, *Red Dreams, White Nightmares: Pan-Indian Alliances in the Anglo-American Mind, 1763–1815* (Norman: University of Oklahoma Press, 2015), 108.

69. Taylor, *Civil War of 1812*, 210 ("twenty"), 245; *Messages and Letters of William Henry Harrison*, 2:283 ("thought").

70. *The Trial of Alpheus Livermore, Before the Supreme Judicial Court of the Commonwealth of Massachusetts* (Boston: Watson and Bangs, 1813), 19 ("Devil take"), 49 ("wild beasts").

71. *ASP, Indian Affairs*, 1:841 ("kill off"), 846; Martin, *Sacred Revolt*, 125–32, 135.

72. *ASP, Indian Affairs*, 1:853.

73. *ASP, Indian Affairs*, 1:848 ("ruin"); Martin, *Sacred Revolt*, 158–63; Susan M. Abram, "Cherokees in the Creek War," in *Tohopeka: Rethinking the Creek War and the War of 1812*, ed. Kathryn E. Braund (Tuscaloosa: University of Alabama Press, 2012), 135; Ostler, *Surviving Genocide*, 168 ("exterminate"), 173; Owens, *Red Dreams*, 215 ("Brave"), 220 ("Exterminating").

74. *ASP, Indian Affairs*, 1:854 ("unite"); McLoughlin, *Cherokee Renascence*, 195 ("prejudice"), 204; Robert V. Remini, *Andrew Jackson and His Indian Wars* (New York: Viking, 2001), 108–29; Sean Wilentz, *The Rise of American Democracy: Jefferson to Lincoln* (New York: W. W. Norton, 2005), 172; Arrell M. Gibson, *The Chickasaws* (Norman: University of Oklahoma Press, 1971), 104–5.

75. Grenier, *First Way of War*, 205; Brian W. Dippie, *The Vanishing American: White Attitudes and U.S. Indian Policy* (Middletown, CT: Wesleyan University Press, 1982), 7 ("menacing"); Treaty of Ghent (1814), archives.gov/milestone-documents/treaty-of-ghent (last accessed November 27, 2022); Keating, *Rising Up*, 199, 232.

76. *ASP, Indian Affairs*, 2:28 ("extermination"), 184 ("independent"), 190 ("emigrate").

77. Claudio Saunt, *Unworthy Republic: The Dispossession of Native Americans and the Road to Indian Territory* (New York: W. W. Norton, 2020), 7; Seeley, *Race, Removal, and the Right to Remain*, 304; Charles Sellers, *The Market Revolution: Jacksonian America, 1815–1846* (New York: Oxford University Press, 1991), 43–44; Daniel Walker Howe, *What Hath God Wrought: The Transformation of America, 1815–1848* (New York: Oxford University Press, 2007), 86, 140, 203–42; *Collected Speeches of Sagoyewatha, or Red Jacket*, 197 ("wicked").

78. Eustace, *1812*, 21 ("looks forward").

79. *ASP, Indian Affairs*, 2:236 ("Humanity").

CHAPTER 4: WHITEWASH

1. The most influential historical argument along these lines is Francis Paul Prucha, "Andrew Jackson's Indian Policy: A Reassessment," *Journal of American History* 56, no. 3 (Dec. 1969): 527–39.

2. Notable recent exceptions are Claudio Saunt, *Unworthy Republic: The Dispossession of Native Americans and the Road to Indian Territory* (New York: W. W. Norton,

2020); Jeffrey Ostler, *Surviving Genocide: Native Nations and the United States from the American Revolution to Bleeding Kansas* (New Haven, CT: Yale University Press, 2019); and Christopher D. Haveman, *Rivers of Sand: Creek Indian Emigration, Relocation, and Ethnic Cleansing in the American South* (Lincoln: University of Nebraska Press, 2016).

3. James Hall, *Sketches of History, Life, and Manners in the West*, 2 vols. (Philadelphia: Harrison Hall, 1835), 1:77 ("frontier"); Thomas McKenney, *Memoirs, Official and Personal, with Sketches of Travel Among the Northern and Southern Indians*, 2 vols., 2nd ed. (New York: Paine and Burgess, 1846), 233 ("Which of us"); Alan Taylor, *The Civil War of 1812: American Citizens, British Subjects, Irish Rebels, and Indian Allies* (New York: Alfred A. Knopf, 2010), 203–4; Adam Jortner, *The Gods of Prophetstown: The Battle of Tippecanoe and the Holy War for the American Frontier* (New York: Oxford University Press, 2011), 190; *On Our Own Ground: The Complete Writings of William Apess, a Pequot*, ed. Barry O'Connell (Amherst: University of Massachusetts Press, 1992), 10–11 ("occasioned"); Walter L. Hixson, *American Settler Colonialism: A History* (New York: Palgrave Macmillan, 2013), 50.

4. Rayna D. Green, "The Indian in Popular American Culture," *Smithsonian Handbook of North American Indians*, vol. 4: *History of Indian-White Relations*, vol. ed. Wilcomb E. Washburn, gen. ed. William C. Sturtevant (Washington, D.C.: Smithsonian Institution Press, 1988), 590 ("I is for Indian"); Kathryn Zabelle Derounian-Stodola and James Arthur Levernier, *The Indian Captivity Narrative, 1550–1900* (New York: Maxwell Macmillan Intl., 1993), 37; Elise Marienstras, "The Common Man's Indian: The Image of the Indian as a Promoter of National Identity in the Early National Era," in *Native Americans and the Early Republic*, ed. Frederick E. Hoxie et al. (Charlottesville: University of Virginia Press for the United States Capitol Historical Society, 1999), 275 ("authentic"); Christina Snyder, *Great Crossings: Indians, Settlers, and Slaves in the Age of Jackson* (New York: Oxford University Press, 2017), 88, 190 ("extirpated").

5. Derounian-Stodola and Levernier, *Indian Captivity Narrative*, 23, 24, 26 ("folly"), 31, 51 ("monsters"); Marienstras, "Common Man's Indian," 282.

6. John Sugden, *Tecumseh: A Life* (New York: Henry Holt, 1998), 396–97; Richard Slotkin, *Regeneration Through Violence: The Mythology of the American Frontier* (Middletown, CT: Wesleyan University Press, 1973), 313–68; Richard Drinon, *Facing West: The Metaphysics of Indian-Hating and Empire-Building* (1980; Norman: University of Oklahoma Press, 1997), 147–64; John Grenier, *The First Way of War:*

American War Making on the Frontier, 1607–1814 (New York: Cambridge University Press, 2005), 222.

7. James Eldridge Quinlan, *Tom Quick, the Indian Slayer* (Monticello, NY: De Voe and Quinlan, 1851), 22 ("young and the old"), 54 ("spared"), 58 ("nits"); legendsofamerica .com/tom-quick (last accessed July 15, 2022); tomquickinnmilford.com (last accessed July 15, 2022).

8. Slotkin, *Regeneration Through Violence*, 369–93; Daniel F. Littlefield, "Washington Irving and the American Indian," *American Indian Quarterly* 5, no. 2 (May 1979): 135–54; Robert F. Sayre, *Thoreau and the American Indians* (Princeton, NJ: Princeton University Press, 1977); Robert F. Berkhofer Jr., *The White Man's Indian: Images of the American Indian from Columbus to the Present* (New York: Alfred A. Knopf, 1978), 86–95.

9. Brian W. Dippie, *The Vanishing American: White Attitudes and U.S. Indian Policy* (Middletown, CT: Wesleyan University Press, 1982), 13–14, 26; Philip J. Deloria, *Playing Indian* (New Haven, CT: Yale University Press, 1998), 65; Sugden, *Tecumseh*, 397; Benita Eisler, *The Red Man's Bones: George Catlin, Artist and Showman* (New York: W. W. Norton, 2013); Berkhofer, *White Man's Indian*, 88; Jean M. O'Brien, *Firsting and Lasting: Writing Indians Out of Existence in New England* (Minneapolis: University of Minnesota Press, 2010); Marienstras, "Common Man's Indian," 295.

10. Vivien Green Fryd, "Imagining the Indians in the United States Capitol During the Early Republic," in *Native Americans and the Early Republic*, Hoxie et al., 297–332.

11. *Adair's History of the American Indians*, ed. Samuel Cole Williams (1775; New York: Promontory Press, 1930), 3–5 ("gluish" on 4).

12. Berkhofer, *White Man's Indian*, 55–66; Ann Fabian, *The Skull Collectors: Race, Science, and America's Unburied Dead* (Chicago: University of Chicago Press, 2010); Robert E. Bieder, *Science Encounters the Indian, 1820–1880: The Early Years of American Ethnology* (Norman: University of Oklahoma Press, 1986), 55–103; Stephen Jay Gould, *The Mismeasure of Man*, rev. ed. (New York: W. W. Norton, 1996), 62–141; Nell Irvin Painter, *The History of White People* (New York: W. W. Norton, 2010), 191–94; Reginald Horsman, *Race and Manifest Destiny: The Origins of American Racial Anglo-Saxonism* (Cambridge, MA: Harvard University Press, 1981), 145; Claudio Saunt, *Black, White, and Indian: Race and the Unmaking of an American Family* (New York: Oxford University Press, 2005), 56–58.

13. David J. Silverman, *Red Brethren: The Brothertown and Stockbridge Indians and the Problem of Race in Early America* (Ithaca, NY: Cornell University Press, 2010); Jill Lepore, *The Name of War: King Philip's War and the Origins of American*

Identity (New York: Alfred A. Knopf, 1998), 191–226; Daniel R. Mandell, *Tribe, Race, History: Native Americans in Southern New England, 1780–1880* (Baltimore: Johns Hopkins University Press, 2008); Silverman, *This Land Is Their Land: The Wampanoag Indians, Plymouth Colony, and the Troubled History of Thanksgiving* (New York: Bloomsbury, 2019), 355–418.

14. William G. McLoughlin, *Cherokees and Missionaries, 1789–1839* (New Haven, CT: Yale University Press, 1984), 14; Joel W. Martin, *Sacred Revolt: The Muskogees' Struggle for a New World* (Boston: Beacon Press, 1991), 87–93, 96–97, 108–10; Lori J. Daggar, *Cultivating Empire: Capitalism, Empire, and the Negotiation of American Imperialism in Indian Country* (Philadelphia: University of Pennsylvania Press, 2022); David Swatzler, *A Friend Among the Senecas: The Quaker Mission to Cornplanter's People* (Mechanicsburg, PA: Stackpole, 2000); Matthew Dennis, *Seneca Possessed: Indians, Witchcraft, and Power in the Early American Republic* (Philadelphia: University of Pennsylvania Press, 2010); Gregory Evans Dowd, *A Spirited Resistance: The North American Indian Struggle for Unity, 1745–1815* (Baltimore: Johns Hopkins University Press, 1992), 134–35; Sami Lakomäki, *Gathering Together: The Shawnee People Through Diaspora and Nationhood, 1600–1870* (New Haven, CT: Yale University Press, 2014), 155–60; James Taylor Carson, *Searching for the Bright Path: The Mississippi Choctaws from Prehistory to Removal* (Lincoln: University of Nebraska Press, 1999), 107; Arrell M. Gibson, *The Chickasaws* (Norman: University of Oklahoma Press, 1971), 108–21; Francis Paul Prucha, *The Great Father: The United States Government and the American Indians*, 2 vols. (Lincoln: University of Nebraska Press, 1984), 164.

15. Carson, *Searching for the Bright Path*, 71 ("cannot expect").

16. McLoughlin, *Cherokees and Missionaries*, 140 ("business").

17. McLoughlin, *Cherokees and Missionaries*, 125; Alexandra Harmon, *Rich Indians: Native People and the Problem of Wealth in American History* (Chapel Hill: University of North Carolina Press, 2010), 98; Carson, *Searching for the Bright Path*, 74, 84 ("not inferior"); Gibson, *Chickasaws*, 122, 131; Anthony F. C. Wallace, *The Long, Bitter Trail: Andrew Jackson and the Indians* (New York: Hill and Wang, 1993), 61; Martin, *Sacred Revolt*, 103, 106; Michael D. Green, *The Politics of Indian Removal: Creek Government and Society in Crisis* (Lincoln: University of Nebraska Press, 1982), 78; Dennis, *Seneca Possessed*, 148–78; Lakomäki, *Gathering Together*, 152–64; Susan Sleeper-Smith, *Indian Women and French Men: Rethinking Cultural Encounter in the Western Great Lakes* (Amherst: University of Massachusetts Press, 2001), 96–140.

18. William G. McLoughlin, *Cherokee Renascence in the New Republic* (Princeton, NJ: Princeton University Press, 1986), 65 ("painful"), 173, 329; McLoughlin, *Cherokees*

and Missionaries, 125; Wallace, *Long, Bitter Trail*, 61; Theda Perdue, *Slavery and the Evolution of Cherokee Society, 1540–1866* (Knoxville: University of Tennessee Press, 1979), 52–53; Theda Perdue, *Cherokee Women: Gender and Culture Change, 1700–1835* (Lincoln: University of Nebraska Press, 1998), 121–22, 161.

19. McLoughlin, *Cherokees and Missionaries*, 114 ("object"), 129, 134–37, 155, 337; Henry Thompson Malone, "The Early Nineteenth Century Missionaries in Cherokee Country," *Tennessee Historical Quarterly* 10, no. 2 (June 1951): 138; Joel W. Martin, "Cultural Contact and Crises," in *Native Americans and the Early Republic*, Hoxie et al., 234–35; Carson, *Searching for the Bright Path*, 83–85, 104–11; J. Leitch Wright Jr., *Creeks and Seminoles* (Lincoln: University of Nebraska Press, 1986), 222–27; Sleeper-Smith, *Indian Women and French Men*, 100–115.

20. *Cherokee Phoenix* 2, no. 3, Apr. 1, 1829, p. 2, col. 1; Ellen Cushman, *The Cherokee Syllabary: Writing the People's Perseverance* (Norman: University of Oklahoma Press, 2011); McLoughlin, *Cherokee Renascence*, 350–65; Sean P. Harvey, *Native Tongues: Colonialism and Race from Encounter to Reservation* (Cambridge, MA: Harvard University Press, 2015), 123–33; Phillip H. Round, *Removable Type: Histories of the Book in Indian Country, 1663–1880* (Chapel Hill: University of North Carolina Press, 2010), 123–49.

21. Perdue, *Slavery and the Evolution of Cherokee Society*, 60; Tiya Miles, *Ties That Bind: The Story of an Afro-Cherokee Family in Slavery and Freedom* (Berkeley: University of California Press, 2005), 124; McLoughlin, *Cherokee Renascence*, 71, 300 ("slaves"); Theda Perdue, *"Mixed Blood" Indians: Racial Construction in the Early South* (Athens: University of Georgia Press, 2003), 65; Gary Zellar, *African Creeks: Estelvste and the Creek Nation* (Norman: University of Oklahoma Press, 2007), 25; "Parsons and Abbott Role—1832 Creek Census," *Native Heritage Project*, native heritageproject.com/2014/07/14/parsons-and-abbott-roll-1832-creek-census (last accessed July 6, 2022); Carson, *Searching for the Bright Path*, 80; Gibson, *Chickasaws*, 163; Saunt, *Black, White, and Indian*, 68–69; Claudio Saunt, "Taking Account of Property: Social Stratification Among the Creek Indians in the Early Nineteenth Century," *WMQ* 57, no. 4 (Oct. 2000): 733–60; *The Collected Works of Benjamin Hawkins, 1796–1810*, ed. H. Thomas Foster II (Tuscaloosa: University of Alabama Press, 2003), 3j ("little farms").

22. Perdue, *Slavery and the Evolution of Cherokee Society*, 56–58; Perdue, *Cherokee Women*, 126, 145, 150–51; Perdue, *"Mixed Blood" Indians*, 65–66; Gibson, *Chickasaws*, 65–66, 134, 149, 206; Carson, *Searching for the Bright Path*, 99, 129; Greg O'Brien, *Choctaws in a Revolutionary Age, 1750–1830* (Lincoln: University of Nebraska Press, 2002),

109–12; Robbie Ethridge, *Creek Country: The Creek Indians and Their World* (Chapel Hill: University of North Carolina Press, 2003), 107, 232; McLoughlin, *Cherokees and Missionaries*, 215–20; Miles, *Ties That Bind*, 71–76, 107–8, 112–13; Fay Yarbrough, *Race and the Cherokee Nation: Sovereignty in the Nineteenth Century* (Philadelphia: University of Pennsylvania Press, 2008), 10–11, 26, 42–43; Kathryn E. Holland Braund, "The Creek Indians, Blacks, and Slavery," *Journal of Southern History* 57, no. 4 (Nov. 1991): 615–16, 624, 625 ("idle"), 629; Saunt, *Black, White, and Indian*, 23–24, 33 ("disgrace").

23. Kenneth W. Porter, *The Black Seminoles: History of a Freedom-Loving People*, rev. ed., ed. Alcione M. Amos and Thomas P. Senter (Gainesville: University Press of Florida, 1996); Kevin Mulroy, "Seminole Maroons," *Smithsonian Handbook of North American Indians*, vol. 14, *Southeast*, vol. ed. Raymond D. Fogelson, gen. ed. William C. Sturtevant (Washington, D.C.: Smithsonian Institution Press, 2004), 465–66; Daniel F. Littlefield Jr., *Africans and Seminoles: From Removal to Emancipation* (Westport, CT: Greenwood Press, 1977); Nathaniel Millett, *The Maroons of Prospect Bluff and Their Quest for Freedom in the Atlantic World* (Gainesville: University Press of Florida, 2013).

24. *ASP, Indian Affairs*, 2:200 ("waste"), 447 ("Indian tribes"); *Collected Works of Benjamin Hawkins*, 1:492 ("extirpation").

25. Timothy Dwight, *Travels in New England and New York*, 4 vols. (New Haven, CT: Timothy Dwight, 1822), 3:28 ("vegetable"); Dippie, *Vanishing American*, 10 ("great mass"), 30 ("Leave him"); Memorial of the subscribers inhabitants of the counties of Oneida and Madison, Dec. 20, 1820, New York Assembly Papers, Rec. Ser. A1823-78, Box 6, Folder 37, New York State Archives, Albany ("fact").

26. Mandell, *Tribe, Race, History*; Colin G. Calloway, *The Western Abenakis of Vermont, 1600–1800: War, Migration, and the Survival of an Indian People* (Norman: University of Oklahoma Press, 1990); John A. Strong, *The Montaukett Indians of Eastern Long Island* (Syracuse, NY: Syracuse University Press, 2001); Strong, *The Unkechaug Indians of Eastern Long Island: A History* (Norman: University of Oklahoma Press, 2011); Dawn G. Marsh, *A Lenape Among the Quakers: The Life of Hannah Freeman* (Lincoln: University of Nebraska Press, 2014); C. A. Weslager, *The Delaware Indians: A History* (New Brunswick, NJ: Rutgers University Press, 1972); Weslager, *The Nanticoke Indians: Past and Present* (Newark: University of Delaware Press, 1983); Helen C. Rountree, *Pocahontas's People: The Powhatan Indians of Virginia Through Four Centuries* (Norman: University of Oklahoma Press, 1990); Rountree and Thomas E. Davidson, *Eastern Shore Indians of Virginia*

and Maryland (Charlottesville: University of Virginia Press, 1997); Malinda Maynor Lowery, *The Lumbee Indians: An American Struggle* (Chapel Hill: University of North Carolina Press, 2018); Laurence M. Hauptman, *Conspiracy of Interests: Iroquois Dispossession and the Rise of New York State* (Syracuse, NY: Syracuse University Press, 1999), 18 ("minister"); Prucha, *Great Father*, 245.

27. Anthony F. C. Wallace, *Jefferson and the Indians: The Tragic Fate of the First Americans* (Cambridge, MA: Harvard University Press, 1999), 224–26, 254, 258–59, 273–75; McLoughlin, *Cherokee Renascence*, 128–67; Dowd, *Spirited Resistance*, 163–66.

28. McLoughlin, *Cherokee Renascence*, 151–55 ("intruders" on 154), 170.

29. McLoughlin, *Cherokees and Missionaries*, 120–21, 272; McLoughlin, "Experiment in Cherokee Citizenship, 1817–1829," *American Quarterly* 33, no. 1 (Spring 1981): 3–25.

30. *ASP, Indian Affairs*, 2:236–40, 709; Donna Akers, *Living in the Land of Death: The Choctaw Nation, 1830–1860* (East Lansing: Michigan State University Press, 2004), 36–37; Carson, *Searching for the Bright Path*, 90, 97–98; Gibson, *Chickasaws*, 146–49, 149–51; Prucha, *Great Father*, 188–89.

31. *Cherokee Phoenix* 1, no. 2, Feb. 28, 1828, p. 2, col. 2 ("peaceably"); Green, *Politics of Indian Removal*, 69–125; Haveman, *Rivers of Sand*, 11–41.

32. Andrew K. Frank, *Creeks and Southerners: Biculturalism on the Early American Frontier* (Lincoln: University of Nebraska Press, 2005), 96–113; Christopher D. Haveman, *Bending Their Way Onward: Creek Indian Removal in Documents* (Lincoln: University of Nebraska Press, 2018), 7; Haveman, *Rivers of Sand*, 11–42, 44; Green, *Politics of Indian Removal*, 69–97; Theda Perdue, ed., *The Cherokee Removal: A Brief History with Documents*, 3rd ed. (Boston: Macmillan, 2016), 125 ("highly oppressive"), 126–27 ("immemorial"); Perdue, *Cherokee Women*, 156; Tiya Miles, "'Circular Reasoning': Recentering Cherokee Women in the Antiremoval Campaigns," *American Quarterly* 61, no. 2 (June 2009): 226.

33. Adam Rothman, *Slave Country: American Slavery and the Origins of the Deep South* (Cambridge, MA: Harvard University Press, 2005), 3–4, 221; Edward E. Baptist, *The Half Has Never Been Told: Slavery and the Making of American Capitalism* (New York: Basic Books, 2014), 113–14; Susan B. Carter et al., eds., *Historical Statistics of the United States: Earliest Times to the Present* (New York: Cambridge University Press, 2006), Series A, 195-209, pp. 24, 30; *Report of a Committee, and Resolutions of the Legislature, of the State of Georgia, in Relation to Certain Lands Occupied by the Cherokee Indians, and Belonging to the Said State, January 28, 1828* (Washington, D.C., 1828), 12 ("tenants").

34. Lewis Cass, "Documents and Proceedings Relating to the Progress and Formation of a Board in the City of New York, for the Emigration, Preservation, and Improvement of the Aborigines of America, July 22, 1829," *North American Review* 31 (1830): 64 ("barbarous"); *ASP, Indian Affairs*, 2:476 ("no alternative"); *Circular Letters of Congressmen to Their Constituents, 1789–1829*, 3 vols., ed. Noble E. Cunningham Jr. (Chapel Hill: University of North Carolina Press, 1978), 1327 ("surrounded").

35. *ASP, Indian Affairs*, 2:475–76 ("scheme"). On such debates see Alexander Keyssar, *The Right to Vote: The Contested History of Democracy in the United States* (New York: Basic Books, 2000), 59; and Deborah A. Rosen, *American Indians and State Law: Sovereignty, Race, and Citizenship, 1790–1880* (Lincoln: University of Nebraska Press, 2007), 117.

36. John Demos, *The Heathen School: A Story of Hope and Betrayal in the Age of the Early Republic* (New York: Alfred A. Knopf, 2014), 153–56 ("nursing mothers" on 154), 161, 181–82.

37. James Sidbury, *Becoming African in America: Race and Nation in the Early Black Atlantic* (New York: Oxford University Press, 2009); Nicholas Guyatt, *Bind Us Apart: How Enlightened Americans Invented Racial Segregation* (Boston: Basic Books, 2016); Samantha Seeley, *Race, Removal, and the Right to Remain: Migration and the Making of the United States* (Chapel Hill: University of North Carolina Press for the Omohundro Institute of Early American History and Culture, 2021).

38. Green, *Politics of Indian Removal*, 48.

39. Perdue, *Cherokee Removal*, 60; McLoughlin, *Cherokee Renascence*, 404.

40. Prucha, *Great Father*, 190 ("good fortune").

41. McLoughlin, *Cherokees and Missionaries*, 247.

42. Mary E. Young, *Redskins, Ruffleshirts, and Rednecks: Indian Allotments in Alabama and Mississippi, 1830–1860* (Norman: University of Oklahoma Press, 1961), 14–17, 38–39; Saunt, *Unworthy Republic*, 37–41, 85, 93–97; Carson, *Searching for the Bright Path*, 115; Gibson, *Chickasaws*, 155, 158; Arthur H. DeRosier Jr., *The Removal of the Choctaw Indians* (Knoxville: University of Tennessee Press, 1970), 100–106.

43. McLoughlin, *Cherokees and Missionaries*, 246–47; Wallace, *Long, Bitter Trail*, 75; Amanda L. Paige, Fuller L. Bumpers, and Daniel F. Littlefield Jr., *Chickasaw Removal* (Ada, OK: Chickasaw Press, 2010), 13; *TPUS*, 21:431, 432; Walter R. Echo-Hawk, *In*

the Courts of the Conqueror: The 10 Worst Indian Law Cases Ever Decided (Golden, CO: Fulcrum, 2010), 87; Snyder, Great Crossings, 127 ("exterminate").

44. *Cherokee Phoenix* 3, no. 14, July 24, 1830, p. 2, col. 3a, and p. 3, col. 3a ("If we are"); Lindsay G. Robertson, *How the Discovery of America Dispossessed Indigenous Peoples of Their Lands* (New York: Oxford University Press, 2005); Robert J. Miller, *Native America, Discovered and Conquered: Thomas Jefferson, Lewis and Clark, and Manifest Destiny* (New York: Praeger, 2006); Echo-Hawk, *Courts of the Conqueror*, 55–122; Stuart Banner, *How the Indians Lost Their Land: Law and Power on the Frontier* (Cambridge, MA: Harvard University Press, 2005), 178–227; *Johnson v. McIntosh*, 21 U.S. (8 Wheat.) 543 (1823), pp. 567 ("civilized"), 569 ("inhabitants"), 573 ("character"), 574 ("occupants"), 588 ("conquest"), 590 ("fierce").

45. Echo-Hawk, *Courts of the Conqueror*, 99; *Cherokee Nation v. Georgia*, 30 U.S. (5 Pet.) 1 (1831).

46. *Worcester v. Georgia*, 31 U.S. (6 Pet.) 515 (1832) ("distinct"); Haveman, *Rivers of Sand*, 179.

47. *Cherokee Phoenix* 1, no. 46, Jan. 28, 1829, p. 1, col. 4, and p. 2, col. 5 ("did not exist"); *Cherokee Phoenix* 2, no. 51, Apr. 14, 1830, p. 3, cols. 2–3 ("would murder"); *Cherokee Phoenix* 2, no. 23, Sept. 9, 1829, p. 2, col. 5; *The Papers of Chief John Ross*, ed. Gary E. Moulton, 2 vols. (Norman: University of Oklahoma Press, 1985), 262.

48. *Cherokee Phoenix* 2, no. 13, July 1, 1829, p. 2, col. 4 ("public opinion"); *Cherokee Phoenix* 2, no. 36, Dec. 16, 1829, p. 2, col. 4 ("plain").

49. *ASP, Indian Affairs*, 2:759 ("country"); *Ross Papers*, 66 ("foreigners"); *ASP, Indian Affairs*, 2:474; Perdue, *Cherokee Women*, 156 ("land was given"); *Cherokee Phoenix* 1, no. 41, Dec. 10, 1828, p. 2, col. 2 ("claims"), *Cherokee Phoenix* 2, no. 11, June 17, 1829, p. 1, col. 2 ("inherited").

50. *Cherokee Phoenix*, vol. 1, no. 42, Dec. 29, 1828, p. 2, col. 2 ("improvement!"), and vol. 5, no. 38, Feb. 8, 1834 , p. 3, col. 4 ("intelligence," rob"); *ASP, Indian Affairs*, 2:722 ("industry"). On other civilizing communities, see *Cherokee Phoenix*: vol. 1, no. 51, Mar. 4, 1828, p. 1, col. 3; vol. 1, no. 6, Mar. 27, 1828, p. 2, col. 2; vol. 1, no. 9, Apr. 17, 1828, p. 3, cols. 3–4; vol. 1, no. 16, June 11, 1828, p. 2, col. 4, and p. 4, col. 3; vol. 1, no. 24, Aug. 13, 1828, p. 3, col. 2; vol. 1, no. 31, Oct. 1, 1828, p. 2, col. 5; vol. 1, no. 33, Oct. 15, 1828, p. 1, col. 5, and p. 2, col. 1; vol. 3, no. 4, May 16, 1830, p. 1, cols. 2–3; vol. 3, no. 52, June 11, 1831, p. 3, cols. 4–5; vol. 4, no. 1, June 25, 1831, p. 2, cols. 1–2.

51. Colin G. Calloway, *First Peoples: A Documentary Survey of American Indian History*, 6th ed. (Boston: Macmillan, 2019), 261 ("improvement"); *ASP, Indian Affairs*, 2:776 ("day would arrive"); *Ross Papers*, 105; *Cherokee Editor: The Writings of Elias Boudinot*, ed. Theda Perdue (Athens: University of Georgia Press, 1996), 69 ("Do what you will"); *Cherokee Phoenix* 1, no. 12, May 14, 1828, p. 2, col. 2; *Cherokee Phoenix* 2, no. 51, Apr. 14, 1830, p. 1, col. 4; *Cherokee Phoenix* 4, no. 18, Nov. 12, 1831, p. 2, col. 2 ("desire").

52. Snyder, *Great Crossings*, 131 ("never saw"); *TPUS*, 19:75; McLoughlin, *Cherokees and Missionaries*, 240–41; *Ross Papers*, 286–87; Silverman, *Red Brethren*; Weslager, *Delaware Indians*; Perdue, *Cherokee Removal*, 147–48 ("a State"); Council with the Oneidas, Letters Received from the Office of Indian Affairs, Green Bay Agency, reel 316, frames 430–32, National Archives, Washington, D.C. ("wherever"); *Cherokee Phoenix* 4, no. 47, June 23, 1832, p. 2, col. 4 ("no resting").

53. Harmon, *Rich Indians*, 124 ("not Indians"), 125; Perdue, *"Mixed Blood" Indians*, 70–103.

54. *ASP, Indian Affairs*, 1:600 ("our blood"); Green, *Politics of Indian Removal*, 70–71; McLoughlin, *Cherokee Renascence*, 141; Perdue, *Cherokee Women*, 147–51; Circe Sturm, *Blood Politics: Race, Culture, and Identity in the Cherokee Nation of Oklahoma* (Berkeley: University of California Press, 2002); Miles, *Ties That Bind*; Saunt, *Black, White, and Indian*.

55. *Cherokee Phoenix Extra*, Jan. 1, 1830, p. 1, cols. 2–3.

56. Mary Hershberger, "Mobilizing Women, Anticipating Abolition: The Struggle Against Indian Removal in the 1830s," *Journal of American History* 86, no. 1 (June 1999): 15–40; Perdue, *Cherokee Removal*, 109 ("helpless"); Constance Owl, "*Tsalagi Tsulehisanvhi*: Uncovering Cherokee Language Articles from the *Cherokee Phoenix* Newspaper, 1828–1834" (master's thesis, Western Carolina University, 2020), 59 ("obligations").

57. Hershberger, "Mobilizing Women," 20 ("white people"); Miles, "'Circular Reasoning,'" 228; Haveman, *Rivers of Sand*, 134; *Cherokee Phoenix* 3, no. 14, July 24, 1830, p. 2, col. 1 ("not a man"); and *Cherokee Phoenix* 4, no. 3, July 9, 1831, p. 2, col. 4 ("cruel").

58. Saunt, *Unworthy Republic*, 145 ("extermination"); Patrick J. Jung, *The Black Hawk War of 1832* (Norman: University of Oklahoma Press, 2002).

59. C. S. Monaco, *The Second Seminole War and the Limits of American Aggression* (Baltimore: Johns Hopkins University Press, 2018); John Missall and Mary Lou Missall, *The Seminole Wars: America's Longest Indian Conflict* (Gainesville: University Press of Florida, 2004), 160; George R. Adams, "The Caloosahatchee Massacre: Its Significance in the Second Seminole War," *Florida Historical Quarterly* 48, no. 4 (Apr. 1970): 368–80.

60. Carter et al., *Historical Statistics of the United States*, Series Ea, 584-587, pp. 5–80; Saunt, *Unworthy Republic*, 298–99.

61. John T. Ellisor, *The Second Creek War: Interethnic Conflict and Collusion on a Collapsing Frontier* (Lincoln: University of Nebraska Press, 2010); Haveman, *Rivers of Sand*, 94–101, 106–9, 148, 176–77, 180–99, 233 ("cross the great river"); Saunt, *Unworthy Republic*, 202, 250 ("whip"), 252–53 ("wild beasts"); Saunt, *Black, White, and Indian*, 50–52 ("kill all"); Wallace, *Long, Bitter Trail*, 86–87 ("destitution"); Jefferson Cowie, *Freedom's Dominion: A Saga of White Resistance to Federal Power* (New York: Basic Books, 2022), 52, 81–93; Ostler, *Surviving Genocide*, 260.

62. Carson, *Searching for the Bright Path*, 124 ("designing"); Saunt, *Unworthy Republic*, 125–26, 202–8; Snyder, *Great Crossings*, 143–44 ("stealing"); Mikaëla M. Adams, *Who Belongs?: Race, Resources, and Tribal Citizenship in the Native South* (New York: Oxford University Press, 2016), 96–131.

63. *Memorial of the chiefs and sachems of the "Indian Party" of the Stockbridge Indians, praying for the repeal of the law of Congress for 1842 for their relief*, H.R. Doc. No. 128, 29th Cong., 1st Sess. (1846); H.R. Repr. No. 447, 9th Cong., 1st Sess. (1846).

64. Silverman, *Red Brethren*, 184–210 ("Civilization" on 210).

65. McLoughlin, *Cherokees and Missionaries*, 305; *Cherokee Phoenix* 4, no. 7, Aug. 13, 1831, p. 3, col. 2 (noose); *Cherokee Phoenix* 4, no. 9, Aug. 27, 1831, p. 2, cols. 3–4 ("Would a white man"); *Cherokee Phoenix* 5, no. 41, Mar. 8, 1834, pp. 2–3; *Writings of Elias Boudinot*, 22–23; Saunt, *Unworthy Republic*, 29 ("whine"), 238.

66. *Writings of Elias Boudinot*, 176 ("cannot exist"); *Cherokee Phoenix* 4, no. 52, Aug. 11, 1832, p. 2, col. 1 ("countrymen"); Wallace, *Long, Bitter Trail*, 93.

67. Perdue, *Cherokee Removal*, 155 ("plunderers").

68. Ostler, *Surviving Genocide*, 256, 260, 263, 274, 361.

69. Ostler, *Surviving Genocide*, 348–52; Saunt, *Black, White, and Indian*, 66; Haveman, *Rivers of Sand*, 133, 149–74, 186, 241; David La Vere, *Contrary Neighbors: Southern*

Plains and Removed Indians in Indian Territory (Norman: University of Oklahoma Press, 2000).

70. Ostler, *Surviving Genocide*, 292.

71. Saunt, *Unworthy Republic*, 308–15.

72. Saunt, *Unworthy Republic*, 315.

73. Volker Depkat, *American Exceptionalism* (Lanham, MD: Rowman and Littlefield, 2021); Ian Tyrrell, *American Exceptionalism: A New History of an Old Idea* (Chicago: University of Chicago Press, 2022); Reginald Horsman, *Race and Manifest Destiny: The Origins of American Racial Anglo-Saxonism* (Cambridge, MA: Harvard University Press, 1981).

74. *Writings of William Apess*, 31.

75. Andrew Jackson, First Annual Message to Congress, Dec. 8, 1829, millercenter .org/the-presidency/presidential-speeches/december-8-1829-first-annual-message -congress (last accessed July 14, 2022).

76. *Writings of William Apess*, 118 ("every white man"), 168 ("bred").

77. *Writings of William Apess*, 157 ("which skin").

CHAPTER 5: "EXTERMINATE THEM!"

1. Robert M. Utley, *The Indian Frontier of the American West, 1846–1890* (Albuquerque: University of New Mexico Press, 1984), 102.

2. *ARCIA* (1864), 255.

3. Elliott West, *The Contested Plains: Indians, Goldseekers, and the Rush to Colorado* (Lawrence: University Press of Kansas, 1998), 75–76; Roger L. Nichols, *Massacring Indians: From Horseshoe Bend to Wounded Knee* (Norman: University of Oklahoma Press, 2021), 71 ("smoldering"). On the Dog Soldiers, see West, *Contested Plains*, 197–200; George Bird Grinnell, *The Fighting Cheyennes* (1915; Norman: University of Oklahoma Press, 1955); Jean Afton et al., *Cheyenne Dog Soldiers: A Ledgerbook History of Coups and Combat* (Denver: Colorado Historical Society, 1997).

4. West, *Contested Plains*, 295.

5. West, *Contested Plains*, 301 ("Damn"); John M. Coward, *The Newspaper Indian: Native American Identity in the Press, 1820–1890* (Urbana: University of Illinois Press, 1999), 98 ("Now boys").

6. *Doolittle Report*, 13 ("depredations"), 30 ("pell-mell"); Ari Kelman, *A Misplaced Massacre: Struggling over the Memory of Sand Creek* (Cambridge, MA: Harvard University Press, 2013), 8–43.

7. Coward, *Newspaper Indian*, 110–12; *Doolittle Report*, 71 ("kill"); West, *Contested Plains*, 331; Kelman, *Misplaced Massacre*, 175–76.

8. West, *Contested Plains*, 308.

9. Nichols, *Massacring Indians*, 91.

10. George A. Custer, "Battling with the Sioux on the Yellowstone," *Galaxy* 22, no. 1 (July 1876), reprinted in *Eyewitnesses to the Indian Wars*, 4:104–14. "Redskins" appears throughout.

11. David Treuer, *The Heartbeat of Wounded Knee: Native America from 1890 to the Present* (New York: Riverhead Books, 2019), 19–98.

12. Among many works, see Elliott West, *Continental Reckoning: The American West in the Age of Expansion* (Lincoln: University of Nebraska Press, 2023); Paul Frymer, *Building an American Empire: The Era of Territorial and Political Expansion* (Princeton, NJ: Princeton University Press, 2017); Richard White, *It's Your Misfortune and None of My Own: A History of the American West* (Norman: University of Oklahoma Press, 1991); Reginald Horsman, *Race and Manifest Destiny: The Origins of American Anglo-Saxonism* (Cambridge, MA: Harvard University Press, 1981); and Frederick Merk and Lois Bannister Merk, *Manifest Destiny and Mission in American History: An Interpretation* (New York: Alfred A. Knopf, 1963).

13. *ARCIA* (1852), 3 ("civilization"), (1859), 130–31 ("beyond"), (1867), 336 ("cannot be"); Francis Paul Prucha, *The Great Father: The United States Government and the American Indians*, 2 vols. (Lincoln: University of Nebraska Press, 1984), 324; *Eyewitnesses to the Indian Wars*, 5:127. Generally, see Merk and Merk, *Manifest Destiny and Mission in American History*; Horsman, *Race and Manifest Destiny*; Brian W. Dippie, *The Vanishing American: White Attitudes and U.S. Indian Policy* (Middletown, CT: Wesleyan University Press, 1982); Walter L. Hixson, *American Settler Colonialism: A History* (New York: Palgrave Macmillan, 2013), esp. 11 and 22; and Donald Yacovone, *Teaching White Supremacy: America's Democratic Ordeal and the Forging of Our National Identity* (New York: Pantheon Books, 2022), esp. xiv, 96, 118, 251.

14. Fergus M. Bordewich, *Killing the White Man's Indian: Reinventing Native Americans at the End of the Twentieth Century* (New York: Doubleday, 1996), 49 ("very lowest"); *ARCIA* (1846), 102–3 ("must seek"), (1869), 185 ("first").

15. *ARCIA* (1850), 78, (1851), 149 ("apathy"), (1852), 154, (1855), 65 ("brute"), (1856), 22–23, 35, 110, (1859), 56, (1866), 173 ("monstrous").

16. Colin G. Calloway, *Pen and Ink Witchcraft: Treaties and Treaty Making in American Indian History* (New York: Oxford University Press, 2013), 176.

17. Craig H. Miner and William E. Unrau, *The End of Indian Kansas: A Study of Cultural Revolution, 1854–1871* (Lawrence: University Press of Kansas, 1978), 16–17 ("slow"), 25–26, 60, 115; Brothertown Indian Collection, Box 50, Folder 2, pp. 32–34, New England Historic and Genealogical Society, Boston; *ARCIA* (1857), 4 ("impossible"), 161, 166, 221–22, (1861), 56.

18. *ARCIA* (1866), 15.

19. *ARCIA* (1853), 32 ("vivid"), (1854), 10; Gov. R. J. Walker's Inaugural Address, kshs.org/km/items/view/3800 ("extinguishment") (last accessed Nov. 1, 2024); John P. Bowes, *Exiles and Pioneers: Eastern Indians in the Trans-Mississippi West* (New York: Cambridge University Press, 2007), 192.

20. Gary Clayton Anderson, *The Conquest of Texas: Ethnic Cleansing in the Promised Land* (Norman: University of Oklahoma Press, 2005), 25–57 ("Indian hunting" and "chasing squaws" on 54), 66–68, 100–101, 157–58, 179, 215.

21. Anderson, *Conquest of Texas*, 10–11, 127, 128, 159–60, 173, 174 ("exterminating war"), 180 ("proper"), 188–90 ("humanity" on 190), 194.

22. *ARCIA* (1847–48), 184–85, (1859), 237; *The White Man* 2, no. 17 (Nov. 14, 1861): esp. p. 2, col. 6; Anderson, *Conquest of Texas*, 236–37, 312, 316.

23. Anderson, *Conquest of Texas*, 228, 234, 317, 319 ("morally right"); *ARCIA* (1859), 237 ("frontier defense"), 318 ("mothers"); "Neighbors, Robert Simpson," Texas State Historical Association, Aug. 24, 2023, tshaonline.org/handbook/entries/neighbors-robert-simpson (last accessed Nov. 1, 2024); "Edward Cornett," Find a Grave, findagrave.com/memorial/48273796/edward-cornett (last accessed Nov. 1, 2024).

24. *ARCIA* (1858), 132 ("wild"), (1859), 19, 227, 237 ("no longer safe"), 247, 251–52; Anderson, *Conquest of Texas*, 317, 319, 326; Utley, *Indian Frontier*, 174–78; Jonathan B. Hook, *The Alabama-Coushatta Indians* (College Station: Texas A&M University Press, 1997).

25. White, *Your Misfortune*, 191; "Oregon. Chapter 1.—Number of Inhabitants," in *Thirteenth Census of the United States: Taken in the Year 1910*, vol. 3 (Washington, D.C.: United States Government Printing Office, 1913), www2.census.gov /prod2/decennial/documents/36894832v3ch4.pdf (last accessed Nov. 1, 2024); David J. Weber, *The Spanish Frontier in North America* (New Haven, CT: Yale University Press, 1992), 265; Steven W. Hackel, *Children of Coyote, Missionaries of St. Francis: Indian-Spanish Relations in Colonial California, 1769–1850* (Chapel Hill: University of North Carolina Press for the Omohundro Institute of Early American History and Culture, 2005); James R. Gibson, *Otter Skins, Boston Ships, and China Goods: The Maritime Fur Trade of the Northwest Coast, 1785–1841* (Seattle: University of Washington Press, 1992); Mary Malloy, *"Boston Men" on the Northwest Coast: The American Maritime Fur Trade, 1788–1844* (Fairbanks, AK: Limestone Press, 1998); James P. Rhonda, *Astoria and Empire* (Lincoln: University of Nebraska Press, 1990).

26. Andrew C. Isenberg, *Mining California: An Ecological History* (New York: Hill and Wang, 2005), esp. 23–51; Albert L. Hurtado, "California Indian Demography, Sherburne F. Cook, and the Revision of American History," *Pacific Historical Review* 58, no. 3 (Aug. 1989): 323–43.

27. Brendan C. Lindsay, *Murder State: California's Native American Genocide, 1846–1873* (Lincoln: University of Nebraska Press, 2012), 70–109, 121; West, *Continental Reckoning*, 13; *ARCIA* (1859), 3 ("atrocious"), (1865), 198; Stuart Banner, *Possessing the Pacific: Land, Settlers, and Indigenous People from Australia to Alaska* (Cambridge, MA: Harvard University Press, 2007), 165 ("lowest"); James J. Rawls, "The Digger Indian Stereotype in California," *Journal of California and Great Basin Anthropology* 3, no. 2 (Winter 1981): 215–23.

28. *ARCIA* (1850), 92 ("shoot"), (1851), 225 ("border"), 234 ("reckless"); Benjamin Madley, "California's Yuki Indians: Defining Genocide in Native American History," *Western Historical Quarterly* 39, no. 3 (Autumn 2008): 317 ("killing," "fifty").

29. Madley, "California's Yuki Indians," 313, 314 ("few children"); Robert F. Heizer, ed., *They Were Only Diggers: A Collection of Articles from California Newspapers, 1851–1866, on Indian and White Relations* (Ramona, CA: Ballena Press, 1974), 1 (Humboldt), 2, 81–82, 85 ("notorious"); *ARCIA* (1861), 149–50, 315, (1867), 117; Albert L. Hurtado, *Indian Survival on the California Frontier* (New Haven, CT: Yale University Press, 1988), 169–92; West, *Continental Reckoning*, 47.

30. Peter Burnett, Inaugural Address, governors.library.ca.gov/addresses/01-Burnett.html (last accessed Nov. 1, 2024); Benjamin Madley, *An American Genocide: The United States and the California Indian Catastrophe, 1846–1873* (New Haven, CT: Yale University Press, 2016), 218, 225, 230, 238, 250, 253, 277, 280 ("However cruel").

31. Madley, *American Genocide*, 170–71 ("no right"), 212 ("fate"), 250–53, 285, 289, 320–21; Banner, *Possessing the Pacific*, 188; *ARCIA* (1862), 311 ("prevent").

32. Robert Aquinas McNally, *The Modoc War: A Story of Genocide at the Dawn of America's Gilded Age* (Lincoln: University of Nebraska Press, 2017), 127 ("Extermination"); Lindsay, *Murder State*, 67–68 ("nothing"), 210 ("prosecute"); Heizer, *They Were Only Diggers*, 48 ("boasted").

33. Lindsay, *Murder State*, 179 ("inoculate"), 199, 248, 320; Heizer, *They Were Only Diggers*, 3 ("use them"), 76; *ARCIA* (1861), 22, (1863), 95–96 ("tied"), (1868), 126, (1872), 375, 376–77; Madley, *American Genocide*, 159 ("no case"), 160–61; Kevin Adams and Khal Schneider, "'Washington Is a Long Way Off': The 'Round Valley War' and the Limits of Federal Power on a California Indian Reservation," *Pacific Historical Review* 80, no. 4 (Nov. 2011): 563 ("wonder").

34. Heizer, *They Were Only Diggers*, 37 ("for fun"); *ARCIA* (1850), 92.

35. Madley, *American Genocide*, 3, 12; *ARCIA* (1864), 161.

36. *ARCIA* (1851), 248 ("little confidence"), (1873), 31 ("remain"); Madley, *American Genocide*, 221 ("lived here").

37. Banner, *Possessing the Pacific*, 242, 249; *ARCIA* (1851), 205 ("fathers"); Gray H. Whaley, "American Folk Imperialism and Native Genocide in Southwest Oregon, 1851–1859," in *Colonial Genocide in Indigenous North America*, ed. Andrew Woolford et al. (Durham, NC: Duke University Press, 2014), 134 ("Exterminators"), 135–36 ("Extermination").

38. *ARCIA* (1854), 15 ("barbarous"), 254–68 ("reckless" and "no act" on 267; "kill all" on 268); Utley, *Indian Frontier*, 53.

39. *ARCIA* (1856), 195 ("without discipline"), 200 ("determination"), (1857), 316 ("impression"); West, *Continental Reckoning*, 64. Alexandra Harmon's *Indians in the Making: Ethnic Relations and Indian Identities Around Puget Sound* (Berkeley: University of California Press, 1998), 86–94, stresses that many Indians and mixed Indian-White couples tried to remain neutral during the war.

40. McNally, *Modoc War*, 39–40, 100; Madley, *American Genocide*, 337; Utley, *Indian Frontier*, 172.

41. *Eyewitnesses to the Indian Wars*, 2:192 ("same law"), 219 ("if you do not"); McNally, *Modoc War*, 185 ("Who will").

42. McNally, *Modoc War*, 220 ("regard"), 284–355.

43. West, *Contested Plains*, xv, 147 ("shiftless"); White, *Your Misfortune*, 189, 192; Utley, *Indian Frontier*, 72; Pekka Hämäläinen, *The Comanche Empire* (New Haven, CT: Yale University Press, 2008), 179, 339–40; David J. Silverman, *Thundersticks: Firearms and the Violent Transformation of Native America* (Cambridge, MA: Harvard University Press, 2016), 279; Richard White, "The Winning of the West: The Expansion of the Western Sioux in the Eighteenth and Nineteenth Centuries," *Journal of American History* 65, no. 2 (Sept. 1978): 330; Peter Iverson, *The Navajo Nation* (Westport, CT: Greenwood Press, 1981), 7.

44. Elizabeth A. Fenn, *Pox Americana: The Great Smallpox Epidemic of 1775–82* (New York: Hill and Wang, 2001); Elizabeth A. Fenn, *Encounters at the Heart of the World: A History of the Mandan People* (New York: Hill and Wang, 2014), esp. 311–26; Colin G. Calloway, *First Peoples: A Documentary History of American Indian History*, 6th ed. (Boston: Macmillan, 2019), 281.

45. Colin G. Calloway, ed., *Our Hearts Fell to the Ground: Plains Indian Views of How the West Was Lost*, 2nd ed. (Boston: Bedford Books, 2018), 64 ("Smallpox"); *ARCIA* (1853), 115 ("cannot"), (1857), 127 ("disease"), (1872), 271 ("healthy"); Jeffrey Ostler, *The Lakotas and the Black Hills: The Struggle for Sacred Ground* (New York: Penguin, 2010), 37; McNally, *Modoc War*, 35 ("Providence").

46. *Eyewitnesses to the Indian Wars*, 1:264 ("medicine"); Thomas Peotto, "Dark Mimesis: A Cultural History of the Scalping Paradigm" (PhD diss., University of British Columbia, 2018), 364 ("utter extermination").

47. Paul Conrad, *The Apache Diaspora: Four Centuries of Displacement and Survival* (Philadelphia: University of Pennsylvania Press, 2021), 189–90 ("war," "destiny"); Utley, *Indian Frontier*, 83–85; Peter Iverson, *Diné: A History of the Navajos* (Albuquerque: University of New Mexico Press, 2002), 48–64; Jennifer Denetdale, *The Long Walk: The Forced Navajo Exile* (New York: Chelsea House, 2007), 49–50.

48. Gary Clayton Anderson and Alan R. Woolworth, eds., *Through Dakota Eyes: Narrative Accounts of the Minnesota Indian War of 1862* (St. Paul: Minnesota Historical Society Press, 2008), 24 ("annihilation"); *ARCIA* (1860), 26, 45–46; Gary

Clayton Anderson, *Massacre in Minnesota: The Dakota War of 1862; The Most Violent Ethnic Conflict in American History* (Norman: University of Oklahoma Press, 2019), 79 ("eat grass").

49. Anderson and Woolworth, *Through Dakota Eyes*, 23 ("whites were always," "better"), 24 ("party," "abused"), 36 ("Kill").

50. Anderson, *Massacre in Minnesota*, 99, 107, 110, 160 ("WAR"), 162, 188 ("must be"), 189–211; Prucha, *Great Father*, 443 ("maniacs").

51. Anderson, *Massacre in Minnesota*, 228, 229–33, 234, 241–50 ("Panthers").

52. Treuer, *Heartbeat of Wounded Knee*, 93; Anderson, *Massacre in Minnesota*, 284.

53. Prucha, *Great Father*, 445–56 ("nature"); Anderson, *Massacre in Minnesota*, 279–80.

54. Nichols, *Massacring Indians*, 58, 61–62, 63–65; Brigham D. Madsen, *The Shoshoni Frontier and the Bear River Massacre* (Salt Lake City: University of Utah Press, 1985), 17, 23; *ARCIA* (1863), 419–20 ("combine").

55. Gregory E. Smoak, *Ghost Dances and Identity: Prophetic Religion and American Indian Ethnogenesis in the Nineteenth Century* (Berkeley: University of California Press, 2006), 93–94.

56. Circe Sturm, *Blood Politics: Race, Culture, and Identity in the Cherokee Nation of Oklahoma* (Berkeley: University of California Press, 2002), 68–72; David A. Chang, *The Color of the Land: Race, Nation, and the Politics of Landownership in Oklahoma, 1832–1929* (Chapel Hill: University of North Carolina Press, 2010), 32–33; Bordewich, *Killing the White Man's Indian* 55; Christina Snyder, *Great Crossings: Indians, Settlers, and Slaves in the Age of Jackson* (New York: Oxford University Press, 2017), 274; Susan A. Miller, *Coacoochee's Bones: A Seminole Saga* (Lawrence: University Press of Kansas, 2003), 73–198; Kevin Mulroy, *Freedom on the Border: The Seminole Maroons in Florida, the Indian Territory, Coahuila, and Texas* (Lubbock: Texas Tech University Press, 1993); David La Vere, *Contrary Neighbors: Southern Plains and Removed Indians in Indian Territory* (Norman: Oklahoma University Press, 2000), 114–17.

57. Tiya Miles, *Ties That Bind: The Story of an Afro-Cherokee Family in Slavery and Freedom* (Berkeley: University of California Press, 2005), 187 ("property"); Laurence M. Hauptman, *Between Two Fires: American Indians in the Civil War* (New York: Free Press, 1995), 41–61, esp. 42; Barbara Krauthamer, *Black Slaves, Indian Masters: Slavery, Emancipation, and Citizenship in the Native American*

South (Chapel Hill: University of North Carolina Press, 2013), 98–100; Claudio Saunt, *Black, White, and Indian: Race and the Unmaking of an American Family* (New York: Oxford University Press, 2005), 88–107; Fay Yarbrough, *Choctaw Confederates: The American Civil War in Indian Country* (Chapel Hill: University of North Carolina Press, 2021); Edwin C. McReynolds, *The Seminoles* (Norman: University of Oklahoma Press, 1957), 289–312; R. David Edmunds et al., *The People: A History of Native America* (Boston: Cengage, 2007), 272; Chang, *Color of the Land*, 36–37.

58. Kevin Mulroy, *The Seminole Freedmen: A History* (Norman: University of Oklahoma Press, 2007), 196 ("presented"); Hauptman, *Between Two Fires*, 59–61; Krauthamer, *Black Slaves, Indian Masters*, 101–18; Edmunds et al., *The People*, 272–76; Chang, *Color of the Land*, 39–40; Sturm, *Blood Politics*, 74; Daniel F. Littlefield Jr., *The Chickasaw Freedmen: A People Without a Country* (Westport, CT: Greenwood Press, 1980).

59. Prucha, *Great Father*, 317, 433, 439 ("in short"), 561 ("vexed"); Dan Flores, "Bison Ecology and Bison Diplomacy: The Southern Plains from 1800 to 1850," *Journal of American History* 78, no. 2 (Sept. 1991): 465–85; Andrew C. Isenberg, *The Destruction of the Buffalo: An Environmental History, 1750–1920* (New York: Cambridge University Press, 2000); *ARCIA* (1855), 11, (1863), 297.

60. Robert E. Bieder, *Science Encounters the Indian, 1820–1880: The Early Years of American Ethnology* (Norman: University of Oklahoma Press, 1986), 96; John S. Haller, *Outcasts from Evolution: Scientific Attitudes of Racial Inferiority, 1859–1900* (Urbana: University of Illinois Press, 1995), 17; Horsman, *Race and Manifest Destiny*, 56–60, 125–29, 139–57; McNally, *Modoc War*, 243; Robert F. Berkhofer Jr., *The White Man's Indian: Images of the American Indian from Columbus to the Present* (New York: Alfred A. Knopf, 1978), 58–59 ("untamable"), Prucha, *Great Father*, 335–36 ("numbered"); Frederick E. Hoxie, *A Final Promise: The Campaign to Assimilate the Indians, 1880–1920* (Lincoln: University of Nebraska Press, 1984), 22–28; Dippie, *Vanishing American*, 138; *ARCIA* (1867), i ("cannot immediately be").

61. Jacqueline Fear-Segal, *White Man's Club: Schools, Race, and the Struggle of Indian Acculturation* (Lincoln: University of Nebraska Press, 2007), 54 ("Today"); *ARCIA* (1859), 129 ("scented"), (1871), 136 ("nothing"); Frank B. Linderman, *Pretty-shield: Medicine Woman of the Crows* (1932; New York: John Day, 1972), 249 ("hate"), 250 ("nobody"); Shepard Krech III, *The Ecological Indian: Myth and History* (New York: W. W. Norton, 1999), 123–50; *Eyewitnesses to the Indian Wars*, 5:154 ("true").

62. Calloway, *Our Hearts Fell*, 139–40 ("white man"), 147 (Sitting Bull); *ARCIA* (1862), 106–7 ("habits"); *Eyewitnesses to the Indian Wars*, 1:15 ("call that slavery"), 5:137 ("absurd"); Robert M. Utley, *The Lance and the Shield: The Life and Times of Sitting Bull* (New York: Henry Holt, 1993), 6–7; Fear-Segal, *White Man's Club*, 56 ("die an Indian"); Peter Nabokov, ed., *Native American Testimony: A Chronicle of Indian-White Relations from Prophecy to the Present, 1492–1992* (New York: Viking, 1991), 192. For other examples of Indians referring to "red people" and "white people," see *ARCIA* (1858), 99, (1869), 54, 61, 63, (1871), 108, 114, 115, (1873), 123–43; *Eyewitnesses to the Indian Wars*, 3:98; and Smoak, *Ghost Dances*, 98. For other invocations of separate divine destinies, see *ARCIA* (1871), 23; and Pekka Hämäläinen, *Lakota America: A New History of Indigenous Power* (New Haven, CT: Yale University Press, 2019), 315; and Luther Standing Bear, *My People the Sioux*, ed. E. A. Brinninstool (1928; Lincoln: University of Nebraska Press, 2006), 130–31. For other examples of Indians resisting farming, see *ARCIA* (1865), 530, (1867), 205, (1871), 35–36. For other predictions of doom if Indians adopted White ways, see *ARCIA* (1854), 68, (1871), 162; and Robert F. Berkhofer Jr., *Salvation and the Savage: An Analysis of Protestant Missions and American Indian Response, 1787–1882* (Lexington: University Press of Kentucky, 1965), 107–8.

63. Linderman, *Pretty-shield*, 46 ("yellow eyes"); Standing Bear, *My People*, 130–31 ("long knives"); West, *Contested Plains*, 47–48 ("spider"); Frederick Webb Hodge, *Handbook of American Indians North of Mexico*, part 2 (Washington, D.C.: United States Government Printing Office, 1912), 349 ("white skinned," "hairy mouths"), 350 ("sun men"); Haruo Aoki, *Nez Perce Dictionary* (Berkeley: University of California Press, 1994), 658 ("crowned"); Lisa Wistrand Robinson and James Armagost, *Comanche Dictionary and Grammar* (Dallas: University of Texas at Arlington, 1990), 22 ("lumberman").

64. James Mooney, *The Ghost-Dance Religion and the Sioux Outbreak of 1890* (1896; Norman: University of Oklahoma Press, 1991), 711 ("new god"), 721, 723–24 ("book Indians").

65. *ARCIA* (1871), 151 ("dogs and rats"), (1865), 434, (1866), 16, 173, (1867) 154, (1868), 32, (1869), 61 ("road"), (1871), 260; Bernd C. Peyer, ed., *American Indian Nonfiction: An Anthology of Writings, 1760s–1930s* (Norman: University of Oklahoma Press, 2007), 210, 264 ("realization"); *Eyewitnesses to the Indian Wars*, 5:152 ("government").

66. *Eyewitnesses to the Indian Wars*, 2:19 ("beg"); *ARCIA* (1866), 118 ("extermination"), (1870), 109 ("suspicion").

67. Charles M. Robinson III, *A Good Year to Die: The Story of the Great Sioux War* (New York: Random House, 1995); Utley, *Indian Frontier*, 155–96; Jeffrey Ostler, *The Plains Sioux and U.S. Colonialism: From Lewis and Clark to Wounded Knee* (New York: Cambridge University Press, 2004), 1–62; Richard G. Hardorff, ed., *The Surrender and Death of Crazy Horse: A Source Book About a Tragic Episode in Lakota History* (Spokane, WA: Arthur H. Clarke, 1998), 205–20; Utley, *Lance and the Shield*, 199–210.

68. Andrew R. Graybill, *The Red and the White: A Family Saga of the American West* (New York: Liveright, 2013); Paul R. Wylie, *Blood on the Marias: The Baker Massacre* (Norman: University of Oklahoma Press, 2016); Calloway, *Our Hearts Fell*, 99 ("cruel"); Karl Jacoby, *Shadows at Dawn: A Borderlands Massacre and the Violence of History* (New York: Penguin Press, 2008); *ARCIA* (1871), 46 ("sacrifice"); *Eyewitnesses to the Indian Wars*, 1:113 ("bloodthirsty"); Peotto, "Dark Mimesis," 368–69.

69. *ARCIA* (1853), 9 ("confederate"), (1854), 17, (1864), 217, 231 (1865), 19 ("fighting"); Frank B. Linderman, *Plenty-coups: Chief of the Crows* (1930; Lincoln: University of Nebraska Press, 1957), 154 ("loved").

70. *ARCIA* (1877), 213; Deward E. Walker Jr., *Conflict and Schism in Nez Perce Acculturation: A Study of Religion and Politics* (Moscow: University of Idaho Press, 1985), 48 ("White men Indians"); *Eyewitnesses to the Indian Wars*, 2:306 ("Great Spirit"), 4:312 ("wounded"); Elliott West, *The Last Indian War: The Nez Perce Story* (New York: Oxford University Press, 2011).

71. *Eyewitnesses to the Indian Wars*, 4:665–66 ("forced"); Treuer, *Heartbreat of Wounded Knee*, 115 ("wild animal"), 122 ("treats").

72. *ARCIA* (1871), 38–39.

73. Prucha, *Great Father*, 479–83, 501–33.

74. *Eyewitnesses to the Indian Wars*, 5:113 ("all Indians"); Angela F. Murphy, "Wendell Phillips and the American Indian," in *Wendell Phillips, Social Justice, and the Power of the Past*, ed. A. J. Aiséirithe and Donald Yacovone (Baton Rouge: Louisiana State University Press, 2016), 239–71. On the reforming class, see Manisha Sinha, *The Rise and Fall of the Second American Republic: Reconstruction, 1860–1920* (New York: Liveright, 2024), 307–46.

CHAPTER 6: "A RACE OF TENANTS"

1. Robert Paschal Nespor, "The Ecology of Malaria and Changes in Settlement Pattern on the Cheyenne and Arapaho Reservation, Indian Territory," and Gregory R. Campbell, "The Epidemiological Consequences of Forced Removal: The Northern Cheyenne in Indian Territory," *Plains Anthropologist* 84, no. 124 (May 1989): 71–84 and 85–97; Peter Iverson, *When Indians Became Cowboys: Native Peoples and Cattle Ranching in the American West* (Norman: University of Oklahoma Press, 1994); Donald J. Berthrong, *The Cheyenne and Arapaho Ordeal: Reservation and Agency Life in the Indian Territory, 1875–1907* (Norman: University of Oklahoma Press, 1976), 29 ("starved"), 31.

2. Robert M. Utley, *The Indian Frontier of the American West, 1846–1890* (Albuquerque: University of New Mexico Press, 1984), 184–86; Jerome A. Greene, *January Moon: The Northern Cheyenne Breakout from Fort Robinson, 1878–1879* (Norman: University of Oklahoma Press, 2020); Berthrong, *Cheyenne and Arapaho Ordeal*, 3–47; *ARCIA* (1878), xxii–xv; Colin G. Calloway, ed., *Our Hearts Fell to the Ground: Plains Indian Views of How the West Was Lost*, 2nd ed. (Boston: Bedford Books, 2017), 152–54.

3. Francis Paul Prucha, ed., *Americanizing the American Indian: Writings by the "Friends of the Indian," 1880–1900* (Cambridge, MA: Harvard University Press, 1973), 14 ("extermination").

4. Angie Debo, *And Still the Waters Run: The Betrayal of the Five Civilized Tribes* (1940; Princeton, NJ: Princeton University Press, 2022), xl ("orgy").

5. Francis Paul Prucha, *The Great Father: The United States Government and the American Indian* (Lincoln: University of Nebraska Press, 1984), 577; *ARCIA* (1862), 278, (1865), 117, (1868), 11, (1871), 157, (1873), 252, (1875), 43–44 ("inadequate"); Berthrong, *Cheyenne and Arapaho Ordeal*, 29 ("ill-humored"), 32; Ryan Hall, "Patterns of Plunder: Corruption and the Failure of the Indian Reservation System, 1851–1887," *Western Historical Quarterly* 55, no. 1 (Spring 2024): 21–37; *Eyewitnesses to the Indian Wars*, 1:320; Prucha, *Great Father*, 586–89; Jeffrey Ostler, *The Lakotas and the Black Hills: The Struggle for Sacred Ground* (New York: Penguin, 2010), 17; *Doolittle Report*, 3, 5, 15, 16, 17, 338–40, 358, 426, 440, 450, 451, 483; Hugh Dempsey, *Firewater: The Impact of the Whisky Trade on the Blackfoot Nation* (Markham, ON: Fifth House, 2002); John C. Ewers, *The Blackfeet: Raiders on the Northwestern Plains* (Norman: University of Oklahoma Press, 1958), 258–62; Paul F. Sharp, *Whoop-Up Country: The Canadian-American West, 1865–1885* (Minneapolis: University of Minnesota Press, 1955), 51, 54, 58–59, 78–106;

Frederick E. Hoxie, *Parading Through History: The Making of the Crow Nation in America, 1805–1935* (New York: Cambridge University Press, 1997), 133; Frank B. Linderman, *Pretty-shield: Medicine Woman of the Crows* (1932; New York: John Day, 1972), 251; Jeffrey Ostler, *The Plains Sioux and U.S. Colonialism: From Lewis and Clark to Wounded Knee* (New York: Cambridge University Press, 2004), 187, including note 57; Robert M. Utley, *Last Days of the Sioux Nation* (New Haven, CT: Yale University Press, 1963), 57; John G. Neihardt, ed., *Black Elk Speaks: Being the Life Story of a Holy Man of the Oglala Sioux* (Lincoln: University of Nebraska Press, 1988), 196 ("power").

6. Hoxie, *Parading Through History*, 133; Linderman, *Pretty-shield*, 252; *ARCIA* (1871), 418–19; *Eyewitnesses to the Indian Wars*, 5:167 ("fine herd"); *ARCIA* (1871), 485 ("neglect"); David H. DeJong, *Paternalism to Partnership: The Administration of Indian Affairs, 1786–2021* (Lincoln: University of Nebraska Press, 2021), 187; Berthrong, *Cheyenne and Arapaho Ordeal*, 130 ("complete farce," "preyed").

7. *ARCIA* (1869), 401–2, (1879), xliv; *Letters and Messages of Rutherford B. Hayes, President of the United States* (Washington, D.C.: United States Government Printing Office, 1881), 177–78. Generally on this ideology, see Jefferson Cowie, *Freedom's Dominion: A Saga of White Resistance to Federal Power* (New York: Basic Books, 2022).

8. Prucha, *Great Father*, 646–48; Sidney Harring, *Crow Dog's Case: American Indian Sovereignty, Tribal Law, and United States Law in the Nineteenth Century* (New York: Cambridge University Press, 1994); Ostler, *Plains Sioux*, 194–203.

9. Calloway, *Our Hearts Fell*, 148–49 ("consider"); Ostler, *Plains Sioux*, 194–98; *Doolittle Report*, 386 ("starving"); Linderman, *Pretty-shield*, 251 ("white men"); Neihardt, *Black Elk Speaks*, 20 ("make us"), 146 ("*Wasichus*"), 196 ("prisoners").

10. Colin G. Calloway, "Sword Bearer and the 'Crow Outbreak,' 1887," *Montana: The Magazine of Western History* 36, no. 4 (Autumn 1986): 38–51; Hoxie, *Parading Through History*, 154–64.

11. Calloway, *Our Hearts Fell*, 157 ("hand"); John M. Coward, *The Newspaper Indian: Native American Identity in the Press, 1820–1900* (Urbana: University of Illinois Press, 1999), 213–14 ("what rights"); Valerie Sherer Mathes and Richard Lowitt, *The Standing Bear Controversy: Prelude to Indian Reform* (Urbana: University of Illinois Press, 2003).

12. David Treuer, *The Heartbeat of Wounded Knee: Native America from 1890 to the Present* (New York: Riverhead Books, 2019), 158; David Wallace Adams, *Education*

for Extinction: American Indians and the Boarding School Experience, 1875–1928 (Lawrence: University Press of Kansas, 1995), 17–18; Michael McNally, *Defend the Sacred: Native American Religious Freedom Beyond the First Amendment* (Princeton, NJ: Princeton University Press, 2020), 33–68; Ostler, *Plains Sioux*, 134, 178–80; Echo-Hawk, *Courts of the Conqueror*, 174; Justin R. Gage, *We Do Not Want the Gates Closed Between Us: Native Networks and the Spread of the Ghost Dance* (Norman: University of Oklahoma Press, 2020), 134; Hoxie, *Parading Through History*, 202–5, 210–13; Deward E. Walker, *Conflict and Schism in Nez Perce Acculturation: A Study of Religion and Politics* (Moscow: University Press of Idaho, 1985), 53–54, 64; Tom Holm, *The Great Confusion in Indian Affairs: Native Americans and Whites in the Progressive Era* (Austin: University of Texas Press, 2005), 34–40; *ARCIA* (1878), 35 ("among the people").

13. *ARCIA* (1874), 273, (1892), 385–90; Utley, *Last Days of the Sioux Nation*, 23 ("disgrace"); William T. Hagan, *United States–Comanche Relations: The Reservation Years* (New Haven, CT: Yale University Press, 1976), 183–84; Berthrong, *Cheyenne and Arapaho Ordeal*, 137; Ostler, *Plains Sioux*, 131; Prucha, *Great Father*, 648–49.

14. Berthrong, *Cheyenne and Arapaho Ordeal*, 65–66.

15. L. G. Moses, *Wild West Shows and the Images of American Indians, 1883–1933* (Albuquerque: University of New Mexico Press, 1996), esp. 5, 8, 34, 131; Richard White, "Frederick Jackson Turner and Buffalo Bill," in Richard White and Patricia Nelson Limerick, *The Frontier in American Culture*, ed. James R. Grossman (Berkeley: University of California Press, 1994), 7–66.

16. Ostler, *Plains Sioux*, 214–15 ("whores"); R. David Edmunds et al., *The People: A History of Native America* (Boston: Cengage, 2007), 341 ("to work").

17. *ARCIA* (1857), 228, (1859), 75, (1863), 470, (1873), 8–9, (1877), 3.

18. Fear-Segal, *White Man's Club*, 1–3; Brad D. Lookingbill, *War Dance at Fort Marion: Plains Indian War Prisoners* (Norman: University of Oklahoma Press, 2006); H. Henrietta Stockel, *Shame and Endurance: The Untold Story of the Chiricahua Apache Prisoners of War* (Tucson: University of Arizona Press, 2004).

19. Fear-Segal, *White Man's Club*, 24 ("similar"), 33 ("thousand years"), 106; Adams, *Education for Extinction*, 46 ("white man"), 326–28.

20. Adams, *Education for Extinction*, 47; Fear-Segal, *White Man's Club*, 26, 163 ("too much").

21. Adams, *Education for Extinction*, 186 ("put aside"), 192; Fear-Segal, *White Man's Club*, 163–64, 171 ("To civilize"); Prucha, *Americanizing the American Indian*, 260–61 ("Kill").

22. Adams, *Education for Extinction*, 58, 66; Fear-Segal, *White Man's Club*, 44, 76, 99; John S. Milloy, *A National Crime: The Canadian Government and the Residential School System* (Winnipeg: University of Manitoba Press, 2017). See also Canada's Truth and Reconciliation Commission Reports, nctr.ca/records/reports/#trc-reports (last accessed Feb. 20, 2025).

23. Margaret D. Jacobs, *White Mother to a Dark Race: Settler Colonialism, Maternalism, and the Removal of Indigenous Children in the American West and Australia, 1880–1940* (Lincoln: University of Nebraska Press, 2009), 57–58. In a vast literature, see Eric Foner, *Reconstruction: America's Unfinished Revolution, 1863–1877* (New York: Harper Collins, 1988); Matthew Frye Jacobson, *Whiteness of a Different Color: European Immigrants and the Alchemy of Race* (Cambridge, MA: Harvard University Press, 1998); Noel Ignatiev, *How the Irish Became White* (New York: Routledge, 1995); David R. Roediger, *The Wages of Whiteness: Race and the Making of the American Working Class* (New York: Verso, 1991); Thomas A. Guglielmo, *White on Arrival: Italians, Race, Color, and Power in Chicago, 1890–1945* (New York: Oxford University Press, 2003); Nell Irvin Painter, *The History of White People* (New York: W. W. Norton, 2010); Nancy Isenberg, *White Trash: The 400-Year Untold History of Class in America* (New York: Viking, 2016); and Lucy Maddox, *Citizen Indians: Native American Intellectuals, Race, and Reform* (Ithaca, NY: Cornell University Press, 2005), 73–74.

24. Adams, *Education for Extinction*, 211 ("children"); Luther Standing Bear, *My People the Sioux*, ed. E. A. Brinninstool (1928; Lincoln: University of Nebraska Press, 2006), 130 ("wild").

25. Adams, *Education for Extinction*, 101–2 ("transformed," "objection"); Calloway, *Our Hearts Fell*, 168 ("imitation").

26. Adams, *Education for Extinction*, 117–19; K. Tsianina Lomawaima, *They Called It Prairie Light: The Story of Chilocco Indian School* (Lincoln: University of Nebraska Press, 1994), 98; Cheryl A. Well, "'Why[,] These Children Are Not Really Indians': Race, Time, and Indian Authenticity," *American Indian Quarterly* 39, no. 1 (Winter 2015), 11–14.

27. Adams, *Education for Extinction*, 115, 125–35, esp. 124–25, and 132; Fear-Segal, *White Man's Club*, 221, 232; Treuer, *Heartbeat of Wounded Knee*, 140; Brenda J. Child,

Boarding School Seasons: American Indian Families, 1900–1940 (Lincoln: University of Nebraska Press, 1998), 12, 58.

28. Peter Nabokov, ed., *Native American Testimony: A Chronicle of Indian-White Relations from Prophecy to the Present, 1492–1992* (New York: Viking, 1991), 220; Treuer, *Heartbeat of Wounded Knee*, 137, 139 ("terror"); Lomawaima, *They Called It Prairie Light*, 112; Adams, *Education for Extinction*, 122–23; Jacobs, *White Mother to a Dark Race*, 257; Dana Hedgpeth, "'12 Years of Hell': Indian Boarding School Survivors Share Their Stories," *Washington Post*, Aug. 7, 2023; Sari Horwitz et al., "In the Name of God," *Washington Post*, May 29, 2024.

29. Adams, *Education for Extinction*, 148 ("Caucasian," "white people"), 192–93.

30. Adams, *Education for Extinction*, 157–63 ("too many" on 162); Fear-Segal, *White Man's Club*, 173, 182, 235–37; Standing Bear, *My People the Sioux*, 183 ("behind"), 189.

31. Berthrong, *Cheyenne and Arapaho Ordeal*, 38 ("Spirit"), 230, 234–35 ("do not desire"); Nabokov, *Native American Testimony*, 217 ("axe"); Hoxie, *Parading Through History*, 205; Adams, *Education for Extinction*, 27, 211; Gregory E. Smoak, *Ghost Dances and Identity: Prophetic Religion and American Indian Ethnogenesis in the Nineteenth Century* (Berkeley: University of California Press, 2006), 187; Gage, *We Do Not Want the Gates Closed*, 31.

32. Fear-Segal, *White Man's Club*, xi ("feeling"), 59 ("conquer"), 142–43 ("not accept"); Standing Bear, *My People the Sioux*, 98 ("fighting"), 151–52; Child, *Boarding School Seasons*, 15, 16; Gage, *We Do Not Want the Gates Closed*, 30.

33. Adams, *Education for Extinction*, 231 ("I do not"); Fear-Segal, *White Man's Club*, 119–20 ("superior").

34. Lomawaima, *They Called It Prairie Light*, 156 ("*stahitkey*"); *Indian School Journal* (Chilocco) 13, no. 1 (Sept. 1912): 12 ("This race"); Fear-Segal, *White Man's Club*, 154 ("nothing more"); Zitkala-Ša, *American Indian Stories* (1921; Lincoln: University of Nebraska Press, 1985), 66 ("iron"), 99 ("real life"); Standing Bear, *My People the Sioux*, 68 (all quotes), 224.

35. Lomawaima, *They Called It Prairie Light*, 24; Child, *Boarding School Seasons*, 46; Adams, *Education for Extinction*, 224–29, 229–31.

36. Adams, *Education for Extinction*, 202–8 ("Indian versus" and "Army" on 208); Child, *Boarding School Seasons*, 4; David Maraniss, *Path Lit by Lightning: The Life of Jim Thorpe* (New York: Simon and Schuster, 2022).

37. Albert H. Kneale, *Indian Agent* (Caldwell, ID: Caxton Printers, 1950), 171 ("dressed"); Nabokov, *Native American Testimony*, 222–23 ("Indian ways").

38. Standing Bear, *My People the Sioux*, 204; Adams, *Education for Extinction*, 280 ("minded"); Calloway, *Our Hearts Fell*, 163 ("English").

39. *Eyewitnesses to the Indian Wars*, 5:392 ("What is there"), 396–97 ("Nobody"); Kneale, *Indian Agent*, 171–72; Arnold Krupat, *Boarding School Voices: Carlisle Indian School Students Speak* (Lincoln: University of Nebraska Press, 2023), 3, 34, 36.

40. *Eyewitnesses to the Indian Wars*, 5:392 ("can't go"); Fear-Segal, *White Man's Club*, 132–33 ("who think"), 145 ("pretty good"); Jacqueline Emery, ed., *Recovering Native American Writings in the Boarding School Press* (Lincoln: University of Nebraska Press, 2017), 111.

41. Adams, *Education for Extinction*, 255–63; Lomawaima, *They Called It Prairie Light*, 71. See also Michael Leroy Oberg's blog discussions of his research on Onondagas and the boarding schools: michaelleroyoberg.com/category/boarding-schools (last accessed Aug. 13, 2024).

42. Adams, *Education for Extinction*, 306; Jacobs, *White Mother to a Dark Race*, 57–58.

43. James Mooney, *The Ghost-Dance Religion and the Sioux Outbreak of 1890* (1896; Norman: University of Oklahoma Press, 1991), 785 ("whites and Indians"), 786 ("hurricane"), 788; Gage, *We Do Not Want the Gates Closed*, 161; Smoak, *Ghost Dances*, 10, 169–70; Standing Bear, *My People the Sioux*, 218–19; Ostler, *Plains Sioux*, 262.

44. Gage, *We Do Not Want the Gates Closed*, 38, 157, 195.

45. Gage, *We Do Not Want the Gates Closed*, 195.

46. *Eyewitnesses to the Indian Wars*, 5:168 ("hasten"); Ostler, *Lakotas and the Black Hills*, 121 ("liable"); Ostler, *Plains Sioux*, 217–39, 308; Herbert T. Hoover, "The Sioux Agreement of 1889 and Its Aftermath," *South Dakota History* 19, no. 1 (1989): 56–94.

47. Ostler, *Plains Sioux*, 301, 313–60; Utley, *Last Days of the Sioux Nation*, 3 ("severe"); S.1073—Remove the Stain Act, 117th Congress (2021–22), congress.gov/bill/117th-congress/senate-bill/1073/text (last accessed Aug. 13, 2024); Davis Winkie, "Medals of Honor for Soldiers Who Perpetrated Wounded Knee Massacre May Be Rescinded," *Military Times*, July 20, 2022, militarytimes.com/news/pentagon-congress/2022/07/20/medals-of-honor-for-soldiers-who-perpetrated

-wounded-knee-massacre-may-be-rescinded (last accessed Aug. 13, 2024); Mark Walker, "Tribes Want Medals Awarded for Wounded Knee Massacre Rescinded," *New York Times*, Apr. 23, 2021, nytimes.com/2021/04/23/us/politics/tribes-medal-honor-wounded-knee.html (last accessed Aug. 13, 2024).

48. Calloway, *Our Hearts Fell*, 175 ("I am"); Smoak, *Ghost Dances*, 188 ("rejected"); Nabokov, *Native Testimony*, 255 ("suppose"); Neihardt, *Black Elk Speaks*, 233 ("despair"). For the traditional view of Wounded Knee, see Utley, *Indian Frontier*, 257–59. The corrective is evident in Ostler, *Plains Sioux*.

49. Treuer, *Heartbeat of Wounded Knee*, 8 ("wipe them").

50. Smoak, *Ghost Dances*, 192–205 ("book" on 195–96).

51. Generally, see D. S. Otis, *The Dawes Act and the Allotment of Indian Lands*, ed. Francis Paul Prucha (1934; Norman: University of Oklahoma Press, 1973).

52. Treuer, *Heartbeat of Wounded Knee*, 148–49; William T. Hagan, *Taking Indian Lands: The Cherokee (Jerome) Commission, 1889–1893* (Norman: University of Oklahoma Press, 2003); Debo, *And Still the Waters Run*, 32–35.

53. *ARCIA* (1876), ix–x ("high degree"); Prucha, *Americanizing the American Indian*, 334 ("intelligently selfish").

54. Frederick E. Hoxie, *A Final Promise: The Campaign to Assimilate the Indians, 1880–1920* (Lincoln: University of Nebraska Press, 1984), 32–33; Otis, *Dawes Act*, 6, 10 ("not a family"). On Cherokees taking care of their own, see Julie L. Reed, *Serving the Nation: Cherokee Sovereignty and Social Welfare, 1800–1907* (Norman: Oklahoma University Press, 2016).

55. On "half-breed tracts," see Anne F. Hyde, *Born of Lakes and Plains: Mixed-Descent Peoples and the Making of the American West* (New York: W. W. Norton, 2023), 143–45, 189, 238, 271–73, 288–89. On Curtis, see William E. Unrau, *Mixed-Bloods and Tribal Dissolution: Charles Curtis and the Quest for Indian Identity* (Lawrence: University Press of Kansas, 1989) ("make something" on 10).

56. Unrau, *Mixed-Bloods and Tribal Dissolution*.

57. David A. Chang, *The Color of the Land: Race, Nation, and the Politics of Landownership in Oklahoma, 1832–1929* (Chapel Hill: University of North Carolina Press, 2010), 57–61, 80; *ARCIA* (1871), 150; Debo, *And Still the Waters Run*, 15–16; Alexandra Harmon, *Rich Indians: Native People and the Problem of Wealth in American History* (Chapel Hill: University of North Carolina Press, 2010), 155–56, 161–62.

58. Prucha, *Americanizing the American Indian*, 128 ("not to help"), 135 ("thirty"), 137 ("despoil"); Otis, *Dawes Act*, 18, 19.

59. Emily Greenwald, *Reconfiguring the Reservation: The Nez Perces, Jicarilla Apaches, and the Dawes Act* (Albuquerque: University of New Mexico Press, 2002), 27–28 ("holding"), 31 ("condition"); Nabokov, *Native American Testimony*, 237 ("God damn"), 238, 242 ("trick"); Harmon, *Rich Indians*, 157 ("graspings"); Otis, *Dawes Act*, 42, 51; Mark J. Swetland, "'Make-Believe White Men' and the Omaha Land Allotments of 1871–1900," *Great Plains Research* 4 (Aug. 1994): 201–36; Judith A. Boughter, *Betraying the Omaha Nation, 1790–1916* (Norman: University of Oklahoma Press, 1998), 96–133; David J. Silverman, *Red Brethren: The Brothertown and Stockbridge Indians and the Problem of Race in Early America* (Ithaca, NY: Cornell University Press, 2010), 184–210; Stuart Banner, *Possessing the Pacific: Land, Settlers, and Indigenous People from Australia to Alaska* (Cambridge, MA: Harvard University Press, 2007), 2–3, 129; Julia Flynn Siler, *Lost Kingdom: Hawaii's Last Queen, the Sugar Kings, and America's First Imperial Adventure* (New York: Atlantic Monthly Press, 2013); James L. Haley, *Captive Paradise: A History of Hawai'i* (New York: St. Martin's Press, 2014); Noenoe K. Silva, *Aloha Betrayed: Native Hawaiian Resistance to American Colonialism* (Durham, NC: Duke University Press, 2004).

60. Berthrong, *Cheyenne and Arapaho Ordeal*, 25–51; Melissa L. Meyer, *The White Earth Tragedy: Ethnicity and Dispossession at a Minnesota Anishinaabe Reservation, 1889–1920* (Lincoln: University of Nebraska Press, 1994), 207; Child, *Boarding School Seasons*, 11; Kneale, *Indian Agent*, 108 ("little land"); Janet A. McDonnell, *The Dispossession of the American Indian, 1887–1934* (Bloomington: Indiana University Press, 1991), 22, 23; Otis, *Dawes Act*, 96, 136–37; Nabokov, *Native American Testimony*, 237, 247; Greenwald, *Reconfiguring the Reservation*, 40, 77–79; James C. Scott, *Weapons of the Weak: Everyday Forms of Peasant Resistance* (New Haven, CT: Yale University Press, 1985); Rose Stremlau, *Preserving the Cherokee Family: Kinship and the Allotment of an Indigenous Nation* (Chapel Hill: University of North Carolina Press, 2011).

61. Chang, *Color of the Land*, 100, 140, 144; Nabokov, *Native American Testimony*, 257–58; Daniel F. Littlefield and Lonnie E. Underhill, "The 'Crazy Snake Uprising' of 1909: A Red, Black, or White Affair?" *Arizona and the West* 20, no. 4 (1978): 307–24; Sidney J. Harring, "Crazy Snake and the Creek Struggle for Sovereignty: The Native American Legal Culture and American Law," *American Journal of Legal History* 34, no. 4 (1990): 365–80; Debo, *And the Waters Still Run*, 53–57.

62. Katherine Ellinghaus, *Blood Will Tell: Native Americans and Assimilation Policy* (Lincoln: University of Nebraska Press, 2017), xi–xii, xxiii, 27 ("admixture").

63. Ellinghaus, *Blood Will Tell*, xi–xii.

64. Anne Hyde, *Empires, Nations, and Families: A New History of the North American West, 1800–1860* (Lincoln: University of Nebraska Press, 2011); Hyde, *Born of Lakes and Plains*; Claudio Saunt, *Black, White, and Indian: Race and the Unmaking of an American Family* (New York: Oxford University Press, 2005), 154 ("serious difficulty").

65. Saunt, *Black, White, and Indian*, 154–60; Chang, *Color of the Land*, 94; Barbara Krauthamer, *Black Slaves, Indian Masters: Slavery, Emancipation, and Citizenship in the Native American South* (Chapel Hill: University of North Carolina Press, 2013), 148–49; Circe Sturm, *Blood Politics: Race, Culture, and Identity in the Cherokee Nation of Oklahoma* (Berkeley: University of California Press, 2002), 172–73; Tiya Miles, *Ties That Bind: The Story of an Afro-Cherokee Family in Slavery and Freedom* (Berkeley: University of California Press, 2005), 191–200; Ellinghaus, *Blood Will Tell*, 31–32; Littlefield, *Chickasaw Freedmen*, 206–11.

66. Meyer, *White Earth Tragedy*, 118–19 ("half-burned"), 181; Miles, *Ties That Bind*, 191–203; Saunt, *Black, White, and Indian*, 155–56; Sturm, *Blood Politics*, 74–78, 98–99, 119, 141; "The Indian: Personal vs. Property," *Indian School Journal* 14, no. 4 (Dec. 1913): 150 ("hundreds").

67. Otis, *Dawes Act*, 87; McDonnell, *Dispossession of the American Indian*, 121; Chang, *Color of the Land*, 152; *Five Civilized Tribes in Oklahoma: Hearings Before the Subcommittee of the Committee on Indian Affairs, House of Representatives*, 68th Congress, 1st Session on H.R. 6900 (Washington, D.C., 1924), 5 ("landlords").

68. Otis, *Dawes Act*, 145.

69. Berthrong, *Cheyenne and Arapaho Ordeal*, 185–86 ("farce"), 188–89 ("fun" on 188).

70. Otis, *Dawes Act*, 102; McDonnell, *Dispossession of the American Indian*, 26–28; Berthrong, *Cheyenne and Arapaho Ordeal*, 185–208, 226–27, 230, 247, 265.

71. McDonnell, *Dispossession of the American Indian*, 60; Greenwald, *Reconfiguring the Reservation*, 31; Otis, *Dawes Act*, 132–33; Chang, *Color of the Land*, 146.

72. McDonnell, *Dispossession of the American Indian*, 58; Debo, *And the Waters Still Run*, 92–125, 183–92; Kneale, *Indian Agent*, 113; Holm, *Great Confusion*, 158–59; Meyer, *White Earth Tragedy*.

73. Berthrong, *Cheyenne and Arapaho Ordeal*, 212–13 ("We have given"); Bernd C. Peyer, ed., *American Indian Nonfiction: An Anthology of Writings, 1760s–1930s* (Norman: University of Oklahoma Press, 2007), 268.

74. Silverman, *Red Brethren*, 184–210; John P. Bowes, *Exiles and Pioneers: Eastern Indians in the Trans-Mississippi West* (New York: Cambridge University Press, 2007), 246–49, 250–51; Stephen Kantrowitz, *Citizens of a Stolen Land: A Ho-Chunk History of the Nineteenth-Century United States* (Chapel Hill: University of North Carolina Press, 2023); Daniel R. Mandell, *Tribe, Race, History: Native Americans in Southern New England, 1780–1880* (Baltimore: Johns Hopkins University Press, 2008), 195–217; Ann Marie Plane and Gregory Burton, "The Massachusetts Indian Enfranchisement Act: Ethnic Contest in Historical Context, 1849–1869," *Ethnohistory* 40, no. 4 (Autumn 1993): 587–618; Ethel Boissevain, "The Detribalization of the Narragansett Indians: A Case Study," *Ethnohistory* 3, no. 3 (Summer 1956): 225–45; Hoxie, *Final Promise*, 74; Chang, *Color of the Land*, 99; Kevin Bruyneel, *The Third Space of Sovereignty: The Postcolonial Politics of U.S.-Indigenous Relations* (Minneapolis: University of Minnesota Press, 2007), 97.

75. McDonnell, *Dispossession of the American Indian*, 95.

CHAPTER 7: VISIONS IN AN AGE OF SYSTEMATIC RACISM

1. Weston La Barre, *The Peyote Cult*, 4th ed., enlarged (Hamden, CT: Shoe String Press, 1975); Thomas Constantine Maroukis, *The Peyote Road: Religious Freedom and the Native American Church* (Norman: University of Oklahoma Press, 2010); J. S. Slotkin, *The Peyote Religion: A Study in Indian-White Relations* (1956; New York: Octagon Books, 1975); Edward F. Anderson, *Peyote: The Divine Cactus* (Tucson: University of Arizona Press, 1996).

2. *Peyote Hearings*, 21, 65.

3. *Peyote Hearings*, 139–40.

4. *Peyote Hearings*, 16–20 (Brosius), 24 (hallucinations), 46–47 (Roe); Maroukis, *Peyote Road*, 82–83 (no visual effects), 106 (Leech).

5. *Peyote Hearings*, 105 (Bull Bear), 113 (La Flesche), 161 (Osage). See also pp. 82, 149–55, 170, 173, 180–81, 182–84.

6. Lee D. Baker, *Anthropology and the Racial Politics of Culture* (Durham, NC: Duke University Press, 2010), 6–7, 9, 15–16, 21, 25–26; Robert F. Berkhofer Jr., *The White*

Man's Indian: Images of the American Indian from Columbus to the Present (New York: Alfred A. Knopf, 1978), 64, 66; Philip J. Deloria, *Playing Indian* (New Haven, CT: Yale University Press, 1998), 91; Hazel W. Hertzberg, *The Search for an American Indian Identity: Modern Pan-Indian Movements* (Syracuse, NY: Syracuse University Press, 1971), 51–52; Lucy Maddox, *Citizen Indians: Native American Intellectuals, Race, and Reform* (Ithaca, NY: Cornell University Press, 2005), 60.

7. *Peyote Hearings*, 141–43 ("brother" on 143), 145, 146, 148 ("light").

8. *Peyote Hearings*, 63; Baker, *Anthropology and Racial Politics*, 2, 89, 116.

9. *Peyote Hearings*, 63. On Warden's background, see his personnel file from Carlisle at carlisleindian.dickinson.edu/sites/default/files/docs-ephemera/NARA_1327 _b004_f0160.pdf (last accessed Feb. 20, 2025).

10. Slotkin, *Peyote Religion*, 49 (messianism), 72 ("only thing"), 157 ("exclusively"); La Barre, *Peyote Cult*, 98, 103.

11. Slotkin, *Peyote Religion*, 72 ("Indian way"); La Barre, *Peyote Cult*, 7–8, 61–62; Anderson, *Peyote*, 52; Maroukis, *Peyote Road*, 11, 69, 72.

12. Slotkin, *Peyote Religion*, 25, 44, 46, 70, 76 ("how to read"); Anderson, *Peyote*, 63–64; La Barre, *Peyote Cult*, 64, 73–74; Maroukis, *Peyote Road*, 72; Slotkin, *Peyote Religion*, 159; Albert H. Kneale, *Indian Agent* (Caldwell, ID: Caxton Printers, 1950), 211, 213.

13. Anderson, *Peyote*, 47–58, 188; Maroukis, *Peyote Road*, 12, 58, 117; Slotkin, *Peyote Religion*, 327 ("except").

14. Maddox, *Citizen Indians*, 83–84.

15. *Indian School Journal* 6, no. 6 (Apr. 1906): 80 ("generation"); *Indian School Journal* 15, no. 5 (Jan. 1915): 255 ("real"); Paul Spruhan, "A Legal History of Blood Quantum in Federal Indian Law to 1935," *South Dakota Law Review* 51 (2006): 41, 44; Katherine Ellinghaus, *Blood Will Tell: Native Americans and Assimilation Policy* (Lincoln: University of Nebraska Press, 2017), xviii–xx.

16. Frederick E. Hoxie, ed., *Talking Back to Civilization: Indian Voices from the Progressive Era* (Boston: Bedford/St. Martin's, 2001), 101 ("no race"); David Martinez, ed., *The American Indian Intellectual Tradition: An Anthology of Writings from 1772 to 1972* (Ithaca, NY: Cornell University Press, 2011), 183 ("school days"); Kenneth R. Philp, ed., *Indian Self-Rule: First-Hand Accounts of Indian-White Relations from Roosevelt to Reagan* (1986; Salt Lake City: Utah State University Libraries, 1998), 43 ("Let the

Indian"); Zoë Burkholder, *Color in the Classroom: How American Schools Taught Race* (New York: Oxford University Press, 2011), 58 ("chiefly"); Ned Blackhawk, *The Rediscovery of America: Native Peoples and the Unmaking of U.S. History* (New Haven, CT: Yale University Press, 2023), 367; Berkhofer, *White Man's Indian*, 109. For similar patterns in later decades, see Jeanette Henry, *Textbooks and the American Indian* (San Francisco: American Indian Historical Society, 1970).

17. "Secretary Lane on the Indian Commissionership and the Indian Policy," *New York Herald*, excerpted in *Indian School Journal* 13, no. 9 (May 1913): 422 ("unscrupulous"); Thomas A. Britten, *American Indians in World War I: At Home and at War* (Albuquerque: University of New Mexico Press, 1997), 167 ("food"); Meriam Report, 569 (two prices), 717 ("We hire"); "Put him to work," *Indian School Journal* 17, no. 9 (May 1917): 472; "Read this everybody," *Indian School Journal* 15, no. 9 (May 1915): 480 ("harsh"); Ellinghaus, *Blood Will Tell*, 116 ("ignorant"); Rosalyn R. Lapier and David R. M. Beck, *City Indian: Native American Activism in Chicago, 1893–1934* (Lincoln: University of Nebraska Press, 2015), 133 ("pitcher"); Philip J. Deloria, *Indians in Unexpected Places* (Lawrence: University Press of Kansas, 2004), 120.

18. Donald L. Fixico, *Indian Resilience and Rebuilding: Indigenous Nations in the Modern American West* (Tucson: University of Arizona Press, 2013), 71; Graham D. Taylor, *The New Deal and American Indian Tribalism: The Administration of the Indian Reorganization Act, 1934–45* (Lincoln: University of Nebraska Press, 1980), 5–6; U.S. Department of Commerce, *Income in the United States, 1929–1937* (Nov. 1938), 33; Britten, *American Indians in World War I*, 167 ("dying").

19. E. B. Linnen, "Increase in Farming Acreage," Apr. 13, 1917, reprinted in *Indian School Journal* 17, no. 9 (May 1917): 447; Ryan Hall, "Patterns of Plunder: Corruption and the Failure of the Indian Reservation System, 1851–1887," *Western Historical Quarterly* 55, no. 1 (Spring 2024): 21–38.

20. Britten, *American Indians in World War I*, 153–54; Nancy Shoemaker, *American Indian Population Recovery in the Twentieth Century* (Albuquerque: University of New Mexico Press, 1999), 4.

21. Alexandra Harmon, *Indians in the Making: Ethnic Relations and Indian Identities Around Puget Sound* (Berkeley: University of California Press, 2000), 156 ("Isn't); Peter Iverson, ed., *"For Our Navajo People": Diné Letters, Speeches, and Petitions, 1900–1960* (Albuquerque: University of New Mexico Press, 2002), 103 ("backward"); Tom Holm, *The Great Confusion in Indian Affairs: Native Americans and Whites in the Progressive Era* (Austin: University of Texas Press, 2005), 173.

22. Blackhawk, *Rediscovery of America*, 397 ("don't want"); Mikaëla M. Adams, *Who Belongs? Race, Resources, and Tribal Citizenship in the Native South* (New York: Oxford University Press, 2016), 30; Malinda Maynor Lowery, *Lumbee Indians in the Jim Crow South: Race, Identity, and the Making of a Nation* (Chapel Hill: University of North Carolina Press, 2010), 21; Brian Klopotek, *Recognition Odysseys: Indigeneity, Race, and Federal Recognition Policy in Three Louisiana Indian Communities* (Durham, NC: Duke University Press, 2011), 141; Arica L. Coleman, *That the Blood Stay Pure: African Americans, Native Americans, and the Predicament of Race and Identity in Virginia* (Bloomington: Indiana University Press, 2013); Laura J. Feller, *Being Indigenous in Jim Crow Virginia: Powhatan People and the Color Line* (Norman: University of Oklahoma Press, 2022); Warren E. Milteer Jr., *North Carolina's Free People of Color, 1715–1885* (Baton Rouge: Louisiana State University Press, 2020); Alleson Herron, "Sovereignty Through Segregation: Indian Schools in North Carolina" (undergraduate honors thesis, George Washington University, 2023).

23. David Grann, *Killers of the Flower Moon: The Osage Murders and the Birth of the FBI* (New York: Vintage, 2017); Donald L. Fixico, *The Invasion of Indian Country in the Twentieth Century: American Capitalism and Tribal Natural Resources* (Niwot: University Press of Colorado, 1998), 35–37, 46–49; Britten, *American Indians in World War I*, 169 ("shamelessly").

24. Meriam Report, 3, 193–94, 198–99, 201, 208–16, 534 ("lift").

25. Michael Hilger, *From Savage to Nobleman: Images of Native Americans in Film* (Lanham, MD: Scarecrow Press, 1995), 24; Holm, *Great Confusion*, 121.

26. Joanna Hearne, *Native Recognition: Indigenous Cinema and the Western* (Albany: State University of New York Press, 2012), 48, 104–5.

27. Hilger, *Savage to Nobleman*, 37; Jacquelyn Kilpatrick, *Celluloid Indians: Native Americans and Film* (Lincoln: University of Nebraska Press, 1999), 19, 34; Deloria, *Indians in Unexpected Places*, 20; Brian D. Behnken and Gregory D. Smithers, *Racism in American Popular Media: From Aunt Jemima to Frito Bandito* (Santa Barbara, CA: Praeger, 2015), 79, 178; Berkhofer, *White Man's Indian*, 103.

28. Michelle H. Rajeja, *Reservation Reelism: Redfacing, Visual Sovereignty, and Representations of Native Americans in Film* (Lincoln: University of Nebraska Press, 2010), 42–43 ("grossly"); Deloria, *Indians in Unexpected Places*, 91–92 ("yelling," "heap bad"), 105; Hilger, *Savage to Nobleman*, 22.

29. Debra Merskin, "Winnebagos, Cherokees, Apaches, and Dakotas: The Persistence of Stereotyping of American Indians in American Advertising Brands," *Howard Journal of Communication* 12, no. 3 (2001–7): 159–69; Elizabeth S. Bird, ed., *Dressing in Feathers: The Construction of the Indian in American Popular Culture* (Boulder, CO: Westview Press, 1996); Behnken and Smithers, *Racism in American Popular Media*.

30. "List of Sports Team Names and Mascots Derived from Indigenous Peoples," *Wikipedia*, en.wikipedia.org/wiki/List_of_sports_team_names_and_mascots_derived_from_indigenous_peoples (last accessed Aug. 13, 2024); Sara Abdelouahed, "UMass Known by Racist Mascot for 24 Years," *Massachusetts Daily Collegian*, Nov. 30, 2021, dailycollegian.com/2021/11/umass-known-by-racist-mascot-for-24-years (last accessed Aug. 13, 2024); "The Redskin Revolution," *Miamian Magazine*, Winter 1993–94, miamioh.edu/_files/documents/about-miami/diversity/miami-tribe-relations/mascot-story/relationship-changes/redskin-resolution.pdf (last accessed Aug. 13, 2024); Denni Dianne Woodward, "The Removal of the Indian Mascot of Stanford," Stanford Native American Cultural Center, nacc.stanford.edu/home/history-timelines/stanford-mascot-timeline/removal-indian-mascot-stanford (last accessed Aug. 13, 2024); J. Gordon Hylton, "Before the Redskins Were the Redskins: The Use of Native American Team Names in the Formative Era of American Sports, 1857–1933," *North Dakota Law Review* 86, no. 879 (2010): 879–903; Colin G. Calloway, *The Indian History of an American Institution: Native Americans and Dartmouth* (Hanover, NH: Dartmouth College Press, 2010), 130–54; Kevin Bruyneel, "Race, Colonialism, and the Politics of Indian Sports Names and Mascots: The Washington Football Team Case," *Native American and Indigenous Studies* 3, no. 2 (Fall 2016): 1–24; C. Richard King and Charles Fruehling Springwood, eds., *Team Spirits: The Native American Mascots Controversy* (Lincoln: University of Nebraska Press, 2001).

31. David J. Silverman, *This Land Is Their Land: The Wampanoag Indians, Plymouth Colony, and the Troubled History of Thanksgiving* (New York: Bloomsbury, 2019), 412–13.

32. W. Jackson Rushing, *Native American Art and the New York Avant-Garde: A History of Cultural Primitivism* (Austin: University of Texas Press, 1995); Daniel H. Usner Jr., *Indian Work: Language and Livelihood in Native American History* (Cambridge, MA: Harvard University Press, 2009), 117–40; Holm, *Great Confusion*, 89–110; Margaret Connell Szasz, *Education and the American Indian: The Road to Self-Determination Since 1928* (Albuquerque: University of New Mexico Press, 1974), 68–70; David J. Wishart, "Kiowa Six," *Encyclopedia of the Great Plains*, plainshumanities.unl.edu/encyclopedia/doc/egp.art.042 (last accessed Feb. 20, 2025).

33. Martinez, *American Indian Intellectual Tradition*, 157 ("disbelief"); Meriam Report, 721 ("never got away"); Joane Nagel, *American Indian Ethnic Renewal: Red Power and the Resurgence of Identity and Culture* (New York: Oxford University Press, 1996), 194 ("there was a time").

34. Hertzberg, *Search for an American Indian Identity*, 31–134, esp. 58 and 142 ("not vanishing"); Thomas Constantine Maroukis, *We Are Not a Vanishing People: The Society of American Indians, 1911–1923* (Tucson: University of Arizona Press, 2021); Paul C. Rosier, *Serving Their Country: American Indian Politics and Patriotism in the Twentieth Century* (Cambridge, MA: Harvard University Press, 2009), 43–44; Christina Stanciu, "Americanization on Native Terms: The Society of American Indians, Citizenship Debates, and Tropes of 'Racial Difference,'" *Native American and Indigenous Studies* 6, no. 1 (Jan. 2019): 116 ("modern Indians").

35. Martinez, *American Indian Intellectual Tradition*, 199–200 ("reservation Indian"); Maddox, *Citizen Indians*, 62, 77–78; Hertzberg, *Search for American Indian Identity*, 23, 73, 306; Stephen Cornell, *The Return of the Native: American Indian Political Resurgence* (New York: Oxford University Press, 1987), 116–17 ("future").

36. Hertzberg, *Search for an American Indian Identity*, 141; Lapier and Beck, *City Indian*, 87, 92–93; Lila M. Teeters, "'A Simple Act of Justice': The Pueblo Rejection of U.S. Citizenship in the Early Twentieth Century," *Journal of the Gilded Age and Progressive Era* 21, no. 4 (Oct. 2022): 301–18; Stanciu, "Americanization on Native Terms," 113; Maddox, *Citizen Indians*, 155 ("hoax"); Blackhawk, *Rediscovery of America*, 383 ("vote"); Frederick E. Hoxie, *This Indian Country: American Indian Activists and the Place They Made* (New York: Penguin, 2012), 261; Philip J. Deloria, "American Master Narratives and the Problem of Indian Citizenship in the Gilded Age and Progressive Era," *Journal of the Gilded Age and Progressive Era* 14, no. 1 (Jan. 2015): 3–12.

37. Hertzberg, *Search for an American Indian Identity*, 65, 67 ("regret"); Maddox, *Citizen Indians*, 97–98 ("the Indian"); Hoxie, *Talking Back to Civilization*, 121–22 ("physique").

38. Raymond Wilson, *Ohiyesa: Charles Eastman, Santee Sioux* (Urbana: University of Illinois Press, 1983); Hertzberg, *Search for an American Indian Identity*, 141 ("red man"); Hoxie, *Talking Back to Civilization*, 65 ("sick").

39. Jeffrey Ostler, *The Lakotas and the Black Hills: The Struggle for Sacred Ground* (New York: Penguin, 2010), 131–32; Peter Metcalfe, *A Dangerous Idea: The Alaska Native Brotherhood and the Struggle for Indigenous Rights* (Fairbanks: University of Alaska Press, 2014), 13–34; Harmon, *Indians in the Making*, 178–85; Hoxie, *This Indian Country*, 254; Britten, *American Indians in World War I*; Ronald Niezen, *The Origins*

of Indigenism: Human Rights and the Politics of Identity (Berkeley: University of California Press, 2003), 31.

40. Britten, *American Indians in World War I*, 73, 82, 84, 85, 99–102, 104, 118–19; Rosier, *Serving Their Country*, 47, 52 ("nature to fight"); Holm, *Great Confusion*, 147, 178.

41. Colin G. Calloway, *First Peoples: A Documentary History of American Indian History*, 6th ed. (Boston: Macmillan, 2019), 438 "(fundamental"); Taylor, *New Deal and American Indian Tribalism*; K. R. Philp, *John Collier's Crusade for Indian Reform, 1920–1954* (Tucson: University of Arizona Press, 1977); Cornell, *Return of the Native*, 92.

42. Szasz, *Education and the American Indian*, 42, 61, 67, 68.

43. Hoxie, *This Indian Country*, 297 ("extinction"); Martinez, *American Indian Intellectual Tradition*, 270 ("training"); Paul C. Rosier, *Rebirth of the Blackfeet Nation, 1912–1954* (Lincoln: University of Nebraska Press, 2001), 83; Philp, *Indian Self-Rule*, 54 ("Bert").

44. Mary Ann Weston, *Native Americans in the News: Images of Indians in the Twentieth Century Press* (Westport, CT: Greenwood Press, 1996), 52 ("mantle"); Hertzberg, *Search for an American Indian Identity*, 289 ("red"); Laurence M. Hauptman, *The Iroquois and the New Deal* (Syracuse, NY: Syracuse University Press, 1981); Taylor, *New Deal and American Indian Tribalism*, 31, 47; Richard White, *The Roots of Dependency: Subsistence, Environment, and Social Change Among the Choctaws, Pawnees, and Navajos* (Lincoln: University of Nebraska Press, 1988), 250–314; Peter Iverson, *The Navajo Nation* (Westport, CT: Greenwood Press, 1981), 23–46; Iverson, *Our Navajo People*, 59–60; Calloway, *First Peoples*, 441; Rosier, *Serving Their Country*, 70.

45. IRA definition of "Indian," uscode.house.gov/view.xhtml?req=(title:25%20section:5129%20edition:prelim) (last accessed Feb. 20, 2025).

46. Lowery, *Lumbee Indians in the Jim Crow South*, 128 ("Indian problem").

47. Spruhan, "Indian as Race/Indian as Political Status: Implementation of the Half-Blood Requirement Under the Indian Reorganization Act, 1934–1945," *Rutgers Race and the Law Review* 8, no. 1 (2006): 32; Lowery, *Lumbee Indians in the Jim Crow South*, 3, 121–43; Malinda Maynor Lowery, *The Lumbee Indians: An American Struggle* (Chapel Hill: University of North Carolina Press, 2018), 118–20.

48. Klopotek, *Recognition Odysseys*, 19–20; Kristy Gover, "Genealogy as Continuity: Explaining the Growing Tribal Preference for Descent Rules in Membership Governance in the United States," *American Indian Law Review* 33, no. 1 (2008–9): 263–64; Spruhan, "Indian as Race," 33–35, 43, 44–45; Ellinghaus, *Blood Will Tell*, xi–xii.

49. Cornell, *Return of the Native*, 102; Gover, "Genealogy as Continuity," 251.

50. Akim D. Reinhardt, *Ruling Pine Ridge: Oglala Politics from the IRA to Wounded Knee* (Lubbock: Texas Tech University Press, 2007), 94 ("white people," "peyote users").

51. Taylor, *New Deal and American Indian Tribalism*, 104–5 ("general trend" on 105).

52. Philp, *Indian Self-Rule*, 104 ("alternative").

53. Blackhawk, *Rediscovery of America*, 411, 415; Rosier, *Serving Their Country*, 72, 120, 134, 150–51, 162; Donald Lee Fixico, *Termination and Relocation: Federal Indian Policy, 1945–1960* (Albuquerque: University of New Mexico Press, 1990), 6, 7.

54. Fixico, *Termination and Relocation*, 14 ("good enough"); Douglas K. Miller, *Indians on the Move: Native American Mobility and Urbanization in the Twentieth Century* (Chapel Hill: University of North Carolina Press, 2019), 57; Rosier, *Serving Their Country*, 104 ("doing our best"), 144.

55. Nagel, *American Indian Ethnic Renewal*, 214 ("no patience"), 215 ("representation"); Roberta Ulrich, *American Indian Nations from Termination to Restoration, 1953–2006* (Lincoln: University of Nebraska Press, 2010), 122 ("You have not").

56. Ulrich, *American Indian Nations*, xiii–xiv (Wasson and Skelton), 17, 21–22, 43 ("demoralized"), 66, 100–101, 129 ("devastation"); Fixico, *Termination and Relocation*, 91, 181; Nagel, *American Indian Ethnic Renewal*, 220; Charles Wilkinson, *Blood Struggle: The Rise of Modern Indian Nations* (New York: W. W. Norton, 2005), 81–85, 183–84; Rosier, *Serving Their Country*, 164; Henry Redman, "Shawano County: 'The Land the Constitution Forgot,'" *Wisconsin Examiner*, Aug. 13, 2020, wisconsinexaminer.com/2020/08/13/shawano-county-the-land-the-constitution-forgot (last accessed Feb. 20, 2025).

57. Shane Day and Sarabeth Anderson, "Determinants of Successful American Indian Resistance to the Establishment of State Government Jurisdiction Under Public Law 280: A Comparative Case Study of the Processes of Exemption and Retrocession," paper presented at the 2011 annual meeting of the American Political Science Association, pp. 8, 11, papers.ssrn.com/sol3/papers.cfm?abstract_id=1902896 (last accessed May 11, 2025); Rosier, *Serving Their Country*, 164; Fixico, *Termination and Relocation*, 112, 148; *NCAI Newsletter* 2, no. 2 (June 1955): 4 ("relocation").

58. Ignatia Broker, *Night Flying Woman: An Ojibway Narrative* (St. Paul: Minnesota Historical Society Press, 1983), 3–4, 5–6 ("I'm sorry"); Fixico, *Indian Resilience*, 132 ("pigs"); Miller, *Indians on the Move*, 139 ("Mexicans"); Cornell, *Return of the Native*, 132; Coll-Peter Thrush, *Native Seattle: Histories from the Crossing-Over Place*

(Seattle: University of Washington Press, 2007), 164–65; Fixico, *Termination and Relocation*, 11.

59. Broker, *Night Flying Woman*, 5 ("sharing"), 6, 7; Lapier and Beck, *City Indian*, 107, 110–11; E. Alan Morinis, "Getting Straight," *Urban Anthropology* 11, no. 2 (Summer 1982): 193–212; Fixico, *Termination and Relocation*, 10, 149, 155–56; Fixico, *Indian Resilience*, 131–32; Miller, *Indians on the Move*, 35, 144; Thrush, *Native Seattle*, 164–65; Cornell, *Return of the Native*, 141; Nagel, *American Indian Ethnic Renewal*, 120–21.

60. Margaret D. Jacobs, *A Generation Removed: The Fostering and Adoption of Indigenous Children in the Postwar World* (Lincoln: University of Nebraska Press, 2014), 33, 59–61, 63–69; Eva Marie Garroutte, *Real Indians: Identity and the Survival of Native America* (Berkeley: University of California Press, 2003), 23.

61. Jacobs, *Generation Removed*, 93–94 ("placements"), 213–14; Blackhawk, *Rediscovery of America*, 429, 431; Wilkinson, *Blood Struggle*, 258, 259.

62. Dina Gilio-Whitaker, *As Long as Grass Grows: The Indigenous Fight for Environmental Justice, from Colonization to Standing Rock* (Boston: Beacon Press, 2019), 74; Rosier, *Serving Their Country*, 97–98, 201; Wilkinson, *Blood Struggle*, 117; *NCAI Newsletter*, June–July 1949, pp. 2–3.

63. Bruce E. Johansen, *Environmental Racism in the United States and Canada: Seeking Justice and Sustainability* (Westport, CT: Praeger, 2020), 11–12; Gilio-Whitaker, *As Long as Grass Grows*, 68.

64. Gilio-Whitaker, *As Long as Grass Grows*, 67–68; Judy Pasternak, *Yellow Dirt: A Poisoned Land and the Betrayal of the Navajos* (New York: Free Press, 2010); Johansen, *Environmental Racism*, 287–88; U.S. Department of Health and Human Services, *Facing Cancer in Indian Country: The Yakama Nation and Pacific Northwest Tribes*, President's Cancer Panel 2002 Annual Report (Dec. 2003); United Church of Christ, Commission for Racial Justice, *Toxic Waste and Race in the United States: A National Report on the Racial and Socio-Economic Characteristics of Communities with Hazardous Waste Sites* (New York: Commission for Racial Justice, 1987).

65. Gilio-Whitaker, *As Long as Grass Grows*, 16, 19; Johansen, *Environmental Racism*, 7, 220–21, 258. See also Rob Nixon, *Slow Violence and the Environmentalism of the Poor* (Cambridge, MA: Harvard University Press, 2011).

66. Environmental Protection Agency, *Environmental Equity: Reducing Risk for All Communities*, 2 vols. (Washington, D.C.: Environmental Protection Agency, 1992), esp. 1:27–28.

67. William A. Brophy and Sophie B. Aberle, comps., *The Indian: America's Unfinished Business. Report of the Commission on the Rights, Liberties, and Responsibilities of the American Indian* (Norman: University of Oklahoma Press, 1966), 67 ("poor"); Loretta Fowler, "Tribal Sovereignty Movements Compared: The Plains Region," in *Beyond Red Power: American Indian Politics and Activism Since 1900*, ed. Daniel M. Cobb and Loretta Fowler (Santa Fe, NM: School for Advanced Research, 2007), 214; Wilkinson, *Blood Struggle*, xii–xiii, 207, 349; Philp, *Indian Self-Rule*, 54 ("sickening").

68. Shoemaker, *American Indian Population Recovery*, 10; Brophy and Aberle, *The Indian*, 163–64; Wilkinson, *Blood Struggle*, xii–xiii; Fixico, *Indian Resilience*, 129; Jacobs, *Generation Removed*, 32.

69. Szasz, *Education and the American Indian*, 192; Brophy and Aberle, *The Indian*, 138, 149–50; *Indian Education: A National Tragedy, A National Challenge*, 1969 report of the Committee on Labor and Public Welfare, United States Senate (Washington, D.C.: United States Government Printing Office, 1969), 157, 159.

70. Robert A. Silverman, "Patterns of Native American Crime," in *Native Americans, Crime, and Justice*, ed. Marianne O. Nielsen and Robert Silverman (Boulder, CO: Westview Press, 1996), 61; "Police Accused by Dakota Tribe," *NCAI Newsletter* 7, no. 1 (June 1962), 1 ("accused"); *Talking Leaf* 1 (1969): 5.

71. Fixico, *Termination and Relocation*, 15, 58; Rosier, *Serving Their Country*, 120–21 ("public prejudice"); Brophy and Aberle, *The Indian*; *American Indian Issues in the State of South Dakota*, hearing held in Rapid City, SD, July 27–28, 1978 (Washington, D.C.: United States Government Printing Office, 1979); Bonnie Matthews, ed., *Indian Tribes: A Continuing Quest for Survival. A Report of the United States Commission on Civil Rights* (Washington, D.C.: U.S. Commission on Civil Rights, 1981); South Dakota Advisory Committee to the United States Commission on Civil Rights, *Native Americans in South Dakota: An Erosion of Confidence in the Justice System* (Denver, CO: U.S. Commission on Civil Rights, Rocky Mountain Regional Office, 2000); Caheidel Berger, "Red Scare: 1954 Chamberlain Mayor Threatens Indian Supporters," *Madville Times*, Dec. 14, 2013, madvilletimes.com/2013/12/14/red-scare-1954-chamberlain-mayor-threatens-indian-office-supporters ("comfortable") (last accessed Aug. 13, 2024).

72. Paul Chaat Smith and Robert Allen Warrior, *Like a Hurricane: The Indian Movement from Alcatraz to Wounded Knee* (New York: New Press, 1996), 42.

73. Alvin M. Josephy Jr., ed., *Red Power: The American Indians' Fight for Freedom* (New York: McGraw-Hill, 1971), 56 ("disappear"), 72–74 ("poverty" on 72); Martinez,

American Indian Intellectual Tradition, 317–18. Generally, see Paul R. McKenzie-Jones, *Clyde Warrior: Tradition, Community, and Red Power* (Norman: University of Oklahoma Press, 2015), esp. 72 and 181; Bradley Glenn Shreve, *Red Power Rising: The National Indian Youth Council and the Origins of Native Activism* (Norman: University of Oklahoma Press, 2011); and Smith and Warrior, *Like a Hurricane*, 36–59.

74. Wilkinson, *Blood Struggle*, 132; Laurence M. Hauptman, *The Iroquois Struggle for Survival: World War II to Red Power* (Syracuse, NY: Syracuse University Press, 1985); Daniel M. Cobb, *Native Activism in Cold War America: The Struggle for Sovereignty* (Lawrence: University Press of Kansas, 2008); Seonghoon Kim, "'We Have Always Had These Many Voices': Red Power Newspapers and a Community of Poetic Resistance," *American Indian Quarterly* 39, no. 3 (Summer 2015): 271–301.

75. Hoxie, *This Indian Country*, 337–92; Vine Deloria Jr., *Custer Died for Your Sins: An Indian Manifesto* (New York: Macmillan, 1969), 175 ("white man"); Kevin Bruyneel, *The Third Space of Sovereignty: The Postcolonial Politics of U.S.–Indigenous Relations* (Minneapolis: University of Minnesota Press, 2007), 152 ("Red Power").

76. Lyndon B. Johnson, "Special Message to the Congress on the Problems of the American Indian: 'The Forgotten American,'" Mar. 6, 1968, presidency.ucsb.edu/documents/special-message-the-congress-the-problems-the-american-indian-the-forgotten-american (last accessed Aug. 13, 2024); Cobb, *Native Activism*, 125–46; Blackhawk, *Rediscovery of America*, 437; David Treuer, *The Heartbeat of Wounded Knee: Native America from 1890 to the Present* (New York: Riverhead Books, 2019), 329, 334–35.

77. Smith and Warrior, *Like a Hurricane*, 18–35, 60–82.

78. Nagel, *American Indian Ethnic Renewal*, 133–34 (all quotes).

79. Smith and Warrior, *Like a Hurricane*, 114–15.

80. Smith and Warrior, *Like a Hurricane*, 194–238 (93 percent on 236); James E. Murphy and Sharon M. Murphy, *Let My People Know: American Indian Journalism, 1828–1978* (Norman: University of Oklahoma Press, 1981), 9 ("last gasp").

81. Anonymous, "Self Hate," *Akwesasne Notes* 3, no. 2 (Mar. 1971): 3.

CHAPTER 8: CHOOSING

1. Richard Nixon, "Special Message to the Congress on Indian Affairs," July 8, 1970, presidency.ucsb.edu/documents/special-message-the-congress-indian-affairs (last

accessed Aug. 13, 2024). For reflections on Nixon's record on Indian affairs, see Duane Champagne, "From Full Citizenship to Self-Determination, 1930–75," in *American Indians, American Presidents*, ed. Clifford E. Trafzer (New York: Harper, 2009), 175–83; Nick Martin, "Indian Country Deserves a Greater Hero than Richard Nixon," *New Republic*, Oct. 21, 2019, newrepublic.com/article/155440/indian-country-deserves-better-hero-richard-nixon; and David H. DeJong, *Paternalism to Partnership: The Administration of Indian Affairs, 1786–2021* (Lincoln: University of Nebraska Press, 2021), 328–38.

2. Nixon, "Special Message to the Congress."

3. David Martinez, *Life of the Indigenous Mind: Vine Deloria Jr. and the Birth of the Red Power Movement* (Lincoln: University of Nebraska Press, 2019), 132–74 ("red man" on 133).

4. Gary Gerstle, *American Crucible: Race and Nation in the Twentieth Century* (Princeton, NJ: Princeton University Press, 2001), 276; Kyle T. Mays, *An Afro-Indigenous History of the United States* (Boston: Beacon Press, 2021), 102–3, 118–20; Raoul Peck, "James Baldwin Was Right All Along," *The Atlantic*, July 3, 2020.

5. Peter Metcalfe, *A Dangerous Idea: The Alaska Native Brotherhood and the Struggle for Indigenous Rights* (Fairbanks: University of Alaska Press, 2014), xxii, 10; Donald Craig Mitchell, *Sold American: The Story of Alaska Natives and Their Land, 1867–1959, the Army to Statehood* (Hanover, NH: University Press of New England, 1997), 11–12; Charles Wilkinson, *Blood Struggle: The Rise of Modern Indian Nations* (New York: W. W. Norton, 2005), 178–89, 239; "American Indian Religious Freedom Act Amendments of 1994," H.R. 4230, Jan. 25, 1994, congress.gov/103/bills/hr4230/BILLS-103hr4230enr.pdf (last accessed Aug. 13, 2024).

6. Alvin M. Josephy Jr., ed., *Red Power: The American Indians' Fight for Freedom* (New York: McGraw-Hill, 1971), 89–92 ("in common"); Alexandra Harmon, *Indians in the Making: Ethnic Relations and Indian Identities Around Puget Sound* (Berkeley: University of California Press, 2000), 230–31; Larry Nesper, *The Walleye War: The Struggle for Ojibwe Spearfishing and Treaty Rights* (Lincoln: University of Nebraska Press, 2002); *NCAI Annual Report*, 2009–10, p. 23; Melinda Janko, "Elouise Cobell: A Small Measure of Justice," *Magazine of the Smithsonian's National Museum of the American Indian* 14, no. 2 (Summer 2016), americanindianmagazine.org/story/elouise-cobell-small-measure-justice (last accessed Aug. 13, 2024).

7. Wilkinson, *Blood Struggle*, 223–24, 229; U.S. Department of the Interior, Indian Affairs, "Petitions Resolved—Acknowledged," bia.gov/as-ia/ofa/petitions-resolved

/acknowledged (last accessed Aug. 13, 2024); U.S. Department of the Interior, Indian Affairs, "Petitions Resolved—Denied," bia.gov/as-ia/ofa/petitions-resolved/denied (last accessed Aug. 13, 2024); "Thomasina E. Jordan Indian Tribes of Virginia Federal Recognition Act of 2017," H.R. 984, Jan. 29, 2018, congress.gov/bill/115th-congress/house-bill/984/text (last accessed Aug. 13, 2024); K. Alexa Koenig and Jonathan Stein, "State Recognition of Native American Tribes," in *Recognition, Sovereignty Struggles, and Indigenous Rights in the United States: A Sourcebook*, ed. Amy E. Den Oden and Jean M. O'Brien (Chapel Hill: University of North Carolina Press, 2013), 115–47.

8. U.S. Small Business Administration Office of Advocacy, "Facts About Small Business: Native American–Owned Business," Nov. 22, 2023, advocacy.sba.gov/2023/11/22/native-american-owned-businesses (last accessed Aug. 13, 2024); Indian Gaming Association, indiangaming.org (last accessed Aug. 13, 2024); National Indian Gaming Commission, "FY 2022 Gross Gaming Revenue Report," nigc.gov/images/uploads/GGRFY22_071923_Final.pdf (last accessed Aug. 13, 2024). Generally, see David Treuer, *The Heartbeat of Wounded Knee: Native America from 1890 to the Present* (New York: Riverhead Books, 2019), 361–406; Wilkinson, *Blood Struggle*, 336–37, 344; Kevin Bruyneel, *The Third Space of Sovereignty: The Postcolonial Politics of U.S.–Indigenous Relations* (Minneapolis: University of Minnesota Press, 2007), 178; Loretta Fowler, "Tribal Sovereignty Movements Compared: The Plains Region," in *Beyond Red Power: American Indian Politics and Activism Since 1900*, ed. Daniel M. Cobb and Loretta Fowler (Santa Fe, NM: School for Advanced Research, 2007), 209–27; and Donald L. Fixico, *The Invasion of Indian Country in the Twentieth Century: American Capitalism and Tribal Natural Resources* (Niwot: University Press of Colorado, 1998), 131–207.

9. *NCAI Annual Report*, 2015–16, p. 8; Wôpanâak Language Reclamation Project, wlrp.org (last accessed Aug. 13, 2024); Joane Nagel, *American Indian Ethnic Renewal: Red Power and the Resurgence of Identity and Culture* (New York: Oxford University Press, 1996), 47; Wilkinson, *Blood Struggle*, 192–93, 281–84, 287, 288, 294. See also the 2007 documentary film by Anne Makepeace, *Tribal Justice*.

10. Donald L. Fixico, *Indian Resilience and Rebuilding: Indigenous Nations in the Modern American West* (Tucson: University of Arizona Press, 2013), 211; Michael McNally, *Defend the Sacred: Native American Religious Freedom Beyond the First Amendment* (Princeton, NJ: Princeton University Press, 2020), 201 ("dream"); Cara J. Chang, "Harvard Holds Human Remains of 19 Likely Enslaved Individuals, Thousands of Native Americans, Draft Report Says," *Harvard Crimson*, June 1, 2022, thecrimson.com/article/2022/6/1/draft-human-remains-report (last accessed Aug. 13, 2024); Kathleen S. Fine-Dare, *Grave Injustice: The American Indian*

Repatriation Movement and NAGPRA (Lincoln: University of Nebraska Press, 2002); Jason Daley, "Massasoit, Chief Who Signed Treaty with the Pilgrims, to Be Reburied," *Smithsonian Magazine*, Apr. 21, 2017, smithsonianmag.com/smart-news/massasoit-chief-who-signed-treaty-pilgrims-be-reburied-180962928 (last accessed Aug. 13, 2024); "Human Remains Task Force Report to the Secretary," Smithsonian Institution, Jan. 10, 2024, si.edu/sites/default/files/about/human-remains-task-force-report.pdf (last accessed Aug. 13, 2024).

11. Margaret D. Jacobs, *A Generation Removed: The Fostering and Adoption of Indigenous Children in the Postwar World* (Lincoln: University of Nebraska Press, 2014), esp. 95–96, 102, 135, 140–41; "Meet the Indigenous Social Workers Who Transformed Tribal Child Welfare," Alliance for Early Success, Oct. 10, 2022, earlysuccess.org/icwa-champions-spotlight (last accessed Aug. 13, 2024).

12. *NCAI Annual Report*, 2010–11, p. 23; Ronald Niezen, *The Origins of Indigenism: Human Rights and the Politics of Identity* (Berkeley: University of California Press, 2003), esp. xii, 3; McNally, *Defend the Sacred*, 22; Walter L. Hixson, *American Settler Colonialism: A History* (New York: Palgrave Macmillan, 2013), 186.

13. Joanna Hearne, *Native Recognition: Indigenous Cinema and the Western* (Albany: State University of New York Press, 2012), 219–20, 225, 249–50, 270–71; Jacquelyn Kilpatrick, *Celluloid Indians: Native Americans and Film* (Lincoln: University of Nebraska Press, 1999), 97, 224; Michael Hilger, *From Savage to Nobleman: Images of Native Americans in Film* (Lanham, MD: Scarecrow Press, 1995), 178, 189, 208; Robert F. Berkhofer Jr., *The White Man's Indian: Images of the American Indian from Columbus to the Present* (New York: Alfred A. Knopf, 1978), 103–4.

14. David Waldstein and Michael S. Schmidt, "Cleveland's Baseball Team Will Drop Its Indians Team Name," *New York Times*, Dec. 13, 2020, nytimes.com/2020/12/13/sports/baseball/cleveland-indians-baseball-name-change.html (last accessed Aug. 13, 2024); Jeremy Bergman, "Washington Will Go by 'Washington Football Team' Until Further Notice," NFL, July 23, 2020, nfl.com/news/washington-football-team-nfl-name-change (last accessed Aug. 13, 2024); David Waldstein, "Amid Pressure, Chicago N.H.L. Team Says It Won't Change Its Name," *New York Times*, July 7, 2020, nytimes.com/2020/07/07/sports/hockey/chicago-blackhawks-stand-by-logo.html (last accessed Aug. 13, 2024); "Celebrating American Indian Heritage," *Chiefs Kingdom*, chiefs.com/americanindianheritage (last accessed Aug. 13, 2024); Matt Bonesteel, "The Braves Have Resisted a Name Change, but Hank Aaron's Death Renews Calls for 'the Hammers,'" *Washington Post*, Jan. 21, 2022, washingtonpost.com/sports/2021/01/22/braves-name-change-hammers (last accessed Aug. 13, 2024).

15. Kenneth R. Philp, "The Indian Reorganization Act Fifty Years Later," in *Indian Self-Rule: First-Hand Accounts of Indian-White Relations from Roosevelt to Reagan*, ed. Kenneth R. Philp (Salt Lake City: Utah State University Libraries, 1986), 24; Troy Johnson, "The Era of Self-Determination: 1975–Today," in Trafzer, *American Indians, American Presidents*, 198–205; Levi Rickert, "Assistant Secretary Newland Touts President Biden's Commitment to Indian Country," *Native News Online*, Mar. 16, 2024, nativenewsonline.net/currents/assistant-secretary-newland-touts-president-biden-s-commitment-to-indian-country (last accessed Aug. 13, 2024); David Montgomery, "What Do Native Americans Want from a President?" *Washington Post Magazine*, May 13, 2019, washingtonpost.com/news/magazine/wp/2019/05/13/feature/what-do-native-americans-want-from-a-president (last accessed Aug. 13, 2024).

16. Briana Theobold, *Reproduction on the Reservation: Pregnancy, Childbirth, and Colonialism in the Long Twentieth Century* (Chapel Hill: University of North Carolina Press, 2019), 1, 80, 159–60; Jacobs, *Generation Removed*, 93; Bonnie Matthews, ed., *Indian Tribes: A Continuing Quest for Survival. A Report of the United States Commission on Civil Rights* (Washington, D.C.: U.S. Commission on Civil Rights, 1981), 38; "Sterilization Report: Congress Finds Indians Sterilized Unknowingly and Used as Guinea Pigs," *Talking Leaf* 42, no. 2 (Feb. 1977): 3.

17. *NCAI Annual Report*, 2010–11, p. 23; Sarah Deer, *The Beginning and End of Rape: Confronting Sexual Violence in Native America* (Minneapolis: University of Minnesota Press, 2015), 1, 4–5, 6; South Dakota Advisory Committee to the United States Commission on Civil Rights, *Native Americans in South Dakota: An Erosion of Confidence in the Justice System* (Denver, CO: U.S. Commission on Civil Rights, Rocky Mountain Regional Office, 2000), unpaginated; *NCAI Annual Report*, 2004–5, p. 9; Nick Estes et al., *Red Nation Rising: From Bordertown Violence to Native Liberation* (New York: PM Press, 2021), 63–65.

18. Deer, *Beginning and End*, 12 ("Imagine"), 99–100; *NCAI Annual Report*, 2011–12, p. 29; Alejandra Dubcovsky, *Talking Back: Native Women and the Making of the Early South* (New Haven, CT: Yale University Press, 2023), 183.

19. John Waliczek, "Civil Rights Said Violated," *Akwesasne Notes* 2, no. 1 (Apr. 1970): 8; "Farmington, New Mexico: 'The Selma, Alabama of the Southwest,'" *Akwesasne Notes* 10, no. 1 (early Spring 1978): 9 ("Selma"); Barbara Perry, *Silent Victims: Hate Crimes Against Native Americans* (Tucson: University of Arizona Press, 2008), 4; Estes et al., *Red Nation Rising*, 38.

20. Estes et al., *Red Nation Rising*, 12, 16, 21, 26, 43–45; Matthews, *Indian Tribes: A Continuing Quest for Survival*, 39, 41; Perry, *Silent Victims*, 53–54, 77, 80–83, 102, 105–6.

21. Fixico, *Invasion of Indian Country*, 110, 113; Matthews, *Indian Tribes: A Continuing Quest for Survival*, 119 (*Time*); Fixico, "Witness to Change: Fifty Years of Indian Activism and Tribal Politics," in Cobb and Fowler, *Beyond Red Power*, 10–11; Wilkinson, *Blood Struggle*, 266; Perry, *Silent Victims*, 77–78, 89–90. An excellent examination of jurisdictional disputes enflaming racial tensions is Thomas Biolsi, *Deadliest Enemies: Law and the Making of Race Relations On and Off Rosebud Reservation* (Berkeley: University of California Press, 2001). See also Matthews, *Indian Tribes: A Continuing Quest for Survival*, 10; "On to Geneva: Indian Delegates Prepare to Bring Their Case to the World Community," *Talking Leaf* 42, no. 9 (Sept. 1977), p. 3, cols. 1–2; and Rennee Ann Cramer, "The Common Sense of Anti-Indian Racism: Reactions to Mashantucket Pequot Success in Gaming and Acknowledgment," *Law and Social Inquiry* 31, no. 2 (Sept. 2006): 313–41.

22. James Clifford, *The Predicament of Culture: Twentieth-Century Ethnography, Literature, and Art* (Cambridge, MA: Harvard University Press, 1988), 277–346; Jack Campisi, *The Mashpee Indians: Tribe on Trial* (Syracuse, NY: Syracuse University Press, 1991).

23. Eva Marie Garroutte, *Real Indians: Identity and the Survival of Native America* (Berkeley: University of California Press, 2003), 14; Joel Lang, "Reading Jeff Benedict: Should You Believe His Revelations About the Pequots and the Making of the World's Largest Casino?" *Hartford Courant*, Dec. 3, 2000, p. 5; Amy E. Den Ouden, "Altered State? Indian Policy Narratives, Federal Recognition, and the 'New War' on Native Rights in Connecticut," in Den Ouden and O'Brien, *Recognition, Sovereignty Struggles, and Indigenous Rights in the United States*, 169–94; Cramer, "Common Sense," 329; Brian Klopotek, *Recognition Odysseys: Indigeneity, Race, and Federal Recognition Policy in Three Louisiana Indian Communities* (Durham, NC: Duke University Press, 2011), 55, 194; "'They don't look like Indians to me': Donald Trump on Native American Casinos in 1993," https://www.washingtonpost.com/video/politics/they-dont-look-like-indians-to-me-donald-trump-on-native-american-casinos-in-1993/2016/07/01/20736038-3fd4-11e6-9e16-4cf01a41decb_video.html (last accessed Oct. 14, 2025).

24. Brian D. Haley and Larry R. Wilcoxon, "Anthropology and the Making of Chumash Tradition," *Current Anthropology* 38, no. 5 (Dec. 1997): 761–94; Martha Sadler, "Authentic Identity in Question," *Santa Barbara Independent*, Jan. 18, 2007, inde

pendent.com/2007/01/18/authentic-ethnicity-question (last accessed Aug. 13, 2024); Jon McVey Erlandson, "The Making of Chumash Tradition: Replies to Haley and Wilcoxon," *Current Anthropology* 34, no. 4 (Aug.–Oct. 1998): 477–510; Kohanya Jessica Ranch, "Changing Perceptions and Policy: Redefining Indigeneity Through California Chumash Revitalization" (PhD diss., University of California, Riverside, 2012), 93–98; Alexandra Harmon, *Rich Indians: Native People and the Problem of Wealth in American History* (Chapel Hill: University of North Carolina Press, 2010).

25. Mikaëla Adams, *Who Belongs? Race, Resources, and Tribal Citizenship in the Native South* (New York: Oxford University Press, 2016), 1–24; Kristy Gover, "Genealogy as Continuity: Explaining the Growing Tribal Preference for Descent Rules in Membership Governance in the United States," *American Indian Law Review* 33, no. 1 (2008–9), 243–309; Garroutte, *Real Indians*, 22, 24.

26. See the note below.

27. Circe Sturm, *Becoming Indian: The Struggle over Cherokee Identity in the Twenty-first Century* (Santa Fe, NM: School for Advanced Research, 2010), 129; Nagel, *American Indian Ethnic Renewal*, 240; Gover, "Genealogy as Continuity," 251, 295–96, 297; Katherine Ellinghaus, *Blood Will Tell: Native Americans and Assimilation Policy* (Lincoln: University of Nebraska Press, 2017), 88; Klopotek, *Recognition Odysseys*, 112; C. Michael Snipp, "Some Observations About Racial Boundaries and the Experiences of American Indians," *Ethnic and Racial Studies* 20, no. 4 (Oct. 1997): 683; Thomas Constantine Maroukis, *The Peyote Road: Religious Freedom and the Native American Church* (Norman: University of Oklahoma Press, 2010), 211; Douglas Kiel, "Bleeding Out: Histories and Legacies of 'Indian Blood,'" in *The Great Vanishing Act: Blood Quantum and the Future of Native Nations*, ed. Kathleen Ratteree and Norbert Hill (Golden, CO: Fulcrum, 2017), 82–83, 91; David E. Wilkins and Shelly Hulse Wilkins, *Dismembered: Native Disenrollment and the Battle for Human Rights* (Seattle: University of Washington Press, 2017).

28. Nancy Shoemaker, *American Indian Population Recovery in the Twentieth Century* (Albuquerque: University of New Mexico Press, 1999), 4; Sturm, *Becoming Indian*, 5; Andrew Van Dam, "The Native American Population Exploded, the Census Shows. Here's Why," *Washington Post*, Oct. 27, 2023, washingtonpost.com/business/2023/10/27/native-americans-2020-census (last accessed Aug. 13, 2024). See also the critique of census definitions by Robert Maxim, "Our Revised Race Standards Still Fall Short for Indigenous Americans," *The Hill*, May 3, 2024, thehill.com/opinion/civil-rights/4639408-our-revised-race-standards-still-fall-short-for-indigenous-americans (last accessed Aug. 13, 2024).

29. Frell M. Owl, "Who and What Is an American Indian?" in *The American Indian Intellectual Tradition: An Anthology of Writings from 1772 to 1972*, ed. David Martinez (Ithaca, NY: Cornell University Press, 2011), 308–10 ("jealous" on 308), 314; Sturm, *Becoming Indian*, 43, 78, 131–32; Malinda Maynor Lowery, *Lumbee Indians in the Jim Crow South: Race, Identity, and the Making of a Nation* (Chapel Hill: University of North Carolina Press, 2010), 204–5.

30. Garroutte, *Real Indians*, 48, 49, 51; Michelle R. Montgomery, *Identity Politics of Difference: The Mixed-Race American Indian Experience* (Boulder: University Press of Colorado, 2017), 62, 94–96, 103. Generally, see Kim TallBear, "Twentieth-Century Tribal Blood Politics," in Ratteree and Hill, *Great Vanishing*, 129–41; Garroutte, *Real Indians*, 51; and Pauline Turner Strong and Barrik Van Winkle, "'Indian Blood': Reflections on the Reckoning and Refiguring of Native North American Identity," *Cultural Anthropology* 11, no. 4 (Nov. 1996): 547–76.

31. Adrienne Keene, "Love in the Time of Blood Quantum," and Leslie Logan, "Good Guidance," in Ratteree and Hill, *Great Vanishing*, 5 ("identity politics"), 25–27, 31; Montgomery, *Identity Politics of Difference*, 101; Garroutte, *Real Indians*, 48.

32. Logan, "Good Guidance," and Suzan Shown Harjo, "Vampire Policy Is Bleeding Us Dry—Blood Quantums Be Gone!" in Ratteree and Hill, *Great Vanishing*, 31 ("current"), 79 ("clever").

33. Circe Sturm, *Blood Politics: Race, Culture, and Identity in the Cherokee Nation of Oklahoma* (Berkeley: University of California Press, 2002), 89.

34. Fowler, "Tribal Sovereignty," 218; Garroutte, *Real Indians*, 22. For an early denunciation of blood quantum, see the letter of Wallace Squires-Popour in *Indian Historian* 7, no. 4 (Fall 1974): 35. For more recent examples, see Garroutte, *Real Indians*, 54; Klopotek, *Recognition Odysseys*, 112; David E. Wilkins and Shelly Hulse Wilkins, "Blood Quantum: The Mathematics of Ethnocide," 210–27, Stephen Cornell and Joseph P. Kalt, "From Tribal *Members* to Native Nation *Citizens*," 289, and Gyasi Ross, "We Chose This, Now What? What Comes After Blood Quantum?," 307–12, in Ratteree and Hill, *Great Vanishing*; Harjo "Vampire Policy," 79 and Kiel, "Bleeding Out," 82–91.

35. Daniel F. Littlefield Jr., *The Chickasaw Freedmen: A People Without a Country* (Westport, CT: Greenwood Press, 1980); Barbara Krauthamer, *Black Slaves, Indian Masters: Slavery, Emancipation, and Citizenship in the Native American South* (Chapel Hill: University of North Carolina Press, 2013); Alaina Roberts, *I've Been Here All the While: Black Freedom on Native Land* (Philadelphia: University

of Pennsylvania Press, 2011); Sturm, *Blood Politics*; Claudio Saunt, *Black, White, and Indian: Race and the Unmaking of an American Family* (New York: Oxford University Press, 2005); Tiya Miles, *Ties That Bind: The Story of an Afro-Cherokee Family in Slavery and Freedom* (Berkeley: University of California Press, 2005).

36. See, for example, Julia Coates, "Race and Sovereignty," in Ratteree and Hill, *Great Vanishing*, 112–18; and the discussions in Circe Sturm, "Blood Politics, Racial Classification, and Cherokee National Identity: The Trials and Tribulations of the Cherokee Freedmen," *American Indian Quarterly* 22, nos. 1 and 2 (Winter–Spring 1998): 230–58; and Philip J. Deloria, "When Tribal Nations Expel Their Black Members," *New Yorker*, July 25, 2022, newyorker.com/magazine/2022/07/25/when-tribal-nations-expel-their-black-members-caleb-gayle-we-refuse-to-forget-alaina-e-roberts-ive-been-here-all-the-while (last accessed Aug. 13, 2024).

37. Deloria, "When Tribal Nations Expel Their Black Members"; Melinda Micco, "'Blood and Money': The Case of Seminole Freedmen and Seminole Indians in Oklahoma," in *Crossing Waters, Crossing World: The African Diaspora in Indian Country*, ed. Tiya Miles and Sharon P. Holland (Durham, NC: Duke University Press, 2006), 121–44. See also the useful update on these cases in "The Long Fight for Freedman Citizenship Continues in Oklahoma Tribal Nations," *NonDoc*, Mar. 4, 2022, nondoc.com/2022/03/04/freedmen-citizenship-fight-continues (last accessed Aug. 13, 2024).

38. Adams, *Who Belongs?*, 44–50; Laura J. Feller, *Being Indigenous in Jim Crow Virginia: Powhatan People and the Color Line* (Norman: University of Oklahoma Press, 2022); Arica L. Coleman, *That the Blood Stay Pure: African Americans, Native Americans, and the Predicament of Race and Identity in Virginia* (Bloomington: Indiana University Press, 2013).

39. Cherokee Open Letter to Elizabeth Warren, Feb. 26, 2020, medium.com/@ewarrenisnotcherokee/open-letter-to-elizabeth-warren-from-cherokee-citizens-ab053578bd95 (last accessed Aug. 13, 2024).

40. Gregory Smithers, "Elizabeth Warren's DNA Disaster," *Politico*, Oct. 18, 2018, politico.com/magazine/story/2018/10/18/elizabeth-warrens-dna-disaster-221607 (last accessed Aug. 13, 2024); Kim TallBear, "Elizabeth Warren's Claim to Cherokee Ancestry Is a Form of Violence," *High Country News*, Jan. 17, 2019, hcn.org/issues/51-2/tribal-affairs-elizabeth-warrens-claim-to-cherokee-ancestry-is-a-form-of-violence (last accessed Aug. 13, 2024); Nick Martin, "Elizabeth Warren's Deception," *Splinter*, Oct. 16, 2018, splinternews.com/elizabeth-warrens-deception-1829755302 (last accessed Aug. 13, 2024); Warren letter to the Cherokees, Feb. 25, 2020: s3.document

cloud.org/documents/6786094/Reply-Letter-From-Elizabeth-Warren.pdf (last accessed Aug. 13, 2024).

41. Sturm, *Becoming Indian*, 15, 18; Darryl Leroux, "State Recognition and the Dangers of Race Shifting," *American Indian Culture and Research Journal* 46, no. 2 (2023): 53–84; Jay Kaspian Kang, "A Professor Claimed to Be Native American. Did She Know She Wasn't?," *New Yorker*, Feb. 26, 2024, newyorker.com/magazine/2024/03/04/a-professor-claimed-to-be-native-american-did-she-know-she-wasnt (last accessed Aug. 13, 2024); Sarah Viren, "The Native Scholar Who Wasn't," *New York Times*, May 26, 2021, nytimes.com/2021/05/25/magazine/cherokee-native-american-andrea-smith.html (last accessed Aug. 13, 2024); Vimal Patel, "Prominent Scholar Who Claimed to Be Native American Resigns," *New York Times*, Aug. 27, 2023, nytimes.com/2023/08/27/us/uc-riverside-andrea-smith-resigns.html (last accessed Aug. 13, 2024); Kathryn Palmer, "Oregon State Professor Accused of Falsely Claiming Native Ancestry," *Inside Higher Ed*, Nov. 7, 2023, insidehighered.com/news/faculty-issues/diversity-equity/2023/11/07/oregon-state-professor-accused-falsely-claiming (last accessed Aug. 13, 2024); Ryan Quinn, "Professor Leaving University After Being Dubbed 'Pretendian' for Years," *Inside Higher Ed*, Aug. 18, 2023, insidehighered.com/news/faculty-issues/diversity-equity/2023/08/18/professor-leaving-after-being-dubbed-pretendian (last accessed Aug. 13, 2024); Cecily Hilleary, "Native, First Nations Scholars: Fake Indians Prevalent in Higher Education," *Voice of America*, Apr. 3, 2022, voanews.com/a/native-first-nations-scholars-fake-indians-prevalent-in-higher-education-/6511681.html (last accessed Aug. 13, 2024); Rosalyn R. Lapier and David R. M. Beck, *City Indian: Native American Activism in Chicago, 1893–1934* (Lincoln: University of Nebraska Press, 2015), 155 ("hot one").

42. Sturm, *Becoming Indian*, 50, 57, 61, 67.

43. Sturm, *Becoming Indian*, 33 ("painful").

44. Philp, *Indian Self-Rule*, 132–33, 248.

EPILOGUE: TRANSITIONS

1. Thomas G. Dyer, *Theodore Roosevelt and the Idea of Race* (Baton Rouge: Louisiana State University Press, 1980), 86.

2. Robb DeWall, *Crazy Horse and Korczak: The Story of an Epic Mountain Carving* (Crazy Horse, SD: Korczak's Heritage, 1982), 56 ("where my dead"); Jeffrey Ostler, *The Lakotas and the Black Hills: The Struggle for Sacred Ground* (New York: Penguin, 2010), 146–47.

3. DeWall, *Crazy Horse and Korczak*; Michael A. Elliott, *Custerology: The Enduring Legacy of the Indian Wars and George Armstrong Custer* (Chicago: University of Chicago Press, 2007), 166–70; Crazy Horse Memorial, crazyhorsememorial.org (last accessed Feb. 3, 2025).

4. Liz Hill, ed., *Past, Present, and Future: Challenges of the National Museum of the American Indian* (Washington, D.C.: National Museum of the American Indian, 2011); Duane Blue Spruce, ed., *Spirit of a Native Place: Building the National Museum of the American Indian* (Washington, D.C.: National Museum of the American Indian, 2004).

5. Spruce, *Spirit of a Native Place*; Jennifer A. Shannon, *Our Lives: Collaboration, Native Voice, and the Making of the National Museum of the American Indian* (Santa Fe, NM: School for Advanced Research, 2014).

6. For criticism of NMAI's approach to the subject of genocide, see Sonya Atalay, "No Sense of the Struggle: Creating a Context for Survivance at the National Museum of the American Indian," Myla Vicenti Carpio, "(Un)Disturbing Exhibitions: Indigenous Historical Memory at the National Museum of the American Indian," and Amy Lonetree, "'Acknowledging the Truth of History': Missed Opportunities at the National Museum of the American Indian," all in *The National Museum of the American Indian: Critical Conversations*, ed. Amy Lonetree and Amanda J. Cobb (Lincoln: University of Nebraska Press, 2008); and Peter D'Errico, "Native American Genocide or Holocaust?" *Indian Country News*, Jan. 10, 2017, ictnews.org/archive/native-american-genocide-holocaust (last accessed Feb. 13, 2025). On the NCAI call for an American Indian Holocaust Museum, see National Congress of American Indians, Resolution #TUL-13-0005, ncai.org/resources/resolutions/national-american-indian-holocaust-museum (last accessed Feb. 13, 2025).

7. "'IndiVisible' Discusses African–Native American Lives," Smithsonian news release, Jan. 6, 2012, si.edu/newsdesk/releases/indivisible-discusses-african-native-american-lives (last accessed Feb. 13, 2025).

8. Paul Chaat Smith, "Critical Reflections on the Our Peoples Exhibit: A Curator's Perspective," in Lonetree and Cobb, *National Museum of the American Indian*, 132.

9. Anna V. Smith, "Trump's Impact on Indian Country over Four Years," *High Country News*, Dec. 16, 2020, hcn.org/articles/indigenous-affairs-trumps-impact-on-indian-country-over-four-years (last accessed Aug. 13, 2024); "Trump Administration Revokes Tribe's Reservation Status in 'Power Grab,'" *Guardian*, Mar. 31, 2020, theguardian.com/us-news/2020/mar/31/trump-administration-revokes-mashpee

-wampanoag-tribe-reservation-status (last accessed Aug. 13, 2024); Associated Press, "Mashpee Wampanoag Tribe Wins Legal Battle over Trump Administration Appeal, Will Keep Legal Status," Boston.com, Feb. 20, 2021, boston.com/news/local-news/2021/02/20/mashpee-wampanoag-tribe-wins-legal-battle-over-trump-administration-appeal-will-keep-reservation-status (last accessed Aug. 13, 2024); Levi Rickert, "Arguably, President Joe Biden Has Been the Best President for Indian Country," *Native News Online*, July 28, 2024, nativenewsonline.net/opinion/arguably-president-joe-biden-has-been-the-best-president-for-indian-country (last accessed Aug. 13, 2024); Darren R. Reid, "How Native Americans Shaped Trump's Presidency—and Helped Bring Him Down," *The Conversation*, Nov. 20, 2020, theconversation.com/how-native-americans-shaped-trumps-presidency-and-helped-bring-him-down-150497 (last accessed Aug. 13, 2024); Kadin Mills, "Five Indigenous Take-Aways from the Republican National Convention," *Source NM*, July 25, 2024, sourcenm.com/2024/07/25/five-indigenous-take-aways-from-the-republican-national-convention (last accessed Aug. 13, 2024). See also the Republican policy blueprint for the Department of the Interior and Indian country proposed by the Heritage Foundation in its Project 2025 report, *Mandate for Leadership: The Conservative Promise* (2023), pp. 536–37, static.project2025.org/2025_MandateForLeadership_FULL.pdf (last accessed Aug. 13, 2024).

INDEX

Note: Page numbers in italics refer to figures.

Abbott, Frederck H., 9
Abenakis, 45, 62–63, 67; 87
Adair, James, 76, 154, 155
Adams, John, 124 130
Adams, John Quincy, 165, 169
agencies, of Indian Department
    Fort Robinson, 242
    Lower Brule, 248
    Quapaw, 266
    Standing Rock, 320
    Upper Platte, 201
Akwesasne Notes, 326, 331
Alabama, 146, 161, 164, 165, 166, 167, 181, 340, 350
Alabama-Coushattas, 209
Alaska (territory and state), 306, 307, 316, 321–22, 326, 338–39, 349
Alaska Native Brotherhood and Sisterhood, 306
Albany, NY, 67, 68
Alcatraz, 328, 336
Alford, Thomas Wildcat, 259, 261, 263
allotments
    early examples of, 164
    leases of, 281–82
    Removal-era examples of, 181, 182, 183

    of reservations, 270–84, *278*
American exceptionalism, 47
American Colonization Society, 168
American Indian Day, 305
American Indian Federation, 309
American Indian Movement, 328–30, *330*
American Revolution, 109–26
    Cherokee campaigns of, 117–18, *118*
    Indian loyalties during, 111
    Iroquois campaigns of, 118–20
    Kentucky campaigns of, 120
Amherst, Jeffrey, 87, 95, 96–97
Anadarkos, 209
Andrews, William, 67–70
Andros, Edmund, 52
anthropology, 3
Apaches, 3, 207, 222, 235, 236, 251, 263, 321
    Aravaipa, 235
    Chiricahua, 251
    Jicarilla, 321
    Lipan, 285
    Mescalero, 222, 255, 259, 321
    Mimbreño, 222
    Pinal, 235
    Yavapai, 303

Apess, William, 151, 189–91
Appalachian Mountains, 21, 72, 85, 95, 102, 105, 111, 138
Arapahos, 193, 194, 196, 197, 198–99, 209, 232, 236, 237, 242, 251, 259, 275, 279, 280, 281, 287, 289, 293, 302, 305, 306, 321
Aravaipa Apaches, 235
Archdale, John, 57
Arikaras, 221
Arizona (territory and state), 219, 220, 222, 235, 236, 307, 317, 341
Arkansas, 164, 175, 207, 245
Armstrong, John, 96
Armstrong, Samuel Chapman, 251, 276
Army Medical Museum, 219
Ashbow, Samuel, 75, 80
assimilation
    Indian approach to, 157–62, 248–49
    policy of, 228–31, *230*, 239, *253*
Assiniboines, 337
Assistant Secretary of Indian Affairs, 327
Auchiah, James, 302
Augusta Boys, 103
Aupaumut, Hendrick, 133
Austin, Stephen, 207

Bacon, Nathaniel, 48–50, 100
Bacon's Rebellion, 48–50
Baker, Eugene M., 235
Baker (Marias) Massacre, 235
Baltimore, third Lord, 52–53
Banks, Dennis, 328
Bannocks, 225, 232, 235, 259
Baptists, 54
Barbados, 55, 58, 59
Battles
    Bad Axe, 178
    Fallen Timbers, 136–37
    Horseshoe Bend, 145
    Point Pleasant, 106
    Thames, 143
    Yorktown, 126
Baylor, John, 208–9
Bear Hunter, 226
Bearskin, Fredline, 318
Belknap, Jeremy, 131–32
Bellecourt, Clyde, 328
Bender, Charles, 294–95
Benezet, Anthony, 125–26
Berkeley, William, 48, 49
Bernard, Francis, 87
Bethlehem, PA, 75, 97
Big Eagle, 223
Big Foot, 267
Big Warrior, 144
bison, 15, 195, *203*, 220, 230, 248, 259, 261, 265, *343*
Black(s)
    colonization of, 168
    enslavement of, 54–57, 58 59, 141, 187, 188
    Indian ideas about, 72, 127–28, 160–61, 360–61
    Indian treatment of, 127–28, 160–61
    inequities experienced by, 17–18
    racial terminology for, 55–56, 58–59, 79, 260–61
    tribal citizenship of, 276–79, 359–62
Black Boys, 103
Black Elk, 234, 246, 268–69
Blackfeet/Blackfoot, 220, 221, 235, 244, 246, 295, 308, *309*, 315
Black Freedmen, 276–79, 359–62
Black Hawk, 178
Black Hawk War, 178, 186
Black Hills Convention, 306
Black Hoof, 138
Black Kettle, 195–200, *196*, *200*

Black Seminoles, 161, 181, 227, 228, 359–62
blood quantum, 176, 276–79, *277*, 310, 355, *356*
Blount, William, 134
Blue Jacket, 136
Board of Commissions for Foreign Missions, 161
boarding schools
   abuse at, 242, 256–57
   Albuquerque, NM, 253
   Carlisle, PA, 252–54, 255–56, 259, 260–61, 288, 289
   Chilocco, OK, 12, 253, 260, 278, *280*, 294
   churches and, 253–54
   curriculums of, 257
   daily routine of, 255–56, 296
   Fort Mohave, 255
   Genoa, NE, 253
   Haskell Institute, 262
   health conditions of, 15, 256
   Indian identity at, 252–53, 257–58, 261–62
   orientation to, 254–56, *256*
   origin of, 251–53
   outing system of, 257–58
   parental resistance to, 258–60
   Pipestone, MN, 293
   policy of, 250–52
Boas, Franz, 294
Bonnin, Gertrude Simmons (Zitkala-Ša), 261, 286, *286*, 287, 289, 290, 292, 305, 306
Boone, Daniel, 120, 152, 154
border towns, 16, 324–24, 350–51
Bosque Redondo, 222
Boston, 45–46, 52, 62, 65, 84, 112, 237–38, 300
Boston Tea Party, 112

Boudinot, Elias, 168, 169, 183–84, 191
Bouquet, Henry, 95, 97
Brackenridge, Hugh Henry, 125–26
Bradford, William, 34
Brainerd, David, 72, 75, 80, 82
Brandon, Gerald, 165
Brant, Joseph, 82, 111–12, 118, 132, 133
Bread, Daniel, 175
Broker, Ignatia, 318
Brookings Institution, 297
Brotherton (NJ), 104
Brothertown (NY and WI), 127, 128, 132–33, 163, 175, 183, 204, 274, 282
Browning, Orville H., 231
Brulés, 9, 245
Bryant, William Cullen, 162
Buffalo Bird Woman, 263
Bull Bear, Jock, 287–88, 289
Bureau of Indian Affairs, x, 156, 201, 254, 281, 286, 293, 303, 314, 329, *342*, *356*
Burke Act, 270
Burke, Charles H., 179
Burlington, NJ, 104
Bushnell, Horace, 211
Butler, Elizur, 184

Caddos, 209, 251, 270, 286
Cahuilla Band of Indians, 315
Calhoun, John C., 147, 156, 162, 165
California, 201, 202, 210–16, *212*, 218–19, 220, 221, 235, 294, 315, 316, 341, 354, 356, 364, 371
Call of the Wild (1908), 398
Calvert, Charles. *See* Baltimore, third Lord
Camp Grant Massacre, 235
Canada, 37, 40, 51, 52, 64, 68, 127, 140, 163, 235, 237, 254, 325
Canasatego, 67, 91

Canyon de Chelly, 222
Cape Cod, 36, 45–46, 78, 189, 352–53
Captain Jack. *See* Kientpoos
Captain Pollard, 132
captivity, 25, 62–63, 64, 125, 143, 151, 222
captivity narratives, 64–65, 143, 151–52
Carleton, James, 222
Carlisle Industrial Indian School, 252–54, *253*, 255–56, *258*, 259, 260–61, 288, 289
Carnegie, Andrew, 5
Carson, Kit, 222
Cass, Lewis, 167
Catawbas, 54, 60, 66, 127
Catlin, George, *138*, 153–54
Caughnawaga, 96
Cayugas, 118, 163
Cayuses, 12, 217
Charles II, 48
Charleston (Charles Town), 54, 56, 60, 79, 88
Cherokee Phoenix, 168, 169, 173–75, 177, 178, 183–84, *184*
Cherokee Nation v. Georgia (1831), 172
Cherokees, 54, 66, 71, 103–4, 231
    American Revolution and, 117–18, *118*, 126
    censuses of, 158
    Christianity of, 159–60
    civilization campaign to, 157–58
    civilized reforms of, 158–62, 169–70, 174–75
    court cases of, 171–72
    Creek civil war and, 145
    Curtis Act and, 271
    diplomacy of, 112, 133–34, 141
    folklore of, 299
    formal education of, 170
    government of, 141, 169–70
    imperial wars of, 87–88
    Keetoowah Society of, 227, 275
    land cessions of, 88, 111, 116–17, 135, 137, 163–64, 184–85
    literacy of, 160
    missions to, 156, 159–60
    "mixed bloods" of, 164, 176–77, 227
    National Council of, 141, 160–61, 170, 174, 175, 184
    Nativism among, 105, 142
    population of, 227–28
    prophesies of, 175–76
    race among, 77, 78, 79, 160–61, 177, 227
    Removal of, 149–50, 165–66, 170, 173–78, 18–85, 186
    reservation of, 271
    slaveholding of, 141, 160–61, 177, 227–28
    syllabary of, 160
    in Texas, 206
    treaties of, 111, 116, 127, 135, 137, 138, 164, 169, 173, 185, 228
    Treaty Party of, 184
    war of 1759–61 and, 87–89, 116
    wars with United States, 117–18, 134–35
    wealth of, 158
    western migrations of, 163, 175, 185, 206
Cherry Valley, NY, 118
Cheyenne River Reservation, 320
Cheyennes, 3, 193–98, *196*, 209, 236, 237, 241–42, 251, 259, 321, 359
Chicago, 142, 249, 253, 289, 300, 318, 347
Chickahominies, 50, 302, 341
Chickamaugas, 117, 160, 165
Chickasaws, 78, 141, 146, 158, 160–61, 165, 170, 174, 176, 186, 187, 206, 227–28, 271, 275
Chief Joseph, 236–37

Chilocco Indian School, 12, 253, 260, 278, 294
Chimarikos, 113
Chiricahua Apaches, 251
Chivington, John M., 196–99, *196*
Choctaws, 61, 141, 145, 146, 157, 158, 160, 164–65, 170, 175, 176, 182–83, 186, 187, 190, 227–28, 271, 275, 278, 296, 340, 348, 354, 359–62
Choptanks, 72
Chota, 112
Christianity
    as binary of paganism, 19, 31, 33–35
    Catholic-Protestant rivalry over, 33, 51–53
    as "White" identity 19, 32–36, 53–58, 59, 67–70, 78, 82–83
    Indian adoption of, 32, 40–42, *54*, 56–57, 68–69, 73, 75, 81, 97
    Indian rejection of, 72, 80–81, 132
    reservations and, 293
    role of in race-making, 18, 22, 32–33, 34–35, 40–44, 45–46, 46–47, 52–53, 54–56, 68–70, 72–73, 80–83, 97–98, 132–33
Church, Benjamin, 46, 152
Church of England, 53–54
Church of Latter Day Saints, 319
Cincinnati, 136
Civilian Conservation Corps, 308
civility, 31–32, 34–36, 54, 67–68, 80–81, 129–30, 132–33, 147, 156, 176–77, 202, 206
civilization policy, 129–33, 148, 156–62, 229–30, 239, 242–43, 250–62, 311–13
Civil War (U.S.), 198, 221–22, 227–28
citizenship, 11, 128–29, 164, 182, 183, 228, 270, 275, 278, 282–83
Clark, George Rogers, 120–21, *121*

Clinton DeWitt, 163
Cody, Buffalo Bill, 2, 249–50, *250*
Cohen, Felix, 312
Colorado, 193–99, 220, 226, *317*
Cold War, 16, 314
Colley, Samuel G., 197, 198
Collier, John, 307–13, *309*, 314
Columbia River, 217, 233, *234*, 321
Comanches, 3, 207, 209, 220, 221, 232, 236, 251
Committee on Civil Rights, 324
Confederate Army, 227
Congregationalists, 75
Conestogas, 77, 98–102
Congress (U.S.), 1, 5, 112, 121, 123, 129, 131, 142, 150, 162, 165, 170, 173, 177, 180, 183, 209, 213, 238, 239, 245–46, 252, 253, 254, 256, 268, 274, 282, 287, 289, 290, 292, 307, 313, 315, 316, 327, 333, 335, 339, 341, 344, 362, 364, 371, 373, 375
Connecticut (colony and state), 29, 62, 72, 75, 81, 83, 167–68, 190, 305, 340, 341, 343, 354, 375
Connecticut River, 45
Connor, Patrick, 226
Constitution (U.S.), 128–29, 130, 137, 169, 172, 173, 326, 334
Continental Army, 110, 119
Continental Congress, 112, 122, 123
Coode, John, 53
Coolidge, Calvin, 283
Coolidge, Sherman, 293, 305
Cooper, John Fenimore, 2, 153, 155, 189
Coosa (town), 145
Coosa River, 117
Coquilles, 216, 217, 316
Cornstalk, 115
Cornwall, CT, 167–68
Coeur d'Alenes, 217

Craig, Joseph, 12
Crawford, William, 116, 124, 125, 126, 147
Crazy Horse, 235, 368, *368*, 369,
Creeks, 54, 59, 60, 66, 78, 79, 105,
    133–36, 137
  civilized reforms of, 156–61, *157*
  civil war of, 141–42, 144–46
  Curtis Act and, 271, 274
  government of, 141–42
  land distribution among, 271
  land loss of, 146, 165, 181
  missions to, 141, 156
  "mixed bloods" among, 60, 141, 145,
    160–61, 176–77, 273–75
  National Council of, 141–42
  Nativism of, 141–42
  race among, 134, 160–61, 227
  Red Sticks of, 145–46
  Removal of, 165–66, 181–82, *182*, 186,
    187
  slaveholding of, 141, 160–61, 227
  Snake faction of, 275
  in Texas, 206
  treaties of, 135, 137, 165, 181, 227–28
  western migrations of, 165–66, 175,
    182–83
Croghan, George, 103
Crook, George, 234, 237
Crosswicks, NJ, 80
Crow Dog, 245
Crows, 3, 4, 221, 232, 246, 248, 259, 321
Crow Creek Reservation, 225
Crow Reservation, 2–3, 244, 246–47,
    259, 264, 321
Curse of Cham, 43, 55
Curse of the Redman (1911), 299
Curtis, Charles, 272–73, *273*
Curtis, Edward S., 4
Curtis Act, 243, 270, 271, 273, 279,
    281, 360

Cusabos, 54
Cussetah Mico, 132
Custer Died for Your Sins (1969), 326
Custer, George Armstrong, 3, 199,
    236, 267

Dawes Act, 164, 243, 270–84, *277*, 311, 360
Dawes, Henry, 271
Daylight, John (Masse-Hadjo), 266
Debo, Angie, 243
Declaration of Independence, 110, 112–13
Delaware (state), 162
Delawares (tribe) 6, 66, 72, 75, 80,
    156, 163
  civilized reforms of, 122–23, 156, 158
  diplomacy of, 73, 76, 77, 112, 154
  in Indiana, 133, 139–40
  intertribal alliances of, 112
  in Kansas, 204
  land cessions of, 88–89
  migrations of, 89–90, 102, 175
  Nativism of, 92–94, 139–40
  peyotism of, 286
  racial ideas of, 78, 92–94, 96, 106, 139
  racial violence against, 97–102, 103,
    115, 122–26, 152
  in Texas, 206
  wars of, 85, 89, 95–97, 105–6, 115,
    122–26, 136
Deloria, Vine, Jr., 326, 327, *327*
Denver, 193–98, *317*
Denver, J. W., 206
Department of the Interior, 10, 295, 321
Detroit, 95, 122
Diné. *See* Navajos
Dixon, Joseph K., 1–13, *4*, *6*, *11*, 23
Dobbs, Arthur, 88
Doctrine of Discovery, 171–72
Dog Soldiers, 195–96, 197, 199
Dominion of New England, 52–53

Downing, Lewis, 231
Dragging Canoe, 116–17, 133
Dull Knife, 235, 242
Dunmore, Earl of (John Murray), 105–6
Duston, Hannah, Dutch, 62–63, *63*
Dwight, Timothy, 162

Eastman, Charles, 260, 268, 287, 289, 292, 303, 305, 306
Ecuyer, Simeon, 97
Edwards, Jonathan, 75
Egushawa, 133
Elder, John, 98–99
Elk Hair, 286
England, 51–52
Eliot, John, 36, 37, 46
Environmental Protection Agency, 322, *322*
epidemic disease, 16, 23–24, 35, 41, 66, 71, 76, 90, 153, 210, 215, 218, 220, 221, 244, 256
ethnology, 231, 288
Evans, John, 196
Everett, Edward, 126
environmental racism, 321–22
Ex parte Crow Dog (1883), 245–46

Federal Indian Territory. *See* Indian Territory
federal recognition, 311, 340–41, 351, 352–54, 364, 365, 375
Field Museum, 289
Fields, Barbara J., 17
Fields, Karen E., 17
fish-ins, 325, 339–40, *340*
Five Civilized Tribes, 227–28, 274, 359. *See also* Cherokees, Chickasaws, Choctaws, Creeks, Seminoles
Five Nations. *See* Haudenosaunees
Fletcher, Alice, 231

Florida (colony and state), 40, 56, 57, 61, 64, 135, 142, 161, 167, 180–81, 201, 251, *251*, 252, 317, 361
Fort Hall Reservation, 259
Fort Randall Dam, 320
forts
    Dearborn, 142
    Duquesne, 87
    George, 88
    Hunter, 68
    Ligonier, 95
    Loudon, 88
    Lyon, 197
    Marion, 251–52, *251*, 260
    Mims, 145
    Niagara, 95, 118, 119
    Pitt, 95, 97, 102, 115, 116, 123
    Randolph, 115
    Reno, 289
    Robinson, 289
    Snelling, 247
    Wadsworth, 1, 5, 6, 10, *11*
Four Mothers Society, 265
Foxes, 2, 140, 186, 206, 262, 351
Fowler, David, 75
France, 40, 52, 61, 94
Francis, Josiah, 144, 145
Franciscans, 40
Franklin (NC), 134–35
Franklin, Benjamin, 99, 101–2, 121
Franklin, William, 104–5
Frelinghuysen, Theodore, 177–78
Friends of the Indians, 239, 242–43, 248, 254, 264, 271–73, 283–84, 287, 305, 377
fur trade, 36, 41, 42, 51, 59–60, 111, 154, 158, 207

Gachradodow, 91
Gage, Thomas, 73, 99

Garrison Dam, 321
Gates, Merrill E., 271
General Allotment Act. *See* Dawes Act
genocide
    American Revolution as war of, 109, 113–26, *118*
    in Arizona, 222, 235–36
    in California, 210–16, *212*, 218–19
    colonial wars of, 3–33, 42–51, 57–58, 61–67, 73–74, 85–90, 95–103, 105–6
    definition of, 14–17
    in Idaho, 225–26
    Indian fears of, 66–67, 73–74, 90, 95–96
    in Minnesota, 222–25, *225*
    in Oregon, 210, 216–17, 218–19
    in Texas, 206–9, 219–20
    U.S. policies of, 135–36, 204–19, 239
    War of 1812 as war of, *139*, *144*, 145
George III, 111, 112–13, 121
George Rogers Clark National Historical Park and Memorial, 121, *121*
Georgia (colony and state), 61, 65, 85, 116, 117, 118, 134, 135, 145, 146, 149, 157, 161, 164–68, 170, 171–74, 176, 178, 181–85
Geronimo, 236
Ghost Dance, *234*, 264–69, *265*, 287, 288
Gibson, John, 123
Glen, James, 85
Glorious Revolution, 52–53
Gnadenhutten, 122–26, 140
Godwyn, Morgan, 55–56, 59
gold strikes, 171, 194, 210, 217, 220
Gookin, Daniel, 46
Goose Creek Men, 54
Gordon, NE, 329
Grand Ronde Indians, 234

Grant, Ulysses S., 234, 238
Great Awakening, first, 75, 83
Great Britain, 61, 71, 80, 94, 109, 111, 113, 118, 126, 129, 130, 142, 146, 171, 201
Great Depression, 307
Great Lakes, 2, 3, 10, 40, 61, 68, 95, 112, 135, 254, 325, 352
Great Plains, 3, 10, 22, 175, 186, 193–96, 207, 220, 221, 231–32, 236, 241, 246, 248–49, 265, 267, 268, 290, 350, 371
Great Sioux Reservation, 235, 263, 267
Gros Ventres, 3
Guales, 61
Guess, George. *See* Sequoyah
Guidiville Rancheria, 316

Hamilton, Alexander, 124
Hampton Agricultural and Industrial School, 251–52, 257, 259–61, 264
Handsome Lake, 138
Hanford Nuclear Site, 321
Hanging Maw, 135
Hannastown, PA, 126
Harjo, Chitto, 275
Harmar, Josiah, 129, 136
Harrison, William Henry, 140, 142, 143, 152, 161
Harvard College/University, 41, 344, 362
Hawkins, Benjamin, 134, 135, 141, 144, 156, 157, *157*
Hawley, Gideon, 75, 81
Hawthorne, Nathaniel, 62, 63, 153
Haudenosaunees, x, 51, 52, 66, 67, 68, 69, 75, 80, 81, 91, 92, 103, 106, 111, 112, 118–20, 126, 133, 137, 305, 310, 326. *See also* Mohawks, Oneidas, Onondagas, Cayugas, Senecas, Tuscaroras
Haverhill, MA, 62, *63*

Hawaii, 274
Hearst, William Randolph, 5
Heckewelder, John, 76, 94, 97, 122, 124
Hendricks, William, 167
Henry, Patrick, 130
Hensley, Albert, 290
Hicks, Charles, 160
Hicks, Elijah, 184
Hidatsas, 221, 263, 343
Hines, Gustavus, 221
History of the American Indians (1775), 154
Ho-Chunks, x, 133, 140, 142, *256*, 290
Hokeah, Jack, 302
Hollow Horn Bear, 9, 274
Hollywood. *See* movies
Hoover, Herbert, 272
Hopis, 296, 302, 321, 326
Hopkins, Samuel, 80
House of Representatives (U.S.). *See* Congress (U.S.)
Houston, Sam, 208
Howard University, 251
Hudson River, 68, 76, 79, 80, 115, 271
Huguenots, 54

Idaho (territory and state), 220, 221, 225–26, 235, 259, 317, 346
Illinois (territory and state), 120, 140, 142, 150, 163, 178, 305
Illinois (tribe), 42
Improved Order of Red Men, 5
Indian Allotment Act. *See* Dawes Act
Indian and his Problem, 293
Indian Civil Rights Act (1968), 327
Indian Citizenship Act of 1924, 283, 305, 307
Indian Claims Commission, 314
Indian Education: A National Tragedy (1969), 323
Indian Historian (San Francisco), 326

Indian New Deal. *See* Indian Reorganization Act
Indian Office. *See* Bureau of Indian Affairs
Indian Relocation Act (1956), 317–18, *317*
Indian Removal
    arguments against, 149–50, 166–67, 172, 173–78
    arguments for, 149, 162–65, 166–68, *170*
    bill for, 170, 173
    Cherokees, 167–71, 172, 173, 183–85
    Chickasaws, 186, 187
    Choctaws, 182–83, 186
    costs of, 186–87
    Creeks, 181–82, *182*, 186
    deaths from, 15, 178–82, 186–87
    early versions of, 163–64
    economic results of, 187
    Foxes, 186
    origins of, 147–48
    Potawatomis, 186
    race wars of, 178–82
    Sauks, 178, 186
    Seminoles, 180–81, *180*, 186
Indian Reorganization Act, 279, 308–13, *309*
Indian Rights Association, 272
Indian Rights Fund, 287
Indian Territory, 149, 183, 186, 199, 204–7, 208, 209, 227–28, 237, 245, 247, 260, 266, 267, 271, 272, 279, *280*, 283
Indiana, 121, 125, 133, 137, 139–40, 142, 163, 167, 175, 261
Indians
    adoption and fostering of, 16, 319–20, 344–45, 376–77
    arrest rate of, 324
    arts of, 302–3, *159*

Indians (cont'd)
    assimilation policy and, 228–32, 237–38, 242–43, 250–58, *253*, 270–79, 314–20
    Black freedmen among, 228–29, 276–79, 359–62
    boarding schools of, 16, 22, 73, 242–43, 250–62, *256*
    border towns and, 16, 324–25, 350–51
    civilized reforms of, 122–23, 141–42, 157–61, *157*, 205–6
    collecting the remains of, 181, 224, 344, 369
    economic status of, 295, 316, 323
    education of, 159–60, 227, 259–60, 293, 296, 323–24, 327, 333, 339, 341–42
    epithets for, 43, 97, 199, 211, 226, 260–61, 351
    enslavement of, 18, 23, 24, 29, 41, 42, 45, 46, 50, 51, 54–55, 56–59, 60–61, 68, 158, 207, 210, 211–12, 214, 215, 222, 226, 376
    environmental racism against, 321–22
    extinction discourse about, 5, 9–10, 16, 20, 21, 23, 29, 30, 132, 149, 153–56, 162, 167–68, 174–75, 187, 292, 293, 294, 308, 341, 367
    federal recognition of, 311, 340–41, 351, 352–54, 364, 365, 375
    health of, 15, 16, 295–96, 321, 323
    identity crises of, 262–64, 331
    land loss of, 46–47, 50, 58, 69, 71–74, 81, 83, 88–89, 91–93, 94–95, 96, 102–3, 105, 106, 116, 126–28, 134, 135–36, 137, 138, 140, 146, 147, 163–65, 178–85, 186–87, 204–6, 210, 216, 222–23, 225, 270–79, 280–82, *280*, 316
    literacy of, 41, 68, 132, 141, 159–60
    mascots of, 300, 346–47, *347*
    "mixed-bloods," 60, 141, 145, 164, 176–77, 188, 272, 273, 276, 278, 279, 289, 293, 310–11, 312–13, 329, 352–54, *356*, 357
    movies about, 297–300, 303, 345–46
    Nativism of, 8, 12–13, 73, 90–97, 138–45, 200, 233
    organizations of, 303–7, 318, 325–26, 328–30
    opposition of to Removal, 169, 171–72, 173–78, 178–85
    police abuse of, 16, 18, 316, 324, 328, 329, 350
    poverty of, 15, 243–44, 246, 260, 314, 316, 323, 341, 369
    racial ideas of, 8–10, 12–13, 35–38, 44, 60, 67, 68–69, 72–74, 74–79, 80–81, 83, 90–97, 111–12, 132–33, 134, 138–45, 173–78, 189–91, 221, 227, 231–35, 259–61, 264–66, 287–88, 289–90, 303–7, 312, 325–31
    racial terminology for, 32, 43–44, 58–59, 77–78, 97, 199, 211, 226, 260–61, 351
    racism toward, 15–16, 43–44, 45–46, 48–49, 50, 57, 61–66, 69–70, 72–73, 76, 80, 82–83, 84–85, 87–88, 99–102, 119, 122, 125, 136–37, 143–44, 150–56, 167–68, 193–239, 243–45, 263–64, 280–82, 295–96, 300–302, *301*, 320–323, 344–54
    Red Power movement of, 325–31, *327*
    relocation of, 317–38, *317*
    Removal of, *170*, 178–86
    reservations of, 194–95, 199, *215*, 228–32, *229*, 241–50
    sexual assault of, 29, 88, 104, 119, 123, 171, 184, 207, 211, 215, 216, 226, 257, 248–50

slaveholding of, 141, 160–61, 177, 227–28
sovereignty of, 23, 161, 171–72, 174, 330, 333–34, 337, 338, 345, 352, 354, 358, 374, 375–76
sterilization of, 16, 347–48, 376
unemployment of, 318, 323, 347
U.S. citizenship of, 11, 128–29, 164, 182, 183, 228, 270, 275, 278, 282–83
voting rights of, 129, 307
wars of, with United States, 117–26, 133–37, 140–45, 180–81, 190–99, 204–19
White views of, 2–7, 33–35, 41, 43, 45–47, 49, 53, 57–58, 61–67, 69–70, 81, 82–83, 85–87, 98–100, 115, 119, 123, 125–26, 129–31, 143, 147–48, 150–56, 167–68, 199–200, 201–4, 208, 213, 224, 226, 230–31, 238–39, 250–51, 270, 272, 283–84, 293–95, 297–302, 314, 318, 330, 333–36, 350–51, 353–54, 373–74
Iowa (territory and state), 170
Iowas (tribe), 2
Inuits, 322
Ironcutter, John, 104
Iroquois. *See* Haudenosaunees
Irvine, William, 123, 124
Irving, Washington, 153
Isleta Pueblo, 12, 341

Jacksboro Rangers, 208
Jackson, Andrew, 21, 145, 146, 148, 149, 152, 164, 169, 170, *170*, 172, 173, 178, 180, 184, 187, 189, 362
James II, 51–52
Jamestown, 31, 36, 48, 49–50
Jay Treaty (1794), 326
Jefferson, Thomas, 121, 124, 130, 138, 163, 168, 368
Jeningo, 80

Jesuits, 36, 52, 62, 68, 75
Jicarilla Apaches, 321
Jim Crow, 24, 350, 361
Johnson, Emma D., 305
Johnson, Guy, 113, 116
Johnson, Joseph, 73, 75
Johnson, Lyndon, 326–27, 333
Johnson, Richard Mentor, 152
Johnson v. McIntosh (1823), 171–72
Johnson, William, 74, 80, 87, 103, 105
Johnston, Adam, 211
Johnston, Gideon, 58

Kabotie, Fred, 302
Kanawalohare, 81
Kansas (territory and state), 149, 183, 204–6, *207*, 227–28, 245, 253, 262, 272–73, 274
Kansas Indian Home Guard, 227–28
Karankawas, 207
Kaws, 2, 206, 272
Kellog, Laura Cornelius, 303
Kenny, James, 93
Kentucky, 106, 111, 116, 120, 125, 126, 138, 141, 143, 151, 152, 168
Keetoowah Society, 275
Kickapoos, 2, 11, 140, 142, 206, 274
Kientpoos, 218–19
Killbuck, 107
King George's War, 65
King Philip's War, 45–47, 52, 53, 55, 62, 64, 76, 152
Kinzua Dam, 320
Kiowa-Apaches, 209
Kiowas, 3, 207, 209, 221, 232, 236, 251, 269
Kiowa Six, 302
Kirkland, Samuel, 72–73, 75, 131
Klamath Reservation, 218
Klamaths, 316
Kneale, Albert H., 262

Knight, John, 125
Knox, Henry, 129–31, 135, 136
Knoxville, TN, 134
Korean War, 314, 324

LaFlesche, Francis, 256, 287
Lake Mohonk Conference, 271
Lakotas, 3, 8, 9, 220, 232, 235, 242, 244, 245, 253, 259, 260, 265, 267–69, 286, 295, 303, 309, 321, 328, 329, 367–69, 373. *See also* Brulés, Oglala, Minneconjous
Lamar, Mirabeau, 208
Lancaster (town), PA, 90, 92, 98–99
Lancaster (county), PA, 74, 99
Lancaster Treaty (1744), 91
land speculation, 20, 130, 135
Lane, Franklin Knight, 294
Last of the Mohicans (1826), 2, 155
Lawson, John, 60
Lea, Luke, 201
Leatherstocking Tales, 153
Le Jau, Francis, 53–54, 56–58, 60, 68
Lenapes. *See* Delawares.
Leupp, Francis E., 293
Lincoln, Abraham, 10, 195, 197, 224, 367
Lipan Apaches, 285
Little Bighorn, Battle of, 3, 9, 236
Little Chief, 259
Little Crow, 224
Little Raven, 197, 237
Little Turtle, 136
Little Wolf, 235, 242
Livingston, William, 122
Logan, 105, 153
London, 41, 49, 69, 77
Lone Wolf, 289
Longfellow, Henry Wadsworth, 1–2, 62
Long Island, 29, 44, 47, 61, 67, 73, 113, 128, 252

Long Walk, 222
Long Warrior, 79
Lord Dunmore's War, 105–6
Los Angeles, 214, 303, 318, 324
Louis XIV, 52
Louisiana (colony and state), 61, 341, 354
Louisiana Purchase, 163, 201
Lovewell, John, 62
Lowery, Major George, 177
Lumbees, 296, 311, 357

Madison, James, 124, 142, 146, 163, 168
Madley, Benjamin, 215
Maine, 40, 45, 53, 62, 65, 84, 85, 340
Major Crimes Act (1885), 246, 376
Mandans, 221, 343
Mangas Coloradas, 222
Manifest Destiny, 2, 16, 22, 47, 188–89, 203, 215, 231, 298, 315, 369
Mankiller, Wilma, 328
Marias (Baker) Massacre, 235–36
Martha's Vineyard, 45, 78
Mary II, 52, 53
Maryland, 52–53, 72, 75, 84, 90, 95, 102, 116, 150, 162
Marshall, John, 171, 172
Mashpee, *302*, 340, 341, 352–54, 375
Massachusetts (colony and state), 31, 35, 41, 45–47, 52–53, 62–63, 80, 84–87, 122, 127, 129, 143–44, 156, 162, 189, 271, 302, 323, 329, 340, 341, 353, 359, 362, 375
Massachusetts (tribe), 37
massacres
    Baker (Marias), 235–36
    Bear River, 225–26
    Camp Grant, 235–36
    Cherry Valley, 118
    Conestoga, 98–99
    Fort Mims, 145

Gnadenhutten, 122–23
Great Swamp, 45
Horseshoe Bend, 145
Mystic, 41
Occaneechis, 49
Sand Creek, 197–98, *196*, *198*
Utter, 225–26
Virginia, 1622, 42–43, *43*
Ward Party, 225–26
Washita, 199
Wiscasset, 84
Wounded Knee, 267–68
Wyoming, 122
Massasoit. *See* Ousamequin
Mather, Cotton, 63, 64
Mather, Increase, 46, 47
Mattaponis, 50, 302, 341
Mayo, William, 225
McCrea, Jane, 122
McGarry, Edward, 226
McGillivray, Alexander, 133, 134
McIntosh, William, 144, 165–66, *166*
McLaughlin, James, 10, 267
McNickle, D'Arcy, 308
Meacham, Alfred, 219
Means, Russell, 328
Meigs, Return J., 158, 163–64
Menominees, 133, 183, 261, 316, 339
Meriam Report, 297, 303
Mescalero Apaches, 222, 255, 259, 321
mestizo, 42, 59
Metamora (play), 153, 156
métis, 42
Mexican-American War, 22, 188–89, 201
Mexico, 208, 227, 285
Miamis, 71, 136, 156, 158, 163, 204
Miantonomo, 44
Michigan (territory and state), 163, 167, 202, 340, 343
Mi'kmaqs, 36

Miles, Nelson, 244, 267
Mimbreño Apaches, 222
Mingos, 71, 85, 97, 105, 106, 136
Minneapolis, 318, 328
Minnesota, 222–25, *225*, 247, 278, 293, 299, 316
Miniconjous, 267–68, 329
missing and murdered Indigenous women, 16
missions
    Anglican, 53–54, 67–70
    Baptist, 156
    Congregationalist, 36, 41, 75, 80, 82, 156, 161
    Florida, 40, 56–57, 61
    Methodist, 156
    Moravian, 75, 76, 80, 92, *98*, 122, 125, 139, 156
    New England, 36, 41
    New France, 40
    New Mexico, 40
    Presbyterian, 72, 75, 80, 131, 156
    Quaker, 156
    role of in race-making, 18, 38–47, 67–70, 72–73, 74–77, 81–83, 99, 122–23, 124, 125
    Spanish, 40
    Virginia, 40–41
Mississippi (territory and state), 146, 158, 165, 166, 182–83
Mississippi River, 147, 154, 178, 181
Missouri (territory and state), 175, 245
Missouri River, 147, 153, 221
"mixed bloods," 60, 141, 145, 160–61, 164, 176–77, 188, 227, 273, 276, 278, 279, 298–99, 310–11, 312, 329, *356*, 357
mob violence, 20, 46, 48–50, 53, 83–84, 87, 88–89, 97–106, 123, 137, 198, 209, 216, 224, 245, 281
Modocs, 213, 216, 218–19, *218*, 237

Modoc War, 218–19, *218*
Mohawks, 29, 61, 67–70, 113, 118, 132, 134, 163, 325
Mohegans, 29, 44, 45, 46, 61, 73, 75, 80, 83, 106, 111, 127, 128, 189–90, 283, 340
Mohicans, 66, 67, 75, 80, 82, 87, 97, 127, 132, 133, 155, 162, 163, 183
Monroe, James, 164, 165, 168
Montagnais, 36
Montana (territory and state), 2, 220, 235–36, 237, 242, 244, 282, 295, 311, 317, 320, 348
Montauketts, 73, 75, 127, 128
Montezuma, Carlos, 303–4
Mooney, James, 234, *265*, 288–89, *288*, *291*, 292
Moore, James, 57
Mopope, Stephen, 302
Moravians, 75, 76, 80, 92, 93, 97, 98, 99–100, 102, 122–25, 139, 156
Morgan, George, 115
Morgan, Henry Lewis, 231
Morse, Jedidah, 131, 132
Morton, Samuel George, 155
Moseley, Samuel, 45, 46, 48
Mountain Chief, 9, 235
movies, 3, 9, 297–300, 303, 331, 345–46, 353
Munsees, 66
Museum of Natural History (NY), 8, 29, 289
mustee, 59, 128

Nairne, Thomas, 57
Nanticokes, 53, 75
Nanziatticos, 50
Napoleon (of Tulalip tribe), 231
Naranjo, Lewis, 315
Narragansetts, 37, 44, 45, 46, 61, 66, 73, 83, 127, 190, 283, 302, 340

Natick, MA, 66
National American Indian Memorial, 1–13, *6*, *11*, 23, 24, 27, 28, 30
National Congress of American Indians, 315, 317, 320, 326, 330, 337, 346–47, *347*, 348, 362
National Day of Mourning, 329
National Indian Association, 272
National Indian Youth Council, 325–26
Native American Church, 292
Native American Heritage Month, 305
Nativism, 8, 12–13, 73, 90–97, 138–45, 200, 233
Navajo Community College, 327
Navajos, x, 11, 220, 222, 223, 260, 296, 310, 321–22, *322*, 327, 343, 350, 362
Nebraska, 247, 253, 274, 305, 316–17, 324, 329
Neighbors, Robert S., 208, 209
Neolin, 92–94, *94*, 106, 233
Nevada, 219, 220, 235, 265, 317, 321
New Deal, 279, 307–313
New England, 34, 35, 40, 41, 44–47, 52–53, 55, 58, 60, 61, 62, 64, 73, 75, 76, 80, 81, 83, 85, 128, 131, 132, 151, 154, 161, 162, 168, 175, 176, 189, 283, 329
New France, 37, 40, 51, 52, 64, 68
New Hampshire, 53, 62, 119, 129, 162
New Jersey, 66, 75, 76, 80, 103, 104, 105, 113, 119, 122, 162, 177
New Mexico, 40, 42, 50–51, *222*, 223, 236, 253, 307, 308, 321, 341, 343, 350
New Orleans, 95, 140, 158, 181
newspapers, 62, 65–66, *212*
  Akwesasne Notes, 345
  Austin City Gazette, 208
  Black Hills Daily Times, 267
  Boston News-Letter, 65–66
  Centennial (Cincinnati), 136

INDEX 491

Cherokee Phoenix, 168, 169, 173, 175, 177, 178, 183–84, *184*
Chicago Tribune, 266
Chico Weekly Courant (CA), 213
Crow Creek Chief, 264
Daily Alta California, 214, 219
Daily Rocky Mountain News (Denver) 196
Denver News, 293
Galenian (Illinois), 178
Hartford Courant, 354
Humboldt Times (CA), 212
Idaho Statesman, 226
Indian Historian (San Francisco), 326
Indian School Journal, 278
Manketo Independent (MN), 224
Maryland Journal, 136
Maysville Appeal (CA), 212
Muskogee Daily Phoenix, 309
Niles Weekly Register (Baltimore), 147
New York Observer, 173
New York Times, 307
Missionary Herald (Boston), 178
Pennsylvania Evening Post, 113
St. Croix Monitor (MN), 224
Salem (NC) *Gazette*, 145
San Francisco Bulletin, 213
Talking Leaf (Los Angeles), 324
Wassaja (San Francisco), 326
White Man (Jacksboro, TX), 208
Yreka Mountain Herald (CA), 213
New York (colony and state), 1–3, 6, 7, 11, 28, 29, 38, 61, 62, 63, 64, 66, 67, 68, 73, 85, 115, 118, 127, 129, 133, 143, 157, 162, 163, 175, 305, 326, 340
New York City, 7, 8, 80, 82, 150, 222, 253, 289, 318, 367, 369
New York Indian Reserve, 204, 206
Nez Perces, 221, 232, 236–37, 248, 275
Niantics, 45, 73, 83

Ninigret, 45
Nipmucs, 41, 45
Nomlakis, 213
Norridgewok, 62, 84
North American Review, 167
North Carolina, 60, 66, 75, 88, 117, 134, 145, 156, 162, 164, 296, 311, 363
Northern Cheyennes, 7, 236, 242, 246, 321, 359
North Dakota, 317, 320, 343
Northwest Ordinance, 135
Northwest Territory, 138
No Shirt, 12–13, 21
Nott, Josiah C., 181, 231

Oahe Dam, 320
Occaneechis, 49
Occom, Samson, 73, 75, 81–82, *82*, 106, 111, 127–28
Ochine, 197
Oconee River, 134, 135
Office of Economic Opportunity, 327
Oglalas, 3, 8, 11, 232, 253, 274, 312, 321, 328, 368, 373
Ohio (territory and state), 71, 89, 90, 91, 92, 94, 95, 102, 122, 127, 133, 135, 136, 137, 142, 163, 175
Ohio Indians, 96, 112, 125, 126, 134, 138, 140, 158
Ohio River, 106, 116, 123, 140
Ojibwes, x, 2, 140, 163, 201, 278, 281, 282, 295, 299, 318, 329, 339, 351, *352*
Okfuskee, 145
Oklahoma, 10, 11, 12, 149, 199, 206, 208, 219, 241, 253, 271, 276, 278, 279, *291*, 292, 296, 297, 305, 321, 327, 343, 357, 358, 360, 361, 362
Omahas, 274, 287, 303
Oneidas, 29, 73, 76, 81, 90, 92, 104, 105, 111, 127, 128, 131, 132, 175, 204, 303

Onondagas, 29, 67, 91, 118–19, 163
Onoonghwandekha, 72
Opechancanough, 42, 44
Oregon (territory and state), 12, 201, 210, 216–17, 218–19, 220, 221, 234, 235, 292, 316
Oregon Donation Act, 216
Oregon Trail, 221
Osages, 11, 245, 262, 288, 296, 325
Ostler, Jeffrey, 186
Ottawas, 51, 95, 112, 133, 136, 163, 340
Ousamequin (or Massasoit), 31–32

paganism, 19, 33–36
Paiutes, 225, 232, 235, 265, 315, 337, 341
Pakantschihiles, 125
Palmer, Joel, 217
Palouses, 217
Pamunkeys, 49, 50, 296, 302, 340
Parker, Arthur C., 9, 12, 293, 294, 303–6
Parker, Ely, 234, 282
Parker, Quannah, 285
Parkinson, Robert, 113
Pawnees, 221, 249, *278*, 281, 326
Paxton Boys, 99–102, 103, 123
Paxton Boys' Riot, 99–102
Peace Policy, 238–39
Pee Dees, 54
Peña, Tonita, 302
Penn, John, 99, 103
Penn, William, 6, *38*, 77, 88, 104, 154
Pennsylvania, 6, 55, 60, 65, 74, 75, 77, 80, 84, 85, 88–90, 91, 95, 96, 97–105, 107, 111, 113, 116, 123, 126–27, 143, 152–53, 162, 173, 252, 260, 320, 362
Penobscots, 84–86, *86*, 340
Peorias, 303
Pequots, 29, 41, 44, 45, 46–47, 61, 73, 83, 127, 151, 189, 283, 341, 343, 353, 354
Pequot War, 41

Peyotism, 285–92
Philadelphia, 1, 3, 38, 75, 76, 89, 95, 98–102, 104, 125, 155, 174, 219, 252, 257, 287
Phillips, Wendell, 237–90
Phips, Spencer, 85, *86*
phrenology, 155
Pickering, Timothy, 132
Piikanis, 235–36, 246
Pilgrims, 6, 154, 344
Pinal Apaches, 235
Pine Ridge Reservation, *247*, 268, *269*, 295, 312, 329
Pipestone Indian School, 293
Piscataways, 53, 66, 75
Pitchlynn, John, 182
Pitchlynn, Peter, 175
Pittomee, John, 66
Pitt River Indians, 294
Pittsburgh, 85, 92, 93, 103, 115, 122–23, 126, 137, 150, 177
Plenty Coups, 9, *11*, 236
Plenty Horses, 268–69, *269*
Plymouth, 32, 34, 45, 46, 329, 344
Pocahontas, 6, 40, 154, 362
polygenesis, 155
Poncas, 248
Pontiac, 95
Pontiac's War, *94*, 95–96, 112
population
    of Alabama, 166
    of Blackfeet, 220
    of California, 210, 220 (Whites), 210, 215 (Indians)
    of Canada, 127
    of Cherokees, 118, 135
    of Cheyennes, 243
    of Colorado, 220
    of Comanches, 220
    of French missions, 40

of Georgia, 166
of Idaho, 220
of Illinois, 163
of Indiana, 163
of Lakotas, 220
of Maryland, 52
of Michigan, 163
of migrants to British colonies, 102–3
of Mississippi, 138
of Montana, 220
of Native Americans, 23, 54, 220, 296
of Navajos, 220
of New Mexico, 40
of New York, 68
of the Northwest Territory, 138
of Ohio, 138
of Oregon, 210
of Pennsylvania, 89
of Prophetstown, 140
of Seminoles, 180
of Spanish missions, 40
of the United States, 23, 127, 201, 231
of Utah, 220
of Virginia, 42–43
Post, Christian Frederick, 93
Potawatomis, 2, 136, 140, 142, 146, 158, 163, 186, 206, 207, 274, 282, 305, 340
Powell, John Wesley, 231
Powhatans, 6, 31–32, 35–36, 40–41, 42–44, 49, 66. *See also* Mataponis, Pamunkeys, Rappahannocks
Pratt, Richard H., 251–53, 256, 257, 262, 288–89, 292
praying towns, 41, 45, 66
Presbyterians, 72, 75, 89, 98, 102
Pretty Shield, 231–32, 246
Pretty Voice Eagle, 4
Proclamation Line of 1763, 111, 130

Prophetstown, 140, 142
Providence, RI, 66
Public Law 280, 317, 376
Pueblo Indians, 12, 50–51, 262, 302, 305, 308, 310, 315, 321, 335, 336, 341, 355
Pueblo Revolt, 50–51
Pumetacom (Metacomet, King Philip), 32, 45, 46, 76
Puritans, 47, 53, 54, 75

Quakers, 54, 89, 99–100, 156
Quick, Tom, 152–53

race
 American Revolution as generator of, 109–26
 art in the creation of, *54, 63, 101, 121, 144, 151,* 154, *155, 299*
 "Black" as a category of, 55–56, 59, 60–61, 276–77
 boarding schools in creation of, 250–62, 296
 captives' assignment of, 96
 Hannah Duston in the creation of, 18, 22, 32–33, 34–35, 40–44, 45–46, 46–47, 52–53, 54–56, *63,* 68–70, 72–73, 80–83, 97–98, 132–33
 definition of, 17
 genocide in the creation of, 14–17, 199–200, 226–27
 historiography of, 24–26
 "Indian" as a category of, 2–7, 9–10, 16, 20, 21, 23, 29, 30, 32, 33–35, 41, 43–44, 45–47, 49, 53, 57–59, 61–67, 69–70, 77–78, 81, 82–83, 85–87, 97, 98–100, 115, 119, 123, 125–26, 129–31, 132, 143, 147–48, 149, 150–56, 162, 167–68, 174–75, 187, 199–200, 201–4, 208, 211, 213, 224, 226, 230–31, 238–39,

race (*cont'd*)
    250–51, 260–61, 270, 272, 283–84, 292–95, 297–302, 308, 314, 318, 330, 333–36, 341, 350–51, 353–54, 367, 373–74
    Indian ideas about, 8–10, 12–13, 35–38, 44, 60, 67, 68–69, 72–74, 74–79, 80–81, 83, 90–97, 111–12, 132–33, 134, 138–45, 173–78, 189–91, 221, 227, 231–35, 259–61, 264–66, 287–88, 289–90, 303–7, 312, 325–31
    Indian Removal arguments based on, 149, 162–65, 166–68, *170*
    instrumentality of, 18, 22, 25, 51, 188, 338, 354, 356, 359
    justice systems in the creation of, 84–85, 103–5, 130–31, 144, 245–46, 296–97, 316, 324, 328, 350
    law in the creation of, 44, 46–47, 50, 56, 149, 167–68, 170, 171
    missions in creation of, 18, 38–47, 67–70, 72–73, 74–77, 81–83, 99, 122–23, 124, 125
    mixing, 60, 141, 145, 160–61, 164, 176–77, 188, 227, 273, 276, 278, 279, 298–99, 310–11, 312, 329, 357
    mob violence in creation of, 20, 46, 48–50, 53, 83–84, 87, 88–89, 97–106, 123, 137, 198, 209, 216, 224, 245, 281
    monuments in creation of, 5–8, 29, 63, 121, 153, 154, 369
    movies in the creation of, 3, 9, 297–300, 303, 331, 345–46, 353
    print media in creation of, 2, 62, 65–66, 155
    Nativism as framework for, 8, 12–13, 73, 90–97, 138–45, 200, 233
    schools' propagation of, 3, 16, 22, 23, 151, *159*, 243, 250–62, 293–94, 296, 316
    "Red" as a category of, 78
    science in the creation of, 17, 25, 154–55, 181, 230–31, 311
    slavery in creation of, 20–21, 23, 24, 25, 33, 45–46, 50, 51, 55–56, 57–58, 160–61, 209, 210, 227–28, 376
    urban experiences of, 317–18
    war in the creation of, 15, 19, 22, 25, 33, 44, 45–51, 52–53, 55, 56, 57–58, 60, 61–64, 65, 66–67, 69, 71–74, 84–90, 94–107, 117–26, 133–37, 140–45, 180–81, 190–99, 204–19
    "White" as a category of, 1, 7, 10, 17–24, 26, 27, 28, 32, 33, 42, 47, 49, 55, 58–60, 62, 64, 65–66, 67, 72, 73, 74–79, 80, 82–83, 84, 90–94, 95–97, 101–2, 104, 109–10, 111–13, 121–22, 124, 125–26, 127, 129, 132, 133, 134, 137, 139–40, 141–42, 143–44, 147, 150, 152, 153, 154–55, 167, 187–89, 195, 203, 282, 298, 315
    White ideas about, 2–7, 33–35, 41, 43, 45–47, 49, 53, 57–58, 61–67, 69–70, 81, 82–83, 85–87, 98–100, 115, 119, 123, 125–26, 129–31, 143, 147–48, 150–56, 167–68, 199–200, 201–4, 208, 213, 224, 226, 230–31, 238–39, 250–51, 270, 272, 283–84, 293–95, 297–302, 314, 318, 330, 333–36, 350–51, 353–54, 373–74
racism
    definition of, 17
    environmental, 16, 321–22
    Indians toward Blacks, 79, 128, 141, 160–61, 177, 227–28, 360–61

Whites toward Indians, 15–16, 43–44,
  45–46, 48–49, 50, 57, 61–66,
  69–70, 72–73, 76, 80, 82–83,
  84–85, 87–88, 99–102, 119, 122,
  125, 136–37, 143–44, 150–56,
  167–68, 193–239, 243–45, 263–64,
  280–82, 295–96, 300–302, *301*,
  320–323, 344–54
Rale, Sebastian, 62
Ramsey, Alexander, 224
Rauch, Henry, 80
Reconstruction, 228, 254
Rector, Elias, 209
Red Cloud, *11*, 232
Red Hawk, Austin, 8
Red Jacket, 147
Red Owl, Amos, 312
Red Power, 325–31, *327*
Red River War, 209, 236
Red Sticks, 145–46
Red Woman (1917), 298
Religious Freedom Act, 339
Republican Party, 228, 271–73, 313–14,
  333, 362, 374, 375
reservations
  allotment of, 270–74, *278*
  "breakouts" from, 236, 242
  Bosque Redondo, 222
  Brazos, 209
  California, 213, *215*
  Cheyenne River, 329
  criminal jurisdiction on, 245–46,
    349, 351
  Crow, 2, 246, 264
  Crow Creek, *12*, 225, 264
  Fort Hall, 259
  Great Sioux, 263, 267
  economic conditions of, 243–44,
    246, 260, 314, 316, 323, 341–43,
    369
  environmental exploitation of, 16,
    321–22
  health conditions of, 15, 16, 295–96,
    321, 323
  Indian criticism of, 9, 244, 246
  justice systems on, 244–45
  Klamath, 218
  leasing of, 270, 272, 281–82
  policy of, 194–95, 199, 228–32, *229*,
    241–50
  Quapaw, 219, 266, 321
  Round Valley, 211, 213
  Rosebud, 245, 275, 309, 323, 324
  Pine Ridge, *247*, 268, *269*, 295, 312,
    329
  Southern Cheyenne and Arapaho,
    241–45, 267, 279, 280–81
  Standing Rock, 244, 320
  Termination of, 313–20
  Tongue River, 312
  Uintah and Ouray, 294
  White crime against, 16, 241–45,
    279–80, 324, 350
  White Earth, 278, 281
  Yankton Sioux, 287
Rhode Island, 34, 46, 302, 340, 344
Rice, John, 324
Ridge, John, 160, 168, 174–75, 178,
  184, 191
Ridge, Major, 184
Riggs, Stephen R., 202
Rio Grande, 40
Rogers, Robert, 152
Rogue River War, 216–17
Rolfe, John, 40
Roman Catholic Church, 40, 50, 52–53,
  56, 57, 64, 68, 210, 248, 257, 319
Roosevelt, Franklin Delano, 5, 279,
  307
Roosevelt, Theodore, 5, 29, 335, 368

Rosebud Reservation, 245, 275, 309, 323, 324
Ross, John, 175, *176*, 177, 185
Round Valley (CA), 212–13, *212*
Round Valley Reservation, 213
Rowlandson, Mary, 64, *65*

Sackquaans, 79
St. Clair, Arthur, 136
St. Lawrence River, 40, 68
Salem, 53
Salish-Kootenais, 308
San Diego, 216
Sand Creek Massacre, *196*, 197–98, *198*
Sandusky, 122, 124, 125
San Idelfonso Pueblo, 302
Santa Clara Pueblo, 315
Santee Sioux, 222–26, 260, 268, 303, 367
Santee Sioux War, 222–26
Sassacus, 4
Sauks, 2, 140, 178, 179, 186, 189, 206, 351
Saunt, Claudio, 186–87
savagery, 19, 34–35, *151*
Savannahs, 54
scalping, 19, 46, 60, 61–64, 84–86, 87, 89, 90, 99, 101, 102, 116, 117, 119, 120–22, 123, 136, 143, 144, *144*, 145, 152, 178, 196, 197, 209, 211, 214, 215, 226, 236
Scaroyady, 90
Schurz, Carl, 242
science, in the creation of race, 17, 25, 154–55, 181, 230–31, 311
Searchers (1959), 298
Seattle, 318
Second Seminole War, 180–81
Seminoles, 142, 161, 180–81, *180*, 186, 189, 227–28, 271, 347, 359–62
Senate (U.S.), 213, 283, 311, 323, 324, 354, 362

Senecas, 29, 53, 72, 73, 115, 118, 132, 138, 156, 158, 163, 204, 274, 358
Sequoyah, 160
Sergeant, John, 75, 82
Settlement Indians, 54, 66, 72
Settler Colonial Studies, 14
Seven Years' War, 62, 65, 71, 85–90, 91, 92, 110, *118*, 148, 152, 155
Seventh U.S. Cavalry, 3, 199, 200, 236, 267–69
Shastas, 213, 216
Shawnee Prophet. *See* Tenskwatawa
Shawnees, x, 66, 71, 73, 75, 77, 85, 89, 92, 95, 96, 97, 101, 103, 105, 106, 112, 115, 120–21, 126, 136, 138–39, 141, 142–43, 156, 158, 163, 175, 204, 206, 259, 274, 351, 367
Sheridan, Philip, 153
Sherman, William T., 199, 230, 239
Shinnecocks, 252
Shoemaker, Nancy, 78
Shoshones, 226, 232, 235, 259, 274, 321
Sioux, 11, 221, 222, 224, 225, 230, 235, 236, 237, 246, 250, 253, 257, 260, 261, 263, 267, 268, 275, 286, 287, 289, 309, 312, 320, 323, 324, 326, 328, 367. *See also* Brulés, Lakotas, Oglalas, Minneconjous
Sitting Bull, 232, 235, 246, 249, 267
Six Nations. *See* Haudenosaunees
Skelton, Gerald, 317
slavery
of Africans, 20, 33, 55–59, 60, 228
by Indians, 141, 160–61, 177, 227–28
of Indians, 18, 23, 24, 29, 41, 42, 45, 46, 50, 51, 54–55, 56–59, 60–61, 68, 158, 207, 210, 211–12, 214, *215*, 222, 226, 376

role of in race-making, 20–21, 23, 24, 25, 33, 45–46, 50, 51, 55–56, 57–58, 160–61, 209, 210, 227–28, 376
Sloan, Thomas L., 303, 309
Slover, John, 125
smallpox, 24, 35, 97, 140, 153, 214, 215, 221, 235
Smith, John, 6, 31, 34, 154
Smithsonian Institution, 219, 344, 369, *270*, 371
    Bureau of Ethnology of the, 288
Smoak, Gregory E., 268
Smohalla, 233, *234*
Snake War, 235
Snow, John Augustus, 156
Snyder Act. *See* Indian Citizenship Act of 1924
Society for the Propagation of the Gospel, 53–54, 67
Society of American Indians, 9, 24, 286, 289, 303–7, *304*, 368
Society of Friends. *See* Quakers
Society of Jesus. *See* Jesuits
Song of Hiawatha (1855), 2
South Carolina, 53–61, 68, 69, 76, 79, 85, 117, 126, 147, 154
Southern Cheyennes, 3, 236, 241–45, 267, 279, 280–81
South Dakota, *247*, 255, 259, 269, 317, 320, 324, 329
Southwest Regional Indian Youth Council, 325
Spain, 40, 61, 95, 129, 135
Spokanes, 217
sports mascots, 300, 346–47, *347*
Squaw Man (1905), 298, *299*
Stagecoach (1939), 298
Standing Bear, 247–48
Standing Bear, Henry, *253*, 303, 368, 369

Standing Bear, Luther, 253, 255, 257, 260, 261, 263, 305
Steele, Elijah, 218
Stewart, Omer C., 292
Stockbridge, MA, NY, and WI, 87, 127, 132, 133, 155, 162, 163, 175, 183, 204, 282
Stone Calf, 237
Stowe, Harriet Beecher, 177
Stump, Frederick, 104
Suckatoby, 78
Sullivan's Campaign, 118–20
Sun Dance, 288
Sun Elk, 262
Supreme Court (U.S.), 149, 168, 171, 173, 245, 292, 355, 361, 362, 363
Susquehannah River, 75, 89, 90–92, 95, 98, 102, 116, 118
Susquehannocks, 48, 49, 66
Sweezy, Carl, 302
Sword Bearer, 246–47
syphilis, 244

Taft, William Howard, 5, 296
Tanaghrisson, 92
Taos Pueblo, 262, *335*, 336
Tar Creek Site, 321
Taylor, Zachary, 152
Tecumseh, 140–44, 153, 259
Teller, Henry M., 274
Tennessee, 117, 134, 138, 141, 145, 163, 164, 173
Tenskwatawa, 138–40, *139*, 144, 233
Termination, 138–40, 144, 233
Texas, 175, 201, 206–9, 212, 219, 236, 245, 280, 364
Thanksgiving, 6, 257
Thom, Melvin, 325
Thoreau, Henry David, 62, 153
Thorpe, Jim, 262, 300

Timucuas, 61
Tippecanoe, 140
Tohono O'odham, 235
Tongue River Reservation, 312
Tonkawas, 207, 209
Tories. *See* Loyalists
Trail of Broken Treaties, 329
Trail of Tears, 149, 185, *185*
treaties
    Canandaigua (1794), 137
    Colerain (1796), 135
    Cusseta (1826), 165
    Cusseta (1832), 181
    Dancing Rabbit Creek (1830), 182
    Doak's Stand (1820), 165
    Fort Atkinson (1853), 194
    Fort Laramie (1851), 194
    Fort McIntosh (1785), 127
    Fort Stanwix (1768), 106, 111, 116
    Fort Stanwix (1784), 126, 135
    Fort Wayne (1809), 140
    Ghent (1815), 146
    Greenville (1795), 137, 140
    Hard Labor (1768), 111, 116
    Hopewell (1785) 137
    Indian Springs (1825), 165
    Lancaster (1744), 91
    Lochaber (1770), 116
    McIntosh (1785), 127, 135
    Middle Plantation (1677), 50
    New Echota, 185
    New York (1790), 135, 137
    Paris (1763), 94
    Paris (1783), 126, 146
    Payne's Landing (1832), 180
    Sycamore Shoals (1775), 116
    Tellico Blockhouse (1794), 135
Treuer, David, 200
Tribes of All Nations, 328
Trinity Site, 321

Troup, George, 167
Truman, Harry S., 324
Tsatoke, Monroe, 302
Tuckabatchee, 145
Tulalips, 231, 296
Tutunis, 216
Tusta Mico, Abihka, 177
Tuscarawas, 92
Tuscarora War, 57–58
Tuscaroras, 29, 66, 69, 75, 118, 127
Tutelos, 75
Types of Mankind (1854), 231
Twiss, Thomas, 201

Uintah and Ouray reservation, 294
Umatillas, 3, 217
United States
    American Revolution of, 109–27
    Army of, 115, 117, 123, 136–37, 142–43, 146, 178–85, 196–99, 209, 217, 218–19, 222, 225–56, 235–38, 242, 267–68
    Capitol of, 7, *155*, 371
    Civil War of, 227–28
    Committee of Civil Rights of, 324
    Congress of, 1, 5, 112, 121, 123, 129, 131, 142, 150, 162, 165, 170, 173, 177, 180, 183, 209, 213, 238, 239, 245–46, 252, 253, 254, 256, 268, 274, 282, 287, 289, 290, 292, 307, 313, 315, 316, 327, 333, 335, 339, 341, 344, 362, 364, 371, 373, 375
    Constitution of, 128–30, 137–38, 149, 169, 172, 326, 334, 338, 345
    environmental policies of, 16, 321–22
    Environmental Protection Agency of, 322, *322*
    expansion of, 116, 135, 149, 194, 201
    Geological Survey of, 321
    historical memory of, 6–7, 109, 150

Indian policies of, 129–30, 147–58, 149–50, 162–70, 194, 230, 250–58, 270–72, 307–20, 326–27, 333–38
Indian Removal by, *170*, 178–89
Indian Reorganization Act of, 308–13, *309*
Indian views of, 108
Indian wars of, 117–26, 133–37, 140–45, 180–81, 190–99, 204–19
mob violence of, 123, 137, 198, 209, 216, 224, 245, 281
population of, 23, 127, 201, 231
Reconstruction of, 228, 254
Relocation policy of, 316–18, *317*
reservations of, 194–95, 199, *215*, 228–32, *229*, 241–50
Senate of, 213, 283, 311, 323, 324, 354, 362
Seventh Cavalry of, 3, 199, 200, 236, 267–69
Supreme Court of, 149, 168, 171, 173, 245, 292, 355, 361, 362, 363
Termination policy of, 138–40, 144, 233
War of 1812 of, 142–46, *144*
White nationalism of, 113
United Tribes of New England, 329
Upper Platte Agency, 201
Utah, 220, 225, 235, 294, 315, 317
Utes, 321

Van Buren, Martin, 173
Van Schaick, Goose, 118
Vaughan, Alfred J., 221
Vermont, 162, 364
Vincennes, IN, 120
Virginia, 6
Indian wars of, 40, 42–44, 47–50
missionary work of, 40

racial terminology in, 43, 47–50
royal charter of, 31
slavery in, 44, 50

Wabanakis, 52, 53, 61, 84
Wabash River, 120, 136, 140
Wacos, 207, 109
Wahunsenacawh (or Powhatan), 31–32, 40
Wailackis, 213
Watkins, Arthur, 315
Walker, R. J., 206
Walla Wallas, 12–13, 217
Wampanoags, 31–32, 36, 37, 41, 45–47, 61, 66, 78, 79, 127, 128, 154, 156, 189, 283, 302, *302*, 340, 341, 343
Wamsutta, 45
Wanapums, 233
Wangomen, 92
Wannamaker Expeditions, 2–4, 10–13
Wannamaker, John, 2
Wannamaker, Rodman, 1–2, 7, 10, 13
Ward, Nancy, 166
wars
American Revolution, 109–27
Anglo-Powhatan War, first, 40–41
Anglo-Powhatan War, second, 42–43
Anglo-Powhatan War, third, 44
Bacon's Rebellion, 47–50
Black Hawk, 178, 186
Cherokee War of 1759–61, 87–88
Civil (U.S.), 198, 227–28
imperial wars, 61–67
King Philip's, 45–47
Korean, 314, 324
Lord Dunmore's, 105–6
Mexican-American, 188–89
Northwest Indian, 136–37
Pequot, 41
Pontiac's, 95–103
Red River, 209, 236

wars (cont'd)
   Removal, 178–80
   Rogue River, 216–17
   Santee Sioux, 222–25
   Second Seminole, 180
   Seven Years', 262, 65, 71, 85–90, 91, 92, 110, 118, 148, 152, 155
   Snake, 235
   Tuscarora, 57–58
   War of 1812, *139*, 142–46, *144*
   World War I, 283, 295, 306, 307
   World War II, 297, 307, 314, 320
   Yakama, 217
   Yamasee, 57–58
Ward Massacre, 225–26
Warden, Cleaver, 289
Warner, Pop, 262
Warrior, Clyde, 325–28, *327*
Washburn, Wilcomb, 313
Washington (territory and state), 12, 201, 216–17, 231, 275, 296, 305, 317, 321, 339–40, 341, 359
Washington, Booker T., 260
Washington, D.C., 4, 7, 9, 149, 195, 219, 237, 289, 329, 336, 369
Washington, George, 118, 120, 125, 129–30, 131, 136, 137, 368
Washita Massacre, 199
Wassaja (San Francisco), 326
Wasson, Wilfred C., 316
Wayne, Anthony, 137
Wayne, John, 298
Weller, John B., 212
Weiser, Conrad, 89
Western Abenakis, 61
Westerns, 297–98
Westos, 54
West Virginia, 105, 106, 111, 115
Wheeler, Burton K., 311

Wheeler-Howard Act. *See* Indian Reorganization Act
Wheelock, Eleazor, 75, 82
Whiskey Rebellion, 137
Whitaker, Alexander, 40
White(s)
   American Revolution and identity of, 109–27
   appropriation of Indigenous identity by, 153
   "Christian" as term for, 18, 33, 41, 55, 57, 59
   conquest ideology of, 188–89, 214–15
   Indian extinction as a principle of, 5, 9–10, 16, 20, 21, 23, 29, 30, 132, 149, 153–56, 162, 167–68, 174–75, 187, 292, 293, 294, 308, 341, 367
   Indian ideas about, 8–10, 12–13, 35–38, 44, 60, 67, 68–69, 72–74, 74–79, 80–81, 83, 90–97, 111–12, 132–33, 134, 138–45, 173–78, 189–91, 221, 227, 231–35, 259–61, 264–66, 287–88, 289–90, 303–7, 312, 325–31
White Antelope, 197
White Eyes, 112, 115
White Mankiller, 134
Wichitas, 207, 237
Wild West Show, 2, 9, 249–50
William III, 52–53
Williams, Roger, 34, 37, 47, 79
Williamson, David, 123
Williamson, Henry E., 146
Williamson, Hugh, 100
Wilson, Dick, 329
Wilson, Jack. *See* Wovoka
Wilson, John, 286
Wilson, Woodrow, 10, 307

Winnebagos. *See* Ho-Chunks
Winslow, Edward, 34
Winslow, Josiah, 46
Winyaws, 54
Wirt, William, 171
Wisconsin, 127, 133, 163, 183, 193, 305, 316, 339, 351
Wokpoeton Sioux, 225
Wolfe, Patrick, 14
Wooden Leg, 7, *11*
Worcester, Samuel Augustin, 172
Worcester v. Georgia (1832), 172
World Columbian Exposition, 249
World War I, 283, 295, 306, 307
World War II, 297, 307, 314, 320
Wounded Knee, 267–69, 287, 329–30, *330*
Wovoka (Jack Wilson), 265
Wright, George, 217

Wyandots, 51, 71, 122, 124, 136, 156, 163
Wyoming (territory and state), 225, 235, 275, 306

Yakamas, 217, 275, 321
Yakama War, 217–28
Yamasee War, 57–58
Yamasees, 54, 57–58, 61
Yanktons, 3, 246, 286, 287
Yellow Robe, Chauncey, 9, 10, *253*
Yellowtail Dam, 320
Yellow Thunder, Raymond, 329
Yellow Wolf, 197
Yukeoma, 296
Yukis, 211, 212, *212*

Zitkala-Ša. *See* Bonnin, Gertrude Simmons